Microsoft® Press

Analyzing Requirements and Defining Solution Architectures

MCSD Training Kit

**For Exam
70-100**

**Scott F. Wilson
KiZAN Corporation**

PUBLISHED BY
Microsoft Press
A Division of Microsoft Corporation
One Microsoft Way
Redmond ,Washington 98052-6399

Library of Congress Cataloging-in-Publication Data

Analyzing Requirements and Defining Solution Architectures : MCSD
   Training Kit / Microsoft Corporation
          p. cm.
     Includes index.
     ISBN 0-7356-0854-7
     1. Electronic data processing personnel--Certification.
   2. Microsoft software--Examinations Study guides   .   3. Application
   software--Development Study guides   .   I. Microsoft Corporation.
   QA76.3.A53   1999
   005.1--dc21   99-33881
                                                                     CIP

Printed and bound in the United States of America.

3 4 5 6 7 8 9   WCWC   4 3 2 1 0

Distributed in Canada by Penguin Books Canada Limited.

A CIP catalogue record for this book is available from the British Library.

Microsoft Press books are available through booksellers and distributors worldwide. For further information about international editions, contact your local Microsoft Corporation office or contact Microsoft Press International directly at fax (425) 936-7329. Visit our Web site at mspress.microsoft.com

Macintosh is a registered trademark of Apple Computer, Inc. ActiveX, BackOffice, JScript, Microsoft, Microsoft Press, MSDN, NetShow, Outlook, PowerPoint, Visual Basic, Visual C++, Visual InterDev, Visual J++, Visual SourceSafe, Visual Studio, Win32, Windows, and Windows NT are either registered trademarks or trademarks of Microsoft Corporation in the United States and/or other countries. Other product and company names mentioned herein may be the trademarks of their respective owners.

The example companies, organizations, products, people, and events depicted herein are fictitious. No association with any real company, organization, product, person, or event is intended or should be inferred.

Acquisitions Editor: Eric Stroo
Project Editor Wendy Zucker

Contents

Part 2   Designing the Product

Part 3   Developing the Product

Part 4   Shipping the Product

Acknowledgments

Many thanks for the tireless support from my family, the entire KiZAN team, and my fellow authors, Bruce and Tim. Thanks for the help from Eric, Wendy, and Vicky from Microsoft Press in publishing this book. Also, thanks to Rod Fergusson for his insightful comments, and the MSF group and Mary Kirtland for the extensive use of their material.

This book could also not have been created without the incredible editing team at OTSI. Special thanks to Joyce Cox and Joan Lambert. If any of this book makes sense, they deserve the credit, and if not, I deserve the blame.

For the undaunted support and love from my wife, Sandy, I'm eternally thankful. You keep my life together, while I do crazy things such as writing—and yes, I'm done with this one.

—*Scott F. Wilson*

First of all, I would like to thank Scott for being such a great person to work with. Doing a big book is no bowl of cherries, but you made it worthwhile, friend. I'd also like to acknowledge all the folks at KiZAN, who have been unfailingly helpful, professional, and pleasant throughout. Thanks to Allan McGuffey, who taught me not to be passive.

Additionally, even though they may not see it, I want to throw a thank-you to the staff at the Steak-and-Shake, without whom much of the late-night authoring would not have been possible! Finally, I want to thank the two most important people in my life: Jesus Christ, and my wife, Nina. Between the two of them, I am about as blessed as any one man can be.

—*Bruce Maples*

Thanks to the KiZAN team for continuing to deliver great products. Special thanks to my wife, Laura, and our daughters, Taylor and Hannah, for their continuing love, patience, and support.

—*Tim Landgrave*

About This Book

Welcome to *Analyzing Requirements and Defining Solution Architectures: MCSD Training Kit for Exam 70-100*. By completing the chapters and associated case studies in this course, you will acquire the knowledge and skills necessary to prepare for the Microsoft Certified Solution Developer Exam 70-100. This self-paced course provides content that supports the skills measured by this exam. Review questions at the end of each chapter recap what you have learned and help you prepare more thoroughly.

Note For more information on becoming a Microsoft Certified Solution Developer, see "The Microsoft Certified Professional Program" later in this section.

Intended Audience

This course is designed for students interested in developing their skills in analyzing requirements and defining solution architectures while developing applications. These skills include developing distributed applications using the the Microsoft Solutions Framework (MSF), building multi-layer and client/ server solutions, and creating Microsoft Transaction Server (MTS) components and custom Component Object Model (COM) interfaces.

Prerequisites

Before beginning this self-paced course, you should be able to:

- Display a basic knowledge of a development language.
- Create and compile a simple application.
- Create a simple database application and possess a basic understanding of relational database concepts.

Getting Started

This self-paced training course is intended to help you prepare for the Analyzing Requirements and Defining Solution Architectures (70-100) exam. You will not need a computer or any hardware or software to complete this course. However, to use and examine the Resource Management System (RMS) Sample Application discussed in the "Case Studies" section, your computer must meet the following hardware and software requirements.

Hardware Requirements for the RMS Sample Application

Although the specific system documentation should be consulted for the minimum requirements to run Microsoft Windows NT Server, Microsoft Internet Information Server, Microsoft Transaction Server, and Microsoft SQL Server, the following server and client minimum configurations are recommended.

The minimum recommendations to run the client and server portions of the RMS Sample Application are:

- Pentium II 266 MHz or equivalent
- 128 MB RAM
- 4 GB hard drive
- Network card and accompanying network components
- CD-ROM drive

Software Requirements for the RMS Sample Application

The RMS Sample Application on the supplemental CD-ROM requires the following server and client software.

Server Software
- Windows NT 4.0 with Service Pack 4
- Windows NT Option Pack 4 with Internet Information Server 4.0 and Microsoft Transaction Server 2.0
- Microsoft Exchange Server 5.5 with Service Pack 2
- Microsoft Collaborative Data Objects 1.21 installed with Microsoft Outlook 98 or higher (must be on machine running Microsoft Transaction Server hosting the RMS business components)
- Microsoft SQL Server 7.0
- Microsoft Data Access Components 2.1
- Microsoft Internet Explorer 4.01 or higher

Client Software

- Windows NT 4.0 Workstation with Service Pack 4, Windows 98, or Windows 95 (must have DCOM95 installed)

- Microsoft Data Access Components 2.1 Redistribution (must have ADOR 1.5) will be installed by client application installation.

- Internet Explorer 4.01 or higher

- Microsoft Outlook 98 or higher

Course Overview

This self-paced course combines text, graphics, and review questions to teach you about analyzing requirements and defining solutions architecture. The course assumes that you will work through the book from beginning to end, but you can choose a customized track and complete only the sections that interest you.

The book is divided into the following chapters:

- **Chapter 1, "Enterprise Architecture"** This chapter examines the need for application and infrastructure guidance at an enterprise level. It begins by suggesting that systems be implemented with an architecture-first process. Next, the chapter introduces the Microsoft Solutions Framework (MSF). Chapter 1 also examines the MSF Enterprise Architecture Model and its Business, Application, Information, and Technology Perspectives. This chapter additionally points out that the four primary goals of an enterprise architecture are that it be integrated, iterative, actionable, and prioritized. Finally, this chapter discusses how to begin the enterprise architecture process and continue to deliver systems and applications while the architecture process is underway.

- **Chapter 2, "Enterprise Applications"** This chapter examines the features of modern enterprise applications, and issues that should be considered. It discusses designing large-scale, distributed, enterprise applications and the need to reduce their complexity. It also recommends managing this enterprise application complexity through abstraction, which involves grouping similar requirements together into a small number of abstract categories. Various architecture descriptions are discussed, such as the Unified Modeling Language (UML), Design Patterns, and AntiPatterns. Additionally, this chapter outlines ten principles for delivering successful applications. Chapter 2 finally suggests that organizations use the several perspectives represented by Microsoft's Enterprise Application Model and discusses the application architecture framework provided by the separate MSF Application Model for Development.

- **Chapter 3, "Project Teams"** This chapter discusses who is responsible for doing what so that all the different parts of an application project are managed properly. The chapter also discusses building a project team within the context of the MSF Team Model for Application Development (MSF Development Team Model). The discussion progresses from understanding the six equally vital team roles to finding and enlisting leaders from different parts of the organization. Chapter 3 also pinpoints specific responsibilities that must be fulfilled for a project to be successful, and assigns these responsibilities to specific team members. It looks at ways to analyze project requirements from the perspectives of different team members and also explores ways to scale the project team to fit the needs and size of the project. Finally, this chapter examines team and leadership characteristics that will help make an organization's use of its project resources more effective.

- **Chapter 4, "Development Process"** This chapter is primarily devoted to the MSF Process Model for Application Development, otherwise known as the *MSF Development Process Model*. Rather than a step-by-step methodology, MSF is a structural framework that an organization can adapt to suit its particular needs. The MSF Development Process Model is the part of this framework that describes the life cycle of a successful software development project. Using a development framework has been successfully proven in the software industry to improve project control, minimize risk, improve product quality, and increase development speed. Also in this chapter, we discuss the Unified Process development framework along with its workflows, stages, and milestones.

- **Chapter 5, "Project Vision"** This chapter describes the dynamics of the MSF Development Process Model's Envisioning Phase. This chapter also discusses what information to gather from the project stakeholders, how to create a product vision, how the MSF Development Team Model's various roles participate in the envisioning process, and what their responsibilities are. In addition, Chapter 5 examines how the envisioning process develops over a period of time. Finally, this chapter presents a detailed discussion of risk management, based on the MSF Risk Management Model.

- **Chapter 6, "Project Plan"** This chapter outlines the process of mapping concepts to actions and explains team roles in the Planning Phase of the MSF Development Process Model. It takes an in-depth look at the MSF Design Process Model and the conceptual, logical, and physical architectures of an application. This chapter also discusses how the MSF Application Model's user, business, and data service layers can be incorporated into the application's physical architecture. The MSF Development Process Model's Functional Specification, Master Project Plan, and Master Project Schedule are all emphasized as key deliverables of the Planning Phase. Finally, Chapter 6 discusses principles of scheduling, as well as the ongoing task of risk management.

- **Chapter 7, "User Service Layer Technologies"** This chapter examines how to create effective and efficient user interface (UI) designs. It also explores legacy, current, and future technologies that affect the user service layer design of the MSF Application Model. Additionally, this chapter discusses the impact of Web technologies on current application design techniques. We complete Chapter 7 with an in-depth look at implementing a Web-based application.

- **Chapter 8, "Business Service Layer Technologies"** This chapter focuses on such issues as using an object context to manage state, using explicitly defined interfaces when possible, composing functionality, maintaining state across transaction boundaries, propagating errors, and programmatically controlling security. In addition, this chapter takes a detailed examination using COM and COM+ within the business service of an application's physical design. This chapter concludes with a detailed look at using COM components with Microsoft Transaction Server.

- **Chapter 9, "Data Service Layer Technologies"** This chapter examines design issues related to data requirements and explores characteristics of different data access technologies. This chapter also discusses best uses for each access technology, and normalization of data and data integrity. In addition, this chapter identifies how business rules can affect application data and where these rules are implemented. Furthermore, Chapter 9 examines technologies that provide data access to legacy data system stores and Enterprise Resource Planning (ERP) applications. Finally, this chapter reviews COM+ In-Memory Database (IMDB) features that can improve data access performance.

- **Chapter 10, "Testing and the Production Channel"** This chapter explains how to build a working environment that supports development, testing, certification, and production. Using real-life examples, this chapter describes the production channel and its goals. Chapter 10 thoroughly examines testing, and recommends several ways to execute and monitor tests. It also discusses ways to scale out an application's production environment by adding servers to the physical implementation. Finally, this chapter examines ways to classify program faults and failures, discuss the larger issue of product bugs, and describe methods of tracking, classifying, and resolving known bug problems.

- **Chapter 11, "Application Security"** This chapter looks at different security-related protocols and the basic security concepts of authentication. It also examines encryption, which stores and passes information from one place to another so that it can't be read by anyone who intercepts it. Additionally, this chapter discusses access control, which determines what users are allowed to accomplish, and auditing, which records what goes on inside the operating system as users request and work with the resources the system makes available to them.

- **Chapter 12, "Development Deliverables"** This chapter examines the creation process, including how the various team roles function during development. This chapter further explores testing, bug tracking, and the "zero-defect mindset," and also shows how the project management team makes effective trade-offs. In addition, this chapter discusses how multi-layer applications are implemented as monolithic or client/server, or distributed in physical form. Finally, Chapter 12 explores the end of the MSF Development Process Model's Developing Phase, when code-complete is reached, and all product features and original code are incorporated into the application.

- **Chapter 13, "Product Stabilization"** This chapter emphasizes the evolutionary cycle the team will progress through to move from the Developing Phase's Scope Complete Milestone to the Stabilizing Phase's Release Milestone. We summarize this phase's effort as four primary steps: Fix the bugs, synchronize all product deliverables, ship the release, and extensively test the release. Leading up to the Release Milestone, the chapter identifies several key interim milestones that are reached by the continual iteration of the phase's steps. This chapter also provides some guidelines for the deployment of an application after the product is released. From the preplanning phases though pilot testing, support, and troubleshooting, we explore efficient ways to deploy the application with as little negative impact as possible on the users and their systems and networks.

- **Chapter 14, "Project Review"** This chapter emphasizes the value of a solid project review, as it both relates to a project just completed and to the ongoing growth and improvement of the organization. The chapter examines the relationship between the project review and the Capability Maturity Model for Software, and also shows the project review's importance in creating a best practice guide for the organization's development teams. This chapter examines the practical considerations of conducting a project review: when to schedule a project review, who should attend, and the proper physical setting for a project review.

Features of This Book

The following features are designed to enhance the usefulness of this course:

- The overall structure reflects the way a development team would progress through the process of creating an application.

- Each chapter contains reference material that also serves as additional recommended reading.

- Each chapter ends with a short summary of the material presented.

- Review questions at the end of each chapter let you test what you have learned in the chapter.

- Case studies provide a different and interesting way to learn development and application design by participating in the complete development life cycle of a multi-layer, distributed application. Although the case study events are purely fictional, they provide fresh insight on how people build applications. See the "Case Studies" section for more information.

Conventions Used in This Book

Before you start reading any of the chapters, it is important that you understand the following notational conventions used in this book:

- *Italic* is used for emphasis when defining new terms. *Italic* is also used for book titles.

- Names of files and folders appear in Title Caps. Unless otherwise indicated, you can use all lowercase letters when you type a file or folder name in a dialog box or at a command prompt.

- File name extensions appear in all lowercase.

- Acronyms appear in all uppercase.

- Monospace type represents code samples, examples of screen text, or entries that you might type at a command prompt or in initialization files.

- Square brackets [ ] are used in syntax statements to enclose optional items. For example, [*filename*] in command syntax indicates that you can choose to type a file name with the command. Type only the information within the brackets, not the brackets themselves.

- Braces { } are used in syntax statements to enclose required items. Type only the information within the braces, not the braces themselves.

About the CD-ROM

The supplemental CD-ROM contains an electronic version of the entire text of this book, as well as the Analyzing Requirements and Defining Solution Architectures 70-100 Sample Exam. You can install this sample exam from Self-Test Software (STS) to practice taking a sample certification exam. Designed to reflect the kinds of skills tested by the actual Microsoft certification exam, this sample exam includes questions to help you assess your understanding of the materials presented in this book. Each question includes feedback and an associated course reference so that you can review the material presented. You can visit the STS Web site at www.selftestsoftware.com for a complete list of available practice exams.

Also included on the supplemental CD-ROM is the RMS Sample Application and its documentation (see the next section).

Case Studies

The concepts taught in each chapter of this book are demonstrated in a series of case studies. These case studies present fictitious scenarios of a company that is using the development process, concepts, and application design strategies outlined in the book to analyze application requirements, define a solution architecture, and create a product. These case studies are designed to help you understand the concepts and goals presented in the chapters, and to offer a clear picture of how this book's development methodology could work in real life for your own company's projects. The "Case Study Background" section below provides the information necessary to understand the structure and context of the case study's fictional organization. Read through this section thoroughly before you begin this book.

The Resource Management System (RMS) Sample Application, which is referred to in the case studies and included on the supplemental CD-ROM, is a complete multi-layer application that uses key Microsoft technologies, such as Microsoft Visual Basic 6.0, Active Server Pages, Dynamic HTML, Microsoft Outlook 98, Microsoft Transaction Server 2.0, Microsoft Exchange Server 5.5, and Microsoft SQL Server 7.0 to manage company resources. The application presents a real-world example of a multi-client, distributed application that accesses two different data stores. Along with the compiled executables and full source code, sample documentation is provided as a simple example of the documentation created by the project team throughout the case studies. The RMS Sample Application provides a basic resource management system for scheduling and tracking individuals and their proficiencies. In reality, two developers coded this application over a two-month period, which speaks to their skill levels and the benefits of the development tools, technologies, and platforms chosen for the application.

The "Getting Started" section earlier in this introduction provides important setup instructions that describe the hardware and software requirements necessary to run the RMS Sample Application.

Case Study Background

To make the case studies both more interesting and more useful, we decided to present them as a story—imaginary, but nonetheless true to life and based on the real experiences of the authors. Our goal is that as you read this story, you will get a clear picture of how the development methodology could work for your own organization and your own projects.

To better understand the issues presented in the case studies, here is some background information about the fictitious company.

The Company

Ferguson and Bardell Incorporated is a Chicago-based engineering, architecture, and project management firm. Founded in 1948 by two WWII veterans, it has grown to over 800 employees with revenues in 1998 approaching $230 million. Corporate headquarters occupy seven floors of a prominent office high-rise in downtown Chicago, with satellite offices in Detroit, Milwaukee, Cincinnati, Indianapolis, and Louisville.

Ferguson and Bardell embraced technology early and often. Unfortunately, consistency and coherence did not always accompany that early adoption. For example, the company stored project data in proprietary formats in a multitude of locations that were connected either by modems or by overnight messenger services. Additionally, until recently the company used three different word processors, including a terminal-based one.

In 1998, the board of directors and senior management came to the conclusion that the firm's IT efforts were inadequate. One board member, who was familiar with studies of effective business uses of technology, contacted the consulting firm responsible for the studies. After examining Ferguson and Bardell's IT practices and accomplishments for two months, the consultants brought a set of recommendations to the board.

The most controversial recommendation was to remove the position of IT Director, which at that time reported directly to the CFO, and to create instead a CIO position within senior management. Several board members, as well as the CFO, wanted to keep the org chart as it was, but the consultants were insistent. "As long as IT is seen only as a cost center," they argued, "you will never get the business value out of technology that you should expect. And, if you keep IT out of the boardroom, you can't possibly learn enough about technology to make informed business decisions about it. You have to include the IT function in your management team and in your management decision-making if you want to see Ferguson and Bardell crawl out of the technology abyss it's in."

The new CIO came aboard in October, highly recommended by his former employer, a regional law firm where he had risen in five years from Network Manager to CIO. The former IT Director, who had decided to leave rather than take on the redesigned position, had spent the previous year putting a new network infrastructure in place and enabling Internet connectivity across the enterprise. As a result, the new CIO had some time to get oriented before starting a major project. He spent the first three months getting to know his staff, learning the ropes of the business, and putting certain processes and procedures in place.

In January, he brought in a Microsoft trainer to introduce Microsoft Solutions Framework (MSF) to his leadership staff, whose response was mixed. Some were enthusiastic, some were skeptical, and a few hinted that they figured this was another management fad that would soon pass. Nevertheless, he pushed ahead, confident in his belief that only a consistent project framework, informed and driven by business-IT interaction, would accomplish what Ferguson and Bardell needed to accomplish.

The Teams

Ferguson and Bardell's new CIO understood that to build an enterprise architecture, he would have to bring together a team that represented several of Ferguson and Bardell's departments. To develop applications within the context of the company's enterprise architecture, he would have to create project teams. He needed people who would take initiative, who were accomplished in their respective fields, and whom he could count on to see a task through to completion. He knew that building any team could be a challenge, as each person would bring his or her own perspective, approach, and personality to the team.

To develop the company's enterprise architecture, the CIO assembled the following team:

- **Dan Shelly, Chief Information Officer** Dan is in his early forties and loves business, technology, and the Chicago Bulls, though not necessarily always in that order. As the new CIO, he is both liked and respected; his peers on the management team appreciate his understanding of business issues, and his staff in IT appreciate that he came up through the IT ranks. As one network engineer put it, "Dan knows what it's like to be on call at 3 in the morning!" Dan is still excited about the potential of technology to make a substantive difference to the company, but he has been around long enough to know how hard it can be to actually make that difference.

- **Jenny Sax, Network Support Technician** Jenny's first job out of college one year ago was with the network support staff of Ferguson and Bardell. In a short time, she has developed a reputation for documenting everything she works on. The company's first help desk guide magically appeared one Monday morning after she spent the previous Friday talking with frustrated users. Detail-oriented, she never misses a chance to learn exactly how things work.

- **Kevin Kennedy, Management Specialist** Kevin is part of Ferguson and Bardell long-range planning committee. In the last year, he has been working directly with the CEO to optimize the planning and budgeting process. Though often brash, he is considered to be on the fast track toward stepping into the shoes of the CEO when he retires in four years. He has worked in most management roles within the company and gathered a reputation for getting the job done, regardless of the cost.

- **Jo Brown, Assistant Chief Operations Officer** When no one else would step up to the plate, Jo took over the stalled Y2K project and succeeded in getting Ferguson and Bardell compliant for the millennium. After completing the Y2K project five months ahead of schedule, Jo has gone back to her normal job of keeping the company's operations running smoothly. Her most recent project was to create a procedure manual to simplify the business process for the company. As long as everyone follows the book, everything works smoothly, but she is known for sending blistering e-mails to the poor souls that try to break the rules.

- **Dick Kaplan, Business Analyst** Every company needs an odd bird, and Dick fills that role for Ferguson and Bardell. In a previous life, Dick was a philosophy professor, and he has a Ph.D and several books to his credit. While looking around for something a little different to do, he stumbled into the consulting business in the early 1980s. Ten years ago, he decided he wanted to work for an architectural firm and chose Ferguson and Bardell. In his current role as business analyst, he is asked to participate on most application design teams because of his easygoing nature and uncanny ability to simplify complex problems.

Even before the company's enterprise architecture was in place, Dan had decided to use the RMS project to test the new development framework. To see this project through, the following team members would need to learn how to work together:

- **Bill Pardi, Director of Development** Bill has been with Ferguson and Bardell since leaving the military in 1978. He has risen through the ranks, beginning with punch-card work and moving through various "heavy iron" systems into PC-based database development using dBase III and Paradox. He was made head of Development in 1996 after leading a 35-person team in a two-year effort to write a new accounting package for Ferguson and Bardell from scratch. Even though the application was six months late and 40 percent over budget, everyone associated with the project agreed that without Bill, it would have been much worse.

- **Jane Clayton, Director of Accounting** Jane knows more about how Ferguson and Bardell actually works than almost anybody else. She started at the company ten years ago as a clerk in the accounting department, and rose to the position of director four years ago. She promotes high-quality work, and she focuses on shielding her staff from obstacles and other distractions, whether those obstacles are people, policies, or technology. She's no computer guru, but she has dealt with software long enough to know what works for accounting purposes and what doesn't.

- **Tim O'Brien, Network Manager** Tim looks ten years younger than his true age of 28. He's interested in all types of technology but has focused his career on Microsoft products by earning an MCSE certification in addition to his EE degree from Northwestern. He's fun to be around, with a ready wit and a smile to match. His tardiness to work and meetings is legendary, as is his knowledge of the Ferguson and Bardell technologies and his ability to troubleshoot problems quickly and effectively.

- **Marilou Moris, Trainer** A favorite of the Ferguson and Bardell staff, Marilou is an independent trainer who lives in downtown Chicago. From there she travels all across the Midwest, doing training for both companies and training centers. She has done a lot of training for Jane's staff in particular, and she and Jane have become good friends. Jane recommended her to Dan when he needed a trainer for the project team.

- **Marta Wolfe-Hellene, Engineer** Both the youngest member of the project team and the newest employee at Ferguson and Bardell, Marta is extremely intelligent, hard-working, and well-spoken. As a result, some people think she is soft until they try to push her. She is quiet, almost to a fault, but can show a quick and dry wit once she is comfortable with the people around her.

Using This Book to Prepare for Certification

The following tables provide a list of skills measured on the Analyzing Requirements and Defining Solution Architectures 70-100 certification exam. These tables list each skill with this book's location in which you will find material relating to that skill.

Analyzing Business Requirements

Skill being measured	Chapter	Section
Analyze the scope of a project. Considerations include: existing applications; anticipated changes in environment; expected lifetime of solution; and time, cost, budget, and benefits tradeoffs.	1 2 4 5	What is Architecture? Enterprise Application Architecture; Guiding Software Principles MSF Development Process Model Principles Overview of the Envisioning Process; Envisioning Process
Analyze the extent of a business requirement.		
Establish business requirements	5	Envisioning Process
Establish type of problem, such as messaging problem or communication problem.	5	Envisioning Process
Establish and define customer quality requirements.	5	Envisioning Process
Minimize Total Cost of Ownership (TCO).	3 5	The MSF Development Team Model Vision Approved Milestone and Its Deliverables

Skill being measured	Chapter	Section
Minimize Total Cost of Ownership (TCO). *(continued)*	6 13	MSF Design Process Deployment Process
Increase Return on Investment (RDI) of solution.	3 5 6 13	The MSF Development Team Model Vision Approved Milestone and Its Deliverables MSF Design Process Deployment Process
Analyse current platform and infrastructure.	1	MSF Enterprise Architecture Model; Creating an Enterprise Architecture
Incorporate planned platform and infrastructure into solution.	6	MSF Design Process
Analyze impact of technology migration.	1	MSF Enterprise Architecture Model; Creating an Enterprise Architecture
Plan physical requirements, such as infrastructure.	6 7 8 9 11	MSF Design Process Entire chapter Entire chapter Entire chapter Entire chapter
Establish application environment, such as hardware platform, support, and operating system.	6 7 8 9 11	MSF Design Process Entire chapter Entire chapter Entire chapter Entire chapter
Identify organizational constraints, such as financial situation, company politics, technical acceptance level, and training needs.	1 3 5	What is Architecture?; MSF Enterprise Architecture Model The MSF Development Team Model Envisioning Process
Establish schedule for implementation of solution	6	MSF Design Process; Project Plan Approved Milestone and Its Deliverables
Identify audience	5	Envisioning Process
Analyze security requirements.		
Identify roles of administrator, groups, guests, and clients.	11	Access Security
Identify impact on existing environment.	11	Entire chapter
Establish fault tolerance	10	Scaling the Production Environment
Plan for maintainability.	11	Authentication Security
Plan distribution of security database.	11	Authentication Security
Establish security context.	11	Authentication Security
Plan for auditing.	11	Auditing
Identify level of security needed.	5 11	Envisioning Process Entire chapter
Analyse existing mechanisms for security polices	11	Entire chapter

Skill being measured	Chapter	Section
Analyze performance requirements. Considerations include: transactions per time slice; bandwidth; capacity; interoperability with existing standards; peak versus average requirements; response-time expectations; existing response-time characteristics; and barriers to performance.	2 10	Enterprise Application Architecture Performance Validation; Scaling the Production Environment
Analyze maintainability requirements. Considerations include: breadth of application distribution; method of distribution; maintenance expectations; location and knowledge level of maintenance staff; and impact of third-party maintenance agreements.	3 10 13	The MSF Development Team Model Managing the Development Environment Product Deployment
Analyze extensibility requirements. Solution must be able to handle the growth of functionality.	10	Performance Validation; Scaling the Production Environment
Analyze availability requirements. Considerations include: hours of operation; level of availability; geographic scope; and impact of downtime.	10	Performance Validation; Scaling the Production Environment
Analyze human factors requirements. Considerations include: target users; localization; accessibility; roaming users; Help; training requirements; physical environment constraints; and special needs.	3 7	The MSF Development Team Model Determining the User Interface; Basics of Interface Design; Creating the UI
Analyze the requirements for integrating a solution with existing applications. Considerations include: legacy applications; format and location of existing data; connectivity to existing applications; data conversion; and data enhancement requirements.	9	What is the Data Service Layer?; Microsoft Data Access Components (MDAC); Choosing the Right Data Access Technology; Accessing Host-Based Data; DCOM Connector for SAP
Analyze existing methodologies and limitations of a business. Considerations include: legal issues; current business practices; organization structure; process engineering; budget; implementation and training methodologies; quality control requirements; and customer's needs.	1 3 4	MSF Enterprise Architecture Model; Creating an Enterprise Architecture The MSF Development Team Model Model for Application Development; Unified Process; MSF Development Process Model
Analyze scalability requirements. Considerations include: growth of audience; growth of organization; growth of data; and cycle of use.	1 3 4 5	MSF Enterprise Architecture Model; Creating an Enterprise Architecture The MSF Development Team Model Model for Application Development; Unified Process; MSF Development Process Model Envisioning Process; Risk Management Process

Defining the Technical Architecture for a Solution

Skill being measured	Chapter	Section
Given a business scenario, identify which solution type is appropriate. Solution types are single-tier, two-tier, and N-tier.	1 2	What is Architecture?; MSF Enterprise Architecture Model Enterprise Application Model
Identify which technologies are appropriate for implementation of a given business solution. Considerations include: technology standards such as EDI, Internet, OSI, COMTI, and POSIX; proprietary technologies; technology environment of the company, both current and planned; selection of development tools; and type of solution, such as enterprise, distributed, centralized, and collaborative.	1 2 7 8 9 11	What is Architecture?; MSF Enterprise Architecture Model Enterprise Application Model Entire chapter Entire chapter Entire chapter Entire chapter
Choose a data storage architecture. Considerations include: volume; number of transactions per time increment; number of connections or sessions; scope of business requirements; extensibility requirements; reporting requirements; number of users; and type of database.	1 2 5 6 9	What is Architecture?; MSF Enterprise Architecture Model Enterprise Application Model Envisioning Process MSF Design Process What is the Data Service Layer?
Test the feasibility of a proposed technical architecture. Demonstrate that business requirements are met. Demonstrate that use case scenarios are met. Demonstrate that existing technology constraints are met. Assess impact of shortfalls in meeting requirements.	5 6 10	Vision Approved Milestone and Its Deliverables MSF Design Process; Project Plan Approved Milestone and Its Deliverables Managing the Development Environment; Testing Enterprise Applications; Performance Validation; Scaling the Production Environment
Develop appropriate deployment strategy.	3 6 13	The MSF Development Team Model MSF Design Process Product Deployment

Developing the Conceptual and Logical Design for an Application

Skill being measured	Chapter	Section
Construct a conceptual design that is based on a variety of scenarios and that includes context, workflow process, task sequence, and physical environment models. Types of applications include: SDI, MDI, console, and dialog desktop applications; two-tier, client/server, and Web applications; N-tier applications; and collaborative applications.	5 6	Vision Approved Milestone and Its Deliverables MSF Design Process
Given a conceptual design, apply the principles of modular design to derive the components and services of the logical design.	5 6	Vision Approved Milestone and Its Deliverables MSF Design Process

Skill being measured	Chapter	Section
Incorporate business rules into object design.	5	Vision Approved Milestone and Its Deliverables
	6	MSF Design Process
Assess the potential impact of the logical design on performance, maintainability, extensibility, scalability, availability, and security.	10	Entire chapter
	11	Entire chapter

Developing Data Models

Skill being measured	Chapter	Section
Group data into entities by applying normalization rules.	9	Data Modeling
Specify the relationships between entities.	9	Data Modeling
Choose the foreign key that will enforce a relationship between entities and will ensure referential integrity.	9	Data Modeling
Identify the business rules that relate to data integrity.	8	Designing MTS Packages
Incorporate business rules and constraints into the data model.	9	Data Modeling
Identify appropriate level of denormalization.	9	Data Modeling
Develop a database that uses general database development standards and guidelines.	9	Data Modeling

Designing a User Interface and User Services

Skill being measured	Chapter	Section
Given a solution, identify the navigation for the user interface.	6	MSF Design Process
	7	Determining the User Interface; Basics of Interface Design; Creating the UI
Identify input validation procedures that should be integrated into the user interface.	9	Data Modeling
Evaluate methods of providing online user assistance, such as status bars, ToolTips, and Help files.	7	Determining the User Interface; Basics of Interface Design; Creating the UI
Construct a prototype user interface that is based on business requirements, user interface guidelines, and the organization's standards.	1	Modern Software Principles
	4	The Four MSF Phases and their Major Milestones
	5	Vision Approved Milestone and Its Deliverables
Establish appropriate and consistent use of menu-based controls. Establish appropriate shortcut keys (accelerated keys).	7	Determining the User Interface; Basics of Interface Design; Creating the UI

Skill being measured	Chapter	Section
Establish appropriate type of output.	7	Determining the User Interface; Basics of Interface Design; Creating the UI

Deriving the Physical Design

Skill being measured	Chapter	Section
Assess the potential impact of the physical design on performance, maintainability, extensibility, scalability, availability, and security.	6	MSF Design Process
	9	Microsoft Data Access Components (MDAC)
	10	Entire chapter
	11	Entire chapter
	12	Development Process
Evaluate whether access to a database should be encapsulated in an object.	8	Designing MTS Packages
	9	What is the Data Service Layer; Microsoft Data Access Components (MDAC); Choosing the Right Data Access Technology
Design the properties, methods, and events of components.	6	MSF Design Process
	8	Designing MTS Packages

The Microsoft Certified Professional Program

The Microsoft Certified Professional (MCP) program provides the best method to prove your command of current Microsoft products and technologies. Microsoft, an industry leader in certification, is on the forefront of testing methodology. Its exams and corresponding certifications are developed to validate your mastery of critical competencies as you design and develop, or implement and support, solutions with Microsoft products and technologies. Computer professionals who become Microsoft certified are recognized as experts and are sought after industry-wide.

The MCP program offers five certifications, based on specific areas of technical expertise:

- **Microsoft Certified Professional** Demonstrates in-depth knowledge of at least one Microsoft operating system. Candidates may pass additional Microsoft certification exams to further quality their skills with Microsoft BackOffice integrated family of server software products, development tools, or desktop programs.

- **Microsoft Certified Professional - Specialist: Internet** MCPs with a specialty in the Internet, who are qualified to plan security, install and configure server products, manage server resources, extend servers to run CGI scripts or ISAPI scripts, monitor and analyze performance, and troubleshoot problems.

- **Microsoft Certified Systems Engineer (MCSE)** Qualified to effectively plan, implement, maintain, and support information systems in a wide range of computing environments with Windows 98, Windows NT, and the BackOffice.

- **Microsoft Certified Solution Developer (MCSD)** Qualified to design and develop custom business solutions with Microsoft development tools, technologies, and platforms, including Office and BackOffice.

- **Microsoft Certified Trainer (MCT)** Instructionally and technically qualified to deliver Microsoft Official Curriculum through a Microsoft Authorized Technical Education Center (ATEC).

Microsoft Certification Benefits

Microsoft certification, one of the most comprehensive certification programs available for assessing and maintaining software-related skills, is a valuable measure of an individual's knowledge and expertise. Microsoft certification is awarded to individuals who have successfully demonstrated their ability to perform specific tasks and implement solutions with Microsoft products. Not only does certification provide an objective measure for employers to consider, but it also provides guidance for what an individual should know to be proficient. And as with any skills assessment and benchmarking measure, certification brings a variety of benefits: to the individual, and to employers and organizations.

Technical Support

Every effort has been made to ensure the accuracy of this book and the contents of the supplemental CD-ROM. If you have comments, questions, or ideas regarding this book or the supplemental CD-ROM, please send them to Microsoft Press using either of the following methods:

E-mail:

tkinput@microsoft.com

Postal Mail:

Microsoft Press
Attn: Analyzing Requirements and Defining Solution
Architectures Editor
One Microsoft Way
Redmond, WA 98052-6399

Microsoft Press provides corrections for books through the World Wide Web at the following address:

http://mspress.microsoft.com/support/

Please note that product support is not offered through these mail addresses. For further information regarding Microsoft software support options, please connect to www.microsoft.com/support/ or call Microsoft Support Network Sales at (800) 936-3500.

About the Authors

Tim Landgrave

Tim Landgrave founded KiZAN Corporation in 1991 as a software development company specializing in client/server development using Microsoft technology. Since then Tim has architected, developed, and deployed systems using key Microsoft technologies. In addition to his role as CEO of KiZAN, Tim has also been active as a Microsoft Regional Director, hosting events such as Developer Days and evangelizing the Microsoft development platform message to companies looking to build robust, multi-layer applications on Microsoft platforms. Before starting KiZAN, Tim was Director of Technology for The Cobb Group, where he started their developer journal group, and served as editor-in-chief of major technical newsletters, including *Inside Visual Basic, Inside Visual C++,* and the *Microsoft Networking Journal.*

Bruce Maples

Bruce Maples' involvement with computers began in 1984 when he got his first Apple II, on which he quickly learned how to write code and hack the operating system. Since that time, he has written applications in languages from dBase to Visual Basic, has taught a wide range of computer classes, and has been active as a consultant and writer. He currently writes for a number of publications and conducts training across the country. He lives in Louisville, Kentucky with his wife, Nina, and his sons, Griffin and Benjamin, where, in addition to his computer work, he is active in church life and community affairs.

Scott F. Wilson

Scott Wilson helped build KiZAN Corporation into a successful systems architecture company specializing in multi-layer development and network services using Microsoft technology. Since then, Scott has designed enterprise architectures, network systems infrastructures, and enterprise applications for KiZAN's clients. For the last three years, he has helped large organizations architect and deploy Web-based applications using Microsoft's MCIS and Site Server Commerce products. In addition to his role as CTO of KiZAN, Scott has been active as a Microsoft Certified Trainer and Microsoft Certified Systems Engineer since 1995. He can be reached at scottw@kizan.com.

KiZAN Corporation

This course was developed for Microsoft Press by KiZAN Corporation. KiZAN was the first Microsoft Solution Provider Partner of the Year in 1995. As a Microsoft Solution Provider Partner and Microsoft Certified Technical Education Center (CTEC), KiZAN works closely with customers to provide the most comprehensive solutions on the market today. KiZAN offers all the Microsoft products and services from desktop applications and packaged applications to advanced enterprise solutions using Microsoft's BackOffice products. These products and solutions are complemented by a full array of services, including system engineering consulting, multi-layer and client/server architectural design, multi-layer application development, project planning, implementation services, and technical and desktop training in public or private classes.

KiZAN has created a number of developer training courses for Microsoft. These include traditional instructor-led courses, self-paced kits, and computer-based (CD-ROM) multimedia titles. In association with their partner company, CustomCourseware.com, KiZAN offers complete conversion and customization services for existing courseware for use in an online or instructor-led training environment.

Contact KiZAN Corporation at:

- E-mail: info@kizan.com
- Web site: www.kizan.com

KiZAN staff members who developed this course include:

Project Editor:	Scott F. Wilson
Authors:	Tim Landgrave Bruce Maples Scott F. Wilson
Application Development:	Kevin Benton Chris Marrow
Technical Contributions:	Damien Kalvar Whitney Roberts John Ross Mark Solomon Steve Staten Craig Stein
Editing Contributions:	Allan McGuffey

Editing, production, and graphic support services were provided by Online Training Solutions, Inc. (OTSI).

P A R T   1

Developing the Framework

C H A P T E R   1

Enterprise Architecture

About This Chapter

The tasks involved with today's enterprise information technology (IT) work require an enterprise architecture. In this chapter, we examine the need for application and infrastructure guidance at an enterprise level. We begin by suggesting that systems be implemented with an architecture-first process. Then we introduce the Microsoft Solutions Framework (MSF). We move on to examine the MSF Enterprise Architecture Model and its Business, Application, Information, and Technology Perspectives. We also point out that the four primary goals of an enterprise architecture are that it be integrated, iterative, actionable, and prioritized. Finally, we discuss how to begin the enterprise architecture process and continue to deliver systems and applications while the architecture process is underway.

The principles and guidelines we provide in this chapter are based on our own experience with the creation of application architectures and the implementation of enterprise applications, together with Microsoft Solutions Framework materials.

Upon completion, you will be able to:
- Describe the merits of architecture-first designs.
- Describe the importance of architecture to IT and application success.
- Describe the four perspectives that make up the MSF Enterprise Architecture Model.
- List the elements of each perspective.
- Describe the benefits of a planned enterprise architecture.

What Is Architecture?

For the purposes of this book, architecture is a coherent, unified technology plan. IT architecture emphasizes a holistic framework of process, interactivity, and technology, intensely focused on achieving business goals and objectives. An IT architect is a person who designs and guides a technology plan that is coherent and unified. In other words, both the architecture and the architect provide direction for IT work. By concentrating on these essentials, an *architecture-first approach* endeavors to achieve results that can be implemented effectively, while minimizing artificial complexity.

A common example of the need for direction is articulated in a scene from Lewis Carroll's *Alice's Adventures In Wonderland*:

> *"Would you tell me, please, which way I ought to go from here?" asked Alice.*
>
> *"That depends a good deal on where you want to get to," said the Cat.*
>
> *"I don't much care where," said Alice.*
>
> *"Then, it doesn't matter which way you go," said the Cat.*

This example directly speaks to the need of an architecture-first approach for planning, building, and managing almost any business activity. So many companies are like Alice, trying to get somewhere without really knowing where they are trying to go.

At the heart of this architecture-first approach are the simple questions we can ask regarding any project:

- How did we get to this point?
- How do we know where we are going?
- Why are we going there?
- What tasks are necessary to get there?
- In what order should we do the tasks?
- How will we know when we have arrived?
- What else do we need to consider?

An architecture-first approach strives to answer these questions early in the life of a project, and to continually provide a reference guide throughout the project. Additionally, an architecture-first approach helps an organization strike the appropriate balance between:

- Business-driven requirements.
- Critical design decisions.
- Human-resource requirements over the life of the project.
- Financial impacts on the organization.

Making a Commitment to Architecture-First Design and Practice

Unfortunately, many organizations honor architecture, as well as project planning, in word but not in deed. Instead of developing a clear idea of where they want to go, they simply go everywhere, hoping that where they wind up will be better than where they currently are. Many senior managers, in fact, feel that the job won't get done if they take time to plan.

The only way to break out of this cycle is if all management within an organization makes a commitment to an architecture-first approach. This approach includes the simple concept that time spent designing and planning up-front will save time in the end.

Note This commitment to planning does not mean that work cannot be started until the architecture is established. As we explain in this and succeeding chapters, we advocate a *plan-while-building approach*. In other words, planning, building, and managing constantly follow one another in an iterative fashion, often overlapping to some extent.

Being committed to architecture-first design and practice means that all three parts of the IT task—planning, building, and managing—are based on a coherent, higher-level architecture; that the architecture has been worked out before the start of the coding work; and that the architecture drives the work. Before this level of architecture can take place for an individual application, higher level architecture and planning must occur for the entire enterprise.

When an organization makes a commitment to architecture-first design and practice, the natural inclination of its IT department is to start at the beginning, designing an architecture for the entire enterprise. Enthusiasm is high, and the IT group thinks nothing is going to stop it from building a completely comprehensive document and then recreating the entire IT environment to match.

When the IT department takes a serious look at what is involved, though, they begin to have second thoughts. The project begins to look more and more daunting. Finally, they have to ask themselves, "Is there any way we can get a handle on this? And considering the work involved, why should we try?"

The majority of our book strives to answer the first question, so let's quickly address the second. Why should busy IT professionals spend the time necessary to design and implement an enterprise architecture? The answer is simple: Every organization has an enterprise architecture whether or not it is planned. The organization can assess and plan, or be a victim of a random enterprise architecture that doesn't necessarily meet its business needs. Only by doing the work involved in building an enterprise architecture can IT professionals gain some control.

Challenges of the IT Environment

Consider for a moment the challenges that characterize the business environment today. We face rapidly changing domestic and global market conditions, accompanied by diverse and complex products and services. Management expects shorter product development cycles and faster times-to-market. To remain competitive, we must continually learn to understand an increasingly complex technology environment. To deal with these challenges, organizations may respond with the following measures (see Figure 1.1):

- Streamlining business processes.

- Flattening organizational hierarchies.

- Introducing complex technologies at a rapid rate.

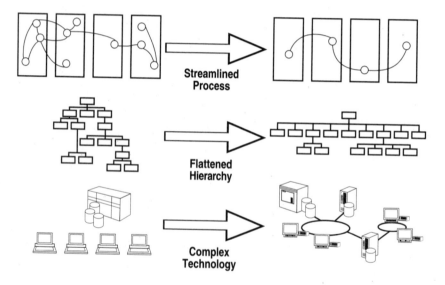

Figure 1.1   Organizational evolutions

As the pace of operational changes accelerates, information systems must be flexible enough to quickly support them. Consider what's expected of the typical IT organization in this new and rapidly changing environment:

- **Dual focus** It must be specific and intensely concentrated on the needs of users, while maintaining focus on the business vision.

- **Flexibility** It must be able to accommodate a constantly shifting technology landscape, at the same time coping with the pressure for "better, faster, cheaper—now!"

For the organization to remain competitive, the IT department must be responsive to changes in business and user requirements. They must be able to create applications quickly, and be able to modify them just as quickly. Flexible, incremental development methods that produce reusable code and reusable components are the key to an organization's success.

The challenge to most organizations is to respond quickly and incrementally to business needs at a relatively low financial cost. Whether an organization is trying to establish a competitive advantage by beating a competitor to market, to increase service levels and responsiveness to customer needs, or to deliver a less expensive product without sacrificing quality, IT plays a vital role. Key organizational functions such as product development, marketing, manufacturing, finance, and sales all require IT as an underlying foundation. These functions also require IT to seamlessly integrate and cooperate across the organization's functional or operational boundaries.

Additionally, organizations face enormously challenging application requirements. New applications are extremely demanding for a multitude of reasons, including:

- **Broad distribution** Applications may be distributed worldwide, via wide area networks (WANs) or the Internet.

- **Broad user base** There are potentially millions of users for these applications. In many cases, these users will be unknown to and outside the control of the company's IT organization.

- **Connection limitations** Connections between users and applications might be temporary or of limited bandwidth. For example, employees might use portable computers that are connected to the corporate network only part of the time. Customers might connect to the application via the Internet over a low-speed modem.

- **Storage limitations** Data required by applications might be stored on multiple computers. These computers might be geographically dispersed and might not be available at all times.

- **Hardware limitations** Existing hardware and software investments must be leveraged. Users might have different types of computers with differing capabilities. Data might be stored in different types of databases. New applications might need to interact with existing applications running on different platforms.

Add all these factors together, along with the number of systems in the environment, and anyone would agree that distributed application development is just plain *hard*. The combination of business problems, technology evolution, and the organization's existing complex applications drives a consistent set of key concerns for senior IT professionals. We can sum up these concerns as three imperatives:

- **Deliver business value** Tightly align IT to business objectives.
- **Control costs** Squeeze every ounce of leverage from existing IT investments and make careful and informed future investments.
- **Sense and respond** Improve the cross-functional capabilities within the organization and extend those capabilities outside the organization to reach customers, suppliers, and partners more effectively.

How Enterprise Architecture Responds to IT Challenges

Technology implementation can either accelerate or impede an organization's ability to adapt to changing business conditions. Today's IT solutions must fully meet business requirements, be sufficiently flexible to integrate new and emerging technologies, and yet not compromise the functionality and daily operations of the existing enterprise architecture. With these concepts in mind, any approach to enterprise architecture should:

- Place first priority on addressing business needs.
- Provide a technical solution that focuses on making the simple things easy and the hard things possible and cost-effective.
- Deliver the flexibility required to adapt to the natural evolution of technology and business.

A key factor in achieving these goals is to establish a comprehensive, high-level enterprise architecture. The enterprise architecture provides the framework for an ongoing process of discovery and refinement. This process is implemented as a series of projects geared towards getting the entire organization's IT infrastructure and application systems to their desired future state. This approach creates a strong framework for aligning IT strategy and day-to-day activities with the overall business strategy.

Goal of Enterprise Architecture

As we noted in the opening discussion about architecture, providing a direction or goal is an important part of the architecture task. The goal when developing an enterprise architecture is:

To provide a logically consistent plan of activities and coordinated projects that guide the progression of an organization's application systems and infrastructure. The plan should move incrementally from the current state to a desired future state based on current and projected business objectives and processes.

Let's examine this goal in more detail:

- **Logically consistent** When two or more parts of the architecture are compared, they fit together logically.
- **Activities and coordinated projects** The architecture addresses both ongoing activities and stand-alone projects.
- **Progression from current state to desired future state** The architecture does more than simply describe the current situation. It also offers a vision of the desired future situation. Most importantly, the architecture articulates a clear path to get from the current situation to the desired situation through versioned releases.
- **Current and projected business objectives and processes** An enterprise architecture plan is ultimately worthless if it is not built upon both the current business situation and the projected business plan and processes. It is possible, however, for the business plan to be shaped by developments in the IT arena, such as global Internet access, which is driving the creation of electronic commerce divisions within companies.

It is important to remember these points while considering the details of enterprise architecture in the rest of this chapter. It's also important to use these points to analyze the completeness of any enterprise architecture plan.

Microsoft Solutions Framework (MSF)

MSF is a collection of models, principles, and practices that helps organizations be more effective in their creation and use of technology to solve their business problems. It helps by providing measurable progress and rigorous guidance that is flexible enough to meet the changing needs of an organization. The core building blocks for this MSF-based solutions guidance are the six major models:

- MSF Enterprise Architecture Model
- MSF Team Model for Application Development
- MSF Process Model for Application Development
- MSF Risk Management Model
- MSF Design Process Model
- MSF Application Model

We describe each model briefly on the following page. In later chapters we show how they can be applied to application development projects.

MSF Enterprise Architecture Model

The MSF Enterprise Architecture Model provides a consistent set of guidelines for rapidly building enterprise architecture through versioned releases. The model aligns information technology with business requirements through four perspectives: Business, Application, Information, and Technology. Using this model helps shorten the enterprise architecture planning cycle.

MSF Team Model for Application Development

The MSF Team Model for Application Development (MSF Development Team Model) provides a flexible structure for organizing project teams. It emphasizes both clear roles and responsibilities and clear goals for team success, and it increases team member accountability through its team of peers approach. Its flexibility means that it can be adapted depending on the scope of the project, the size of the team, and the skills of the team members. Using this model and its underlying principles and practices helps produce more engaged, effective, resilient, and successful teams.

MSF Process Model for Application Development

The MSF Process Model for Application Development (MSF Development Process Model) provides structure and guidance through a project's life cycle that is milestone-based, iterative, and flexible. It describes the phases, milestones, activities and deliverables of an application development project and their relationship to the roles of the MSF Development Team Model. Using this model helps improve project control, minimize risk, improve quality, and shorten delivery time.

MSF Risk Management Model

The MSF Risk Management Model provides a structured and proactive way to manage project risks. It sets forth a discipline and environment of proactive decisions and actions to continuously assess what can go wrong, determine what risks are important to deal with, and then implement strategies to deal with those risks. Using this model and its underlying principles and practices helps teams focus on what is most important, make the right decisions, and be better prepared for when the unknown future becomes known.

MSF Design Process Model

The MSF Design Process Model provides a three-phase, user-centric continuum that allows for a parallel and iterative approach to design for the greatest efficiency and flexibility. Three different phases—Conceptual Design, Logical Design, and Physical Design—provide three different perspectives for three different audiences—users, the project team, and developers. Moving from Conceptual Design through Logical Design to Physical Design shows the translation of user-based scenarios to services-based components so that application features can be traced back to user requirements. Using this model helps ensure that applications are created not just for the sake of technology, but to meet business and user requirements.

MSF Application Model

The MSF Application Model provides a logical, three-tier, services-based approach to designing and developing software applications. The use of user services, business services, and data services allows for parallel development, better use of technology, easier maintenance and support, and the greatest flexibility in distribution, because the services that make up the application can reside anywhere from a single desktop to servers and clients around the world.

Presentation of MSF in This Book

Throughout this book, we use the basic concepts of MSF to provide a foundation for our discussions of enterprise architecture and enterprise application development. The MSF models and their key principles originate within the MSF team at Microsoft. In this book, we draw heavily on materials provided by the MSF team. Rather than limiting ourselves to these materials, however, we also draw on other sources and our own application development experience to round out these concepts and show how they can be applied in practical ways within an organization. When discussing MSF concepts, we try to distinguish information drawn from places other than official MSF sources wherever it is possible to do so in a way that does not detract from the readability of the text and the cohesiveness of the approach to application development we are trying to present.

MSF Enterprise Architecture Model

How does the enterprise function today? Many organizations can only tentatively answer this question. The MSF Enterprise Architecture Model gives current systems a context that can provide a rationale for the systems' existence, both current and future. Additionally, the MSF Enterprise Architecture Model can provide the foundation for the implementation of business solutions by using technology. Not only do different systems provide features and functionality of their own, but these systems can be logically combined to create an overall system that is greater than the sum of its parts. This overall effect is the desired future state of the organization's enterprise architecture, which the evolutionary implementation of the MSF Enterprise Architecture Model can provide.

As illustrated in Figure 1.2, the MSF Enterprise Architecture Model is a framework composed of four architecture perspectives: Business, Application, Information, and Technology.

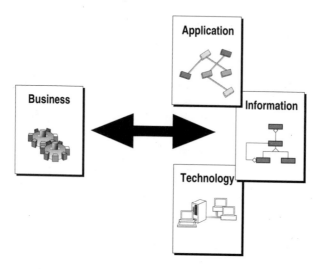

Figure 1.2   The four enterprise architecture perspectives

Business Perspective

The Business Perspective includes broad business strategies and plans for moving the organization from its current state to its desired future state. The Business Perspective describes how the business works. It includes:

- The organization's high-level goals and objectives.
- The organization's products and services.
- Business processes that embody the functions and the cross-functional activities performed by the organization.
- Major organizational structures.
- The interaction of all these elements.

Application Perspective

The Application Perspective represents the services, information, and functionality that cross organizational boundaries, linking users of different skills and functions to achieve common business objectives. It defines the enterprise application portfolio and includes:

- Descriptions of the automated services that support the business processes presented in the business architecture.

- Descriptions of the interaction and interdependencies of the organization's application systems.
- Priorities for developing new applications and revising old applications based directly on the business architecture.

Information Perspective

The Information Perspective describes what the organization needs to know to run its business processes and operations. It includes:

- Standard data models.
- Data management policies.
- Descriptions of the patterns of information consumption and production in the organization.

The Information Perspective also describes how data is bound into the workflow, including structured data stores such as databases, and unstructured data stores such as documents, spreadsheets, and presentations that exist throughout the organization. Often, the information most critical to an organization resides not only in database servers, but on the thousands of desktop computers that comprise the enterprise's active working environment.

Technology Perspective

The Technology Perspective lays out the hardware and software supporting the organization. It includes:

- Desktop and server hardware.
- Operating systems.
- Network connectivity components.
- Printers.
- Internet connectivity.
- Other necessary peripheral devices.

The Technology Perspective provides a logical, vendor-independent description of infrastructure and system components that is necessary to support the application and information perspectives. It defines the set of technology standards and services needed to execute the business mission. These standards and services include, but are not limited to:

- Topologies.
- Development environments.
- Application Programming Interfaces (APIs).

- Security.
- Network services.
- Database management system (DBMS) services.
- Technical specifications.

Four Perspectives, One Architecture

Although the MSF Enterprise Architecture Model has four perspectives, there is only one enterprise architecture. As an organization builds an enterprise architecture, it is important to remember that the architecture's value is not in any one individual perspective but in the relationships, interactions, and dependencies between the perspectives.

The development of these four architecture perspectives and the examination of their individual and collective interactions should reveal the information that an organization requires to make rational decisions about its IT priorities, projects, policies, standards, and guidelines. This information is critical for IT implementation and purchasing decisions, and provides a powerful communication tool between the organization's IT and business units.

Alignment of Business and IT Goals

Two significant problems arise for IT managers when facing software deployment and development of business applications:

- **After the fact** By the time the IT group gets involved, the fundamental business processes are already established, and the IT group misses a major opportunity to effectively apply technology.
- **Out of the business decision-making process** Because IT is disassociated from the line of business, myriad miscommunications and poor decisions are made about technology.

Organizations should focus on forming a partnership between IT and the line of business. People and processes must rest on a solid foundation before new technology that provides true business value can successfully be deployed.

When confronted with the rate of change and innovation that are inherent in high-technology industries, IT departments may become so consumed with keeping up with new technology, or so frozen with indecision, that they lose sight of the organization's purpose and vision. As a result, they may lose credibility and relevance within the entire organization. To maintain credibility and relevance, IT departments must constantly focus on applying new information technologies in ways that consistently support the organization's purpose and business vision.

The MSF Enterprise Architecture Model is a tool for ensuring the alignment of IT activities to the business operations of the organization. Business unit managers should never doubt that the IT group, and all information technologies under it, exist to support the business. On the other hand, the IT group cannot be expected to align its plans with the business units if it is not given the opportunity. It is critical that the IT and line-of-business managers share a cooperative and reciprocal relationship.

Artificial Wall

Often, an artificial wall exists between the IT and business units of an organization. We say "artificial" because it primarily results from two false assumptions made by both the business and IT communities:

- **Business false assumption: "They don't need to know"** Many business people think that they should be able to list requirements outside of a specific business context and have the IT group produce valuable solutions based solely on those requirements. An abundance of empirical evidence suggests that requirements are very difficult to meet without a contextual frame, and that generating requirements should involve a number of organizational perspectives, especially that of IT departments.

- **IT false assumption: "We already know"** Many IT people believe that, even with their limited exposure to the front-line business activities, they can "do it better." Again, empirical evidence suggests that until people actually carry out the functions of a job, they don't understand all its nuances.

For the IT group to successfully support the business groups, both groups must work to tear down this artificial wall. The IT and business groups must forge a partnership based on recognition of their common goal: satisfying the business objectives of the organization. Crucial to this objective are these considerations:

- **Business-driven requirements first** The MSF Enterprise Architecture Model's Business Perspective provides a framework for determining the impact a project must have to meet the business needs of the organization. These business needs serve to justify each project.

- **IT's understanding of business** The IT group must have an understanding of the organization's business drivers and opportunities, core processes, and business goals so that it can make rational and informed decisions about IT support activities.

- **Business's understanding of IT costs** Business unit managers must recognize that when considering the value proposition for altering existing processes or undertaking the development of new ones, true IT costs, including the cost implications of using specific information technologies, must be part of the equation.

- **IT's involvement in business decisions** Business units should involve the IT group in the development of their business cases and in the definition of changes to business processes.

- **Business's involvement in IT decisions** Investments in IT infrastructure should be presented and approved based on business, not technical, grounds.

Both business and IT managers must let go of the notion that only those people trained in their own respective disciplines can truly understand their needs. The more each group understands and experiences the "realities" of the other group, the less likely they are to perceive the other as being on an "opposing side" and the more likely they are to find common ground.

Dangers to Avoid During the Enterprise Architecture Process

As an organization defines an enterprise architecture, significant issues can seriously impede its chances of successful implementation.

"Buy" List Focus

The idea of enterprise architecture is not new. Most large organizations claim to have an enterprise architecture in place, but often what they have is no more than a simple "buy" list of approved products. A list of approved products, however, does not constitute or guarantee an effective enterprise architecture. The organization must go beyond the product list to specify the overall strategy and migration steps, as well as provide guidelines on how individual project teams should use the listed products to achieve the IT goals of the enterprise.

Lack of a Clearly Articulated Future State

Without adequate planning and a clear vision of where an organization needs to be, based on business drivers and other reasons specific and internal to the organization, introducing an enterprise architecture will not help the organization arrive at the future state it strives to reach.

For clarity, look again at the definition outlined earlier. The only way to have a *progression* is to be making *progress toward a clearly defined goal*. The opposite of progression can be regression, but it can also be walking in circles. It is imperative that an enterprise architecture plan include a clearly defined description of the desired future state.

Too Big and Too Complex to Achieve

Another common problem lies in attempting to define *all* the details of an enterprise architecture, no matter how wide or deep. The enterprise architecture can become so large that individual and enterprise-wide IT projects suffocate under the weight of their own paper. Because the architecture takes so long to develop, the problem changes before the organization can produce a solution.

Enterprise architecture debates are problematic. A typical enterprise architecture plan can be hundreds or even thousands of pages long, and take one to two years to complete. Remember that this is the time frame for the plan itself, and does not include the implementation. The size and complexity of the resulting enterprise architecture, and the time frame in which it is developed, often make it difficult to identify and prioritize key, organization-wide IT needs. The resulting projects fail to address real business problems, and the IT unit still has the problems it originally set out to solve.

No Provision for Feedback and Course Correction

Building an enterprise architecture should be a collaborative process between the users of the architecture (the project teams), the business owners, and the enterprise architecture team. Enterprise architectures are often built without any provision for feedback from individual project teams. At some point, the architecture must be moved from planning to implementation, and it is the individual project teams that drive the implementation. Without clear communication and a mechanism for feedback from the people actually doing the work, an architecture might be put into place that looks good on paper but is inappropriate or unstable.

All too frequently, business conditions and priorities change over the course of developing an enterprise architecture plan. Additionally, newer and more powerful technologies often supersede the technologies originally proposed as solutions to problems identified in the plan. If there is no opportunity for periodic feedback and course correction, the entire architectural effort is jeopardized.

Lack of Integration and Stability

Even when individual IT solutions work, they often stand alone without being an integral part of the overall enterprise architecture. Frequently, power users bring in unsubstantiated, or "cool," technologies or application features that can destabilize the architecture. This in turn causes other technologies or application systems that could significantly improve operations to suffer, because the environment is too chaotic to introduce them effectively.

Lack of Focus on Implementation

A true enterprise architecture encompasses not just the plan, but also the implementation. Application systems must be built and infrastructure must be deployed. Everything that is defined in the architecture must be implementable within reasonable constraints. Often, however, enterprise architecture efforts are not firmly based in reality.

It is acceptable to have goals that "push the envelope" within the architecture, but the basics must come first. For example, if the architecture specifies that systems consolidate onto specific platforms, it should also put into place specific migration assistance or incentives for individual project teams to support and implement the architecture.

Failure to Deliver on Immediate Business Needs

Many enterprise architecture plans lose sight of the fact that business operations must be maintained and projects must be delivered while the architecture is under development.

If the IT department offers no assistance for the organization's business requirements, the business units will implement technology and systems on their own in an attempt to survive and thrive in any way they can. Any approach to enterprise architecture must stress the delivery of key application system functionality to meet immediate business needs during the development of the architecture.

Objectives of the MSF Enterprise Architecture Model

The MSF Enterprise Architecture Model consists of a suggested process augmented with discussions of techniques and key principles. The process is designed to quickly deliver benefits to the organization and to take advantage of rapid advances in technology and changing business conditions, by using versioned project releases. A dynamic MSF Enterprise Architecture Model facilitates learning from feedback and rational decision-making. This approach improves an organization's ability to adopt and internally apply innovative technology that provides direct business value.

Note As an organization implements the MSF Enterprise Architecture Model, it's important to remember that this approach provides a roadmap that can and should be appropriately customized to reflect the specific needs of the organization or situation.

The MSF Enterprise Architecture Model has the following characteristics:

- **Integrated** Specific needs of business stakeholders, the architecture team, and individual project teams are balanced. Project teams understand both the whole system and the individual parts of the technology within their organization. Business stakeholders understand where technology objectives are aligned with business needs.

- **Iterative** The enterprise architecture is built through a succession of versioned releases.

- **Actionable** The primary goal of all enterprise architecture development is to quickly reach an interim release that can be implemented. In the meantime, project teams work to advance the architecture to the desired future state. This approach provides ample opportunity for feedback and course correction.

- **Prioritized** Efforts focus on where they can provide the most value to the business while improving overall IT efficiency. Architectural decisions are always framed to maintain support for critical business processes.

Creating an Enterprise Architecture

We have examined the four perspectives of the MSF Enterprise Architecture Model (Business, Application, Information, and Technology), and we have looked at some of the difficulties organizations encounter when using an enterprise architecture process. We have looked at the four enterprise architecture objectives (to be integrated, iterative, actionable, and prioritized), and we have pointed out the artificial walls that business and IT people often construct around themselves. At this point, these questions often arise: "How do we accomplish these goals? What steps do we need to take, and in what order?" As one exasperated IT manager exclaimed, "Just tell me where to download the Project file and Excel templates so I can get started!"

Unfortunately, it's not that simple. The enterprise architecture process is more than just a list of steps for achieving a goal. Rather, enterprise architecture is built on certain *key principles* that allow organizations to tailor the architecture to their unique business needs. Keeping the following principles in mind ensures that an enterprise architecture design will be both valued and valuable.

The Myth of an Enterprise-Wide, Project-Deep Architecture

It is not reasonable to expect to put in one massive, collective effort to produce an enterprise architecture that:

- Specifies all levels of detail, from business processes through technology selections and application functionality.
- Covers all individual projects (project-deep).
- Spans the entire enterprise (enterprise-wide).

Despite how unreasonable these expectations are, many approaches to enterprise architecture attempt the impossible. They use a horde of architects and consultants who closet themselves away for years at a time and then deliver "the answer." The problem with this approach is that by the time the answer is delivered, it is out of date. In attempting to define all things for all people, this approach severely compromises the value of any decisions.

We recommend recognizing these limitations when going into the process and taking appropriate measures to build the enterprise architecture in *successive iterations*. This approach allows the architecture to provide business value quickly, allows the gathering of feedback from actual use, and allows adjustments to be made through subsequent iterations.

Milestone-Driven Process

The MSF Enterprise Architecture Model promotes an iterative, milestone-driven process based upon a series of versioned releases to advance the organization to the desired future state. As shown in Figure 1.3, the organization can pass through different stages, which we will discuss in more detail later, as it adopts an enterprise architecture for development projects.

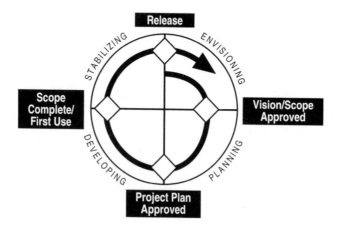

Figure 1.3   Stages of enterprise architecture adoption

Getting from Current State to Future State

Organizations are constantly forced to re-create their business processes and re-write their business rules. Business application systems must be equally adaptable and responsive to these changes. Successful architectural teams must move beyond the "big bang" approach to enterprise architecture. We have found that teams employing an ongoing, iterative approach—implicitly assuming that the architecture is never finished but remains a work-in-progress—have greater long-term success.

The enterprise architecture is established by framing the definition of an organization's current state (as-is) and where it wants to be in the future (to-be). Teams establish priorities and then undertake individual projects in order to incrementally move toward that future state. As they deliver systems and services, they constantly update the enterprise architecture plan based on feedback and an ongoing assessment of business and technology changes (see Figure 1.4).

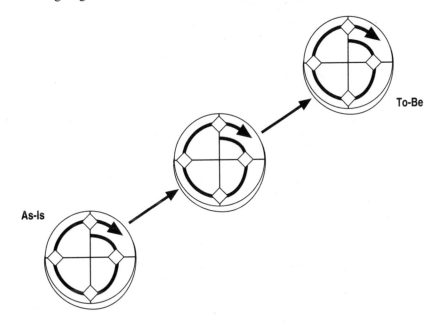

Figure 1.4   Evolution through multiple versions

Caution Stating that the enterprise architecture is never finished can kill both the hope of ever reaching implementation and the satisfaction of reaching a milestone. Applying the concept of versioned releases prevents this from happening. Each release is a part of, or a continual improvement in, the overall capabilities of the organization, and each release is a logically coherent and achievable milestone.

Value of an Iterative Enterprise Architecture

The concept of versioned releases recognizes that most enterprise architectures are too big to effectively produce at one time. It is better to prioritize the implementation of successive product versions based on business needs and then deliver completely working subsets of the envisioned future state in rapid succession.

The versioned release approach has several advantages:

- **Elimination of unnecessary requirements from the plan** Because business units and individual project teams know that there will be subsequent releases, they do not feel compelled to "throw in everything but the kitchen sink" into the first version. Each version can remain tightly focused on key issues while rapidly delivering value to the organization.

- **Ability to respond to feedback on each release** Requirements and priorities for the "complete" architecture often change once a working version of the architecture is in place and some of the infrastructure and business application development issues are solved.

- **Discovery of answers** Many organizations abhor uncertainty so intensely that they attempt to magically convert ignorance to knowledge by stating something as fact, when in reality it is unknown. This self-deception can lead to poor decisions. It can be avoided by using versioned releases and by operating under the principle of "Get it out there; get it validated; don't make it up."

Value of a Dynamic Process

An enterprise architecture is never static. It is an organic system in which each element has the following life cycle:

- Creation (some functionality, low stability).
- Development (growing quickly, not fully realized).
- Maturity (running smoothly, stable).
- Decline (struggling to maintain pace).
- Death (retirement, disposition).

To make appropriate changes to an enterprise architecture, constant attention must be paid to changes in the business and technology environment so that teams can respond accordingly by:

- Understanding which elements of the enterprise architecture must be changed.
- Recognizing where those elements are located in the architecture life cycle.

Versioned releases allow adjustment over time, responding in a controlled manner to changes in the environment. Implementing small elements of the overall architecture in successive releases allows for better management and budgeting, while still providing something useful at each release.

Philosophy of Versioned Releases

For versioned releases to work, the team must produce a first release of the architecture and then frequently produce subsequent releases that are directly responsive to the changing needs of the organization.

We can summarize the approach of versioned releases as follows:

- Smaller is better than larger.
- Understood is better than unknown.
- Progress is better than promises.

Reactive and Proactive Flows

One of the most significant problems that IT may encounter in developing an enterprise architecture is that all of the fundamental business processes have been defined and established by the time IT becomes involved. As a result, the business may miss significant opportunities to use existing technology more effectively or in new ways.

Developing an enterprise architecture is not just a reactive activity. A reactive flow is a one-way flow of decisions and input that determines how technology will be implemented in the organization. As shown in Figure 1.5, a reactive flow includes the following steps:

- Define business processes.
- Identify applications and information.
- Implement technology.

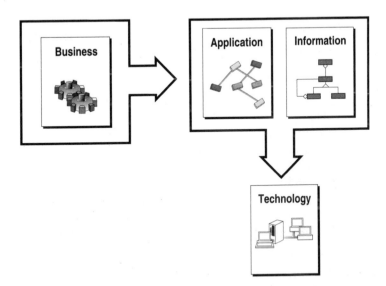

Figure 1.5   A reactive flow of decisions and input

Reactive flow is important, but it should be coupled with a proactive flow of input from the technology side to the definition of business processes. As shown in Figure 1.6, a proactive flow includes the following steps:

- Analyze technology.
- Identify applications and information.
- Define business processes.

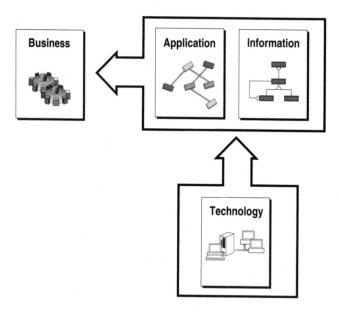

Figure 1.6   A proactive flow of decisions and input

Note Technology by itself doesn't provide value, but applying technology in innovative ways to business opportunities can provide important value. Deciding where and how to apply technology is another area where business and IT cooperation is essential. Electronic commerce is a good example of a proactive flow beginning with the Technology Perspective.

Maintaining Focus

The MSF Enterprise Architecture Model focuses IT efforts on defining and prioritizing core processes that drive the business and that are therefore critical to the organization. Support for these processes should form the foundation of the enterprise architecture. Many architectures existing today have grown without proper focus. The result is an increase in activities that are more supportive of peripheral and administrative processes than of the core processes that truly drive the business. Core processes are left languishing and are often never adequately addressed.

By focusing first on the core processes of critical areas, the MSF Enterprise Architecture Model maintains the proper perspective as the architecture is first established and then begins to evolve. Each versioned release is driven by the need to be implementable. This requirement reduces the time spent on "ivory tower" dreaming, and recognizes the need to look to the future and plan accordingly.

Enterprise Architecture and Individual Projects

The enterprise architecture, as illustrated in Figure 1.7, coordinates every project the organization undertakes. The enterprise architecture defines opportunities and constraints that:

- Achieve consistency.
- Leverage resources.
- Align infrastructure and application systems with business goals across the enterprise.

The enterprise architecture should therefore be the basis for IT strategic planning. It helps define the domain of application systems and infrastructure development by addressing core business processes and the technologies available to automate them. This big-picture view is especially critical when applications will run concurrently or share resources.

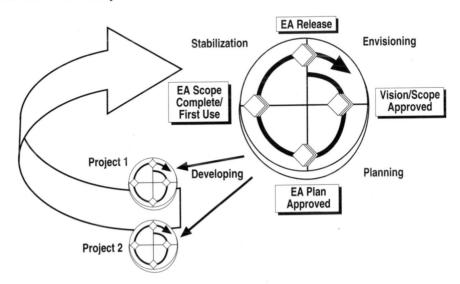

Figure 1.7   Coordination of individual projects by the enterprise architecture

The enterprise architecture is more than a planning tool. It also defines the development and operation of applications and the deployment of infrastructure. This can greatly benefit the organization by assuring that:

- Proposed applications are aligned with broader business objectives.
- The targeted technology is among those supported.
- Applications can be operated efficiently after a technology is deployed.

The enterprise architecture establishes the business and technological domains within which individual projects should be designed and deployed.

Planning While Building and Building While Planning

Organizations by their very nature often dictate top-down decision-making, especially where it relates to establishing business policy or strategic planning. When developing an enterprise architecture, the organization can impose standards from above, but as shown in Figure 1.8, the architecture should also be refined and expanded from below, using input from specific individual projects.

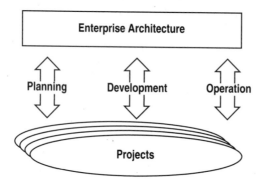

Figure 1.8   The enterprise architecture planning structure

It was once conventional wisdom to construct a model of the entire enterprise before proceeding with individual IT projects. To assure consistency of data definitions, interfaces, and business processes across the enterprise, each project would be neatly carved out of the enterprise model. However, this approach to architecture planning often broke down because it assumed that all the details were attainable and known at the start of the planning process. We now know from experience that this assumption is false. The enterprise architecture should not be defined in a vacuum, but should reflect information discovered by actually building solutions. Using versioned releases that incorporate feedback from teams and users must result in progressive refinement of the architecture. Otherwise, a rapidly changing business environment could quickly overtake an organization's ability to both complete models at the enterprise level and deploy projects before business changes make the models invalid.

Summary

In this chapter, we began by describing *architecture* as a coherent, unified technology plan. We noted that architecture should focus on business goals and objectives and provide direction for IT. We then discussed the need for both business unit and IT managers to make a commitment to architecture-first design and practice.

We examined the challenges facing the IT organization in today's rapidly changing business environment and concluded that the only sane response to such an environment is a well-designed enterprise architecture. We gave this definition of enterprise architecture:

> *A logically consistent plan of activities and coordinated projects that guide the progression of an organization's application systems and infrastructure. The plan should move from the current state to a desired future state based on current and projected business objectives and processes.*

We introduced MSF and discussed the MSF Enterprise Architecture Model, which is based on four perspectives (Business, Applications, Information, and Technology) and has four goals (to be integrated, iterative, actionable, and prioritized). We noted the importance of aligning enterprise architecture with the business goals of the organization and discussed the wall that can exist between IT and the business units.

Finally, we discussed the relationships between the organization's strategic plan, its enterprise architecture, and individual application projects.

Review

1. What common IT challenges can an enterprise architecture address?
2. What are the primary goals of an enterprise architecture?
3. List the phases of enterprise architecture adoption.
4. Describe the four perspectives of the MSF Enterprise Architecture Model.
5. How can applications be delivered while an enterprise architecture is under development?

Developing an Enterprise Architecture

Tim O'Brien, the Network Manager for Ferguson and Bardell, poked his head into the CIO's office. "You wanted to see me, Dan?" he started to say, and then realized that the office was empty.

He was turning to leave when he heard a scuffling noise, followed by grunting and more scuffling. Either Dan Shelly had trapped a gorilla under his desk, or there was someone in his office.

Tim advanced into the room slowly, not wanting to be too far from the exit because of the gorilla possibility. He heard the grunting again and realized it came from between the desk and the credenza. He moved around the desk, and there, sitting on the floor, was his boss.

Dan pulled a cardboard box from the bottom of the credenza, then grunted as he lifted out a stack of manila folders and dropped them into his lap. He scanned the titles of the folders and glanced into some of them, but apparently couldn't find what he was looking for. With a gesture of disgust, he added the folders to a growing pile beside him and reached for another set.

Tim couldn't remember when he had ever seen a CIO in such a position. "But, that's Dan," he thought. Not much for pretense when there was work to be done. Tim leaned against the wall and grinned. "I've already cleaned all the lottery tickets out of there, if that's what you're looking for."

Without looking up, Dan replied, "Huh! Wish what I was looking for was as easy to find as a winning lottery ticket." He looked at the last folder in the box, made another sound of disgust, and threw it onto the stack on the floor. Getting up and brushing himself off, he turned to Tim. "Is there anywhere else in this building where they might have stashed information about EA?"

Tim prided himself on keeping up with the industry and its acronyms, but this one stumped him. He knew ET, CNA, and a bunch of others that were close, but EA? Not a clue. He decided to play along. "Uhm, which EA would that be, Dan?"

"The one for Ferguson and Bardell, of course," replied Dan as he put the folders away and kicked the box back into the credenza. Straightening up, he saw the confusion on Tim's face and said, without condescension, "Enterprise Architecture, Tim. I'm looking for something on Ferguson and Bardell's Enterprise Architecture."

"Oh, *that*," said Tim, relieved he didn't have to guess anymore. Of course, he still had to pretend that he knew what it meant. "I don't think we have one of those."

Dan laughed. "No, Tim, we have one. We just don't seem to have it documented anywhere. Which, by the way, I suspected all along, and which is why I asked you to stop by."

He shut the credenza door and sat down at his desk, motioning for Tim to sit opposite him. "Here's the situation, Tim. We're going to be starting some major projects around here over the next year or so. Before we can start, though, we need to get an idea of what we have and why we have it. In short, we need to document our enterprise architecture, or at least make a first cut at it."

Dan pulled a folder out of his desk and opened it. "I'm putting together an interdisciplinary team that is going to take no more than two months to do a first draft of our EA and to recommend our first set of projects." He glanced at his calendar and said, "Today is February 22. The kickoff is next Monday, March 1. I want someone from your area, someone sharp who knows our technology infrastructure well, and whom you would like to put on an important project—either because he or she needs the experience, or likes a challenge. Can you think of someone who meets those criteria?"

Tim grinned. "Well, I know one guy who fits that profile exactly: sharp, knows the place, likes a challenge—me!"

But Dan shook his head. "No, Tim, you're not the right person for this team. I want someone else from your group." Seeing the crestfallen look on Tim's face, Dan continued in a more gentle tone, "Don't be too disappointed, Tim. I've got another project coming up that's going to be both big and important, and your name is already on the list."

Tim brightened up somewhat when he heard that. "That's good. I wouldn't want the young bucks to get all the credit around here!" He and Dan both laughed; Tim's youth was a regular source of kidding around the department.

Tim thought a moment and then said, "There's that woman we added last fall, about the time you came aboard. You know, the one whose name you never can get right."

"You mean Jenny? Jenny Flute, or Jenny Alto, or … shoot, what is her name?"

"Jenny Sax, Dan—Sax, like saxophone. She's doing good work with the network on her shift, and I've noticed that she has already memorized almost all the fixed IP addresses we have. She seems to have a knack for detail and for documentation, and—well, her *brain* just seems better organized than most of ours. If I understand what you're looking for, I think she would be perfect."

"She sounds like it," said Dan. "Can you spare her for this? It will mean about ten hours a week, possibly more."

"It'll mean some adjustments, but we'll handle it. Besides, it'll make her a better resource later on, and it's only for two months."

Dan was pleased at Tim's response. It was exactly what he had hoped his young Network Manager would say. Tim was already showing the kind of take-care-of-your-people attitude that made good leaders. Dan stood and walked Tim to the door of his office. "Thanks for your willingness to help out, Tim. Ask Jenny to stop by later today so I can go over the assignment with her. And be watching your e-mail as well. I'll be announcing the other big project within the next week or so."

As Tim said goodbye and left, Dan stood in the doorway of his office, thinking. "That's one good one on the team," he mused. "Sure hope the other managers see the value in this and send me good people as well. Otherwise," he reflected as he turned back to his desk, "this EA project is going to be like lots of others I've seen—all technology and no business."

EA Kickoff

By the kickoff meeting for Ferguson and Bardell's Enterprise Architecture Project, Dan had stopped worrying about whether he was going to get good people for the team. Apparently, the other department heads had wanted to impress the new CIO, and as a result, sent Dan some of their best and brightest. In fact, Dan's new worry was whether all the egos and opinions would fit around the table in his office.

Jenny showed up early. "Not like her boss!" thought Dan with a grin as he welcomed her. Next in the door was Kevin Kennedy, a management fast-tracker sent over by the CEO. Kevin was on the firm's long-range planning committee, where he'd established a reputation for both insightful analyses and the willingness to share them.

Right behind Kevin came Jo Brown, the Assistant COO for Ferguson and Bardell. Jo had been heavily involved in the firm's Y2K effort, and as such had extensive knowledge of the firm's application portfolio. In addition, she was known for her sharp wit and even sharper memos, especially if someone wasn't following the Procedures Manual.

As the group was taking their places around the table, in strolled Dr. Richard Kaplan, who was somewhat of an enigma at Ferguson and Bardell. Dick's first contact with the company had been as part of a consulting team in the late 1980's, doing an analysis of the firm's data storage. Something about him had impressed the IT Director at the time, who had later hired him and stuck him in the development area as an "analyst." Dick had proceeded to teach himself data modeling and data warehouse technology and was often used in the early stages of development projects. He was something of a loner, and seen by some as not too bright because of it. Dan, intrigued to find a Ph.D. working in development, had once asked to borrow Dick's dissertation, which was titled "The Epistemology of Kant: Based on Etymological Studies of His Later Writings." After reading only a few pages, Dan knew that Dick Kaplan was no dunce.

"Morning, all," said Dick, casually putting his pipe in his jacket pocket as he took the last chair. "Sorry if I've held things up."

"No, we were just starting, Dick. Glad you could make it," replied Dan, handing Dick the last of the notebooks he had been passing around. "Did Bill have any problem letting you go to work on this?"

"Well, he groused about it a little, but I gauged the level to be about a 1 on the Bill-O-Meter, so I think it's okay."

Dan laughed. "Jo and Kevin, I hope you had no problems either, taking this assignment."

Jo spoke first. "Not a bit, Dan. They just told me to show up here at 10:00 A.M. for an important project and to give you whatever amount of time you needed." Kevin nodded in agreement.

"Excellent," said Dan as he took his place at the table and opened up his notebook. "Since none of you are up to speed on what we are doing here, I'd like to begin by outlining what this project is about. If you'll open your notebooks, you'll find an agenda. At the top of the agenda, you see that the name of the project is Ferguson and Bardell's Enterprise Architecture Project, or F-BEAP for short. Our job, briefly, is to discover and document our current enterprise architecture and to develop a direction for the future."

Kevin had been listening to Dan closely and taking some notes. Now he stopped and asked, "Okay, I'll bite—what is an *enterprise architecture*, anyway?"

Dan smiled. "Take a look further down your agenda, Kevin. Our first task is to define EA. Normally, I would have written it on the agenda, but I wanted all of us to write it out manually, so that we could get it locked in our brains a little better and so that we could discuss it as we went."

FERGUSON AND BARDELL
ENGINEERING • ARCHITECTURE • PROJECT MANAGEMENT

The Ferguson and Bardell Enterprise Architecture Project
Meeting Agenda

Meeting Date: March 1, 1999   **Purpose:** Project Kickoff

I.   Enterprise Architecture defined

II.   Four Perspectives
- Business
- Application
- Information
- Technology

III.   Proactive versus Reactive

IV.   Versioning

V.   Q&A

VI.   Wrap-Up: Path-Forward Assignments

CHICAGO • DETROIT • MILWAUKEE • CINCINNATI • INDIANAPOLIS • LOUISVILLE

He stood and moved to the whiteboard behind the table. "I'm going to write the definition out one phrase at a time, and I want you all to copy it onto your agenda. We'll discuss it as we go. Here's the first phrase." Dan turned and wrote *A logically consistent plan of activities and coordinated projects* on the board and waited while the others copied it down.

"First of all," Dan began, "it's a plan. It's not just a document about what we are doing; it's also a plan of what we're going to do. Within the plan, it is logically consistent. In other words, if we take any two random sections of the plan, they make sense together. And, it covers both activities—things we do over and over—and stand-alone or one-time projects. Everybody got that much?"

While everybody was still writing, Jo asked, "Dan, that's awfully broad. Are we trying to document every activity and every project going on at Ferguson and Bardell?"

Dan shook his head. "An EA is primarily concerned with an organization's Information Technology plans. We're not trying to document everything throughout the company."

Kevin asked, somewhat curtly, "Then why are we all here? I don't know very much about your area."

"As you'll see in a moment, Kevin," Dan said evenly, "each of you has a viewpoint that is valuable and necessary for our EA." He turned back to the board. "Okay, let's keep going." He added *that guide the progression of an organization's application systems and infrastructure.* to the definition on the board. "See, this is the point of the plan. We will use the document this team creates as a guide for our work in the IT department, both for applications we build or buy, and for any infrastructure work we do. Any questions?"

There were none, so Dan wrote the next part of the definition on the board. *The plan should move from the current state to a desired future state...* He finished writing and then waited until the others had also finished. "This is an important point. The EA document must both describe where we are now and where we want to be. Implied in this is that we should also put a timetable on that future state; in other words, we have to lay out some goals for reaching wherever it is we want to be. Does that make sense?" Everyone nodded in agreement, so Dan continued. "Alright. This last phrase begins to explain why you are all here." He turned and completed the definition with *based on current and projected business objectives and processes.* He turned back to the group.

"You see," he said, putting down the marker and sitting back down at the table, "we in IT cannot write our own EA document. We need input from other parts of the firm so that we base our document on the business, not just on what we want to do." He turned to Kevin. "So you see, Kevin, you are here because of your work on the strategic plan of the firm. We have to know those strategic plans before we can develop both our own strategic plans for IT as well as our own tactical plans."

"What about the rest of us, Dan?" said Jo. Dick Kaplan added, "Yes, Dan, I can see the need for Kevin here, but I'm not sure I see where an Assistant COO and a jack-of-all-trades analyst are needed."

Dan replied, "Good questions, you two, but I think the next item on the agenda will help explain each of your roles more fully. Look under the first tab in your notebook."

Four Models with Perspective

In their notebooks, they saw a drawing that showed a triangle subdivided into four sections labeled Business, Application, Information, and Technology. "To be complete, an enterprise architecture is based on four models that each present a different perspective," Dan said. The descriptions of each one are on the following pages. Let's walk through them and look at what each of you are responsible for."

He turned to Kevin. "The Business Perspective is yours, Kevin. We want to know Ferguson and Bardell's broad business strategies along with the plans for carrying out those strategies. Basically, you've got to tell us both how the business works today and how the planning group envisions it working tomorrow. You've also got to help us understand the business processes we follow to run the business. It's all there in the bullet points on that page. Does this make sense to you?"

Kevin seemed somewhat more subdued as he studied the Business Perspective page in the notebook. Finally he looked up and said, "This is a big task, but I think my background with the planning group will help. I can do this."

Dan nodded. "It *is* a big task, but you wouldn't have been assigned to this team if we didn't think you could do it. And, as you'll see in a minute, we're going to cut it down to size before we leave today."

He then turned to Jo. "Your area, Jo, is the Application Perspective. You are responsible for identifying and documenting the applications and functionality that Ferguson and Bardell uses to carry out the processes that Kevin identifies. In addition, you have to find and document the interaction and interfaces *between* applications and functions. Again, it's laid out there on the page. Does it make sense to you?"

Jo nodded. "I can see now why I was chosen for this role. My work on the Y2K project, along with the application inventory we did, will be a good jumping-off point for this project."

"Absolutely," Dan said. "Don't limit yourself with that thought, though. Even without the Y2K project, your credentials speak for themselves. I suspect your knowledge of the operations of the firm would have put you here anyway."

Dan then turned to Jenny. "I bet you already know which of these is yours, Jenny," he said, smiling.

Jenny smiled back and said, "Yes, I think I do." She became more serious and continued, "And, as I look over the Technology Perspective bullets on this page, it looks like an excellent job for some sort of asset discovery tool, which, of course, we don't have. So, do I have to gather all this data by hand?"

Dan noted the frustration in her voice. "Jenny, you're right. That sort of tool would make this much easier. But I think that if you check with Jo, you'll find her Y2K hardware inventory will make a good base document for your work. Beyond that, you may be able to gather much of what you need with a well-designed e-mail questionnaire. And I'll talk with Tim about adding the asset management tool to the budget for this year." He leaned back in his chair and continued, "Make sure you don't limit your thinking to just auditing the current situation, though. Look at the definition again and match it up with the bullet points on your page. You have to document the current environment—this is true, but, you also have to plan for the environment the company should have in the future. You're responsible for thinking through and proposing whatever technologies we will need to take this firm where it wants to go strategically. Granted, all of us, including me, are going to have to agree on those technologies, and you are going to have to make a business case for them, but considering the amazing capabilities that technology is bringing us, I'd say you have the most 'fun' position on this project team."

Jenny thought about that a moment and was about to say something when Jo leaned over to her and started singing "Blue Skies." Jenny laughed and said, "Okay, okay, I guess I'm sold. I'll do the grunt work now so that I can do the soaring work later." She looked at Dan and smiled. "And when we break up here today, I'll tell Tim you want to see him about a budget adjustment."

"Fair enough," said Dan. He then turned to Dick, who had been observing the interactions with an amused expression on his face. "So, Dick, you've got the sheet that's left. What do you think of being the one to bring us the Information Perspective?"

Dick studied the Information Perspective page in his notebook and then said, "Well, it looks to me to be the most abstract of the four. I'm supposed to document what the firm 'needs to know' to carry out its processes and operations. I suppose the best way to do that will be to take the output of Kevin's and Jo's work, and then transform it into models showing the information and data needed to make it work.

"I'm also supposed to make a note of all the places we store information and what our data management policies are, if any. This sounds as if it needs to be based on what Jenny does, to some extent. So, all in all, my work is dependent on theirs to start out with. But, as we make plans for the future, their work will be somewhat based on my work, because they will have to consider what data models and data stores we already have in place and how their work will interact with those. Does that cover it, in a nutshell?"

Dan shook his head and smiled. "Dick, I asked for you because of your ability to look at disparate concepts and combine them into a coherent whole. Once again, you have explained it better than the official material did. But even though you ultimately have to base your work on the output of the others, I think you already know enough about the firm's business, processes, and technology that you can begin work on your section now. Do you agree?"

Dick nodded and then asked, "Do you want me to use UML to document this?"

"Ultimately, I will," said Dan, as the others looked puzzled. "For now, though, just begin with some simple tables of data structures and the processes they relate to. Those will be easier for us to grasp on this first version."

Proactive, Reactive, and Versions

Dan turned to the next page in the notebook. "Let's take a moment to look at the direction of process and priorities on this team. Everyone turn to page 6 in the first section."

On that page, a diagram showed the Business Perspective on one side, with an arrow flowing through the Application and Information Perspectives into the Technology Perspective. "This is how EA work is often carried out," Dan said. "First we understand and document the business strategic plans and processes, and then we build applications and information stores to carry out those plans. Finally, we implement the technology necessary to support the applications and information we need."

Kevin leaned back in his chair and said, "Cool! So I bring in the gospel from the business side, and all the rest of you use that to do your thing while I sit back and relax." He smiled smugly and said, "I'm liking this project better by the moment."

Dan thought to himself, "And I'm liking you less by the moment." Concealing his thoughts, he said to Kevin, "That's part of the picture, Kevin. But let's look at the next page for another take on it." They all turned the page and saw a drawing similar to the first, except that now the arrow flowed back from the Technology Perspective, through the Information and Application Perspectives into the Business Perspective. Dan continued, "In today's world, technology is changing so rapidly, with such important implications for business, that only a foolish business planner ignores the impact technology can have on his or her plans. In short, what we want is to have a two-way flow of information throughout all four perspectives, but especially between Technology and Business." He looked directly at Kevin. "One of your tasks, in fact, will be to take the technology possibilities we discover and feed them back into the long-range planning process of the firm. To do that, you will have to listen carefully and learn thoroughly as Jenny, Jo, and Dick share their insights. Do you think you can do that?"

Noticing the tone in Dan's voice in this last sentence, Kevin said in a somewhat more subdued manner, "I certainly will try."

"Good!" said Dan emphatically. He looked at the rest of the group. "I hope you can all see how your part fits into the whole and how important each of you is to the success of this project. Any questions about roles and perspectives?" There were none, so Dan turned the page in his notebook and said, "Alright then, let's take a look at schedule."

When the team looked at the calendar page, there were muttered expressions of disbelief. Finally, Jenny looked at Dan and said, "Dan, I know you said this was a two-month project, but after looking at the tasks before each of us, and at the overall task of the team, I don't see any way we can do this in two months. Two years, perhaps; but two months? No way." There were nods of agreement all around the table. Dan waited a moment and then responded.

"Jenny, if we were going to produce a complete EA this first time, you would be exactly right. But you see, that is the trap that so many firms fall into. They try to document everything in the first cut. In other words, they try to achieve both 100 percent breadth and 100 percent depth. What happens is that by the time they finish, much of the architecture has changed, and they have to go through the process all over again. And because they spend so much time documenting the current state, they never get to plan the future state." He paused, then stated firmly, "This team is going to avoid both mistakes. And here is how."

He moved to the whiteboard, erased it, and then drew a line across the middle. "If we draw what I just said, this line represents 100 percent breadth." He drew another line at the bottom of the board, then drew arrows between the two lines. "And this box represents 100 percent depth." He then drew a line about an inch below the top line. "This is how we keep from drowning in detail. We only shoot for about 10 percent depth this first time around." He put the marker down and continued. "For our documentation of the current situation, we aim for a fairly high level of abstraction—major processes, major infrastructure resources, primary strategic plans. It is up to each one of us to identify the key elements in our area, the ones we absolutely have to pay attention to." Moving back to the board, he then drew three boxes above the middle line. "Once we have a big picture of our current situation, we can pick out two or three big projects or processes that we want to implement, and we make those our priorities for this planning 'season.' That's the end of Version 1 of the F-BEAP."

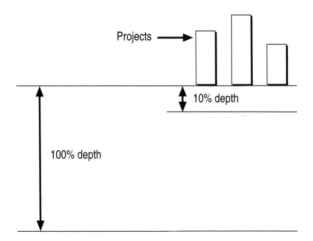

"How can we do 10 percent and still carry out our tasks?" asked Jo. "I am beginning to see the value of this work, and I'm beginning to get excited about being part of this team. But if we're going to produce some half-baked document that is too general to be of any use to anyone, I want out now. And, if all we're doing is some fuzzy justification for projects you want to do anyway, I don't want to be a part of that either."

Dan realized that Jo's reputation for forthrightness was well-deserved. He thought about her comments for a minute, thinking how to respond. Finally he said, "Jo, I'm with you. My time is too valuable to waste on a project or a document that is just fluff. And, I don't need cover for my pet IT projects. I'm a big enough boy that I can ask for what I want without help from you or anybody else." He noticed that Jo didn't seem fazed by this last comment. "Well, I'm glad to see she takes it as well as she dishes it out," he thought.

Dan went back to his place at the table. "Let me see if this analogy will help. Let's say we need to do some extensive remodeling work on our house. First we'd probably get a high-level picture, an architectural drawing or something to that effect, of the area we need to work on—the current state. Then we'd compile a list of the things we want to change, and based on what seems the most important and cost-effective, we'd decide what we should focus on first. We'd pick out two or three of the projects on our list—the ones that had to be done right away or those that we could actually do in a reasonable time frame, and we'd move forward on them. We'd get whatever additional documentation we needed; but otherwise, we'd do the process well enough to enable us to move forward *intelligently*."

"That's the key here, everyone. We want to work at a high level so we can get the first version complete in a reasonable amount of time. But the goal is to document the current state just well enough to enable us to plan for the future state, without tripping over any 'gotchas' along the way." He turned to Jo. "Does that make sense to you, Jo?"

She nodded slowly. "Yes, it does. In fact, it's an excellent analogy. When we're remodeling, we're not building a new house. We don't have to do extensive planning just to start. We're already *living* in our house. It's already built. We could go back and recreate all the plans necessary to build it again, but why? We're better off simply understanding what we have well enough that we can mold our vision of the house in the future based on the reality of the house we have today. Then, we plan how to get from here to there, with some feedback along the way from our friendly neighborhood contractor and her pal the architect," she concluded, smiling at Jenny and Dick.

"By George, I think you've got it!" said Dan, looking around at the others. "Is everybody clear on our goals for Version 1, then?" When everyone nodded, Dan turned back to the agenda in the front of his notebook. "Alright, then, we're ready for assignments."

Getting Started on F-BEAP

Dan pulled some handouts from his notebook and passed them around the table. "What I am giving you now is a listing of the things that I think are part of your EA perspective. Some of them are from the diagrams you've already seen; others I've added based on my months here at Ferguson and Bardell. You may think some are unnecessary; you may think of others you want to add. We can deal with either possibility as long as you can justify your decision to the team.

"Before our next meeting, I want each of you to make a list of all the primary items you can think of under each thing. Keeping in mind our 10% depth goal, go back and rank the items in terms of importance and whether they help to form the foundation of the element. In other words, you want to be sure to include the absolute fundamental items that must be included for Ferguson and Bardell to run. Other items may not be fundamental, but if they're important, include them, too.

Finally, make a first cut at identifying any relationships you see between the items you've listed. The more relationships you identify, the more fundamental that item probably is to the EA. Of course, there is also the possibility that an entire process or two may be unnecessary, which we hope we will see as we move through the project."

"Dan, when is our next meeting?" asked Dick, taking out his personal digital assistant to note the date and time.

"Next Monday, a week from today. That should give each of you plenty of time to write up your first draft. I'd like you to send those documents to everyone by Thursday afternoon so that we can all review them before Monday. Is that okay with everyone? Yes? Good." Dan paused and looked at each member of the team. "I know you know that this is important, and I'm looking forward to seeing what you come up with. I'll see you back here next Monday, and in the meantime, if you have any questions or need any help, just call or come by."

"Oh, I almost forgot." Dan added as everyone rose to leave. "Everyone needs to keep in mind that we are not holding off on developing projects until this EA is completed. We will continue to create new systems and refine our existing systems. Other groups will need to work with us as we architect a solution, to make sure our initial visions for the enterprise converge. Don't forget, we'll continue to refine our environment to reach the desired state and revise the vision as we go along."

C H A P T E R   2

Enterprise Applications

About This Chapter

One of the greatest challenges facing IT departments is that of quantifying and measuring improvements in software design and implementation. As a result, there has been continual disagreement among experts within the software industry about how to tackle this task, and unending pontifications and complexity measurements have been published in various journals and texts.

We start by looking at the features of modern enterprise applications, and issues that should be considered. Then we recommend ten principles that help developers create and deliver successful applications.

We move on to discuss designing large-scale, distributed, enterprise applications and the need to reduce their complexity. We recommend managing this enterprise application complexity through abstraction, which involves grouping similar requirements together into a small number of abstract categories. We suggest that organizations use the several perspectives represented by Microsoft's Enterprise Application Model, and discuss the application architecture framework provided by the separate MSF Application Model for Development.

The principles and guidelines we provide in this chapter are based on our own experience with the creation of application architectures and the implementation of enterprise applications, together with the following sources:

- Microsoft Solutions Framework
- Walker Royce's *Software Project Management: A Unified Framework*
- Adele Goldberg and Kenneth S. Rubin's *Succeeding with Objects*
- William Brown, Raphael Malveau, Hays McCormick III, and Thomas Mowbray's *AntiPatterns: Refactoring Software, Architectures, and Projects in Crisis*
- Grady Booch, James Rumbaugh, and Ivar Jacobson's *Unified Modeling Language User Guide*
- Mary Kirtland's *Designing Component-Based Applications*

Upon completion, you will be able to:

- Understand key features of enterprise applications.

- Understand modern architecture techniques.

- Identify architecture perspectives to use within a typical enterprise application project.

- Identify key principles that guide the development of enterprise applications.

- List characteristics of the MSF Application Model for Development.

Features of Enterprise Applications

An enterprise application is a business application, but more specifically, it is a *big* business application. In today's corporate environment, enterprise applications are complex, scalable, distributed, often component-based, and mission-critical. They may be deployed on a variety of platforms across corporate networks, intranets, or the Internet. They are data-centric and they typically meet stringent requirements for security, administration, and maintenance. In short, they are highly complex systems.

Designing and developing enterprise applications means meeting many separate requirements. Every development decision made to satisfy a requirement affects many other requirements, often in ways that are difficult to understand or predict. The failure to meet *any* of these requirements can mean the failure of the entire project!

Like any modern application, an enterprise application should be reliable and perform well, in addition to providing an intuitive and efficient user interface. But beyond these common qualities, it can be characterized by these three specific attributes:

- **Complex** It is a multi-user, multi-developer, multi-component application that can utilize substantial data, employ extensive parallel processing, affect network-distributed resources, and require complex logic. It can be deployed across multiple platforms and inter-operate with many other applications, and it is long-lived.

- **Business-oriented** Its purpose is to meet specific business requirements. It encodes business policies, processes, rules, and entities; is developed in a business organization; and is deployed in a manner responsive to business needs.

- **Mission-critical** It is robust enough to sustain continuous operation. It must be extremely flexible for scalability and deployment, and allow for efficient maintenance, monitoring, and administration.

These qualities clearly make the task of enterprise development challenging, and the trend is toward ever-increasing demands. The rapid improvement of computer hardware and software, combined with global economic competition—and opportunities—has created an environment in which business systems must respond quickly and deliver unparalleled levels of performance. As these demands continue, organizations must automate even more of their processes, build their software even faster, serve more and more users, and process a rapidly growing mass of data.

Aside from these challenges, the power, complexity, and rate of change of the technology used in building these corporate solutions make efficient development ever more difficult. Designing an enterprise application requires the weighing and balancing of an enormous array of application requirements, such as:

- Its business goals.
- How soon it must be delivered.
- Its budget.
- The number of people who will develop, test, and maintain it.
- The number of concurrent users it must support.
- The importance of performance and ease of use.
- The hardware it must run on.
- Where it will be deployed.
- What security is required.
- How long it will be used.

Without a systematic way to understand the relationships among these complex and often conflicting requirements, it's hard to know where to begin. What is needed is a straightforward method of reducing this complexity and providing an organized way to design and build applications that chart an optimum course among the many requirements.

Enterprise Application Architecture

As we mentioned in Chapter 1, one of the principles of modern application development is that an architecture-first process should be used to create systems. The term *application architecture* has different meanings for different people. It has been called a science, an art, and many other things that aren't quite as nice. Primary drivers behind the modern application architecture movement, including Grady Booch in his "Software Architecture and the UML" presentation at UML World 1999, have defined application architecture as encompassing a set of significant decisions about the organization of a software system. These decisions include:

- The selection of the structural elements and interfaces comprising the system.
- The system's behavior as determined by collaborations among those elements.
- The combining of structural and behavioral elements into larger subsystems.
- The architectural style that guides the system's organization.

Booch's architecture definition combined with Mary Shaw's definition of architectural style provide insight into what architecture is. In *Software Architecture: Perspectives on an Emerging Discipline* (Prentice Hall, 1996), Shaw notes that architectural style defines a family of systems in terms of a pattern of structural organization. The architectural style definition is:

- A vocabulary of components and connector types.
- A set of constraints that determine how they can be combined.
- One or more semantic models that specify how a system's overall properties can be determined from the properties of its parts.

With Booch and Shaw's concept of architecture in mind, we can gain additional insight from Booch's identification of the following characteristics of a good architecture:

- Resilient
- Simple
- Approachable
- Clear separation of concerns
- Balanced distribution of responsibilities
- Balanced economic and technology constraints

Without a doubt, constantly evolving new technologies, rapidly growing organizations and markets, ever-shrinking IT budgets, and the incredible expansion of the Internet raise new concerns and create new priorities for developers of application architectures. In this section, we look at these concerns and at ways to address them when creating an application's architecture.

Component Reuse

Given the size of enterprise applications, it makes sense to develop an application architecture that reuses as many components as possible. Reuse is an underlying assumption in most application models and should not be treated as a new technology or a technical breakthrough. Developers have been reusing code since the early days of application development. Categories of reuse include:

- Source code segments.
- Code libraries.
- Resource libraries.
- Object interfaces.
- Objects, extending objects, and so on.

The reuse principle should not be limited to application code. Following a standard development process on multiple projects or leveraging the artifact structures created during one project in another project are examples of the efficiencies to be gained through reuse. Some of the best examples of reuse are internal applications that later made the transition to commercial products and were released as toolkits, systems, or environments. Examples of this type of reuse include COM/COM+, network directory services, and Microsoft products such as ActiveX Data Objects (ADO), Microsoft Transaction Server (MTS), Microsoft Message Queuing Services (MSMQ), Exchange, and SQL Server. These products now provide developers with significant advantages when creating applications.

The cost of creating reusable object components within an organization is significant. The additional overhead of creating and supporting object components over the long-term makes object reuse an expensive proposition for most non-commercial organizations. The cost of designing for reuse is often the primary driver behind the "buy it, don't build it" mindset.

Figure 2.1, which is based on a diagram in Walker Royce's *Software Project Management: A Unified Framework*, provides general statistics on the cost and schedule impact of creating reusable object components.

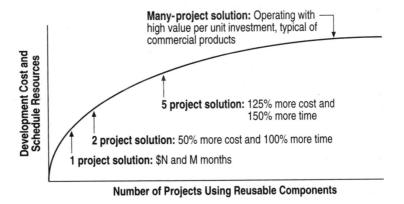

Figure 2.1 Cost and schedule investments necessary to achieve reusable components

Reuse can also occur at the level of the application itself. As we discuss later in this chapter and throughout Part 3 of this book, the N-tier, or multi-layer, architecture model provides the basis for solid internal application reuse. Separating services into multiple tiers provides interface points between the lower and upper portions of an application that can be used by any portion of the application functioning at a given layer. One of the benefits of this internal application reuse is that, as particular services need to be modified, maintaining the services interface means that other portions of the application will not require modification.

With the development of new application modeling techniques, another form of reuse has become possible: design reuse. Application logic and algorithm reuse have existed for many years. Many developers remember implementing their first search algorithms. Although they did not invent the algorithm, they were quickly able to implement the code based on someone else's intellectual work. With most software reuse, developers typically reuse specific code after the application architecture has been decided and the code is being implemented. The developing science of software patterns has led to design reuse and object class reuse that may or may not entail code reuse, depending on the origin of the pattern.

Application Size

Because today's enterprise applications are so big, controlling their size has become an issue. The most efficient way to reduce the size of an application is to reduce the number of lines of human-generated source code. An important distinction here is reducing the amount of human-generated source code vs. reducing the total amount of source code. With today's modern development tools, the number of source code lines in an application often increases and therefore requires additional computer processing. However, component-based development models decrease the number of human-generated lines of code by incorporating reuse of objects and code, object-oriented systems, high-level development languages, and automatic code-generation tools.

Over time, as the use of higher-order application languages has increased, the efficiencies of these languages and their libraries has resulted in fewer lines of human-generated code. In his book *Software Project Management: A Unified Framework* (Addison-Wesley, 1998), Walker Royce compares the number of lines of code needed to write the same routine with various programming languages and tools, stating that

> *these values represent the relative expressiveness provided by various languages, commercial components, and automatic code generators.*

Table 2.1 summarizes this comparison.

Table 2.1   Lines of code produced by various languages and tools

Human-generated lines of code	Programming language and tools
1,000,000	Assembly Language
400,000	C
220,000	Ada 83
175,000	C++ or Ada 95
75,000	Integration of third party commercial systems/components and C++ or Ada 95

Object-oriented technologies and visual modeling tools also decrease the amount of source code that must be created by individuals. There has been much discussion on the efficiency of complex modeling languages, such as Unified Modeling Language (UML) and new visual modeling systems. Although these systems help to decrease the number of human-generated lines of code, they require significant investment in training to be used efficiently.

Software Performance

An application's architecture needs to take performance requirements into account and set steps in place to ensure that the application meets those requirements now and in the future. The application must be tested to determine whether it meets requirements, and if it doesn't, ways to tune the performance must be found. Performance requirements are rarely met without some tuning, so performance must be considered up-front and throughout the application project's life cycle.

Considering performance does not mean micro-optimizing every component. What is important to the application's users is overall system performance, not the performance of each individual component. Distributed applications have many variables that can influence performance—hardware, communications links, system software configuration, application topology, and so on—regardless of how components and applications are coded. Tradeoffs will always exist between ease of development, deployment, maintenance, and performance. The key to performance tuning is to do the minimum amount of work required to identify and eliminate—or at least reduce—bottlenecks in the overall system so that the application meets its performance requirements.

During performance validation, the conditions in which the application will be deployed can rarely be exactly duplicated, especially early in the project's life cycle. Thus, validation is a matter of extrapolating expected performance from the results of a series of controlled tests in environments resembling the deployment environment. The more closely the test environment resembles the deployment environment, the more likely that the application will meet performance requirements. However, the cost of creating such a test environment can greatly outweigh the benefit of reducing the risk that test results might be incorrect. Again, the key is to do only as much work as necessary to meet performance goals with an acceptable degree of confidence and then stop. Performance validation is about reducing the risk that the application will not achieve a necessary level of performance, not about tuning the application to the ultimate level of performance.

Application Scaling

An application's architecture must accurately describe not only the size of the application but also the hardware setup, or *distribution topology*, necessary to meet the application's user requirements. An application's distribution topology defines the type, number, and configuration of server machines the application will run on. The key to building scalable, reliable applications is location transparency. Location-transparent applications can run on multiple servers to handle additional load, with no loss in performance. Applications, or portions of an application, can also be replicated across a cluster to provide better reliability in the event that a server fails. (A *cluster* is a group of physical computers that logically acts as a single computer.) The appropriate topology is selected based on the existing corporate computing infrastructure and policies, results of performance tuning, and any implementation-specific constraints on location transparency.

Most distributed applications are deployed into an existing computing infrastructure, so certain aspects of the topology might be predetermined. For example, an application might use an existing database running on a dedicated database server, and corporate policy might prohibit applications from being installed on that server. In such a case, the application's architecture must allow for its deployment on a different server and ensure that the appropriate communications protocols are in place, that connectivity exists between the servers, that the application can access the remote database with appropriate security credentials, and so on.

Corporate computing policies can also have a big impact when deploying applications that will be accessible to external users over the Internet. Typically, most servers will run behind a firewall to prevent random external users from accessing confidential information. There may be multiple levels of firewalls, each with different restrictions on who can penetrate the firewall and what type of communication is permitted. Web servers, applications, and database servers might need to be deployed behind different firewalls. Here again, appropriate communications protocols, physical connectivity, and security credentials must be available between the computers.

Although the existing computing infrastructure and policies might impose some constraints on how the application is scaled, the results of performance testing and tuning can influence the topology. For example, performance goals might be achieved with a single server that meets minimum processor speed, memory, and disk access speed requirements, or testing might indicate that the only way to meet performance goals is by scaling out. *Scaling out* means adding servers to the topology to distribute the client load. Applications can also be scaled out by adding additional business object servers, adding database servers, or partitioning data access.

Scaling out is often an attractive solution to the challenge of meeting performance goals because it improves performance without requiring any code changes to the application. The cost of adding hardware to the application topology is usually much less than the development and testing costs associated with changing application code, especially relative to the performance gains. Scaling out might increase administrative overhead, but the performance benefits will typically outweigh the administrative costs.

Architecture Forms

One of the great difficulties involved in developing an application architecture is finding a common terminology to express new concepts and apply existing concepts. Communication difficulty exists on both the development and organization levels and can be addressed using the tools discussed in this section.

Unified Modeling Language

As we've said, one of the most important factors in delivering successful applications is being able to communicate process, business, and technical information to all the people involved. The Unified Modeling Language (UML) can provide the common language with which to communicate and build understanding. Its primary purpose is to help organizations visualize, specify, create, and document the artifacts of a software system.

UML evolved from several primary modeling languages that were prevalent in the late 1980s and 1990s. Version 0.8 began as a combination of the Grady Booch method and James Rumbaugh's OMT method; Version 0.9 saw the incorporation of Ivar Jacobson's OOSE method; and Version 1.0 evolved when a large group of partners built upon the previous versions and incorporated new pieces. Further additions and approval by Object Management Group (OMG) have increased UML's status as a strongly supported, industry-standard modeling tool.

A complete description of UML is beyond the scope of this book, so this discussion serves only as a reminder of its key features. UML can be separated into four sections:

- **Modeling elements** These elements are categorized into four primary groups:
  - Structural
  - Behavioral
  - Grouping
  - Other

- **Relationships** These elements are also categorized into four groups:
  - Dependency
  - Association
  - Generalization
  - Realization

- **Extensibility mechanisms** These elements provide a mechanism to add capabilities to models.
- **Diagrams** These elements provide graphical representations of the system. Each diagram is one of two types of views: static or dynamic (see Table 2.2). Different views provide different perspectives of a problem, and each view is represented by a specific model within UML.

An understanding of UML is critical to the development and communication of successful application architectures. Several good textbooks are available on this topic, including *The Unified Modeling Language User's Guide* (Addison-Wesley, 1998) and *Tried and True Object Development: Practical Approaches with UML* (Cambridge University Press, 1999) by Ari Jaaksi, Juha-Markus Aalto, Ari Aalto, and Kimmo Vatto.

Design Patterns

Another approach to describing and communicating complex application architectures involves the use of design patterns. The principles of design patterns were first applied to building architecture by Christopher Alexander, Sara Ishikawa, and Murray Silverstein in *A Pattern Language: Towns, Buildings, Construction* (Oxford University Press, 1977). In 1995, Erich Gamma, Richard Helm, Ralph Johnson, and John Vlissides applied these principles to software engineering in their foundation book *Design Patterns: Elements of Reusable Object-Oriented Software* (Addison-Wesley, 1995), where they stated that the technique:

> ...*identifies the key aspects of a common design structure that make it useful for creating a reusable object-oriented design.*

Table 2.2   Static and dynamic UML diagram views

View	Model	Characteristics
Static	**Use case**	Built in the early stages of development to capture system functionality as seen by the user. Their purpose is to specify the context of a system, capture the requirements of a system, validate a system's architecture, drive implementation, and generate test cases.
		Typically generated by analysts or experts in a particular problem or industry domain.
	Class	Captures the vocabulary of a system. Once built, continually refined throughout the application's development. They exist to name and model system concepts, specify collaborations, and specify logical database schemas.
		Generated by systems analysts, designers and implementers.
	Object	Shows specific instances and links to others. Created during the analysis and design phase. Illustrates data and object structures and provides specific snapshots of system occurrences. Typically generated by systems analysts, designers, and implementers.
	Component	Captures the physical structure leading to implementation. Created as part of the architectural process before development, thus the architecture-driven approach. They exist to organize and structure source code, lead the construction of an executable release, and specify a physical database structure.
		Created by the systems architects and programmers.
	Deployment	Captures the actual topology of a system's installation and hardware. They exist to specify the distribution of components and identify system performance bottlenecks.
		Created as part of the architectural process by systems architects, network engineers, and systems engineers.
Dynamic	**Sequence**	Captures time-oriented, dynamic behaviors. Represent application's flow controls. Describes what the system does in typical scenarios.
	Collaboration	Captures message-oriented dynamic behavior. Also represents flow controls, as well as demonstrating the coordinated behavior of the object structures.
	Statechart	Captures event-oriented behaviors. Can represent the life cycle of the objects as well as their reactive nature. Often used to help model the user interface, as well as devices.
	Activity	Captures movement-oriented behaviors. Primarily used to model the business workflow, the application's interaction with business workflows, and general operations.

Today, the term *design patterns* has achieved buzzword status. Anything and everything must follow a pattern, and everyone has identified his or her architectural design as a pattern. In an article in the *Theory and Practice of Object Systems* journal, Dirk Riehle and Heinz Zullighoven provide a definition that represents the practices of the pattern community:

> *A pattern is instructive information that captures the essential structure and insight of a successful family of proven solutions to a recurring problem that arises within a certain context and system of forces.*

This definition provides some pointers on how to identify a pattern. As noted by James Coplien in *Pattern Languages of Program Design* (Addison-Wesley, 1995), a pattern has the following characteristics:

- It solves a problem.
- The solution is not obvious.
- It is a proven concept.
- It describes a relationship.
- It has a significant human component.

Another way to identify a design pattern is to remember that it is a reoccurring phenomenon and is subject to the *rule of three*; that is, it can be identified in at least three separate systems or solutions within the same problem domain.

Design patterns can be either generative or non-generative. Generative patterns can be used to solve engineering problems, whereas non-generative patterns are merely observed. In his book *The Timeless Way of Building* (Oxford University Press, 1970), Christopher Alexander discusses the difference in these terms:

> *...in one respect they are very different. The patterns in the world merely exist. But the same patterns in our minds are dynamic. They have force. They are generative. They tell us what to do; they tell us how we shall, or may, generate them; and they tell us too, that under certain circumstances, we must create them. Each pattern is a rule which describes what you have to do to generate the entity which it defines.*

Fortunately, a number of patterns have already been identified that can be applied to common problems. These patterns typically are defined within a template. Some patterns have been identified for a particular industry segment, and some patterns address specific technical design problems. Although an organization can identify its own patterns for its applications, we recommend first following the patterns that have successfully provided solutions within the software industry. To apply a pattern to an application, the technical and business requirements for the application must first be identified. Then the design pattern that best fits the needs of the application can be selected. (In this respect, design patterns get to the heart of reusability, because they enable entire system architectures to be reused.) A good generative design pattern supplies the rationale for the solution as well as the solution itself. However, most software development design patterns stop at the architectural level and do not suggest specific code implementations.

As with any immature science, disagreement abounds on what should be included in a properly defined pattern. However, several common elements exist between many patterns. The general consensus regarding these elements has been summarized by Brad Appleton in his paper *Patterns and Software: Essential Concepts and Terminology* (www.enteract.com/~bradapp/docs/patterns-intro.html) and is paraphrased below:

- **Name** A meaningful single word or short phrase that identifies the pattern and the structure it describes. (In some cases, patterns are identified by their classifications in addition to their names.) Good pattern names form a vocabulary for discussing conceptual abstractions. When more than one name has been assigned to the same pattern, the alternative names are documented as aliases.

- **Problem** A statement of the problem that describes the goals and objectives it wants to reach within the given context and forces. Often the forces oppose these objectives as well as each other.

- **Context** The preconditions under which the problem and its solution seem to occur and for which the solution is desirable. It can be thought of as the initial configuration of the system before the pattern is applied to it.

- **Forces** A description of all the relevant forces and constraints and how they interact or conflict with one another and with the goals to be achieved. A concrete scenario may be used. Forces reveal the intricacies of a problem and define the kinds of tradeoffs that must be considered.

- **Solution** A description of how to realize the desired outcome. Instructions may provide pictures, diagrams, and text to show how the problem is solved. The solution should describe not only the static structure (the pattern's form and organization) but also the dynamic behavior, which may provide guidelines (as well as pitfalls to avoid) when attempting a concrete implementation of the solution.

- **Examples** One or more sample applications of the pattern that illustrate a specific initial context; how the pattern is applied to and transforms that context; and the resulting context left in its wake. Easy-to-comprehend examples from known systems usually are preferred.

- **Resulting context** The state of the system after the pattern has been applied, including the consequences (both good and bad) of applying the pattern, and other problems and patterns that may arise from the new context. When a pattern is just one step toward accomplishing some larger task or project, the resulting context of the pattern is often correlated with the initial context of other patterns.

- **Rationale** A justifying explanation of steps or rules in the pattern and also of the pattern as a whole in terms of how and why it resolves its forces in a particular way to be in alignment with desired goals, principles, and philosophies. The rationale provides insight into the deep structures and key mechanisms of the system and explains how the pattern works, why it works, and why it is "good."

- **Related patterns** The static and dynamic relationships between this pattern and others within the same pattern language or system. Related patterns often share common forces and have compatible resulting or initial contexts, provide alternative solutions to the same problem, or are codependent.

- **Known uses** The known occurrences of the pattern and its application within existing systems. This verifies that the pattern is a proven solution for a recurring problem. Known uses of the pattern often serve as instructional examples.

A typical design pattern has a brief abstract that summarizes all these elements and presents a clear picture of the forces and the solution that the pattern addresses.

Design AntiPatterns

Generative design patterns provide complete solutions to business and technical problems. They are primarily geared toward "green field" designs, meaning they are applied to new designs. Design antipatterns are geared toward solving problems for which an inadequate solution is already in place. The best way to differentiate patterns and antipatterns is to say:

> *Patterns lead to an original solution for a set of criteria and forces.*
> *Antipatterns lead to a new solution when the current design is not working.*

Thus patterns are used when starting from scratch, and antipatterns are used to fix things that are broken. Figure 2.2, which is from William Brown, Raphael Malveau, Hays McCormick III, and Thomas Mowbray's book *AntiPatterns: Refactoring Software, Architectures, and Projects in Crisis* (John Wiley and Sons, 1998), illustrates this concept.

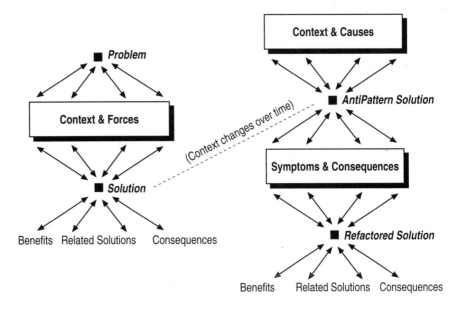

Figure 2.2 Differences between design pattern and antipatterns

Design patterns and antipatterns are similar in their structure and underlying principles. Thus, antipatterns:

- Have a structured description that provides a common language for communicating with everyone involved in an application development project.
- Require the *rule of three.*
- Begin with a recurring problem.

Existing antipattern definitions can be leveraged as solutions, or as the starting point for the process of creating organization-specific antipatterns. They can provide a structured way for new or inexperienced software developers to learn how to solve the complex application development problems they will encounter.

Guiding Software Principles

The practice of developing software has changed dramatically over the last 20 years. Many of the more traditional management techniques have been updated to reflect recent experience. The driving forces behind this shift have been the ability to develop more features over less time, and as a result, the increased complexity of current software products. Competitive pressures, growing customer influence, constant increases in technology company stock values, and constantly evolving technology have all combined to force organizations to streamline their development process. But above all, the driving factor behind the streamlining of the development process is that too many projects have failed. The motivating goal of today's software developers is to successfully build better software with less money. The new mantra is "Ship the right product at the right time."

For this section, we have compiled a list of software management principles on which to base the development of enterprise application architectures. The principles are not listed in any particular order, because they are all important to a successful application development process. These are the keys to shipping the right product at the right time.

Alignment with Business Goals

Every project must justify its capital resource requirements. The organization's business goals form the basis of this justification. Thus, the vision for each development project is driven by the business needs of the project's stakeholders.

A project's return on investment is not always measured in strict financial terms; the project may provide strategic value to the organization that is difficult to quantify monetarily. However, the business values the project addresses must align with the stated business goals of the entire organization. As the organization's goals change, the project team must reassess the underlying business goals to confirm that the project is still in alignment with the organization's goals. At the very least, the project must not conflict with any new goals.

Because business goals are critical to the project's success, it's not enough for the project team to be technically competent only in the ways of software development. Many a great product has been shelved because it did not meet the customer's business goals, even though it was well-written and technically sound. To prevent this kind of disconnection between product and goals, the project team needs a clear understanding of the business problem it is trying to solve.

Product Mindset

The product mindset is not about shipping commercial software products as Microsoft does, or about developing applications for internal customers. It's about treating the results of labor as a product. Having a product mindset means focusing more on execution and what is being delivered at the end of the project and less on the process of getting there. The application development process is not unimportant, but it should be used to accomplish the end goal and not just for the sake of using a process. Adopting a product mindset means that everyone on a project team feels responsible for the delivery of the product. Everyone's primary job is to ship the product; all other responsibilities are secondary.

Architecture-First

In *Software Project Management,* Walker Royce states that "architecture-first" is the single most important principle of modern software management. Using an architecture-first approach achieves a demonstrable balance between the business requirements, the architecturally significant design decisions, the customer's expected ship dates, and the product's life cycle plans, before resources are committed for full-scale development. Prototypes and proof-of-concept systems can be used to help determine the appropriate design decisions. The project team must make the appropriate trade-off decisions between resources, ship dates, and features, as well as create a product vision that is shared by all project stakeholders.

Design Within Context

Today's complex applications don't exist in a closed environment. Applications interact with business needs, other applications, network and system infrastructure, and data systems. Just as applications involve other systems, current and future systems interact with applications. So applications must be designed to integrate into the entire enterprise environment. Project teams must be sure they understand the product's inherent interaction with and reaction to the environments in which it will run.

Different Languages for Different Project Phases

Using specialized languages for the different phases of development is a well-recognized best practice in the software industry today. For example, various print and electronic forms can be used to communicate business requirements; UML provides notations for stating requirements and excellent design-modeling capabilities; and modern programming languages, such as Visual Basic, C++, and Java, provide robust application development platforms.

Project Success Factors

Each application project has different priorities and must work with different constraints. Just as each project is different, the specific goals that measure each project's success are different. Success cannot be defined for a particular project without first determining the expectations of the project's stakeholders.

Team Approach

Today's enterprise applications are too complex for any one person to grasp completely. Ensuring that all the critical success factors are addressed requires a team approach that assigns critical success factors to different team roles. Assigning ownership of key success factors also significantly improves project success rates.

Individual Commitment to Project Goal

The success of a project team resides in the commitment of the team members to the project's goals. Everyone must agree on these goals and accept success as an all-or-nothing proposition: "We will get it done, period." In addition, team members and the customer must commit to a common project vision—that is, to a clear understanding about the goals for the project. Team members and the customer bring with them assumptions and hidden agendas concerning the project and what the product should do for the organization. To mitigate these risks, the team must commit to the common goal. Ultimately, all members of the team must be working to ship the right product at the right time.

Early Product Demonstrations

The project team must understand the interests of the customer and help the customer identify and prioritize the features of the product, determining which features must appear first and which can wait for a later release.

During the initial project phases, prototypes can be used to give the customer, the users, and the team a better understanding of what the product will do. These prototypes can consist of user screens that demonstrate product concepts and system progression. Without fail, the customer and users will change their priorities or identify new needs after seeing the prototypes. These changes are not motivated by greed, but result simply from a better understanding of what can realistically be accomplished.

During the middle phases of a project, architects and developers can use proof-of-concept systems to test critical designs before large code segments that rely on unproven designs or technology are written.

Finally, during the early stages of the development process, alpha and beta product releases can be used to solicit additional input from the stakeholder community. More importantly, beta product releases address system-integration and deployment issues before the development is completed.

Risk Management

Risk is the possibility of suffering loss. For any given project, the loss can be in the form of diminished quality, increased cost, missed deadlines, or complete failure to achieve the goal of the project. These risks must be addressed, either proactively or reactively. Good project management proactively identifies and manages project risks throughout the entire project life cycle. Managing risks as a formalized process raises awareness of the risks and provides a common tool set that all project participants can use and review.

A solid risk management process:

- Identifies the risk.
- Determines its potential impact on the project.
- Determines the probability of occurrence.
- Determines the risk exposure to the project.
- Proactively mitigates the risk.
- Designates a contingency plan to be followed if the risk materializes.

If effective risk management is practiced from the beginning of a project, the probability that risks will materialize during the late stages of a project is significantly reduced.

Component-Based Development

Mary Kirtland's book *Designing Component-Based Applications* (Microsoft Press, 1998) summarizes the component-based approach. Traditionally, an application's services have been exposed through application programming interfaces (APIs). The learning curve for a development team to make effective use of APIs is significant.

Object-oriented frameworks are another popular way to expose services, but they also have a significant learning curve. Additionally, object-oriented frameworks are usually specific to one programming language.

Components provide a standard model for packaging services and exposing the services to other applications. These components act as "black boxes," hiding all their data and implementation details. Component services are exposed via public interfaces and a common programming model. As an additional advantage, component models provide facilities to enable communication with components regardless of their development language or deployment location.

Change Management

Each project needs a change control process and system, and committing to the change control process is everyone's responsibility. Developers have used source-code control systems for years, but these systems are typically only revision control systems for project artifacts, such as documents, agendas, functional specifications, source code, compiled code, and so on. Revision control is only part of change management. A change control system incorporates additional steps, such as how changes affect other components, who implements a change and how, the impact on project constraints, and the creation of a new product baseline that includes the change. Following a change control process decreases the entropy of a project.

Product Versions Based on Customer Priorities and Expectations

No matter how fast the project team advances, the market, the technology, the competition, or the customer's business advances faster. Releasing versioned product updates enables the project team to respond to continuous changes in scope, schedule, and project risk. Frequently updating the product allows the team to communicate with the customer as well as collect suggestions for future product releases directly from the customer's use of the product.

The team should deliver a core set of features in the first release and add features incrementally in later releases, until the full vision for the product is achieved. As later product versions are delivered, the product vision can be validated and updated to reflect any changes to business requirements.

After the development team establishes a pattern of making good project trade-off decisions and shipping products, it's important to cycle through versioned releases as rapidly as possible.

Flexible, Scalable Framework

No one process works for all application development projects. A practical process must provide a flexible framework to address the needs of different projects. This process framework should be scalable to large and small projects.

As projects are completed using the framework, a collection of proven best practices can be compiled. These best-practice experiences can improve the development process and increase the likelihood that the right product will be delivered at the right time; in other words, that projects will be successful.

Enterprise Application Model

Application architecture is the high-level plan for building an application to solve a specific business problem. The Enterprise Application Model is an orderly summation of all the requirements for the implementation of any enterprise application, divided into six specific submodels. Table 2.3 lists the requirements as items to define or deliver within each submodel.

Figure 2.3 shows not only the categories of requirements that an enterprise application must meet, but also the relationships between the various requirements. The arrows show that successful application development begins with determining the business requirements and results in the physical architecture of the completed system. Between these two stages, the user, logical, and technology requirements are fulfilled, with each category depending on inputs from both the business requirements and its neighboring submodels, and with each model's outputs directly contributing to the physical architecture that is finally implemented. The Development Model (the teams and processes applied to developing the application) permeates and coordinates all of the other requirements.

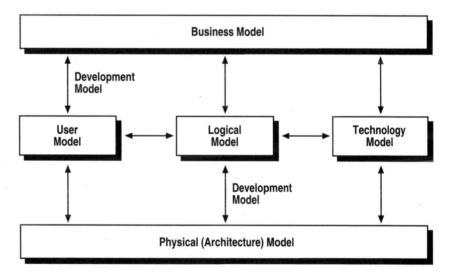

Figure 2.3   Enterprise Application Model

Table 2.3   Submodel requirements of the Enterprise Application Model

Submodel	Requirements
Business	Business goals Development cost Return on investment Resources needed Time constraints Security and maintenance Existing infrastructure investment Business rules and policies
User	User interface Ease-of-use requirements Training and documentation Application support User's desktop configuration and network connection
Logical	Logical application structure Object and data modeling Business objects and services Interface definitions
Technology	Component development or reuse Development tools Deployment platforms System and database technologies Clustering, pooling, and messaging technologies
Development	Development team Development process Project management Source code control Testing Application milestones and deliverables
Physical	Physical application architecture Distribution and interconnection of components End product of the iterative inputs of each of the other submodels

The view of the Enterprise Application Model shown in Figure 2.3 immediately provides important insights into the requirements for successful enterprise application development, some of which are listed here:

- **Importance of relationships** Understanding the relationships between the different requirements provides a way to move through the process of designing and building the application without neglecting the many dependencies that each design task has on other parts of the overall design. We'll explore this iterative development style at length in the section titled "Enterprise Development Teams and Processes."

- **Importance of requirements** All of the requirements embodied in each of the submodels are a part of the overall Enterprise Application Model and contribute to the success or failure of an application, whether or not they are consciously addressed in the development process.

- **Importance of submodels** Each submodel can be treated in a relatively stand-alone manner, much like software components. Each submodel has its own set of concepts, requirements, techniques, processes, tools, state storage, and input/output (deliverables). In most cases, the output of each submodel becomes a critical part of the overall functional specification for the project, and this specification is in turn used to define the project's physical architecture and to produce the project test plan.

These insights suggest a development process that is iterative and incremental rather than linear. Such a process involves working on each set of requirements a little bit at a time, pausing at frequent intervals to assess the impact of each model on its neighbors. It helps to identify conflicting requirements early so that necessary design tradeoffs and adjustments can be made *before* they require re-implemention of major portions of the application.

Designing with the Enterprise Application Model

First and foremost, the Enterprise Application Model is a design tool. It guides application architects through the process of designing and building a large-scale application, by organizing its design requirements into submodels and showing how the submodels fit together. It shows how to balance the competing requirements of every design decision. As a result, the application can be built in small incremental steps, working in any order that seems appropriate, with the confidence that every design choice integrates smoothly with the overall application architecture.

Designing with Submodels

A big advantage of using the Enterprise Application Model as a design guide is that the process can start anywhere. The context and priorities of the project, rather than an arbitrary linear order, determine the correct sequence for traversing from one submodel to another, ultimately fulfilling the requirements of all the submodels. For new projects, the preferred direction is top to bottom, with the needs of the business driving the middle submodels and the needs of the middle submodels driving the physical architecture that is finally implemented. However, good reasons may dictate starting elsewhere—for example, an existing application context that needs re-deployment, or a usability problem that must be fixed.

As the arrows in Figure 2.3 show, the requirements and output from neighboring submodels directly affect each other. These arrows are used to balance and resolve the competing requirements between the submodels while creating the application's Functional Specification.

Regardless of which submodel is worked on first, the general pattern for traversing the model during application design is:

- Make some design choices in any submodel.
- See what effect those design choices have on the neighboring submodels, and make any necessary design adjustments in those models.
- Repeat step 2 until the change has been fully accounted for through the entire Enterprise Application Model.

Note To give a high-level view of how submodels work, the following example uses some concepts of distributed component-based architecture, such as pooling and scalability, that are not covered until later chapters. If necessary, check the definitions of these concepts in the Glossary.

Suppose that the User Model for an online sales system requires the system to accommodate a twenty-fold increase in the number of users during the holiday season compared with the rest of the year. How does this requirement affect the other models? With each arrow in Figure 2.3, the effects of this requirement ripple through the model as follows:

- **The Business Model** This model must provide the justification and resources for changes to be implemented. The impact of technology on support, operations, and other groups within the organization must be assessed. The implementation or acquisition of technology should be considered for all systems. If a project doesn't integrate with the organization's Business Model, it should not be undertaken.
- **The User Model** This model provides the user perspective of each project. Each new application released to the user community should provide a common and consistent method of use. When application interfaces are consistent, user productivity can increase.
- **The Logical Model** This model must respond by encapsulating the services that interact directly with the user and defining interfaces for them so that they can be implemented as components that can be easily pooled.
- **The Technology Model** As a result of changes in the Physical, Logical, and Business Models, this model has to build the pooled components and choose an appropriate scaling technology, such as Microsoft Transaction Server, to coordinate them.
- **The Development Model** This model needs to organize the teams that will build and test the pooled components, to allocate resources, and to schedule the development milestones. In the Enterprise Application Model, the Development Model is the glue that ties together the submodels, specifying the overall project resources and defining how the work and deliverables flow from one submodel to another.

- **The Physical Model** This model needs to accommodate scaling quickly to a great number of users without degrading performance. Meeting this requirement usually means that a clustering or pooling strategy must be employed so that more instances of the critical components can be made available to the system simply by adding additional servers.

All important submodel output—business requirements, user requirements, business rule logic and algorithms, database schema, performance, and so on— is described in the project's *Functional Specification*. This is a living document that is continuously changed and updated throughout the development cycle. At each design stage, it's important that any significant change percolate through the other submodels, following the arrows between neighboring submodels until the impact of the change has been fully accounted for throughout the entire Enterprise Application Model. Many iterations of feedback between neighboring submodels might be needed before a change has been completely assimilated.

Balancing Interactions Between Submodels

The Physical Model for an enterprise application is the final outcome of the design process and can be directly derived from the requirements of its neighboring submodels. Because of this, the design process is, to a great extent, a process of balancing the natural contentions between the various submodels.

For example, the Business Model's interest in reducing administration costs might push the Technology Model toward remote processing on central servers. At the same time, the most efficient User Model might suggest local processing on the user's desktop. The process of defining the Physical Model necessarily involves finding an acceptable compromise between these two competing goals.

Understanding these interactions helps determine the order in which design decisions should be made, and can help prevent ill-considered changes to one aspect of the overall design that may unacceptably impact the requirements described in other submodels.

Note Because the Development Model permeates the entire Enterprise Application Model, this submodel has no "typical" interactions with the other submodels. Every design and implementation decision must be accounted for in the Development Model.

Examples of the common submodel interactions that can occur within the Enterprise Application Model are presented in the following sections. For each submodel, we briefly cover:

- The major application design questions the submodel answers.
- The major relationships between it and other submodels.

- Examples of how it is affected by the Internet.
- References to more complete information given later in the book.

Note The Internet is a major new technology and deployment platform for enterprise applications. For this reason, it is less familiar to many developers than other technologies for component-based design and delivery. Its impact is discussed in these brief summaries. Singling it out in this manner is not meant to imply that the Internet is always, or even usually, the best platform for enterprise applications. It is simply an attractive new option that may be the right choice in some situations.

Business Model

The Business Model defines the organization's goals and its reasons for funding the application. Questions about the application that this model answers include:

- What are the business requirements for this project?
- What business objectives and features must it provide?
- What level of investment will provide the best financial return?
- How fast must the project be delivered?
- How expensive will it be to deploy?
- What platforms must it support?
- How many users must have access to it concurrently?
- How important is security?
- How reliable must it be?
- When will this release be replaced or updated?
- How quickly must new business policies or user needs be incorporated into new updates?

In an ideal scenario, implementing an enterprise application architecture begins by defining the business requirements embodied in the Business Model. If other models are implemented outside the Business Model context, the business goals supported by the project may not be appropriate for the organization.

How the Business Model Interacts with Other Submodels

Figure 2.3 illustrated that the Business Model directly interacts with the User Model, the Logical Model, and the Technology Model. Table 2.4 characterizes these interactions and gives brief examples of each.

Table 2.4   Interactions of the Business Model

Submodel	How the Business Model relates to it	Example
User	Determines who will use the application, their skill levels, and their desktop configuration.	An application that will be used by inexperienced personnel must be highly intuitive and well-documented.
Logical	Sets policies about how business assets must be managed. These policies are reflected in logical business rules.	Business policies determine how shipping, inventory, and sales must respond to new orders.
Technology	Determines or constrains the technology needed to satisfy business requirements.	A business requirement to directly market the organization's products through electronic commerce mandates Internet technology.

Note Each of these interactions works both ways. For example, the cost and capacity of new modems may limit the number of customers an organization will be able to serve with its new Internet-based direct marketing application. In this case, the Technology Model might force a reassessment of the goals and requirements of the Business Model.

How the Internet Has Impacted the Business Model

Examples of the way the Internet has impacted the Business Model include:

- The opportunity to write software that can run without changes on multiple platforms (although with varying degrees of compatibility and reliability).

- The cost of testing an application on many platforms, virtual machines, and Internet browsers.

- The opportunity to publish vast amounts of information very inexpensively, increasing product visibility and sales while providing a powerful mechanism to decrease product support costs.

- The ability to deploy some kinds of "lightly interactive" applications by using the capabilities of Internet servers, thereby reducing deployment costs.

- The need to protect the organization from malicious attacks on Web servers and the risk of Internet-delivered viruses or non-sanctioned components.

User Model

The User Model defines the target user of the application. Questions about the application that this model answers include:

- Who are the users and what are their skills, experiences, and use cases or scenarios?

- What are the user requirements for task sequencing, usability, training, responsiveness, performance, and interoperability with external applications and data?

- Are users dedicated employees who can tolerate usability quirks or inconveniences, or are they consumers who may not buy the product if its user interface is not easy, reliable, and efficient?

- How much feature documentation and help will users need? Will they have the patience to read documentation?

- Will users require product support? Will they pay for it?

- How many users will be accessing the application at any one time?

- How powerful are the users' computers, and how fast are their network connections?

- What is required to ensure proper security?

Note In larger or more formal environments, the User Model itself can be separated into four relatively independent submodels: the Usability Model, the Documentation Model, the Support Model, and the User Security Model.

How the User Model Interacts with Other Submodels

Figure 2.3 illustrated that the User Model directly interacts with the Business Model, the Logical Model, the Technology Model, and the Physical Model. Table 2.5 characterizes these interactions and gives brief examples of each.

Table 2.5   Interactions of the User Model

Submodel	How the User Model relates to it	Example
Business	The number of users, their skill levels, and desktop configurations determine the cost of training and supporting them.	A retail order-entry application must be fast to accommodate busy clerks. This may require additional hardware or infrastructure investments.
Logical	How the user thinks about the tasks and works at them determines how the functionality must be logically encapsulated.	If a customer's credit can be checked while the order is being taken, the credit-checking functionality must be in a separate, asynchronously processed component.
Technology	User requirements determine the technology needed to meet them.	An application deployed on the Internet must use platform-independent technology for the user-interface elements.
Physical	The number of users and their locations affect the component architecture needed to reach them effectively.	An application that will be used by a rapidly changing number of users must deploy its user-intensive services in an easily scalable configuration, such a component pool or queue.

How the Internet Has Impacted the User Model

Examples of the way the Internet has impacted the User Model include:

- Access to an enormous wealth of professionally published HTML-based information.

- A huge growth in the opportunity to reach untrained consumers directly from enterprise applications.

- A significant fear of "Big Brother-like" Web applications gaining access to personal desktop resources.

- A loss of some user interface form-rendering techniques.

- Slower user-interface responsiveness in applications, based on slow network links.

- Unreliable information and application access over relatively fragile Internet links.

Logical Model

The Logical Model defines the business entities that will be rendered by the application, and what policies and rules will be used to operate on those entities. The questions this model answers are very specific to the business for which the application is being developed. Questions about the application that this model answers include:

- When should a customer be given a purchase discount?
- When should inventory be restocked?
- How much sales tax should be charged on an out-of-state order?

The Logical Model itself is made up of two relatively independent submodels:

- **The Logical Data Model** This submodel is responsible for documenting the business entities that the system manages (for example, products, customers, and orders) and the rules for maintaining them (for example, "All new orders must be represented in the Orders Table as well as the Shipping Table").

- **The Logical Object Model** This submodel is responsible for documenting the rules and algorithms that operate on the data entities, determining how these rules are grouped into interfaces and classes, and assessing how the various objects interact among themselves to solve macro-level requirements. The Logical Object Model is also used to specify how each object fits into an N-tier application design.

How the Logical Model Interacts with Other Submodels

Figure 2.3 illustrated that the Logical Model directly interacts with the Business Model, the User Model, the Technology Model, and the Physical Model. Table 2.6 characterizes these interactions and gives brief examples of each of the interactions.

Table 2.6   Interactions of the Logical Model

Submodel	How the Logical Model relates to it	Example
Business	Determines how business policies can be encapsulated.	An application that must accommodate rapidly changing tax rates and rules must isolate these rules in separate, easily maintainable components.
User	Defines the logical entities users act on to perform various business tasks.	Logical customer and order objects and credit-checking services are needed to enable users to carry out typical sales tasks in the application.
Technology	Specifies the features and services that must be packaged into the chosen technology's components.	A credit-checking component must use technology capable of interfacing with credit reporting agencies.
Physical	Determines the features and services that must be deployable using the chosen physical architecture.	A funds transfer component must be deployed upon an infrastructure that supports reliable security protocols.

How the Internet Has Impacted the Logical Model

Examples of the way the Internet has impacted the Logical Model include:

- Increased use of N-tier application designs that separate business logic from user-interface behavior, as organizations strive to encode business functionality on powerful Internet application servers.

- An aggressive push by corporations and third-party software vendors to implement their new functionality with objects that can be more easily maintained and reused, improving responsiveness.

For the most part, the Internet is a physical phenomenon. It will not have a significant impact on the Logical Model of those organizations that have already moved to object-oriented, LAN-based development.

Technology Model

The Technology Model defines the technology services that are available to solve the application's requirements. The Technology Model is used to identify, acquire, or create the necessary technical resources that support the requirements. Questions about the application that this model answers include:

- What operating system features can be assumed to be on the desktop, on the server, and on the database?
- What network protocols will be supported?
- What security technology will be used?
- How will technology be used to assist with high-end scalability?
- How will database integrity be maintained across multi-component and multi-database transactions?
- How will large, asynchronous requests be handled?
- What technology will be used to access legacy systems?
- How will UI forms be rendered?
- What technology will be used to access data on a remote database?
- What technology will be used to replicate data across database servers, or on the desktop?
- Considering the needs of the business (such as schedules, resources, skills, and costs) and the capabilities of the available technology (such as objects and components, data access, graphical user interface forms, distributed transactions, security, design tools, programming tools, and bug tracking), how should the product be built?
- What tools should be used to help build, debug, integrate, or deploy the application?

Note Code written and compiled for the project becomes part of the Technology Model, just like controls or operating system services picked up from external sources. Similarly, the source code for the project is part of the Technology Model, in the same way that usability test reports are part of the User Model.

How the Technology Model Interacts with Other Submodels

Figure 2.3 illustrated that the Technology Model directly interacts with the Business Model, the Logical Model, the User Model, and the Physical Model. Table 2.7 characterizes these interactions and gives brief examples of each.

Table 2.7   **Interactions of the Technology Model**

Submodel	How the Technology Model relates to it	Example
Business	Implements the application's business objectives into the physical system.	New Internet technologies create business opportunities that were previously unavailable.
Logical	Implements the logical structure of the application as physical components.	Business rules are encapsulated in components that run on the application's infrastructure.
User	Delivers application functionality with technology appropriate to the user's skills, desktop configuration, and connectivity.	If an Internet application gives users remote database and business-processing services, the development team must acquire the tools to program, debug, and test multi-user, asynchronous, distributed applications.
Physical	Provides the technology to deliver the application functionality on the chosen physical architecture(s).	If an Internet application must run on servers that use different operating systems, the development team may have to use multiple programming languages and tools.

How the Internet Has Impacted the Technology Model

Examples of the way the Internet has impacted the Technology Model include:

- The availability of Hypertext Markup Language (HTML), Java, Hypertext Transfer Protocol (HTTP), Internet servers, LAN firewalls, component signing, and desktop-based Web browsers.

- The need for fast application servers to remotely process business rules.

- The possibility of adding additional new end-user platforms to the test and development support list.

Development Model

The Development Model defines the process and resources used to develop an application, and is the "glue" that allows all the submodels to work together. Questions about the application that this model answers include:

- Who should work on what part of the overall development problem?

- In what order should submodel tasks (such as logical object design, usability testing, database design, programming, and testing) be performed, and how should progress be measured?

- How many developers are assigned to the project and what are their skills?

- What specialized activities should be employed to optimize development efficiency and final quality of the deliverables?

- How should the project be managed and coordinated with other projects?

- How important is software reuse and componentization? (The answer to this question influences coordination, the importance of standards, the time spent on design, and the value of a general-purpose architecture.)

- How should work in progress be shared and promoted for other developers and testers to use?

- How should the application be deployed into the final production environment?

- How will administration be managed?

- How will updates be deployed?

The Enterprise Architecture Development Model can effectively use two additional MSF models. However, these models can also stand alone and should be considered peers.

- **MSF Team Model for Application Development** This model, which is concerned with the organization, coordination, and management of development teams, is discussed in Chapter 3.

- **MSF Process Model for Application Development** This model, which addresses issues of planning, scheduling, and milestones, is discussed in Chapter 4.

How the Development Model Interacts with Other Submodels

Figure 2.3 illustrated that the Development Model permeates all the other submodels, guiding the process of development through them and coordinating their requirements and deliverables. In this respect, there are no "typical" interactions, because every design and implementation decision must be taken into account in the Development Model.

How the Internet Has Impacted the Development Model

Examples of the way the Internet has impacted the Development Model include:

- An enormous increase in the importance of server-based (UI-less) logic.

- An increase in the complexity and resource requirements for testing and debugging complex, multi-user, distributed, continuously running applications.

- An emphasis on the value of location-independent components, and all the processes involved in their development, coordination, and sharing.

- An extension of the developer or programmer roles to include the roles of author and publisher.

- The creation of a strong commercial demand for a universal, scalable, and component-oriented enterprise application architecture.

Physical Model

The Physical Model defines where the physical resources to support the requirements of the other submodels of the application are deployed. It also specifies the process through which competing interests of the submodels are resolved. The completed Physical Model of an enterprise application is the application's architecture. Questions about the application that this model answers include:

- How will the physical resources of computers, network bandwidth and protocols, databases, components, operating system and back-office services, and third-party features be used to meet the overall needs of the business (such as scalability and robustness)?

- How will existing deployments migrate to desired deployments?

- How can resources be accessed most efficiently (for example, local machine versus the Internet)?

- How can usability and throughput performance requirements be met in execution environments that include slow LAN or WAN access times, intermittently disconnected network servers, and unreliable Internet connections?

Application Architectures

An application architecture is a conceptual view of the structure of an application. As shown in Figure 2.4, each application has three distinct layers: the user layer, the business layer, and the data layer. Each application also contains presentation code, business-rule processing code, data processing code, and data storage code. Application architectures differ in how this code is packaged to form a particular application product.

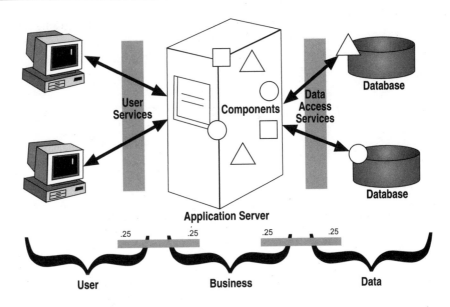

Figure 2.4 Physical Model and its application layers

Many current applications have a *two-tier architecture*, also known as *client/ server architecture*. In a two-tier architecture, a client process handles the data processing and presentation parts of the application. Data is stored on centrally administered server machines. Clients connect directly to the servers they need, often for the lifetime of the application's use.

Client/server applications work well in controlled environments in which the number of users can be estimated and managed, and resources can be allocated accordingly. However, when the number of users is unknown or very large, the client/server architecture breaks down. Because each client connects to data servers directly, the number of available data connections limits scalability. Opportunities for reuse are limited because the clients are bound to the database formats. Each client application contains data processing logic, making the applications relatively large. (This type of client is sometimes called a *fat client*.) If the data processing logic ever needs to change, new applications must be distributed to every client computer.

A slight improvement comes from moving parts of the data processing, or business logic, to the data servers—for example, by using Microsoft SQL Server stored procedures. This architecture is sometimes called "two-and-a-half tier." Applications built on this model are somewhat more scalable, but not scalable enough to meet the needs of highly distributed applications. In addition, opportunities for reuse are limited.

Scalability and reuse can be improved significantly by introducing a third tier to the application architecture. With *multi-layer architecture*, also known as *N-tier architecture*, the user, business, and data tiers are logically separated, as illustrated in Figure 2.5.

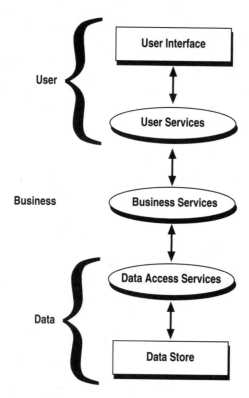

Figure 2.5   Multi-layer application architecture

The three tiers perform the following functions:

- **User tier** The presentation tier presents data to the user and, optionally, lets the user edit data. The two main types of user interfaces for PC-based applications are native and Web-based. Native user interfaces use the service of the underlying operating system. On the Microsoft Windows platform, for example, native user interfaces use the Microsoft Win32 API and Windows controls. Web-based user interfaces are based on HTML and Extensible Markup Language (XML), which can be rendered by a Web browser on any platform. We look at the user tier more extensively in Chapter 7.

- **Business tier** The business tier is used to enforce business and data rules. The presentation tier uses the services of the business tier. However, the business tier is not tied to any specific client; its services are available to all applications. Business rules can be business algorithms, business policies, legal policies, and so on—for example, "Users get a 10 percent discount for ads placed before Tuesday night" or "Six percent sales tax must be collected for all orders delivered to the Commonwealth of Kentucky." Data rules help to ensure the validity and occasionally the integrity of the stored data—for example, "An order header must have at least one detail record" or "Money must not be lost or generated during transfers between bank accounts." Business rules are typically implemented in isolated code modules, which are usually stored in a centralized location so that multiple applications can use them. (This code isolation embodies the software management principle of component-based development, discussed earlier in this chapter.) The business tier is discussed further in Chapter 8.

- **Data tier** The business tier has no knowledge of how or where the data it works on is stored. Instead, it relies on the data access services, which perform the actual work of getting and putting the data. The data access services are also implemented in isolated code modules, encapsulating knowledge of the underlying data store. If the data store moves or changes format, only the data access services need to be updated. Each data access module typically is responsible for the integrity of a set of data—for example, data placed in relational tables or Microsoft's Active Data Object (ADO) and OLE DB technology. We discuss data access technologies more extensively in Chapter 9. For the purpose of N-tier design, the data store is simply the database management system (DBMS)—the systems required to serve data from tables, as well as optimize information retrieval, such as database indexes. Examples of data stores will be provided in Chapter 9, but include SQL Server, Exchange Server, In Memory Database (IMDB), and Microsoft Access.

It may be slightly confusing to talk about logical architecture as part of the Physical Model. It is important to understand that logical architecture encompasses a wide range of physical architectures and implementations that specify where services are deployed. In other words, applications are constructed as logical networks of consumers and suppliers of services. Services are merely units of application logic that provide well-defined functionality.

The terms *multi-layer* and *N-tier* don't imply separate computers. The N-tier application architecture promotes scalable applications. To create highly scalable applications, resources such as database connections must be shared. Instead of each client application consuming resources to access data servers directly, client applications communicate with business services. One instance of a business service can support many clients, reducing resource consumption and improving scalability, as shown in Figure 2.6 and Figure 2.7. Because business services do not manage data directly, it's easy to replicate these services to support even more clients. Services can often be designed and implemented independently of any particular client applications, providing flexibility and the potential for reuse in many applications. By encapsulating application logic behind well-defined public interfaces, developers create a body of reusable services that can easily be combined in new ways to create new applications. In addition, common functionality can easily be updated in response to changing business requirements, without impacting the client applications that rely on the functionality. This reduces the management and deployment costs of changing requirements.

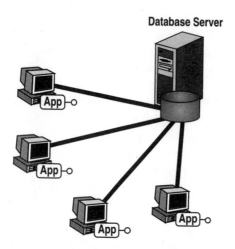

Figure 2.6   Client/server systems

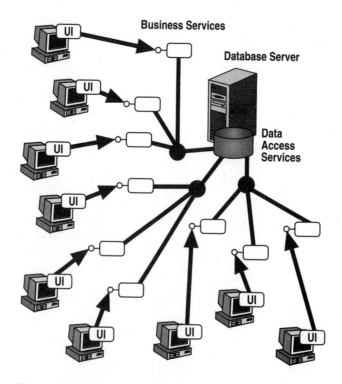

Figure 2.7   N-tier systems

The multi-layer application architecture can also help developers deal with existing, or legacy systems. Developers can "wrap" access to existing systems within business logic, data access, or data store services. Client applications need to worry only about how to access the business logic, not about how to access all the different legacy systems they might rely on. And if the legacy system is modified or replaced, only the wrapper needs to be updated.

How the Physical Model Interacts with Other Submodels

Figure 2.3 illustrated that the Physical Model directly interacts with the User Model, the Logical Model, and the Technology Model. Table 2.8 characterizes these interactions and gives brief examples of each.

Table 2.8   Interactions of the Physical Model

Submodel	How the Physical Model relates to it	Example
User	Provides the means by which the application is made available to users.	The physical architecture must be able to support users' desktop configurations and scale efficiently to the number of users and their processing requirements.
Logical	Determines the extent to which logical constructs can be mapped to the physical infrastructure.	An application that provides online transaction processing must define components that can interface with a transaction management infrastructure.
Technology	Limits the technology that can be supported on the physical infrastructure.	An application deployed to the public on the Internet must use "least common denominator" technology for user-interface elements that must run on a variety of platforms and browsers.

How the Internet Has Impacted the Physical Model

Examples of the way the Internet has impacted the Physical Model include:

- An enormous increase in the importance of using highly scalable architectures to support unknown or unlimited numbers of Internet users.

- A requirement to access application functionality (business logic) from many different client platforms.

- An enormous increase in the use of distributed, asynchronous resources.

- The enabling of new application types, including simple informational applications (simple HTML) and active informational applications (interactive HTML, ActiveX, and Java).

- The introduction of traditional desktop-oriented applications embedded in Web pages.
- The availability of installation-free user interfaces (browser-based HTML).
- The need for corporate firewalls between internal LANs and the public Internet.
- The need for on-demand, server-based application installation (ActiveX components and Java applets).
- The introduction of the packaging (.cab and .zip files) and digital signing of components.

MSF Application Model for Development

The MSF Application Model for Development (MSF Application Model) provides a multi-layer services-based approach to designing and developing software applications. MSF views an application at a logical level as a network of cooperative, distributed, and reusable services that support a business solution. Application services are units of application logic that include methods for implementing an operation, function, or transformation. These services should be accessed through a published interface, driven by the interface specification, focus value toward the customer not the provider, and map directly to actions. As mentioned in Chapter 1, the MSF Application Model describes applications as using three services: user, business, and data. These services allow for parallel development, better use of technology, easier maintenance and support, and flexibility in distributing the application's services. These user, business, and data services can reside anywhere in the environment from a single desktop to servers and clients around the world.

User Services

User Services are logic that provides an application with its user interface. The user interface is not necessarily visually conveyed; it can be programmatic, as the user may be a person or another application. User Services seek to hide or isolate information views from the application's user interface structure.

Business Services

Business Services are logic that controls the sequencing and enforcing of business rules. These services provide transactional integrity as well as transform data into information through the application of business rules.

Data Services

Data Services are logic that provides the lowest visible level of detail used to manipulate data. Data Services seek to maintain consistent application data, as well as separate the application's design and implementation from the location and structure of the data store. Most Data Services provide the ability to define, create, read, update, and delete data.

The MSF Application Model establishes the definitions, rules and relationships that form the actual structure of an application. It is designed to influence the approach the team takes for building applications.

Summary

We began our chapter by looking at application architecture. We discussed various methods that can be applied to create an architecture. Additionally, we identified several key characteristics of modern applications. Then we identified the modern software management principles that allow consistent delivery of successful applications, and moved on to discuss the Enterprise Application Model and its six submodels: the Business Model, the User Model, the Logical Model, the Technology Model, the Physical Model, and the Development Model. Each of these submodels was examined in turn. Finally, we looked briefly at the MSF Application Model for Development. This MSF model discussed three-tier application architecture with User Services, Business Services, and Data Services.

Review

1. What is software architecture and what are the characteristics of a good architecture?
2. What are three ways to document software architecture?
3. What are the features of an enterprise application?
4. What are design patterns and antipatterns?
5. Identify five guiding software management principles.
6. List the six submodels of the Enterprise Application Model.
7. What is the MSF Application Model for Development?

C H A P T E R 3

Project Teams

About This Chapter

A common question asked about many application development projects is
"Who is supposed to do all the things that have to be done to make a project successful?" This chapter discusses who is responsible for doing what so that all the
different parts of an application project are managed properly. We discuss building a project team within the context of the MSF Team Model for Application
Development (MSF Development Team Model). The discussion progresses from
finding and enlisting leaders from different parts of the organization, to understanding the six equally vital team roles. We talk about specific responsibilities
that must be fulfilled for a project to be successful, and assign these responsibilities to specific team members. We also look at ways to analyze project requirements from the perspectives of different team members. We explore ways to
scale the project team to fit the needs and size of the project. Finally, we look at
team and leadership characteristics that will help make an organization's use of
its project resources more effective.

The principles and guidelines we provide in this chapter are based on our own
experience with the creation of application architectures and the implementation
of enterprise applications, together with the following sources:

- Microsoft Solutions Framework
- Microsoft Consulting Services
- Jim McCarthy's *Dynamics of Software Development*
- Steve McConnell's *Rapid Development: Taming Wild Software Schedules* and *Software Project Survival Guide*
- Barry Boehm's *Software Engineering Economics*

Upon completion, you will be able to:

- Understand the challenges of the hierarchical resource model.
- Understand the rationale behind using the MSF Development Team Model for application development.
- Understand the MSF Development Team Model's roles and responsibilities.
- Understand how to scale the MSF Development Team Model for large and small projects.
- Understand the risks involved in combining team roles.
- Identify the characteristics of effective leaders.
- Identify the means of improving team effectiveness.
- Identify subject areas in which the team must be trained.

Team Model vs. Hierarchical Model

Most developers fondly remember the first time they saw "Hello World" displayed on their screen—an indication that their first programming effort was successful. Although many of us relish the memory of that rather simplistic achievement, the fact is that the complexities of enterprise applications and systems make them nearly unmanageable. In addition, the deployment of those applications and systems to hundreds of desktops at many different sites has significantly expanded the scope of the development process.

As we noted in Chapter 1, today's enterprise applications are too complex for any one person to grasp completely. No one can hold all the requirements, options, and design choices in mind at one time. Several people, and several minds, need to work together to hold them all. In today's enterprise environments, responsibility for application development must be assigned to a team rather than a single person.

People sometimes have difficulty adjusting to working in teams. They are expecting to know "Who's in charge?" A hierarchical model, such as an organization chart, describes who is in charge and who reports to whom. However, in today's enterprise environments, assigning a single project manager to oversee all aspects of a development project and make all critical decisions creates many points where the project could fail. The challenges of a single manager approach can include:

- An information bottleneck.
- Insufficient perspective to address all the project's needs.
- Increases in miscommunication as information is filtered up the management hierarchy.

- Difficulty in grasping the vast technical knowledge required of multiple-application platforms.

- The overwhelming breadth of knowledge required to integrate the project with current internal systems.

- Difficulty in prioritizing business requirements against technical requirements.

- A single experience, which limits the ability to quickly solve problems based on historical, more broad-based experience.

In addition, communication is more difficult in organizations that adhere to strict hierarchies, which by definition imply indirect communications. A hierarchical group's communications may be "filtered" by three or four managers, thus significantly increasing the likelihood that the true message and intent will be lost. Often the greatest miscommunication occurs between upper management's vision and the actual practical work on a project, four managers removed. This miscommunication can lead to the disengagement of individuals from the project, decreased productivity, and increased likelihood of project failure.

To combat many of the difficulties with a single manager approach, a team model describes the key roles and responsibilities of a project team. No single person is in charge of the overall project. Instead, each team member is in charge of a specific role that must be performed in order for the project to be successful.

The team model does not define the management structure of the team from a personnel-administration perspective. A multi-disciplined team acquires project resources from many departments within the organization and from the organization's vendors. Project teams are specifically designed to address project goals and assign project responsibilities to different roles. The leaders of each role are responsible for executing their role's activities given the resources assigned to their part of the team. The daily management tasks they perform within the roles are specifically related to project activities, not to particular human-resource (HR) activities. The HR management of the organization's employees continues to be handled by each individual's current manager. Such activities can include compensation plans, benefits, vacations, and performance reviews. The team provides performance information about individuals to their managers but doesn't oversee the individual's adherence to employment policies.

The team approach has its challenges. Potential pitfalls that need to be understood and continually mitigated include:

- Lack of a single point of contact for external communication.

- An inconsistent vision applied to different aspects of the project.

- Team members with different agendas for the project.

- Inexperience that prevents an effective team implementation.

In this chapter, we'll look at ways to avoid these pitfalls.

Project Responsibilities

Rather than being a methodology, MSF is a framework that can be adapted to suit the particular needs of any organization. The MSF Team Model for Application Development (MSF Development Team Model) is one aspect of this framework. The model describes how teams should structure themselves and what principles they should follow in order to be successful at developing software.

The MSF Development Team Model is specific in nature, but as part of the framework, it should be viewed as a starting point. Different project teams may implement aspects of the framework differently, depending on the scope of their project, the size of their team, and the skills of their team members.

Specific responsibilities must be carried out and specific goals must be met in order for any project to be successful. These responsibilities and goals serve to provide continual direction for all the team members. Key project responsibilities and goals include the following:

- **Customer satisfaction** Projects must meet the needs of their customers and users in order to be successful. It is possible to meet budget and time goals but still be unsuccessful because customer needs have not been met.

- **Delivery within project constraints** Most projects measure success using "on time, on budget" metrics.

- **Delivery to specifications based on user requirements** The Functional Specification describes in detail the deliverable to be provided by the team to the customer. This specification represents an agreement between the team and the customer as to what will be built, and constitutes the basis for "Doing what we say we will do."

- **Release after identifying and addressing all issues** All software is delivered with defects. The team's goal is to ensure that those defects are identified and addressed before the product is released. Addressing defects can involve everything from fixing the defect in question to documenting work-around solutions. Delivering a known defect that has been addressed along with a work-around solution is preferable to delivering a product containing unidentified defects that may "surprise" the team and the customer later.

- **Enhanced user performance** For a product to be successful, it must enhance the way that users work. Delivering a product that is rich in features and content but can't be used is considered a failure.

- **Smooth deployment and ongoing management** The effectiveness of deployment directly affects the perceived quality of a product. For example, a faulty installation program may imply to users that the installed application is similarly faulty. The team must do more than simply deploy the product; it must deploy smoothly and then support and manage the product.

Note Many factors can affect a project, some of which will constrain it. When the project team focuses on meeting the agreed-upon goals of the project and delivering the product on time, it ensures that the organization receives the right Return on Investment (ROI), which is the right product for the right price.

The MSF Development Team Model addresses the need to meet these key goals by assigning tasks to six team roles: Product Management, Program Management, Development, Testing, User Education, and Logistics Management. Each goal requires a different discipline, so each team role embodies a different discipline. The people who carry out the team roles must have the unique perspective and set of skills necessary to meet each goal.

Table 3.1 shows the correspondence between the six roles of the MSF Development Team Model, which we discuss in detail later in this chapter, and the six key goals of an effective project team. Because each goal is critical to the success of a project, the roles that correspond to these goals are seen as peers with equal say in decisions. There is no project master, but simply a team that knows what to do and is properly equipped to do it.

Table 3.1 Goals and corresponding team roles

Goal	Team role
Customer satisfaction	Product Management
Delivery within project constraints	Program Management
Delivery to product specifications	Development
Release after identifying and addressing all issues	Testing
Enhanced user performance	User Education
Smooth deployment and ongoing management	Logistics Management

How does a team get started on a project when it doesn't know how long it will take, how much it will cost, and what it is going to create? Answering these questions is the core function of the MSF Development Team Model discussed in the next sections of this chapter and the MSF Development Process Model discussed in Chapter 4. These models involve a bottom-up scheduling process, a top-down design process, and separation of responsibilities, so at first glance, they don't seem to answer these questions at all. But in fact, they lend themselves well to minimizing risk and exposure in the early phases of a project. Making the correct decisions early in the process and avoiding changes late in the process significantly decreases a project's overall time and costs.

The MSF Development Team Model

Because a large number of activities must be performed and several perspectives must be addressed in each project, assigning ownership of key project-success factors to specific team roles significantly improves project-success rates. As shown in Figure 3.1, MSF identifies six distinct roles that comprise the MSF Development Team Model. Each role has clearly defined responsibilities, and when all roles are combined at the completion of a project, all critical success factors will have been covered.

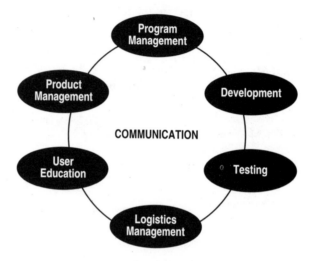

Figure 3.1   MSF Development Team Model's roles

Usually, each role has a team of people assigned to it to carry out that role's responsibilities, with one person acting as the role team's leader. Assigning a leader to each role creates a single point of contact to represent that role on the project team.

Caution Assigning responsibility to teams of people can mean that no one takes responsibility for anything. But with MSF, each team role has specific responsibilities for critical portions of the development process. The overall success of the project is the primary shared responsibility of all the team members.

For project teams to be successful, they should have:

- Experienced leaders.
- Self-motivated team members, empowered to make decisions and accountable for the success of their team's role.
- A focus on shipping the product.
- A commitment to a shared project vision.

To facilitate communication, a project team should be a small, multi-disciplined group that has the following characteristics of good teambuilding:

- **Trust** People can rely on each other, and each person exhibits repeatable patterns of consistent behavior. "We do what we say we will do."

- **Respect** People have regard for each other's abilities. "We all add value to the team."

- **Commitment** Everyone agrees on the project's goals and accepts success as an all-or-nothing proposition. "We will get it done, period."

- **Accountability** People act on clearly defined goals, responsibilities, and expectations. "I'll do this, you'll do that, and by Tuesday we'll have built our house."

These fundamental characteristics will lead the team to what's known as the "right" principle: "It's everyone's responsibility to ship the right product at the right time."

Product Management

The job of the Product Management role is to respond to the customer's need or problem. The key contribution of this role is to drive the team to a shared vision of how to meet the need or solve the problem. Product Management answers the business-driven question "Why are we doing this?" and ensures that all members of the team know and understand the answer.

The key external goal of this role is customer satisfaction. Product Management can achieve this goal by acting as the customer advocate to the team and as the team advocate to the customer. (Here, it's important to distinguish between the customer and the users: The customer pays for the product, while the users use it.) Product Management works with Program Management to determine the "tradeoffs" between what the project will deliver, the project development time, and the amount of money it will cost.

As the customer advocate to the team, the leader of the Product Management role is responsible for understanding customer requirements, creating the business case, establishing the shared project vision between the team and the customer, and ensuring that any solution that the team develops meets the needs of the customer by solving the particular business problem.

As the team advocate to the customer, the leader of this role is responsible for high-level communications and managing customer expectations. High-level communications include public relations, briefings to the customer and senior management, marketing to users, demonstrations, and product launches.

Product Management also communicates the initial ship dates the customer expects the team to target. However, successful projects employ a bottom-up scheduling process determined by other team roles, and Product Management must then communicate the achievable ship dates to the customer.

Note The customer (the person paying the bill for the project) will have a set of expectations for the project. Meeting these expectations creates a satisfied customer, which helps define a successful project. Once a project's vision is set, the key role for Product Management is to manage customer expectations. Thus, the Product Management role often defines what success and failure are for a project.

Product Management should continually manage customer expectations by asking the question "Did we do what we said we would do?" Suppose a project had an initial goal of delivering five features for $10,000 in two weeks, but instead delivered three features for $7,000 in one and a half weeks. Was this project a successful one for the customer? From a Product Management view, we would say, "We agreed with the client on the second day which of the most important features could be done within the budget and the time frame. We met those goals, so the project was successful. We've started a second project for the other two features and two additional features." Product Management included the customer in the tradeoff, demonstrated the decision-making process, and informed the customer of the changing risks and challenges. (The standard challenges are cost control, resource allocation, product features, and the product completion date.) When everyone involved with the project can say, "Yes, we did what we said we would do," trust and respect are built among team members and with the customer.

Note Poorly communicated expectations are the primary reason so many projects fail. When a project's features, resources, or ship date change, whether planned or not, the expectations of the customer, the users, and all project team members should be reset.

The Product Management team represents the interests of the customer and helps the customer identify and prioritize the features of the product. Because the customer has final signoff on which features can wait for a later release and which features must appear in this release, Product Management facilitates this decision by ensuring communication between the customer and the team. Program Management may be asked to remove features from the current release to meet the product ship deadlines, because Program Management is responsible for the schedule and for determining how long it takes to deliver the agreed-on feature set. If Program Management determines that a feature must be cut to maintain the schedule, the customer and Product Management can agree or not agree. However, if the customer and Product Management decide that the feature must stay in this version, they must also agree that Program Management can change the schedule and the ship date. Alternatively, the customer and Product

Management may choose to spend more money to allow the addition of members to the project team. Program Management will determine where and how the money is spent, as well as whether the addition will in fact improve the schedule. The customer and Product Management will approve the overall cost of the project.

Caution Applying additional resources to projects does not always decrease time schedules, because communication and management overhead increases.

Within the project team, the term *Product Champion* might be used to describe the leader of the Product Management role. Often, the Product Champion will be a member of the organization's senior management team. The other people assigned to the Product Management role will be the individuals with the strongest understanding of the organization's structure, business, and strategic goals.

Note If the project team is a consulting group or vendor for a project, Product Management will have two sets of customer expectations to meet: those of the consumer, who sponsors the project and foots the bill, and those of the customer, who is typically the IT person who engages the consulting group and pays for its services. Typically, the consulting group will need to rely on its expertise to explain the organization's use of MSF and how both the consumer and the customer will work with the project team within this framework.

Program Management

The job of the Program Management role is to own the development process and to drive the process to ensure the product is delivered within the project constraints. The leader of this role must understand the difference between being a leader and being a boss. In his book *Dynamics of Software Development* (Microsoft Press, 1995), former Microsoft Program Management team director Jim McCarthy writes:

> *Keep in mind that the goal is to endow each person on the team with the fullest possible authority, not to rake it in for yourself.*

The primary responsibility of the leader of the Program Management role is to move the project through the development process to ensure that the right product is delivered at the right time. Through leadership, facilitation, and consensus building, this leader coordinates all the other team leaders and their particular responsibilities. Although occasional scheduling pressures may mean the Program Management leader must prod the team firmly back on track, he or she should forget the dictatorial management style.

The leader of Program Management owns the overall schedule for the project, which has been built from the bottom up by the other roles within the project team.

He or she coordinates the creation of the project's master schedule with the other team leaders. Any overrun or buffer time for the project is owned by and applied at the appropriate time by Program Management. When individual portions of the project are completed ahead of or behind schedule, Program Management determines the impact on other roles and coordinates schedule changes.

The skills needed for the Program Management role include a strong understanding of the business side of the organization as well as a solid understanding of the technology currently used by the organization and the technology needed for the project. The leader of the Program Management role must possess strong organization skills and strong communication skills.

In organizations that are new to MSF, Program Management often requires a much deeper understanding of the framework and processes that enhance the efficiency of the rest of the team and its leaders. Although leadership characteristics are important for all roles, this expertise is particularly important in Program Management. To be most effective, the Program Management team should have the respect of the other team members before the project begins, including the business, technical, and senior management groups. Typically, the Program Management team will include the administrative resources used by other team roles, as well as support for scheduling and coordinating various meetings among the different team roles.

As the owner of the project's feature set, Program Management defines which features will be delivered in order to meet the agreed upon requirements. Product Management may determine critical requirements, but Program Management determines which particular product features meet those requirements. Additionally, Program Management recommends to the customer which features may be negotiated for future versions given time and money constraints. Program Management owns the features outlined in the Functional Specification (what will be built) and the Master Project Plan (how it will be built). Program Management also coordinates and facilitates the creation of these documents by getting input from each of the team members. It's essential that each member contribute his or her input and approve the Functional Specification and Master Project Plan.

Caution It's important for the Program Management leader to remember that team members have a much deeper knowledge of their particular responsibilities than he or she has. Program Management needs to rely on them, trust their expertise, and yet still provide the overall framework to deliver the whole product within all project constraints.

As the owner of the project's budget, Program Management facilitates the creation of the planned cost by gathering resource requirements from all of the roles on the team. Program Management must understand and agree with all resource decisions (hardware, software, people, and so on) and must track the actual costs against the planned costs. However, the Program Management leader will need to provide regular status reports to the team and key stakeholders throughout the project. Another symptom of failed projects is the delay of status report delivery until after the budget has been exceeded. It's important to remember that adding additional funding is a tradeoff and is therefore a decision that should be made by Product Management and the customer.

Development

The job of Development is to be technology consultants and product builders. As technology consultants, Development provides input into high-level designs, evaluates technologies, and develops prototypes and proof-of-concept systems to validate potential solutions and to mitigate development risks early in the development process. To succeed in meeting its quality goal, it is important that Development focus not only on coding certain aspects of the project according to the Functional Specification, but also on solving the business problem. As a result, Development must innovate, but only to solve the customer's problem, not just for the sake of implementing interesting features. Often to improve envisioning and communication, Development will create prototypes, and to test technology that is new to the organization, the group will create proof-of-concept systems. These systems may also provide ways to communicate architectural decisions to the rest of the team.

As builders, Development provides a low-level product and feature design, estimates the effort required to deliver that design, and then builds the product. In many organizations, a few senior members of the Development team drive the architecture for the product. These architects are involved in the early phases of a project, fleshing out the details of the Functional Specification and determining the appropriate internal and external system interactions for the product.

Development estimates its own schedules because it is responsible for the daily coding work. This MSF concept of schedules being created by those responsible for the work is called *bottom-up scheduling*. It is an important factor in delivering the right product at the right time. The goal is to achieve a higher quality schedule and to increase accountability for the estimates and for the work.

Development's responsibility for the technical implementation of the project's features primarily falls within the Logical Model and Physical Model of the Enterprise Application Model discussed in Chapter 2. Development determines exactly how to implement each feature, the actual architectural implementation, and how long the coding portion of the project will take to implement. Development does not determine which features to implement, but how to write the code for the product.

In addition, during the Planning Phase of a project, Development must be able to determine the impact on the schedule of adding and removing features. During the late phases, Development is not specifically responsible for the actual deployment of the product, but it must work closely with Logistics Management to understand what installation and setup routines will be needed.

Caution The person assigned as the leader of the Development role should not be assigned to any other roles. The goal is to let the developers do what they do best: write "killer code."

Testing

The job of the Testing role is reality induction. Testing must be able to clearly articulate both what is currently wrong with the product, and what is currently right with it, so that the status of the product's development is accurately portrayed. Performing a valid test requires a good grasp of the needs of the users and a clear understanding of what the product will do to meet those needs. Testing develops test strategies, plans, schedules, and scripts.

The goal of Testing is to make sure that the team knows and addresses all issues before releasing the product. An issue is anything that prevents the product from meeting its requirements. It can be a fault in the Development team's code (known as a bug), a deviation from the Program Management team's specification, or a defect in the User Education team's documentation.

Note It's important to distinguish between Testing and total quality assurance (TQA). Testing has a project focus and involves detailed technical work. TQA, on the other hand, is often a corporate function organized under a Director of Quality, whose responsibility is process compliance with corporate, government, or other regulatory standards.

The same people should not be assigned to the Testing and Development roles. Two key reasons for such a separation are:

- Better, independent assurance that coded products truly meet the requirements.
- The ability to exploit the concurrency of two working teams.

Testing's independent assessment should verify that Development has met its quality goals, but it is everyone's responsibility, not just Testing's, to ship a good product.

> **Caution** It is the Development team's responsibility to write quality code. Separating the Testing role from the Development role does not remove the responsibility of code quality from the Development team.

Change Control

The project will need a change control process and system. Committing to the change control process is everyone's responsibility, though implementing the change control system often falls to Testing. Developers have used source code control systems such as Microsoft Visual SourceSafe for years, but this type of system provides only revision control. All project artifacts, such as documents, agendas, functional specifications, source code, and compiled code, must be placed under revision control, but revision control is only a portion of change management. As an example, simply turning on revision marks in Microsoft Word does not ensure that the correct edits are made and that the correct information is presented. Thus, change management incorporates many additional steps, including:

- Creating a baseline.
- Determining which elements should change.
- Determining how the change will affect existing systems, processes, or documents.
- Identifying how the change will be implemented.
- Identifying who will implement the change.
- Determining the impact the change will have on project constraints, budget, schedule, and politics.
- Determining who makes the change-approval decision.
- Implementing the change.
- Creating a new baseline that includes the change.

> **Caution** Change proposals should be evaluated in batches to prevent the project team from being overwhelmed or distracted from daily work plans.

Compiling Source Code

A few important responsibilities of Testing are often overlooked:

- **Bug reporting and tracking** As with change management, implementing the bug reporting and tracking system is also the responsibility of the Testing team.
- **Building the product** Someone must be responsible for building (compiling) the product, and often this *Build Meister* is a member of the Testing

team. The Build Meister should use only the source code that is stored in the revision control system. Compile scripts can automate much of the tedium of building code; however, ensuring that the build occurs properly is important.

- **Risk tracking and management** Ongoing risk tracking and management are the responsibility of all teams. Program Management should provide a common method for tracking risks, such as using Microsoft Excel spreadsheets. The Testing team's role is "reality induction," meaning that it provides an outside view of development risks and schedule.

Caution Risk plans that are created or updated five minutes before a project review meeting are useless. Teams should be managing risks as a continuous, ongoing process to help ensure that quality products can be delivered on time.

User Education

The job of the User Education role is to enhance user performance so that users are as productive as possible with the product. To accomplish this goal, User Education acts as the advocate for the users of the product, much like Product Management acts as the customer advocate. However, this is a two-way street, because User Education also acts as the team's advocate to the users of the product.

As the user advocate to the project team, User Education participates in the design process to ensure delivery of a product that is useful and usable, and that needs as little performance support material as possible. User Education is responsible for usability testing, tracking usability issues, and ensuring that those issues are addressed in the product's user interface (UI) design.

By actively participating in UI design as well as other user enhancements, User Education can have a direct impact on a project by helping to reduce the costs of supporting it in the operations/delivery channel. These ongoing support costs are often not adequately considered for many software products. However, the cost-benefit calculation is very simple: The easier a program is to use, the lower the ongoing user support costs.

Caution Do not fall into the budgetary trap of assigning unrealistic user productivity gains that grossly overestimate the total ROI for a project.

Too often projects roll into production without a training plan or consideration of how the users will actually learn to use the product. Where user performance support materials are required, User Education designs, builds, and tests the materials that will enable easier use. These materials can include reference cards, keyboard templates, user manuals, online help, wizards, Web pages, and even full-featured courseware. Once the support materials are created, User Education coordinates the appropriate training for the user community.

Just as it is important for Product Management to manage the expectations of the customer, it is important for User Education to manage the expectations of the user community. However, users shouldn't be expected to be able to understand the language of the Functional Specification. Using prototypes to communicate business and technical requirements to the user community greatly improves the success of the project. Additionally, users will feel progress is being made when they actually see screens and working portions of programs. Although marketing is the responsibility of Product Management, it is important to keep users informed. Randomly posted signs, e-mails about new features or functionality, and beta test programs are excellent methods of communicating with the user community.

Note In cases where an application is being developed for another organization, the User Education role is still important. The consulting organization can't expect the IT person who is paying the bill to adequately represent or interact with the user community. Just as Product Management manages customer expectations, User education manages those of users. Successful projects never spring new products on users and expect that they will love the features. Adequate preparation and training are always essential.

Logistics Management

The job of the Logistics Management role is to serve as the advocate for the operations, product support, help desk, and other delivery channel organizations, and to focus on the smooth deployment and ongoing management of the product. Logistics Management participates in the design process to help ensure that the product is deployable, manageable, and supportable. This role is responsible for creating the deployment schedule. Logistics Management, Product Management, and Program Management work together to determine which users and sites will receive the product in what order. Logistics Management then prepares the sites to receive the product.

For large projects, the Logistics Management team leader should have experience with large-scale product deployments to several thousand desktops. Logistics Management is responsible for the entire deployment of the product to all desktop systems, and requires both a strong technical background and excellent communication skills. Logistics Management also oversees the technicians or contractors who install, configure, and migrate the users' systems. Additionally, this role requires experience in estimating and coordinating software installations.

Logistics Management is responsible for understanding the product's infrastructure and its support requirements. All installation sites, as well as all user systems, must meet those requirements before the product can be deployed. Typically, this is facilitated through the creation and implementation of rollout, installation, and support plans. Significant advances in Microsoft Windows 2000, the Active

Directory, and System Management Server have greatly decreased the deployment effort required to target and touch user systems.

Although Logistics Management's primary responsibility is to smoothly deploy the product to all users, the leader of this role also needs to create an ongoing support plan and ensure that existing support groups are able to help users. Just as important as training the user community is providing training to the operations and help-desk personnel. The training process must involve these groups early in the product's life cycle and during the beta-test phase. Formal support documentation, backup and restore requirements, and disaster-recovery plans must be created for the product before it is handed off to the operations group. For a fixed period after turning a product over to operations, Logistics Management should plan on providing the operations group with technical support. It is difficult to anticipate all the problems and issues that will arise from a fully deployed application, so Logistics Management must plan for the unexpected.

Other Logistics Management activities include supporting interim operations and supporting the product during the development process. Logistics Management will often be required to assist in monitoring the applications' behavior within the test environment. Additionally, this role provides initial support for the software during the production process in the form of development systems, test systems, certification, and production systems. Product support for the quasi-production process used during the beta-testing phase must also be provided.

Many organizations have specific systems that provide real-time monitoring for performance and stability. The Logistics Management team should provide the Development team with the appropriate information and technical contacts to integrate the new product into current and future management tools. For example, incorporating ongoing product management into Microsoft Management Console (MMC) will help support organizations easily integrate the product with other Microsoft systems.

The aggressiveness of the deployment schedule, the automation level of the installation, the use of automated software delivery tools, and the migration processes created by the Development team will determine the size of the Logistics Management team.

Adapting Team Size to Project Size

For project teams, at least one person is usually assigned to each role to ensure that someone looks after that role's interests. The greatest challenge with large-scale projects is setting up and maintaining effective communication. For smaller projects or in smaller organizations, the same person may be assigned to multiple roles. In that case, the greatest challenge is to successfully wear multiple hats and to ensure that all the issues are looked at with each hat.

Large-Project Scaling

In his book *Rapid Development* (Microsoft Press, 1996), former Microsoft software developer Steve McConnell states:

> *Large projects call for organizational practices that formalize and streamline communication. ... All the ways to streamline communication rely on creating some kind of hierarchy; that is, creating small groups, which function as teams, and then appointing representatives from those groups to interact with each other and with management.*

To scale large projects, the project team can be divided into two kinds of subteams: feature teams and function teams.

Feature Teams

Feature teams are small subteams that organize one or more members from each role into a matrix organization. These teams are then assigned a particular feature set and are responsible for all aspects of that feature set, including its design and schedule. For example, a feature team might be dedicated to printing.

Steve McConnell writes in *Rapid Development*:

> *Feature teams have the advantages of empowerment, accountability, and balance. The team can sensibly be empowered because it contains representatives ... from each of the concerned parties. The team will consider all necessary viewpoints in its decisions and thus there will hardly ever be a basis for overriding its decisions.*
>
> *For the same reason, the team becomes accountable. They have access to all the people they need to make good decisions. If they don't make good decisions, they have no one to blame but themselves. The team is balanced. You wouldn't want development, marketing, or quality assurance alone to have ultimate say over a product's specification, but you can get balanced decisions from a group that includes representatives from each of those categories.*

Function Teams

Function teams exist within a role. They arise when a team or project is so large that it requires the people within a role to be grouped into teams based upon their functionality. For example, it is common at Microsoft for a Product Management team to have a Product Planning team and a Product Marketing team. Both jobs form an aspect of Product Management, but one focuses on getting the features the customer really wants and the other focuses on communicating the benefits of the product to potential customers.

As another example, the Development role might need to be grouped by service layer: user, business, or data. It is also common for developers to be grouped based on whether they are solution builders or component builders. Solution builders build enterprise applications by "gluing" together the separate parts of the product produced by the component builders. Solution builders usually work with higher-level languages such as Microsoft Visual Basic, whereas component builders usually work with low-level C code to create reusable components that can be leveraged by the enterprise for multiple projects.

Small-Project Scaling

Although the MSF Development Team Model consists of six roles, a team doesn't need a minimum of six people. In other words, it doesn't require one person per role. The key point is that the six goals have to be represented by the six roles on every team. Having at least one person per role helps to ensure that someone looks after the interests of each role, but not all projects can be approached in that fashion.

On smaller teams, one team member might have more than one role. Two principles guide this type of role sharing:

- **Single role for Development** Development team members should never be assigned to another role. The developers are the builders, and they should not be distracted from their main task. To give additional roles to the Development team only makes it more likely that schedules will slip due to these other responsibilities.

- **Conflict of interest** Roles that have intrinsic conflicts of interest should not be combined. For example, Product Management and Program Management have conflicting interests. Product Management wants to satisfy the customer whereas Program Management wants to deliver on time and on budget. If these roles are combined and the customer requests a change, the risk is that either the change will not get the consideration it deserves to maintain customer satisfaction, or that it will be accepted without understanding the impact on the project. Having different team members represent these roles helps to ensure that each perspective receives equal weight.

Figure 3.2 illustrates risky and synergistic combinations of roles. The role combinations marked N should not be combined because of conflicting interests. The role combinations marked U are unlikely combinations, as the skills required for each role differ. For example, the skills and focus of Product Management vary greatly from those of Logistics Management. The role combinations marked P are possible combinations, because they represent compatible interests. For example, Testing and User Education both focus on users and try to ensure that the users' needs are met.

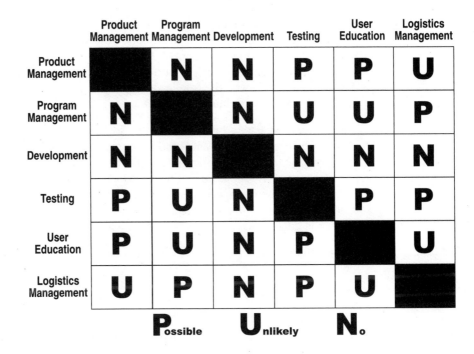

	Product Management	Program Management	Development	Testing	User Education	Logistics Management
Product Management		N	N	P	P	U
Program Management	N		N	U	U	P
Development	N	N		N	N	N
Testing	P	U	N		P	P
User Education	P	U	N	P		U
Logistics Management	U	P	N	P	U	

Possible   **U**nlikely   **N**o

Figure 3.2   Risky and synergistic role combinations

As with any teaming exercise, successful role sharing comes down to the actual team members themselves and what experience and skills they bring to the project. Some projects successfully share roles even though the table indicates a risk. The point is that if a team needs to share roles, the goals of the roles must be kept in mind so that the amount of conflict that could arise because of the role sharing is controlled. Otherwise, some aspect of the key goals might be over-looked, or risks might be in some way mismanaged.

Building Successful Teams

The MSF Development Team Model provides a team structure for tackling enterprise application projects, but the quality of the people that make up the team is a huge factor in the project's success. In this section, we examine some of the ways to ensure that quality.

Finding Effective Leaders

For the person in charge of putting together a project team, the first task is to decide who will work on the project. This seemingly simple (but more often complex) decision can dramatically affect the project's outcome.

Finding leaders within an organization is not a difficult process. By definition, leaders are recognized by those they work with. It's important to remember that we are talking about leaders here, not bosses. Every organization has its share of managers, directors, and so on, but the hierarchical structure of an organization does not determine who the true leaders are. Actions and characteristics, rather than job titles, identify leaders.

Why do we need leaders? Because we have so many followers. It's important to realize that labeling people as leaders and followers does not imply a value judgment. We must have leaders to be successful, but we must also have followers. Leaders provide direction for the team. Followers get the work done. The team needs to strike a balance between its leaders and followers. It must decide what to do and then must do it, so both leaders and followers are equally important and valuable. An absence of either leaders or followers will hinder the project's success.

Certain characteristics are present in many leaders. Common qualities of leaders include:

- Understanding and meeting the needs of others.
- Communicating well with groups and individuals.
- Earning the respect of internal and external customers.
- Displaying commitment to well-defined purposes.
- Making a positive difference.
- Having confidence in his or her abilities.
- Practicing good problem-solving skills.
- Helping others to develop their skills.

Many people will read this list and say, "I do those things." More people will read this list and say, "I intend to do those things." But being a leader also means knowing the difference between *intent* and *impact*. When measuring their own success, people measure their intent; when measuring other people's success, they measure their impact. The impact that leaders have on others may or may not be their intent, and leaders' intent may not have the impact they were striving for. The proper way to measure people's leadership skills is by the impact they actually have, not by their intent. We can summarize this concept by saying, "Other people's perceptions are reality."

Improving Team Effectiveness

We view teams as progressing through the following stages:

- Awareness/concern
- Hope/optimism, willingness
- Identification of needs and solutions

- Supportive/caring behaviors
- Trusting/respectful relationships
- Team cohesiveness

The goal is to have all teams move to the last stage, team cohesiveness, where productivity is the highest.

To be successful, a team has to do more than just define roles and responsibilities. Along with the team structure, there must also be some underlying practices and principles that help to ensure the success of the team. Following is a discussion of "best practices and principles" that have helped to make the MSF Development Team Model a success internally at Microsoft and with customers and partners who have implemented MSF.

Shared Project Vision

Fundamental to the success of any project is getting team members and the customer to share a project vision—that is, a clear understanding of the project's goals and objectives. Team members and the customer all bring with them assumptions and hidden agendas regarding what the project and the product are going to do for the organization. The process of establishing a shared vision brings those assumptions and agendas to light and ensures that all project participants are working to accomplish the same goal.

The vision should be formalized as a Vision Statement that is the basis for the first project deliverable. An effective Vision Statement:

- Describes not only what the product is, but also what it is not.
- Provides guidance for defining the product (for example, features are included or omitted to suit the vision).
- Motivates the team to achieve the vision.
- Is achievable so that both the team and customer can commit to it.

Note Writing a Vision Statement doesn't guarantee that the project team, customer, and users will all share it. The vision must be effectively communicated so that everyone understands it.

Without a shared vision, project participants will invariably have competing drives, making it much more difficult to reach the project's goals as a cohesive group. The most effective tool for communicating the vision is to talk about what the goals are and why the project has been undertaken. This discussion provides an opportunity to gain real commitment from the project participants. Commitment is not simply an agreement: "Yes, we'll work on the project." Commitment is motivation: "Let's get going. We can make a difference." The

Product Management or Program Management teams will often need marketing experience to get project participants truly committed to the project early in the development process.

Caution Never assume that others understand what the project team is doing or why it is doing it. The team and the customer should discuss the project's vision thoroughly.

Team of Peers

In a team of peers, each role has equal value. This peer approach enables unrestricted communication between the roles, increases team accountability, and reinforces the concept that all six goals are equally important and all must be achieved. For a team of peers to be successful, all roles must have ownership of the product's quality, must act as customer advocates, and must understand what business problem they are trying to solve.

Although each role has an equal value on the team, the team of peers exists between roles and should not be confused with consensus-driven decision-making. Each role requires some form of hierarchy for the purposes of distributing work and managing resources. The leaders of each role are responsible for managing, guiding, and coordinating the role's effort, while the other members of each role focus on meeting their individual goals.

Product Mindset

The product mindset is not about whether the organization ships commercial software products or develops applications for internal customers. It's about treating the results of people's labor as a product.

The first step to achieving a product mindset is to look at the work being done either as its own project or as contributing to a larger project. MSF advocates the creation of project identities so that people see themselves less as individuals and more as members of a project team. One effective technique Microsoft uses to accomplish this step is to give projects code names (such as "Chicago" for Windows 95 and "Memphis" for Windows 98). The code name helps to clearly identify the project, clearly identify the team, raise the sense of accountability, and serve as a mechanism for increasing team morale. Printing the team's project code name on T-shirts, coffee mugs, and other group gift items are ways to create and reinforce team identity and spirit.

Having a product mindset means being more focused on execution and what is being delivered at the end of the project, and less focused on the process of getting there. That doesn't mean that the process is bad or unimportant, just that it should be used to accomplish the end goal and not for its own sake. A strict adherence to process should never get in the way of delivering a product. With the adoption of the product mindset, everyone on the team should feel responsible for product delivery.

Former Microsoft program manager Chris Peters describes the product mindset as applied to software development in the following excerpt from a 1991 presentation:

> *Everybody ... has exactly the same job. They have exactly the same job description. And that is to ship products. Your job is not to write code. Your job is not to test. Your job is not to write specs. Your job is to ship products. That's what a product development group does.*
>
> *Your role as a developer or as a tester is secondary. I'm not saying it's unimportant—it's clearly not unimportant—but it's secondary to your real job, which is to ship a product.*
>
> *When you wake up in the morning and you come in to work, you say, 'What is the focus—are we trying to ship or are we trying to write code?' The answer is, we are trying to ship. You're not trying to write code, you're trying* not *to write code.*

Zero-Defect Mindset

The zero-defect mindset is a commitment to quality. It doesn't mean delivering a product with no defects; it means that the product meets or exceeds the quality bar that was set by the team's project vision. Additionally, it means that the goal of the team is to work at the highest quality level possible all the time, so that if a working product has to be delivered tomorrow, the team has one to deliver. It's the idea of having a nearly shippable product every day.

In a successful team, every member feels responsible for the quality of the product. Responsibility for quality cannot be delegated from one team member to another. In this sense, every team member is a customer advocate.

Understanding the Business

To be successful, it's not enough for a team to be technically competent in the ways of software development. Many a great product did not meet the business objectives of the customer and, although well written and technically sound, was shelved. To avoid this pitfall, the team members need a clear understanding of the business problem that they are trying to solve.

One way to achieve this understanding is to have active customer participation and feedback throughout the development process. This includes customer participation in establishing the product vision, signing-off on what is going to be built, taking part in tradeoff decisions, and adding feedback through usability studies and beta releases.

Overlapping Roles and Shared Responsibilities

As Chris Peters humorously put it in a 1991 presentation:

> *It's extremely important to move responsibility very low in the organization. Your goal is not to be working on a project where you can't sleep at night. Your goal isn't to have it so that the project leads can't sleep at night. Your goal is so that nobody sleeps at night. And when nobody is sleeping at night, you have pushed responsibility to the proper level.*

To encourage team members to work closely with each other, they should be given broad, interdependent, and overlapping roles, and they should all share responsibility for shipping the right product at the right time. This approach discourages specialization among team members, which often leads to isolated, rather than collaborative, effort.

Total Participation in Design

Jim McCarthy summarizes the concept of total participation in design in *Dynamics of Software Development*:

> *The goal in any product design is to have the best ideas become the basis of the product. Everybody on the team should be working to accomplish that goal.*

Each role participates in the generation of the Functional Specification because each role has a unique perspective of the design and tries to ensure that the design meets their role's objectives, as well as the project team's objectives.

Learning from Current and Past Projects

For project success to be more than just luck, a work environment must encourage teams to make a deliberate effort to learn from current and past project successes and failures. Creating a learning organization is fundamental to ongoing improvement and the continued success of projects. One method for structuring this type of behavior is post-milestone reviews, or postmortems. After the team reaches a milestone, it reviews the lessons it learned. This review allows the team to make midcourse corrections to avoid repeating mistakes, and to highlight what went well so that best practices can be created and followed.

Note It is very important that best practices be shared both within and across teams throughout the organization.

Summarizing the principles of project staffing in Barry Boehm's *Software Engineering Economics* (Prentice Hall, 1981), we offer these guidelines:

- **Top talent** Use better and fewer people.
- **Job matching** Fit the tasks to the skills and motivation of the people available.

- **Career progression** Help people self-actualize.
- **Team balance** Select people who will complement and harmonize with one another.
- **Phase out** Cull misfits.

Educating the Team

For a team to be effective, it must understand what it's doing. Many organizations pay only lip service to this simple guideline. Having both a formal and an informal training plan for the project team will smooth the process of shipping the right product at the right time.

Process Education

The process of developing software, as we refer to it throughout this book, is much more than the process of writing code. Formal education about the development process for the team leaders, major stakeholders, and significant project contributors will decrease the overall cost and time schedule for most projects.

Improving communication should be a goal for every project. Training in MSF or other development processes provides the common language for communicating responsibilities and project status. The ideas behind the process have existed for years, and most developers have used some or all of these practices in many of their development projects. Using the common language of MSF, experienced developers can effectively teach others what they know, and team members can relate their own experiences within an easily understood framework.

Technical Education

Creating great products is a difficult task. Technical training must be provided for the Development team, the Logistics Management team, and possibly the Program Management team. New forms of training are created on a daily basis to explain new technologies, but the key to implementing those new technologies is not just to learn about their features, but also to understand best practices.

As an example of the range of technical skills and knowledge that might be required for a project, the following is the skill set needed for working with all aspects of the application code for the Resource Management System (RMS) described in the case studies that are scattered throughout this book:

- HTML
- Dynamic HTML
- Microsoft Active Server Pages (ASP)
- Microsoft Visual Basic Scripting Edition (VBScript)
- Microsoft Internet Information Server (IIS)

- Microsoft Windows NT 4.0
- Microsoft Windows 2000
- Microsoft Systems Management Server 2.x (SMS)
- Microsoft Outlook 2000 programming
- Microsoft Visual InterDev
- Microsoft Visual Basic 6.0 (VB)
- Microsoft Visual C++ 6.x (C++), ATL, STL libraries
- Microsoft Transaction Server 2.0 (MTS)
- Microsoft SQL Server 7.x
- Creating COM objects using VB and C++
- Using the ActiveX Data Objects (ADO)
- Using the Collaborative Data Objects (CDO)

Often forgotten on the training front is a method for understanding the support of the application in the organization's current environment. Successful projects aren't just about getting the code written. The project team needs to consider how the product will affect and be affected by the rest of the environment. What will be the future impact on the product of introducing a new operating system, a new version of the existing operating system, or new base applications used by the product?

The team should also expect software vendors to release new technology products and product revisions during the project, and should be able to determine the impact of new features and support issues with new product revisions during the project's lifecycle. The team should include training sessions in the overall project schedule before committing to any ship dates.

Coordinating with Outside Teams

For a team to be successful, it must interact, communicate, and coordinate with external groups, ranging from the customer and users to other product development teams. Program Management, Product Management, User Education, and Logistics Management are the primary coordination facilitators. These roles are both internally and externally focused, whereas Development and Testing are internally focused and insulated from external communications. (Insulating the Development and Testing teams from external interruptions provides more efficient project delivery.)

It is important that the interfaces with any external groups be explicit and well understood. Figure 3.3 illustrates how coordination occurs with either a business focus or a technology focus. The diagram represents a high-level perspective.

Teams typically have to coordinate with many more external groups, such as quality assurance, finance, and legal.

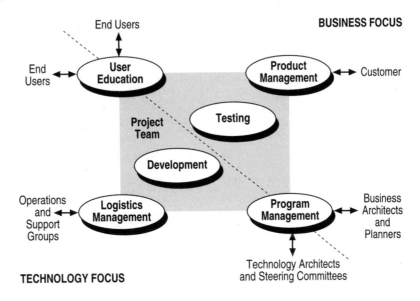

Figure 3.3 Internal and external team communications

Team Management Tools

To effectively manage a strong team, team leaders must possess a range of skills and characteristics that promote communication and teamwork. Continually building and monitoring these skills can help leaders establish a set of best practices for their organization. Below is a list of simple statements that identify several key leadership characteristics and constitute a Leadership Evaluation Checklist as created and distributed by Microsoft Consulting Services. As we discussed at the beginning of this chapter, how a person responds to these statements about himself or herself represents the person's intent; how others respond to the statements about that person represents his or her actual impact.

- I have a long-range view of things.

- I promote innovation and new ideas, and I engage stakeholders in the planning/creative process.

- I encourage people to consider how things could be better, and I enjoy communicating the possibility of a better future.

- I have a clear understanding of how the overall organization works and where it is going.

- I think about "what and why" more than "how and when."
- I have a firm sense of purpose and commitment, and I act on my commitments.
- I am action-oriented, and I can mobilize people and resources.
- I cultivate mutual respect and trust, and I share decision making where appropriate.
- I tell the truth, and my values and beliefs are clear to others.
- I let people know when they've done a good job.
- I let people know I care about what they are doing, and I work to bring out the best in people.
- I promote teamwork, and I foster team goals and commitment.
- I keep channels of communication open, and I communicate plans and goals to the stakeholders.
- I continually evaluate progress against plans.
- I deal with problems in proportion to their importance.
- I make sure people understand their responsibilities, I hold them accountable, and I provide honest and timely feedback.

These traits can turn a team from a loose group of individuals into a team capable of achieving goals much greater than any individual alone can accomplish. It is important to remember that these traits, along with education in the development process and training in technical issues, must be considered integral tools for effective teams.

Often, both customers and product developers see themselves as misunderstood by the other. As a quick reminder of the important relationship between these two groups, project teams can use the Customer's Bill of Rights and the Developer's Bill of Rights provided below to guide their interactions and communications:

- **Customer's Bill of Rights** The Product Management team might want to bear in mind the following customer's rights, taken from Steve McConnell's *Software Project Survival Skills:*
  - To set objectives for the project and have them followed
  - To know how long the project will take and how much it will cost
  - To decide which features are in and which are out of the product
  - To make reasonable changes to requirements throughout the course of the project and to know the costs of making those changes
  - To be apprised regularly of risks that could affect cost, schedule, or quality, and to be provided with options for addressing potential problems
  - To have ready access to project deliverables throughout the project

- **Developer's Bill of Rights** Steve McConnell provides a similar bill of rights for the Development team in *Software Project Survival Skills:*

  - To know the project objectives and to clarify priorities

  - To know in detail what product is to be built and to clarify the product definition if it is unclear

  - To have ready access to the customer, manager, marketer, or other person responsible for making decisions about the software's functionality

  - To work each phase of the project in a technically responsible way, and especially to not have to start coding too early in the project

  - To approve effort and schedule estimates for any requested work, including the right to provide only the kinds of cost and schedule estimates that are theoretically possible at each stage of the project; to take the time needed to create meaningful estimates; and to revise estimates whenever the project's requirements change

  - To have the project's status reported accurately to the customer and upper management

  - To work in a productive environment free from frequent interruptions and distractions, especially during critical parts of the project

Summary

The MSF Development Team Model and principles for application development that we've outlined in this chapter aren't a guarantee for project success. Factors other than team structure help determine the success or failure of a project. However, team structure is critical. Proper team structure is fundamental to success, and implementing the MSF Development Team Model and utilizing its underlying principles will help make teams more effective and, therefore, successful.

In *Rapid Development*, Steve McConnell illustrates this point by saying:

> *Even when you have skilled, motivated, hard-working people, the wrong team structure can undercut their efforts instead of catapulting them to success. A poor team structure can increase development time, reduce quality, damage morale, increase turnover, and ultimately lead to project cancellation.*

The MSF Development Team Model for application development is meant to address exactly the point McConnell makes.

In examining the qualities that make teams successful, we identified key leadership traits and effective team traits. Then we discussed some simple individual and team evaluation tools.

Review

1. What are the six roles of the MSF Development Team Model for application development?

2. What are the focal points and responsibilities of each role?

3. How can the MSF Development Team Model be scaled for large and small projects?

4. What are the stages of development through which a team can progress?

5. What two types of education improve a team member's effectiveness?

C A S E S T U D Y 2

Introducing the RMS Project Team

Bill Pardi looked again at the agenda memo in his hand. *The RMS Project* was the title across the top. "I can't believe I'm here at 8 A.M. for some silly meeting," he muttered to himself. He had known this was coming ever since Dan Shelly, the new CIO, had made Bill and all the other IT leaders attend a training session in January. At the time, Bill had joked about it, saying something about seeing circles in front of his eyes. Dan had smiled, but it became apparent that this Microsoft Solutions Framework stuff was serious business with him, and they were all going to have to deal with it at some point. "Looks like that time is here. Might as well get it over with," Bill thought. He threw a notepad in his bag and headed for the conference room.

On the other side of the building, Dan Shelly sat at his desk, sipping his third cup of coffee and going over the presentation notes for the fourth time. He had been there since 6 A.M. He already had the handouts in everyone's chair and the overhead projector in place. He knew the importance of this project, and the importance of this meeting. "If Ferguson and Bardell is ever going to get maximum value from IT, they'll have to do a better job of integrating the business and IT processes and goals, and MSF is the key," he thought, getting to his feet. "Bill is going to be a tough one to bring around, but once he sees the value to his people, as well as to Ferguson and Bardell, he'll get on board." Putting his notes in his portfolio, he glanced at his watch. "Show time," he said aloud, and started down the hallway.

On the way to the conference room, he saw Tim O'Brien hurrying from the other direction. When Tim saw Dan, he broke into one of his trademark grins and shouted down the hall, "Look at this, Dan! I'm actually here before 10 A.M.!"

"Yes, but all brownie points get taken away if you're late for the meeting," Dan said amiably.

"As long as I'm there before you, I'm not late, big guy." Tim jumped in front of Dan so that he would enter the room first. "See, I made it!" he said triumphantly.

As Dan entered the conference room, he noticed Jane Clayton, Director of Accounting, sitting at one end of the table, engaged in an animated conversation with Marilou Moris, a training contractor they had used on and off over the years. Jane had brought Marilou in to train some of the accounting staff, and the results had been so positive that other units within Ferguson and Bardell used Marilou for training as well. In fact, many people at Ferguson and Bardell thought Marilou was an employee, so well did she fit into the company.

The two women glanced up at Dan and smiled. "You know you have to pay us contractors time-and-a-half for meetings this early, don't you?" Marilou asked. Jane affected a look of mock consternation. "Wouldn't that be offset by the long lunch break you gave your classes when they offered to take you to that new restaurant?" Marilou turned to Jane. "You try docking me for that and I'll start charging you double every time you send one of those executive types to my classes!" she said, grinning.

At the other end of the table, Marta Wolfe-Hellene smiled slightly. Marta was the newest addition to the Engineering division in Chicago. A recent master's graduate of MIT, she was already known to be a bright, organized, and detailed worker, but one who kept to herself for the most part. Dan noted approvingly that she had already written a number of questions at the bottom of the agenda memo. "She's going to be perfect for the team role I chose her for," he thought.

Just then, Bill Pardi walked in and sat down, taking a middle seat at the table. "Good morning, Chief," Dan said, but Bill just grunted. "Shaping up to be an interesting meeting," Dan thought.

"Thank you all for agreeing to be a part of this project team," Dan began. "As I discussed with each of you individually when I asked you to join the team, this project is going to be both highly visible within Ferguson and Bardell, and highly significant for the firm. Each of you has been chosen because I believe you will bring something unique to the team, something that makes you especially well suited to the task I have in mind for you. In a moment, we'll examine those tasks and how each of you fits into the project.

"Thank you also for being on time this morning." Tim beamed. "We've got a lot to cover, as you can see by the agenda I sent out a few days ago. So let's start at the top."

Agenda Overview

"First of all," Dan continued, "let's look at some elements that may be new to you. Three items on this agenda will be on every meeting agenda for this project. The first is Agenda Building. This is an opportunity, right at the beginning of the meeting, for the team to adjust the agenda as it sees fit. Normally, I will construct and distribute an initial agenda a few days before a team meeting. It's possible—indeed, likely—that you will want to discuss items that I either don't know about or that I forgot to include. So, the Agenda Building item is your chance to add or subtract items from the agenda as a team.

FERGUSON AND BARDELL
ENGINEERING • ARCHITECTURE • PROJECT MANAGEMENT

The RMS Project
Meeting Agenda

Meeting Date: March 22, 1999   **Purpose:** Project Kickoff and Team Building

I.   Agenda Building

II.   Introduction of Team Members
- Dan Shelly
- Bill "Chief" Pardi
- Jane Clayton
- Tim O'Brien
- Marta Wolfe-Hellene
- Marilou Moris

III.   Review of MSF

IV.   Brief Introduction to the RMS Project

V.   Explanation of Team Roles
- Product Management
- Program Management
- Development
- Testing
- User Education
- Deployment

VI.   Q&A

VII.   Wrap-Up: Path-Forward Assignments

CHICAGO • DETROIT • MILWAUKEE • CINCINNATI • INDIANAPOLIS • LOUISVILLE

"At the end of the agenda, there will always be questions and answers. This is your last chance for clarification or information before we move to the Wrap-Up item. Your questions do not have to be about items on the agenda, but they do have to relate to the project and be pertinent to the group. We don't want to waste team members' time with questions about other projects or with specifics about this project that the team as a whole is not involved in.

"The final item on the agenda will always be the Wrap-Up. This is where we re-cap any decisions we made in the meeting and make sure everyone is clear on what we did. This is also where we confirm any assignments made during the meeting, along with deadlines. You'll notice I use the term Path-Forward Assign-ments. It may be that during a meeting we will have to analyze a situation, possi-bly taking apart a problem and figuring out what went wrong. That's okay; we need to learn from our mistakes. At the end of the meeting, though, we want to focus on where we go from here. What is our path forward for the current project? What are our immediate next steps? That's how we want to conclude our meetings. Any questions?"

At this first meeting, no one wanted to be the first to ask a question, so Dan pressed ahead. "Does anyone have any adjustments to the agenda that they would like to propose?" Everyone looked around the table to see who might be the first to break the ice. Finally, Marta raised her hand slowly.

"Pardon me, Mr. Shelly, but in your opening remarks you mentioned how impor-tant this project is to the company, and how visible it will be. I appreciate the invitation to be a part of the project team, but I'm not sure why I'm here. Might it be worthwhile to add an agenda item for you to explain why each of us has been included?"

"First of all, Marta, it's Dan, not Mr. Shelly. Secondly, your question is an excel-lent one. My plan is to match up team members with roles in item 5 on the agenda, where I think it will become clear why each of you is on the team. Does that work for you?" With another small smile, Marta nodded, and Dan looked at the others around the table. "How about the rest of you? Does it make sense to you to proceed this way?" Everyone nodded in agreement. Tim leaned over to Marta and whispered loudly, "Thanks for asking, Marta. I was wondering the same thing, but the last time I asked a question in a meeting, I got made project lead!" Everyone laughed, and the tension level in the room dropped noticeably.

Dan turned to Jane. "Jane, why don't you move us into our next agenda item by introducing yourself? We'll just go around the table. Tell us your title, how long you've been at Ferguson and Bardell, and what your responsibilities are." He looked at the rest of the team. "We six are going to be working closely together over the next couple of months, so the sooner we get to know one another, the better. Start now to get a good sense of each other's abilities, as well as each other's blind spots. To be a good team, we'll want to use each person's strengths and help each person work around their weaknesses and preconceptions. Honest communication is a must, so begin by listening and learning as we do the introductions." He turned back to Jane. "Okay, Jane, tell us all about yourself."

Team Introductions

"After a motivational sermonette like that, Dan, are you sure I shouldn't stand up and sing instead?" she said, smiling. Jane proceeded to tell about her years at Ferguson and Bardell and her rise to Director of Accounting, and to give a brief description of her areas of responsibility. She concluded by noting that she was accountable to the management team for all aspects of the accounting function. "So if something isn't working or it's working too slowly, I catch it from above. That makes me highly motivated to find answers that work."

Dan nodded. "Good. We'll need that focus as we move forward. Glad you're here, Jane. Marilou, how about you?"

"Well, I've been doing training here at Ferguson and Bardell, and at other firms around Chicago, for about four years. Most of my work for your firm has been teaching end-user applications such as Office, along with a smattering of operating system classes and such. Haven't done any technical training for Ferguson and Bardell, though."

"She's really good, too," Jane added. "Every time I send some of my staff to one of Marilou's training classes, they always come back more enthusiastic about both the application and their work. She seems to understand what's involved in their day-to-day tasks, and is able to incorporate that into her teaching."

"As any good trainer should," replied Dan. "It's that user savvy that made you a candidate for this team, Marilou. It will be the key to your work here."

"And just when are we going to learn what that work is?" Bill interrupted.

"Hang on, Bill—it's items 4 and 5 on the agenda. Okay, Tim, let's hear your life story."

Tim grinned. "It'll be pretty short, I guess, since I've only been here a few years. Of course," he continued, turning to Bill, "since I'm also the youngest one here, the percentage of my life that I've spent at Ferguson and Bardell is about the same as an old-timer like you, huh, Bill?"

Bill grunted in reply, but his face also softened with a slight smile. In the time Tim had been at the firm, he and Bill had had more than one run-in, and Bill had learned that behind the boyish grin was an excellent network and systems engineer. Improbably, Bill and Tim had developed a fairly good relationship. In fact, Tim was one of the few people at Ferguson and Bardell who could kid Bill Pardi and get away with it.

Tim turned back to the group. "Well, I came here right out of college as the Assistant Network Manager. Basically, all that title got me was a pager and the 'privilege' of being on call 24/7. A few things happened along the way, and—well, I don't know, I was just in the right place at the right time, I guess, and I wound up as Network Manager for the entire company."

Jane leaned forward and looked at Tim. "There's more to it than that and you know it!" Turning to Dan, she continued, "The 'few things' he's referring to happened about six months after he got here. We had moved to NT, and it wasn't going well at all. Tim tried to make a few suggestions, but the consultant doing the work ignored him because he was so young. Finally, after two weeks of the network going up and down every day, your predecessor told the consultant and the Network Manager to step aside, turned to Tim, and asked him, 'Can you fix it?' Tim started working, and in about a day-and-a-half we were up, it was stable, and it's been stable since." As Tim blushed slightly from the praise, Bill muttered "fine work" under his breath.

Dan smiled at Tim. "So, when the manager job came open last spring, you got off third shift and onto the hot seat, right?" Tim nodded while everyone else chuckled. "Well, guy, that seat may get hotter before this project is over. But Tim, I want you to know something: I heard about your expertise when I interviewed for this job, and nothing I've seen since has made me think the reports were exaggerated." Tim started blushing again until Dan added, to general laughter all around, "Just buy an alarm clock, okay?"

Dan then turned to Marta on his right. "Marta, you're the newest one here, so many of us in the room haven't even met you before today. You're an MIT grad. What brought you to us, and what should we know about your work and what you do?"

"I graduated with a master's in Electrical Engineering last spring. I had already done a co-op for Ferguson and Bardell in the Louisville office, and enjoyed both the work and the people. About a month before I graduated, I was contacted by the Director of Engineering here in Chicago about a job, and after some negotiations about the job description, I accepted the job offer and began work here in the summer."

Dan already knew about the negotiations Marta had mentioned, because the Director of Engineering had recommended her to Dan in the first place. He thought it was important for the project team to know something of Marta's interests, though, so he asked her, "Just what issues were you negotiating, if you don't mind my asking?"

Marta laughed. "No, it's certainly not something personal or earth-shattering. I just told him that I wanted to be involved in some cross-discipline project work. One of the attractions of working for Ferguson and Bardell is the opportunity to work with architects and project managers as well as engineers. I'm not sure yet how I want to use my degree, so I want exposure to a wide range of issues and projects."

"I think you'll certainly get some of that on this project," said Dan. "Glad you're with us, Marta, and welcome aboard." There was a murmur of agreement around the table.

All eyes then turned to Bill Pardi as Dan said, "Okay, Bill, I've saved you for last. As Tim has already pointed out, you've been here longer than any of us, and you've probably forgotten more about technology than most of us know. As we build this team, what do we need to know about the Chief?"

Bill looked up, seeming not to know what to say, to be at a loss for words. He wasn't comfortable talking about himself, at least not in this "warm and fuzzy" manner, and it showed. Finally, shrugging slightly, he said, "I guess being ex-military explains a lot about me. When I went in the Navy, I was a young jerk with a big mouth and an attitude to match. The Navy taught me that big talk had to be backed up with big action. Ever since, I've put more stock in getting things done than in talking about it. The Navy also taught me about computers, and how to crank out code. Some of the projects we did! Churning out line after line for hours, days at a time. Excuses didn't work, talking didn't work, meetings didn't work; the only thing that counted was how many lines you got in and compiled that day. We built stuff that's still running today, still slamming data through, and we put in the hours to do it. Now I can't find anyone willing to burn some midnight oil to get projects out. It seems like it takes longer and longer to get stuff out the door, even though this Visual Whatever stuff is sup-posed to make it easier. Some days, I wish I was back writing VAX code on a green-screen terminal, rather than managing a bunch of mouse-clickers." Then, as if exhausted by his sudden burst of autobiography, Bill slumped back in his chair and stared at the conference table.

No one spoke for a moment. Finally, Dan broke the silence. "Bill, we've all felt that way, one time or another. Managing others is often much harder than simply doing the work yourself. I'm hoping that as we all work together on this project, the processes and models we use will make the work of managing a little bit easier."

After another pause, Jane spoke up and said, "Okay, Dan, you've put all of us on the hot seat. How about you? What brings you to Ferguson and Bardell, and to this project that is so important, none of us know anything about it?"

Dan smiled at the question, and thought for a moment before replying. "Well, I came from a law firm, as you know. What you probably don't know is that tech-nology was not my first career choice. I began my work life as a teacher—his-tory, in fact—and I'm not sure I've ever completely left that field. I enjoy helping people: helping them learn, helping them grow, helping them succeed. That's one of the reasons I got involved in computers. Technology should be an enabler, not a barrier, and that's what I want to make it. That's also how I see my job: helping my staff and the rest of the company become more adept at their jobs through the intelligent use of technology. Remember, technology should never be the end; it should always be the means to the end. In the case of Ferguson and Bardell, that end is providing the best architecture work, engineering work, and project management to our clients that we possibly can. The business goals should both drive and inform our technology goals. Which brings us to MSF."

MSF Revisited

At the mention of the acronym, the other members of the team realized that they were moving to the next item on the agenda and got out notepads and pens. Dan turned down the room lights and laid his first transparency on the overhead projector's glass. It showed an arrow going in a circle, divided into three different sections.

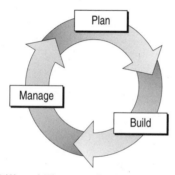

"Bill and Tim, you both took the MSF training we held in January, so some of this will just be review. Marilou, I seem to remember that you borrowed the material from the IT library in February. Were you able to go through it?" Marilou nodded. "Good. So, Jane and Marta are the only ones who haven't seen this before. I'll get both of you a copy of the basic material, so you can look it over before the next meeting. For now, I want to go over some of the key points that apply to today's agenda. As we move through this project, we'll spend part of each meeting reviewing the pertinent MSF material for that phase of the project.

"MSF stands for Microsoft Solutions Framework, and it is just that: a framework. It is a set of principles, models, and processes on which we can build our own project-management framework, metrics, and procedures. It is both conceptual and pragmatic, and comes out of the experiences of Microsoft and many other firms as they struggle with using technology to further business goals.

"This arrow represents the ongoing work of the IT department. That work falls under one of these three rubrics: Plan, Build, or Manage. Notice that the arrow is going in a circle, indicating that the work is iterative. In other words, we never stop planning, building, and managing."

He replaced the first transparency with the next one. It showed another arrow going in a circle, but this time the circle was divided into four sections instead of three.

"This diagram shows one of the models of MSF, the Development Process Model. This is a model of the process we are going to follow as we work through our project together. The process has four phases: Envisioning, Planning, Developing, and Stabilizing. In other words, first we have to get a vision for what the problem really is and what our solution might be. Then, we have to do the hard, detailed work of building plans to carry out the solution. Once the plans are complete, we have to develop the solution. Finally, we have to deploy the solution and make it stable and usable. There are many more details to this model which we will fill in as we go along, but that's the gist of it for now."

Jane squinted at the image on the screen. "What are those diamond-looking things at the points of the compass? They look like bases on a baseball field."

"Glad you asked, Jane. Those are milestones. Each phase of the project concludes with a milestone, which is a time for all the members of the team to review progress, resynchronize objectives, and make any mid-course corrections needed. There are also milestones within each phase. We'll cover these as we move through the phases."

Dan turned off the overhead projector and turned the lights back up. He pointed to a box on the credenza. "I have gotten each of you a binder for this project, and I'll be handing out various MSF materials for you to review as we move through the work. One of your assignments for the next meeting will be to review the sections I've already put in the binders. They are the parts of MSF that are specific to developing new software applications. Which leads us to RMS."

RMS Application

Dan leaned back against the credenza. "RMS stands for Resource Management System. It is a new application that we are going to develop for use throughout Ferguson and Bardell, including all the branch offices. As I've already said, RMS is both a critical and a highly visible project. In fact, all the employees of the firm are resources that RMS will manage, and RMS will handle the scheduling and time tracking of those employees as well. In other words, every person at Ferguson and Bardell will be able to see and use the results of this team's work. And, since RMS will provide the means we'll use to gather time and billing information, everyone's paycheck will depend on RMS being both effective and stable."

As the significance of the project began to sink in, the room became very quiet. Dan waited a moment and then continued. "Normally, developing such an application would have been handled exclusively by the Chief and his crew. In thinking about the RMS project, though, I decided that it was the perfect project for introducing MSF to Ferguson and Bardell. I think, as you begin to understand the value that MSF can bring to a company, you'll see what I mean.

"Let me make one thing very clear from the beginning: My decision to involve all of you, and to do the RMS project using MSF methods, does *not* mean that I don't trust the Chief or his team. He and I have already discussed RMS and why I wanted to tackle it this way."

Jane interjected, "But Dan, you said this was a project to develop a new piece of software. How can that involve me? I haven't the slightest clue how to—what was that you called it, Bill?—'crank out code.' I barely know how to record a macro in Word. What good am I to a project that is supposed to write a new time and billing system?"

"I am wondering why you asked me to be part of this team, too," Marta added. "It is true I did some programming in college, but I suspect you are not going to write this application in either GBASIC or Fortran. Therefore, my question is the same as Jane's: What am I doing here?"

"Excellent questions, and certainly understandable," Dan replied. "Let me explain what you both are doing here—indeed, what each of us is doing here—by way of these next few transparencies." And with that, he turned the projector back on.

Review of the MSF Development Team Model

The next transparency, titled Team Goals for Success, had six bullets. "I want us to shoot for these six goals for project success," said Dan. "See what you think of them." He read the goals out loud. "Satisfied customers. Delivery within constraints. Delivery to specifications based on user requirements. Only release the software after addressing all known issues. Enhanced user performance. And finally, smooth deployment and ongoing management." He turned to the group. "The contention of MSF is that no project can be called a success unless *all six* of these goals are met. My question for all of you is, are these valid goals?"

"Sure, they're great goals, Dan, but I've never seen any project come close to meeting all six of them!" Jane exclaimed. "Aren't these just a little too optimistic?"

"Not only that, but some of them seem contradictory," Tim added. "How do you satisfy your customers, deliver within constraints, and deliver to specifications that you got from the users? It's not possible to do all of those on the same project, is it?"

"That's the beauty of the framework," Dan answered, taking a step out from behind the projector. "I've *seen* this work. I've seen a project team use MSF on a large project and succeed because of it. At my last firm, we put in a client tracking system and used the MSF approach to do it. If you asked anyone associated with that project, they would tell you that all six goals were achieved. I'm telling you, it *can* be done. And here's how we're going to do it." He switched to a transparency that displayed six ovals arranged in a circle.

Dan turned to the group. "This model represents the six roles on an MSF project team. Each of you is here to fill one of these roles. Before I tell you what the roles are and which role is assigned to each of you, I want to point out something about this diagram.

"There are two types of project teams. The kind you are probably familiar with is the *hierarchical* type, where one person is the Project Manager and everyone else reports to him or her. The problem with that is that the only person on the team who is ultimately responsible, and who therefore is highly motivated to make the project a success, is the Project Manager.

"The model we are going to use is represented by these ovals. You'll notice that all of them are the same size and that they are all related to each other in the same way. In other words, they are equals. This is a *team of peers*. Each person on this team is equally important, and each is equally responsible for the success or failure of the project. You'll also notice that each oval is a different color. Each person on the team has a role and a responsibility. As we move through the project, responsibilities will become clearer, but for now, just understand that each one of you has a role on the team that only *you* can fulfill. Now, let's look at the roles."

Team Roles

Dan placed a new transparency on the projector. It was the same as the previous one, except that each oval had a title. He pointed to the top oval, titled *Product Management*. "Jane, Product Management is your role. You represent the customer to the team and the team to the customer. Your main task is to make sure we meet the needs of the customer."

Jane had been writing, but she looked up to ask, "And just who is the customer that I am representing?"

"Often, the customer and the user may be the same person, but many times they aren't. The best way to identify the customer is to look for the person or persons whose direct needs you're trying to meet. So, within the Ferguson and Bardell organization, who is directly concerned with the firm's ability to track time and billing effectively?"

Jane thought for a moment. "I started to say 'me,' because I certainly have an interest in it. But it seems to me that the CFO is the person whom the management team holds ultimately responsible for time and billing, so I'd say he's also the customer."

Dan nodded. "Exactly right. As the Product Management person on the team, you represent both your department, Accounting, and our ultimate customer, the CFO. Your goal is first, to understand completely the needs of the customer, and then, to lead the team to a shared vision of both those needs and a way to meet them. Now you see why your ability to write code is not the issue. You are here because of your ability to understand the customer's needs, to communicate them to us, and to keep us focused on meeting those needs."

Jane nodded that she understood, so Dan moved on to the next oval on the circle. "Program Management is next, and that is my role. I am responsible for delivering the right product at the right time. This means that my Program Management role owns and drives the schedule, the features, and the resources for the project."

"That sounds just like the old role of Project Manager!" Tim said.

"It is similar, but there are some key differences. Remember, this is a team of peers. Everyone is responsible for the success of the project, not just me. In addition, because everyone's viewpoint is equally valid as they fulfill the work of their particular role, I can't simply dictate what I think or want. To accomplish the goals of Program Management, I have to act as a leader, facilitator, and coordinator of the project, but not the boss."

"So in other words, you can't throw your CIO weight around in here," Tim commented, smiling.

"That's right. Only within the tasks of my role do I have the authority." He turned to the transparency and pointed to the next oval down. "This is the role of Development. Bill, this is your baby, as you might expect. Your tasks are to participate in the design phase as technical consultant, helping us to see what is doable, and then to build the application based on the design and vision the team comes up with."

"So in other words," Bill said, "I listen to the requirements from Jane, then get my guys and gals together, build it, and give it to her, right? That sounds pretty similar to what we are doing now."

"That's only part of the picture," said Dan. "There are other pieces, other roles, that you also have to relate to, which will make the process different than the one you are used to. One of these," he continued, pointing to the next oval, "is the Testing role. Marta, that's your job." Marta began writing as Dan listed her tasks. "It is up to you to design and carry out testing plans and to track the status of the application in terms of quality. We should be able to ask you at any time for a list of issues remaining in the application, and you should know what they are. The bottom line is, your goal is to portray the status of the product accurately, at any time, by clearly stating what is wrong and what is currently right with the product."

Before Marta could respond, Bill exploded. "Do you mean to tell me that *Marta*, who is new to Ferguson and Bardell and who doesn't write code herself, is going to be testing what my folks write?"

Dan nodded. "That's exactly what I mean, Bill, and if you think about it, you'll see it makes good sense. The same person can't be in charge of both coding and testing, simply because of the inherent conflict of interest. You need the independent verification—someone to tell you the unvarnished truth, someone who hasn't been involved in the coding so they don't miss something through familiarity. As for not being able to write code—that doesn't matter. *Your* people will write the code; Marta's job is to figure out ways to test what you write. That's where her engineering background, as well as her organization and attention to detail, will be invaluable."

Turning to Marilou, Dan pointed to the next oval. "Marilou, this is you—User Education. Just as Jane is the go-between in the team-customer relationship, you are the link between the RMS team and the users of the application. You will take part in the design phase, helping us to understand what the users need and what the feature set should be. Your primary responsibility, though, will be to design and develop the support systems for the product, including the Help system, and to plan and carry out the training."

Making some notes, Marilou asked, "I think I know already, but tell me: What is the difference between the customer and the user?"

Jane spoke up, "That's easy. The customer pays for it, while the users use it!" Everyone laughed, including Dan. "Actually, that's correct, Jane, at least partially. The customer typically has a business problem that the application is designed to fix. So, the customer is willing to throw resources of some sort—money, time, labor—at the problem. The users themselves may not have the need, at least in the same way as the customer, but the users are the ones who will actually be using the application to meet the need. The requirements of the customer and the users may be very different, and perhaps even contradictory. That's why we have two roles on the team to deal with them."

Tim had been fidgeting impatiently in his chair, and finally could wait no longer. "Okay, Dan, everyone else has an assignment, a role. What's mine?"

Dan pointed to the last oval. "This is you: Logistics Management. You're our link to the operations staff. It will be your task to plan and manage the deployment. With that in mind, you should be watching for support and management issues as we do the design work. You will support the product during the beta phase, and then you will train the help desk folks to support the product once it is deployed." His expression turning serious, he continued, "Tim, this is a growth opportunity for you. This is more management than hands-on work. I picked you to do it because I think you have what it takes to be an excellent manager some-day, and I want you to begin understanding and using MSF now." Tim nodded.

Dan displayed the last transparency. "Remember the six goals for the project? I'm sure it occurred some of you that the six goals and the six roles might be re-lated. Here's how they interact.

"Jane, in the Product Management role, you are responsible for satisfied custom-ers. In the Program Management role, I am responsible for delivering RMS within project constraints. Bill, you and your group are responsible for delivery to product specs. Marta, your role keeps us from releasing until all known issues have been addressed. Marilou, your role ensures enhanced user performance. Finally, Tim, you are responsible for smooth product deployment." He turned back to the group. "Any questions?"

Bill had been alternately rearranging his papers and tapping his pencil, seeming to get more and more agitated as the assignments were handed out. He burst out, "I don't get it, Dan. It looks to me like you've taken everything that the develop-ment staff is used to doing and parsed it out to non-developers. We've got an ac-counting person setting the vision, a newbie engineer overseeing testing, and an Excel-clicker-turned-trainer gathering user requirements! What's left for me and my staff to do, for heaven's sake?"

"In one word, Bill—*develop*," Dan replied, keeping his voice level. This was the fight he'd expected, the tooth that had to come out, and better he did it quickly and calmly, rather than slowly and loudly. "In the MSF materials, the point is driven home again and again that many of these roles can be assigned to the same person, doubling up roles if necessary. The one role that must stand on its own is Development. 'Leave the developers alone so they can develop.' That's the goal.

"Bill, by moving these responsibilities to other team members, you and your staff can do what you do best: write killer code. Your job is to write an applica-tion that meets the vision, the customer requirements, the user requirements, the deployment requirements, and the maintenance requirements, and to do it in such a way that we don't notice your work at all—like a finely balanced hand-tool that feels so right we just pick it up and go to work. Or, if we do notice it, we are innately pleased at the craftsmanship of it. Frankly, Bill, MSF may be the best thing that's ever happened to developers."

Still not convinced, Bill replied, "Well, I sure hope you've planned about six months for this, because with all this 'teamwork' stuff and all that requirements junk, it'll take us at least that long to get this thing designed and written."

Dan smiled. "Make it one-third of that, Bill. Two months." Bill's jaw dropped open as Dan continued, "We're going to have a tested, working application on line in two months. And we're going to walk the entire MSF process along the way."

Bill spluttered, "That can't be done! There's no way we can meet all those requirements you listed earlier—customer, user, whatever else it was—and get it done in two months!"

Dan paused and recalled having the same conversation with the Enterprise Architecture team. "Bill, that's a very common reaction with those new to MSF. My honest answer is, you're right. We can't. So part of our process is going to be learning what to do with that reality. That comes later." He turned to the agenda. "For now, we have two final agenda items. First, questions and answers. Are there any questions?" Everyone looked somewhat shell-shocked, and Dan hadn't expected any questions at this point. The questions would come as the team warmed to the project and to each other.

"Great. Then our last item is Path-Forward Assignments. For now, those are fairly simple. Each of you is to take the binder I've given you, and by our next meeting, you are to review the Development Team Model material that we outlined today and study the Development Process Model material. I expect you all to know the responsibilities of your role and how they relate to the project as a whole. I may also make some individual assignments, so watch your e-mail. We will meet back here Thursday morning, same time, ready to move into the first phase of the project as laid out in your materials. See you then."

As the members of the newly constituted RMS Project Team gathered up their things and moved to the credenza to pick up their binders, Dan called Bill over. "Bill, you remember when you called Marilou an—let's see, how did you phrase that? Oh yes—an Excel-clicker-turned-trainer?" Bill nodded, slightly embarrassed. "Well, Marilou's a little more than just an Excel-clicker. She actually has both her CNE and MCSD. She does training because she loves it. So when you talk about 'cranking out code,' she's done a little bit of that herself. Thought you'd like to know."

Bill's face dropped as he digested this information. Watching Marilou as she was leaving, he said, "Thanks for telling me privately, Dan. That could have been embarrassing if you or she had corrected that stupid remark I made in the meeting."

"Not a problem, Chief. Wouldn't ever want to embarrass one of my staff in public. Just wanted you to have the real picture." Dan gathered up his materials and the last binder, and turned back to Bill. "In fact, my goal in this is to make you look good, Bill. If we work together on this MSF thing, I think you'll be pleasantly surprised at how good it will make your developers look when it's done."

"If it can do that," he said, "then I guess even this old Navy dog can learn a new trick or two." The two men smiled at each other as they parted ways, binders in hand.

C H A P T E R   4

Development Process

About This Chapter

Successful management of a development project requires two important qualities. The first is *rigor*, which ensures that a process is followed. The second is *flexibility*, which allows the process to adapt to a changing environment. In this chapter, we first look at two traditional models for application development: the Waterfall Model and the Spiral Model. We then discuss another model that is widely used today: the Unified Software Development Process (UP or Unified Process).

The majority of this chapter is devoted to the MSF Process Model for Application Development, which we call the *MSF Development Process Model*. Rather than a step-by-step methodology, MSF is a structural framework that an organization can adapt to suit its particular needs. The MSF Development Process Model is the part of this framework that describes the life cycle of a successful software development project. This model allows a project team to respond to customer requests and to change product direction midcourse. It also allows a team to deliver key portions of the product faster than would otherwise be possible. The MSF Development Process Model is a flexible component of MSF that has been successfully proven in the software industry to improve project control, minimize risk, improve product quality, and increase development speed.

The principles and guidelines we provide in this chapter are based on our own experience with the creation of application architectures and the implementation of enterprise applications, as well as information from the following sources:

- Microsoft Solutions Framework
- Walker Royce's *Software Project Management: A Unified Framework*
- Grady Booch, James Rumbaugh, and Ivar Jacobson's *The Unified Modeling Language User Guide*
- Ivar Jacobson, Grady Booch, and James Rumbaugh's *The Unified Software Development Process*

Upon completion, you will be able to:

- Understand the characteristics of the Waterfall and Spiral Models and list their disadvantages.
- List the workflows of the Unified Process.
- Identify the primary models of the Unified Process.
- List the four phases of the MSF Development Process Model.
- Understand the benefits of versioned releases and the impact of an iterative approach on development projects.
- Relate team roles and responsibilities to the MSF Development Process Model.
- Understand the relationships between project variables and constraints, and the concept of managing tradeoffs.
- Analyze projects to determine goal-driven milestones.
- Analyze development projects to determine process iteration goals.

Models for Application Development

Every software development effort goes through a process, called a life cycle, that includes all the steps and activities that lead to the product's initial release. It is possible to build a model of this life cycle that illustrates the activities at some level of abstraction, and that serves to establish the order in which a project specifies, implements, tests, and performs its activities. A well-built life cycle model can streamline a project and ensure that each step moves the project closer toward its goal.

Modern processes for application development have evolved over time from best practices derived from very traditional processes, such as those represented by the Waterfall Model and the Spiral Model. As a way of providing background information for the rest of this chapter, we first take a look at the main characteristics of these two models. Then we look at the Unified Process and the MSF Development Process Model.

Waterfall Model

The common metaphor of building a house is often used to describe the traditional approach to application development. The builder first gathers information from the customer about his or her needs and desires, determines what needs to be built, designs the structure, and constructs it from the plans. The builder must ensure that the building holds together and that all the components, from the electricity and plumbing to the doorbell, are fully functional. The customer then tests everything to ensure that all elements meet expectations. Even after the customer moves into the new home, the builder must occasionally come back to fix minor problems.

The stages of building a house are similar to the stages of the Waterfall Model of application development. As shown in Figure 4.1, the tightly defined Waterfall Model is an orderly, highly structured process based on the following well-defined development steps:

- Gathering system and software requirements
- Analysis
- Program design
- Coding and unit testing
- System integration
- System testing
- Operation acceptance

Each step is completed and thoroughly documented before the next step can begin.

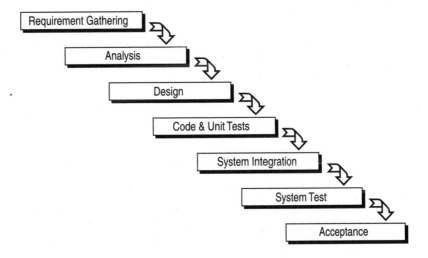

Figure 4.1 Waterfall Model

Strict use of the Waterfall Model is declining. Following this model causes several problems throughout the product life cycle, which are summarized below.

- **Extra time** Typically more time than was initially scheduled is needed to integrate subsystems into a complete, working application.
- **Late design changes** Design flaws that require significant changes to the product are discovered late in the software coding process. Rarely is tangible design validation performed in the project's early stages.

- **Inadequate risk resolution** The project's risks are not resolved until late in the product life cycle.

- **Lack of requirement revisions** The project's requirements must be stated and frozen at the first stages of the development process. Often, the project's stakeholders don't completely understand the business and product requirements at the beginning of project. With most software projects, requirements are clarified and changed throughout the project, which dramatically increases product cost and delays ship times. If the changes are not integrated into the product, the stakeholders don't think the product they receive is the one they requested.

- **Limited opportunities for input** The traditional practice allows a single review process to finalize each project stage. This single opportunity to voice concerns and suggest changes produces an over-sensitized focus on details that can lead to adversarial relationships between project stakeholders.

- **Lack of review** The first four stages of the Waterfall Model are paper-based exercises, and to prove that the project is progressing, reams of paper may be produced as each stage is completed. As volumes of system documentation are presented, the most understood portions are often the ones that are reviewed, while the more complex portions are simply assumed to be correct.

Spiral Model

More recent management techniques have resulted in an iterative approach to application development known as the Spiral Model, as seen in Figure 4.2. The stages of application development that make up this model are typically characterized as:

- **Inception** Application planning and analysis
- **Elaboration** Application design
- **Construction** Application implementation
- **Transition** Application assessment and stabilization

Walker Royce in *Software Project Management: A Unified Framework* notes that each stage typically involves five activity phases: requirements, design, implementation, deployment, and management. The Spiral Model's process is a continual circle through the stages of development, with each stage requiring multiple revolutions through the five phases. For example, the inception stage may require four iterations through the five RSIDM phases. The development life cycle is designed to define the product more tightly over time so that each iteration brings the product closer to the point of delivery.

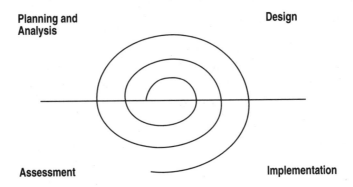

Figure 4.2 Spiral Model

Like the Waterfall Model, the Spiral Model can run into problems, such as the following:

- **Feature postponement** Complex features—important to the customer and users—are moved to later iterations of the project. Postponing important features delays and decreases the project's ROI.

- **Never-ending projects** Individuals and organizations need to reach closure on projects, but a project can take on a life of its own, with work being done solely for the sake of the project, and not directed toward achieving business goals. If the project's business goals change after multiple project iterations, there is a tendency for team members to continue to work to get the next feature set completed, without addressing the changed goals. But the changing business goals directly affect the viability of the project, and best practices are often lost if those goals are not addressed.

- **Unknown costs** The continual iteration, which moves and postpones features, makes feature cost/benefit analysis difficult. The historical costs and benefits of the project are difficult to identify and use for future project justification.

- **No sense of stability** When systems are in a constant state of flux, the customer and users often feel that the product is unstable. Constant updating requires additional resources for product maintenance and significantly increases product deployment costs.

- **Lack of automation** Most organizations fail to invest adequate capital in the automation of the software development process. Significant up-front costs for automation and productivity tools are viewed as project expenses rather than capital investment. Without an automated development process, however, the number of iterations required to deliver a product can significantly delay its ship dates. Additionally, when the product is ready for deployment, lack of automated software deployment tools makes it difficult to continually update all users' computers with new product versions.

Unified Process

The information in this section is based primarily on Walker Royce's *Software Project Management: A Unified Framework* (Addison-Wesley, 1998), and Ivar Jacobson, Grady Booch, and James Rumbaugh's *The Unified Software Development Process* (Addison-Wesley, 1999). Although we try to summarize this model accurately, this brief discussion nevertheless reflects our interpretation of the Unified Process, which is based on our development experience. For a strict definition of the Unified Process, refer to the source texts.

One commonly used model for the analysis, design, and implementation of enterprise applications is the Unified Software Development Process (Unified Process or UP). The Unified Process, which requires extensive use of the Unified Modeling Language (UML) modeling, is:

- Use-case driven.
- Architecture-centric.
- An iterative development process.
- An incremental development process.
- Risk-confronting.
- An object-oriented and layered design approach.
- A repository for object-oriented system development patterns, objects, and code.

Workflows

The heart of the Unified Process is five core workflows that are continually executed during the four phases of the development process until the application is completed. Each completion of the five-workflow steps is called an iteration, and each iteration culminates in an internal product release. The workflow names are descriptors that simplify communication; they contain no magic or hidden meaning. These core workflows are:

- **Requirements** The Requirements Workflow is done to gather business, application, and technical requirements.
- **Analysis** The Analysis Workflow provides business and application modeling derived from requirements.
- **Design** The Design Workflow uses object-oriented design techniques to complete the application architecture.

- **Implementation** The Implementation Workflow is execution of the designed work including prototypes.
- **Testing** The Testing Workflow verifies the proper work has been done.

The next iteration begins the cycle again with the Requirements Workflow. We will briefly summarize the main workflows of the Unified Process.

Requirements

The main purpose of the Requirements Workflow is to aim the iteration toward developing the right application for the customer and users. The underlying goal is to describe the application in enough detail that agreement can be reached between the customer, user, and development team on what the application can and cannot do. Information can be gathered from many sources; the project stakeholders, an existing system, or occasionally an existing requirements document created by the customer.

As the team gathers the information, it develops a list of candidate requirements. These requirements can be structured with a brief name, description, status (proposed, approved, incorporated, or validated), estimated cost to implement, priority, and associated level of risk to implement the feature. The context of the application is also part of this workflow. The Unified Process suggests that the context be described using business modeling or domain modeling. Functional requirements detailing who does what to the application are noted in the use case model. It is also important to capture nonfunctional requirements regarding things such as performance, extensibility, and reliability. These nonfunctional requirements can be tagged to specific use cases as well as appended to the use case model as nonfunctional system requirements.

Note The use case model is in the language of the customer and user.

The team can also deliver a set of UI designs or prototypes that represent the interaction of the roles conducted by the users. Ivar Jacobson *et al.* summarize the high-level deliverables of the Requirements Workflow as:

- *A business model or a domain model to set the context of the system.*
- *A use case model that captures the functional requirements and the nonfunctional requirements that are specific to individual use cases. The use case model is described by a survey description, a set of diagrams, and a detailed description of each use case.*
- *A set of user interface sketches and prototypes for each actor representing the design of the user interfaces.*
- *A supplementary requirements specification for the requirements that are generic and not specific for a particular use case.*

Analysis

During the UP's Analysis Workflow, the application requirements are examined and described in the terms of the application's developers. This description is a refinement and structuring of the functional requirement captured by the use case model in the Requirements Workflow. The Analysis Workflow is an interim step that serves as an abstraction of the requirements and leads to the actual design of the application. Ivar Jacobson *et al.* summarize the Analysis Workflow as:

- *A more precise specification of the requirements than we have in the results from requirements capture, including the use case model.*

- *An analysis model is described using the language of the developers, and can thereby introduce more formalism and be used to reason about the internal workings of the system.*

- *An analysis model structures the requirements in a way that facilitates understanding them, preparing them, changing them and in general, maintaining them.*

- *An analysis model can be viewed as the first cut at a design model (although it is a model of its own), and is thus an essential input when the system is shaped in design and implementation. This is because the system as a whole should be maintainable, not just the description of its requirements.*

The high-level deliverable of the Analysis Workflow is the architectural view of the analysis model. This view consists of:

- **Analysis classes** These consist of border, entity, and control classes. Border classes are situated between the user roles (actors) and the internal working of the application and are often candidates for presentation layer or user services. Entity classes describe long-lived and persistent information. Control classes describe the application behaviors that handle the sequencing, transaction, and control of the application, excluding those described by border and entity classes.

- **Use case realization analysis** Ivar Jacobson *et al.* define this as:

    ...a collaboration within the analysis model that describes how a specific use case is realized and performed in terms of the analysis classes and their interacting analysis objects.

    This combination, or *collaboration*, of use case diagrams and analysis class diagrams depicts their interaction. The team can then determine how to group the use cases by the classes, their objects and iterations.

- **Analysis packages** These seek to organize the analysis classes, use case realizations, and potentially other analysis packages. They represent the grouping of functional requirements described by use cases. Thus, analysis packages can be based on use cases that support a specific business process, a specific user role (actor), or related use cases noted by generalization or extended relationships.

Design

Following the analysis of the application, the lower-level Design Workflow can begin. The design classes and their behaviors are developed and assigned to one of four layers: standard user interface (presentation view), business, access, and data.

The Design Workflow consists of the following activities:

- Define the structure into subsystems (design model).
- Distribute the subsystems to layers (design model).
- Define the class and object interfaces (design model).
- Mapping active classes into deployment nodes (deployment models).

At the conclusion of the Design Workflow, the application's architecture is complete. The design model, which is the representation of the application's physical model, is also complete. Unlike the analysis model, the design model should be maintained throughout the application's life cycle. The design classes are fully described including their state, properties, and methods, as well as their relationship to other classes.

Implementation

The Unified Process is strongly based on the Spiral Model and features incremental prototyping and development until the development team is satisfied with the product and all required features are implemented. The Implementation Workflow is the actualization of the Design Workflow. There should be a one-to-one correspondence between the design classes and the code that is developed during this workflow. Each class can be compiled into an executable or many classes can be combined into a single executable, depending on the implementation language and analysis package design. The steps for this workflow, which are fed by the Design Workflow, are:

- Implement architectural prototype.
- Implement the components (classes and objects).
- Unit test the components.
- Integrate the components.
- Build the application.
- Derive tests from use cases.
- Evaluate architecture.
- Plan the next build.
- Iterate development.

Testing

The Testing Workflow verifies the expected results against the actual results of the Implementation Workflow. Testing is conducted upon conclusion of the Implementation Workflow regardless of whether the iteration's release is internal, intermediate, or external. Through each iteration, the testing model is refined to remove obsolete test cases, generate regression test cases, and create new test cases for future builds. Test cases specify a particular way of validating the application including the conditions of the test, the required input, and expected output. Test cases should be derived from use cases. In addition to testing the application as a whole, further test cases should be executed to verify the installation on the given application platform and verify the application is correctly configured. Finally, test components can be developed to automate the execution of the test cases.

Project Phases

Because the Unified Process is based primarily on the Spiral Model, like that model, its four phases of development are Inception, Elaboration, Construction, and Transition. Each phase strives to achieve specific goals:

- Inception Phase iterations focus on producing the business case.
- Elaboration Phase iterations are responsible for developing the baseline architecture.
- Construction Phase iterations focus on creating the product with incremental releases of product builds and features.
- Transition Phase iterations ensure the product is ready for release to the user community.

Requirements and the analysis, design, and implementation architecture represent the majority of the work within the Inception and Elaboration Phases. The completion of each phase describes the application in a level of detail using the Unified Process models. In addition, movement from one phase to the next is the result of accomplishing the goal for the phase and reaching the milestone for the phase. At each phase's major milestone, a critical go/no-go business decision is made about whether the project should continue, thus approving the next phase's requirements for budget and schedule. These major milestones are the synchronization points between the technical portions and business portions of the project.

Inception

Although no specific number of iterations can be associated with the Inception Phase, typically this phase does not exceed two workflow iterations and relies primarily on the Requirements Workflow. The Inception Phase is defined strictly by its goals, which are to set the scope of what the product should do, reduce the probability that the worst project risks will materialize, and prepare the project justification via the initial business case. The four steps used to make the business case are as follows:

- **Delimit the scope of the proposed system** This is the identification of the applications boundaries and its relationship to other systems.

- **Describe the candidate architecture** These contain more detail on the new, difficult, or risky portions of the application with the goal of creating confidence that the team can create a stable architecture.

- **Identify the critical risks** In addition to simply identifying the risks, a management plan is created to mitigate the risks at the appropriate time.

- **Demonstrate that the proposed system is capable of supporting the business case** An application prototype along with the initial use case can generate this agreement from the application's customer and user.

The Inception Phase's milestone is the Life-Cycle Objective Milestone.

Elaboration

Like the Inception Phase, the Elaboration Phase is typically limited to at most two or three workflow iterations. The Elaboration Phase maintains a focus on "do-ability." The primary goals of this phase are to deliver the application architecture baseline, to estimate in some detail the cost and the schedule, and to plan for the Construction Phase. The main steps of this phase are as follows:

- **Create an architectural baseline** This covers significant functionality and features important to the project stakeholders.

- **Identify significant risks** These should take into account the plan, its cost, and the schedule of later phases.

- **Specify quality attributes** These include reliability, defect rates, and performance (response times).

- **Capture use cases** These should include 80 percent of the functional requirements.

- **Prepare a project bid** This encompasses the schedule, staff requirements, and cost within the limits set by business practices.

The Elaboration Phase's milestone is the Life-Cycle Architecture Milestone.

Construction

In relation to the other phases, the Construction Phase consumes the longest time period and requires the highest resource requirements. It also requires the greatest number of workflow iterations. The Construction Phase is focused on creating the application. Its primary goal is to complete development of the application and ensure that it can begin transition to customers. This transition means the application has achieved initial operational capability and is ready to begin beta testing. Incremental development provides ongoing feature releases with each additional application build. The Construction Phase activities include the following:

- **Extend use cases** This includes identification of details, descriptions, and realization for all use cases.
- **Finish the first three workflows** The Analysis, Design, and Implementation Workflows should be completed.
- **Start testing** About 15 percent of the Testing Workflow should be completed.
- **Maintain the integrity of the architecture** Changes and updates should be carried out as needed, but within the context of the application's architecture.
- **Manage risks** Continue managing the risks identified in the earlier phases.

The Construction Phase's milestone is the Initial Operation Capability Milestone.

Transition

The Transition Phase is denoted by the initial beta release of the application to the customer and limited release to the user community. The two primary goals of this phase are to ensure that the product is ready to be released and to train users how to use the product. The additional burden placed upon the application by the user community and the application's true environment provides the necessary testing to determine whether the development process has reached its final milestone: the Product Release Milestone. The Transition Phase activities can include the following:

- **Prepare for deployment** This includes environment and site preparation and advising the customer on necessary environment updates.
- **Prepare documentation** This includes operation, user, and other manuals that will accompany the product when it is released.

- **Tune the application** The product must be prepared for the production environment.

- **Correct defects** All bugs found during the beta tests must be addressed.

- **Modify the application** The software might need modification to accommodate problems that were unforeseen earlier in the process.

Iterations

As development of the product continues through its phases, each workflow iteration brings the product closer to its final release. Iterations are continued within a specific phase until the goal for the phase has been reached. The emphasis of each iteration changes as time progresses through the four phases. Figure 4.3, which is based on a diagram in *The Unified Software Development Process* by Ivar Jacobson *et al.*, shows the amount of effort needed to execute each workflow over the project's life cycle.

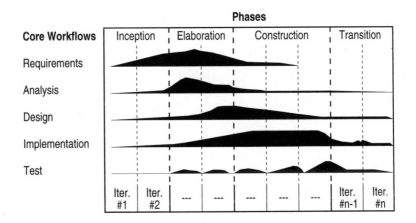

Figure 4.3 Workflow emphasis over the project life cycle

Additionally, heavy emphasis is placed on managing the project and creating a development environment during the Inception and Elaboration Phases.

Over the course of time, the amount of detail displayed within each Unified Process model grows, and the models are gradually completed. Figure 4.4, which is also based on a diagram in *The Unified Software Development Process* by Ivar Jacobson *et al.*, shows that the six primary Unified Process models are almost complete by the end of the Construction Phase, though some fine tuning is usually required to finish the models during the Transition Phase.

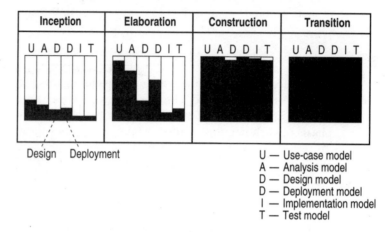

Figure 4.4   Detailed model completion over the project life cycle

Ivar Jacobson *et al.* also note that the important consequences of a Unified Process iterative and incremental approach are as follows:

- *To make the business case in the Inception Phase, the organization has emphasized reducing critical risks and demonstrating proof-of-concept.*

- *To make a business-worthy bid at the end of the Elaboration Phase, the organization has to know what it is contracting to build (represented by the architecture baseline plus requirements) and be confident that it contains no hidden risks (i.e., insufficiently explored cost and schedule expanders).*

- *To minimize costs, defects, and time-to-market, the organization has to employ reusable components (an outgrowth of early architectural development based on study of the domain in which the proposed system falls).*

- *To avoid delivery delay, cost overrun, and poor-quality product, the organization has to "do the hard stuff first."*

- *To avoid building a product that is out-of-date at delivery, the organization can no longer stubbornly say no to all changes. The phased, iterative approach enables it to work changes into development much further along the development trail.*

MSF Development Process Model

Traditional approaches to software development, such as the Waterfall and Spiral Models, often cannot meet the needs of today's enterprise application development environments.

With the Waterfall Model, a project progresses through sequential steps, from the initial concept through system testing. This model identifies milestones along the course of the project and uses them as transition and assessment points. This approach works well for a project in which requirements can easily be specified at the beginning, but may not work well for a complex project where requirements can change during the project's life cycle. Additionally, practitioners of this model rely heavily on volumes of documentation and a single review process for each stage. These two Waterfall practices usually lead to overextended "analysis paralysis" and adversarial relationships between developers, customers, and users.

Using the Spiral Model, the application evolves over a number of iterations. Early passes through the Spiral life cycle provide increasingly tight definitions of the product, with middle and later iterations adding features and functionality to the application. The Spiral Model seeks to confront project risks early in a software project and address them in early product releases. Due to its iterative nature, the Spiral Model supports creative adjustments along the way, thus evolving and hopefully improving the quality of product. The highly iterative Spiral process requires significant amounts of process and documentation automation to become efficient. In practice, customers and users may develop a general sense of instability because the product can change too rapidly for them to grasp. Finally, many Spiral projects lack a known ending point, so they continue to iterate indefinitely with no financial or business end within site.

As shown in Figure 4.5, the MSF Development Process Model combines the strengths of these two models, providing the benefits of milestone-based planning from the Waterfall Model and the benefits of the iterative creative process from the Spiral Model.

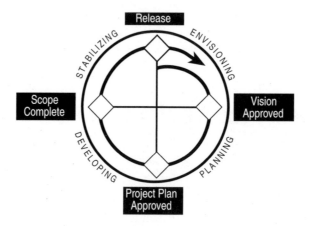

Figure 4.5   MSF Development Process Model

The MSF Development Process Model has three primary traits:

- A phased process (the four wedges of the diagram in Figure 4.5).
- A milestone-driven process (the diamonds separating the phases).
- An iterative process (the process arrow aiming back into the first phase).

Although Figure 4.5 shows the four phases as quarters, the phases do not necessarily require equal amounts of time to complete. Different business and technological environments will require different time and resource ratios for the various phases.

Phased Process

The MSF Development Process Model consists of four interrelated phases. Each of these phases represent deliverables for which a baseline should be established before the development process can move to the next phase of the project. The four phases and their primary tasks are:

- Envisioning, which must produce a shared vision.
- Planning, which must produce a detailed project plan and application architecture.
- Developing, which must produce a well-built, complete product.
- Stabilizing, which must produce a stable, deployed product.

Milestone-Driven Process

The MSF Development Process Model is based on milestones that are points for review and synchronization, rather than points for freezing the application or its specifications. They enable the team to assess the project's progress and make midcourse corrections, such as adjusting the scope of the project to reflect changing customer requirements, or reacting to risks that may materialize during the course of the project.

The MSF Development Process Model uses two types of milestones: *major milestones* and *interim milestones*. Each milestone, whether major or interim, is marked by one or more *deliverables*. Deliverables are physical evidence that the team has reached a milestone.

Major Milestones

Each phase of the development process culminates in an externally visible major milestone. *Externally visible* means that the milestone and its deliverables are visible to entities outside the project team, such as the customer or operations personnel.

A major milestone is a point in time when all team members synchronize their deliverables. Additionally, those external to the project team such as the customer and users; operations, support, and help desk personnel; the distribution channel (commercial software); and other key project stakeholders, should be updated on the project status.

A significant role of major milestones is to allow for a stage-by-stage assessment of the project's viability. The project team and the customer, having reviewed the deliverables for the current phase, jointly make the decision whether or not to move into the next phase. Thus, major milestones serve to move the project from one phase to another.

Interim Milestones

Within each phase of the MSF Development Process Model are various interim milestones, which, like major milestones, are review and synchronization points, rather than freeze points. Unlike major milestones, however, interim milestones are *internally visible*—that is, visible only to members of the project team.

Interim milestones indicate early progress and break large work assignments into smaller pieces that are easier to address.

Versioned Process

The MSF Development Process Model is a versioned process in the sense that it is designed to be repeated during the life cycle of a given product. Each succeeding completion of the MSF Development Process Model allows for the addition of features and functionality in order to satisfy changing business requirements.

The Four MSF Phases and Their Major Milestones

Each of the four phases of the MSF Development Process Model concludes with a major milestone. In this overview, we examine each of the phases briefly with the goal of establishing the basic tasks of each phase and their relation to each other. In later chapters, we'll explore the phases in more depth and suggest interim milestones for each one.

Envisioning Phase

The purpose of the Envisioning Phase is to build a shared vision of the project among all the key stakeholders. This vision should include:

- **A mutual understanding of the business needs being addressed** Many times, developers build an application for a customer (either internal or external), only to discover upon completion that the application solves the wrong problem. This situation arises for a variety of reasons, including poor communication by the customer or poor understanding by the developers. It's critical that the project team members understand the business needs thoroughly *before* attempting a solution.

- **Clearly identified solutions that meet the customer's expectations** Developers often deliver a solution and then learn too late that it is not the solution the customer expected. In today's rapidly evolving computing world, customers are more technologically sophisticated than in times past and may have certain solutions in mind before the project begins. Part of the purpose of the Envisioning Phase is to make certain the customer communicates any specific expectations early in the project. As discussed in Chapter 3, this setting and resetting of the customer's expectations is the primary responsibility of Product Management.

- **A solid estimation of the project constraints** During the Envisioning Phase, the critical project variables—schedule, resources, and features—begin to take shape. In this phase, team members may have only a general idea about these project variables. For example, they may create schedules in terms of quarters or fiscal years instead of weeks or months.

Defining the variables more exactly and establishing their triangulated balance is an iterative process. As analyzing, prototyping, and planning activities proceed, the team may revise the scope because of:

- A better understanding of user requirements.
- A change in business requirements.
- Discovery of technical issues or risks.
- Tradeoffs among the project variables (schedule, resources, and features).

By creating a broad but intuitive view of the project's goals and constraints, the Envisioning Phase begins to define the scope of the project, and sets the stage for the more formal and detailed planning effort that will come later, in the Planning Phase.

Vision Approved Milestone

The Envisioning Phase culminates in the Vision Approved Milestone. This first milestone represents the point at which the project team and the customer agree on the overall direction for the project, including what features and functionality the product will and will not include.

Reaching this milestone meets one of the most fundamental requirements for project success—unifying the project team. The team must have a clear vision of what it wants to accomplish for the customer, and must be able to state that vision in terms that will motivate both the team members and the customer.

The deliverables of the Vision Approved Milestone are:

- A Vision Document.
- A Master Risk Assessment Document.
- A Project Structure Document.

We also recommend that a prototype system be included with the deliverables for this milestone.

As explained earlier, the completion of major milestones results in a synchronization between the customer and the project team, and provides an opportunity for determining whether or not to proceed. Smaller function teams, as described in Chapter 3, must also synchronize with the main project team at major milestones. The Vision Approved Milestone is the first point in the process where the individuals involved may decide that the project does not make sense and should not continue. It is imperative that everyone agrees to move forward at this point in order to prevent misunderstandings later in the project. The creation of application prototypes during the Envisioning Phase can help the team reach a clear understanding of the product vision.

Vision approval signals that members of the project team, the customer, and key stakeholders agree on:

- A broad understanding of the business needs that will be met by the product.
- The vision of the product.
- The design goals for the product.
- The risks that may be incurred by undertaking the project.
- Program Management's initial concept of the business solution.
- How the project should be run and who should be part of the team.

In summary, the true goal of the Envisioning Phase is to create a clear consensus on the product vision between all team members and project stakeholders. Once the product vision is understood, the team and stakeholders can agree and commit to it. Understanding, agreement, and commitment to the vision will place the team in an excellent position to move into the Planning Phase.

Planning Phase

We've all heard the saying "Plan the work, then work the plan." However, daily pressures and deadlines often preempt adequate planning. Proper planning is ensured by following the MSF Development Process Model.

Why is planning so important? For a very simple reason: It costs less to fix design defects early in the development process. Figure 4.6 illustrates the relative costs of fixing design defects during the four phases of the MSF Development Process Model. As the diagram clearly illustrates, early planning pays off in the end, by reducing the cost in time and resources of fixing defects caused by a lack of good planning.

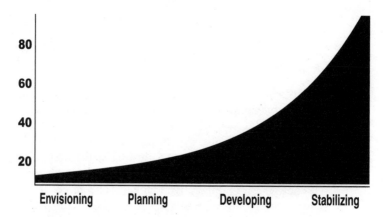

Figure 4.6   Repair cost of design defects by phase

Although some teams risk failure by planning too little, others risk failure by planning too much. It is important to avoid "analysis paralysis." Good planning is necessary, but it's also important to know when to stop planning and move on. As a general rule, the amount of planning necessary for a given project is a function of both its size (lines of code or function points) and the critical nature of the project.

The application's architecture is defined during the Planning Phase. This application architecture, as noted in Chapter 2, is based on the Conceptual, Logical, and Physical Design Models, which we discuss in detail in Chapter 6. Additionally, the modern approach of multi-layer or N-tier architecture provides a solid and scalable product design that can be implemented as a monolithic, client/server, or N-tier application.

Tradeoff Triangle

As we mentioned in our discussion of the Envisioning Phase, every project presents three variables with which the team must work. These three variables—schedule, resources, and features—are illustrated in the tradeoff triangle shown in Figure 4.7. These variables are more clearly defined during the Planning Phase, and by the end of that phase, the team has determined the schedule it will meet, the resources it will use, and the features it will build.

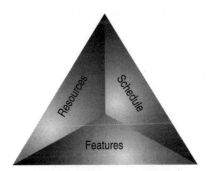

Figure 4.7   Tradeoff triangle

During the Planning Phase, the initial balance of the three tradeoff variables is set. The challenge while moving forward into the Developing Phase is to maintain this balance. We discuss the tradeoff triangle in greater detail later in this chapter.

Project Plan Approved Milestone

The Planning Phase culminates in the Project Plan Approved Milestone, which is the point at which the project team, the customer, and key project stakeholders agree on the project deliverables. This milestone provides an opportunity to establish priorities and set expectations, and serves essentially as a contract between the project team and the customer. Upon completion of this step, the team can move forward to build a solution.

The deliverables at this milestone are:

- The Functional Specification.
- The Master Project Plan.
- The Master Project Schedule.
- An updated Master Risk Assessment Document.

For most projects, another deliverable of this phase might be a proof-of-concept system that helps the team and stakeholders understand the application's architecture. Additionally, any significant design concerns can be tested with the proof-of-concept system before the Project Plan Approved Milestone is reached.

Reaching this milestone means that the project team, the customer, and key project stakeholders agree on:

- What should be built to meet the business needs.
- Prioritization of features.
- How long it should take to complete the project.
- How the product will be built and who will build it.
- The product architecture.
- The risks of building the product.
- The milestones and deliverables along the way.

Developing Phase

By now, some developers will be eager to "crank out some code." As we'll demonstrate in a moment, that's just what the team has been preparing to do in both of the preceding phases. In the Developing Phase, however, the most important task is to build the application.

Part 3 of this book is devoted to the Developing Phase and the various ways and means of approaching it. For now, let's just say that the work of the Developing Phase should be much more straightforward as a result of the work done in the Envisioning and Planning Phases. It's common wisdom that it's much easier to build an application when a clear set of expectations and a properly defined and tested product architecture exists.

Versions, which have been used during the earlier phases, become even more important during the Developing Phase. The team can expect to do multiple versions of the application during this phase. These application versions, which are typically named alpha, beta, and scope-complete release, will be discussed in detail later.

Additionally, all known bugs should have been addressed by this phase. Addressing known bugs does not necessarily imply that all the bugs have been fixed; merely that they have been investigated. The goal of the Developing Phase is to deliver an application that meets all stated expectations and is ready for external testing.

Scope Complete Milestone

The Developing Phase culminates in the Scope Complete Milestone, when all features are complete and the product is ready for external testing and stabilization. This milestone is the opportunity for the customer, users, operations and support personnel, and key stakeholders to evaluate the product and identify any remaining issues that need to be addressed before it ships.

The deliverables of at this milestone are:

- A revised and completed Functional Specification.
- An updated Master Project Plan and Master Project Schedule.
- An updated Master Risk Assessment Document.
- Source code and executables.
- Initial performance support elements.
- A Test Specification and test cases.

At this point in the project, the team should have completed development and functional testing for all the product's features. Additional optimization of feature code can continue, and new bugs can be discovered and addressed, during the Stabilizing Phase.

Reaching this milestone means that the development team will create no new features and that the project team, the customer, and all key stakeholders agree on:

- The fact that the planned feature set has been developed.
- The baseline materials needed to support user performance.
- The fact that development and functional tests have produced a baseline scope-complete release.
- How the product will be tested and deployed throughout the organization, including beta releases and testing.

Stabilizing Phase

Good development teams have known for years that testing should be a major part of any project. Unfortunately, many developers don't adequately test their solutions. They may believe that their code is so good that it needs no testing, or they know that their work was so rushed or ill-conceived that they are afraid of testing it.

Experienced developers realize that software is never error-free. They also know that only good testing procedures can minimize software errors. Experienced developers not only expect testing, they demand it.

Caution It is important to properly set the expectations of the user community at the beginning of this phase. Pilot deployments should be designed to identify performance and environment issues. After these issues are addressed in subsequent bug fix releases, the final product will be deployed.

The functionality of the code is tested during the Developing Phase. However, significant performance and environmental testing occurs during the Stabilizing Phase. During this phase, all known issues are resolved before delivery, and any tasks needed for support and ongoing maintenance of the product are completed. This phase seeks to tie up the loose ends. Documentation, release notes, final "bug stomping," product hand-off, and product deployment are all part of this phase.

The Stabilizing Phase starts when the team shifts its focus from code development to stabilizing and shipping the product and ends when the customer accepts the product as complete. A significant aspect of this phase is that the customer and users begin significant testing of the product. This phase is also the training ground for the organization's operations and support teams. During this time, Logistics Management works to ensure a smooth transfer of product support to the organization's internal support groups, with the product release completing the transfer.

Release Milestone

The Release Milestone is reached when the team has addressed all outstanding issues and ships the product, placing it in service. At the Release Milestone, responsibility for ongoing management and support of the product officially transfers from the project team to the operations and support groups.

The deliverables of this milestone are:

- Golden release.
- Release notes.
- Performance support elements.
- Test results and testing tools.

- Source code and executables.
- Project documents.
- Milestone review.

By now, the product is fully operational and ready to ship. The Release Milestone signifies agreement by the project team, the customer, and all key stakeholders on:

- Product stability and resolution of all known bugs.
- Customer acceptance of the product.
- Transfer of ownership for long-term management and support.
- A change in team focus to the next release.

Importance of All Phases

Immature development organizations often minimize the first and last of the four phases of the MSF Development Process Model. Early analysis of the development task noted that two essential steps are common to the development of computer programs: analysis and coding. These steps correspond almost directly to the second and third phases of the MSF Development Process Model: the Planning and Developing Phases.

For a development organization, or any specific project team, to move from an immature state to a mature one, the organization must pay adequate attention to the Envisioning and Stabilizing Phases. Both of these phases feature increased interaction with the customer and others outside the traditional development team. A development team that does not relate to non-developers will never realize its full potential.

One of the advantages of the MSF Development Team Model discussed in Chapter 3 is that certain team roles are responsible for customer and user interaction. Use of that model ensures that the project team cannot gloss over the Envisioning and Stabilizing Phases. Use of the MSF Development Process Model also ensures that interaction with non-developers is approached in a professional and organized manner. The team should be motivated by the simple fact that the success or failure of the project depends on the attention given to each phase, not just to analysis and coding.

MSF Development Process Model Principles

The MSF Development Process Model fulfills a key function of project development by specifying which activities should be performed and when. The model has two other important aspects: its close relationship with the MSF Development Team Model and the benefits to the organization of using them together;

and the MSF Development Process Model's underlying practices and principles. The latter include:

- Using versioned releases.
- Creating living documents.
- Scheduling for an uncertain future.
- Managing tradeoffs.
- Managing risks.
- Maintaining a fixed ship date mindset.
- Breaking large projects into manageable parts.
- Performing daily builds.
- Using bottom-up estimating.

Using Versioned Releases

We recommend a product development strategy that divides large projects into multiple versioned releases, with no separate product maintenance phase. After the project team establishes a pattern of making good tradeoff decisions and shipping the right products at the right time, it's important to begin cycling through versioned releases as rapidly as possible. Versioned releases enable the project team to respond to continuous changes in scope, schedule, and project risk. In the process of frequently updating the product, communication is maintained with the customer, and the customer's suggestions for future releases of the product can be taken into consideration.

The team should deliver a core set of features in the first release and add features incrementally in later releases until the full vision for the product is achieved. For later versions, the product vision can be reshaped as business requirements change, and the product can be updated accordingly.

To summarize, using versioned releases has the following benefits:

- **Communication** Promotes frequent and honest communication between the team and the customer. Each release reflects the best ideas of everyone involved.
- **Earlier delivery** Enables the project team to deliver critical functionality earlier and to obtain feedback from the customer for future releases. When the customer knows (or senses) that future product releases will be delivered in a timely manner, the customer is much more receptive to deferring features to later releases.
- **Closure** Forces closure on project issues. Using a versioned release allows the team to deal with a manageable number of issues during the Stabilizing Phase and to address all the issues before release.

- **Goals** Sets clear, motivating goals for all team members. The team can easily manage each version's scope and quickly achieve results, so team members see rapid progress. Their role in determining the schedule helps ensure that their tasks are manageable, specific, and associated with a tangible result.

- **Freedom and flexibility** Allows freedom and flexibility in the design process, enabling the team to be responsive to changes in the business environment. This freedom and flexibility reduces uncertainty and helps to manage the changes in project scope by allowing the team to vary features and schedules in relation to the overall plan. Features that become critical as a result of business changes can be designated as high priority for the next release. The early release becomes stable as the team starts work on the next one.

- **Continuous and incremental feature delivery** Dictates a new set of features immediately following the release of the completed set. As a result, the team continues to add value for the project's customer and users.

In *Rapid Development*, Steve McConnell explains:

> *One of the keys to users and customers agreeing to the version-2 approach is that they have some assurance that there will in fact be a version 2. If they fear that the current version will be the last version ever built, they'll try harder to put all their pet features into it. Short release cycles help to build the users' confidence that their favorite feature will eventually make it into the product.*

Another way to reassure the project's customer and users is to create a multi-release product plan from the beginning of the project. This plan involves the articulation of both current *and* future versions of the product so that the team and the customer can trust in the product's future.

Creating Living Documents

Although a sufficient amount of good planning is crucial to project success, too much planning is harmful. As we've said, an over-emphasis on planning can create "analysis paralysis." To avoid endless spinning in the Planning Phase, the team needs to establish a baseline in its planning efforts as early as possible, so that it can move on to developing the solution even if some questions are left unanswered. On the other hand, because of the ongoing need for change, planning and other documents should be frozen only when leaving them unfrozen poses an unacceptable project risk.

This concept of "baseline early, freeze late" is the essence of creating living documents that change and grow throughout the development process.

One mark of a mature project team is that it admits when a document needs to be changed to reflect new or updated information. Another mark is that it has implemented a good change control process, so that documents are changed only when necessary.

Scheduling for an Uncertain Future

The future is inherently uncertain. Teams need to address future uncertainties in project scheduling and management by planning for them, using two primary approaches: adding buffer time and using risk-driven scheduling.

Buffer Time

Typically, the project team determines the product's ship date by simply adding up all the time estimates along the critical path. In some cases, the team then increases all the estimates by a given percentage in an attempt to allow for delays. This practice is not the same as buffer time.

To use an analogy, buffer time is what a military commander gains by holding back reserve troops to account for variations in the results of an attack plan. In the world of software development, buffer time is a period added by Program Management to the end of a project timeline. Program Management owns the scheduled buffer time and applies it as needed. As shown in Figure 4.8, this period is not factored into the individual tasks, and the goal is still to complete the tasks within the time allotted for them. Buffer time is not an allowance for poorly defined tasks. In almost all cases, having to use the buffer period comes at a cost, even if it is nothing more than a required explanation and justification for using the buffer and a plan for avoiding the problem that caused the buffer use in the future.

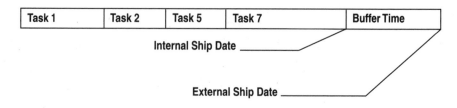

Figure 4.8 Critical-path timeline

The addition of buffer time to the timeline creates two ship dates: an internal ship date and an external ship date. The internal ship date is the summation of the critical-path time estimates, and the external ship date is the internal ship date plus the buffer time.

Risk-Driven Scheduling

Risk-driven scheduling assigns a high priority to high-risk tasks and takes into account risk priorities assigned by the customer. If the high-risk tasks require more time than planned, risk-driven scheduling increases the amount of required reaction time. Risk-driven scheduling:

- Encourages early proof-of-concept prototypes.
- Determines which features will be shipped and when.
- Prioritizes tasks based on technical and business risk.
- Encourages developers to aggressively shoot for the early deadline.
- Signals a warning if the early deadline is missed, pinpointing the need to make adjustments and tradeoffs earlier.
- Gives the customer a better view of the riskier areas of the project and manages customer expectations in a more productive manner.

Managing Tradeoffs

In *Dynamics of Software Development*, Jim McCarthy confirms that every project balances three critical elements:

> ...*you're working with only three things:* resources *(people and money)*, features *(the product and its quality), and* the schedule. *This triangle of elements is all you work with. There's nothing else to be worked with. And changing one side of the triangle has an impact on at least one other side, usually two.*

The relationship between these three variables tends to be hazy at the beginning of the development process. At that point, the team has a rough idea of what to build, an estimate of available resources, and an approximate target delivery date. During the Planning Phase, the project elements represented in the triangle become more distinct. By the time the Planning Phase is complete, the team knows the nature of available resources, the product features, and the fixed ship date.

It's important to keep in mind that the three variables are interrelated. Changes on one side of the tradeoff triangle affect the other two sides. If the team understands and utilizes this concept, the team has both the rationale and the motivation to take corrective action as changes occur during development.

For example, suppose that a triangle shows that 10 resources will deliver 20 features by June 1. During the development process, the customer discovers a new critical feature that was not included in the original Functional Specification. Adding this new feature to the triangle creates an imbalance in the other sides. As noted in Figure 4.9, the team must correct this imbalance by dropping features, adding resources, changing the ship date, or some combination of all three actions.

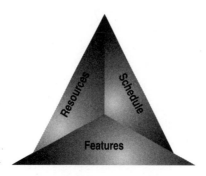

Figure 4.9   Unbalanced tradeoff triangle

The power of the triangle lies in its simplicity. It's simple enough that it can be drawn on a napkin during lunch with a customer to explain the types of tradeoffs that must occur in order for the project to succeed.

Although the triangle is a simple and effective tool, it does not convey the project's priorities with regard to the three variables. One way to document these priorities and to manage the expectations of the team and the customer is to create a tradeoff matrix like the ones shown in Table 4.1 for the project variables and the levels of constraint. This matrix allows the team and the customer to indicate the manner in which tradeoffs should occur.

Table 4.1   Sample Tradeoff matrixes

Project 1				Project 2			
	Optimize	Constrain	Accept		Optimize	Constrain	Accept
Resources		✓		**Resources**	✓		
Ship Date	✓			**Ship Date**			✓
Features			✓	**Features**		✓	

Working together, the team and the customer select an exclusive level of constraint for each of the project variables. No row or column in the project tradeoff matrix may have more than one check mark, because hybrid combinations pose serious risks to the project and must be accounted for explicitly in the risk management plan. The columns are defined as follows:

- **Optimize** The optimized variable is the one that should be as good as possible at the end of the project. To optimize resources is to seek the lowest possible allocation of resources (minimum cost strategy). To optimize the ship date is to seek the earliest possible ship date (early to market strategy). To optimize features is to seek the most complete product possible (maximum benefit strategy).

- **Constrain** The constrained variable has been assigned a fixed value. To constrain resources is to set a ceiling for them (not-to-exceed strategy). To constrain the ship date is to time-box the project (not before and not after strategy). To constrain features is to ship at least the essential set of functionality (minimal acceptable benefit strategy).

- **Accept** When one variable has been constrained and another optimized, the third variable must simply be accepted. To accept resources is to acknowledge that the product will take whatever resources it takes (time and materials strategy). To accept the ship date is to acknowledge that the product won't ship before it's finished (it's done when it's done strategy). To accept features is to achieve one or more of the other project tradeoffs by dropping features immediately before the ship date (it's done when it ships strategy). The check mark in the "accept" column designates the variable that is owned by the team and ensures that the team is empowered to manage change and risk, and is therefore positioned to succeed, not fail. For example, if the customer says that the feature set must be as rich as possible (features are optimized) and that the project must be done by a certain date (the ship date is constrained), the customer needs to give the team whatever resources are necessary to meet those two conditions (resource costs are accepted).

The team should use the tradeoff matrix as a reference when making decisions. The matrix is not intended to show absolute priorities; it is merely a tool to facilitate communication and understanding. Most important for the project team is that the matrix defines areas in which the customer is willing to compromise.

Managing Risk

For most projects, the ability to manage risk is the key to project success. For a project team to be successful, it must:

- Learn from its environment.
- Adapt to the environment rapidly.
- Predict accurately what will happen next.
- Take actions based on the above.

When the team understands and implements actions that minimize uncertainty and maximize stability and predictability, it can operate equally well in either a volatile or a stable environment. Preparedness for uncertain events is the goal of risk assessment and management.

There are two inherently different approaches to managing risk. Most teams practice *reactive* risk management; that is, they react in some way after the risk has already caused a problem. We advocate practicing *proactive* risk management, which we discuss in detail in Chapter 5. Proactive risk management means that the team has a visible process for managing risks before they are realized.

The process should also be measurable and repeatable. With proactive risk management, risks are assessed continuously, and this assessment information is used to make decisions in all phases of the project. The risks are then carried forward until they are resolved or, if they emerge as problems, until they are handled.

Maintaining a Fixed Ship-Date Mindset

A fixed ship-date mindset means that the team treats its projected ship date as unchangeable. Essentially, the team builds the project schedule and then agrees that the schedule side of the triangle is fixed in place. Once the ship date is fixed, the team cannot use this side of the triangle for making corrective decisions unless there are no other options available.

Adopting a fixed ship-date mindset has the following advantages:

- **Forces creativity** Creativity is necessary to implement features in as timely a manner as possible, because the option of delaying the ship date has been removed.

- **Prioritizes tasks according to importance** Features are prioritized so that lower priority features can be dropped if necessary to ship on time. If features must be dropped in order to make the ship date, the features that are most important to the customer will be delivered.

- **Empowers the team by providing an effective decision-making tool** The team makes decisions on the basis of how they will affect the ability to deliver on the fixed ship date.

- **Provides a motivational goal for the team** A constantly slipping ship date creates team morale problems and can ultimately lead to a developmental "death march," in which team members lose interest in a project because it seems as if the product will never ship.

The team arrives at a fixed ship date through bottom-up estimation and the use of buffer time. This estimation process is fundamental to the success of implementing a fixed ship date mindset, because the team must be willing to commit to the date as a realistic and achievable goal.

Breaking Large Projects into Manageable Parts

For large projects or complex projects, the feature set should be broken up into smaller, somewhat independent pieces. These pieces should then be treated as internal releases or subprojects. This process can be thought of as versioned releases within a single project, where only the final version is released at the end of the project life cycle.

Teams can spend approximately two to four months on an internal release. Each release has time allocated for feature development, optimization, testing, and stabilization. In addition, approximately one-third of the total development time is added as buffer time for unplanned contingencies.

For each internal release, Development delivers a cluster of features for testing. Assuming that the release is testable, the team goes through a full test/debug/retest cycle, as if it was going to ship the product with just these features. When the code meets or exceeds the quality bar for the internal release, the team can proceed to develop the next set of features. This internal-release approach also helps solve the significant problems that can arise when applications are integrated only in the late stages of product development.

Breaking a large project into subprojects:

- Allows the team to focus on delivering a smaller and more easily definable aspect of the project.

- Provides a sense of completion for the team as it achieves each internal release milestone.

- Provides early warning signs of project health, because each internal release milestone is an assessment point with its own postmortem review. If internal releases slip, then the team can take corrective action earlier to keep the larger project on track.

- Increases the overall quality of the product, because each internal release has its own quality bar.

- Allows the team to practice shipping with each internal release so that the actual shipping of the product at the end of the project is more predictable.

In *Debugging the Development Process* (Microsoft Press, 1994), Steve Maguire states:

> It's not the two-month period alone that creates the wins and fosters enthusiasm. It's the thrill of finishing an interesting subproject.
>
> "Finishing all top-priority items" may be important, but the top-priority items don't make up a subproject. They're just a random list of things that happen to be important. There's no motivating theme behind such a list.
>
> For example, "Implementing the charting subsystem" is a subproject. All of the tasks that would be involved would relate to that common theme. You might use a task list to remind people of the known charting issues they'd have to handle, but ultimately the theme of the subproject would drive development. The goal wouldn't be for the team to finish 352 unrelated tasks. The goal would be to do everything necessary to fully complete—to "ship"—the charting subsystem, regardless of whether the tasks it would take were on a list somewhere. The subproject would be in "ship mode" from the outset.

Performing Daily Builds

A typical software development project involves "building" an executable program from up to thousands of different files. Some software development teams practice the "daily build and smoke test" process in which they compile every file, combine them into a single executable program, and put the program through a smoke test, or simple coverage test, to see if it runs. The smoke test is a quick-pass test of the entire system to expose any major problems. The daily build is not valuable unless accompanied by a smoke test. We discuss coverage testing further in Chapter 12.

Performing daily builds and smoke tests provides a number of important benefits including:

- Minimizing code integration risk by identifying incompatible code early and allowing the team to make debugging or redesign decisions.
- Supporting improved defect diagnosis, making it easier to pinpoint why the product may be broken on any single day.
- Reducing the risk of low quality.

The daily build and smoke test must be performed each day—not weekly or monthly—to produce the greatest benefits. The software being built must work; otherwise, the build is viewed as broken, and it must be fixed. Performing daily builds and smoke tests is like trying to ship a product every day, which enforces a sense of discipline.

Standards for daily builds and smoke tests vary from project to project, but at a minimum the standards should include:

- Compiling all files and components successfully.
- Linking all files and components successfully.
- Finding no "showstopper" bugs that would make the program hazardous to operate or prevent it from launching.
- Passing the smoke test.

Using Bottom-Up Scheduling

Simply put, those who will be doing the work should schedule the work.

Two fundamental benefits result from requiring the individuals who actually perform the work to develop their own work estimates are:

- **Accuracy** The estimates tend to be more accurate because they are based on experience. A person asked to perform a particular task is expected to have previous experience in executing this or other similar tasks.

- **Accountability** Because team members have developed their own estimates, they are more accountable for the success of meeting those estimates. Initial estimates may be high, but with milestone reviews, project knowledge, and also estimating practice, the estimates will begin to more accurately reflect the tasks and will provide the right task-level motivation.

As shown in Figure 4.10, the estimating process is the responsibility of the entire team. As the low-level estimates are rolled up into the Master Project Schedule, buffer time is added to ensure that the schedule is attainable. It's this technique that makes the fixed ship-date mindset possible.

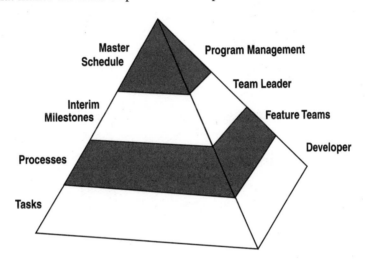

Figure 4.10   Bottom-up scheduling

Using Versioned Processes

Throughout this book, we emphasize the concept of using versioned releases. As Figure 4.11 illustrates, using versioned releases means repeatedly going through the MSF Development Process Model, delivering increasingly feature-rich versions of the same product. In this part of the chapter, we'll expand on the concept of versioning by first giving some additional guidelines for creating versioned releases. Then we'll discuss how our experience takes the concept even further, by suggesting that the project team can create multiple iterations of the MSF Development Process Model *within* each versioned release.

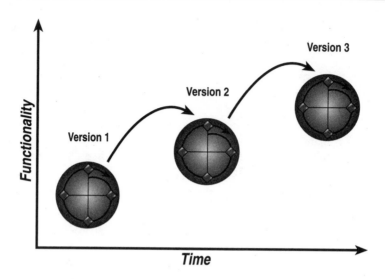

Figure 4.11   Versioned releases within the MSF Development Process Model

Guidelines for Versioned Releases

As soon as the project team begins work on the first version of a new software application, it should already be planning the creation of the second version. This iterative process is helpful throughout all four phases of the MSF Development Process Model. For one thing, the team can assign feature requests to various versions, which in turn enables it to deliver the core functionality in the first version, and subsequent features in later versions. In addition, the realization that decisions made for the first version will have to be revisited for subsequent versions motivates everyone to make well-considered decisions the first time!

There are six overall guidelines for creating versioned releases:

- **Adopt a product mindset** Constantly keep in mind the ultimate goal of building the version that delivers the complete feature set. Having a product mindset helps the team think beyond the current version by focusing on execution and on what is being delivered at the end of the project.

- **Create a multi-version release plan** Be sure the product release plan takes the various versions into account.

- **Cycle rapidly** Remember that the customer and users will be more willing to accept that certain features won't appear until later versions if they are confident that the team can deliver those versions.

- **Analyze each feature request for impact, feasibility, and priority** Think beyond the current version to increase the team's capacity to make sound decisions about what to build now and what to defer until a later version.

- **Deliver core functionality first so that there is a solid first release to build on** Address the primary business issues the product is supposed to address. If the team demonstrates the ability to plan and execute the delivery of the software based on the business issues, customer and user confidence in the team will increase.

- **Stop building new versions when they no longer address business needs** Know when to stop adding versioned releases. If a new release isn't supported by a strong business need, another version isn't necessary.

Phases and Living Documents

Earlier we described living documents as documents that change throughout a project. The flexibility of the development process is the reason living documents are necessary.

For example, one of the deliverables of the Envisioning Phase is the Vision Document. A traditional Waterfall-like approach to project management insists that the Vision Document be complete in all respects before the Planning Phase can begin. By contrast, the MSF Development Process Model assumes not only that the document is not complete before the Planning Phase, but that although the document has a baseline, it will not be complete until the project is complete. The Vision Document delivered during the Envisioning Phase is the *baseline* version of the document, but the document won't be *finished* until the end of the project. The document is refined more and more with each phase of the MSF Development Process Model.

Development Tasks During Other Phases

In our opinion, by executing limited development tasks outside the Development phase, the team gains two major advantages:

- **Forward movement** Immature development teams typically do very little analysis and planning. The drive is to simply "get to coding." When the team members realize the errors of their ways—often through a painful failure— the members move to the opposite extreme and determine to write code only when every detail of the plan is complete. If the team can keep moving through the plan/build cycle using development tasks where appropriate, it won't get stuck in either planning or building mode. Additionally, executing portions of the application code gives the entire team a sense of accomplishment and progress. No one task seems to go on forever; the team is meeting deadlines, accomplishing goals, and identifying and managing problems. It is moving forward through the process, with a growing sense that the project will be successful. This sense of success feeds back into the team system, generating exponential improvement.

- **Early warning system** One of the major objections to the traditional Waterfall Model is that mistakes and errors are not identified until the end of the process. However, having development tasks early in a project gives the team an early warning system for identifying errors much sooner in the process, so that they can be fixed when the cost is low.

For example, suppose the team is planning a distributed application: the bandwidth requirements have been calculated on paper, and the network demands appear acceptable. As part of the Planning Phase, the team decides to build a proof-of-concept working version of the application to test the architecture. (Note that the Developing Phase hasn't begun yet; a task of development occurs *within* the Planning Phase.) The proof-of-concept system reveals that the application seems to take much more bandwidth than the team had calculated. In fact, if the application is built and deployed as designed, it will saturate the organization's current network. The team rethinks its approach and finds a better design. A second working version is built, and this one is much more frugal with network resources. There is no need to ask ourselves, "Where would we rather discover such a problem: during the Planning Phase, at the end of the Developing Phase, or even when the application is actually deployed?" Obviously, an early discovery is better than a late one. The only way to gain this early warning system is to execute limited development tasks as needed within each phase of the project.

Development Task Goals

As we noted earlier, the team can avoid the pitfalls of the Spiral Model by determining the development tasks for each phase early in the project life cycle. Each phase normally has a primary purpose, one for each of the Envisioning, Planning, Developing, and Stabilizing Phases.

All the goals set for a development task should flow out of the goals for the parent phase. For example, the goals of the Envisioning Phase are agreement on business needs, a common vision, a set of design goals, and so on. The goals of any development tasks within the Envisioning Phase should relate to that phase's goals. Any goal that doesn't should be delayed or dropped.

Aligning development tasks with phase goals keeps the team from working on a task before its time. A common failing is to begin doing extensive development work before the architecture is established. Establishing the architecture is done as part of the Envisioning and Planning Phases; the extensive development work is part of the Developing Phase. Doing such work any sooner may turn out to be wasted effort.

In many projects, the goals of the development tasks follow this pattern:

- **Prototype** During the Envisioning Phase, a prototype can be a useful means of communicating and refining the vision. A prototype is a non-functional, visual version of the product. Often it is nothing more than a series of linked screens. If the application is to be Web-based, the prototype may be a series of Web pages. If the application is desktop-based, a simple mock-up can be constructed in Visual Basic or Access. The point is that the prototype is simply a way to get agreement between the project team and the customer on the overall vision of the product and the user interface.

- **Proof-of-concept system** In contrast to the non-functional prototype, the proof-of-concept system is a functional application used to ensure that the design is achievable. While the prototype is primarily concerned with concept and user interface, the proof-of-concept system is primarily concerned with design and technology. Can a stable, useable application be built with the envisioned design? Typically, a proof-of-concept version of the product is built during the Planning Phase.

- **Alpha, beta, and subsequent interim releases** During the Developing Phase, the development team often creates alpha and beta releases. These interim releases demonstrate the gradual melding of the prototype's user interfaces and the proof-of-concept's technologies. A large project may have many such releases during the Developing Phase. We recommend the release of at least an alpha and a beta version for all but the smallest projects. The alpha release says, "Here is our first cut at putting interface and technology together. What are the major issues?" The beta release says, "We think we've dealt with all the major issues and most of the minor ones. What have we missed?" This phase culminates with the creation of the golden release candidate.

- **Golden release** During the Stabilizing Phase, the golden code is pilot-tested by the user community. Additionally, bug fix releases are tested and deployed as performance or environment problems are determined. The final golden release at the end of the Stabilizing Phase signals the completion of the project and transfers all product deliverables to the customer.

Some development teams resist creating prototypes or proof-of-concept systems because they see them as a waste of time. In reality, the opposite is true. Even for smaller projects, a prototype and a proof-of-concept system can ultimately save the team much wasted time and effort by clarifying the customer's needs and by testing the design. It's better to spend a little time on an earlier version that gets discarded than to spend a lot of time on a later version that gets discarded.

Team Roles in the MSF Development Process Model

Although Program Management oversees the overall development process, achieving each milestone requires attention from different team roles, as shown in Table 4.2. Aligning a team role, or collection of team roles, with each of the four major milestones makes it clear who is responsible for achieving each milestone. This strategy creates clear accountability.

Table 4.2   Responsibility of team roles for milestones

Phase	Milestone	Primary driver
Envisioning	Vision Approved	Product Management
Planning	Project Plan Approved	Program Management
Developing	Scope Complete	Development, User Education
Stabilizing	Release	Testing, Logistics Management

At each major milestone, the responsibility for the next phase is handed to the appropriate role or roles. The transition is acknowledged by the receiving roles so that everyone is clear that the project is now moving to the next phase. The visible transitioning of responsibility is the hallmark of a healthy project.

Artifacts and Deliverables

Throughout the project, the team generates various artifacts and deliverables. *Artifacts* are documents of all kinds that are generated as part of the project, and *deliverables* are the specific documents and applications required by each phase of the project.

Some product information remains internal to the project team. Not all project artifacts are customer deliverables; for example, meeting agendas are not deliverables. However, all artifacts are important as either documentation or aids to the process. Usually, artifacts should be kept after the project is complete, as part of the project documentation.

Deliverables are the key elements that must be developed, built, and handed off throughout the project, and are externally visible to people in the organization who are not involved in the project. Some deliverables are documents; some are code or applications. All deliverables are important and should be kept for future reference after the project is complete.

Each artifact or deliverable should be communicated in the most effective way. For example, not all documents have to be printed. Distributing an agenda through e-mail or on the organization's intranet may be just as effective and less time-consuming. If a prototype is not executable, developing it as a Web site and thereby making it available to all interested parties at the same time, no matter where their location, might be the most effective way to communicate it.

Everyone should remember that the objective is to deliver a completed, useable application that meets the stated needs, not to generate mounds of paper. The team should be creative in its use of technology to communicate artifacts, to share results, and to move the process forward.

For example, imagine that a PowerPoint presentation is e-mailed in advance to all the participants in an online progress meeting, who are located in five different countries. The PowerPoint presentation is cued up on a projector at each location. The online meeting is then started and cued up on the same projector. Finally, a Web browser attached to the Web server at the home office navigates to the Web prototype on that server and loads the home page. During the online meeting, the participants alternate between the presentation and the browser, making comments and suggestions. Meanwhile, a developer incorporates as many suggestions as possible into the prototype and then instructs everyone to refresh their browsers to see the changes. In this manner, the group moves through the prototype, and at the end of the online meeting the group agrees that the prototype meets the stated needs. Such a scenario, considered the stuff of fantasy only a few years ago, brings an entirely new meaning to the phrase "rapid application development."

Although the team might not have access to such technology, or a given project might not warrant using it, team members should nevertheless take a close look at their assumptions about communication. They should think creatively in order to deliver effectively. Above all, they must be sure everything they do is moving them *through* the process model and *toward* the project's goal: a stable, useable product that meets the stated customer needs.

Relationships Between Models

Much of this book is concerned with various models. (As we said earlier, a model is an abstraction used to simplify or represent a process or concept.) It is important to remember that many of these models are interrelated. As we conclude Part 1 of this book, we need to examine the relationships between models at three different layers of abstraction.

The MSF Enterprise Architecture Model discussed in Chapter 1 should exist at the highest level of abstraction within the IT environment. In other words, it is the top-level model or artifact for IT design and practice. It should be related to, and driven by, the organization's strategic plan. In turn, the MSF Enterprise Architecture Model should be the driver for any Enterprise Application Models that are developed.

The information captured in a higher-level model or document should inform and flow into the appropriate area of the lower-level model or document. The plans and processes outlined in the organization's strategic plan and operations manual should, for example, be the basis for the Business Perspective of the MSF Enterprise Architecture Model. In turn, the Business Perspective of the MSF Enterprise Architecture Model should form the Business Model of specific enterprise applications. In other words, each application's architecture must also cohabit with the organization's enterprise architecture.

In this chapter, we discussed the MSF Development Process Model, which describes the process for building an application. A part of this model is the development of a Design Model for the application's conceptual, logical, and a physical architecture. Although it is not a step-by-step process, the MSF Development Process Model helps provide the steps for a project team to get where it wants to go.

It is sometimes difficult to show a clear-cut information flow between parts of one model and parts of another.

It is also important to clearly understand terms from different models that are similarly named. Table 4.3 helps keep the terms in their correct "home" model.

Table 4.3   Related terms from different models

MSF Enterprise Architecture Model	Enterprise Application Model	MSF Design Model
Business Perspective	Business Model	Conceptual Design
Application Perspective		
Information Perspective		
Technology Perspective	Technology Model	
	User Model	
	Logical Model	Logical Design
	Physical Model	Physical Design
	Development Model	

Summary

Developing software is a complex and dynamic undertaking. As Jim McCarthy observes:

> *Shipping ordinary software on time is damned hard. Shipping great software in any time frame is extraordinary. Shipping great software on time is the rarest of earthly delights.*

Shipping great software is increasingly difficult because of the burgeoning growth of Internet applications and enterprise-wide multi-tier applications. In this chapter, we briefly reviewed the Waterfall Model, the Spiral Model, and the Unified Process, and then focused on the MSF Development Process Model.

Rigor and flexibility—the two most essential qualities needed to successfully develop these application types—are provided by the MSF Development Process Model: rigor through milestone-based planning, and flexibility through its creative, iterative process. In this chapter, we examined the four phases of this model: Envisioning, Planning, Developing, and Stabilizing. We discussed the concept of versioned releases and looked at the importance of doing complete iterations of the model within each of its phases. We discussed living documents and the idea of "baseline early, freeze late." Finally, we described how to set goals for each iteration.

Review

1. Briefly describe the Waterfall Model and the Spiral Model.
2. What are the workflows of the Unified Process?
3. What are the phases and milestones of the Unified Process?
4. Discuss the objectives and purpose of each MSF phase.
5. List the deliverables for each phase of the MSF Development Process model.
6. Discuss the benefits of versioned releases.
7. Explain the concept of tradeoffs and the tradeoff triangle of project variables.

C A S E   S T U D Y   3

Introducing the RMS Project

"Good morning, everyone."

Thursday morning, 8 A.M. Only three days had passed since the kickoff meeting for the RMS project team, but Dan Shelly noticed that the mood in the conference room was much different from the last meeting. The team members were in place, binders open in front of them, pens at the ready. They were all eager to get down to business on the new project, and they were all eager to begin applying their new knowledge of MSF.

Everyone, it seemed, except Tim O'Brien. "Alright, where's Tim?" asked Dan, his voice a mixture of exasperation and amusement. "I hope he didn't oversleep."

"No, I didn't oversleep!" came a voice from down the hall. "In fact, I didn't sleep at all."

"Tim, you look awful!" exclaimed Jane Clayton as Tim came into the room. "What happened?"

Tim slid into the seat beside Dan. "Well, you know that new server we were bringing up on the 24th floor, the one for the CAD drawing storage? It came in a couple of days ago, and I told one of my guys to bring it up, get it on the network, assign the proper rights—you know, the whole deal. We had promised it by today for that group of designers, and I told him when it came in to get right on it.

"Anyway, at about 10 last night he paged me. When I called in, he told me that he had been working at it for two days and still couldn't get it on the network. I tried to walk him through some stuff, but he didn't seem to understand me. So I piled into my truck and got here about 11. We finally got it on the net and useable about 30 minutes ago."

"Thanks for going to the mat, Tim." Dan's gratitude was genuine. "I know the CAD folks were anxious to get that box running, and I especially appreciate that you did what you had to do to keep IT's word to a business unit." Everyone gave Tim a good-natured round of applause, and he smiled through his blushing.

"Before we move into the agenda," Dan continued, "I'd like to introduce the new face at the table. Most of you already know Jim Stewart, our CFO. I asked him to join us this morning as a resource for the second part of the meeting. His insights will be valuable to us, both today and as we move through our project. Jim, welcome."

"Glad to be here, Dan," Jim replied. Only Dan seemed to notice a note of caution in his tone. "I'm looking forward to hearing the information your people have gathered."

"Yes, I think it will be informative, if not necessarily heartening." Dan looked at the agenda for the meeting, then back at the group. "As always, our first item is Agenda Building. Does anyone have adjustments or additions they would like to make to our agenda today?"

Marilou Moris spoke up. "I thought we were going to go over the materials you gave us last time, Dan. This agenda doesn't mention them at all."

"That's true, Marilou, it doesn't. Before I respond, does anyone else have a change to the agenda?" No one spoke, so Dan continued. "As Marilou has said, I gave you the MSF Development Team Model and MSF Development Process Model materials in our last meeting and asked you to study them. After hearing some of your questions in the last meeting, though, I decided that we needed a background meeting on the current situation before we could move forward effectively.

Current State

"As most of you know, this project is concerned with possibly building a new application called the Resource Management System, which we call RMS for short. This application will take the place of our current processes for scheduling resources and reporting and billing time. I've asked some of you to prepare background information so that we all know how we do these things today. I realize that two days is short notice, so I gave this assignment to the people who are already familiar with how we do things."

Dan glanced at Tim with a smile. "Considering what you went through last night, Tim, it's probably fortunate that I didn't ask you to prepare anything extra for this meeting." Tim nodded. "Only too glad to be a spectator this time, boss."

Scheduling Resources

Dan turned to Marta Wolfe-Hellene, who was sitting at the end of the conference table. "Marta, even though you are fairly new to Ferguson and Bardell, I knew that you had already had some experience with how resources are scheduled. Why don't you begin?"

FERGUSON AND BARDELL
ENGINEERING • ARCHITECTURE • PROJECT MANAGEMENT

The RMS Project
Meeting Agenda

Meeting Date: March 25, 1999   **Purpose:** Background of RMS

I.   Agenda Building

II.   Current State
        Tell both how the task is accomplished and any negative issues associated with the methodology
        as it currently stands.

        • Scheduling Resources (Marta)
        • Completing Timesheets (Bill)
        • Recording Time (Jane)
        • Generating Invoices (Jane)

III.   Business Implications
        • Scheduling Resources
        • Completing Timesheets
        • Recording Time
        • Generating Invoices

IV.   Q&A

V.   Wrap-Up: Path-Forward Assignments

CHICAGO • DETROIT • MILWAUKEE • CINCINNATI • INDIANAPOLIS • LOUISVILLE

Marta stood to speak, referring to the neatly written notes in her binder. "The week I started with Ferguson and Bardell, the Director of Engineering called me into his office. We talked about a number of things, primarily what I would be doing and how the work was done here. One of the things he showed me was his Master Scheduling Sheet.

"This was nothing more than a very large Excel spreadsheet, with dates across the top and names down the left side. The names were all the various resources he was responsible for—the engineers, designers, secretaries, and administrative people. They were listed alphabetically, by last name then first name.

"He explained that whenever a project needed resources, he would open this spreadsheet and scan it to see who was available during the time frame of the project. If someone who was competent to do the work was free, he would block out that person's time by filling in the appropriate dates with the name of the project. If nobody was available, he would have to either juggle resources or ne-gotiate with the salesperson who sold the job to see whether the dates could be adjusted.

"The system is fairly straightforward, and I've seen it used in many small firms," commented Dan. "However, Ferguson and Bardell is not a small firm, which leads me to think that our Director of Engineering might have some issues with this system. Am I right, Marta?"

Marta smiled. "He told me he gave you an earful about it last week on the golf course and that he wasn't taking you golfing again unless you got it fixed. So I think that's a safe assumption," she said to chuckles all around the table. "I've made a list of the issues that he and I discussed. Shall I put them on the whiteboard?"

"That's a good idea," replied Dan. "In fact, put up a Scheduling Resources head-ing, and we'll list all the issues as we go along."

Marta walked to the whiteboard, wrote *Issues List* at the top, and then put *Sched-uling Resources* underneath.

The Issues

"The first problem," she began, "is that nothing on the spreadsheet tells you the abilities of the various resources." She wrote the problem on the board. "Because it's a spreadsheet, you can't list a varying number of facts about a resource. So there's no way to search or to sort on abilities. I know all about this problem, be-cause it has already happened to me."

"How so?" asked Tim.

"One of my areas of concentration in graduate school was programmable logic controllers. Unfortunately, the Director didn't know this and it didn't show up on the scheduling sheet, so when he had a PLC job come up, he didn't think of me as a resource. We lost the job even though I was available, because he didn't think he had anyone to do it." Jim squirmed uncomfortably in his chair but didn't say anything.

"A second issue," continued Marta, adding it to the list on the whiteboard, "is that the scheduling sheet is disconnected from the calendar system. Ferguson and Bardell uses Outlook and Exchange as its calendar system, but very few people have any reason to keep their Outlook calendars up to date.

"As a result, managers can't check the availability of resources via their calendars. When managers plug people into a schedule, they either send an e-mail to them, telling them what they are doing and when, or they try to page or call them. Often, managers get back an e-mail saying that so-and-so is not actually available. There is no link back from anyone's calendar to the resource spreadsheets, so someone might look free on the spreadsheet when he or she is actually out on vacation or already committed to a meeting. When this happens, the manager has to go back to the spreadsheet and start over.

"Finally, the scheduling system is basically unmanageable. It worked OK when each manager was responsible for, say, 30 people. With Ferguson and Bardell's drive to create a flattened organization, some managers are scheduling as many as 100 resources. It's simply not possible for them to keep track of everyone's skill set, much less everyone's calendar. To put it simply, we have outgrown the spreadsheet method of scheduling." Marta sat down, and all eyes turned back to Dan.

"Good job, Marta," said Dan. "Succinct and accurate."

Completing Timesheets

Next Dan turned to Bill Pardi. "Chief, I asked you to tell us about timesheets for two reasons: because you've been doing them for years, and because I know you've had problems with your staff's timesheets. So, what can you tell us?"

Bill grunted, "Hope you don't expect me to stand up. I'm worn out from filling out timesheets." Nods and smiles came from the rest of the group around the table.

"Our timesheet system is basically a manual process," Bill began. "We have a Word template that people use to create a new timesheet each week. At the top is a place for the employee's Name, ID Number, Department, Title, Status, and Supervisor. Below that is a table, with columns for Date, Job Number, Category, Phase, Total Hours, Billable Hours, Mileage, Meals, Lodging, and Description." He passed a sample timesheet to the other members of the team, even though most of them were already familiar with it.

"There are some things to notice about the sheet," he said. "The employees fill in, line by line, how they spent their work time during the week. Each line is supposed to have a Job Number. This is the ID number for the job or project, and is assigned by the accounting office."

"How do they know the Job Number?" asked Marilou, who, as an independent contractor, kept her own timesheet and was not familiar with the Ferguson and Bardell system.

"They ask what it is, or they're told, whenever they get a work assignment," replied Bill. "Unfortunately, sometimes they get the wrong one, or one hasn't been created yet because the project is so new. That's one of the problems with this."

Dan interrupted, "We'll get to the issues for this section in a minute, everyone. In the meantime, let Bill finish laying out the current system as it is." He turned back to Bill. "What are Category and Phase used for?"

"Well, they aren't always used, Dan. They are primarily for larger projects. Phase refers to the part of the project they are working on, and Category is the generic type of activity." Bill looked at Jane. "For smaller jobs, there is no Phase. And on jobs where it seems obvious what the activity is, we often leave the Category blank and assume that Accounting will fill it in. Right, Jane?"

Jane grinned. "Absolutely right, Bill. Of course, you know the old saying about *assume*, right?" Everyone laughed, and Jane continued, "I especially enjoy how every time-entry for your department shows Development as the Category. How do you do Development during lunch?"

Before Bill could say anything, Tim interrupted. "That's easy! If you eat where Bill eats, you *develop* heartburn during lunch!" This got a good laugh from everyone, even Jim. Bill growled back, "I can't help it if you've got a pansy stomach," but it was obvious he was joking.

Although the team had a lot to accomplish during the meeting, Dan wasn't in too much of a hurry to pull them back on track. These moments of good-natured ribbing were part of the process of becoming a team, and he was glad to see the interaction between the members. He paused to allow the laughter to die down and then said, "Perhaps we can all go to lunch with Bill and judge for ourselves." He turned back to Bill. "I see places for Total Hours and Billable Hours. Why is that?"

"Obviously, not all of the work done by everyone in the company is billable," Bill answered. "Even billable resources go to training, for instance. And we occasionally have a situation where a resource decides that a piece of work took longer than it should, and they list the time but don't consider it billable. We try to minimize that sort of thing, but if it is in good faith, we allow it."

He continued, "The Mileage, Meals, and Lodging columns are for employees to turn in expense items. Of course, for meals and lodging they also have to turn in receipts. The last column, Description, is important because it is the column that actually goes onto the invoice for the customer."

Marilou interrupted again. "What if someone has an expense that isn't listed on the form—say, a book they purchase?"

"Well, it depends," said Bill. "If the expense is billable back to the client as part of a project, the employee lists it under one of the three expense columns and then explains what it really is in the Description column. If the expense is not billable to a client but is an internal expense, it doesn't go on the timesheet at all. Instead, it's handled through an internal purchase-order system." Marilou nodded that she understood, and Bill continued. "Once the employee finishes filling in the timesheet, it's e-mailed to the central office. We have a Time alias set up in Exchange so that timesheets can be e-mailed either through Outlook or via the Internet."

"At which point it becomes Jane's problem," Dan said. "Alright, Bill, what are the issues with this system?" Dan moved to the whiteboard, picked up the marker, and turned back to the group. "And, since you are worn out from doing your timesheets, I'll do the writing for you."

The Issues

"My part of the process will probably win the prize for having the most issues," said Bill. "One of the largest issues is the possibility of error because people enter their own time. The Word table can't check the data as it is entered, so people often miscalculate or misenter their hours, especially if their time is so chopped up that the table runs to two or three pages. We also get wrong project numbers or no project numbers all the time. If the project number is wrong, the time gets billed to the wrong project. Sometimes we catch it before it goes to the customer, but occasionally we don't, and the customer gets billed incorrectly.

"Another issue is the fact that the timesheet is static data. In other words, there is nothing on the screen that changes as people enter the data to give them feedback about what they have entered. Sure, they can add it up manually, but often they are hurrying to get their timesheet done and e-mailed before the deadline, and they just don't take the time to check it thoroughly. As a result, they leave out an entire day, or they enter something twice. If something updated a total every time they completed a line, they would be more likely to get it right the first time.

"A third issue—Marta already mentioned this one—is that people's timesheets are disconnected from their calendars. Some people use their Outlook calendar, and others use various other calendar programs and hand-held things. Whatever time-tracking method they use, they have to open it up, read the data from it, and re-enter the data into their timesheets. There's no quick-and-easy method for dumping their calendar data into their timesheets, even as a starting point that they could then edit.

"Which leads to another issue," Bill said as Dan continued to write. "This may seem esoteric to some of you, but our current system encourages duplication of data. One of the primary principles of data management is to store data once and only once, and preferably in a central location that is easily accessible to everyone who needs it. Currently we have time data stored in various user devices and documents, which is then rekeyed into the timesheets, which are then entered again somewhere else. We need to cut down on the number of places this data is kept."

"We hear you, and we agree," said Dan as he finished noting the issue on the board. "We may not solve this problem completely, especially in the first RMS release, but we can certainly put it up here as a target." He turned back to the board. "What else?"

Bill looked at his notes and then at the group. "All of the above come together to make the system a pain to use." There were nods of agreement around the table. "So most of our employees do their timesheets at the last minute because they hate the hassle. And as a result of *that*, the timesheets are often late, which makes the rest of the process late." He looked at Jim, the CFO. "I'm assuming that when the billing process runs late, it causes some other issues that you would know about, right?"

Jim nodded vigorously and started to say something, but Dan interrupted him. "Jim, would you mind dealing with those further implications as part of item III on the agenda? I would rather give you a block of time all together than piece it out as part of item II, because I think what you have to say will be valuable and I don't want to dilute its impact." Jim thought about that for a moment, then said, "I think that's a good plan, Dan. I'll make some notes as we go along, and deal with them when we get to item III."

Recording Time

Dan turned to Jane. "Alright, Jane, we've scheduled the resource, done the work, filled in the timesheet, and e-mailed it in. What's next?"

Jane opened the manila folder in front of her and pulled out copies of a flowchart, which she passed to everyone around the table. "I thought it might be easier to follow this part of the process if I charted it out for you." Murmurs of appreciation followed as the team members looked at the chart.

"As you can see, Accounting's part of the process begins in the upper left, when the timesheets are received in the Time alias in Exchange." She looked up at the group. "Because of the volume of timesheets, we have eight different clerks with access to that alias. We rotate the task among them, because if we assigned it to anyone full-time, he or she would quit." Looking back at the chart, she continued. "No matter who's doing the work, the process is the same. We open each e-mail and save the attached timesheet in a directory named for the employee. We use the date the e-mail was received as the name of the file when we save it. Then we open the file and print it.

"Once we have the paper copy, we enter the data into the time and billing add-on for our accounting package. We then print a summary of the time for the week, by team, and fax or hand-deliver the summary to the appropriate manager for approval. The manager reviews each employee's time totals and either approves or disapproves the time for that employee. He or she then faxes or hand-delivers the signed summary back to us, along with any notations of approval or disapproval."

While Jane paused, Marta asked, "How often is a timesheet not approved?"

"About 5 percent of the time," Jane answered. "Usually it's because people haven't entered all their time, or they've miscalculated it in some way, and the manager knows it." Marta nodded that she understood, and after waiting to see if there were any other questions, Jane continued.

"If a timesheet is disapproved, we e-mail it back to the employee with a note about what the manager said, and we ask the employee to redo the timesheet and resubmit it. We also delete the one we saved so that two timesheets don't cover the same time period. Then all the approved timesheets are posted into the time and billing system."

"Let's stop there, Jane, and list the issues just for what you've covered so far," said Dan, moving to the whiteboard. "What are the issues, as you see them, with the way we record the timesheets currently?"

The Issues

"There are two big issues, but they are caused by a third issue, so which one should I start with?" asked Jane.

"Let's do the primary one first, then we'll list the problems it causes," replied Dan. "What in your mind is the 'driver' issue?"

Jane said emphatically, "Just the fact that it's a large, cumbersome, manual process. It has multiple steps, most of which involve keying, printing, and keying again. There are too many hands and too few computers in it for me."

Dan wrote *Manual Process* on the board. "I think we can all agree that anything manual associated with 800 timesheets has to be both large and cumbersome." He drew an arrow downward from Manual Process. "So what are the two issues caused by this one?"

"The first is the number of errors we get in data entry. The second is the amount of time this process takes each week."

As he wrote, Dan said over his shoulder, "Elaborate for us, please."

Warming to her subject, Jane responded, "Some weeks we enter over 10,000 line items into the time system. Even excellent data-entry people, which we have, make mistakes when that much work is involved. We catch most of them in the review process, but even so, some get out to the customer. I've worked hard to get the mistake rate down, and we've cut it substantially, but our eyes and fingers can only take so much.

"The other thing is the way this process eats up my resources! I could get much more done, even with fewer people, if we didn't have to deal with this monster each week. And it never stops. Every Monday, you know as you walk through the door that you are going to spend the entire day keying in time. I'm telling you, it's a killer." Realizing she was getting too excited, she paused and took a deep breath. Letting it out, she concluded, "Anyway, those are the three issues."

"I think there's a fourth," said Marta.

"And a fifth," added Marilou.

"OK you two, let's hear them," said Dan, turning back to the board. "Marta, you first."

Marta looked at Jane. "Didn't you start out by saying that you rotate the time-entry task among eight different resources, because if you assigned anyone permanently to it they would quit?" Jane nodded. "And didn't you also say that when people *are* assigned to it, they dread it?" Again, Jane nodded, and Marta continued, "Then I would say another issue with this part of the process is the effect it has on employee morale and retention, wouldn't you, Jane?"

Jane thought about it a moment. "You know, I hadn't considered that as an issue, because I was mainly focusing on the technical or data pieces of the problem. But come to think of it, the biggest gift I could give my staff would be to take weekly time-entry off their plates." She turned to Dan. "Are we allowed to consider quality-of-life issues like these, Dan?"

"Absolutely," Dan replied. "Sometimes they are harder to quantify, as we'll see when we look at return-on-investment issues later on. But Marta's point is a good one. Making Ferguson and Bardell a good place to work is important, especially when you consider the cost of recruiting and training a new hire." He turned to the board. "Let's list it just as Marta said it: 'Employee morale and retention.'" Looking at Marilou, he asked, "And what's your issue, Marilou?"

Pointing to Bill, Marilou said, "It's the same problem Bill talked about in his section. We've got duplication of data again. By my count, we've got time data in at least three locations: the employee's machine where the timesheet is created, the central directory where the sheet is stored, and the time and billing system where it is entered." She looked at Bill. "Kind of tough to guarantee data integrity, not to mention concurrency, wouldn't you say?"

"Sure would!" Suddenly Bill realized he was agreeing with the person he had called an Excel-clicker-turned-trainer in their last meeting. He looked up at Dan, who had set him straight about Marilou's technical background and who now had a slight smile on his face. "If it were up to you to redesign this monster, Marilou, what would you do?"

"Get a central data store to start with, that's for sure," she said firmly. "Try to cut down on the number of places time data is kept and analyzed. We might not be able to get it all the way to one, but we could get pretty close if we thought it through carefully." Bill nodded his agreement.

"That's the right direction, Marilou," Dan interjected, "but it's a topic for a later meeting. Hang onto it, because we'll need it soon."

Generating Invoices

Dan turned back to Jane. "There's more to your flowchart, Jane. Tell us about this last section."

"It's actually fairly simple," said Jane, looking down at the chart in front of her. "As you can see, once the timesheets are posted to the time and billing system, we run trial invoices and print them. The trial invoices are then sent to both management and sales for review. After both of them sign off on the invoice, the trial invoices are posted to the main accounting system, which runs the actual invoices."

"Are there any issues with this part of the process?" Dan stood at the board, marker ready.

The Issue

"I've given it some thought, and the only issue I can come up with is not so much an issue with this process as it is with the way Ferguson and Bardell is structured."

"And that is?"

"Well," Jane answered, "some of our work is billed on a project basis, and some of it is strictly hourly. The hourly work is managed through this process. The project work is billed the same no matter how much time we spend on it. When we go over the amount of time allotted to a project, we lose money. But because of the way we track time, we often don't know we are over until we do the invoice."

"So the issue is that there is no way to track time by project and compare the amount of time we actually spend with the amount of time the bid allows for?" asked Tim.

"That's right," said Jane. "It doesn't happen often, because most of our sales people and managers work together to make sure we have good estimates for our larger projects. Typically, it happens on smaller jobs where the work is only going to last a few weeks. By the time we catch it, the project is already over the estimate and there's no room to make it up."

"Alright," said Dan, "let's put it on the issues list, and perhaps as we move through the process, we can come up with a good way to deal with the problem as part of the overall RMS project." He moved away from the whiteboard and back to his place at the table.

Business Implications

"As I said earlier," Dan said, "I asked Jim Stewart, our CFO, to sit in with us today and share any insights he might have about the business implications of the current time and billing system. He's been taking some notes as we talked, and I'm sure he would like to share them with us." He turned to the CFO. "Jim, you've been here longer than I have, which is one reason I wanted you to be here today. We'll need your insights into what matters from a *business* standpoint as we begin finding solutions to these issues. More than anything, we want to plan a product that makes good business sense. Take as long as you need and tell us what you see as the business implications of the issues we have listed." Dan sat down, and all eyes turned to Jim.

When Dan had invited him to attend the meeting, Jim hadn't been sure what to think. Early on, he had resented the fact that Dan wasn't reporting to him but was instead part of the senior management team. He had worried that the new CIO would spend money wildly and not really care about what made Ferguson and Bardell the successful business it was. Over the past six months, however, he had come to realize that Dan was interested in far more than just computers, and was primarily concerned with the same things he was: how to use his area and his skills to make Ferguson and Bardell the best it could be for its customers, its employees, and its stockholders.

Being invited to share his opinions in what was primarily a technology meeting was a new experience for him. It seemed, though, that Dan and the others really wanted to hear what he had to say. Taking a moment to gather his thoughts, he began.

"I appreciate the opportunity to join you today," he said, looking at Dan and then the others. "It has been good for me to hear your analyses and to see the issues list you have developed." He looked at Jane, with whom he had worked for the past four years. "I especially appreciated your section, Jane, and the self-control you showed. I have heard you describe our time and billing system in the past in somewhat more, shall we say, graphic terms."

Jane blushed and smiled, and everyone else laughed knowingly. The tension broke, and everyone, including Jim, relaxed noticeably.

Jim continued, "I made some notes as you all spoke, and I'd like to share with you what I see to be the primary business issues caused by the current system. I was going to follow Dan's agenda, but now that I think about it, I'd like to simply list the business issues, because they actually cross more than one area. Is that acceptable to everyone?" When the group nodded, Jim moved to the whiteboard.

"Basically," he said, "you can affect the profit picture of a company in only two places: the top line or the bottom line. In other words, you can increase profits either by increasing revenues or by cutting costs. There are an infinite number of means to either of those ends. I'm being fairly simplistic, but this is a good way to begin considering business implications of a problem. Does it affect either the top line or the bottom line?

"It seems to me that four basic business issues relate to the current time and billing system. Two are top-line issues, and two are bottom-line issues.

"The first issue is inefficient use of resources. The example Marta gave is perfect: We have a resource that has a certain skill set, but we are not aware of that skill set. Or we might have one person who is marginally competent at a given task and another person who is exceptionally competent at the same task, and we send the marginal person because we don't know that the exceptional person is, in fact, free at that time.

"Ultimately, of course, an inefficient use of resources leads to loss of revenue. Customers want a resource adequate to the job at hand, but only adequate. The point is to send the appropriate resource to the customer. If we send a $200 resource to do a $50 task, either we bill the customer $50, in which case we lose money, or we bill them $200, in which case we lose a customer.

"Of course, there is also the other situation Marta mentioned: where we lost a job entirely because we believed we didn't have the resource to cover it, when in fact we did and didn't know it. This sort of situation sends salespeople and management absolutely over the edge. In fact, I happen to know that we lost a salesperson over that particular incident. She had spent six months trying to get into that company, and when she finally got us a shot at some work for them, we didn't have our internal systems together well enough to deliver, even though we could have.

"Those are the two top-line issues I see. Now, what about bottom-line issues? Again, I see two. The first is the cost of the time associated with filling out, entering, and reviewing timesheets, and then generating, reviewing, and mailing invoices. Although spending a certain amount of time is inevitable, we should still look for ways to reduce it. If we can cut 15 minutes a week from the time spent filling out timesheets, that adds up to over ten hours of time saved a year. Multiply that by 800 resources and you have saved over 8000 employee-hours a year.

"The biggest area of improvement I see, though, is in data entry. Jane mentioned that if the process were even partially automated, she could possibly cut one or even two positions in her department. Considering the loaded cost of even one of those positions, that alone could be enough to justify the cost of writing a new piece of software.

"But let's say we don't cut the two positions but instead assign the people to other, more productive work. What that means is that as we grow, we don't have to hire two new people but can instead use people who already know Ferguson and Bardell and who already understand the work and what we do here. We get productivity from the beginning."

Jim paused to let his comments sink in. Looking around the room, he could see that some of these concepts were new to most of the members of the team. Dan seemed unfazed by the discussion, and Jane had heard some of this before, but the others clearly weren't used to working through the business implications of technical issues. He continued.

"There's another business implication that is a little more esoteric. But it's one that I deal with every day, and in some cases it can have a major impact on the bottom line. That is the cost of money."

"Here is the problem," Jim explained. "Like all companies, Ferguson and Bardell works with a certain cash flow. We have money flowing in from invoices, and money flowing out to payroll and other expenses. If more comes in than goes out in a given time period, we have a positive cash flow, and if more goes out than comes in, we have a negative cash flow.

"If we expect to be profitable, over time, we should always have a positive cash flow. But much of our work is on large projects for other large companies, and a lot of our invoices are milestone-based. So at any given moment we may have only a very small positive cash flow or even a negative cash flow.

"A contributing factor is our current invoice cycle. Jane, how often do we send out invoices?"

"Twice a month," replied Jane, wondering where this was headed.

"What are our invoice terms?" Jim asked.

"We do net-30 for almost all of our clients, but most of them actually pay around net-45."

"And what do we typically do to cover payroll, if we are having a tight month while we wait for large invoices to come in?"

"We move money out of the line of credit and into the payroll account."

"Exactly!" Jim exclaimed. "We hit the credit line while we wait for our cash flow to catch up. That's the cost-of-money issue."

Jim seemed pleased that he had managed to explain something as complex as the cost of money to a group of techies. But, realizing that many members of the team hadn't quite grasped the connection, Dan decided to act as if he didn't understand. "Jim, I understand that we have to take money out of our line of credit to cover bills whenever our receipts are slow coming in. But why do you call that the cost of money, and what is the relationship to our time and billing system?"

The group looked relieved that Dan had been the one to show his ignorance. Catching on, Jim smiled slightly. "Alright, here is the point. When we hit the line, it costs us interest. The rate isn't that high, but over time it can certainly add up. That interest cost is the 'cost of money' I've been referring to.

"Here's how it relates to time and billing. We currently do invoices twice a month because it takes us two weeks to walk the entire time and billing cycle. If we could shave enough time off the process to do invoices every week, then the money would come in one week sooner, we would use the money from the line one week less, and we'd pay one week's less interest. Over the course of a year, that can really add up."

"How much?" the group demanded, almost in unison. Jim looked startled by the response, so Dan repeated calmly, "How much money do you think we might save in a year, Jim, if we were able to go to once-a-week invoicing?"

Jim thought a minute, seeming to debate with himself about what to say. Finally, he did some calculations on his pad. "If I've figured this correctly, moving to weekly billing would save Ferguson and Bardell approximately $500,000 a year."

Dan whistled, and Tim muttered "Holy moly!" Jim was quick to interject, "Now, those are just preliminary figures, based entirely on our current line of credit and what we've had to do over the past year. It could be less, if our work cycles evened out so we wouldn't have to hit the line as often."

"But, it could be more if the Fed raises interest rates, right?" Jane asked. Jim nodded in agreement.

Wrapping Up and Assignments

Dan stood up. "Thanks, Jim, for your help with this. I think you certainly opened our eyes to some of the implications of this system and why we are considering writing a replacement for it." He turned to Marta, Bill, and Jane. "Thanks also to the three of you for giving us a good idea of both the process and the issues in your areas. I think we have a very clear picture of how time and billing works and of what the issues are with it. Alright, any questions? Tim?"

Tim was tapping his pencil on the table. "You just said we were 'considering' writing a replacement for time and billing. Sounds to me like we don't need to 'consider' it. We just need to *do* it!"

"I know it seems that way, but remember, all we've heard is the current situation. We haven't done any work to find out the cost of writing a replacement, and we can't do that until we agree on what the replacement will look like. We have to agree on a vision for the solution and then come up with a cost for that vision. Then we'll be able to decide whether it makes sense to build something. That's part of the beauty of MSF. If we follow it properly, we won't start any projects that should never have been started, or commit significant resources to something before we are sure it warrants them.

"Any other questions? No? Alright, then, here are our assignments.

"I will capture what we've written on the whiteboard and add it to the project directory. You'll find it listed as 'Initial Issues' in the 'Envisioning' directory.

"Jane, would you please work with Jim over the next few days to put a finer point to that cost-of-money figure? If we decide we can design a solution that will enable us to cut our invoice cycle to one week, we're going to need a solid number as part of our cost analysis. Jim, is that OK with you? Do you have the time?"

"How about it, Jane? Do you have some time to work on this with me?" Jim asked.

"We've got a few people out tomorrow, so it may be tough, but I think I can move things around to free up some time. How about this afternoon?"

"Two o'clock?" Jim suggested, and Jane nodded.

"Good," said Dan. He began handing out packets of paper, already punched for the team's binders. "Here is your reading material for our next meeting. Be sure you've already covered the MSF Development Team Model and MSF Development Process Model material. The new stuff is about goal-setting and iterative design. Be ready to use it on Monday morning. Same time, same place. We're just about ready to get creative with time and billing."

As the group filed out of the conference room, Marta turned to Tim. "I've used the term 'iterative' before, but I'm not sure it means the same in an IT setting like this."

"The best definition I can think of is the one I read on the wall of the computer lab in school, Tim replied. "It said 'Iterative, noun; see iterative.'" They both laughed and headed to their offices.

CASE STUDY 4

Determining Goals

"Wow, look at this place!"

Tim O'Brien turned completely around as he came through the door of the Oak Room, where Ferguson and Bardell held its board meetings. His eyes wide, he said, "Look at that picture on the wall. It's bigger than my desk!"

"Talk about a big desk—take a look at that conference table," said Jane Clayton as she followed Tim into the room.

The rest of the RMS project team entered the room, with all but Dan Shelly and Bill Pardi doing their fair share of rubbernecking. Dan had already been working in the room for two days, getting things ready for the Monday morning team meeting. Bill had helped install the networking and communications equipment when the Oak Room was remodeled a few years earlier, so he was neither surprised nor intimidated by it.

"Alright, people, it's just a big board room. Let's move to this end of the conference table and get started." Dan was already beginning to feel the pressure of the project timeline, and he was anxious to get started. Over the weekend, he had laid out the project calendar, and its time limit had come into sharp focus. As the team moved to join him, he wondered if he had bitten off more than he and the team could chew.

"Where do you want us, Dan?" asked Marilou Moris, moving toward a chair beside Jane.

"Yes, do you have a seating plan or preference?" added Marta Wolfe-Hellene, debating whether to sit next to Bill, who seemed not to like her, or by Marilou, who usually talked only to Jane.

"I do have a seating plan, but it's only for one of you, and we'll get to that later. For now, just grab a spot near this end." He sat at the head of the table and motioned for the others to take a seat. Jane noticed all the diagrams on the walls and the easels with flip-charts spread around the room. She turned to Dan and said, "Boy, you've been busy as a beaver this weekend!" She waved a hand at the room and said, "What's all this about?"

Dan finished laying out some papers on the table in front of him before addressing the others. "Alright, folks. I'll explain. Last week, after our meeting, I went to Mike Adamley, our Chief Operations Officer, and explained to him what we are trying to do. I told him we needed a big space to work in. In short, that we needed a "war room." He gave us permission to use this room. It'll be our home for the next two months."

"We get to use the Oak Room for two months? Wow, we must be important!" said Tim, leaning back dangerously far in his chair, a smug smile on his face.

"Don't get a big head, Big Head," said Jane as she pretended to push his chair over. "*We're* not important; it's the *work* that's important."

"That's exactly right, Jane," said Dan. He flipped on the overhead projector and laid a transparency on it. "And it's time to get that important work moving. So, if everybody will turn to the agenda I sent you over the weekend, we'll get started." Sensing the edge in Dan's voice, the team quickly quieted down and opened their binders.

"Okay," Dan continued, "the first item on the agenda, as always, is Agenda Building. Does anyone have any changes they'd like to suggest?"

"I've got one," said Tim. Everyone looked at him with surprise. Tim admired Dan so much that it was unusual for him to question or add to anything Dan did. Even Dan seemed surprised. "Alright, Tim, that's what this is for. What do you want to change?"

Tim suddenly looked a little sheepish. "Well, some of you know that I'm usually on the run to make these meetings on time." There were grins of acknowledgement from the other team members. "I know we have coffee and juice when we meet, but I was hoping we could have something more substantial."

"Like, breakfast?" said Jane, laughing. "What do you want us to do, cater in a brunch for you?"

Tim blushed and said, "No, not like that. I'd just like something to nibble on. I was thinking of something like—well, doughnuts."

This brought hoots from the rest of the team. Tim's fondness for pastries was well known. Dan said, "And who, pray tell, do you think should provide these delicacies?"

Tim said, "Well, I thought we should take turns." Then, reaching into his backpack, he brought out a box full of doughnuts. "And I decided to take first turn." To his team members' delight, he placed the box on the table, and asked Dan, "Can I have one now?"

FERGUSON AND BARDELL
ENGINEERING • ARCHITECTURE • PROJECT MANAGEMENT

The RMS Project
Meeting Agenda

Meeting Date: March 29, 1999   **Purpose:** Goal-Setting

I.   Agenda Building

II.   Review of the MSF Development Model

III.   Team Responsibilities for Phases
- Envisioning
- Planning
- Developing
- Stabilizing

IV.   Multiple Iterations Within a Version

V.   RMS Project Calendar and Initial Goals

VI.   Q&A

VII.   Wrap-Up: Path-Forward Assignments

CHICAGO • DETROIT • MILWAUKEE • CINCINNATI • INDIANAPOLIS • LOUISVILLE

Dan just laughed and said, "Tim, I can always count on you to help me remember what is really important in this work." The edge was gone from his voice. "Alright, everyone grab a napkin off the credenza and get your doughnut."

Once the team had settled back down, happily munching on Tim's doughnuts, Dan said, "Normally, agenda changes have to be voted on, but I think Tim's addition is approved by acclamation. Good idea, Tim. We'll add munchies to the meetings from now on. Alright, let's move on."

Review of the MSF Development Process Model

Dan looked at his agenda. "The first thing we need to do is to review your reading assignments. Who can tell me what the first phase is in the MSF Development Process Model, and its purpose?" Dan held a transparency in his hand, waiting. "Marilou?"

"It's called Envisioning. Its purpose is first, to understand the problem you are trying to solve, and then to build a high-level vision that everyone agrees with." Dan nodded, and put the transparency on the projector. It was the MSF Development Process Model diagram they had seen in their first meeting.

"The MSF Development Process Model has four phases: Envisioning, Planning, Developing, and Stabilizing. Each has a set of deliverables, and each concludes with a major milestone. Within each phase are interim milestones. Who can tell me the difference between a major and an interim milestone?"

"That's easy," said Tim, reaching for a doughnut as he spoke. "The interim milestones are seen by only the project team; the customer doesn't have to know about them. The major milestones, on the other hand, are sign-off points at the end of each phase, where the customer and the project team agree that it makes sense to proceed with the project." He took a bite and continued, "All milestones are times for the people involved to check their progress and to re-synch their efforts."

"Good work, Tim," said Dan. He reached out and picked up the doughnut box just as Tim reached for another. "Now, for a bonus doughnut, can you tell me the four major milestones, by phase?" Everyone laughed as Tim grinned at Dan. Tim went to the nearest easel, picked up a marker, and drew the MSF Development Process Model's four phases. He labeled each phase, then wrote the names of the four milestones and drew arrows to connect the names with the diamonds at the end of each phase. Affecting a sing-song voice like a six-year-old, he recited, "The Envisioning Phase concludes with the Vision Approved Milestone. The Planning Phase concludes with the Project Plan Approved Milestone. The Developing Phase concludes with the Scope Complete Milestone, and the Stabilizing Phase concludes with the Release Milestone." He then bowed in an exaggerated manner as the group, including Dan, applauded, and went back to his chair as Dan slid the box of doughnuts across the table.

"Excellent!" Dan said with a smile, pleased that his young network manager had risen to the challenge. "Let's hope that everyone else knows it as well as you do." He turned to the rest of the group. "So, who can tell me some of the principles of the MSF Development Process Model?" Marta quietly raised her hand. "Yes, Marta?"

Marta ticked the principles off on her fingers as she listed them out loud. "Use versioned releases, create living documents, schedule for an uncertain future, manage tradeoffs, manage risks, maintain a fixed ship-date mindset, break large projects into manageable parts, perform daily builds, and use bottom-up estimating." Finished, she sat back and looked at Dan with a small smile.

The rest of the group stared at her, stunned. Finally, Tim whistled, low and long. "Wow, Marta, you're good." He slid the box of doughnuts across the table. "Here, you deserve all of them."

Marta simply laughed and slid the box back to Tim. "No, thanks, Tim. I'm not really into doughnuts like you are. Keep them for later."

After a pause, Dan said, "Quite impressive, Marta. I'm not sure I could list them all in order like that, at least not without writing them out as I went."

Team Roles and Their Phase Responsibilities

Dan put another transparency on the projector that showed a table with the four phases on the left and blank boxes beside each phase "We've already spent some time on the MSF Development Team Model, and each of you has studied the material explaining what your roles and responsibilities are. Now I want to tie those roles to the MSF Development Process Model." He moved to where he could write on the transparency and continued. "As Program Management, I'm responsible for the overall progress of the project. But each of you is individually responsible for driving a certain phase to completion. Based on what you know about your roles, who do you think is responsible for the Envisioning Phase?"

"That would be me, wouldn't it?" answered Jane, copying the transparency's diagram into her notes for the day. "I mean, since Envisioning is where the project team and the customer build a common vision, and since I am the one responsible for dealing with the customer, my role as Product Management should be responsible for the Envisioning Phase and the Vision Approved Milestone."

The rest of the team was nodding as Dan said, "Exactly right, Jane. The Product Management role is responsible for leading the team forward to the first milestone." He wrote *Product Mgr.* in the first box, then continued, "Do you all remember what I said about special seating plans—that I had one, but it was for only one person? This responsibility is what I was referring to. Beginning next time, Jane, I want you to sit at the head of the table and to run our meeting."

Marilou leaned over and said, "Hey, you're moving up in the world, girl!"

Jane looked doubtful. "I don't know about that, Dan," she said, looking around the room at the other team members. "I'm not sure I should do that. I don't know very much about some of these areas."

"Yes, but you know the customer better than any of us, and that makes you eminently qualified to help us build the vision we need. Don't worry, Jane; I'll be giving you some help and pointers as we go along. And don't forget, this is a good team."

He wrote his own name in the second blank box on the transparency, next to Planning. "The Program Management role has the overall responsibility for the project, but also has the specific responsibility for the Planning Phase. A good Program Manager actually starts planning the day he is enlisted to run the project."

Dan turned back to the transparency. "Let's jump to the third phase, Developing. I think we can all name at least one person who is responsible for that phase."

Bill Pardi stirred in his seat. "Guess that would be me, now wouldn't it?" he said gruffly. "Since this is a *development* project, glad we finally got the developers involved." It was obvious to the rest of the team that Bill still wasn't convinced of the value of using the MSF Development Process Model. The other team members looked at Dan, who answered Bill with a tight smile.

"Actually, Bill, you'll see in a moment that you and your folks are involved much sooner than you think. However, first, we need to finish assigning roles to phases." Bill shrugged, and Dan continued. "We've got six roles on this team, and only four phases, which means some phases have responsibilities that are carried out by more than one role. Which role do you think works with you on Developing, Bill?" Bill and the rest of the team looked around, trying to figure out who else would be needed in the Developing Phase. "I'll give you a hint," said Dan. "It's someone that mature developers always want to hear from."

Bill furrowed his brow as he thought through the possibilities. Finally he said, "It seems to me that us code jockeys should listen to every one of the groups you people represent. Customers, operations folks, testers—they're all important to the work."

Dan nodded approvingly and said, "That's true, Bill, and that's one of the reasons MSF is structured the way it is—to make sure each of those groups is represented. But, when you are actually building the application, there is one group whose concerns should be paramount in your mind as you work."

Again, Bill's face showed his concentration. "Users! We're supposed to work with the users as we build it!" Suddenly he realized that Marilou represented users on the team, and he turned to face her. "That means you and I will be working together." The memory of calling her an "Excel-clicker-turned-trainer" flashed through his mind, and he wondered if she remembered also.

Marilou just laughed and placed a hand on his sleeve. "Don't worry, Bill. Even we 'Excel-clickers' can help you 'code jockeys' when it comes to users. I promise not to write any code unless you ask me to." The rest of the team laughed, and Tim stage-whispered to Bill, "She got you, old man." Bill just looked flustered.

"Actually, it makes sense for the User Education and Development roles to work together in the Developing Phase," said Dan as he wrote the role names in the box on the transparency. "Marilou will take early versions of the application to begin training the users, and she will bring their feedback back to Bill and his team so they can incorporate it into their work as appropriate." He turned to Bill. "Your work will be better, Bill, with the users involved as you build, rather than having them simply send you complaints once the app is rolled out."

Tim said to Bill, "Hey, this is a good deal for you, guy. You've got someone like Marilou to deal with the users, rather than having to do it yourself. They love her, and they'll talk to her. She meets with them, brings you back the info, and you put their ideas in as you go. You're a hero, and you didn't even have to stop being your old grumpy self." Everyone laughed good-naturedly at that, and even Bill smiled.

Tim then said to Dan, "Based on what's left, I bet my Logistics Management role and Marta's Testing role take the lead for the last phase, right?"

Dan wrote the two roles in the last block and said, "That's right, Tim. First we test the app, and then we deploy it. It's Marta's job to make sure the app is ready for the users, and it's your job to figure out how to get it to them. When you are both done, this version will be finished."

"Cool," said Tim, leaning back in his chair again. "I guess that means Marta and I can take it easy till then."

"Not so fast," said Dan, placing another transparency on the projector. "You've forgotten about iterations within a single version." Tim's chair came down with a thud, and he looked up at Dan with a puzzled expression, as did the rest of the team.

Iterations Within Versions

"Look at this," said Dan, pointing to the transparency. "This is the MSF Development Process Model, unrolled out of its circle into a straight line. What does it remind you of?"

Marilou said, "Hmm—get the requirements, make a plan, build the app, test it and deploy it." Suddenly it struck her, and she exclaimed, "Why, it's just ..."

"The Waterfall Model with another name," said Bill flatly. "I told you this MSF was just the 'same old same old' under a new name."

"Hold on, Bill," said Dan, making some marks on the transparency. He had drawn the MSF Development Process Model circle in miniature above each of the phases on the straight line. "Does this look like the same old Waterfall?"

"Dan, I did not understand this when I read the material you gave us, and I do not understand it now," said Marta, clearly puzzled. "Are you saying that we do an entire turn through the Process Model *within* each phase?"

"That's *exactly* what I'm saying, Marta. And here we're departing somewhat from the strict MSF way of doing things" replied Dan. "In each phase, we are going to do some Envisioning, some Planning, some Developing, and some Stabilizing. In some phases, we might loop around more than once."

"Do we do a miniature version of the milestones, too?" asked Jane.

"No, this isn't like one of those photographs of two mirrors, where the images keep repeating smaller and smaller to infinity. These smaller iterations aren't full-blown versions of the MSF Development Process Model, with interim deliverables inside of interim deliverables and such.

"All that 'iterations-within-iterations' means is that we are planning and building throughout the project. We do some testing and deployment early, in the Envisioning Phase, rather than wait until the very end."

"So," said Marilou, speaking slowly as she worked through the idea, "this means that the vision may not be complete, may not be final, until the very end, even though it gets approved at the end of the first phase."

"Exactly," Dan replied. "That's the whole point behind the Living Documents concept in your materials. All the deliverable documents are open to revision as we go through the project, based on new or changed information we gather along the way."

"What's to keep you from iterating right out of control?" asked Bill with irritation in his voice. "Looks to me like you could just do iteration after iteration until you blow away your time and your budget."

"You limit the number of iterations up front," replied Dan. "And, you set goals for each iteration up front as well, so everyone on the team knows what each iteration is supposed to accomplish."

"How many iterations are we going to do in the RMS project?" asked Jane.

"That number is determined largely by our calendar," said Dan. "Since that's next on our agenda, let's take a look at it." He put a new transparency on the projector. "What do you think?" There was a collective gasp as the team looked at Dan's proposed calendar.

RMS Project Calendar and Initial Goals

"Boy, when you said two months, you weren't kidding, were you?" said Bill. He continued, "Do you honestly think there is any way we can make these deadlines?"

"Bill, we won't know the definitive answer to that until we get further into the planning process. Remember, scheduling belongs in the Planning Phase. But we can set up a high-level, tentative schedule now, simply to give us a framework on which to base our planning. That's what I've done here."

"Let's see," said Jane, as she sketched the calendar on her notepad. "Looks like you've got a week and a half for Envisioning, another week and a half for Planning, three weeks for Developing, and two weeks for Stabilizing. I bet that boils down to one iteration for Envisioning, one for Planning, two for Developing, and one for Stabilizing. How close am I?"

Dan smiled and said, "Exactly right, Jane. Your accounting background serves you well."

Marta asked, "What about the goals for each iteration, Dan? You mentioned we needed to set those up front."

"Yes, and I've got a tentative set of goals right here," Dan answered as he handed out a paper diagram to the team. Looking at the copy in front of him, Dan continued, "I've listed the development goals for each iteration first, as those are probably the easiest to grasp.

"In the first iteration—the one done during the Envisioning Phase—our development goal is to build a prototype. A prototype is a visual mock-up of what we think the app should look like. It is a tool for communicating with the customer, and is only the interfaces. Bill, do you think your team can do a prototype in roughly a week?"

"With all the visual tools we have, are you kidding? Interfaces we can do," said Bill.

"Great. So our primary goal for the first iteration is to build the prototype and use it as a vehicle to create a vision of what the RMS product can be. Now, on to the iteration done within the Planning Phase. Here, our development goal is to build a proof-of-concept version of the application. This version is where we work out the critical design and architecture questions, and prove that our design is doable. The proof-of-concept version is almost the functional opposite of the prototype. The prototype was all interfaces; the proof-of-concept is all the critical guts of the app: data access, back-end products, things like that."

"I get it," said Bill, warming to the discussion. "Then in the iterations done during the Developing Phase, we build an alpha version and a beta version of the application, right? That's just like we've done before, *but* "—Bill was beginning to get excited—"this time our alpha is really way ahead because of the work we've already done! We can simply take the interfaces from the prototype and the technical design of the proof-of-concept and put them together with some connecting objects. Using this MSF Development Process Model, our alpha will be almost like our first beta in past projects."

"Exactly, Bill. You've got the idea," said Dan. "Then, in our final iteration, we incorporate any issues that Testing and Logistics have found, and we're at our golden release. And then we're done."

Everyone was silent for a moment. Finally, Jane spoke up. "Well, if I'm going to start driving this process forward, I guess the first question is, where do we go from here?"

"Good question, Jane," Dan replied. "That's the Path-Forward Assignments at the end of the agenda. Before we go there, let's see if anyone has a question." He paused. After a moment, Tim raised his hand. "Yes, Tim?"

Tim said, "Dan, this looks great. I mean, the idea of turning a project this quickly is so exciting, I know *I* am already pumped. But, it's also a pretty radical departure from our past practices, and I'm still struggling to get a handle on it. I bet the others are, too." There were nods of agreement around the table. Tim continued, "Do you have any examples of this process, any sample documents, for instance? Something showing how a particular team laid out its goals would be helpful."

Dan nodded and said, "Tim, one of the best ways to understand the MSF Development Process Model and the iterations within it is to watch another project team work through it. That's why the handouts I've prepared this time are the deliverable documents from another team's project. I happen to know the program manager on that project, and he said I could share them with you."

As Dan said this he began to smile, and Tim exclaimed, "*You* were the program manager! These are documents from your old law firm!"

"Yes, and I haven't cleaned them up very much, so you'll get to see just how green I was then," said Dan. "We were all new at it, but we were still able to turn a project in six months when most people thought it would take three years. Granted, we wound up doing two more versions over the next year before we got the application where we wanted it, but we still delivered the core functionality in the first version. I got permission from the directing officer of the law firm to share these with you, and I hope that they help you get a grasp of these concepts."

He noticed that Marta seemed troubled. "Marta, you look like something is bothering you. Is there something I can clear up?"

"No, not right now. I want to look over the documents you mentioned; then I may want to come and talk with you."

Everyone noticed the tone of her voice, but Dan decided to act as if he hadn't. "That's fine. My door is always open to you or anyone on this team. Just stop by, and we can set something up." She nodded and remained silent.

Dan turned back to the group. "Any other questions? No? Then let's move on to our Path-Forward assignments.

"Everyone should pick up a set of documents from the box on the credenza and read them before our next meeting on Wednesday morning. Based on your reading and on what you know of RMS at this point, each of you should come up with at least one goal for your area for each iteration. I want you to e-mail those goals to me by tomorrow morning so that I can give you some feedback on them before the Wednesday meeting. They won't be our final goals, but they'll be a start.

"Bill, you need to line up people to help you with the prototype. We'll want to start it after the work we do on Wednesday. And Jane, would you stay for just a moment? I want to explain use cases to you, so you can work on them for the next meeting. Everyone understand? Okay, we're done. Next meeting is Wednesday morning, same time and place. Marilou, your turn for the doughnuts, okay?"

As the meeting broke up, Dan couldn't help but notice the contrast between Marta and the rest of the team. Everyone was talking about RMS, sharing ideas, discussing possible goals, getting excited about the work—everyone, that is, except Marta. After picking up her packet from the credenza, she had looked at the others for a moment before walking silently out of the room. Dan thought, "Great! Just when I finally get Bill Pardi to buy in, I get a new problem on the horizon. I sure hope she talks to me before the next meeting so we can deal with whatever it is."

Unfortunately, she didn't. As a result, the meeting on Wednesday took a direction no one could have anticipated.

P A R T 2

Designing the Product

C H A P T E R   5

Project Vision

About This Chapter

Without a well thought out, clearly communicated, business-driven vision, a project will not be successful. In this chapter, we describe the dynamics of the MSF Development Process Model's Envisioning Phase. We discuss what information to gather from the project stakeholders and how to creating a product vision. We discuss the participation of the MSF Development Team Model's various roles and what their responsibilities are within the Envisioning Phase. We also discuss how the envisioning process develops over a period of time. Finally, we present a detailed discussion of risk management, based on the MSF Risk Management Model. This risk management process starts at the beginning of the project and is incorporated into the entire development process.

The principles and guidelines we provide in this chapter are based on our own experience with the creation of application architectures and the implementation of enterprise applications, together with the following sources:

- The MSF *Principles of Application Development* course #1516
- *Creating a Vision for Your Product,* a white paper written by Laurie Litwack, Senior Program Manager, Microsoft Small Business Solutions (BackOffice)

Upon completion, you will be able to:

- Explain the roles that individual team members play during the Envisioning Phase of the development process.
- Describe the Envisioning Phase of the MSF Development Process Model.
- Understand the concept of risk, and why continual risk management is important.
- Describe the process of risk assessment.
- Understand the differences between risk mitigation and implementing risk contingency plans.

- Describe the deliverables required to achieve the Vision Approved Milestone.
- State the contents and purpose of the Vision Document.
- Discuss the best methods of communicating vision.

Overview of Project Envisioning

A project's success depends on the ability of project team members and the customer to share a clear *vision* of the project's goals and objectives. Usually, these goals and objectives stem from the mission or purpose of the organization. The concept of vision has broad-reaching implications beyond the implementation of technology, and effectively aligning a project with an organization's mission requires careful thought.

Before a team begins any other part of a project, it must develop a vision that describes a unified aim and direction for the project. During the process of developing the vision, the team must have the freedom to brainstorm about the elements of a perfect project and how it relates to the business needs of the organization. Otherwise, members of the team who are well aware of business constraints may be discouraged from using their creative talents and abilities to dream of the "ideal" goals and objectives for success.

Although a project's vision definition may go through iterative cycles of refinement, by the end of the envisioning process, those directly and indirectly responsible for the project must have accepted the vision and be able to communicate it. The process of defining and accepting the vision helps team members and the customer clarify the project's goals and objectives, and provides everyone involved with a sense of purpose and direction that they can carry with them to project completion. Without a properly defined vision, it is simple to become lost in project details.

A properly defined vision promotes success by giving the team a clear path for the future. In practice, the power of a shared vision must be harnessed. As shown in Figure 5.1, MSF does this by including an *Envisioning Phase* in the MSF Development Process Model, and defining the vision created in this phase primarily for this version's product release. A long-term vision for all versions of the product can also be developed to provide guidance for future releases. Each incremental product release represents a vision of a specific aspect of the long-term vision, also called a *product scope*, which is used to measure success by tying project and organization goals to an achievable outcome.

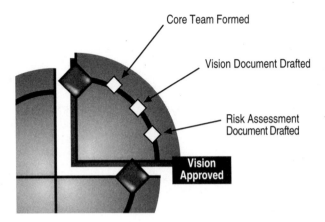

Core Team Formed

Vision Document Drafted

Risk Assessment
Document Drafted

Vision
Approved

Figure 5.1   MSF Development Process Model Envisioning Phase

MSF uses a *Vision Document* to help define and quantify the Envisioning Phase. The Vision Document details the following elements:

- Project vision
- Project scope
- Background information
- Business requirements
- Project requirements
- Deliverables
- Risks

In this chapter, we describe the Envisioning Phase and the Vision Document, as well as the relationships between its interconnected components. Keep in mind that throughout the Envisioning Phase, the team uses documents to communicate among its members. However, this documentation is not the end result of envisioning; communication is the goal. Documents are merely some of the tools used to reach that end result.

The Envisioning Phase is complete when the team reaches the Vision Approved Milestone. This milestone is the point where the project's team and stakeholders jointly approve the product's vision and determine to move into the planning process.

Why Establish a Vision?

Developing a product without a vision is like sailing a ship without a compass: The ship is going somewhere, but where? Do the crew members know where they're going? Are the passengers going where they paid to go?

Although developing a vision for a product is absolutely essential, it's a step in product development that is all too often skipped or undervalued. Most people involved in application development projects have had much more practice doing the tasks necessary to release a product than they have in creating a vision for it. Many find the idea of a product vision unstructured or vague and of little value, especially those new to product development. However, it's important to understand that envisioning:

- Serves as an early form of planning.
- Establishes clear communication and consensus from the beginning of the project.
- Helps the team pull different perspectives into a common understanding.
- Provides the basis for future planning.
- Identifies what the customer and key stakeholders deem essential for success.

At a time when more and more organizations are focusing on "delighting the customer," building a vision is more important than ever. It is the first and most critical step in development, because it describes where the project team is headed and the landscape everyone is traveling in. In an interview with Laura Litwack, Steve Sinofsky, at the time Vice President for Microsoft Office products, noted:

Visions are important because they help a team make decisions at the right level—closest to where the issue is. In that sense, a good vision statement is a tool that empowers the entire organization to work together to build a great product. If there are 10 people working on a project, you can always ask each other everything and there is a shared understanding of what to do. When there are 1,000 people working on a project, you need a way for people to make decisions that move the whole project in the same direction without each person having to talk to all 999 others.

A solid vision builds trust and cohesion among team members, provides perspective, improves focus, and eases decision-making. A common vision fuels the highest team performance and provides the following:

- **Clarification** Team members need to know what they are trying to build before they can build it. In addition, they need to understand why Program Management, Product Management, and the customer decided to include some features and not others. A vision details not only what will be done, but also what won't.
- **Prioritization** There is never enough time to include all the features and elements a team can dream up. During the product's life cycle, the team needs

criteria to guide them through a host of decisions. Development decides how to code the specification and how to lay a foundation for future versions of the product. Testing prioritizes bugs. User Education decides which features to emphasize and how to explain them. Program Management works with product designers to decide how the features should work and how the user will interact with each feature. To make appropriate decisions, the team needs to understand not only what and why, but also in which order. A good vision provides the necessary priority framework for making future decisions.

- **Integration** The vision of this product must complement and support the vision and functionality of other products in the organization. Many other products may serve the same customer and users as this one, and some may have overlapping feature sets. Any long-term duplication of features across different products should be examined to ensure that it makes good business sense.

- **Future investment** Not only should the vision guide today's product, but it should lay a foundation for the future. For example, if Development knows that business-to-business commerce will be included in the next version of the product, Internet delays and low bandwidth issues can be taken into account in the architecture for this version. This foresight can save time in the future.

Pitfalls

We have been using MSF and the MSF Development Process Model for some time now, and have found that it has increased both our team's productivity and customer satisfaction. But there are hazards. In this section we describe some of the pitfalls our team has occasionally fallen into during the Envisioning Phase.

- **Pitfall #1: Not taking advantage of the dynamic nature of the MSF Development Process Model** Initially, we went through the envisioning process as if it were set in stone, not daring to deviate from the MSF documentation. However, as our team began to mature, we learned to tailor the process and its deliverables to our organization's needs and strengths. The Envisioning Phase is a tool, not a law, for encouraging communication and establishing expectations.

- **Pitfall #2: Not being thorough in the Envisioning Phase** We needed to be disciplined about working through the entire envisioning process before beginning a project. With time and budget constraints, it is tempting to begin a project using traditional methods and only use envisioning when it's convenient. We needed to resist that urge and stay with the framework, because the details of the Envisioning Phase are critical to the success of any project.

- **Pitfall #3: Not understanding how the Envisioning Phase establishes a foundation for complex concepts** Envisioning encourages the project team to sort through information and ideas that may be difficult to fathom. This process helps to ensure that the Envisioning Phase is as easy as possible to implement in order to accelerate and streamline the ongoing process of development.

Envisioning Process

The guidelines we give here are modified versions of those outlined by Laurie Litwack, who has worked on operating systems, server applications, and networking subsystems.

Who Does What During Envisioning?

At the beginning of the Envisioning Phase, the project team is selected and members are assigned to lead the six team roles. (Refer to Chapter 3 for guidelines about how to choose a team and how to work with large and small teams.) Each of the team roles plays an important part in the Envisioning Phase, so each must be represented.

Table 5.1 identifies some specific team role responsibilities for the Envisioning Phase. The lead for each team role ensures that these responsibilities are carried out and communicates with the rest of the project team.

Table 5.1   Team roles and Envisioning Phase responsibilities

Role	Responsibilities
Product Management	Deliver Vision Document
	Manage customer expectations
	Involve customer in prototype development
	Manage project risks
Program Management	Develop design goals
	Describe solution concept
	Outline project structure
	Manage project risks
Development	Design prototypes
	Outline development options
	Identify implications
	Manage project risks
User Education	Identify user performance needs and implications
	Manage user expectations
	Involve user in prototype development
	Manage project risks
Testing	Develop testing strategies
	Specify acceptance criteria
	Design bug-tracking system
	Design risk management system
	Manage project risks
Logistics Management	Identify deployment implications
	Identify support implications
	Manage project risks

As the table shows, each role is involved in the task of managing project risks. The process of risk identification and management is discussed later in this chapter.

Several steps can be identified to help the team during the Envisioning Phase. These steps are similar to the Unified Process workflows, discussed in Chapter 4. We don't mean to imply that following these steps is the only way to complete the Envisioning Phase, but to provide a guideline for those new to the MSF Development Process Model. The headings are for descriptive purposes only; they are not intended as formal declarations of procedures or workflows. Additionally, these steps are sequential but should be followed in a flexible manner. For example, if the team is working on Step #4 (the implementation step) and realizes additional use cases are needed, it can return to Step #2 to develop the new set of use cases.

Step #1: Research

For the vision to be complete, the team needs to do some research, focusing its efforts on the customer and on other similar products being developed by or used by the organization. The goal of this step is to identify and record as much information as possible. Sources for this information should include the project customer, users, current applications and their documentation, as well as experts in the application's area or focus (domain), such as distribution or manufacturing. The team should limit notations about priorities to those obtained from these sources; additional prioritization will occur later. Using this information, the team can ultimately create a vision that outlines priorities, identifies dependencies, and roughs out a schedule.

Researching Other Enterprise Applications

If a previous version of this product exists, the team should start by understanding that version's vision. It's likely that the previous vision will include long-term goals for future versions that can and should be leveraged. Likewise, the team needs to understand the visions of any other applications concurrently under development.

Some of the questions to be asked when creating a vision for the new product include:

- Is the new product expected to be a big leap or a small step for the organization?
- Are the concept and the architecture being considered new to the organization?
- What new features does the product bring to the organization?

Researching the Customer and Users

Throughout this book, we continually stress the importance of knowing and understanding the customer and the customer's business requirements before beginning any kind of development work. The Envisioning Phase is the time when the team focuses on the customer's problem and how users will work with the product to solve that problem. Areas the team should address include the following:

- **Business initiatives** What business initiatives is the organization undertaking? How will these new initiatives affect the product?

- **Existing information** What have other people discovered about this customer? Where can the team take advantage of any previous work? What customer information will need to be confirmed or clarified?

- **New hardware** What new hardware products will impact the customer? How can new hardware be used to this project's benefit? For example, can features be included to take advantage of touch screens?

- **New technologies** What new technologies will impact the customer? How can new technology be used to help the customer? For example, how will improved search capabilities or speech recognition affect users?

- **Support issues** What problems did users have with other products like this one? What are the "Top 10 Support Issues" for the organization? What are the most requested features for new applications? What do the operations and support groups think of this product's vision?

- **User Education plans** What are User Education's plans for documenting the product? What features and concepts from previous applications are difficult to grasp? What features from previous applications have been difficult to document? (Usually a feature that is difficult to document is difficult to use.)

- **Global issues** What groups in other countries rely on the English language version of this product? How well will the new product meet the needs of foreign users? What research will be needed to ensure that the product can be used worldwide? Will a foreign (localized) version of the product be needed?

Researching Similar Products

The vision the team develops for this product must fit with the visions already developed for the other products used by the organization. In some ways, this is the easiest type of research, because it's a matter of leveraging existing knowledge and working with existing contacts within the organization to ferret out information that already exists. Questions the team should ask include the following:

- **Leverage points** What were the visions of other products developed for the same customer? What can be done to leverage and support the work done for those products?

- **Operating system** What do the current operating systems provide for this product? What will future versions of the operating systems provide? How will changes in the operating systems affect this product's architecture? How can new operating system features be leveraged and supported?

- **Schedule** What other products, systems, or applications is the organization implementing during this product's time frame?

Step #2: Analysis

Synthesizing the business and user requirements gathered in the research step is by no means an exact science. One of the ways to boil down the information is to group it into simplified statements or questions with their solutions. For example, "The consulting group must enter hourly data in three different locations" and "The consulting group wants to enter data only once." Often one side of the equation can be stated, and the team has to determine the other side. The concepts presented on one side represent the current state, and the concepts presented on the other side represent the future state. Looking at a list of the organization's overall business goals can also help the team requirements for a project.

In Chapter 6 we discuss noun-verb concepts for determining logical and physical designs. Looking for key noun phrases and verb phrases can also be useful in identifying project requirements. If project stakeholders repeatedly use the same nouns and verbs when talking about the project, those phrases are probably important requirements for the project.

Business and user information can be analyzed to create product feature lists. As with requirements, the derived features should not have a scope or version applied to them at this point. The team will determine the current product's actual feature set, and some feature sets for future releases, in the implementation step discussed below.

To help document business and user requirements, UML use case and activity diagrams are very helpful for concisely communicating information. The use case model of the Unified Process can be used to describe the requirements in the language of the users. Additionally, simple word descriptions (typically in sentence form) of the specific use cases, as well as descriptions of usage activities and usage scenarios, provide good communication of requirements. When this step is complete, the team should have an exhaustive list of use cases, which will be the foundation of the entire development process.

Step #3: Rationalization

After the use cases and feature lists are created, those features that are similar in nature can be grouped into *feature buckets*, or sets of features, based on user actions, application actions, the data being used, or any other grouping that applies to the application's domain. At this point, the team is still working with features that describe current state as well as future state. For current state activity descriptions, the team can apply process re-engineering techniques to determine whether the activity can be modeled more efficiently in another manner. The design patterns discussed in Chapter 2 can provide examples of different and better ways to model processes in an application.

Step #4: Implementation

As each step of research, analysis, and rationalization is completed, and as any prototypes related to the category are developed, what has been learned is recorded so that over a period of time, a body of documentation about the project accumulates. In the research step, the team's job was not to analyze the information, but simply to record the information as it was encountered. During the analysis step, the research was refined into actual business and user requirements described by use cases, and candidate features were listed. The rationalization step grouped features into feature buckets. The final step is to determine what specific feature buckets will be implemented for the current product version.

At this point, the team prioritizes the feature buckets, with their corresponding features. The future-state use cases, use case diagrams, activity diagrams, and usage scenarios that describe this release of the product are gathered together, and a project vision is drafted. This draft includes the long-range goals for the project and validates that the current product version is moving in the right direction. At this point, enough information is known to determine how the product's tradeoff triangle of resources, features, and ship date is constrained, optimized, and accepted. The initial high-level project schedule can also be determined to provide guidance and reference for the Planning Phase.

Step #5: Validation

As mentioned, the team created the draft of the Vision Document during the Implementation step. The team now reviews and modifies this document. The Envisioning Phase's validation step is the point where the team members need to take a step back and look at their progress and deliverables to ensure that they are adequately prepared for the Vision Approved Milestone.

Communicating

The envisioning process in not about creating documents; it is about communicating the vision of the project within the project team and with the project stakeholders. Prototypes are an excellent method of communication. At the heart of any prototype concept is the old adage "A picture is worth a thousand words." The level of detail in a prototype application is typically very shallow. It may consist of nothing more that screen shots or examples of typical screens. However, the application flow can be described by stepping users through a prototype that follows one of the use cases or usage scenarios defined by the team.

Caution Don't expect to reuse significant amounts of code from a prototype. Reuse often leads to jumbled "spaghetti" code that limits the application's design process.

Risk Management Process

A key factor in the success of any application development project is the identification of the risks a project might encounter, and the development of a system for managing those risks should they materialize during the project's life cycle. We include a discussion of risk management in this chapter because it begins in the Envisioning Phase. However, the process of managing risks continues throughout the entire project.

Many IT professionals have misconceptions about risk management. At best, they think it is a necessary but boring task to be carried out at the beginning of a project before the real work of writing code begins. At worst, they think it is another form of bureaucratic red tape that prevents the organization from achieving its objectives. Every project has its risks, and taking risks is essential to progress. However, that doesn't mean that attempting to recognize and manage risks is a useless activity or that it will stifle creativity.

Risk is the *possibility of suffering loss*. For a given project, this loss could be in the form of:

- Diminished product quality.
- Increased costs.
- Missed deadlines.
- Complete failure to achieve the project's goals.

Because risk is a problem waiting to happen, not one that has occurred, effective risk management is a dynamic process rather than a static project management chore.

Team members usually know the risks associated with their project, but often communicate these risks poorly. Typically, communicating risks down the chain of command is easy, but communicating risks up the chain of command is difficult. At every level, people want to know the risks identified at the lower levels, but are wary of communicating the risks they have identified to the people above them. For the risk management process to succeed, the organization must create an environment in which people who identify and communicate project risks are safe from retribution. In a "don't shoot the messenger" environment, team members feel free to express tentative or controversial views, which significantly improves the scope and quality of risk management.

On some projects, reporting new risks can be viewed as a form of complaining or troublemaking. Often the reaction to the risks is seen as a problem with the person making the report rather than a problem with the product. If the organization's unspoken message is to "soften the risk," critical information that would result in better risk mitigation and contingency plans might be stifled.

Caution Remember that risk is the possibility, not the certainty, of loss. Team members might erroneously view a project with a list of 15 to 20 identified risks with skepticism, even though the total risk exposure is modest.

Sources of Risk

Effective project risk management must take into consideration the business environment in which the project will be carried out. Many IT projects fail not because of faulty technology or bad project management, but because larger organizational pressures were ignored. These organizational pressures come in many forms, such as competition, financial health, and organizational culture. Potential risk sources include:

- Mission and goals.
- Decision drivers.
- Organization management.
- Customer and users.
- Budget and costs.
- Schedule.

- Project characteristics.
- Development process.
- Development environment.
- Personnel.
- Operational environment.
- New technology.

Possible consequences for the project include:

- Cost overruns.
- Schedule slips.
- Inadequate functionality.
- Project cancellation.
- Sudden personnel changes.
- Customer dissatisfaction.
- Damage to the organization's image.
- Demoralized staff.
- Poor product performance.
- Legal proceedings.

It is important to remember that different types of projects pose different kinds of risks, and each project's risks must be addressed individually.

Types of Risk Management

Risk management can be approached in three ways:

- **Waving the magic wand** The project team assesses the risks only once during initial project planning. Major risks are identified, but are never explicitly reviewed or acted upon.
- **Reactive** The project team reacts to the consequences of risks (actual problems) as they occur.
- **Proactive** The project team has a visible process for managing risks that is measurable, repeatable, and addresses the conditions that cause the risks.

Obviously the "magic wand" approach is not an example of good risk management. But neither is the reactive approach, because it has no prevention component. Preventing the risks identified for a project from materializing is the hallmark of a good risk management process. Prevention begins in the Envisioning Phase and continues until the product is released at the end of the Stabilizing Phase. For most risks, the goal is to take certain actions to prevent the risks from materializing as problems, as well as to determine in advance what actions will be taken if a particular risk does in fact materialize. To reach mature levels of proactive risk management, the project team must be able to unemotionally evaluate the risks and take actions that address their root causes, not just their symptoms.

It's important to emphasize that no matter how good a job the team does of risk assessment, it is the team's ability to manage risks that will be a determining factor in the project's success.

The risk management process consists of proactive decisions and actions that continually:

- Assess what risks might occur.
- Determine what risks need to be acted upon.
- Specify what strategies should be implemented to mitigate those risks.

An effective project team assesses risks throughout the life cycle of the project and uses them for decision-making in all project phases. As shown in Figure 5.2, the team carries the risks forward until either they are resolved or they turn into problems and are handled as such.

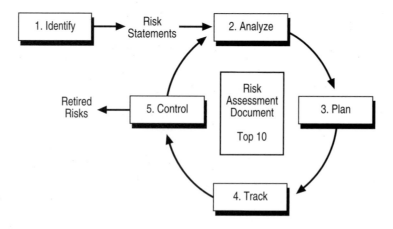

Figure 5.2   Proactive risk management process

Step #1: Risk Identification

Risk identification is the first step in the proactive risk management process. Risks must be identified before they can be managed. Risk identification provides the opportunities, cues, and information that allow the team to expose the major risks that might adversely affect the project.

To identify risks, team members and key stakeholders hold a series of brainstorming and open discussions to identify and rank the risks for the project. To facilitate this process, risk factors can be grouped by focus area, such as custom software development, infrastructure deployment, packaged software deployment, enterprise architecture planning, and component-based development. Within each focus area, risk factors can be further grouped into categories, such as mission and goals factors, decision drivers, organizational management factors, and budget and cost factors.

For example, Table 5.2 identifies three mission and goals risk factors. Each factor has low, medium, and high risk cues. If the low risk cue is in evidence for the project fit risk factor, the project directly supports the customer's mission and goals; if the factor's high risk cue is in evidence, the project does not support or relate to the customer's mission and goals.

Table 5.2   Sample risk factors chart

Risk factor	Low risk cue	Medium risk cue	High risk cue
Project fit	Directly supports customer's mission and goals	Indirectly impacts one or more goals	Does not support or relate to customer's mission or goals
Customer perception	Expects team to provide this product	Believes team is not working on expected product	Believes desired product is mismatched with prior team products
Workflow	Causes little or no change to workflow	Changes some aspect of workflow or has small effect on workflow	Significantly changes workflow or method of organization

For any risk the team discovers as a result of working through the risk factors chart, it should develop a risk statement and enter the risk on a master list. A risk must be clearly expressed before it can be managed. In stating a risk, the team should consider not only symptoms, but also causes and results. As Figure 5.3 shows, each risk statement should include the problem (the condition), what is causing the problem (the source), and the expected result for both the problem and the project (the consequence).

Figure 5.3   Sample risk statement

The process followed during this step is a powerful way to expose the assumptions and differing viewpoints of various team members and stakeholders. It's unlikely that everyone will agree on the ranking of all risk factors. Depending on their level of experience and area of concern, different team members will see the project differently. If no agreement can be reached, the best approach is a majority vote technique. If the votes are tied, caution dictates that the worst case be used for the risk assessment.

Step #2: Risk Analysis

Risk analysis is the process whereby risk data is converted into risk decision-making information. Thorough analysis ensures that the team is working on the right risks.

Risk is primarily composed of two factors:

- **Risk probability** Risk probability is the likelihood that an event will actually occur. A simple percentage from 0 to 100 can be used for ranking risks. Only risks with a probability that is greater than 0 percent pose a threat to the project. Only risks with a probability of 100 percent are certainties—in other words, they are known problems. The team might find it more efficient to consistently use a 1 to 3 scale that corresponds to 25 percent, 50 percent, and 75 percent, because too many arguments are often waged over the difference between a 60 percent and 70 percent probability.

- **Risk impact** Risk impact measures the severity of adverse affects, or the magnitude of a loss, if the risk materializes. Deciding how to measure sustained loses is not a trivial matter. If the risk has a financial impact, the team can use a dollar value to quantify the magnitude of loss. The financial impact can be long-term costs in operations and support, loss of market share, short-term costs in additional work, or lost opportunity cost. When the financial impact is understood, the risk impact can be classified on a simple 1 to 5 scale, 5 being the greatest impact. Additionally, other risks might have the type of impact where only a subjective rating from 1 to 5 is appropriate. This scale essentially rates the viability of project success. High values indicate serious loss to the project, and medium values show loss to portions of the project or loss of effectiveness.

To evaluate a list of risks, the team must understand the overall threat each risk poses to the project. Sometimes risks that are high in probability are low in impact and can be safely ignored. At other times, risks that are high in impact are low in probability and can again be safely ignored. Risks that have high exposure (high probability and high impact) are the ones worth managing. Reducing the risk exposure can be accomplished by reducing either the risk probability or the risk impact.

To help communicate project risks, team members and stakeholders typically maintain the following items of information in a spreadsheet or database:

- **Risk identifier** This name uniquely identifies a risk statement for reporting and tracking purposes.
- **Risk source** The source can be identified from a focus area (custom software development, infrastructure deployment, packaged software deployment, and so on), or a category (mission and goals, decision drivers, organizational management, and so on), and or factors (project fit, political influences, organization stability, and so on).
- **Risk condition** This natural language statement describes the existing condition that might lead to a loss for the project.
- **Risk consequence** This natural language statement describes and quantifies the loss that can occur if the risk materializes.
- **Risk probability** This expression represents the likelihood that a risk that results in a loss will materialize. The probability is typically stated as a value of 1, 2, or 3, representing a percentage of 25 percent, 50 percent, or 75 percent respectively.

- **Risk impact** The effect on the project, should the risk materialize, is measured as a dollar value or a number, on a scale of 1 to 5, that indicates relative magnitude.

- **Risk exposure** The overall threat of the risk to the project is calculated by balancing the likelihood of actual loss with the magnitude of the potential loss. The result of multiplying risk impact by risk probability is used to rank risks. (Note that to rank risk exposure, all the risk impact values must be in the same unit of measurement: either dollars or relative magnitude.)

- **Risk context** This paragraph contains additional background information that helps clarify the risk situation.

- **Related risk** This list of risk identifications is used to track interdependent risks.

Risk analysis weighs the threat of each risk and determines which risks require preventive action. After the risks are ranked by risk exposure, the team should focus on a risk management strategy and how to incorporate risk action plans into the overall project vision. Because managing risk requires time and effort, the key is to identify a limited number of major risks that must be managed. A simple but effective technique is to develop a list of the ten highest risks for the project. This top-ten risk list should be visible to all project team leads. An additional list of major project risks, to raise awareness with the project stakeholders, should be included in the Vision Document created during the Envisioning Phase and the Master Project Plan created during the Planning Phase.

Step #3: Risk Action Planning

Risk action planning turns risk information into decisions and actions. Planning involves developing actions to address individual risks, prioritizing risk actions, and creating an integrated risk management plan that forms the basis of the *Master Risk Assessment Document* delivered as part of the Vision Approved Milestone.

During risk action planning, the team should consider four facets of each identified risk:

- **Research** Does the team know enough about this risk? Is further study necessary to acquire more information and better determine the characteristics of the risk before decisions are made about what action to take?

- **Accept** Can the team live with the consequences if the risk actually occurs? Can the risk be accepted and no further action taken?

- **Manage** Can the team do anything to mitigate the impact of the risk should the risk occur?

- **Avoid** Can the risk be avoided by changing the product's scope?

When the team identifies a risk that needs management, team members have three options:

- Reduce the probability of occurrence.
- Reduce the magnitude of loss.
- Change the consequences of the risk.

For those risks within the team's control, the action plan consists of applying the resources needed to reduce the risk. For those risks outside the team's control, the action plan consists of finding workarounds. It may also be possible for the team to transfer the risk by:

- Moving to different hardware.
- Moving a software feature to another part of the system that is better able to handle it.
- Subcontracting the work to a more experienced player.

As a safety net, the team should also develop a *contingency strategy*, which is a fallback plan that can be activated in case the action plan fails to contain the risk. For example, suppose a particular commercial product is needed so that software can be deployed on desktop systems, but the release date of the commercial product is uncertain. The team's contingency strategy might be to use an alternate product. In this case, during Planning Phase's design, the team would identify an alternative product to be used if the original commercial product does not meet the release date.

Deciding when to resort to the contingency strategy is a matter of watching the strategy's *trigger value*. Often the team can establish a trigger value for each contingency plan based on the identified type of risks or the type of project consequences. Table 5.3 shows some typical risks and consequences and their trigger values. When a trigger value is exceeded, the corresponding contingency strategy can be put into action to help mitigate the risk.

Table 5.3 Sample risks and contingency plan trigger values

Type of risk	Trigger value
Schedule slips	Latest date to use contingency strategy Latest date to select another vendor
Additional resources required	Latest date to allow time to find resources Greatest amount of penalty or fine to incur Greatest amount of effort available for overrun
Extra cost to customer	Dollar limit
Learning time	Time limit

To begin creating the Master Risk Assessment Document, several key items must be identified for each risk. These items are typically entered into an automated risk action form to assist communication between the team members and stakeholders:

- **Risk identifier** This name uniquely identifies a risk statement for reporting and tracking purposes.

- **Risk statement** This natural language statement (explained earlier) describes the condition that could possibly lead to a loss for the project, and describes the loss that will occur if the risk materializes.

- **Risk management strategy** In a paragraph or two, the team describes its strategy for managing the risk, including any assumptions it has made.

- **Risk management strategy metrics** The team will use the following metrics to determine whether the planned risk management actions are working:

- **Probability** The likelihood that the risk will occur. Represented as a number between 1 and 3.

- **Impact** The severity of the impact on the project. Can be represented as a relative number between 1 and 5. Consistent impact measures should be used for all risks.

- **Exposure** The overall threat to the project. Calculated by multiplying the probability by the impact.

- **Action items** This list describes the actions the team will take to manage the risk. Any actions taken will be logged in the risk tracking system.

- **Due dates** This is the date by which the team will complete each planned action item.

- **Personnel assignments** These people are assigned to perform the listed actions.

- **Contingency strategy** In a paragraph or two, the team describes the contingency strategy to be followed in the event that the action plan fails to manage the risk.

- **Contingency strategy trigger values and metrics** The team will use these trigger values to determine when the contingency strategy should be put into effect and these metrics to gauge whether the contingency strategy is working.

Step #4: Risk Tracking

Risk tracking is essential to effectively implement an action plan. It is the process by which the project team monitors the status of risks and the actions it has taken to mitigate them. It includes devising the risk metrics and trigger values needed to ensure that the planned risk actions are working. Tracking is the watchdog function of the risk action plan.

Note It is a good practice to include a risk review during regular project reviews and debriefings. Risk review should include an assessment of progress made toward mitigation of the project's top ten risks.

During each project review, the team should report on the major risks for the project and the status of any risk management actions. Ranking risks over time is useful, as well as keeping a record of the number of times a risk appears in the top-ten risk list.

Risk status reporting can identify four possible risk management situations:

- The risk is resolved, and the risk action plan is complete.
- Actions are proceeding as planned, in which case the risk action plans can continue.
- Actions are not proceeding as planned, in which case corrective measures should be determined or the contingency plan can be implemented.
- The situation has changed significantly with respect to one or more risks, and reassessment is necessary.

As the team takes actions to manage risks, the total risk exposure for the project should decrease.

Step #5: Risk Control

After the team has defined the risk trigger values and metrics, the difficult part of risk management is over. Risk management melds into project management processes that:

- Control risk action plans.
- Correct for variations from plans.
- Respond to trigger values.
- Improve the risk management process.

As suggested by Ron Higuera and Yacov Haimes in the Software Engineering Institute paper *Software Risk Management*,

> *If the risk management process is not integrated with day-to-day project management, it will soon be relegated to a background activity.*

Vision Approved Milestone and Its Deliverables

The goal of the Envisioning Phase is to reach the Vision Approved Milestone, which is the culmination of the team's work during this phase and signifies agreement between the customer and the team on critical project issues.

Four deliverables are required to meet the Vision Approved Milestone. They are:

- A Vision Document, which outlines the product being developed, the needs it will meet, its features, and initial schedule

- A Project Structure Document, which outlines who is responsible for each role in the MSF Development Team Model and identifies the team lead for each role

- A Master Risk Assessment Document, which lists possible risks to the project and outlines how the team plans to deal with each one

We also recommend that a prototype system be included with the deliverables for this milestone to show how the team initially plans to execute the project, and to present concrete visual evidence of the product vision.

Note The goal of any deliverable is that it serves as an efficient communication tool. In this context, a deliverable does not necessarily result in a paper artifact. A deliverable can take whatever form is appropriate (a document, a diagram, a screen shot, e-mail, and so on) as long as it facilitates communication.

Every major milestone in the MSF Development Process Model signifies an agreement between the customer, the project team, and any other key project stakeholders. Reaching the Vision Approved Milestone indicates agreement on the points listed in Table 5.4.

Table 5.4   Agreement achieved by the Vision Approved Milestone

Point of agreement	Documented in
Business needs that will be met by the project	Vision Document
The project vision	Vision Statement
The product design goals	Vision Document
The product team	Project Structure Document
The initial concept of the business solution	Vision Document and Prototype
Risks of building the product	Revised Master Risk Assessment Document

The Vision Approved Milestone provides the initial opportunity for the customer and the project team to decide whether to proceed with the project. After reviewing the deliverables from the Envisioning Phase and fully understanding the product vision, the customer or the project team may decide that the product does not provide enough benefits to justify its costs. This decision represents a critical point in the beginning of the project. A well-executed Envisioning Phase enables the team and the project stakeholders to proceed with confidence, knowing that there is sufficient information about the remaining development phases to maximize the chances for success.

Vision Document

To be effective, the Vision Document developed by the end of the Envisioning Phase should include at least these elements:

- A vision statement
- User research
- Competitive information
- Feature buckets and features
- A rough schedule

Writing a Vision Statement

During the 1960s, when the United States was trying to place a man on the moon, President John F. Kennedy created a vision for everyone in the country to rally behind. We can paraphrase that vision as:

In the next decade, we will send a man to the moon and back safely.

This vision statement illustrates many of the attributes of SMART goals, which are:

- Specific
- Measurable
- Achievable
- Relevant
- Time-based

To bring this discussion down to earth, another example of a solid vision statement is:

Quickly create the fastest spreadsheet on the planet.

Presented with that vision statement, every member of the project team would instantly know that performance issues were more important than any other factor. In fact, a good rule for concise vision statements is to make them so clear that a new employee will stand as a good chance of working toward a solution that is consistent with the project's goals as a current employee.

Reporting on User Research

What the team learns about its customer and users is the underpinning of everything else it does. Site visits, contextual research, market research, focus groups, and international visits will help gather the information needed to describe the primary customer and the users. Additionally, this research provides information for creating usage scenarios that describe how users currently work and how they will work in the future with the product.

Providing Competitive Information

Will the product provide an appropriate return on investment in both today's and tomorrow's competitive landscapes? What other solutions are available to meet the customer's needs? The team must make sure that the product it envisions solves the customer's problem better than any other available solution and that it does so in a way that justifies the investment. The best solution to a problem doesn't have to be a software solution. For example, it may be simpler and more cost-effective to hire the services of a person, such as an accountant, instead of using financial software. Even if a software solution does fit the needs, it should not be assumed that the software must be built from scratch. Research about other systems that provide the required functionality might identify a commercial solution. Even if the solution is not purchased, insight can be gained from the commercial software that will lead the team toward creating a stronger internal product.

Sometimes a project must compete with other demands on the organization's resources. For example, in the latter part of the 1990s, many companies spent a significant portion of their software budgets evaluating the threat of the Year 2000 problem, which directly affected many other software projects.

Describing Feature Buckets and Features

Feature buckets are the categories into which all the product's features will fit. Program Management uses these categories to test whether the proposed features meet the goals of the product. If a feature doesn't fit into any of the buckets, it's probably not important enough for the current release.

Feature buckets should be specified with an eye to the future. Some people maintain that each release of a product can provide only three categories of features. Even so, it's a good idea to create as many as five feature buckets to allow for a product's current and future needs. This practice builds a foundation now for the features that will be postponed until a later version of the product.

Specifying Priorities and the Schedule

By the end of the research, analysis, and rationalization steps in the envisioning process, the team usually has a rough idea of the schedule and of the tradeoffs necessary to meet it. Additionally, the team will choose the appropriate tradeoff triangle setting for the project and will use the triangle to communicate how the project's resources, features, and ship date will be constrained, optimized, and accepted. Including this information in the Vision Document shows that the team is thinking about the tangible realities of development, and gives some structure to the other elements of the vision.

Prototype System

Clearly communicating the information learned from the customer and users is difficult. Information about business requirements must be communicated to team members with varying degrees of technical and business background, and information about how the product will solve the business problem must be communicated to the customer and users.

To more easily accomplish this communication, a prototype application that demonstrates portions of the product's vision should be developed during the envisioning process and included in the Vision Approved Milestone deliverables. The prototype may be a working application, or it may be a series of sample application screen shots. This prototype helps clarify existing ideas and helps draw out additional ideas from the team, the customer, and the product's users.

Project Structure Document

Whereas the Vision Document describes what will be done, the Project Structure Document describes who will do it. This document simply identifies:

- Each team role.
- Who the lead is for each role.
- Who is assigned to each team and their contact information.
- Who the project stakeholders are.
- How the project will be managed, such as change control systems and status reporting.
- Project meeting schedules, e-mail aliases, and web sites.

It can also be helpful to include a short description of the team leads' background and experience and to provide contact information for stakeholders such as the product's customer and key users.

Master Risk Assessment Document

An important deliverable of the Vision Approved Milestone is the Master Risk Assessment Document, which provides an analysis of the project's risks and plans to manage them. The bulk of the Master Risk Assessment Document consists of the itemized risks with their descriptions that were gathered in the risk action planning step of the MSF Risk Management Process described earlier. These are typically summarized into a top-ten list, both for an executive overview and to raise additional awareness. This list describes the risks, their contingency plans, and who is responsible for executing those plans. Finally, a simple chart of risks with their management metrics can quickly communicate which risks have the greatest probability of occurrence and greatest impact on the project.

Communicating the Vision

After the team has created the first draft of its Vision Document, it's time to start communicating the vision, obtaining buy off from upper management, incorporating other people's expertise, and getting everyone excited about delivering on the vision's promises. This process involves the following steps:

- **Validating the vision** The team should review the vision with everyone inside and outside the group. This is a time to gather feedback, verify agreement, incorporate the feedback into the next revision of the vision, and justify why issues are not incorporated into this product vision, as appropriate.

- **Selling the vision** The Vision Document should be reviewed with the key players so that they understand why the product is important and what it will do for them. Additionally, they should understand that only the features that are part of the vision will be included in the product. This is a good opportunity to reinforce stakeholder training about tradeoff decisions, prioritize feature sets, and determine product versioning. This multi-stage communication should begin with those who have the most knowledge about the product's area, and should work outward to other more tangential groups and stakeholders.

Caution Communication is a two-way street. The team should continually incorporate stakeholders' feedback into the vision. Team members should not only tell stakeholders what the product will do, but should continually validate that the product meets the stakeholders' needs.

During validation and selling of the vision, the team creates revised drafts of the vision document. When the team believes it is time to move on to the planning process, the product vision is agreed upon by the team and stakeholders, and the Vision Approved Milestone is reached. This milestone is the identification of a baseline vision that will be used throughout this release of the product. Although the baseline vision may undergo slight changes during the remaining project phases, they nevertheless constitute a foundation for this product release.

At this stage of the envisioning process, it's important to remember that the vision does not belong to any one person. To deliver the vision, the team must own it, not a single individual. The whole team must nurture the product vision to life, so the whole team must clearly understand and be committed to it.

Expanding the Envisioning Process

After seeing the benefits gained from the envisioning process, it is tempting to try and incorporate the process throughout an organization. However, for most organizations, envisioning requires a change in culture and in the way of doing business. We recommend that envisioning be expanded in small, incremental, and manageable steps within an organization. Over time, using not only envisioning but the entire MSF Development Process Model can significantly improve the success of any project—application development or otherwise. Some examples of starting in small, manageable steps are:

- Use envisioning principles with the people closely associated with the project chosen as the starting point for implementation of MSF and the MSF Development Process Model.

- Create a Vision Document to communicate how envisioning will be implemented and set an example for using a Vision Document as a standard communication mechanism.

- Host whiteboard and other sessions to discuss the MSF Development Process Model in general and the Envisioning Phase in particular.

- Videotape a discussion of project visions that can be shown at group meetings or delivered via an intranet using Microsoft NetShow technology.

- Design and use templates to proliferate envisioning in a consistent fashion.

Once again, the primary goal is a shared understanding of what a product should do and how to proceed with its development. By incorporating this goal into all its projects, over time an organization can provide the additional structure needed to increase the efficiency of its projects and to improve any given project's chances of success.

Summary

Developing a clear understanding of the business reasons for undertaking an application project and what the application will accomplish is the goal of the Envisioning process.

By creating a vision that documents a project's feasibility, goals, constraints, opportunities, and risks, the project team reaches the Vision Approved Milestone, which marks the end of the Envisioning Phase of the MSF Development Process Model. The Vision Document:

- Points all the team members in the same direction.
- Simplifies the decision-making process.
- Ensures consistent decisions.
- Motivates the team and reinforces the product goals.
- Directly impacts the quality of the product.
- Measures project performance and effectiveness.

In addition to generating a Vision Document as the primary deliverable for this milestone, the team can create prototypes that help ensure:

- Comprehension of important features by less-technical project stakeholders.
- Rapid visual understanding of the product's vision.

Knowing who is responsible for each critical portion of a project helps ensure that all project success factors are met. To meet this goal, the Project Structure Document identifies:

- The team leads for the six MSF Development Team Model roles.
- Expected staffing requirements for the six teams.

The team also begins the ongoing process of managing the project's risks to ensure success and documents these efforts in a Master Risk Assessment Document. The Master Risk Assessment Document:

- Identifies the highest risks for the product.
- Begins the project's risk management process.

The culmination of the Vision Approved Milestone is the cementing of the team's understanding of the vision, as well as that of the project's stakeholders.

Review

1. What are the primary goals of the Envisioning Phase?
2. What team roles are responsible for accomplishing envisioning goals?
3. What are the primary components of a Vision Document?
4. What are the benefits of using prototypes?
5. What are project risks?
6. What is risk management?

CASE STUDY 5

Envisioning RMS

The RMS team's goal-setting meeting started out well. On Monday the team met in the Oak Room for the first time and really got going on the MSF Development Process Model. Even Tim's doughnuts didn't throw them off track. As the team moved through the four phases, they outlined who was responsible for each phase and went over the preliminary calendar Dan had drawn up. They were making real progress. Then toward the end of that Monday morning meeting, Dan started talking about iterations within versions. Little did he know that such a simple concept would cause so much trouble.

Round One

The Wednesday meeting started badly and went quickly downhill. To begin with, Tim was late. Being late had been normal for Tim in the past, but Dan had been working with him on it and was proud of the progress Tim had made. When Tim didn't show up at 8:00 A.M., Dan delayed starting for a few minutes, thinking Tim would walk in any moment. Finally, when it became obvious Tim wasn't going to show, Dan sent Jane out to phone him. She returned in a few minutes and said, "I got him at home. He just overslept, plain and simple. Said he'd be here as soon as he could."

"Let's get started, then. He'll just have to catch up," Dan was disappointed, and just a little angry, but tried not to let it show. At least Marilou had remembered the doughnuts. Of course, Tim wasn't there to enjoy them, so Marilou seemed somewhat miffed, too.

FERGUSON AND BARDELL
ENGINEERING • ARCHITECTURE • PROJECT MANAGEMENT

The RMS Project
Meeting Agenda

Meeting Date: March 31, 1999   **Purpose:** Envisioning 1

I.   Agenda Building

II.   Iteration Goals

III.   Envisioning Deliverables

IV.   Introduction of Golden Triangle

V.   Vision Document – first draft

VI.   Q&A

VII.   Wrap-Up: Path-Forward Assignments

CHICAGO • DETROIT • MILWAUKEE • CINCINNATI • INDIANAPOLIS • LOUISVILLE

Dan looked at his agenda. "OK, folks, as usual the first item is Agenda Building. Does anyone have any items to add or remove from the agenda, or any adjustments to make?" Marta raised her hand. "Yes, Marta?"

She stood up, and Dan noticed a slight tremble in her hand as she placed it on the conference table to support herself. "Uh-oh," he thought. She had seemed upset at the end of the meeting on Monday, and he'd hoped she would come by his office to talk about it, but she hadn't. He wondered if she would now share whatever was bothering her.

"I've been reading the material you've given us, Dan, and listening to you explain it. I liked the Team Model; it made me excited to be working on this project. When we talked about the background of RMS, I realized that not only was this going to be an enjoyable project, it was also going to be an important one.

"But last meeting, when we worked through the Process Model, I started having my doubts about the work. The concept of iterative planning just doesn't make any sense to me. How can you build something when your plans aren't complete? You put up the Waterfall Model and talked about the MSF method being better, and all I could think about was all the bridges and buildings that have been built over the centuries using the Waterfall method. I'm an engineer by training, and I'm used to doing high-level plans, mid-level plans, detailed drawings, all the way down to subassembly drawings. Only when *all* the drawings are done and approved do you begin building the bridge or whatever you are building. How can software engineering be different?

"Frankly, the whole process looks horribly flawed to me. I read the documents from your last project, and I think you were lucky that the project came together as well as it did." Marta paused, then took a breath as if gathering herself for a final sprint in a race before continuing. "Dan, I'm just starting out in my career, and I can't trust luck. I think the MSF process is flawed, and I think this project will fail. I can't afford to be associated with such a large failure so early in my career. You need to find someone else to fill the Testing role on the team."

And with that, she gathered up her things and walked out of the conference room.

No one spoke for what seemed like a long time. Everyone looked at Dan to see what he would do, but he simply stood there, looking at the doorway through which Marta had made her exit. Finally, Bill cleared his throat and said, "Do you want me to go after her?"

Dan seemed to shake himself as if coming out of a trance, then looked down at the table for a moment. Finally, without looking at Bill, he said, "No, Chief, it's not your place and it's not your problem. I'll deal with it." To himself he thought, "Not that I have any clue at this moment how I'm going to do that." Again he seemed to shake himself, but this time he looked up at the rest of the RMS team. "Alright, Marta has raised some interesting points. Even though she's not with us to hear the discussion, let's deal with her objections before moving on. Does anyone have a response, either agreeing with her or answering her?"

The rest of the group appreciated the opportunity to talk after the shock of Marta's departure, and a lively discussion ensued. Most of the group was sympathetic to Marta's objections, but wondered if there wasn't something she was missing in her analysis. Jane mentioned the space program. "They surely used the Waterfall Model to do the moon shot, didn't they? Perhaps it's the size of the project that makes it necessary to use that method."

"That's part of it, Jane," replied Marilou. "I think there's another factor, though—the clarity of the goal. In the case of a bridge, or a shot at the moon, you know exactly what your final goal is. You can do all that planning and know it's not a waste of time, because you are all aiming at the same thing, and the target isn't going to change. The bigger and more certain the goal, the more you should use the Waterfall method. Our RMS project isn't like that at all: it's not big, and we're not real sure what we are going to build."

Dan began to answer Marilou when suddenly Bill interrupted. "No, you're both wrong." He jumped up and moved to the whiteboard. Grabbing a marker, he turned to the group to say something and noticed the looks of irritation and hurt on Jane's and Marilou's faces. Realizing what he had done, he stopped. "Sorry, ladies—I didn't mean to be so abrupt. I've just got some background here that may shed some light on this."

He turned to Dan. "You probably didn't know I worked on the space program while I was in the Navy. Nothing big; just part of the data processing team. But I've been thinking back on that, and about what Marta said, and I think I see something I didn't see before."

Bill moved to the whiteboard and drew a rough diagram of the Waterfall Model. "Marta was saying that all engineers know big projects like the space program use this model. We just went along with her on that, but you know what? She's wrong." At the end of the diagram, he wrote *moon landing*. "If you think about just the moon shot, it looks like a classic Waterfall Model." He drew three MSF Development Process Model circles above the diagram, then said excitedly, "The problem is, we're forgetting the other space shots. We did Mercury, then Gemini, and then Apollo. Each was a 'versioned release,' if you will. And you know what? Inside each of those versions, we did prototypes, and proof-of-concepts, and models for wind tunnels. And every time we did one, we went back and re-did the project plan, and the schedule, and the subassemblies, and whatever else needed redoing." Bill was drawing all over the board now, talking while he drew. "All we had when we started was Kennedy's vision statement. We had no idea what 'putting a man on the moon' would look like when we got done. We took what we learned along the way and incorporated it into the next version. It was absolutely an iterative process, and we used that process to carry out one of the most complex, massive development projects ever attempted."

He put down the marker, turned, and looked right at Dan. "You know, I've been something of a skeptic about this MSF stuff. After our meeting on Monday, I went back to my office, shut the door, and went through the documentation from the MSF project at your old law firm. I struggled with it, I admit. When I read that you put out that first version with half the features cut and some of the buttons actually inoperative, it made me cringe. But then I read your user evals."

Bill moved to his chair and sat down. "I was amazed. Your users loved you! I kept reading, trying to figure out why, and then it hit me. Because you locked in the ship date, and then got everyone to buy into the idea of versions. You delivered a product that was both on time and on function. That first win showed the users they could trust you, so they were willing to wait on the second and third versions for the rest of the features.

"The clincher for me, though, was lunch yesterday. You had asked me to line up a team for the prototype, so I took Sam and Beth to lunch. When I explained the approach we were going to use for this project, they couldn't wait to get started. I asked them why, and they said how cool it would be to get a product to the users before the users forgot why they wanted it." Bill smiled wryly and said, "My folks sure know how to tell it straight."

"They learned from the master, Bill," said Jane, laughing. Dan and Marilou couldn't help laughing too, and Bill just shook his head, smiling. Finally he continued, "So I guess you could say I'm coming around to your way of thinking, Dan. I want to see it happen, of course, but I'm actually looking forward to the process of trying to figure out how to make it happen."

"Well," thought Dan to himself, "you win some, you lose some."

Just then Tim walked in. Looking around the room, he asked, "Where's Marta? And where are the doughnuts?"

"And some are rained out," thought Dan, grinning.

"Here, O Sleepy One," Dan shoved the doughnut box across the conference table. "Throw some sugar into your system so you can catch up with the rest of us."

After that, the meeting went fairly smoothly. The team listed their goals for the five iterations Dan had discussed at the last meeting by filling in a chart on an easel. Dan had to help out a few times, but overall it was obvious that everyone had read the material and understood iterations within versions.

		Env	Plan	Dev 1	Dev 2	Stab
Prod Mgt	Env	Vision doc	Concept design; validate vision doc	Consult on features for alpha	Consult on features for beta	Check response of users
Prog Mgt	Plan	Check feasibility of schedule	Complete all plans	Validate plans	Plan end-game	??
Dev	Dev	Prototype	Proof-of-concept	Alpha	Beta	Final
User Ed	Dev	User feedback on prototype	Assist concept design	Document user interaction	Trial user ed plan	Final user ed plan
Testing	Stab	Test plan for prototype	Test plan for POC	Bug mgt	Performance testing	Use testing
Logistics	Stab	Install prototype	Install POC, measure impact	Pilot 1	Pilot 2	Rollout

Next he went over the MSF concept of a "tradeoff triangle" and showed how to use it to balance resources, schedule, and features. The team grasped this immediately and was able to give examples of constraining, optimizing, and accepting. He showed them the project matrix, asking them to indicate where the checks should go for RMS. After a moment, Tim had figured out all three checks—optimize schedule, constrain resources, and accept features.

Finally, Dan put a transparency on the overhead projector showing the interim milestones for the Envisioning Phase. The first one, Core Team Formed, drew a chuckle when Dan said, "Well, up to about 30 minutes ago I thought we at least had this one covered." Dan left the milestone checked, though, and moved to the other two milestones.

"We'll do the first draft of the risk assessment document on Friday. Be sure to read the material on risk management that's in your packet." He paused. "I had planned on doing the first draft of the vision statement today, but I think I want to postpone that until Friday." Everyone nodded, and Dan realized that they were all hoping he could persuade Marta to rejoin the team. "Looks like you've got your own interim deliverable," he thought as the meeting broke up.

When he returned to his office, his secretary informed him that the Director of Engineering had already called twice and that he "seemed somewhat upset." Dan returned the call.

"What have you done to Marta, Dan?" the man almost shouted. "She came in and told me she quit the RMS team—something about SMF, or FMS, and iterations. Now she's in her office, and it sounds like she's cleaning out her desk! You want to tell me what's going on?"

Dan hurried to the engineering department and explained briefly to the Director what Marta was upset about. They went to her office to persuade her to stay with both the company and the RMS project. The company was winning, but the project didn't have a chance until Dan brought up Bill's space shot example. Marta thought for a long time, and then finally asked her boss, "What do you think?"

"Marta," he said, wiping his glasses as he talked, "I don't know a lot about the designing end of software. I *do* know something about the user end, though, and if rapid iterations will get us users a product we need in a shorter amount of time, then I'm all for it. And, I'll tell you one other thing—"

He leaned forward as if about to share a very special confidence. "Frankly, I envy you being on this RMS project. Over here in Engineering, we design the way we do because we *have to*. Once we put all those rivets in that steel, it takes a lot of work to change it. But with Dan, it's different. You can make changes so much faster, and for so much less money. In a few hours, one programmer can change an entire screen, or even create a new one." He sighed. "If I was younger, I'd jump at a chance to be a part of that, if only for the experience." He put his glasses on and stared at Marta over the top of them. "Marta, you *are* young. You should jump at this chance."

In the end, Marta changed her mind and agreed to stay with the project. Dan knew beyond a shadow of a doubt that it was the director's comments that had convinced her.

Round Two

When Dan got to the Oak Room on Friday, Tim was already there, looking over the packet from Wednesday. Dan noticed that the coffee was also made, so he tried a cup. Knowing that Tim was not a coffee drinker, Dan was pleasantly surprised to find that the coffee actually tasted pretty good. "Thanks for the coffee, Tim."

"Well, after being late on Wednesday, I figured I'd better get some brownie points today," Tim said with a grin. "Of course, I had some help."

Dan looked up, surprised, as Marta came into the room with the other coffeepot in her hand. Marta looked at him and smiled slightly as she crossed to the coffee maker. "So did we both get enough points to at least be back at zero, or do we have to make coffee for a month, Dan?"

"I'll need to double-check the figures on my brownie-point chart, but I think you are both well in the positive range." Dan took another sip of coffee. "Of course, another meeting like the last one, and I'll skip the coffee and go straight to the embalming fluid."

Tim and Marta both laughed, and Marta came over and sat down across from Dan. "I'm sorry, Dan. I was feeling both trapped and unsure of myself; trapped into a project that I just didn't think was going to make it, and unsure whether I could keep up technically. I overreacted, and I'm sorry."

"Apology accepted, Marta," Dan paused and then said, "What can we do to help you feel better about RMS?"

Just as she was about to answer, the other three members of the RMS team entered the conference room. Marilou and Bill were arguing. Dan looked at Jane, who wore a knowing smile. "Seems that Development and User Education are already interacting on the users' behalf. I'm glad to see such a highly professional discussion." At that moment Marilou shouted "Web-based!" to which Bill replied, equally loud, "Windows-based!" Jane just shrugged and smiled even more.

"Here, you two, stuff a doughnut in it and sit down," said Dan as he shoved the doughnut box across the table. Marilou, Bill, and Jane took their places, and Dan continued, "Before we hit the agenda, would you two like to tell us what you were arguing about? Marilou?"

Marilou put down her doughnut. "When I realized that I was responsible for representing the users of RMS throughout the process, I decided to talk to a few of them to see what they were thinking. You know, just some of the people I've had in my classes. Well, a number of them are on the road a lot, and they all said they wanted some way to put their time in over the Internet. So I told Bill that we needed RMS to be Web-based."

"And I told her she's nuts," Bill replied, half to Marilou and half to Dan. "It would mean we'd have to build two applications: one for the Web, one for the desktop. We'd have security issues, authentication issues, access issues—it's a development nightmare! I say a Windows app only, and they'll just have to come in on Saturday to fill out their time sheets." He turned back to Dan. "So, which one of us is wrong?" he asked with a smug look.

"You both are." Marilou and Bill looked shocked, and Jane laughed.

"See?" she said, pointing at them both. "I said you were jumping the gun. We don't make final technology decisions until the Planning Phase, isn't that right?"

"You've been reading ahead, Jane," said Dan. He turned to Bill and Marilou. "I'm glad you're uncovering these issues, but Jane's right—it's much too soon to decide on a front-end technology. Doing so will limit our vision." Addressing the group, he continued, "And vision is what we're about today. Let's move to the agenda.

FERGUSON AND BARDELL
ENGINEERING • ARCHITECTURE • PROJECT MANAGEMENT

The RMS Project
Meeting Agenda

Meeting Date: April 2, 1999   **Purpose:** Envisioning 2

I.   Agenda Building

II.   Risk Assessment Document—first draft

III.   Work on Vision Document

IV.   Start Conceptual Design

V.   Q&A

VI.   Wrap-Up: Path-Forward Assignments

"As you can see, we have a full plate today. Since we cut our meeting short on Wednesday, we didn't draft the vision statement as I had planned. So, under Agenda Building, I'd like to add that as our first item for today. Is that acceptable to everyone?"

The rest of the team nodded and began writing in the new item. "Does anyone else have something to change on the agenda?" Dan asked.

Marta raised her hand. "It doesn't warrant an agenda item, but I would like to take this moment to apologize to the group for my departure Wednesday. It was immature and unprofessional, and I'm sorry I handled it that way."

Smiles and nods came from the members of the team, and Dan said, "Marta and I talked later, and I think we've addressed her concerns about iterative processes. In fact, Marta, the argument that Bill and Marilou were having is a good example of why we do iterative designing. By gradually working through the iterations, we 'home in' on the best solution using real implementations and real test data from our own environment. Basically, we 'circle the drain,' finally getting to an agreeable solution that meets all our needs. Does that make sense to you?"

Marta nodded and then smiled. "And it's my testing work that ensures we don't go down the drain, right?"

"Exactly. That's why we're all glad you're still part of the team." He waited a moment to see if there were any other comments, and then went on. "Alright, let's begin work on the Vision Document." He put a transparency on the projector. "Here are the six parts of the document, which you should already know from your reading. Who is supposed to be driving right now?"

"Jane is," said Tim. "Product Management is the owner of the Envisioning Phase and drives the Vision Document."

"Right, Tim," Dan said, rising from his chair. "So, Ms. Product Management, you get to sit at the head of the table and run the show."

"Jane Clayton, come on down!" said Marilou, as the rest of the team applauded and laughed. Jane laughed, too, but determination was in her eyes. She put some notes in front of her and then looked at the group. "Alright, folks, let's look at this Vision Document. First, what's the problem we're trying to solve?"

Dan nodded approvingly as Jane moved the group through the discussion. "She might not know a lot about software design," he thought, "but she sure knows how to run a meeting."

The group agreed fairly quickly on the problem statement, which centered on replacing the manual time keeping system and improving the process of assigning resources to projects. The vision statement was harder because Bill, Tim, and

Marilou wanted to describe the product using specific technologies and products. Finally, Jane turned to Marta. "Can you describe a fundamental goal for the RMS product?"

"Sure. How about this: 'RMS will allow supervisors to assign resources to projects based on the resource's ability and availability, and will allow all users to enter time into a common data store so that analysis, reporting, and billing can be done from that single store.'"

"But that's so *generic*, so *broad*!" Bill spluttered.

"That's the point," Jane answered. The Vision Document and all of its parts are supposed to be high-level. We don't get to the specifics until the Planning Phase. As long as we agree that Marta's statement describes what we want RMS to be, we can use that for now. So, do we think her statement describe what we want RMS to be?"

After more discussion, the team agreed that Marta's single sentence did a good job of laying out the goals of RMS, and they adopted it as the vision statement. Jane then jumped to the user profiles. "What about the solution concept?" Bill asked. Jane replied, "Let's move through the user profiles and business goals first, because I think the solution will become clearer if we do." Bill frowned, but nodded, and Jane went on.

"I've prepared some profiles of the potential users of RMS, which I'd like you all to look at. Marilou helped me with them, since she has already taught many of the folks in my area. The rest of you need to tell me if you think these profiles are accurate."

Jane's profiles were short but succinct. Across the top of a table, she had outlined four types of users: Resources, Supervisors, Clerks, and Admin. Then, down the left side of the table, she had listed two subtypes: Mobile and Fixed. In the cells of the table, she had listed the standard computer available to each user type, the average skill level of each type, and each type's basic RMS needs.

"Jane, why is there an NA in the Mobile Clerks cell of the table?" Dan asked.

"Because we don't have clerks working from motels or from home," replied Jane. "And we won't. Those job classifications are not allowed to work off-site."

"Nice work, Jane," said Dan. "We need to keep these ability ratings in mind as we think through the design later." Jane nodded, and proceeded to lead the group in a discussion of possible business goals.

She began by writing *$412,000* on the board and asking the group, "Does anyone know what this figure means?" No one spoke until Tim said, "The total of my student loans?" After everyone finished laughing, Jane said, "That may be, but I was thinking of something RMS could help with. It's actually the figure Jim Stewart and I came up with for the savings we would generate by moving to weekly billing."

"That looks like a pretty good business goal to me," said Bill.

"Yes, but what if we don't make that goal? Are there other business goals or business needs that would be met by RMS even if we stay with our current billing cycle? Let's brainstorm for a minute." Jane picked up a marker and wrote on the whiteboard as various members of the team called out ideas. She then led the group through the process of combining some and discarding others, until they had a short list of significant business goals.

"Now," she said, "keeping in mind everything we've done so far—the problem statement, the vision statement, the user profiles, and the business goals—tell me in two or three sentences what your concept of a solution is."

Again she worked at the whiteboard, and again some of the group kept trying to cast the solution in terms of products and technology. Finally Dan intervened. "Look, folks, quit trying to describe something only another developer would understand. Describe it so that someone who thinks "You've got mail!" comes from a cassette tape in the computer can understand it. After that, the business solution statement came together quickly.

"Now," said Jane, "What are our design goals for RMS? What do we think, at this point, it has to fit with, and are there any constraints we want to identify at this time?"

"Well, for starters, we can't add any network capacity to accommodate it," said Tim emphatically. "Why not?" Marilou asked. "Because, we just spent buckets of money last year to move everyone to 100-meg Ethernet and give them Internet access, and I don't want to go to that well again this year! I want to save my asking power for other things next year," Tim replied.

"Along with that," Dan added, "I'd say that RMS has to fit in with our current technologies. We can't change network software or messaging software, for example. I don't think there's enough business value to justify that."

"Well, I've got a selfish goal, "said Bill gruffly. "Y'see, I've got these new code slingers that are just itching to try out some of the new stuff they've been learning. I understand some of it, and it sounds like it might work. So, I guess I'd like us to turn them loose on this design stuff to see if these new distributed application techniques fit the bill like my programmers think they will."

"That's not selfish, Bill," said Dan, "that's just taking care of your folks. Any good manager wants his people to have the opportunity to grow and branch out. The question, of course, is whether these technologies can do the job we need. I think everyone here will leave that up to your judgement, because we know that ultimately you'll do what's right." Everyone agreed, and Bill just nodded his thanks.

"Okay, then," said Jane, "I think we've got a draft Vision Document. I'll type it up and distribute it via e-mail later this morning. Everyone feel free to e-mail me back with any changes you think of, so we can discuss them on Monday." She turned to Dan. "Anything else from me, boss?"

"One other thing, Jane. Be sure you send a copy of the draft over to Jim Stewart for his review. He's coming to our meeting on Monday, and I want him to see the draft before then. Remember, he is the customer for this project, and he has to sign off on the Vision Document as well." Jane nodded and started to move out of the head chair, but Dan motioned for her to stay seated. "Just stay there while we draft the risk assessment document, Jane. You did such a good job leading us through the vision process, I'd like you to facilitate our first look at risks." He slid a manila folder across the table. "Here are the transparencies you need."

Jane looked though the transparencies in the folder until she found the one showing the five-step risk management process. She put it on the projector and said, "Well, it looks to me like the first thing we have to do is identify risks." She erased the whiteboard, picked up a marker, and said, "Who's got a risk to start us off?"

The group brainstormed for a while and then spent some time organizing the list of risks they had come up with. Finally, Dan said, "That's good enough for today. I'll put these into a matrix and send it to you. You'll need to fill in your opinion of probability and impact for each one and come to the meeting Monday prepared to discuss them." He stood up and looked at Jane. "Since we've drafted the vision statement, Jane, it's time to start the conceptual design process. How are you coming on those use cases we discussed?"

Jane pulled out a stack of papers out of her bag. "Looking good," she said. "It wasn't that hard, once you showed me what we needed."

"Excellent." Dan moved to the head of the table and began marking on his copy of the agenda. "Okay, time for Q&A and Path-Forward Assignments. Does anyone have any questions? No? Let's do the assignments, then. Bill, you and your folks are on for Monday. Will you have something to show us by then?"

"Absolutely. Sam and Beth are already working on it, and they've got some good ideas. I'll take the draft Vision Document back to them so they can make sure they're on the right track. They'll have to do some work this weekend, but they understand the schedule we're working on, and they both said they could pull the extra time."

"Remember, Bill, this first prototype doesn't have to be especially high fidelity," Dan cautioned. "Storyboard, flow charts, maybe a drawing of the interface—nothing fancy."

Bill nodded. "I know we said that, but Sam is so quick at Visual Basic, I think he may have some screen shots ready. Beth is already working on a first cut at program flow, so that will probably be ready also."

"Wow, that's great, Bill. More than I had hoped, with such short notice." Dan looked at his notes and continued. "Jane, you're going to make sure the draft Vision Document gets to Jim Stewart for his review before Monday. I'm going to send out the risks matrix, and each of you is going to fill in your own opinion of the probability and impact for each one. Jane's going to send each of you the draft Vision Document for you to review and edit over the weekend. You'll e-mail both your risk work and your edits of the Vision Document to me by Sunday at 6:00 P.M.

"On Monday morning, we're going to see the first prototypes, try to wrap up the risk assessment, finalize the Vision Document, and meet with our customer, Jim Stewart, to see how he feels about where we're going with the project. Is that it, everyone?"

"Who's bringing the coffee and munchies?" Tim asked, as he finished off the last doughnut.

"I guess it's my turn," Bill growled. "I sure wouldn't want you to waste away, Tim." He punched Tim lightly in the stomach, and Tim fell across the table, as if mortally injured. While everyone was laughing, Jane said, "Forget it, Bill—you've got enough to do this weekend. I'll bring the goods on Monday. Besides, the last time you made the coffee it tasted like something you'd find on a ship."

"Yeah, in the bilge!" yelled Tim, as he ran from the room with the Chief in hot pursuit. Marilou turned to Jane and Marta. "Come, girls, let us leave these boys to their childish pursuits," she said, wryly.

Dan smiled to himself. "Certainly is nice when meetings are both productive and pleasant," he thought as he gathered up his things. "Of course, sometimes the best work comes out of conflict." He turned out the lights and went to his office, already looking forward to the meeting on Monday.

Client Perspective

Monday morning dawned clear and early—*too* early for Dan, who had just gotten to sleep, it seemed, when the alarm went off. "At least I've got everything ready so I can just grab it and go," he thought as he stumbled toward the shower.

Forty-five minutes later he pulled into the parking garage, grabbed his bag, and headed for his office. A sudden growl from his stomach reminded him he hadn't eaten yet. "I sure hope Jane remembers the food," he thought as he picked up the packets of material he had run off the night before and headed for the Oak Room.

Ahead of him he saw Bill and two younger workers heading for the conference room, one with a laptop under his arm, and all three engaged in an intense discussion. Dan heard references to "COM" and "Visual Modeler" and realized that the people with Bill were Sam and Beth, the two programmers working on the prototype.

Dan quickened his pace so he could catch up, and asked, "So, guys, you got something good for us today?" Sam and Beth both nodded and smiled, and then looked at Bill. "Absolutely! Dan, these two are wonders when it comes to this stuff. I'm amazed at what they've been able to do since last Wednesday." Bill shook his head ruefully and said, "I dunno, Dan. Looks like us old COBOL cowboys are getting left behind."

"Don't let him kid you, Mr. Shelly," Sam said as they turned into the conference room. "He was right there with us, turning out screens and cleaning up our work as we went along. In fact, when Beth showed him the program flow chart, he made some really good suggestions. He knows his databases, that's for sure."

"I already told you, Sam, no money left for raises this year, so quit your brown-nosing," Bill growled. Dan could tell, though, that he was pleased at the compliments from this hotshot programmer.

Grabbing a doughnut and coffee as he moved to the front of the room, Dan offered a silent prayer of thanks for Jane's memory. He piled the packets of new material on the credenza, put the meeting's agenda on the projector, and then turned to the group. "Good morning, all."

FERGUSON AND BARDELL
ENGINEERING • ARCHITECTURE • PROJECT MANAGEMENT

The RMS Project
Meeting Agenda

Meeting Date: April 5, 1999   **Purpose:** Envisioning 3

I.   Agenda Building

II.   Work on Risk Assessment Document

III.   Work on Vision Document with Jim Stewart, CFO

IV.   First Prototype

V.   Q&A

VI.   Wrap-Up: Path-Forward Assignments

CHICAGO • DETROIT • MILWAUKEE • CINCINNATI • INDIANAPOLIS • LOUISVILLE

As the murmurs of "G'morning" died down, Marilou added, "My, we're chipper this morning!"

Dan smiled. "All an act, Marilou. I'm actually just running on nervous energy and excitement." He looked over the agenda. "Is everybody ready to begin?"

"Hey, where's Mr. Stewart?" Tim asked. "I thought he was joining us."

"He's coming later, Tim," Dan said as he handed out the packets he had prepared the night before. "I thought we could knock out the risk assessment fairly quickly, so I asked him to join us around 8:45." Dan replaced the agenda with another transparency.

"I appreciate all of the hard work you people did on the risk matrix I sent you. The opinions of probability and impact were surprisingly similar across the group. I've averaged them, calculated the exposure, and ranked them. Let's take a look and see if we agree with the group wisdom."

As Dan had expected, "scope creep" was a clear choice for the project's primary risk. Because of the tight schedule, missing the ship date was next. Tim argued strongly that the team needed to consider the project's impact to the network and that concern wound up as the third biggest risk. The risk of exposure ratings dropped substantially, and the remaining seven risks were ranked by only one or two team members.

The group worked through each of the risks, building mitigation plans, contingency plans, and contingency triggers. In most cases, assessing the risks required no further research. When Bill and Tim began to argue about the impact RMS might have on the network, however, the group decided that Tim should do further research on the risk of network saturation before they could adequately address the issue.

They were just wrapping up the risk assessment when Jim Stewart came into the conference room. "Welcome, Mr. CFO!" said Dan. "Pull up a doughnut and have a chair—there's plenty of both to go around."

Jim sat across from Dan and ignored Dan's offer. "I hope I'm on time," he said in a somewhat brisk manner. Something in his tone made Dan eye him closely but he could read nothing on the man's face. Dan thought to himself, "Get a grip! Quit projecting your own exhaustion onto others." He retrieved the doughnut box, moved it to the credenza, and looked squarely at Jim. "You're right on time, as usual. We were just wrapping up the risk assessment document, and we're ready to go through the draft Vision Document with you. I hope you got a copy?" He looked at Jane, and she nodded.

"Yes, I received a copy," Jim replied. He took off his glasses and wiped them slowly. Dan had seen him do this before in management meetings, and it always bode ill for whomever was in the line of fire.

"Yes, I received a copy," Jim repeated. By now, everyone on the project team had picked up the tone in Jim's voice, and they were all looking at him, wondering what it meant. "I have my copy right here, and it seems somewhat incomplete, I must say."

"Here it comes," thought Dan. "Incomplete in what way, Jim?" he asked.

Jim began thumbing through the document. "I see the vision statement, and the user profiles, and the rest. All very interesting. Especially the proposed solution." He put the document back on the table and looked directly at Dan. "I don't see anything in the solution about project management. Not a word. Why are we going to all this trouble, reinventing the entire time and billing system, if we don't give our supervisors a better way to manage projects and control costs?" By this time, he was jabbing his glasses in Dan's direction.

Trying to keep his voice level, Dan answered, "What did you have in mind, Jim? This is a draft document, after all. We asked you here to get your input and feedback, and that's what we want. So, tell us how you think project management should be included in RMS."

"Why, it's as plain as the nose on your face," replied Jim heatedly. He stood up and began pacing as he talked. "We've got projects that go over budget all the time. We have to eat thousands of dollars on some of them because they are fixed-bid projects. Because of the way we do time tracking, most of the project managers complain that they can't get good data on how much time has been spent and how much is left. Before they even realize it, they are over the allotted hours on part of the project, or even on the entire project.

"Now here you are, proposing to put all the time data into a central data store. You've written this nice Vision Document, but there's not one word about giving the project managers a tool to track time by project. How hard can that be? As the person who is authorizing the budget for this, I demand that you add it to the project!"

At that, Bill jumped up and shouted, "That's a load of bull, Jim! Where do you get off coming in here and throwing your weight around! Here we are, busting our tails to get this app out the door in two months—two months!—and you've got the nerve to ask for more! I don't know why your precious project managers can't track project time manually, just like we do. We can manage our projects in IT just fine, thank you, without any extra tools."

Jim glared at Bill. "Yes, I've seen how well you manage development projects, Bill. Just how late were you last time—six months, I believe?"

Bill's face turned red, but before he could say anything else, Dan slammed his hand on the table. "That's enough! Sit down, Bill, and shut up before you say something we'll all regret. And Jim, it's not fair to throw that project back in Bill's face, because it suffered from the very thing we're trying to avoid with this project."

Dan moved to the head of the table and put the risk matrix back on the overhead projector for everyone to see. "Jim, we were working on this before you got here. I want you to look at it for a moment while I explain what happened to the project time-tracking feature."

Dan pointed at the first row of the matrix. "These are risks we've identified for this project. What is the absolute number one risk we identified?"

Jim squinted at the screen and then remembered to put his glasses back on. Reading the first item, he recited, "Scope creep. Sounds like a horror movie disease."

"It is, Jim, it is," said Dan. "Scope creep wrecks more project plans than almost any other risk. It happens when well-meaning customers insist on adding features to the scope of the project, without adjusting anything else." Dan turned to Jane. "Jane, did we identify tracking time by project as a potential feature for RMS?"

"Absolutely, Dan," replied Jane. "In fact, a number of users mentioned it while I was working on the use cases. So we discussed it in our last meeting."

"And what happened to it?" Dan asked, glancing at Jim to see his reaction to her response.

"We decided to delay it until Version 2."

"But why?" Jim exclaimed. "What Version 2? Why not put it in the program this time?"

"Because of the tradeoff triangle," replied Marilou, moving to the whiteboard. She drew the triangle on the board and explained to Jim the relationship of resources, features, and schedule. "So you see, we decided that the only way to include this feature was to slip the ship date, and we don't want to do that. We want to get this version of RMS out on time so that our users will begin to trust our word. Even though the project management feature is important, we didn't feel it was a core feature of the product, so we decided to hold it until Version 2."

"And how do I know there will be a Version 2?" asked Jim, skeptically. "Promises are cheap, but they're sometimes hard to keep."

"You'll know there will be a Version 2 when we deliver Version 1 on time," said Dan, "because you'll see that we keep our word. We'll start on Version 2 immediately after we deliver Version 1 and we'll follow the same process we did for the first version."

Jim thought about all this for a moment and then said, "Dan, you came to us with high recommendations from the law firm. One thing they noted was that almost all of your projects came in on time and on spec." He paused, looked at Bill, then continued. "No offense meant this time, Bill, but I've never seen our development staff deliver either on time or on spec, much less both at once. I guess I'm just skeptical. If you and Dan and all the rest of you can deliver what's in this document within the time frame you've outlined, then I can wait for Version 2 for my project management feature."

The room fell silent for moment, until Tim looked at Dan and said, "So, did we mitigate that risk, or just avoid it?" Everyone froze and looked at Jim, wondering how he would take Tim's comment. Jim stared at Tim for moment, then started laughing, and everyone relaxed.

Jim turned to Bill. "I'm sorry I came on like that. I guess I think I can make software happen just by fiat." He stuck out his hand, and after a pause, Bill slowly took it.

"Yeah, I guess I sorta lost my cool, too. Sorry."

"I hope," said Dan, "that in about seven weeks, you'll both can shake hands again. That will mean we delivered Version 1 on time, and we can all start work on Version 2 with Jim's feature added. To get there, though, we've got to get going on the rest of today's agenda, so let's move forward."

The team worked through the draft Vision Document, making some minor changes, but basically keeping it intact. When they finished, Dan said, "Alright, Bill, show time! Are you guys ready to give us a glimpse of the RMS of the future?"

"Sure," Bill said, as Sam and Beth moved into position. Beth put her flowchart on the easel at the head of the table, while Sam set up a monitor at the other end. "First, we're going to look at Beth's chart of the data flow and program flow for the application. Then, we'll see what Sam's done with the major screens for RMS and get your feedback."

Working through the flowchart didn't take much time at all, as RMS was a fairly simple application. When Sam turned on his monitor and navigated through several well laid out screens. Marilou whistled. "Wow, Sam, you got this done since last Wednesday?"

"Actually, after Bill brought us the draft Vision Document, I didn't like what we had, so I redid most of it over the weekend," Sam replied. He minimized the Visual Basic application that contained the screens. "Watch this."

Sam started up the browser on his laptop, loaded a file from his local hard drive, and suddenly they were looking at a time-entry table inside the browser. "I thought you might like to see what a Web-based client might look like," he said, grinning.

"How'd you get that laid out so quickly, Sam? That's pretty good work." Dan looked at the various tables and links, obviously impressed. "Why, it even looks like the spreadsheet I've seen some of our folks using to calculate their time."

"That's because it's based on that spreadsheet. With Office being so HTML-capable, I simply did a spreadsheet the way I wanted it, saved it as HTML, and then tweaked it a little bit. Didn't take very long at all."

"Yes, but making it actually do something would take a lot longer," said Bill, frowning. "Don't go getting any ideas about your Web-based client, Marilou."

Marilou just grinned. "I'll just save this little demonstration till the Planning Phase, when we get to arm-wrestle over which client to build."

The team took some time to examine each screen in detail, affirming some and making suggestions about others. Sam and Beth both took notes, and Sam promised that the final prototype would be ready by Wednesday's meeting.

Finally, Dan said, "I think we've covered it as well as we need to. Good work, Beth and Sam. I think we've all got a much better feel for what RMS could be." He looked at his watch—almost 10:00 A.M. Time to wrap it up. "Does anyone have any questions? No? Okay, here's the plan for Wednesday.

"Wednesday is our final Envisioning Phase meeting. We'll finalize our Vision Document and our risk assessment document, and look at the revised prototype. By then I'll have finished the project structure document, which is basically a background document about the project and the team. Finally, we'll make a go/no-go decision at that meeting." He picked up one of the thick packets he had passed out earlier. "In here is your reading material for Wednesday. This is the outline of the Planning Phase, including information about the MSF Design Process. It's a lot, I know, but you need to read it between now and Wednesday morning. Once we finish Envisioning, we want to be ready to move right into Planning and start mapping out the design. Everyone understand?" The team nodded, and everyone rose from the table and began to pack up.

As they did so, Tim turned to Jim with the box of doughnuts. "Ready for one of these now?" Jim looked first at the box and then at Tim. Laughing, he took one, and they walked out together, confectioner's sugar dusting the floor as they went.

FERGUSON AND BARDELL

ENGINEERING • ARCHITECTURE • PROJECT MANAGEMENT

The RMS Project
Meeting Agenda

Meeting Date: April 7, 1999   **Purpose:** Vision Approved Milestone

I.   Agenda Building

II.   Review and Approval of Project Structure Document

III.   Review and Approval of Risk Assessment Document

IV.   Review and Approval of Vision Document

V.   Review and Agreement on Key Points

VI.   Go / No-Go Decision

VII.   Q&A

VIII.   Wrap-Up: Path-Forward Assignments

CHICAGO • DETROIT • MILWAUKEE • CINCINNATI • INDIANAPOLIS • LOUISVILLE

Wrap-Up

After the fireworks of the previous meetings, the final Envisioning Phase meeting was somewhat anticlimactic.

First, Dan presented the some documents describing the basic project structure. Most of it was informational: who filled what role, the team's contact information and e-mail addresses, and so forth. There was a section on change control that explained the process the team would use to manage changes to documents. There was also a schedule showing when status reports were due and to whom, which Jim Stewart liked.

Next, the team looked at the risk assessment document. "Do you have any more information on the risk of saturating the network with the RMS application?" Dan asked Tim.

Tim put a transparency on the overhead projector. It showed a graph of network traffic over the past two weeks. "I went back and pulled the logs off our monitoring software, put them into Excel, and created this graph," Tim began. "As you can see, on most days we have two usage peaks: around 10:00 A.M. and around 1:30 P.M. Typically, we run around 55 percent load during those times, with bursts up to 85 percent. If all 800 of our employees try to hit this application at the same time, we could have a problem, depending on where the app is located and what sort of activity they are working on. On the other hand, the odds that all 800 will be updating their hours at the same time are pretty small, so I think we'll be okay."

"But Tim," Marilou interjected, "doesn't it also depend on how the application accesses the database? If the application has to reconnect for every record it sends, then even if only 250 people send 50 records at the same time, it could be a real mess." It was obvious to everyone in the room that Tim hadn't thought about that, and he looked concerned. "Bill?" he said, turning to the director of development. "What about it?"

Bill passed the question off to Sam and Beth. "What about it, you two?"

Sam was grinning when he replied, "How would it be if no matter how many users access the system at the same time, they look like only one user to the database? Would that solve part of our network traffic problem?" Everyone was surprised except Bill, who suddenly seemed to think of something significant. He winked at Sam and then turned to Tim. "Don't worry, Mr. Network Manager, I think Sam's onto something that will save your network from exploding."

"How can you have multiple users look like only one to the database? That's not possible," said Marilou. Bill turned to Dan. "Didn't I read something about building proof-of-concept systems in the Planning Phase?" Dan nodded. "Well, then, everyone, let's just leave this problem for the proof-of-concept folks to deal with. Then we'll know for sure."

Dan looked around the group. Everyone seemed content with that approach except Marilou, who just shrugged and said, "I'll believe it when I see it, but I'm willing to wait. Let's move on."

Following that, the team walked through the Vision Document one last time. Dan had sent everyone the changes from the last meeting, and then had incorporated the feedback into a final document. After some minor adjustments, the team approved the document. Dan turned to Jim. "Does it have your approval as well?" he asked.

Jim paused a moment. "Yes, it does. I feel like I'm going out on a limb here, because I've always had to push to get features I wanted into the software, and you all are asking me to trust you on this. But, I'm intrigued with the process you're following, and I want to give you enough room to either succeed gloriously or fail miserably. I'm in."

"Good," said Dan, as the team members looked at one another with grins of success. "I think I speak for the entire RMS team when I say that, as our customer, we want you to hold us to our commitments. In return, we want you to be fair in your acknowledgement when we have met or exceeded a goal. Is it a deal?"

"Absolutely," said Jim emphatically.

"Then, the Vision Document is approved," Dan said, as he put a final transparency on the projector. "The Vision Approved Milestone is the first major milestone in the Development Process Model. We have completed the deliverables, and all that is left is to be sure we all agree on these six points."

He read each point in turn—the reason for RMS; the expected outcome; the feasibility, goals, and constraints for the project; the opportunities and risks; and the structure—and asked each person to state his or her agreement. As the team moved through the six points, Dan tried to ensure that everyone was heard and that everyone was in solid agreement on each point.

When the entire team had expressed agreement on all the points, Dan turned off the projector and leaned against the credenza. "Alright, gang, last question. And this same question will conclude each of our other major milestone meetings. Do we go ahead, or not?"

The group obviously hadn't been ready for such a question. Jane seemed to speak for all of them when she said, "I thought that was already decided when we went through the agreement questions."

Dan shook his head. "No, Jane, it's possible to work through those agreement questions and still come out realizing that the cost/benefit ratio isn't there, or there is some overriding concern that is a showstopper. Plus, we've got to have a positive commitment from each of you, not just a de facto commitment based on simply not disagreeing. So, I ask again—should we go forward with RMS?"

One by one, the team members and Jim Stewart said, "Yes." When they were finished, Dan summarized. "We each agree, then, that we should move into the Planning Phase for the RMS project." He made a note. "I'm documenting the group's decision to go to the Planning Phase. We are now beginning that phase."

The RMS project team and its customer exchanged smiles, handshakes, and high-fives all around as Dan began gathering up his notes and handouts. "Enjoy it now," he thought. "The real work is about to begin."

CHAPTER 6

Project Plan

About This Chapter

During a project's planning process, the team turns concepts and requirements into solid action plans, goals, and schedules. In this chapter, we outline the process of mapping concepts to actions and explain the roles of the team in the Planning Phase of the MSF Development Process Model. We take an in-depth look at the MSF Design Process Model and the conceptual, logical, and physical architectures of an application. We also discuss how the MSF Application Model's user, business, and data service layers can be incorporated into the application's physical architecture. We emphasize the MSF Development Process Model's Functional Specification, Master Project Plan, and Master Project Schedule as the key deliverables of this phase. Finally, we discuss principles of scheduling, as well as the ongoing task of risk management.

The principles and guidelines we provide in this chapter are based on our own experience with the creation of application architectures and the implementation of enterprise applications, together with the following sources:

- Microsoft Solutions Framework
- Walker Royce's *Software Project Management: A Unified Framework*
- Mary Kirtland's *Designing Component-Based Applications*

The majority of information in this chapter is from three MSF models: the MSF Development Process Model, the MSF Design Process Model, and the MSF Application Model for Development.

Upon completion, you will be able to:

- Describe the interim milestones and deliverables that lead to the Project Plan Approved Milestone.
- List and explain the purpose of various Planning Phase deliverables.

- Explain the roles that individual team members play during the Planning Phase.
- Understand the stages of application design.
- Analyze business requirements and their mappings to an application's design.
- Explain the importance of a Functional Specification.
- Explain the underlying principles of MSF scheduling practices.

Overview of Project Planning

The second of the four phases of the MSF Development Process Model is the Planning Phase, shown in Figure 6.1. It follows the Envisioning Phase, which culminated in the Vision Approved Milestone.

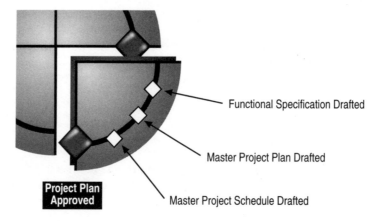

Figure 6.1   MSF Development Process Model Planning Phase

The Envisioning Phase asks the question "Can we use technology to solve this business need, and if so, how?" The result is a common understanding of the problem and a common vision of the solution. The Planning Phase asks the question "Realistically, what will it take to reach the vision developed in the Envisioning Phase?" The result is a detailed plan that both the customer and the project team agree to.

Of all the phases in the MSF Development Process Model, the Planning Phase can be the most difficult to accomplish. The Envisioning Phase is a time of "blue-skying," or exploring possibilities, that is usually exciting, invigorating, and full of energy and enthusiasm. The Developing Phase is a time of hands-on activity, full of the energy of creation, of building, and a feeling of "Now we're getting somewhere!" In between is the Planning Phase, where the dreams of the Envisioning Phase are tested against reality. This phase can be the most emotionally draining of the four phases. It's here that the hard questions are asked: "Which features will get delayed until the next version?" "Which technology isn't yet mature enough to release?" "What cost is too high to justify?" The Planning Phase involves difficult, detailed work, and as a result a project team may be tempted to avoid it or rush it.

The truth is that the work done in this phase will determine the success or failure of the project. It is better to face the truth now, on paper, than to face it later in a failed implementation. The common vision established in the Envisioning Phase has to go through the refining fire of the Planning Phase for the team to be sure that the vision is strong enough to bear up during the Developing and Stabilizing Phases.

Planning Phase and the MSF Design Process

The Planning Phase is the "home phase" for the MSF Design Process, which is outlined later in this chapter. Even though parts of the MSF Design Process can extend outside the Planning Phase, its baseline is established during the Planning Phase. This design baseline is the foundation for the Functional Specification, which is the primary deliverable for the Planning Phase.

Who Does What During Planning?

Although the team works as a whole to achieve the Project Plan Approved Milestone that marks the end of the Planning Phase, individual roles on the team have individual focuses during this phase. Because the primary emphasis is on the MSF Design Process, every role focuses on something to do with design.

Table 6.1 identifies some specific team role responsibilities for the Planning Phase. The lead for each team role communicates these responsibilities to the rest of the project team, and ensures that these responsibilities are carried out.

Table 6.1   Team roles and Planning Phase responsibilities

Role	Responsibilities
Product Management	Drive the requirements-gathering process and the conceptual design process. Work on a communications plan and schedule.
Program Management	Drive overall design, specifically the Logical Design. Draft the Functional Specification. Take the overall lead and drive the process of determining whether the team can achieve the plans and schedule.
Development	Drive the physical design portion of the Functional Specification. Determine the time and effort required to build and stabilize the product, resulting in the development plan and development schedule. Develop any necessary proof-of-concept systems.
User Education	Analyze user needs. Create performance support strategies. Evaluate the completed design for usability. Estimate the time and effort to develop user support systems. Conduct usability testing for all user interface deliverables.
Testing	Evaluate the design to determine whether the features test properly. Provide a plan and schedule for testing features. Devise methods and metrics to use in tracking bugs. Develop testing strategies.
Logistics Management	Evaluate the design for deployability, manageability, supportability, and total cost of ownership. Devise and set a schedule for deployment plans and support plans.

Thus, every role on the team is responsible for developing both a plan and a schedule for its particular part of the project. These plans and schedules are then aggregated into two of the Planning Phase deliverables, the Master Project Plan and the Master Project Schedule.

MSF Design Process

Ultimately, the aim of the Envisioning and Planning Phases is to do what's necessary to build an effective and useful application. Part of that work is to actually "architect," or design, the application. Although it is possible to use the MSF

Development Process Model with any number of design methodologies, the MSF Design Process is a thorough, effective tool that ensures that the architecture of an application reflects the needs of the users and the business. At the same time, the MSF Design Process integrates the application with the existing enterprise architecture and with other applications. The MSF Design Process is especially effective for N-tier development, and is, in fact, aimed at that type of application.

Because the task of design resides primarily in the Planning Phase, we will take some time in this chapter to examine the MSF Design Process. First we'll present an overview of the three parts of the process. Then we'll explain how this process relates to the Planning Phase and how certain deliverables of the Planning Phase are dependent on the output of the Design Process. Finally, we'll examine in detail the three parts of the process, including their own internal deliverables.

Overview of the MSF Design Process

The MSF Design Process consists of three distinct types of design work: conceptual, logical, and physical. Each of these generates a model of the same name: the Conceptual Design Model, the Logical Design Model, and the Physical Design Model.

Each part of the process approaches the design task from a different perspective and defines the solution differently, as shown in Table 6.2.

Table 6.2   Design task approaches to the three parts of the MSF Design Process

Type of design work	Perspective	Action
Conceptual	Views the problem from the perspective of the user and business	Defines the problem and solution in terms of scenarios
Logical	Views the solution from the perspective of the project team	Defines the solution as a set of cooperating services
Physical	Views the solution from the perspective of the developers	Defines the solution's services and technologies

The output of each part is used as the input for the succeeding part, as Figure 6.2 illustrates.

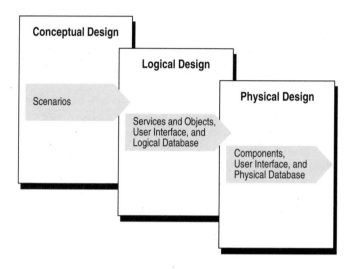

Figure 6.2   Outputs of the three interdependent design process models

The goals of the three parts are:

- **Conceptual Design** Identify business needs and understand what users do and what they require. Conceptual Design generates scenarios that reflect complete and accurate requirements, by involving the customer, users, and other stakeholders.

- **Logical Design** Organize the solution and the communication among its elements. Logical Design takes the business problem identified in Conceptual Design scenarios and formulates an abstract model of the solution. Following the workflow in Figure 6.2, Logical Design takes the scenarios from Conceptual Design and produces objects and services, user interface prototypes, and a logical database design.

- **Physical Design** Apply real-world technology constraints, including implementation and performance considerations, to the outputs of Logical Design by specifying the details of the solution. The outputs of Logical Design are used to produce components, user interface specifications, and physical database design.

The MSF Design Process moves from tangible requirements (use cases) to an abstract application design (Conceptual Design), then to a rationalized application design (Logical Design), then to a concrete application design (Physical Design), and finally, to the tangible product. Conceptual Design is the initial translation of the use cases (the language of the users) to the application design (the language of the application developers). Logical Design is the developers' perspective and serves as a translator between the high-level application concepts—the business and user requirements—and the detailed application design.

Conceptual Design does not take into account the approach or the technologies needed to build the solution. Rather, Conceptual Design corresponds to rough sketches and scenarios for building a house. These are easily understood models jointly created by the customer, the user, and the architect. It is the translation of the business and user requirements from the language of the users to the language of the developers.

Logical Design starts to get into the details of the application that the team will build to fulfill business needs and user requirements. Logical Design thus corresponds to the floor plan and elevation of a house, where elements such as spatial relationships are organized. In this part of the process, the architect's team lays out the design's relationships and communication paths.

Physical Design addresses the technology that will be used. This design adds detail to the architecture and reflects real-world implementation constraints.

Essentially, the different parts of the MSF Design Process address the needs of different "readers" while still serving as parts of a functional whole. Instead of forcing readers to digest what may be a very large and detailed document, this model allows readers to focus only on the information—the part of the whole—that is pertinent to them. The model also allows the use of formal or informal techniques as appropriate.

The design evolves as each step in the process contributes more detail to the Functional Specification. And as the design evolves, every aspect is traceable from any point back to the original business problem, for verification and testing purposes.

Although the MSF Design Process resides primarily within the Planning Phase of the MSF Development Process Model, the work of design often begins before the Planning Phase is officially started, and it continues to some extent up to the point when the code is frozen (near the end of the Developing Phase). The baselines for each of the three parts of the process are established during the

Planning Phase. As shown in Figure 6.3, the three design activities occur in a staggered, parallel manner, with the early output of one activity signaling that the next activity should begin.

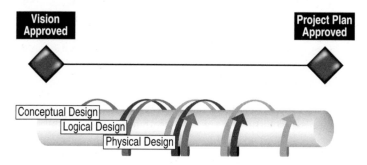

Figure 6.3   Overlapping, iterative, and spiral qualities of the MSF Design Process

The Conceptual Design activity begins when the team agrees upon a vision statement, which may occur before the team reaches the formal Vision Approved Milestone. The Logical Design and Physical Design activities parallel those of Conceptual Design, and all three sit squarely in, but are not limited to, the Planning Phase of the MSF Development Process Model.

It is the parallel execution of all three design activities that allows the product's conceptual, logical, and physical design to have the following three qualities:

- **Overlapping** The activities are parallel, with Conceptual Design typically starting first, followed by Logical Design and then Physical Design. They are not sequential, so one doesn't have to finish before the next can begin. In fact, Logical Design and Physical Design may begin even before the baseline for Conceptual Design is established.

- **Iterative** The activities have their own cycles of validation, design testing (as opposed to code testing), and redesign.

- **Spiral** Each iteration of all three activities represents progress toward the Project Plan Approved Milestone of the Planning Phase.

Obviously, a minimum degree of sequencing must occur as a practical matter. Conceptual Design must start before Logical Design, which must start before Physical Design. Similarly, the baseline for Conceptual Design must be established before the baseline for Logical Design, which must be established before the baseline for Physical Design. From a bigger perspective, the baseline output of the entire process is required to complete the Functional Specification.

Conceptual Design

The first part of the MSF Design Process, Conceptual Design, is defined as the process of acquiring, documenting, validating, and optimizing business and user perspectives of the problem and the solution. Its purpose is to capture and understand business needs and user requirements in their proper context. The output of Conceptual Design is a set of information models, use cases, and usage scenarios that document the current and future states of the system.

As we've said, Conceptual Design may be likened to the first stage of designing a house, when the client and the architect collaborate on a rough sketch and on a short list of needs and requirements. Using the Conceptual Design Model facilitates the gathering of complete and accurate requirements by involving the customer, users, and other stakeholders. Without a good conceptual design, the project team may end up with a wonderful solution...to the wrong problem.

In application design and development, it is critical that products be "user-centric" or attuned to users' true requirements. User-centric means having an awareness of how users view the current environment and what they would like to see in a new product. Whereas gathering requirements has traditionally meant compiling a list of desirable features, the aim in Conceptual Design is to understand and document the relationships between the users, the application, and the business. It is vital to uncover what users truly care about.

The goals for Conceptual Design are:

- **A design based on real data from the customer and users** These are the business needs and user requirements for the solution.

- **A coherent, integrated picture of the product** The project team needs to understand exactly how the proposed application affects the business and the users of the application.

- **Useful levels of abstraction or classification** Conceptual Design uncovers information about the business itself. Understanding users and their requirements in the context of business activities eliminates unnecessary or extraneous requirements, and increases the visibility of those that remain.

- **A common set of expectations among the customer, users, and the project team** Agreement is important early-on in the process, not only because of the obvious danger of divergent expectations (which can only increase with time), but also because of the importance of these three parties to the success of the product.

- **Group consensus in design** Consensus ensures the success of the implemented system.

- **Synchronization with the enterprise architecture** Conceptual Design represents one of the earliest opportunities for the customer, users, and project team to validate the application architecture, and to validate the proposed application against the business models included in the enterprise architecture.

- **A basis for team communication** Including the customer and users as project participants fosters open communication, in turn reducing the possibility of future design changes due to an ongoing understanding of the evolving solution.

Conceptual Design consists of three steps: research, analysis, and implementation. Each step ends in its own baseline, which contributes to the overall Conceptual Design baseline.

Research involves:

- Getting answers to key questions.
- Identifying key business processes and activities.
- Prioritizing processes and activities.
- Identifying users and creating profiles.

Analysis involves:

- Reviewing in-depth user and business research.
- Creating scenarios to depict context, workflow, task sequence, and environmental relationships.

Implementation involves:

- Improving workflow and the solution that supports it.
- Validating and testing the work redesign.

The Conceptual Design baseline includes the implementation baseline, and is the culmination of the research, analysis, and implementation steps.

Step #1: Research

Before starting the Conceptual Design process, the team must first determine the focus of its investigation. For example, the team might start by describing the core operational processes of the appropriate business area, rather than the organizational function. These descriptions might include:

- Descriptions of core business processes and their boundaries, along with the functional elements of the business.
- High-level descriptions of business transactions within those processes.
- A description of the customer and the users.

More specific details can include business process maps and their interdependencies, information structure and usage, and measurements and metrics (such as revenue per unit, expenses, operational locations, forecasts, and projections). Much of this information can be obtained from the enterprise architecture documentation, if it is available. When using UML or the Unified Process Model, these activities can be related to the use case, activity, and collaboration model.

During the research step, the project team conducts a high-level evaluation of existing business processes and activities in the context of enterprise strategy, goals, and objectives in the focus area. It should identify core corporate processes that support the business's objectives and goals. These may be product, service, or managerial processes, and in most cases, they are cross-functional in nature and move horizontally across the organization rather than vertically within the business's traditional departments or "silos."

A core process:

- Runs the business.
- Directly addresses strategic directions and competitiveness.
- Has identifiable owners and customers.
- Has a definition that makes as much sense to external customers or suppliers as it does to internal staff.
- Has discrete and minimal dependencies on other core processes.

After the team has identified and prioritized business processes and activities, it should conduct additional investigations to complete its understanding, such as tapping into the corporate culture, gathering artifacts, and so on. The point is to gain a complete, accurate picture, with the quality of information being more important than the quantity of data.

In addition to researching business processes, the team can also conduct research on users and user groups. The first step is to identify as many groups as possible, including the organization's owner, users within the organization, and users outside the organization such as suppliers and consumers. After the various constituencies have been identified, a user profile must be created for each one, detailing the group's role in the organization, as well as its department, location, and involvement in specific activities. Any background data appropriate to the scope of the project should be included. Finally, the user roles must be related to the activities and processes documented earlier.

The research step is complete when the following tasks have been performed:

- Identify inputs to Conceptual Design, including appropriate enterprise architecture information, business processes and activities, and users and user profiles.
- Gather data, including business and user requirements.

Step #2: Analysis

The first task of the analysis step is to validate the results of the research step, usually at a group debriefing. After a data-gathering activity is completed, the interviewer's findings, which might include diagrams and notes, are presented to the team. Comments from team members help the interviewer interpret the results, and the session helps the team to better understand the user requirements.

It's important to involve as many team members as possible in the debriefing sessions, especially Development, Testing, User Education, and Logistics Management. All team members have some involvement in the design of the application, and each member needs to understand and accept a common view of the users. Team members contribute different perspectives to the sessions, and walk away from these debriefings with information that is important to their role in the project.

When the research is deemed credible, the next task is to build information models to capture context, workflow processes, and task sequences. These information models are of two types: use cases and scenarios.

Use Cases

A *use case* is defined as a behaviorally related sequence of interactions performed by an actor in a dialogue with a system to provide some measurable value to the actor.

An *actor* can be a person, a group of people, another system, or even a piece of equipment. The defining characteristic of an actor is a role, or set of roles, performed in relation to the business or system. Use cases serve the following purposes:

- Identify the business process and all activities, from start to finish.
- Document the context and environmental issues.
- Trace a path between business needs and user requirements.
- Describe needs and requirements in the context of usage.
- Focus users and the project team.

Use cases have the following benefits:

- Provide the context for all business and user requirements.
- Facilitate "common" understanding of the application.
- Provide the basis for user work-flow scenarios.
- Facilitate objectivity and consistency in evaluating user suggestions.
- Provide organization for the Functional Specification.
- Enable paths to be traced between user needs and logical design.

Scenarios

A *scenario* is defined as a single sequence of interactions between objects and actors.

A scenario illustrates a particular instance of a use case and can show either the current state of the process or a desired future state. Four types of information are captured within a scenario:

- **Context** This includes cultural norms, policies, procedures, rules, regulations, and standards that constrain and support the business and the user.
- **Workflow process** This process depicts the flow of products and information within a business process, and among departments and customers. Note that business processes can cut across organizational boundaries.
- **Task sequence** This sequence documents the activities and tasks within a discrete part of a process. Included in the task sequence are the tasks that trigger the sequence; the activities, tasks, and steps involved in the task sequence; any decisions and loops within the sequence; and both typical and atypical paths.

- **Physical environment** This illustrates the physical, environmental, and ergonomic conditions that constrain or support the work. The physical environment could include geographic maps of sites; personnel or other resources; work area schematics or floor plans; or photographs showing equipment, computers, furniture, and lighting.

Scenarios document the sequence of tasks performed by a specific role. Because each scenario represents only one particular instance of the use case, many scenarios are needed to document all the tasks comprising the workflow process in a given use case.

Scenarios can be easily documented in narratives, pseudocode, and task sequence diagrams. They are also easily prototyped for verification with users.

There are positive and negative aspects to building current-state scenarios. On the positive side, current-state scenarios:

- Provide reference points for proposed development.
- Educate users and project team on the current environment.
- May reveal additional justification for the new system.
- May reveal intersystem dependencies.

On the negative side, though, current-state scenarios:

- Take time, resources, and money.
- May not provide added value if the solution is small or well understood, or is not critical.
- May not be relevant.

On every project, the team must evaluate the negative and the positive aspects of the project's current-state scenarios, considering the resources required to construct them. Risk assessment brings a degree of objectivity to this process, by asking the questions "What is the risk of taking the time to create scenarios versus not doing so?" and "What is the risk of misunderstanding if we don't create scenarios?"

The analysis step is complete when the following tasks have been performed:

- Synthesize business and user data, integrating the four categories of information—context, work-flow process, task sequence, and physical environment—needed for scenarios.
- Create scenarios, to whatever extent the team has deemed appropriate.

The scenarios at this point are current-state. We discuss how the scenarios can be changed to depict the desired future state in the next section.

Step #3: Rationalization

In this step, the goal is to include business processes as part of the design process, and to make improvements where possible. The scope of Conceptual Design includes not only the system under evaluation, but also the broader context of business processes, information, and goals that a new system will support.

The project team will not necessarily make all the improvements alone, but may coordinate with other efforts already underway, or with consultants brought in specifically for the work. Depending on the scope of the project and the depth of the team's understanding of the business, the team may be able to optimize one or more processes without any outside help.

What should be optimized? The goal is to eliminate as many of the following as possible:

- Inefficiencies
- Bottlenecks and unnecessary steps
- Redundant and ineffective practices and processes
- Unnecessary paperwork
- Dysfunctional policies
- Transport and delay time

The team should begin by asking questions: "How can we improve productivity?" "Where can we optimize?" "Are there places where we can integrate entire processes?" It's not enough to simply identify weaknesses. The team must also be able to imagine and describe the desired future state. Once the desired future state has been clearly visualized and described, the team can build appropriate new scenarios.

The following design basics can be used to optimize the processes involved in the project:

- **Break the rules** Question assumptions. Ask why there are principles and rules such as "In this company, travel requests must be approved at the unit, departmental, and divisional levels."
- **Align with performance goals** Ensure that goals chosen at the outset are truly aligned with projected results. Think of performance in terms of meeting customer requirements and not just short-term needs.
- **Design work around products and services** Design a person's job around the goals and objectives of the process, not around a single task.
- **Eliminate bureaucracies and other obstacles** Replace bureaucratic hierarchies with self-organized teams working in parallel.

- **Improve productivity** Move away from fragmentation and specialization, and move toward task compression and integration.
- **Ask where technology can enable and support** Consider the availability of appropriate technology that will support and enable the redesigned process. Question activities and roles that simply relay information and that can be handled more easily with technology.
- **Be aware of the risk of taking on too complex a process at the outset** Break the process into subprocesses that can be addressed sequentially.

After new scenarios are created, the final rationalization step is to validate the new scenarios; that is, to assure that they solve the business problem. The team accomplishes this by completing these steps:

- Build a proof-of-concept version of the system.
- Use the proof-of-concept version to represent the user interface design.
- Get usability and business feedback.
- Repeat until both the customer and users are satisfied.

Early in the design process, proof-of-concept systems should show only the main features, user interface design and overall structure of the system. With this proof-of-concept level, the team is open to quickly reworking the design, because it has not invested a lot of effort in one "solution." Proofs-of-concept at this stage can take some of the following forms:

- Applications displaying basic functionality
- Storyboards (either paper-based or screen-based)
- Paper prototypes of the overall structure and user interaction
- Microsoft PowerPoint slides that illustrate the main elements of the system and demonstrate the navigation through the system for one or more tasks

As the design process progresses, prototypes are likely to become more high fidelity, allowing the team to evaluate the visual style and some details of the design, particularly the user interface.

Validation using scenarios is preferable to producing a generic requirements document, because a scenario contains the larger context of the requirements. It's much easier to validate a scenario with a walk-through, role play, or proof-of-concept. One objective of validation is to uncover, before user sign-off, any missing pieces or incorrect interpretations of the design goals. Divergent views among the users over any aspect of the solution will also become starkly apparent and should immediately raise concerns.

It's important not to try and re-engineer the entire business process with the initial releases of the applications. Later product releases can introduce more future-state scenarios that may provide additional streamlining of the modeled business processes. Often, users will be hesitant to change how they do everything with one application release, and the phasing of future states into the application can be a compromise for the user community.

The rationalization step is complete when the following tasks have been performed:

- Build future-state scenarios that will improve the work.
- Validate desired future state scenarios with an update to the organization's enterprise architecture.

Logical Design

Logical Design is defined as the process of describing a solution in terms of the organization, structure, syntax, and interaction of its parts from the perspective of the project team.

The purpose of Logical Design is to apply the services-based organizing principles of the MSF Application Model, which we discussed in Chapter 2, and to lay out the structure of the solution and the relationship among its parts. The output of Logical Design is a set of business objects with corresponding services, attributes, and relationships; a high-level user interface design; and a logical database design.

Logical Design can be likened to the second stage of designing a house, during which the architect concentrates on creating the floor plan and elevation. Here, architectural elements like doors, windows, roofs, patios, rooms, and spatial relationships are organized into a harmonious whole.

Logical Design is the project team's view of the solution. The team paints a picture of the solution's behavior and logical organization, which is required for Physical Design. Logical Design helps the team refine the requirements specified in Conceptual Design and manage the complexity of the whole solution.

In the Logical Design stage, the team:

- Manages and reduces complexity by defining the structure of the solution, describing the parts of the system, and describing how the parts interact to solve the problem.
- Sets boundaries and describes interfaces to provide an organizational structure for interaction between multiple groups.
- Uncovers any errors and inconsistencies in Conceptual Design.
- Eliminates redundancy and identifies potential reuse.
- Provides a foundation for Physical Design.
- Improves the operation between the various parts of the system, and of the system itself.
- Articulates a common view of the solution among project team members.

Note that Logical Design is independent of physical implementation. The primary focus is on what the system needs to do, as explained by an organized set of cooperating elements. It is important to understand the solution completely before making a commitment to specific technologies.

Logical Design has two steps: analysis and rationalization. (There is no research step, because the output of Conceptual Design is the input to Logical Design.)

Analysis involves:

- Identifying business objects and services.
- Identifying attributes and relationships.

Rationalization involves:

- Verifying business objects.
- Identifying implied business objects and scenarios.

Step #1: Analysis

The goal of the analysis step is to convert the scenarios from Conceptual Design into modules for use in Logical Design. *Modules* are the core use cases of the system, the services or activities that occur within them, and the paths between them. A module is a logical unit used as an abstraction for the use cases and scenarios created in Conceptual Design. For each module, the team identifies its services, objects, attributes, and relationships.

To identify services, business objects, attributes, and relationships, the team refers to the work flow and task sequence information of scenarios, focusing on its appropriate aspects, as follows:

- Services focus on the actions (verbs).
- Business objects focus on the people or things (nouns).
- Attributes focus on the properties.
- Relationships focus on the properties.

The team can also derive useful information from the context and physical environment.

Services

A *service* is a unit of application logic that implements an operation, function, or transformation. Services can be relatively straightforward and can provide algorithmically simple functions—such as Create, Read, Update, and Delete—or algorithmically complex calculations or transformations—such as Pay, Validate, and Reserve.

The capabilities and responsibilities of a service should be stated as generally as possible, using only active verbs. A service should be identified by a clear, unambiguous name. Difficulty identifying and naming a service often indicates that its functionality or purpose isn't clear and that additional Conceptual Design investigation may be necessary.

The example in Table 6.3 shows a sample task sequence and the services within it.

Table 6.3 Sample task sequence and its services

Sample task sequence	Candidate services
Front desk clerk **looks up** guest reservation	View reservation
System **retrieves** room **assigned to** confirmed guest	Retrieve room Assign room
Front desk clerk **issues** a key	Issue key

Business Objects

A *business object* is an encapsulation of services and data used to organize the solution and reduce its complexity. Business objects are the people or things that are described in the scenarios. These objects then become the "anchor points" for attributes and relationships. (Note that this definition is different than that of an object from a COM perspective, which is the instance of a class definition.)

Some business objects might not be specifically stated in a scenario, even though these objects might be necessary to complete the business activities that the scenario describes, which are often noted as non-functional requirements. To identify business objects look for structures, other systems, devices, things or events remembered but not actually physically present in the scenario, roles played, operational procedures, locations or sites, and organizational units. To identify missing objects, the team must look for behaviors that have no apparent object associated with them.

The example in Table 6.4 shows the same sample task sequence as that of Table 6.3 with its business objects.

Table 6.4 Sample task sequence and its business objects

Sample task sequence	Candidate business objects
Front desk clerk looks up **guest reservation**	Front desk clerk Guest reservation
System retrieves **room** assigned to confirmed **guest**	System Room Guest
Front desk clerk issues a **key**	Key

Attributes

Attributes (called *properties* in COM) are the elements of an object that the business needs to know about and keep track of. Attributes are the definitions of data values that are held by an object. Each instance of an object maintains its own set of values based on the corresponding definition. For example, an attribute might be First Name, and the value that the attribute takes in a certain instance might be John. Attributes can also show ownership of an object by another object. The set of values for an object's attributes at any given point is known as its *state*.

As the team attempts to discover attributes, it must be sure to note any attributes that are derived—that is, computed—from other attributes. The derivation of this type of attribute becomes a service of the object, and the calculation or manipulation is maintained as part of the interface contract for that service. For example, if the Reservation Number attribute of the Room Reservation object is derived from the Reservation System object, then a Create Reservation Number service needs to be identified within the Reservation System object.

Also, the team must look at the total set of attributes for an object. If some of an object's attributes are very different from its other attributes, a new object might need to be created.

Notice that our definition points out that attributes are properties *that the business needs to know about and keep track of.* Conversely, some attributes might be present but be *irrelevant* to the task at hand. Such attributes should be noted, in case they are later deemed relevant. (Note that attributes that are relevant today may become irrelevant in the future, as business and process needs change.)

Table 6.5 shows the same sample task sequence as that of the two preceding tables with some candidate attributes. Examples of irrelevant attributes for this sample are age, height, religion, ethnicity, and Social Security number. Note that the same object can have many states.

Table 6.5   Sample task sequence and its attributes

Sample narrative	Candidate attributes	Values at one state
Guest **has a name and address**	First name Last name Address	Dan Shelly 100 Microsoft Way
Guest must **have a type of reservation**	Type	Gold Club
Depending upon type of reservation, guest can **have a company**	Company	Microsoft
Guest can be a **smoker or nonsmoker**	N/smoker	Nonsmoker

Relationships

A *relationship* is a logical association between objects. Recognizing relationships is required for determining effective design and assembly of the system parts.

Relationships, or associations, illustrate the way in which objects are related or linked to one another. Relationships fall into one of three types: whole/part, interaction, or generalization/specialization. As the team looks for relationships, it should consider any whole/part relationships that can be identified, any interactions that must be identified to maintain context, and any generalizations or specifications that can be made.

As the example in Figure 6.4 demonstrates, the *guest* object might be a specialization of the more generic *person* object; a *guest* can be part of a *guest list*, and a *guest* stays at a particular *hotel*.

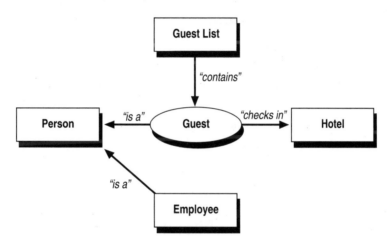

Figure 6.4   Example of identifying relationships

To summarize, the analysis step is concerned with identifying the objects, services, attributes, and relationships comprising the scenarios. The diagram in Figure 6.5 illustrates this process. Note that in some methodologies, this process is called *noun-verb analysis*.

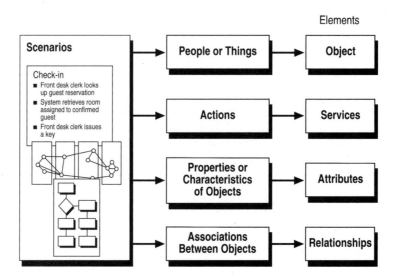

Figure 6.5   Identification process

The anaysis step of Logical Design is complete when the following tasks have been performed:

- Identify services and prepare a list of services.
- Identify objects and prepare a list of objects.
- Identify attributes and prepare a list of attributes.
- Identify relationships and prepare a list of relationships.

Step #2: Rationalization

The first task of the rationalization step of Logical Design is to create any needed services and objects that have not been created to this point. New services and objects are created either because their existence is implied, or because they are needed for control. The team then refines the design. Finally, the Logical Design must be verified.

Creating Implied Services and Objects

This stage consists of creating objects and services that seem to be missing from Logical Design. For example, a guest (represented by an object) has company affiliations (also represented by an object). However, the relationship might not always exist. (For example, the guest might or might not use a company credit card for discounted rates.) Creating a new *type of stay* object effectively handles the missing, implied object and records the relationship between a guest and his or her company if one exists.

Control

At this point, the team should concern itself with matters of *control*. Control means ensuring that services are conducted in the right sequence at the right time. In distributed systems, transactions can be used as a means for determining effective sequencing and the dependency relationships of objects, such as MTS packages. Otherwise, control objects might be needed to ensure the transactional integrity of a scenario, to coordinate services across multiple objects, or to manage cross-object dependencies.

For example, the hotel check-in scenario is a business transaction, or a collection of objects, that have dependency and sequencing relationships. An object or service would need to be created that ensures those relationships are honored and that takes corrective action (such as canceling the reservation) if one of the relationships is broken.

The team must always consider the need for additional business objects to handle control, sequencing, and dependency. The team can also isolate services that are likely to change from those that are stable.

Iterating and Refining Objects

After the team has identified the objects, it needs to refine the design by:

- Eliminating objects that are irrelevant or out of scope.
- Combining redundant objects.
- Refining vague or implicit objects.
- Distinguishing between attributes and objects.
- Considering transactional control.
- Distinguishing actors and roles from objects.

The first attempt at specifying objects using noun-verb analysis usually requires some refinement. Not all of the nouns will be relevant for describing the solution. The remaining candidates might consist of physical entities such as customers, employees, and pieces of equipment, as well as concepts that indicate business transactions such as room assignment, payment authorization, or promotion.

As part of the refinement process, services can also be used to discover objects. For each service that was identified in the analysis step, the team might ask, "What does this service act upon?" and "Is there an entity, individual, or organization that has the responsibility of carrying out this service?" Any objects with zero services or only one service defined might need further investigation.

Verification

Verification refers to testing the functional completeness and correctness of the design at the object level. The objects are tested in both an individual and cooperating context. Verification of independent objects makes the task of integration much easier because the independent parts have been rigorously tested prior to assembly. Verification of cooperating objects ensures that the work specified in the scenario is accomplished as a whole.

For individual objects, the team should examine the pre-conditions feeding into the object and the post-conditions coming out of the object. The question to ask is "For a given set of pre-conditions, do the post-conditions match the scenario's requirements?"

However, this testing will not uncover assembly issues. The team also needs to look at the combination of objects that can solve the higher-level problems that were captured in the scenarios. A collection of modules that are interdependent in solving a problem can be complex. A simple way to verify multi-object scenarios is to conduct a full walk-through of the scenario as shown in Figure 6.6, ensuring that all the needs of the scenario are met by some combination of objects.

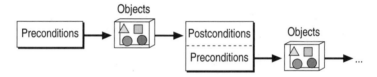

Figure 6.6   Tracing the objects back to the scenario

The team can walk through a scenario and determine which object's services are required in which sequence to move through to a successful completion. From a starting trigger to an object, the team must determine what other objects' services are needed for the scenario to be complete.

The rationalization step of Logical Design is complete when the following tasks have been performed:

- Identify implied objects and services and refine control.
- Verify objects and services and refine the object module.

Physical Design

Physical Design is defined as the process of describing the components, services, and technologies of the solution from the perspective of Development. Its purpose is to apply real-world technology constraints to Logical Design, including implementation and performance considerations. The output of Physical Design is a set of components, a user interface design for a particular platform, and a physical database design.

Physical Design can be likened to the third and final stage of designing a house. Once the basic architectural plan is complete, the contractors, like the Development team, create their wiring plans, plumbing plans, heating and ventilation plans, and so on—as "components" of the internals of the house.

In the Physical Design stage, the team:

- Breaks down the system requirements to simplify the segmenting and estimating of the work needed to create the system, and to provide developer focus and clarity.
- Provides a bridge between Logical Design and implementation, by defining the solution in terms of implementation—a bridge "by developers for developers."
- Evaluates implementation options.
- Provides a flexible design based on services.
- Seeks compatibility with the organization's enterprise architecture.
- Traces back use cases and scenarios through Logical Design.

Physical Design provides the basis for the Functional Specification, which Development, Testing, and Logical Management can use for quality assurance. Why is this important? Because Physical Design represents the last chance to validate the design before writing the code. Once the team has begun code development, design changes can still be made, but the cost to the project in time and resources becomes much higher than in the Planning Phase.

The Physical Design baseline can be established when enough information is available to start developing or deploying. Thus development and deployment can be started before the baseline is frozen. The Physical Design baseline can be frozen well into the Developing Phase to take advantage of opportunities for refinement, but it must be frozen before the solution can be stabilized.

As the Physical Design is being completed, it provides input into other tasks of the Planning Phase by:

- Creating the basis for cost, schedule, and resource estimates.
- Mapping the solution to the MSF Development Process Model for interim milestones or internal releases.
- Refining and updating the earlier risk analysis.

It is important to note that the deliverables of the Physical Design Model help to form the deliverables of the Project Plan Approved Milestone, as follows:

- Topologies and component specifications become part of the Functional Specification.
- Tasks and estimates become part of the Master Project Plan and the Master Project Schedule.
- Risk assessment items update the Master Risk Assessment Document.

When developing, reviewing, and approving the Master Project Plan and the Master Project Schedule, issues will arise that require tradeoff changes to Physical Design. For example, time and resource constraints might require changes to the application's scope or features.

The Physical Design segment of the MSF Design Process consists of four steps: research, analysis, rationalization, and implementation. (The research step is required in order to identify possible technologies to be used in the application.) Each step ends with its own baseline except for the implementation step, whose baseline is included in the overall Physical Design baseline.

Research involves:

- Determining physical constraints of the infrastructure.
- Determining physical requirements of the solution.
- Managing risks from this conflict between physical constraints and requirements.

Analysis involves:

- Selecting candidate implementation technologies.
- Drafting a preliminary deployment model composed of network, data, and component topologies.

Rationalization involves:

- Determining a packaging and distribution strategy.
- Decomposing objects into services-based components.
- Distributing components across topologies.
- Refining packaging and distribution.

Implementation involves:

- Determining the programming model.
- Specifying the component interface.

- Specifying the components in the development language.
- Understanding component structure considerations.

The Physical Design baseline includes the specification baseline and constitutes the culmination of the research, analysis, rationalization, and implementation steps.

Step #1: Research

The goals during the research step of Physical Design are twofold:

- Determine the physical constraints of the infrastructure and the physical requirements of the application.
- Manage the risks from conflict between the physical constraints of the infrastructure and the physical requirements of the application.

By this point, the physical requirements of the application should be well known in a general sense—the application must serve so many people, it must carry out this many transactions per day, and so on. Fairly specific research may be necessary to determine detailed physical requirements, including building proof-of-concept trial applications and testing them.

The physical constraints of the infrastructure, on the other hand, are rooted in the organization's enterprise architecture. As we pointed out in Chapter 1, the organization's enterprise architecture may not be formally documented. If it isn't, this is an opportunity to establish its baseline.

As the team endeavors to list both the requirements of the application and its matching constraints, beginning with the application will yield one list, while beginning with the infrastructure will yield a somewhat different list. Building the list from both viewpoints ensures that nothing is missed. Examples of the constraints and requirements the list might include are:

- Performance
- Cost versus benefit
- Deployment
- Supportability
- Technology choices
- Reliability
- Availability
- Security

One means of examining the current physical infrastructure is through *topologies*, which are maps showing some aspect of the infrastructure. For purposes of planning an application at the physical level, it is helpful to produce network, data, and component topologies. Examples of these are included in the following section on analysis. Infrastructure topologies produced during the research step of Physical Design are of the *current* state of the infrastructure.

Once the physical constraints and requirements are listed, the next task is to manage the risks presented by any conflicts or gaps that have been identified between the three topologies. This is a five-step process:

1. **Identify where infrastructure constraints conflict with application requirements** When the physical requirements of the application are compared with the physical constraints of the infrastructure, some will be in conflict, some will not be in conflict, and some will be immaterial. For example, the infrastructure might require use of TCP/IP across the enterprise. The application might require some other protocol (conflict or gap), might require TCP/IP (no conflict or gap), or not care which protocol it uses (immaterial).

2. **Perform a preliminary assessment to highlight the gaps or conflicts** Is it a gap (a deficiency which could possibly be overcome) or a conflict (implying some sort of choice or crossroads)? How big is the gap or conflict?

3. **Prioritize the tradeoffs to determine which aspects are more important** Which requirements are absolutely necessary? Which constraints are the result of enterprise architecture decisions? When prioritizing, the team must be sure to examine the business case, if any, for either the requirement or the constraint.

4. **Brainstorm initial solutions with the team** Fundamentally, only two things can be done with a gap or conflict:
   - Accept it without doing anything (move ahead and see what happens later).
   - Change one side or the other (requirement or constraint).

5. **Identify associated risks branching from the original list** It is important not to make the mistake of dealing with a risk, only to have the chosen solution cause new and unforeseen issues.

The result of this process is a preliminary risk assessment and mitigation plan for the Physical Design of the application, which will become part of the project's Master Risk Assessment Document.

The research step of Physical Design is complete when the following tasks have been performed:

- Determine constraints and requirements.
- Identify the current network, data, and component topologies and physical application requirements.

- Manage risks resulting from conflicts or gaps between constraints and requirements.
- Produce a risk assessment and mitigation plan.

Step #2: Analysis

The focus in the analysis step of Physical Design is on selecting candidate technologies for the implementation, based on an understanding of the application requirements. Note that these are *candidate* technologies. The final choice will be made later. Once the potential technologies have been chosen, the team can draft a preliminary deployment model, taking into consideration these technologies.

In evaluating candidate technologies, the team should address business considerations first, then take into account enterprise architecture considerations, and only then address technology considerations. The technologies should not be evaluated on their technological merits until the first two steps have been completed.

Business considerations include the following:

- **Ability** Establish whether the technology will actually meet the business needs.
- **Product cost** Understand the complete product cost. Consider developer, server, and reseller licenses, and upgrade costs.
- **Experience** Understand that experience (or lack thereof) can have a large impact. What experience is available in terms of training (costs or time), consultation (costs or availability), and comfort level?
- **Maturity or innovation** Understand that maturity is a fine line and decisions must be made based on risks. A mature product is accepted in the market, is well understood, is a revision of something done before, is stable, and has knowledgeable resources available. An innovative product is the "latest and greatest" or is "ahead of the curve." Ideally, the product should cycle quickly to stay as current as possible with new technologies.
- **Supportability** Understand that this technology must be supported just as the solution built with it must be supported. What are the implications of that support for the project and the enterprise? A supportable product has support options such as vendor, outsourcing, and help desk, and also accumulates support costs such as incidental costs and maintenance.

Other points to consider include deployment, competitive advantage, time to market, and industry perception.

Enterprise architecture considerations include the following:

- **Alignment with enterprise architecture goals** The application can fit within the goals and principles outlined by the enterprise architecture. These goals will be based on the four perspectives and models of enterprise architecture: Business, Application, Information, and Technology.

- **Adherence to the enterprise architecture** The enterprise architecture will identify the current-state and future-state plans. Specifically, the application should fit within the detail architectures of the application, information, and technology models of the enterprise architecture.

- **Opportunity for growth** Scalability of the application can be considered within the business growth plans for the organization, as well as the addition of people and markets through acquisition.

- **Interoperability** The application must work with the other systems within an organization. Not only can the application not interfere with other systems, but a communication interface can be defined so that other applications can easily interact with the new application.

Technology considerations include the following:

- **Languages** When selecting a language for component development, different languages should be considered for different tasks within a project. When choosing a development language, it is important to evaluate whether it supports the design and implementation of loosely coupled components that can be replaced and upgraded as necessary.

- **Component interaction standards** Platforms and interaction standards are related. When selecting a component interaction standard (how components connect and communicate with each other), cross-platform integration must be weighed against power and performance. More than one technology should be considered for the "plumbing."

- **Data access methods** When selecting a data access method (how components interact with data stores), performance, standardization, and future direction should be considered, as well as the diversity of supported data stores and data access management. When selecting a data store, more than one type should be considered, and the decision should be based on structure and location of information.

- **System services** When selecting system services ("plumbing" for distributed solutions), the types of services required by the solution must be identified, as well as which of those services can be provided natively by system software.

- **Operating systems** When selecting the operating system, the services that are provided by the operating system can significantly reduce the coding requirements of the application. Additionally, security and scalability needs can be met by the operating system; however, different operating systems provide different methods of access to their services.

With the candidate technologies in mind, the team can now draft a preliminary deployment model consisting of network, data, and component topologies. At this stage in Physical Design, these topologies are proposed but are not yet the selected topologies.

The *network topology* is an infrastructure map that indicates hardware locations and interconnections. A current-state version of the infrastructure map was developed in the research step. At this point, it might require changes to support the new Physical Design. A sample network topology diagram is shown in Figure 6.7.

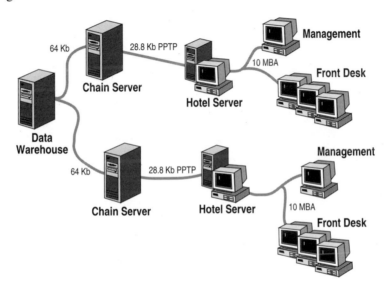

Figure 6.7   Sample network topology

The *data topology* is a data distribution map that indicates data store locations in relation to the network topology. Again, a current-state version was constructed in the research step, but a new data distribution strategy or new data technologies might need to be considered to support the new Physical Design. Figure 6.8 shows a sample data topology.

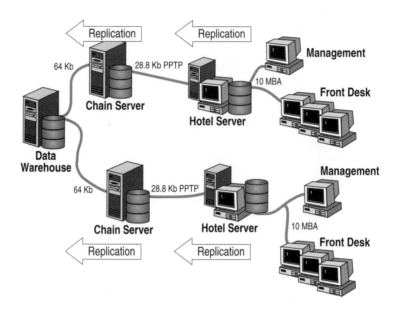

Figure 6.8   Sample data topology

The *component topology* is a component distribution map that indicates the locations of components and their services in relation to the network topology. The current-state version should already exist from work in the research step. Any new components and services required by the new application should now be added, and any updating required to reflect changes in the other topologies should also be carried out. Figure 6.9 shows a diagram of a sample component topology.

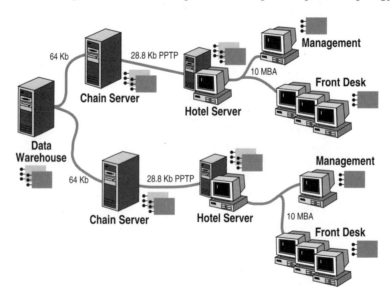

Figure 6.9   Sample component topology

The analysis step of Physical Design is complete when the following tasks have been performed:

- Select and list candidate implementation technologies.

- Draft a preliminary deployment model to include the proposed network topology, the proposed data topology, and the proposed component topology.

Step #3: Rationalization

The team has done its research and has analyzed that research. At this point, it is time to begin solidifying the design. Determining a packaging and distribution strategy is part of this process.

The team might be thinking, "We can't plan for packaging and distribution when we haven't solidified the component model," and the team would be right. By the same token, the team cannot complete the component model without a firm packaging and distribution plan. The tasks involved in the rationalization step are both interactive and iterative. In some cases, it may make more sense to begin with the component model, while in others the packaging considerations will take precedence. One possible guideline is to begin with the task that seems the most complex or the most critical.

When determining the packaging and distribution strategy, the team should follow three basic steps. The first is to consider various packaging rationales, or reasons to choose a particular strategy. These could include any of the following:

- Service category
- Scalability
- Performance
- Manageability
- Reuse
- Business context
- Granularity

The second step is to align the strategy with the programming model. Because the programming model is not firm at this point, this step is inherently interactive in nature.

The third step is to determine the design tradeoffs that impact the strategy, based on the rationales used in the first step. For example, the team might have based its strategy primarily on the performance needs of the application. In doing so, any necessary scalability might have been compromised, and if it has, the team needs to decide what it will do about this tradeoff.

The team is now ready to begin defining components. Although there are many ways to do this, we recommend that the first cut at the component model be based on the MSF Application Model's three logical service layers: user, business, and data. As shown in Figure 6.10, the services are distributed throughout the topology. The team can then package candidate components from the same logical service located in the same place in the topology.

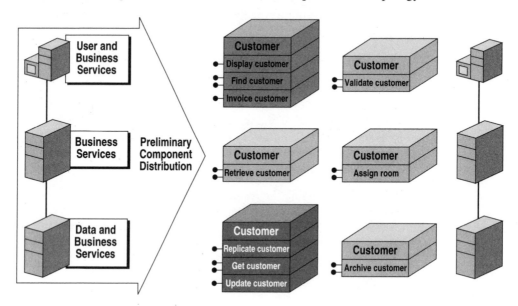

Figure 6.10   Sample component model

When the component model is complete, the team is ready to finalize the distribution of those components. Again, the first cut at distribution should be based on the three logical service layers: user, business, and data. Note, though, that the use of three logical services does not in any way imply a distribution of three physical locations. It is entirely possible to build an N-tier application that runs on a single computer. By the same token, a distribution strategy for a multi-site, complex application may involve 10, 20, or more physical locations.

Throughout the rationalization step, the team should be validating the proposed components and their packaging and distribution. Questions to ask include "Do the components fit the packaging strategy?" "Are we meeting the design goals and application requirements we outlined earlier?" "Do the components we have derived actually match up with the logical design?" and "Are we fitting into the enterprise architecture?"

One way to validate the design is to build prototypes and proof-of-concept test applications. As the team defines more and more components, they should be included in these trial applications and the results should be observed.

Although the development team has been doing validation work throughout the rationalization step, it should carry out formal component refinement and validation at the conclusion of this step. This validation task should be done by the Development and Testing roles. In some cases, it may be worthwhile to schedule a formal Quality Assurance review of the component design, carried out by an outside expert with component design expertise.

What would such an expert be looking for? Here are some attributes of a good component plan:

- The identified components contain all the services identified in the Logical Design Model.
- All component/service dependencies have been taken into account.
- The distribution of the components across the topologies matches the rationales on which it is supposedly based.
- Services are grouped into components based on a good balance of physical location, packaging rationale, and technology constraints.
- The component plan demonstrates high cohesion and loose coupling.
- The component plan addresses both upward and downward scalability. (Both are important!)

Cohesion and Coupling

One of the design goals noted above is high cohesion and loose coupling. *Cohesion* is the relationship among different internal elements of a component, whereas *coupling* is the relationship of a component to other components.

A component whose internal elements—primarily its services—are closely related is said to have high cohesion. Cohesion can be both beneficial and non-beneficial, depending on the cause of the cohesion.

Beneficial types of cohesion include the following:

- **Functional** A component does one and only one thing. This is the strongest type of cohesion.

- **Sequential** A component contains operations that must be performed in a specific order and must share the same data.

- **Communicational** Operations in a component use the same data but aren't related in any other way. This type of cohesion minimizes communication overhead in the system.

- **Temporal** Operations are combined because they are all done at the same time.

Non-beneficial types of cohesion include the following:

- **Procedural** Operations are grouped together because they are executed in a specific order. Unlike sequential cohesion, the operations do not share any of the same data.

- **Logical** Several operations are grouped into a single unit that requires some control flag, such as a large or highly nested **IF** or **CASE** statements, to be passed to select the appropriate operation. The operations are related only by artificial selection logic.

- **Coincidental** Operations are grouped without any discernible relationship to one another.

Metrics that can be used to determine the amount of coupling include the following:

- **Size** Minimize the number of connections and the complexity of interfaces.

- **Intimacy** Use the most direct connection.

- **Visibility** Define all connections explicitly.

- **Flexibility** Use arm's-length interfaces.

Ultimately the arm's-length flexibility goal should be to have high cohesion and loose coupling. The high cohesion provides a better definition of the component's function and behavior. An example would be organizing services by business function so that each component has only the services that pertain to its function. The loose coupling provides more flexibility and independence, and leads to better-defined and simpler interfaces. An example would be organizing relationships among components by business function so that each component interfaces with the minimum number of other components for access to data.

Even though the team carries out a formal refinement process at the end of the rationalization step, it can expect refinement to continue during development and stabilization. Packaging and distribution will change as the team tests for the results of the determining criteria, such as performance. Thus, if the system fails to meet performance objectives during testing, the team may have to revisit the packaging and distribution plan that was supposed to provide the expected performance levels.

The rationalization step of Physical Design is complete when the following tasks have been performed:

- Determine a packaging and distribution system.
- Transform objects into services-based components to create a services-based component model.
- Distribute components across topologies to produce a final deployment model that includes the future network, data, and component topologies.
- Use strategies and prototypes to refine packaging and distribution, resulting in a baseline deployment model.

Step #4: Implementation

The last step of Physical Design is implementation. During this step, the team specifies the programming model that Development will use, the interfaces for each component, and the internal structure of each component.

The programming model, which could also be called the programming specifications or standards, does the following:

- Prescribes how to use the selected technologies.
- Sets design guidelines for component specifications, which helps to ensure consistency across the project.
- Uses different considerations to address different aspects of the solution, such as stating that all business services will be stateless while client-side services will be stateful.

Several aspects need to be considered when building a programming model, some of which are highlighted in Table 6.6 and discussed at length in subsequent chapters.

Table 6.6   Programming model aspects

Aspect	Considerations
Implementation technologies	Programming language; API; servers and server technologies; and other technologies affecting implementation. Implementation technologies are a consideration because some technologies require a specific programming model to take full advantage of them. For example, Microsoft Transaction Server requires single-entrant, single-threaded, in-process components.
Stateful vs. stateless objects	A stateful object holds private state accumulated from the execution of one or more client calls. A stateless object does not hold private state. Typical questions to be addressed include where state will be kept and tradeoffs such as scalability, complexity, and performance.
In-process vs. out-of-process function calls	In-process is fast and direct. Out-of-process on the same machine is fast and offers secure interprocess communications. Out-of-process across machines is secure, reliable, and offers a flexible protocol based on Distributed Computing Environment, Remote Procedure Calls (DCE-RPC).
Connected vs. connectionless modes	In connected application/component environments, the various components participating in the service of a task must have real-time, live connections to each other to be able to function. If the connection is severed because of problems at run time, the components involved in the interaction fail. Real-time applications typically must be run in connected mode. Applications/components that are written to run in a connectionless environment are able to reestablish a connection as and when needed.
Synchronous vs. asynchronous programming models	A synchronous programming model blocks the calling component from proceeding with other work until the called interface completes the requested service and returns control to the calling component. An asynchronous programming model allows components to send messages to other components and continue to function without waiting for a reply. A component designed to use an asynchronous programming model is harder to program, but it lends itself to more scalability. Each component isn't blocked and doesn't have to wait for a spawned process to complete before proceeding.
Threading model	Choosing the threading model for a component is not a simple matter because it depends on the function of the component. A component that does extensive I/O might support free-threading to provide maximum response to clients by allowing interface calls during I/O latency. On the other hand, an object that interacts with the user might support apartment threading to synchronize incoming COM calls with its window operations.
Error handling	Certain programming and deployment model decisions will constrain the number of error handling options available.
Security	A given component or service has four security options: component-based, at either the method level, the interface level, or the component level; database-based; user-context based, in either an interacive method using system security, or a fixed security within the application; or role-based, such as a night clerk or general manager.
Distribution	Having three logical tiers does not necessarily translate into three physical tiers. The logical tiers will be spread among the physical tiers. For example, some business services reside on the client.

Note There typically is not just one programming model for all components. There may be many programming models for an application, depending on the different requirements of the different components.

Although not a part of the programming model itself, an important consideration is the skill set and experience of the technical people who will implement the programming model.

When the programming model has been outlined, the team is ready to specify the external structures of the components. These are outlined in the component interface, which:

- Is a contract that represents the supplier-consumer relationship between components.

- Is a means to access the underlying services.

- Represents one or more services.

- Includes underlying object attributes.

The specification of the component interface must include all the different ways the component can be accessed and, if possible, include examples of how the component can be used for each way it is accessed. A sample is shown in Figure 6.11. Note that the interface must be documented and understandable to the developers who will be using the components.

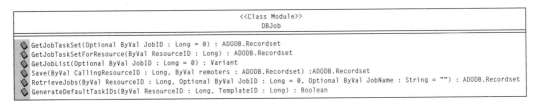

Figure 6.11   Sample component interface specification

There are three implications to consider when creating component interfaces:

- A published interface is an interface contract and should be considered permanent.

- A modification of an existing interface should be published either as a new component or an entirely new interface.

- The data types of published attributes must be supportable by the service interface consumer.

The interface contract defines the parameters, the data types, any interaction standards, and a description of the interface. The degree of specificity depends on user needs—ultimately, the degree of reuse.

Finally, the team is ready to specify the internal structure of the components. (Note that internal structure is important only when building the component itself. When assembling components, the interface is the important factor.) Many factors come into play when defining the internal structure of a component. The most significant factor is the language or tool used to implement the component. The other factors are used as criteria to determine the component's internal structure. For example, when writing the first N-tier application for a large organization that plans to develop other applications that will use many of the same services, the internal structures of the components should be designed so as to enhance their reusability.

When the internal structures have been specified, the baseline for the implementation step is established. This baseline is merged into the overall Physical Design baseline. The implementation step of Physical Design is complete when the following tasks have been performed:

- Determine a programming model.
- Specify the external structures of components, including interfaces, attributes, and services.
- Specify the internal structures of components.

The design process is now complete, having moved from the reality of user requirements, through Conceptual Design, through the abstraction of Logical Design, and back to the reality of Physical Design and the completed application design. The output of the process will become the basis for the Functional Specification, which feeds the Master Project Plan, the Master Project Schedule, and a revision of the Master Risk Assessment Document.

Ongoing Risk Management Process

During the Envisioning Phase, the team began identifying and managing risks using the five-step process shown in Figure 6.12. As part of the Vision Approved Milestone, the Master Risk Assessment Document was prepared. This document was fairly high-level, because in the Envisioning Phase, the details of the project had not yet been worked out.

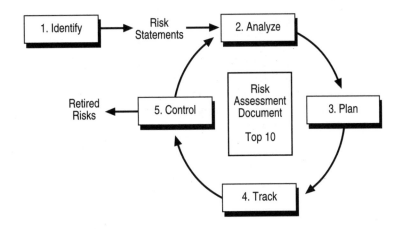

Figure 6.12   Five steps of risk management

One deliverable for the Planning Phase is a revised version of the Master Risk Assessment Document. At this point in the project, the team is ready to work through the risk management process again, adding necessary details to the plan and perhaps changing some of the original assessments. As the team moves through the project, it will continue to loop through the risk management process, retiring some risks, controlling others, and even identifying new ones. In fact, when the revised Master Risk Assessment Document is complete, it's a good idea to include a risk management section in each subsequent meeting agenda. Doing so ensures that the team will continue to use the five steps shown in Figure 6.12 to manage risk.

When creating the original risk document in the Envisioning Phase, the team identified as many risks as possible. As part of its analysis, the team calculated each risk's *exposure rating* by multiplying the risk's *probability* by its *impact*. The team also developed preliminary plans to address the Top Ten risks, based on that analysis. For each plan, the team considered five key areas:

- **Research** Do we know enough about the risk?
- **Acceptance** Can we live with its consequences?
- **Avoidance** Can we avoid the risk?
- **Mitigation** Can we reduce the probability or impact?
- **Contingency** What can we do of the risk is realized?

The team then developed subplans either to mitigate the risk or to create contingency trigger values and strategies if the risk occurred.

The problem with the risk management approach of some project teams is that they create a risk management plan and then believe that their work is done. In fact, the risk tracking and risk control steps are just as critical to risk management as the risk action planning step, and are the key steps during the Planning Phase of a project.

After creating the Master Risk Assessment Document, the team should begin tracking the status of the various risks and progress as far as controlling each risk is concerned. For each risk, the team should ask:

- Have we done anything to mitigate the risk?

- Has the risk changed due to forces outside our control?

- As a result of either our efforts or outside forces, has there been a change in either the probability or the impact of the risk?

- If anything has changed, what is the corresponding change in the risk's exposure rating and therefore in its priority?

- Have any of the contingency triggers been "pulled"?

- Based on the above, what should be our response?

The risk tracking step leads to the risk control step, in which the project team reacts to the tracked changes. This reaction may include new mitigation plans, activation of contingency plans, re-analysis of the risk, or retirement of the risk if the risk has occurred or been resolved.

Risk management is an ongoing, dynamic process. Practicing risk management throughout the project is a vital part of the MSF approach to project management.

Project Plan Approved Milestone and Its Deliverables

The goal of the Planning Phase is to reach the Project Plan Approved Milestone, which is the culmination of the team's work during this phase and signifies agreement between the customer and the team on critical project issues.

Four deliverables are required to meet the Project Plan Approved Milestone. They are:

- A Functional Specification, which outlines the product being developed and the needs it will meet.

- A Master Project Plan, which shows how the team plans to execute the project and includes any subsequent milestones and deliverables the team intends to meet.

- A Master Project Schedule, which outlines the time required for each subsequent milestone and deliverable.

- A revised Master Risk Assessment Document, which identifies possible risks to the project and outlines how the team plans to deal with each one.

We also recommend including proof-of-concept systems to demonstrate and validate the team's design choices.

Note The goal of any deliverable is to serve as an efficient communication tool. In this context, a deliverable does not necessarily result in a paper artifact. A deliverable can take whatever form is appropriate (a document, a diagram, an application, a screen shot, e-mail, and so on) so long as it facilitates communication.

Every major milestone in the MSF Development Process Model signifies an agreement between the customer, the project team, and any other key project stakeholders. Reaching the Project Plan Approved Milestone indicates agreement on the points listed in Table 6.7.

Table 6.7 Agreement achieved by the Project Plan Approved Milestone

Point of agreement	Documented in
What to build to meet the business needs	Functional Specification
What features have priority	Functional Specification
How long it will take to complete the project	Master Project Schedule
How to build the product and who will build it	Master Project Plan
Risks of building the product	Revised Master Risk Assessment Document
Milestones and deliverables	Master Project Plan

The Project Plan Approved Milestone also provides an opportunity for the customer and the project team to decide whether to proceed with the project. After reviewing the deliverables from the Planning Phase, the customer or the project team may decide that the product does not provide enough benefits to justify its costs. This decision represents a critical point in the project and is one of the reasons why the Planning Phase is so significant. A well-executed Planning Phase enables the team and the customer to proceed with confidence, knowing that the necessary up-front work has been done to maximize the chances for success.

Interim Milestones

To break the Planning Phase into manageable chunks, interim milestones can be set throughout the phase. Because the plans and schedules are developed by the various team roles based on the Functional Specification, it makes sense to create a draft version of the specification first. Team members can then create draft versions of their own plans and schedules, which can be "rolled up" into an overall master version. The team will probably revise and expand these draft documents as it moves through both the design process and the Planning Phase.

Functional Specification

The Functional Specification is the primary deliverable of the Planning Phase. It is a detailed set of specifications for the product, and serves as a contract between the customer and the project team. It is not an exaggeration to say that all the work of the project team to this point has been leading up to the Functional Specification, and all subsequent work of the team will flow from and be based on it. Out of the Functional Specification flow the remaining deliverables for the Planning Phase: the Master Project Plan, the Master Project Schedule, and the revised Master Risk Assessment Document.

Program Management is the owner of the Functional Specification and is responsible for its ultimate completion. This is not to say that Program Management must write the entire document. Indeed, the Functional Specification should reflect the entire team's understanding of the product, and should be based on information contributed by various team members.

As the team creates the Functional Specification, certain pitfalls should be avoided, including:

- Failing to provide enough detail.
- Providing too much detail.
- Creating an unrealistic design.
- Freezing the Functional Specification too early.
- Spending too much time updating the Functional Specification.
- Failing to communicate changes in the Functional Specification to the customer, project team members, or other key project stakeholders.
- Failing to involve the whole team in design.

Although most of these pitfalls seem obvious, many teams find them easy to overlook. The team might want to post them in a prominent place while it develops the project's Functional Specification.

Functional Specification Contents

The Functional Specification should contain all the items or sections listed in Table 6.8. The project team may decide to include additional items in the document to suit the demands of a particular application development project.

Table 6.8   Key components of the Functional Specification

Item	Description
Vision summary	What the team wants the product to be, justification for it, and key high-level constraints. Based on the vision document from the Envisioning Phase.
Design goals	What the team wants to achieve with the product. Development will use these goals to make decisions on such issues as performance, reliability, timeliness, and possibly usability and accessibility. These goals were originally developed during the Envisioning Phase.
Requirements	What the customer, users, and stakeholders think the product must do. The requirements should be prioritized. Conflicting requirements should either be resolved or balanced in some way.
Usage summary	When the product will be used and who will use it. This is a high-level aggregation of the usage scenarios that were defined during the design process.
Features	What exactly the product does. A prioritized list of each of the product features, including such things as potential user interface, application navigation, and detailed functionality.
Dependencies	What the product depends on. A description of external entities upon which the product might depend, including both high-level issues (such as interfacing to corporate systems) and low-level issues (such as a shared component).
Schedule summary	What the schedule is. A summary of the Master Project Schedule, identifying key interim milestones, deliverables, and the product ship date.
Risks	What the risks are. A list of risks that require external visibility or escalation.
Appendixes	What remains. A collection of the design process output that the team used to develop the Functional Specification.

Functional Specification Review and Consensus

An important step in developing the Functional Specification is its review by the project team. The Functional Specification review:

- Allows everyone with a stake in the Functional Specification to take part in creating it.
- Involves a variety of people in making sure that requirements are met.
- Serves as a method of communicating what is going to be built.
- Provides a forum for negotiating and for achieving buy-in.

The primary purpose of reviews of the Functional Specification is to get the input of all the team roles. If all team roles participate in these reviews, the specification will describe a much better product that will meet the needs of each of the roles. Holding reviews is one way to ensure that team members actually read the document.

Note the use of "reviews" (plural) in the preceding paragraph. Because one of the interim deliverables noted earlier is the draft Functional Specification, the Planning Phase should include at least two reviews of the Functional Specification. Ideally, the Functional Specification will be reviewed and updated regularly throughout the Planning Phase.

The goal at the end of the Functional Specification process is *consensus*. Everyone directly involved with the project—the project team, the customer, and any other key stakeholders—should concur that the Functional Specification accurately and adequately documents their expectations of the product. Specifically, the customer and each team role should agree with the items shown in Table 6.9.

Table 6.9   Agreements required for the Functional Specification

Role	Agrees that
Customer	Solution meets business needs. The customer is willing to accept development schedules and resource estimates based on the scope specified in the Functional Specification.
Product Management	Solution meets known requirements. Product Management believes the Functional Specification reflects a product that will meet known requirements when delivered.
Program Management	Team responsibilities and schedules are realistic. Program Management believes that it is clear who is responsible for each specified function and that the committed schedules are realistic.
Development	Solution is implementable. Development has sufficiently investigated development risks throughout the Planning Phase and believes the risk in meeting delivery dates is manageable. Development is willing to commit to schedules based on the state of the Functional Specification at this time.
Testing	Solution is testable and can be stabilized. Testing has a defined strategy for test platforms, scripts, and data and commits to testing all aspects of the Functional Specification.
User Education	Solution is usable, and user support needs are defined. User Education has a clear idea of who the users are and how the product will be used and supported. It commits to developing the user support systems outlined in the Functional Specification.
Logistics Management	Solution is supportable and deployable. Logistics Management has a clear idea of all the organizational, application, and system interfaces and can commit to deploying the system.
All roles	Everyone agrees to the ship date.

Master Project Plan

The Master Project Plan tells how the product will be built by gathering detailed plans from members of the project team. The team then uses this collection of more detailed deliverables to synchronize its work throughout the remainder of the project.

The purpose of a Master Project Plan is to:

- Consolidate feature team and role work plans.
- Describe how feature teams and roles will execute their tasks.
- Synchronize the plans across the team.

The overall owner of the Master Project Plan is Program Management, because this role is the primary coordinator of planning and process for the project. However, each role on the team is responsible for developing and maintaining its own realistic project plan within the overall plan.

The Master Project Plan should include the items listed in Table 6.10.

Table 6.10   Components of the Master Project Plan

Plan	Description
Development	Tells how Development will build what's described in the Functional Specification. It describes such things as tools, methodologies, best practices, sequences of events, and test methods.
Test	Includes a testing strategy, the specific areas to be tested, and the resources (hardware and people) Testing will require to do its job.
Training	Includes a strategy and a plan for developing any necessary training materials.
User support	Includes a strategy and details for developing anything that users will need for performance, such as wizards and user manuals.
Communications	Includes a marketing strategy and promotional activities for users.
Deployment	Includes a strategy and a detailed plan for preparing end users and operations personnel before and during deployment.

Note The Master Project Plan is not typically used for direct project management, because it is too cumbersome and at too high a level. Instead, each team role should manage its responsibilities according to its own project plans and merely synchronize any necessary changes with the Master Project Plan.

Master Project Schedule

We are discussing the Master Project Schedule as the *third* deliverable because it's important for both the customer and the project team to understand that the schedule comes *after* the Functional Specification and the Master Project Plan. The team can't prepare the schedule until it knows what the feature set is and how the team plans to deliver those features.

This is not to say that these three deliverables fall like dominoes. This process can be, and often should be, iterative. The team prepares the feature set, then the project plan, and finally the schedule, and then realizes that the current feature set will push the ship date too far into the future. So the team revises the Functional Specification, revises the Master Project Plan, and revises the Master Project Schedule, iterating through these steps until all three are acceptable.

The point to remember is that while it is legitimate for the team to include the ship date in its planning, it's not good management practice to prepare the schedule *first* and then try to fit the Master Project Plan and Functional Specification into it. The schedule must flow out of the other two deliverables. The original ship date identified in the Envisioning Phase acts as a design guideline.

The owner of the Master Project Schedule is Program Management, but Program Management does not prepare the schedule as much as consolidate the more detailed schedules prepared by each of the other team roles. Program Management uses this aggregated version of those lower-level schedules as an overall project schedule.

Of all the schedules in the Master Project Schedule, the development schedule is the most crucial. All the other schedules will be based on it.

The Master Project Schedule includes:

- Development schedule.
- Product ship dates, both internal and external.
- Test schedule.
- Training schedule.
- User support schedule.
- Communications schedule.
- Deployment schedule.

Principles of Scheduling

Although covered throughout the book, we have summarized these MSF-based principles for project scheduling here for easy reference. As the team develops plans and schedules, it should keep certain principles of scheduling in mind.

These four principles from the MSF Risk Management Model will help build schedules that are realistic and attainable.

Bottom-Up Scheduling

The people who will do the work should also plan the work. Their task-level estimates should be rolled up into the Master Project Schedule. This principle not only increases the accuracy of the estimate, but also fosters team acceptance of the schedule.

Fixed Ship-Date Mindset

Fixing the ship date eliminates easy excuses and limits tradeoff decisions to resources and features. It's a way of heightening the importance of shipping on time. It also drives the engineering decisions about what will be built and to what extent. Note that a fixed ship-date mindset means *realistically* setting a ship date, not *arbitrarily* setting one. Achieving a fixed ship date requires using the other three scheduling principles.

Risk-Driven Scheduling

Risk-driven scheduling essentially means doing the most difficult and most risk-laden tasks first. There are several significant advantages to this approach:

- The greatest risks tend to be those with the highest level of unknowns, and addressing them first gives the team more time to work on mitigation where mitigation is feasible.

- If the team attacks a show-stopping risk early in the project and realizes there is no mitigation, the project can be canceled much earlier, minimizing wasted resources.

- Working through the process of understanding what's important to the customer and explaining what is most risky to the project helps to manage customer expectations.

- Mitigating show-stopping risks (those severe enough to end the project) often means developing proof-of-concept systems during the planning process to prove or disprove the probability or impact of those risks.

Obviously, for the team to practice risk-driven scheduling, it must be prioritizing risks through some sort of risk management.

Scheduling for an Uncertain Future

Scheduling something uncertain seems like a contradiction in terms. The point of this principle is that, because the future *is* uncertain, the team must create schedules that are designed to adjust to the unexpected. The three methods illustrated in Figure 6.13 can help create such schedules.

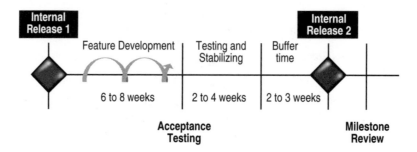

Figure 6.13   Methods of scheduling for an uncertain future

- **Add buffer time** Program Management adds buffer time to the end of the schedule to accommodate project slippage. Although buffer time is often controversial and disliked by management, it is an essential part of an effective schedule. A project without buffer time is a project set up for failure. The amount of buffer time that Program Management adds to a schedule directly depends on how much confidence Program Management has in team estimates. Bottom-up scheduling determines the internal ship date. Adding buffer time to that date determines the externally communicated ship date. However, buffer time should be owned and managed at the Program Management level, not at the individual resource level, because resources must stay focused on their estimated dates.

- **Use interim development milestones** These development milestones are alpha and beta releases within a single project. Breaking projects into smaller pieces provides more indicators that tell the team earlier and more often how the project is progressing. The product will also be more stable, and the schedule will be more predictable. Using practice releases with their own Stabilizing Phases allows the team to practice shipping and also indicates the health of the project.

- **Use discrete tasks** The team can keep the project on track by using visible deliverables over short intervals. It is much easier to define and manage short tasks. Also, the shorter the duration of the task, the smaller the margin of error. For example, it would be difficult for a one-week task to slip by six weeks. The team should break down the product functions into associated tasks that are clearly defined, with a beginning and ending point, a single output, and a single owner. Task size should be limited to efforts that require, at most, one to two weeks. Then, each task should be tracked as the project progresses, and schedules should be adjusted accordingly.

Revised Master Risk Assessment Document

By the end of the Planning Phase, the team should have a much clearer picture of the risks associated with the project, and also of their relative impact and priority. This revision of the Master Risk Assessment Document should reflect increased insight into these risks.

Again, Program Management is the owner of this document and is responsible for ensuring that the revision is complete and accurate. The revised Master Risk Assessment Document represents a collection of more detailed risk assessments from the various team members. The team can use this aggregated version of those lower-level assessments to get an overall view of risks.

This document helps synchronize risk assessments across the team. It also drives the team's decisions about risks and aids in prioritization of risk-management effort. Risk management is still handled by the individual team roles responsible for the given risk, because it is difficult to manage risks from the level of the Master Risk Assessment Document.

Summary

The Planning Phase truly gets to the heart of an architecture-first development process. The project team gathered the requirements and created the application vision within the MSF Development Process Model's Envisioning Phase. Now with the MSF Development Process Model's Planning Phase, the team has designed the architecture for the application. This architecture provides the foundation to begin the creation of application code and executables. Having reached the Project Plan Approved Milestone, the team now knows how it is going to build the application and how long each step will take.

In this chapter, we looked at application architecture steps through the MSF Design Process's Conceptual, Logical, and Physical Designs. Each design represented the different level views for the application's layers, based on the MSF Application Model's user, business, and data service layers. We also identified specific deliverables of the Planning Phase, such as the Functional Specification, Master Project Plan, and Master Project Schedule.

Review

1. Why do we need a Planning Phase?
2. Describe the three designs of the MSF Design Process.
3. What information is presented in a Functional Specification?
4. What is a Master Project Plan?

CASE STUDY 6

Planning RMS

"Alright, everyone, confession time. Did you read the material for today?"

Dan was standing at the head of the conference table, sipping a cup of coffee. He had just put a transparency on the overhead projector showing the MSF Development Process Model, with the Planning Phase highlighted. The first meeting of the Planning Phase had started about fifteen minutes earlier, and the team had already worked through Agenda Building and a review of the Envisioning Phase.

After a moment of silence, Tim piped up, "I cannot tell a lie, Dan. I didn't touch it. We had that server go down, and that virus problem in Cleveland, and I just didn't get to it."

Jane grinned at him. "What, you didn't pull one of your patented all-nighters to be ready for today?"

"I could have, but I figured putting all that info in my head wouldn't do any good if my head was on the table all through the meeting."

After the chuckles died down, Marta broke in timidly, "Well, I read all of it, but it was slow going. Frankly, I didn't understand most of it." Across the table, Jane nodded in agreement.

"That's understandable, Marta," said Dan. "After all, application development isn't your area of expertise, nor is it Jane's, or even Tim's. That's why we're going to review some of the information as we go along." He turned to Bill. "On the other hand, Bill, development *is* your area, so it should have been an easier read for you. Were you able to get through it?"

"Scanned the whole thing Wednesday night," said Bill gruffly, opening his project notebook. "It looks to me like a lot of make-work. Putting out reams of paperwork doesn't make a program appear out of thin air. And another thing: I grant you that RMS is important, but it's not really *big* as applications go. Why are we doing all this planning work when we could just cut to the chase and crank the thing out?"

Before Dan could respond, Marilou jumped in. "Oh, you're just grumpy because you're planning on taking off early today, and you're afraid all this planning work

FERGUSON AND BARDELL
ENGINEERING • ARCHITECTURE • PROJECT MANAGEMENT

The RMS Project
Meeting Agenda

Meeting Date: April 9, 1999   **Purpose:** Planning 1

I.   Agenda Building

II.   Overview of Planning Phase
- Design Phase
- Functional Specification
- Master Project Plan
- Master Project Schedule

III.   Overview of Design Process
- Conceptual Design
- Logical Design
- Physical Design

IV.   Conceptual Design for RMS

V.   Q&A

VI.   Wrap-Up: Path-Forward Assignments

CHICAGO • DETROIT • MILWAUKEE • CINCINNATI • INDIANAPOLIS • LOUISVILLE

is going to cut down on your fishing time." Bill asked how she knew he was leaving early. "Because when I pulled into the parking garage," Marilou answered, "There was your big blue truck with a fishing boat taking up five parking spaces!"

Everyone laughed except Bill, who looked sheepish. Tim leaned over and said, "She got you again, old man."

"That's OK, Bill. If we work hard, we should play hard too." Dan said, "I've seen your car here before mine most mornings, and after mine most evenings. When we get done here, go catch a few for me." He walked to the whiteboard. "Bill has raised some important questions, though, and I think we ought to consider them for a moment before we look at the planning materials." As he drew the MSF Development Process Model on the board, he said, "Bill's right—we could skip some of the MSF work and probably get the RMS application out the door sooner. So why am I insisting we do this project 'by the book'? Because we have some much bigger projects in the pipeline, ones that absolutely require a framework like MSF. I don't want to introduce MSF on one of those because of the risk of failure. I want a high-profile, quick-hit win for MSF so that everyone understands its value and buys into it as the way Ferguson and Bardell does development. This project fits that bill perfectly. So even though it may be overkill, we're going to walk the MSF process step by step, both to learn it ourselves and to sell it to the rest of the organization."

"Like Jim Stewart?" asked Tim, devouring a doughnut.

"Like Jim, and Bill's development team, and the head of engineering, and any number of other people who are watching this project closely. They know what we've promised, and they are watching to see if we make it. I want them to know that they can make a request of the IT department and get a response in a reasonable amount of time. I also want them to understand, through their interactions with Jane, Marilou, and Marta, just what a reasonable time frame truly is. I want this project to have some ROI other than the benefits of the project itself."

Dan turned back to the board and drew a triangle beside the model diagram. "There's another reason we're going to do this exactly by the book, and that is its impact on Ferguson and Bardell's enterprise architecture." He wrote *EA* inside the triangle and drew a looping arrow between the triangle and the model. "The work we do for this project is based in part on our enterprise architecture. In the end, though, the architecture will be changed by our work. So, the two are interactive in an ongoing, dynamic way." He wrote the word *documentation* on top of the arrow and turned to Bill. "That's one of the reasons for the paper work. The artifacts we produce during the RMS project will be incorporated into the documentation of our EA."

"I've been hearing about EA," said Marilou. "Someone was saying that that smart-aleck Kevin Kennedy was working on a project to create our enterprise architecture. As if his ego needed any boosting."

Ignoring the personal commentary, Dan replied, "The rumor mill has it only partly right, Marilou. You don't *create* an enterprise architecture, because it already exists on its own. What Kevin and the others on that team are doing is *documenting* our existing EA and planning the next revision of it. The RMS project is related to their planning, and they will incorporate the output of our Planning Phase into their work. In addition, we will be coordinating with them later in the process."

Dan moved back to the table and sat down. "There are two keys to not getting bogged down in planning and documentation in MSF. The first is *balance*. You want to cover all the bases at a level of detail that is appropriate to the scope and importance of the project. The bigger or more important the project, the more planning and documentation you need to do.

"The second key is *scheduling*. At the beginning, we put together a tentative project schedule showing when we wanted to hit certain major milestones. By keeping our eyes on those deadlines, we keep ourselves from spending too much time on one step. We have to keep moving to hit those deadlines." Dan paused, then asked, "Is everyone OK with this? Do you understand why we have to do all the pieces of the Planning Phase?"

"Makes me feel like the neurotic in the old joke," said Jane. Seeing Dan's puzzlement, she continued, "My husband's a therapist, and he once asked me if I knew the difference between a psychotic and a neurotic. When I said 'No,' he told me that the psychotic says, 'Two plus two is five.' The neurotic says, 'Two plus two is four, but I don't like it!'" After the chuckles died down, Jane continued, "I'm like that neurotic. I understand why we have to do it, but I don't like it. It looks like a lot of work."

"It is, Jane," said Dan with a nod. "The Planning Phase is detailed, sometimes tedious work. It is also the key to the success of the project. The quality of the planning work we do directly affects the quality of the application we deliver."

"And the sooner we get going, the sooner my folks can start building that application," said Bill with a hint of impatience. "We're all convinced, Dan, even me. I'd rather be coding, but I see the need. So let's move to the next agenda item."

"Good idea, Bill," said Dan. They all refocused their attention as he changed the transparency. "Let's take a look, then, at what we've got in front of us."

Overview of the Planning Phase

"As you can see, the Planning Phase lies between the Envisioning and Developing Phases. The purpose of Planning is to take the common vision we built in Envisioning and transform it into concrete plans for Developing. It's one thing to say, 'We want an application that does thus-and-so.' It's another thing entirely to be able to say, 'And this is how we're going to build it.'

"To get from the vision to the plans, here is the process we will follow." The next transparency showed a flow chart. "First, we'll work our way through the MSF Design Process, which I'll talk about in a minute. The output of that work goes into the main deliverable for Planning, the Functional Specification. Based on the Functional Spec, we then develop a Master Project Plan and a Master Project Schedule. Those three documents—the Specification, the Plan, and the Schedule—drive the Developing Phase. Any questions so far?"

"So the Functional Spec is where we get down to the nitty-gritty detail of the application?" asked Marta.

"That's right," said Dan. "Only when we've agreed on that can we finalize our plans for the remainder of the project, and only after we've finalized our plans can we do the final schedule." He turned to a new page in his project notebook. "Does anyone remember where the plan and schedule come from?"

Marta and Marilou both began thumbing furiously through their notebooks, and Marta mumbled, "I seem to remember something about 'top-down versus bottom-up scheduling,' but I can't find it."

Tim leaned over to look at Dan's notebook, then leaned back toward Marta and stage-whispered, "Try page 56." He grinned at Dan as everyone else turned to the correct page, and Marta said triumphantly, "The project plan and schedule are a compilation of our individual plans and schedules."

"Exactly right," said Dan, smiling, "even if you did get help from the peanut gallery over here." He put a new transparency on the overhead. "Let's take a look at what each of you is supposed to focus on during this phase, and what plans and schedules you each deliver."

Role	Focus	Plan	Schedule
Product Management	Requirements gathering; in charge of conceptual design	Communications	Communications
Program Management	Overall design; in charge of logical design; Functional Spec	Master Project Plan	Master Project Schedule
Development	In charge of physical design; proof-of-concept work	Development	Development
User education	Analyzes user needs; user support plans; evaluate design for usability	User education and support; usability testing	User education and support; usability testing
Testing	Evaluate design for testability; methods and metrics for bug/ issue tracking	Testing; bug/issue tracking	Testing
Logistics	Evaluate design for deployability, manageability, supportability, and total cost of ownership	Deployment; support	Deployment; support

Dan explained the deliverables each of them was responsible for. "The final deliverable is a revision of the Master Risk Assessment Document, which we'll do toward the end. Any questions?"

Marta and Marilou raised their hands at almost the same time, but Marilou put hers down again. "I bet you're going to ask the same thing I am, so you go ahead." Marta turned to Dan. "Looking at these deliverables, I'm not sure I know how to pull this off. I'm not a developer. How do I evaluate the design for testability, for instance? And how does Marilou evaluate for support?"

"Good questions, Marta. The short answer is that I've got some extra material for both of you, along with some books for you to look through. I'll also be working with both of you individually, just as I have with Jane on her conceptual design work, which we'll see in a moment. And I'll give you the contact information for the people who filled these roles on the project at my old law firm. They said you could call them if you needed to."

Marilou gave a thumbs-up. "I figured you'd have planned ahead, Dan. Thanks!"

"Not a problem. Remember, I want you all to be successful. Now let's take a look at how we design an application."

Overview of the Design Process

Dan's next transparency showed a circle similar to the one in the MSF Development Process Model, except it had three sections instead of four. "This is the MSF Design Process. It has three parts: Conceptual Design, Logical Design, and Physical Design. The three parts are staggered, parallel processes. In other words, before we finish Conceptual Design, we can begin Logical Design and work on them in parallel. The three are also interrelated, which means that if we decide to change something in Logical Design, for example, we need to go through Conceptual Design again to make sure the change is reflected there."

"What are the differences between the three parts?" asked Marilou.

"There are a number of differences, but basically, they are three different ways of looking at the same application. Conceptual Design is from the viewpoint of the user, Logical Design is from the viewpoint of the project team, and Physical Design is from the viewpoint of the developers.

"Another difference is the level of abstraction. The MSF Design Process is sort of like morphing software. We take something concrete—the users' needs, wants, and ways of doing things—and put that in at one end of the process. As this input goes through the process, it becomes transformed into an intermediate step, Logical Design, which is fairly abstract. Then we take that abstract model and transform it back into something concrete and physical—the final application. As we move through this concrete-abstract-concrete process, we have to ensure that the two ends of the process correlate; in other words, every feature of the application that comes out of Physical Design should be traceable through Logical Design back to something in Conceptual Design, and vice versa."

Jane was shaking her head. "This is beginning to sound like some of the philosophy courses I had in college. I'm getting lost already, and we haven't even gotten to the hard stuff. How about an example?"

"OK. This will be greatly simplified, but perhaps it will give us all a better grasp of the concepts involved. Let's take a small task that we should all do every day: backing up our data files. Jane, you do this manually. Tell us what you do."

Jane looked at Tim, somewhat embarrassed. "It's not because I don't trust your backups, Tim. When it comes to money and accounting, I'm just a belt-and-suspenders kind of gal."

Tim tried to look hurt. "I'm devastated. Hmm…think I'll drown my sorrows in another doughnut."

Jane laughed and then turned to Dan. "Well, it's pretty simple, really. I open up the data folder for our accounting package, sort by date, and copy all the files changed today to my Zip drive. Then I take the disk home with me."

"OK," said Dan as he made some notes. "Remember that in the conceptual part of the Design Process, we see the application from the viewpoint of the user. We do this by creating use cases and scenarios to describe everything the user does and how they do it. Later on, we'll see how use cases and scenarios interact. For now, let's describe Jane's backup process so that we can write an application to do it for her."

"Are we going to do a batch file, or a Visual Basic app, or what?" said Tim.

"At this point, we don't know and don't care," said Dan. "The choice of technology comes much later." He went to the whiteboard. "OK, someone take a shot at describing what Jane does."

Marta raised her hand. "It sounds like a two-step process: First she selects the files, and then she copies them to the Zip disk."

"You're leaving out a step," Bill said. "How does she select the files?"

"By date, of course," said Marta. "Oh, I see. She already knows the date, but the application would have to get it. So, we need to add an earlier step to get the date."

"Good." Dan added the step on the board. "Now, would everyone agree that this is a fairly accurate description of the application from the user's viewpoint?" Everyone nodded. "Since we agree, we can move on to Logical Design. If this application were larger, we might continue doing conceptual work on other bits of it. However, even though we were still working on Conceptual Design, as soon as we finished a description, we would send it on to Logical."

He erased the whiteboard. "Our job in Logical Design is to turn the descriptions we get from Conceptual Design into abstract entities called *objects*. We also need to discover what *services* are needed, what *attributes* are needed, and what the *relationships* are among the various services. You'll find definitions of these in your materials." While the rest of the team studied the definitions, Dan drew some boxes on the board and turned back to the group. "Now that you know what entities we're looking for, tell me some of the objects you see in our example."

"There are the files themselves," said Marta, drawing on her notepad as she spoke. "And the files have a Date Modified attribute that we're going to need."

Marilou added, "There's the User object, although I can't think of any services or attributes to go with it. There's the Get Date service. And, somewhere we're going to have to have a Copy Files service, but I can't figure out what object it belongs with."

Dan continued drawing on the board. "That's OK, Marilou. As you'll see in a moment, sometimes we create objects simply to hold the services we need." He finished what he was doing, then turned to the group. "Any other candidate objects or services?"

Bill had been sketching continuously since the discussion had begun. "It seems to me there are some other objects and services that are implied by the use cases we wrote," he said. "For example, the files themselves are part of a larger data store called the *file system*, which has its own services and attributes. Also, we need a Select Files service before we can use the Copy Files service. And what about error checking in case there's no disk in the drive, or something to make sure the files copied completely?"

Dan added Bill's descriptions to the board. "All excellent points, Bill. One of the steps in Logical Design is to discover any implied objects or services, which you've helped us to do. Now, let's take a moment to trace the use cases to the objects we've described and make sure we've covered everything."

The team spent a few minutes cleaning up the diagram, including drawing object boxes to hold some of the "orphan" services. They then drew arrows to show the flow of the application and to make sure their diagram worked properly. Finally, Dan said, "Does everyone understand, roughly, how the Logical model comes from the Conceptual model?" The team members nodded, so he continued.

"OK, at this point we're ready to move into Physical Design. Now we identify possible technologies for the application and consider their tradeoffs. The tradeoffs come from the differences between the physical requirements of the application and the physical constraints posed by the enterprise architecture and the current technologies. Who's got a candidate technology for our BJF application?"

"BJF?" asked Tim.

"Backup Jane's Files. We seem to run to acronyms for project names around here, so I wanted to be consistent. How about it, folks? What should we use to write this massive, enterprise app?"

Marilou spoke up immediately. "I vote for Visual Basic."

"Too much overhead," said Bill. "I'd do it with a batch file, preferably using 4DOS, which is a command.com substitute. It allows you to choose files by date within a batch file using a single command."

"Close, but no cigar, Old Man of the Sea," said Tim, grinning. "Batch file is the right track, but it needs more error-checking than 4DOS can give you, at least without going far out of your way. Besides, 4DOS isn't approved technology here. WinBatch is. It gives you a true Windows application, it's simple to write, it's easy to debug, and it can even be compiled!"

"Sounds like a winner," said Dan. "Tim's considered the tradeoffs, *and* he's locked into the enterprise architecture. What do you think, Bill?"

"I've never heard of this WinBatch, but if it does what he says, I agree it's probably the best candidate." Bill turned to Tim. "What I want to know, though, is how you know so much about it!"

"I use it all the time for automating little tasks around the office; been using it for years." Tim grinned. "Just because your folks have "Programmer" in their title, doesn't mean you're the only ones who know how to program! Some of us used to dabble in it, 'til we saw the light." He ducked as Bill's paper napkin whizzed over his head.

Dan laughed. "OK, Bill, don't wipe out our Network Manager. We might need him some day." Turning to Jane and Marta, who had been observing the technology discussion with bemused expressions, he said, "I know this may have been hard to follow, but don't let that worry you. Remember, Physical Design is from the viewpoint of the Development team, so they have to take the lead in working through the candidate technologies. When we come to Physical Design in RMS, I'll have some high-level material for you both so that you can follow the discussions and prepare your own deliverables."

Dan erased the whiteboard. "At this point, if we were really building the BJF app, we'd finalize the Physical model and then use it to complete the Functional Specification. Finally, we'd ask Development to do a project plan and a project schedule, then each of us would do our own project plan and schedule based on the one from Development. We'd put them all together, work out any conflicts or issues, meet with the customer to finalize and approve them, and we'd be done with the Planning Phase and ready to begin the developing Phase. Any questions or comments?"

Marta held up her hand and ticked off the steps. "Conceptual, Logical, Physical, Functional Spec, Project Plan, Project Schedule, done. Is that it?"

"Don't forget the revision of the Risk Assessment Document," added Jane.

"Got it," said Marta.

Conceptual Design

"Moving right along," said Dan, looking at his agenda. "In some cases, the design process can take weeks or even months. For RMS, we're going to try to complete it in three meetings. Today, we've got to complete Conceptual Design to stay on schedule. Fortunately," he continued, as Jane stood up, "Jane has done some of the work ahead of time, so we have a good chance at completing this today."

Jane passed out stacks of papers to each team member. "The first step under Conceptual Design is research, which includes key processes and activities, as well as user profiles. I gathered this information and tried to organize it as best I could." She sat back down. "The second step is analysis, which involves reviewing the research information and coming up with scenarios to cover all the use cases discovered in the research step, as well as descriptions of other data, like the physical environment in which the process takes place. I've tried to write the scenarios, but I'm sure they need some refinement."

"Wow, Jane, this is a bunch of work!" exclaimed Tim. "You've sure saved us a lot of time."

"Marilou helped, especially with the user profiles," said Jane.

Dan flipped through the well-organized documents. "You both deserve a big thanks. When I started you on this a few weeks ago, I had no idea you'd be able to take the work this far. Excellent job." Jane and Marilou both smiled.

"OK, folks, let's dig into this." The team spent the next 45 minutes working through the material and finalizing the scenarios. At the end of that time, Dan said, "That's the last one—I think we're done," and everyone sat back, relaxing.

Finally Marta said, "I hate to mention this, since it seems as if we're at a stopping point, but isn't there another step in Conceptual Design? Something about optimization?"

Dan nodded. "Yes, there is. I'm sitting here, debating whether or not to do it now. Let me describe it, and then you can tell me if you think there is more work to do." Briefly, he explained the optimization step. "Do any of the scenarios need optimization?" he asked. "In other words, do you want to do a future-state version in addition to the current-state scenario we just completed?"

For a moment, no one spoke. Then Tim said, "Well, the only one I can think of is the one for generating a time sheet. I think the current process is unwieldy, and it could be much better. If RMS doesn't deal with that, I think most people will see it as a failure."

Bill nodded. "Let's do it now, folks. Better now while the use cases are still fresh." The team spent another 20 minutes working through not only the time sheet scenario, but also the scenarios for resource assignment and invoice printing.

Dan asked for the tenth time, "Any more changes?" No one spoke up. "Alright, then, we're done with that for now." Dan pushed himself up from his chair and moved to the credenza.

"What do you mean, for now? Will we have to come back and do this again?" said Tim, his voice rising slightly.

"I doubt that we will on this project, Tim," said Dan as he laid out stacks of material on the credenza. "RMS isn't that complex, even though it *is* important. But there is always the possibility that we'll learn something later that will force us to come back and redo this part. If we have to, we have to. Remember, we'd rather spend the time getting it right in the Planning Phase than starting over Developing or Stabilizing." Dan finished putting out material and turned to the group. "Here's your reading material for the weekend. It explains Logical Design and Physical Design in greater detail. Be sure to read it before Monday morning's meeting. And for those of you who haven't yet read the first set, you need to read that, too, just so you're on the same page as the rest of us." He looked pointedly at Tim.

"It's going to be a long weekend," sighed Tim, putting his head down on the table.

"Not for me," said Bill, standing to gather his things. "I'm going *fishing*." He patted Tim on the shoulder as he moved to the credenza to pick up his material. "I'll just prop that pole on the transom, prop my feet on the rail, and read this stuff while I catch my limit."

"Sounds like a plan, Chief," said Dan, handing material to the others as they left. "By the way, don't forget our meeting Monday afternoon with the EA team."

"I can't hardly wait—and I hope you caught the double negative."

"I see he's met Kevin Kennedy," said Marilou to Jane as they walked out of the room.

Logical Design

Dan spent much of the weekend preparing for the Monday morning meeting. When the team members began arriving, they found a new stack of papers at their places, along with new binders. Fresh coffee and doughnuts were already in place on the credenza.

"I know somebody who was busy this weekend, and he wasn't catching fish," said Marilou as she sat down and looked over the papers.

"Yes, I put in some extra hours this weekend," said Dan as he filled his coffee cup and sat down. "I wanted to get us ready to move into the Logical Design step, and that meant doing some preliminary work on the objects and services."

"I came in Saturday afternoon to pick up something," said Marta as she handed Tim a doughnut. "Was that your car I saw in the parking lot?"

"Yes, but I wasn't here for RMS," replied Dan, quietly. "We had an executive management team meeting." Everyone looked up at the tone in Dan's voice, but he was busy moving some papers from his old binder to the new one and didn't see the questioning looks.

"The new binders," said Dan, "are for your MSF materials. I thought it might make more sense to keep them separate from the project materials. You'll eventually want to file the RMS folder away, but I hope you'll keep the MSF binder handy for other projects."

Everyone took a few moments to shift papers back and forth between the two binders. While they were doing that, Jane leaned over to Marilou and said in a low voice, "When we get done here, come by my office. Have I got some news for you!"

"What's up?" said Marilou. "It'd better not be more gossip about Jeff over in Legal."

"No, this is something else. Got an e-mail right before I came to the meeting."

"Everyone done?" asked Dan. "OK, open your MSF notebook, and let's take a brief look at the Logical Design step, which is our entire agenda for today." Everyone turned to the new Logical tab in their binder while Dan wrote *Analysis* and *Rationalization* on the whiteboard.

FERGUSON AND BARDELL
ENGINEERING • ARCHITECTURE • PROJECT MANAGEMENT

The RMS Project
Meeting Agenda

Meeting Date: April 12, 1999   **Purpose:** Planning 2

I.   Agenda Building

II.   Logical Design for RMS
        • Analysis
        • Rationalization

III.   Q&A

IV.   Wrap-Up: Path-Forward Assignments

CHICAGO • DETROIT • MILWAUKEE • CINCINNATI • INDIANAPOLIS • LOUISVILLE

"Alright," he said, turning to the group. "We don't have a research step in Logical Design like we did in Conceptual Design. Can anyone tell me why?"

"Because we use the output of Conceptual Design as the input to Logical Design, so we don't need to do any research," said Tim, leaning back in his chair.

"Bravo, Tim," said Dan. "I'm glad to see you covered the material this weekend."

"Well, a few of us formed a study team," said Tim, smiling a little broader. "Always makes it easier when you study in teams."

Knowing that Tim and Bill were good friends, Dan wondered how much studying they had done between casts. However, he kept his thoughts to himself and continued, "Tim's right, everyone. We take the work we did Friday on the conceptual model and use it as the basis for our analysis step. The goal is to identify all the objects, services, attributes, and relationships, both explicit and implicit. Does everybody remember the definitions of those terms from our work last week? Then turn to the materials I prepared over the weekend, and let's get started."

The group worked hard for a little over an hour, thankful for Dan's advance effort on the logical model. When they stopped, Jane said, "That wasn't as bad as I thought it would be. Are we really finished?"

"Not yet, Jane." Dan moved to the whiteboard. "We've done a good job defining our objects and services, but there is one more step. We need to assign the services to layers. After we do that, we may want to redo some of the objects or services."

"I knew it was too easy," moaned Tim.

"Are these the 'user-business-data' layers that were in the material, Dan?" asked Marta. "I don't really see the purpose of them. Why split your application into pieces like that?"

"To deal with problems of flexibility, scalability, and reuse, like the ones we identified in RMS a few meetings ago," said Bill before Dan could answer. He walked to the board, picked up a marker, and asked Dan, "May I?"

Somewhat surprised, Dan nevertheless stepped back. "Absolutely, Chief. Go for it."

Bill spent about 10 minutes explaining N-tier development, including a brief explanation of packaging objects and services into components. "So you see, N-tier has so many advantages that we have decided as a company to write all our applications this way, even stand-alone ones."

"You mean that even if an application is going to run on only one machine with its own local database, you still write it using multi-layer principles?" asked Marta.

"Almost always," said Bill. "It gives you so much more flexibility. For example, you write a simple application for a single user that uses a VB front end against a local Access database. The specs clearly say that the app is never going to be multi-user and the data set is never going to grow beyond a certain size. After you deliver it, though, other users see it and want their own copy, or they want access to the same data. Before you know it, you've got 10 or 20 users, and the data set has grown way too big for Access. If you write it properly using multi-layer, it's a fairly simple thing to change the data services so that they point to SQL Server.

"One of the best features, though, is that you can design different front ends that hit the same business and data services. For example, you can have both a Win32 client and a Web-based client working with a single set of business services. The Web-based client is especially appealing because it's easy to deploy. You put the necessary pieces on your Web server, and the first time a user accesses the page, the necessary components are downloaded to their machine and registered automatically. No more walking from machine to machine to install software 800 times, or even messing with automatic software installers. The time savings can be phenomenal in an organization as large and dispersed as ours."

"Wow," thought Dan, "The Chief has been doing some big-time reading." Out loud he said, "Bill, it sounds to me as if you have made a real commitment to MSF."

"Not necessarily to MSF, Dan," said Bill with a tight smile. "I'm still in wait-and-see mode on that. But I started studying multi-layer and components about a year ago when I ran across an old COBOL buddy and asked him what he was doing. He told me he was doing multi-layer applications using Microsoft technologies, and all I could do was grunt and say something inane like 'That's nice.' I realized the development world was passing me by—and not only me, but also all the folks under me. I decided it was time to learn some new tricks so that I could teach them to the rest of the crew. Turns out many of them were way ahead of me and just waiting for me to catch on. I talked with them about doing multi-layer on RMS back during the kick-off, and they convinced me that it was time to make the switch. We've been doing a few smaller things in multi-layer over the last six months, but this is the first major application we've done this way. So, Dan, I would say I am absolutely committed to multi-layer development and to the Microsoft methodology for doing it. As for MSF, this old sea dog is still trying to decide if it's a wonderful new bone or simply bilge."

Everyone laughed, including Dan. "Well, Chief, you'll never be accused of hiding your feelings. That's fine; I think you'll come around before we're through. Let me say for now, though, that you just gave an excellent overview of multilayer development. Thanks."

Jane nodded as Bill went back to his chair. "He's right, Bill. Even *I* understand it. Maybe you should have been a teacher."

"Nah," said Bill, smiling. "They don't let you go fishing on Fridays."

"All right, everyone, Bill has pointed the way. Let's take our earlier work and finish for today by putting things into layers." The team worked for another 30 minutes, moving objects and services into user, business, and data layers. As Dan had suspected, they had to change some items slightly, and a few items had to be split into two new objects for different layers.

Finally, Dan said, "I think that's got it. Now, let's verify our work by doing some walk-throughs. Start at the user layer and see if we can carry out all the use cases using the objects and services we've designed." After the team had walked through all the use cases, Dan sat back. "Good work, all. I think this is a good working version. It may change some as we get into Physical Design, but for now, we're done."

He stood up. "I'll get these drawn up nicely this afternoon and e-mail them to you by tomorrow morning. Bill and the other developers are meeting this afternoon with the EA team, and we'll begin work on the Physical Design then. The rest of you need to be prepared on Wednesday with draft versions of your parts of the Functional Spec, Project Plan, and a tentative schedule. We'll send you a development schedule to use after we meet this afternoon. Any questions? No? Then, Bill, I'll see you and Beth and Sam this afternoon at 2, and I'll see the rest of you on Wednesday morning."

Development and EA Team Meeting

When Dan came into the conference room, he was struck by the seating arrangement. The EA team was on one side, and Bill and his two developers were on the other. "Looks like disarmament talks of some sort—which is not a bad comparison," Dan thought to himself as he took his place at the head of the table.

"Hope everyone's lunch was satisfactory, and that you are all ready to work together on this," he said as he opened his notebook. "Has everyone looked through the materials I sent around last week?"

"I sure did, and there's something I just don't understand," said Bill, obviously irritated. "We've been busting our tails on the RMS project team, but it seems like the EA team is setting our IT direction. Before you came in, Mr. Kennedy here was telling us about all the great new technologies we're going to implement at Ferguson and Bardell. Since when does someone from Long-Range Planning dictate our technology choices?"

Before Dan could answer, and before Kevin Kennedy could open his mouth, Richard Kaplan said in a calm voice, "Now, Bill, don't act so surprised. I've been sending you weekly updates on the work of the EA team, so what Kevin said shouldn't have come as a shock. As for Kevin, he sometimes likes to assume airs, but that doesn't mean we should discount either his intelligence or his contributions. If we all take a look at the agenda, we'll see that this meeting is about the mutual feedback loop explained in the materials Dan sent around." Although Dick's words were fairly blunt, neither Bill nor Kevin seemed offended. In fact, they both looked somewhat sheepish.

"As usual, Dick has brought us to a moment of clarity," said Dan. "Our purpose here is not to endorse one team's views over the other's. As we used to say in graduate school, the work of both teams should be *informed* by the work of the other team. The EA team has spent the past six weeks putting together an excellent first cut at both documenting our current EA state and at planning the high-priority projects for the coming year. As you might expect, RMS is one of those projects. So before we complete the design process for RMS, we need to synchronize the two efforts. That is the purpose of our meeting today."

"Frankly, Bill, because the RMS project is so important, it may have more impact on us than we on it," said Jo Brown. "We've seen in our research into other companies how high-priority projects have a tendency to reshape a company's EA."

"Yes, but even if that's the case here, we still want to validate the direction of the RMS project against the stated business direction of Ferguson and Bardell," said Kevin. "Ultimately, what we build for RMS should fit into the long-range plans of the company." He looked at Dan. "Don't worry, Dan. I haven't forgotten the two-way information flow you've been pounding into my head." Kevin turned to Bill. "Our technology plans and discoveries have to be part of the input to our business plans, as well."

Bill shook his head. "I never thought I'd hear someone on the business side say something like that." He smiled wryly at Kevin. "I guess there's hope for you after all." Kevin just laughed. "Some would not agree with you, Bill, but thanks for the vote of confidence, anyway."

Dan was glad to see signs of willingness to cooperate and was grateful to Dick Kaplan for his influence. "OK, folks, now that we've established the relationship between our two teams, let's get going on the agenda. First, I'd like the EA folks to share the highlights of their individual perspectives that might relate to the RMS project."

FERGUSON AND BARDELL
ENGINEERING • ARCHITECTURE • PROJECT MANAGEMENT

The RMS Project
Meeting Agenda

Meeting Date: April 12, 1999   **Purpose:** Sync of EA and RMS

I.   Agenda Building

II.   F-BEAP Highlights
- Business
- Application
- Information
- Technology

III.   RMS Project Highlights

IV.   Coordination and Recommendations

V.   Q&A

VI.   Wrap-Up: Path-Forward Assignments

CHICAGO • DETROIT • MILWAUKEE • CINCINNATI • INDIANAPOLIS • LOUISVILLE

The four EA team members took a few minutes each to point out findings or plans that they felt could have an impact on RMS. Bill, Sam, and Beth took notes and asked questions, and a lively discussion ensued. Jo told them that the RMS project was already a key component of their plans for the year, and that a project to build a training and skills tracking system might begin after RMS was complete. Sam noted that tying into the training and skills system might be a good feature for RMS Version 2.

Jenny Sax discussed the company's intention to narrow its approved technologies list to decrease support and training costs. She also mentioned that a pilot group was working with Windows 2000, but that it wouldn't be deployed across the enterprise until well into the fall of 2000, if then.

Beth turned to Sam. "Do we need any COM+ features for RMS Version 1? Do we need Windows 2000 sooner for either Version 1 or Version 2?"

Sam shook his head. "It might make certain parts of the business layer easier, but not enough to change the deployment schedule for Windows 2000. We can make do with what we have, and simply rewrite those components whenever we get 2000 deployed and stable."

Dick talked about some of the information gaps he had discovered. "One of the key gaps is good scheduling and resource information. In fact, almost every project and department manager has complained about the inability to match resources and projects across the enterprise. I'd say there are a number of people hoping RMS is going to take care of that." He pulled a packet of papers from his bag and passed them over to the development team. "As part of my work, I've put together a proposed data model and dictionary for Ferguson and Bardell. It's not completely approved yet, but I thought you might want to look at it and see if it is in agreement with your work on RMS."

The three developers looked over the data documentation sheets. "Dick, this is great!" Beth exclaimed. "There's a lot of overlap, but you've thought of some fields we hadn't considered. We'll take a look at this more closely later, and I'll send you our comments."

"Kevin, what about the business direction?" asked Dan. "What key strategic plans does the RMS team need to know about?"

"The biggest one is expansion," said Kevin as he shared his own handouts. He pointed to the first bullet point. "As you can see, we're going to go from six offices to ten over the next 18 months. We're also going to add approximately 250 people, which is more than a 30-percent increase in staff."

"Wow! That's some growth rate," exclaimed Sam. "And all those folks will be doing time sheets, right? That certainly changes some things—or at least, locks in some plans we were already considering." He looked at Beth and Bill, who both nodded.

"That sounds like a good transition to the next item on the agenda," said Dan. "What does the RMS team have to share with the EA team? Bill, why don't you take some time to bring the EA folks up to speed on the RMS project and the technologies you are considering."

Bill outlined the various design paths the development team was considering, including the question of whether to use Win32 clients or Web clients. The EA team spent some time asking questions, trying to be sure they understood the implications of various decisions on their EA work. Finally Dan said, "It sounds to me as if both teams understand each other's work pretty well. Let's move on to coordination and recommendations." He turned to the development team. "What have you heard from the EA folks that has an impact on your design choices?"

"I think the biggest impact will come from the expansion plans Kevin talked about earlier," said Sam. "In our original design work, we were planning on no more than 300 concurrent users. We thought that was a safe number, given the time differences between the offices and the fact that people update their time sheets throughout Friday and Monday. That left the options open between a Web client and a Win32 client. Now, with the number of concurrent users shoved up another 100 to 200, I think we've got to go with a strictly Web client, keeping as much functionality as possible on the application servers to minimize network traffic."

"But Sam," said Dan, frowning, "if I remember correctly, some of the most important functionality for the managers was in the Win32 client, and you hadn't put it into the Web client. In fact, a few of the features strike me as being fairly difficult to pull off in a Web client. Won't doing a pure Web client increase your development time?" Sam and Beth both nodded, and the group fell silent as they considered the dilemma. Dick Kaplan stopped doodling on his legal pad. "Do you have the Logical Design with you?" he asked Bill.

Bill tapped his bag. "Sure, it's right here. Why?"

"Let me see it a minute," Dick said. Bill passed it across the table, and Dick studied it for a minute. Then he looked at the group. "I think I see a way we can get off the horns of this dilemma." He laid the drawings out on the table for the EA team to see. "These drawings are representations of the various functions of the RMS application. Look first at the user services, then the business services, and finally the data services, and tell me if anything strikes you."

The group, including Bill, Beth, and Sam, spent some moments looking over the various drawings in silence. Finally, Jo said, "I'm not a developer, but from what I can tell, it almost looks like two separate applications using a common database."

"What do you mean?" asked Beth.

Jo picked up the drawings and rearranged them on the table. "See? This set over here is all concerned with entering time, verifying the time entered, submitting time, and approving the timesheet." She pointed to the second group of drawings. "And these are all about resources: knowing their skills, assigning them to projects, and checking on their availability." She stood up and folded her arms. "There's some common data, obviously, because in both instances we're working with the same resources and the same projects. But the purposes seem separate." Dick slowly nodded his head as he listened to the discussion with his eyes closed.

Suddenly Sam snapped his fingers. "That's it!" He turned to Bill and Beth. "We build *both* clients! A Web client for time entry for everybody, and a Win32 client for just the managers. Most of the managers are in the office when they assign resources, anyway, and there's a limited number of them." He was getting more excited as the pieces fell into place in his mind. "And we can use Transaction Server with it, to make sure that the time sheets get across even if the server is clogged up."

Sam seemed pleased with the vision he had just articulated, but Bill was aghast. "*Two* clients? I wasn't even sure we could get one done in time, and now you want to do two? There is no way we can hit the deadlines that way!"

"Sure there is, Bill!" Beth said. "If we split the services up like that, we can divide the work along both tiers and clients and work in parallel. Some of the other people in the department want to work on this project, anyway. We can get more done in less time, *and* meet our scalability requirements as well!"

Looking dubious, Bill turned to Dan. "What do you think?"

"I think it might work, Bill. I like the idea of the single-purpose Web client, and it will be easier to write. As for the parallel development effort—that's a management problem, not a technical one. I know a pretty good development manager who's probably up to the task."

Bill could see that Beth and Sam were excited about the solution, and he threw up his hands in mock surrender. "Alright, alright—we'll try it! But if it doesn't work, we write it my way: terminal emulation and assembler language." Everyone laughed.

"Remember, Bill, the Planning Phase can include proof of concept work, said Dan. "It might be worthwhile to have a certain pair of eager-beaver programmers put something together before committing completely to the two-client concept. No fancy interface, not fully functional; just something showing the effect of that many Web clients on our servers."

"Can you two do that?" asked Bill. They looked at each other and then nodded.

"Good, then that's a plan. And a good example of letting our company's enterprise architecture inform our development work." Dan turned to the EA team. "What about you four? Is there anything that the RMS development team has shared that you'll need to consider as you wrap up your EA work?"

Jenny nodded. "Absolutely. For one thing, we have been considering whether or not to make a stronger commitment to our intranet. It's served some good purposes, but it needs to be more than a source of static information. We have been debating whether it made sense to move some of our business processes onto the intranet, and I'd say that decision is now made. Our task is going to be identifying other candidates for that technology."

Kevin added, "Another area the long-range planning group has been looking at is expanding our service area even further outside our offices. In fact, we're looking at a national advertising campaign in about nine months. One of the concerns we've had, though, is connectivity issues involved with having that many people on the road. Jenny and Tim have already worked with us, showing us various ways we might deal with these issues. I think this meeting today has helped us to see we need to consider not only the pipes, but also what runs across those pipes. I, for one, am much more confident in the ability of our IT group to come up with creative solutions to business needs."

"Kevin, I think that's the nicest thing I've ever heard you say about a group you weren't part of!" said Jo with a sly grin. "We need to get you away from the CEO more often." The room got quiet as everyone waited to see how Kevin would take such a jab, but he said simply, "Sometimes a fast-tracker needs to do some growing to stay on the fast track." The few appreciative murmurs made Kevin smile.

Dan waited a moment, before continuing. "I think this has been a productive meeting for both teams. The EA team will be wrapping up Version 1.0 of the EA plan for Ferguson and Bardell in about a week, and I'm sure they would like to see the Functional Spec for RMS when it is done. Before we finish, are there any questions or comments?"

Dick Kaplan had been staring into space for the past few minutes, seemingly oblivious to the conversation of the others. Now he looked at Dan. "I'd like to meet with you and the development team after we're done, if the four of you have a moment. I've got an idea that might be helpful for the RMS work."

"Can you three stay for moment?" Dan asked Bill. All three nodded. "Good. If no one has anything else, we're adjourned."

As the rest of the EA team gathered up their things to leave, Dick joined Dan and the developers, who were standing together discussing the idea of two clients. "OK, Dick, we're all ears," Dan said. "You've already helped us with your insight into the work flows of RMS. What else have you got?"

Dick turned to Beth. "What were you considering for your back-end data store?"

"SQL Server, of course," she said. "That's the corporate standard."

Dick shook his head. "I think you should reconsider. There's a better choice for the application you have in mind."

"Dick, I know you're not as committed to the Microsoft product mix as the rest of us, but I'm not going to let another database in the door." Bill was slightly irritated. "I just got rid of the last dBase III application four months ago. We standardized on SQL Server for a number of good reasons, and I don't want another database that I have to train for, program for, and support."

"Bill, you're not hearing what I am saying," Dick said calmly. "I didn't say anything about another database. I said you should consider another data store. There's a difference."

Bill was getting visibly irritated. "Dick, you're talking in riddles again. Stop being the Socratic professor and spit it out."

Dan interrupted. "He's right, though, Bill—there is a difference. We tend to think of databases as the only place to store data, but it's too narrow a concept. We store data in file systems, e-mail, scanned documents, the Internet, any number of places that are not traditional databases."

"Exactly," said Dick. He turned to Beth and Sam. "What three primary data elements are common across both application threads in RMS?"

Sam and Beth answered almost simultaneously, "Resources, projects, and time."

Dick nodded and continued, "And what data store do we already have in place that everyone has access to and that already deals with people and time?"

Dan and the developers thought for a moment. Suddenly Sam said, "Exchange! Our Exchange server stores every user and their calendar!"

"I think you might consider Exchange as one of your data stores for RMS," said Dick, "especially when you add in its ability to replicate across the enterprise, and the fairly rich set of objects and services it exposes."

"Not to mention its integration with Web technologies," said Dan. "Excellent suggestion, Dick. You're two for two today."

Bill's initial irritation had melted during this conversation. "I didn't realize you know so much about day-to-day programming issues, Dick," he said as the group moved out of the conference room.

"Each of us has abilities and interests that are hidden, just as one side of an object is hidden when you look at the other side," said Dick calmly. "No one can know another person completely. Don't worry about it."

They had arrived at Dick's office door. Bill asked, as if on an impulse, "Do you keep a copy of your dissertation in your office? If so, I'd like to borrow it. It sounds like it might be interesting reading."

"I never would have thought of you as someone interested in Kant," Dan said in surprise.

"I think the man said something about hidden interests and abilities. Besides," Bill continued, "I hear Kant was a killer fisherman."

Physical Design

Bill and the rest of the development team spent most of Tuesday working through the Physical Design process, trying to get a working document ready for the RMS team meeting on Wednesday. Dan was with them at the beginning of the day but got called away by Jim Stewart at about 10:30.

After lunch, Dan stopped by the small conference room in the development team area where Bill and the others were still working. "So, how's it coming?"

"Pretty well, actually." Bill replied. "We've got two data stores defined—SQL Server and Exchange. We've worked out their data elements and normalized as much as possible. Most of the components are sketched out, along with their interface contracts. We're working on packaging now."

"What about deployment strategies?" asked Dan.

Sam looked up from his laptop. "We've got some ideas, but we want to test the prototypes a bit more before we commit to a final deployment plan."

"You have new prototypes?"

Bill nodded. "Yes. Sam and Beth stayed late last night to write some quick-and-dirty proof-of-concept applications, and we're using some of their work in our planning."

"Wow, I'm impressed," said Dan. "Think you'll have something for us tomorrow? How about a schedule?"

Beth grinned. "Oh, we'll have something, all right. *What* we'll have is another question."

"As for the schedule," Bill added, "I've been working on that with input from Sam and Beth, and I'm afraid I've got some bad news, Dan. We just don't see how we can make that tentative deadline we set in the Envisioning Phase."

"Even with the buffer time?" asked Dan.

Bill nodded. "Even with the buffer time, and even with some pretty fancy footwork around parallel development paths. The two clients, the two data stores, the integration with the accounting package to do the invoice work—it's just too much to pull off in that time. We'll need another month, at least."

Dan looked as if he'd been hit in the stomach. "Just what I needed to hear after my meeting this morning," he thought grimly. He took a deep breath. "Bill, I told you and the team we will practice bottom-up scheduling. If you and your people say that the current feature set will take an extra month, then I'll back you up. We'll just have to tell the customer and the users that to get the feature set they want, they'll have to wait. I just have one question: Is the one month firm, or do you really need two?"

The three developers looked at one another for a moment. Then Sam said, "It's firm, Dan. Our prototypes haven't turned up any problems that are showstoppers. One month."

Dan nodded. "I'll count on it." he said quietly and walked away.

"What's with him?" said Sam to Bill. "I've never seen Dan look like that."

Bill gave a noncommittal grunt, but he, too, wondered what was wrong. "Guess we'll find out tomorrow morning," he thought, and turned back to the calendar sheets in front of him.

The next morning found the RMS team in their usual chairs, waiting. Dan's car was in the parking garage, and his office light was on, but he was nowhere to be found. Finally, at 8:15, just as Tim was dialing Dan's pager for the second time, the CIO came into the conference room with notebooks in his hands and a frown on his face. He put his notebooks down and then sat and stared at the others for a moment.

When Tim said, in a cheerful, sing-songy voice, "And good morning to you, too, Dan!" Dan looked at him blankly. Then he shook his head. "Sorry, folks. Guess I was still mentally in my last meeting. I apologize."

"We were beginning to get worried, Dan," said Jane.

"Yes," said Marta, "we were worried you'd been taking lessons from Tim!" The others laughed as Tim stuck out his tongue at her. She got up and moved to the credenza. "Would you like some coffee and a doughnut?"

"That would be great," said Dan as he opened his project notebook and handed out materials to the others. "I had a 7 o'clock this morning and didn't have time for breakfast." Marta handed him some coffee, and he took a sip. "Thanks, Marta—that really hits the spot. Yes, that meeting not only kept me from eating, it also made me late. We just couldn't come to any agreement. In fact, they were still discussing things when I left. I just said I had to be here, and walked out."

"Nothing bad, I hope," said Marta as she put a couple of doughnuts in front of Dan and sat down.

"Well, Marta, one thing I learned long ago is if you don't have any problems, you're either out of business or dead. This problem has already happened, unfortunately, so what we're really trying to do is keep it from happening again." He took a bite of doughnut, chewed thoughtfully for a moment, and continued talking to the group between bites. "There's a chance we may have to deal with the problem in this group before all is said and done. But I think that's down the road a ways." He brushed the sugar from his hands. "In the meantime, we have a project to complete, a design to finalize, and an agenda for today. So let's get started."

FERGUSON AND BARDELL

ENGINEERING • ARCHITECTURE • PROJECT MANAGEMENT

The RMS Project
Meeting Agenda

Meeting Date: April 14, 1999   **Purpose:** Planning 3

I.   Agenda Building

II.   Physical Design
    • Client Decisions
    • Workflow
    • Data Stores

III.   Development Schedule

IV.   Draft of Functional Specification

V.   Draft of Project Plan

VI.   Draft of Project Schedule

VII.   Revision of Risk Assessment

VIII.   Q&A

IX.   Wrap-Up: Path-Forward Assignments

CHICAGO • DETROIT • MILWAUKEE • CINCINNATI • INDIANAPOLIS • LOUISVILLE

Dan stood and moved down the table. "Bill, the Development role drives Physical Design, so why don't you come up here and drive?"

Bill came to the head of the table and handed out sets of documents showing the various pieces of the proposed design. "Our meeting with the EA team on Monday afternoon was very fruitful. In the process of working out some issues with scalability, we decided we needed both a Web client..."

"Yes!" interjected Marilou, pumping her fist.

"...*and* a Win32 client," finished Bill, returning Marilou's look of triumph.

"Wait a minute," exclaimed Jane, "you're going to build *both* clients? What in the world for?"

"If you'll turn to the second and third pages, which show the overall process flow and the technologies used, I think it will make sense," replied Bill. He waited as the rest of the team traced through the drawings.

"Wow, you're using Exchange as the primary data store for the assigning of resources and the tracking of time," said Marilou as she studied the documents. "That'll make some of the worker-bees unhappy."

"Why?" asked Jane.

"Because, some of them don't keep their calendar in Exchange. They use paper calendars, or stand-alone organizers, or whatever works for them. They aren't going to want to switch."

Tim spoke up. "I guarantee you that my folks would gladly trade their paper calendars, or Post-It notes, or their faulty memory, for an automated tool that would cut their two-hour time sheets down to a few minutes. And if they could do it from home over the Web, they'd think they had died and gone to heaven."

"And Jim Stewart would be ecstatic to think we might get some value other than e-mail out of Exchange," said Jane. "We sold it to him as an enterprise-wide solutions base, but other than our room reservation folder, we haven't produced much."

"So, what we're saying is that we considered the tradeoffs and decided that this particular technology made the best business *and* technological sense," said Tim, leaning back in his chair and smiling.

"Why, Tim," said Dan, "I do believe you've caught up on your reading!"

"Had some help—again," said Tim, putting his hands behind his head.

"Well, however you're getting it done, I'm glad you're up with the rest of us. And you're right: This was one of a number of tradeoffs the development team made in working through Physical Design. Let's get back on focus and let Bill take us through the rest of the design."

The group spent the next 20 minutes working through the design, examining the various components and the objects and services they contained. When Bill explained how using multi-layer design, along with certain Microsoft technologies and design practices, would allow the pooling of connections to the data stores, Marilou sat up. "So *that's* what Sam had in mind that day! That's a significant boost to scalability, which is like giving us a gift of time before we have to deal with growth issues."

"Exactly," said Dan. "In addition, because we're building RMS this way, we can change pieces of it without disrupting the whole thing. And we can use some of the components in other applications as well, cutting our development time in the future."

"Speaking of time, Chief," said Tim, "How does your schedule look, now that you're writing two clients and hitting multiple data stores? And didn't I see some Transaction Server stuff in there as well? Even with all the people you've got writing—I saw the names beside the components—I just don't see any way you can be done by deadline."

"The short answer is, we can't," said Bill, frowning. "I already told Dan. No matter which way I slice it, I can't find a way to hit the delivery target we originally set. We're going to have to have an extra month."

"You can't have it!" boomed a voice from the hall, and in strode Jim Stewart.

"Jim, what a surprise," said Dan, without rising from his chair. The edge in his voice, even though he spoke evenly and without shouting, was palpable, and everyone except Jim noticed it. Ignoring Dan, he turned to Bill. "I'm telling you, Bill, there is no way we can wait an extra month for the RMS application. You and your guys have got to deliver it on time, if not early!" The CFO was growing more and more agitated as he leaned over the table in Bill's direction. He banged his fist on the table and almost shouted, "And if you can't deliver on time, I'll find someone who can!"

"Enough!" interrupted Dan sharply. He moved back to the head of the table. "First of all, sir, this is my meeting, and you don't come busting in here without asking. Secondly, Bill works for me, not you, and it's not your place to threaten any of my employees with termination. And finally, I don't work *for* you, but *with* you. If you don't understand what I'm saying, then you and I have our own issues to work out in private, not in front of the employees. Do I make myself clear?"

The room was suddenly very quiet. After a long moment, Jim passed his hand across his face and slumped against the credenza. "Dan, I'm sorry," he said.

Tim stood up. "Here, Mr. Stewart, take my chair." As Jim sat down, Tim got him some water. Jim sighed and said again, "I'm sorry, Dan. I guess I just lost it." He took a drink, then continued, "I was coming down to see if you were done. The executive committee finished its meeting, and I wanted to tell you how it came out. But when Bill mentioned needing another month for RMS, something just snapped." He sighed again. Turning to Bill, he said, "It looks like all I do is say ugly things to you, and then have to apologize. If I keep this up, you'll need tracking software to keep up with it all. Sorry, Bill."

"As long as the software reports an equal number of insults and apologies, I guess we'll be okay," said Bill gruffly. He put out his hand, and Jim took it.

Leaning on the credenza with his arms folded, Dan said, "Well, Jim, I'd say our agenda is pretty well shot. So why don't you take a moment to calm down and then tell the team why the RMS project is suddenly so important to you that a slippage of a month sends you into conniptions."

"'Conniptions'—I like that. Perfectly describes what I just did." He sighed again and then asked, "How many of you know what happened this past Friday in the sales department?"

Marilou and Jane looked at each other, and Jane said, "A few of us heard something about it, but we don't know many of the details. Wasn't it something about losing a potential project?"

"Yes, but it was what we lost and how we lost it that caused such a stir," said Jim. He got up and started pacing.

"Here's the scoop. One of our sales guys has been working for six months on a big construction project, right down the street from here. We were up for architecture, engineering, project management—the whole cahuna.

"Well, if you've ever been in sales, you know how these things go. Our guy put the proposal and bid together two months ago and then didn't hear anything for a month. He got some hints that we were in the finals, but these folks weren't going to do any further interviews, or rebidding, or anything. So, our guy was pretty much in the dark. Until Friday, that is.

"When he got in to the office on Friday morning, there was a voice mail waiting from the CEO of the firm doing the project. We had the project *if* we could begin work a week from Monday. Seems they had some sort of financing that was about to fall through, and they had to show progress by that date. To make matters worse, we had to accept it *in writing* by 3 PM on Friday. *And* we had to guarantee that we could put a full project team on the project on that Monday, no later. *And* there were substantial performance penalties if we didn't have the team in place."

Jim stopped pacing, put his hands on the back of the chair, and faced the group. "Well, the sales guy was frantic. He only had about five hours to pull together his response, and he had to be absolutely sure we could perform. He went to the head of each division, trying to line up resources. People started scrambling— after all, everyone likes business, and this was both high-profile and big. But in the end, we couldn't do it. We had enough architects and almost enough engineers. But we didn't have enough project managers with the experience to pull this off, and we were short on civil engineers. We hated to do it, but when 2:30 came and it looked like we couldn't do it, the sales guy sent them a formal refusal by messenger, and we all said what a shame it was."

Everyone had been following Jim's story with rapt attention, but Bill was confused. "So we lost some business because we didn't have the resources! What's the big deal? It's happened before, and it'll happen again. And anyway, they were nuts to think we could jump that high on such short notice."

"Wait, Bill, there's more," Dan said quietly. "The story's not over, not by a long shot."

Jim nodded. "Isn't that the truth!" He sat down and continued. "You're right, Bill; we've lost work before when we didn't have the resources. What made this such a disaster is..." he paused a beat "...we actually *did* have the resources. We just didn't know it."

"Whoa, I hate it when that happens," said Tim, grimacing.

"Turns out," said Jim, "we had two project managers coming off other projects, but there was no record of that anywhere in the office. Their original project schedules showed they were going to be on those projects at least another month, but there had been some problems with supplies on one project and the other had finished early. They had sent e-mails to the head of the PM department, telling him they would be back in town this week, but he was out sick and didn't see their messages. The only way we track our projects managers is on the chart on his wall, and he wasn't there to update it."

"And the civil engineers?" asked Marta.

"Turns out that the spreadsheet your boss uses only shows each resource's latest degree. Five of our electrical engineers have Master's degrees in EE, but their Bachelor's degree was in civil engineering. Two of them had actually done civil engineering work for a number of years before going back for their Master's. But nothing we use now was capable of telling us that."

"And when did we discover we could have done the work, Jim?" Dan prompted, still leaning against the credenza with his arms crossed.

Jim sighed. "The secretary called the head of PM at home around 2 in the afternoon. After she called, he decided to check his e-mail and found the messages from his two managers. He called back in about 2:45."

"And the hidden civil folks?" asked Marta again.

"One of them walked by while we were moaning about the fact that we didn't have enough CEs. He told us about his own background and mentioned two of the others. Then one of them told us of the others. By then it was about 4:45. That's when it really hit the fan." Jim shook his head, apparently still amazed at the mess.

"Just how big was this contract that we lost because we have no idea what's going on in our own company?" Jane asked quietly.

Jim looked down at the table. "Four point two million." His voice was barely audible.

Tim whistled, "Whew! We could buy a whole roomful of new servers with that!"

"That's still not all of it," said Dan grimly. "Go ahead and tell them the rest, Jim. Tell them about this past weekend. It's OK."

"You'll all hear about it in a day or two, anyway, so I guess there's no harm in telling you now." He paused and then continued. "When word got upstairs about losing a contract of that size and prestige, things started popping around here, and I do mean popping. The executive management committee met over the weekend, as well as Monday morning and this morning. They weren't pleasant meetings, let me assure you.

"The bottom line is that the COO is 'leaving to pursue other interests' at the end of this month. Apparently this screw-up was the last straw. Jo Brown is going to take his place, but not until she wraps up some other work. In the meantime, I've been made interim COO as well as CFO. Those are the major changes in people, but there are other shakeups coming as well, including the guy over in project management. The management committee—which includes Dan—has no more than two weeks to turn in the first draft of a completely documented procedure manual for their departments. We tried telling the CEO that he couldn't just dictate a deadline for a project like that, but he was in no mood to listen to arguments about bottom-up scheduling."

"And after you left this morning, Dan, the discussion turned to RMS. There's some confusion about who is in charge of it, and since you are still the fair-haired child, you got away without catching any of it. But the last thing the Old Man said to me was, 'Stewart, we've got to get that RMS thing up and working, so we don't ever lose a contract like this again. I'm holding you personally responsible for getting it done. And if you can't do it, I'll find somebody who can!'"

The team members winced at the harsh words. The CEO's temper was legendary. "So when you heard me delaying the project, it just took you over the edge, right?" Bill said quietly.

Jim nodded, without looking at either Bill or Dan. "It's really unfortunate, because I actually trust both of you—*all* of you—more than I've ever trusted any tech folks. But I just don't know what I'm going to do. If we don't get RMS built and put in place on schedule, I know someone else who's going to be 'pursuing other interests.'"

Dan walked purposefully to the whiteboard and drew a triangle. He wrote the words *Features*, *Resources*, and *Schedule* on the three sides of the figure. Then he turned back to the group. "Jim, do you remember this?"

Jim looked up and smiled wanly. "Absolutely—the Golden Triangle. One of the best concepts I've ever learned, even if it was from a techie."

"It's not just for the beginning of a project, Jim. It's for use anytime something changes." Dan drew a big minus sign beside the *schedule* side of the triangle. "To write the application we originally planned, our development team tells us it is going to take a month longer. You're saying we don't have that month. So our schedule is less than it needs to be. To bring the Golden Triangle back into balance, we've got to change something. Either we have to drop features, or add resources, or change the design, or adjust the schedule somewhere else."

Dan moved back to his spot at the credenza. "I like the design we have, and I'd rather not change it. So we can either drop features or add resources. And keep in mind the mythical man-month. Adding resources, especially to a project as short and as small as RMS, may not produce what you want.

"You are the customer. Ultimately, it's up to you to determine the best way to rebalance the Golden Triangle. We can make suggestions, but you have to decide. So what's it going to be?"

All eyes turned to Jim as he stared at the table. Finally, without moving or looking up, he said, "Drop the accounting."

"What?" exclaimed Jane. "That was one of the main features of RMS! We can't drop the accounting interface! How do you expect us to generate invoices?"

"The same way you do now," said Jim with an edge creeping back into his voice. He stopped, took a deep breath, turned to Jane, and continued. "Jane, the accounting interface and features are important to you and your people, but look at the big picture. We still save the time-sheet data entry. We still get the resources database, and the resource tracking, and the automated time-sheet generation. And we get it all in place within the original deadline. That's the right business decision for Ferguson and Bardell, and as the customer for RMS as well as the acting COO, that's the decision I'm making. Whatever heat comes from it, I'll just take." He turned to Dan. "Didn't we talk earlier about doing a Version 2? Can't we make the accounting interface that version's top priority?"

Dan nodded. "Our plan is to begin work on Version 2 as soon as we finish this version."

"Then that's what we should do," said Jim, getting up and crossing the room to shake Dan's hand. "Thanks for your help and your insights. Sorry to meet and run, but I've got some other fires to put out, and this one looks pretty well under control." He turned to the rest of the team. "I believe we have a major milestone scheduled for Friday morning. I'm looking forward to it. Good luck!" And he was gone.

"Wow, I sure wouldn't want to be in his shoes," Tim said.

"Yes, I believe his moccasins have some hard paths to walk in the next few months." Dan moved back to the head of the table. "It's our job to do all we can to get RMS delivered on time and not be a rock inside those moccasins."

Dan looked over his agenda. "Tell you what—I want to adjust this. I had wanted to develop draft versions of our other deliverables today, but we're now significantly behind schedule for this meeting, so let's can some of it. Here's what we're going to do. We're going to go over the parts of the Functional Spec. Then I'll assign different parts to different people. As you complete your section, e-mail it to the rest of us for comment. I'll put the sections together for a final document that we can approve on Friday.

"Bill, I know your development plan and schedule is toast after these changes, and the rest of us rely on that as a basis for our own work. So there's no reason to work on the Master Project Plan or the Master Project Schedule until you have a chance to make your changes. I want you to adjust your plan and schedule as quickly as possible and e-mail them to the rest of us. Then we can adjust our own documents, and everyone will submit their final versions to me for compilation. Does that make sense to everyone?"

Everyone nodded, and Bill said, "Subtracting is easier than adding. I should be able to have the revised documents to everyone by this afternoon."

"Excellent," said Dan. He started making notes as he spoke. "Let's assign the Functional Spec sections. Jane, I want you to take the vision summary and design goals. Marilou, you've got the requirements and the usage summary. Bill, you and Tim work together on features and dependencies. I'll do the schedule summary, and Marta, you make a first cut at risks. We'll use your work to jump-start our work on Friday on the Master Risk Assessment Document."

"So on Friday we'll go over the three design models, the Functional Spec, the Project Plan, and the Project Schedule, and make any changes we need to. Then we'll go through the Master Risk Assessment Document together, using Marta's work as a guide. Finally, Jim will join us and we'll work through the milestone questions, just like last time. Any questions?"

Everyone seemed anxious to get started, so Dan concluded the meeting by saying, "Remember, everyone, I need your documents as soon as possible so that I can compile them and get them back to you by tomorrow afternoon. Let me know if you have anything else pending that I can move to someone else. I need you to be free to concentrate on this."

"How 'bout my laundry?" asked Tim as the others laughed.

"That's why we gave you a laptop, Tim," said Dan with a grin. "Take it and your clothes to the laundromat and do some multi-tasking. Who knows? Maybe watching your stuff spin-dry will remind you of the Process Model."

"Nah, when I do laundry, it's more like a living example of risk management," said Tim, grabbing another doughnut as he prepared to leave.

"You keep eating those doughnuts," said Marta over her shoulder as she walked out, "and you won't need to worry about laundry for a while, because you'll have to buy a whole new wardrobe!"

Tim just grinned as he followed her out the door.

Project Plan Approved Milestone

"Alright, everyone—does that cover everything?"

The RMS team had been meeting for an hour, working through the sections of the Functional Specification. There had been some minor changes, but most of the work the team members had done remained intact. Jane commented, "You know, I was worried about assigning pieces of the Functional Spec to individuals. But when I worked on my sections, they just seemed to flow right out of the work we'd already done. And it looks as if that was true for the rest of you as well."

Tim nodded. "We had discussed the project so much already that putting it on paper almost seemed like an afterthought." He looked at Dan and quickly added, "But it's not, of course."

Dan smiled at the correction. "Good recovery job, Tim." He turned to the group. "I thought it might work that way, especially since one of the guidelines I gave you for Functional Specs was that they should only be as long as necessary to document the project, and no longer. I appreciated the fact that none of you tried to impress me with your ability to churn out verbiage." He smiled at Jane. "Did the project plan and project schedule go as smoothly, once you got Bill's revised plan and schedule?"

"No, those were much harder," said Jane emphatically. Several of the others nodded their agreement. "The Functional Spec covered items we had discussed in here. Our own plans and schedules are about areas that are unique to each of us. I have never had any project management training, so I found it very difficult to estimate the effort needed to carry out my tasks. Also, I've never done a communications plan before, so I wasn't even sure what sort of things to include. The examples from the project at your old law firm were good, but that project was different and it was hard to extrapolate to this project."

"The same was true for me," said Marta. "I appreciated your help with the testing plan, Dan, but it was still a radical departure from what I am trained to do. I'm not at all sure that what I turned in to you is adequate."

"Actually, all of your plans were very good for first efforts from people who are new to MSF," said Dan. "I made some comments and suggestions, and printed them out again. Take a moment to look through what I wrote, and then let's work through them together."

The group spent another hour going through each of the project plans and schedules, beginning with the ones for Development. Dan had prepared a Master Project Schedule, and when he handed it out, everyone immediately saw a number of conflicts and issues. They worked through the schedule step by step, adjusting various activities and deadlines and consulting the company master calendar as they worked.

When they were finished, Tim stretched. "Boy, that's hard work! I never thought project planning would wear me out like this." He stood up to get some water from the credenza. "I thought Jimbo was joining us this morning."

Dan was busy copying the last of the changes onto his copy of the Master Project Schedule. He didn't look up as he said, "I have to send over the finalized documents first. He's going to review them while we work through the Risk Assessment Document, and then he'll join us at the end. He should be here about 11 o'clock." Dan made a final mark with a flourish. "There! That's got it." He called his assistant to take the documents to Jim. "Let's take a ten-minute break, everyone. Oh, and Tim, don't eat any more doughnuts. Jim is taking us all to lunch, and Ferguson and Bardell is buying."

"Don't worry," Tim said, grinning. "I haven't met a doughnut yet that could keep me from my lunch. Servers, yes; doughnuts, no way!"

After the break, Marta led the team through the Risk Assessment Document. They changed some assessments and then added a new risk of unrealistic expectations from management, which they assigned Jane the task of mitigating with her communications plan. Jane pretended to be indignant. "Gee, thanks a lot, guys! I get to deal with the pointy-hairs." When she realized what she had said, she looked sheepishly at Dan. "Oops! Sorry, Dan, I didn't mean you. You're part of that crowd, but your hair hasn't changed. At least not yet."

Amidst the chuckles, Dan waved off the comment. "That's okay, I know just how you feel. But if there is anyone who is secure enough to deal with PHMs, it's you, Jane."

"PHMs?" whispered Marta to Tim.

"Pointy-haired managers," said Tim. "Just look for the cartoons on most of the cubicles."

Dan looked at his watch. "Let's get going, folks. I know where Jim is taking us, and it would be good to get there early." He turned to Bill. "One of our risks is performance. How are the proof-of-concepts coming?"

"Actually, they're done." Bill announced proudly. "Beth is a whiz at writing components, and she had the basics of the ones we were concerned about done by yesterday morning. We spent yesterday hitting on them and running some load tests." He smiled. "It looks as if we can handle up to 500 simultaneous users with our current topologies, and perhaps more if we add some boxes and distribute the components a little more."

"I wonder if your testing was what made my print job so slow," said Marilou. "When were you testing?"

Bill's smile faded. "From about 10 to noon, then again at about 2:30," he said, somewhat defensively.

Marilou nodded. "Yep, that was it. I printed ten pages at 1:30, and they came right out. When I sent over five pages at 2:45, they took forever to print."

"Here's a problem just waiting to happen," Dan thought to himself, but he decided against saying anything to Bill in the meeting. He made a mental note to ask Bill about his testing environment next week. Then he smiled at Bill and said, "Chief, those numbers sound great! Did you actually simulate that many users?"

"Yes. Sam wrote a test script, and we were able to work the application pretty well," said Bill, smiling again. "Beth pointed out some tweaking we needed to do in the component model, and we squeezed another 12 percent out of it before we were done."

"Excellent work, Bill," said Dan. "And the same for all of you. You've all put in extra hours, I know, getting this project plan ready, especially with the changes we got at the last minute. I appreciate your hard work."

Just then, Jim Stewart poked his head into the room. "Request permission to come aboard, Admiral."

"Permission granted." Dan and Bill had spoken at the same time. They looked at each other in surprise and laughed. Bill said, "Sorry—force of habit."

"That's all right, Chief. I should have yielded to my first mate, anyway." He turned to Jim, who had moved to the head of the table. "What did you think of the final version of the project documents I sent over?"

"I thought they were very good," said Jim emphatically. "In fact, this is one of the best-documented projects we've ever had in this company. If your execution is as good as your planning, we should be in very good shape when you're finished." He pulled the documents out of the folder he was carrying. "I do have a few suggestions. Shall we look at them now?"

"Absolutely," said Dan, and the team listened as Jim outlined four proposed changes. A brief discussion followed, during which three of the four changes were adopted and the fourth was dropped. "Are we ready to go to lunch, now?" Jim asked.

"Not quite yet," said Dan. He pulled a flip chart from its place in the corner and turned to a page where he had written six bulleted points. "It's time to see if we have hit the Project Plan Approved Milestone. Remember, major milestones are points in the life of the project where the customer and the project team agree on certain major questions. Here are the six for the Planning Phase. Tell me whether we have agreement on these points, and where that agreement is documented."

The team looked at the six points in silence. Then Jane got up, took the marker from Dan, and went through the bullets, writing beside each one.

"Details of what to build to meet the business need? That's in the Functional Spec. Features of the application, in priority order? Again, the Functional Spec. How long? Master Project Schedule. How to build it, and who builds it? Master Project Plan. Risks of building? The revised Master Risk Assessment Document. And the milestones and deliverables for the rest of the project? In the Master Project Plan." She looked around. "I think we're done," she said.

"No, you're wrong," Bill growled. "We've got one more thing to do before we're finished with the Planning Phase." Everyone looked at him as he continued, "We have to decide whether or not to proceed."

Everyone nodded, remembering the end of the Envisioning Phase. Jim said, "Things sure can change in a hurry, can't they, Dan?"

Dan smiled. "Yes, but that's why we do this the way we do, so we can respond." He paused and then said, "I think we're all ready to move forward, Jim, but you're the one with your neck on the line. What do you want to do? Do you want the RMS that these documents describe to move into the Developing Phase?"

Jim didn't hesitate. "Let's do it. Even though we've cut back somewhat, it still brings a lot of value to the table. And besides," he said, standing up, "I'm seeing what good leadership and teamwork can accomplish, and it's exciting to watch. I want to see what sort of product you can turn out."

"Actually," said Dan, "so do I." He turned to the rest of the team. "It's agreed, then. We have decided to move to the Developing Phase." Shaking hands with Jim, Dan continued, "I think I heard something about lunch. Are we ready to go?"

Jim put on his jacket and straightened his tie. "They've got a table waiting for us. The sooner we get there, the sooner we can start eating."

"Then let's get moving!" said Tim, heading for the exit. Just then, Beth and Sam stuck their heads into the conference room. "Glad you could join us, you two," Dan said.

"Bill said he thought we'd had enough pizza and soda, and it might be time to try some of the other major food groups," Sam explained.

Dan turned out the lights, and the group headed for the elevators.

Developing the Product

C H A P T E R   7

User Service Layer Technologies

About This Chapter

This chapter examines how to create effective and efficient user interface (UI) and user service designs. We explore legacy, current, and future technologies that affect the design of the user service layer of the MSF Application Model. We also determine the impact of Web technologies on current application design techniques.

We start our discussion of user service design issues by examining different types of user interface applications. We also study the effects of application requirements and design on development implementation choices. We briefly discuss creating and accessing native user interface applications while taking an in-depth look at creating and accessing Web-based user interface applications.

Finally, we look at some techniques and configurations developers can use in their implementations to connect the user service layer to the business service layer.

The principles and guidelines we provide in this chapter are based on our own experience with the creation of application architectures and the implementation of enterprise applications, together with the following sources:

- Mary Kirtland's *Designing Component-Based Applications*
- *Microsoft Visual Basic 6.0 Programmer's Guide*

Upon completion, you will be able to:

- Use basic user interface guidelines to create effective user interface designs.
- Analyze user interface requirements to derive the appropriate user interface technology model.
- Understand different technologies that can be used to implement a user service layer.
- Understand the effects of user service technologies on the deployment of applications.

Determining the User Interface

The *user interface* (UI) is the portion of an application that displays and receives information from the application's users. Typically, the application users are people that perform particular activities to accomplish their intended work. Although another application could be considered a user of the new application, we primarily refer to user interface as the interaction point for humans not other applications.

Many times project teams have said "Why bother with designing and creating a user interface—doesn't everyone know how to use computer? This is simple, and if someone can't figure it out, they shouldn't be using the program anyway!" Although these statements can be argued forever without convincing some team members, a good user interface design and implementation will significantly improve the efficiency and productivity of the application's users.

Before setting out to determine the look and feel for the application, which is primarily called the UI, it is important to determine how the UI will be presented. This manipulation to provide information to the users is provided by the user service layer. Although the user service layer does not contain the actual UI, for simplicity we will refer to the user service layer as also including the UI.

The user service layer displays data from business objects, displays data objects to users, and retrieves data from these users. The Microsoft Windows Distributed interNet Applications (DNA) Architecture supports a wide range of user service layer architectures, from native Win32 applications to pure HTML Web-based applications. In all cases, the user service layer uses COM to access services from business layer components.

An application's business logic is encapsulated in its business service layer (middle-tier) components, rather than in the user service layer. This arrangement makes the business logic easier to reuse if the user service layer needs to be changed. The user service layer communicates with the business logic using COM method calls. The user layer might also use COM-based ActiveX controls to display the actual UI. The same ActiveX controls can be used in native and Web-based applications running on Microsoft Windows, so it is possible to reuse user service layer code among applications with different types of UIs.

User Service Layer Considerations

Several factors should be considered when choosing the architecture for the user service layer:

- Do any application requirements specify the type of UI?
- Do security issues such as firewalls impact communication between user workstations and server-side computers?

- Which operating systems must be supported on user workstations?
- Which Web browsers must be supported?
- Can COM components install and run on user workstations?
- Are remote COM components accessible from user workstations?

The answers to these questions will help the development team determine which type of UI architecture is most appropriate for the application.

Application Requirements

Whether the application will use a native or a Web-based UI might be dictated by business or use requirements for the application, relieving the team of responsibility for making this decision. Often, diverse user needs determine the presentation platform that must be implemented. For example, if users must be able to access the application over the Internet, a Web-based architecture is almost always the logical choice. Developers can write native applications that communicate with server-side code over the Internet; however, users must logically be able to access a particular application through a Web browser to use it over the Internet.

In enterprise applications, application UIs often have some common characteristics. A corporate policy may even dictate the type of interface the application must use. For example, to reduce costs, some organizations have standard UI styles for all their in-house applications.

Many organizations are standardizing on Web-based applications because employees can access Web pages more easily than they can run multiple native applications with which they may not be familiar. Additionally, the cost of maintaining Web-based applications will likely be lower than that of maintaining native applications.

Security Issues

Security issues in three primary areas must be addressed:

- Authentication of users
- Control of access to application components and data
- Encryption of application information

Chapter 11 is devoted to the issues surrounding application security, but we'll discuss them briefly here because firewalls and security policies that have an impact on communications between user workstations and server-side computers also have an impact on the architecture choices available to the development team. Firewall and security issues primarily affect Web-based applications, in which users access applications over the Internet. However, similar issues can also apply to applications running on a wide-area network (WAN).

We suggest the following four options for resolving problems caused by firewalls and proxy servers:

- **Reconfigure the firewall** Firewalls can be configured to permit Distributed COM (DCOM) traffic and to allow the proxy servers to show user workstation IP addresses. Normally, this is not a practical solution, because proxy servers are not likely to be under the development team's control, and corporate policy may not permit modifications to the firewall.

- **Implement Internet tunneling** DCOM traffic can be sent over encapsulated in Hypertext Transfer Protocol (HTTP), which is sent via TCP/IP. This Internet tunnel of DCOM traffic over TCP/IP typically uses HTTP's port 80. As most firewalls permit HTTP traffic through the firewall, using the TCP/IP protocol helps avoid the firewall issue. However, to penetrate proxy servers, the team must configure the proxy servers to permit tunneling on port 80. Again, this solution might not be practical, because the proxy servers are not likely to be under the development team's control.

Note Internet Tunneling via TCP/IP is included with Microsoft Windows NT 4.0 Service Pack 4 and Microsoft Windows 2000. Client-side support is also available for Microsoft Windows 95 and Microsoft Windows 98.

- **Use Remote Data Services (RDS)** RDS can be used to marshal ActiveX Data Objects (ADO) **Recordset** objects over DCOM or HTTP. Generally, RDS can marshal calls over HTTP from client-side code to any server-side business object that exposes an **IDispatch** interface. This option allows the use of the COM programming model, but avoids firewall and proxy server issues. This technique can be used from either native or Web-based applications. (We discuss using RDS to access remote business objects later in this chapter.)

- **Redesign applications** Applications can be structured so that they don't need to make COM calls through a proxy server or firewall. This option normally implies a Web-based application, typically implemented using Active Server Pages (ASP), to allow users to access the applications through a Web browser. ASP pages use server-side scripting to create and use business objects, and subsequently generate Web pages to return via HTTP to users' computers. These pages might contain client-side scripts and components, but they would never reference remote COM objects through a firewall. (We look at how to access business objects from ASP pages later in this chapter.)

Network traffic from server computers may pass through firewalls that permit only certain communication protocols to access the server. User workstations may need to use proxy servers to access remote computers. In such situations, it may be difficult to use DCOM components to communicate between the user and business layers. Although DCOM can work through a firewall, this normally involves modifying the firewall to permit DCOM traffic to pass through. Access through proxy servers presents an additional challenge, because most proxy servers hide user workstation IP addresses. Normally, DCOM network protocols need workstation IP addresses to establish proper communication between workstation and server computers.

Desktop Operating System Constraints

It's important to determine in the early phases of a project which operating systems must be supported by client-side code. If the user layer needs to run only on Win32 operating systems, all of the technologies discussed in this chapter are available.

One constraint involves COM's possible unavailability on certain target platforms. If COM is not available, the application cannot use client-side COM objects, nor can it communicate with remote COM objects. Even if the development team can access COM, DCOM may not be available with such operating systems as Microsoft Windows 3.1 or Macintosh. With Windows 95, DCOM95 must be installed on client computers to use DCOM. If DCOM is unavailable, the application cannot communicate with remote COM objects. In this case, a distributed user layer that uses a server-based ASP page to generate Web pages for a client is probably most suitable.

Another constraint is that COM components are normally distributed as platform-specific binary executables. To use client-side COM objects, components must be available for each target platform. Otherwise, special versions of the user layer must be created that don't use such components.

Finally, UI or Web browsing services supported on each platform can vary. To work around platform differences for native applications, a platform-neutral UI framework can be used. To work around platform differences for Web-based applications, it may be necessary to use a restricted subset of HTML and scripting languages. Otherwise, platform-specific user layer applications must be written.

Web Browser Constraints

It may be necessary to support multiple Web browsers even when supporting only a single operating system. When writing a Web-based application, it's important to determine early in the development process which HTML tags, scripting languages, object models, components, and so on are supported by the targeted browsers. Application developers must either find a common feature subset supported by all browsers, or write browser-specific presentation layer applications.

The browser detection capabilities provided with Microsoft Internet Information Server's (IIS) ASP lets developers dynamically generate Web pages that use the highest possible level of browser functionality. Developers can find out which browsers request ASP pages, and what feature set is supported by those browsers. Because the Browser Capabilities component determines supported features using an .ini file indexed by the browser's HTTP user agent string, developers can easily customize the .ini file to provide information about any desired browser features.

Because browsers have different capabilities, deciding which browser(s) to support helps determine how the team will implement certain Web features. Different browsers implement slightly different object models, so the team will need to watch for incompatibilities among these models that may break the script code. In general, if client-side scripting is being used, European Computer Manufacturers Association (ECMA) script (Microsoft JScript) should be used for browser-neutral applications.

Note Server-side scripts can be written in any scripting language supported by the Web server, because those scripts are never sent to the browser.

It is important to know which browsers are available to the application's primary users. If the application is to be distributed over a corporate intranet and the organization has implemented a single browser standard, such as Microsoft Internet Explorer 5.0, the development team can confidently utilize the innate capabilities of the browser. Otherwise, the team may have to design for a much broader range of browser capabilities. For example, an organization that utilizes electronic commerce cannot afford to turn away customers just because they don't have the latest browser. In such cases, developers must plan their designs to accommodate older browsers and HTML versions to capture the largest possible user audience. (This is referred to as *degrading gracefully*.) Users with older browsers should be able to view a text-only version of the site, or at least see a notification that they need to upgrade their browser, along with a link to the appropriate download site.

Note In the United States, Canada, the European Union, and Japan, users generally have a robust browser—typically a minimum of Internet Explorer 4.x or Netscape Navigator 4.x.

If developers code to the HTML 3.2 standards, they may not have all the layout or data manipulation tools they need, but their Web pages will work across virtually all platforms, even on mobile operating systems such as Microsoft Windows CE. However, coding with HTML 3.2 does not ensure consistent visual display across platforms or browsers, at least not with pinpoint accuracy. User display sizes can vary from 640 x 480 pixels to 1600 x 1200 pixels, drastically affecting browser window size and thereby affecting on-screen page rendering. Visual display can also be affected by color depths, which range from 16 colors to millions of colors. The rendering engines themselves visually build pages that can vary by several pixels from browser to browser, with some older browsers not properly rendering certain features at all. Developers should test on every screen size, platform, and browser version possible to work around hurdles posed by HTML 3.2. Once this version of HTML renders appropriately on all target systems, developed applications will usually operate smoothly. The truth is, if developers don't know or can't control the variety of platforms and browser versions on which users will run the application, they can't be completely sure how the application's pages will display.

Client-Side COM Components

If the UI is a native application, installing and running COM components on user workstations probably isn't an issue. A Win32 application needs to be installed, but the COM components are simply treated as part of the application's installation routine. Things are somewhat more complicated for Web-based applications. Providing that a particular browser supports client-side COM components, the components usually download and automatically install on users' computers the first time the component is accessed.

ActiveX Controls

ActiveX controls are COM objects that are sent from a Web server to execute on users' desktop with their browser. Some users, or the organizations for which they work, might worry about the security of automatically downloading and installing executable code on client computers. Some users might not allow any components to be downloaded to their computers. If Web-based applications must support such users or organizations, it is best not to use any client-side COM components (including ActiveX controls) unless the components already exist on the users' computers. Some users want to decide on a case-by-case basis whether to download and install particular components on their computers. In this case, developers might choose to use client-side COM components. (Later in this chapter, we examine ways to make client-side COM components available to user computers.)

Distributed COM Components

To be able to access remote components, the users' computers must be able to make remote COM calls, using either DCOM or RDS. Client-side browsers must also support the creation and scripting of COM objects. In addition, accessing remote components usually requires the installation of some code or registry entries on the users' computers. If an application uses vtable-binding or early-binding to access COM components, proxy/stub DLLs or type libraries must be installed on the users' computers. (We explore binding methods and COM in greater detail in Chapter 8.)

Most applications rely on registry information to locate remote server computer names, and remote components might also present a perceived security issue to users. (Later in this chapter, we examine methods of making remote components available to user computers.)

Note When producing a Web-based application, it is important to verify that needed functionality is exposed via the **IDispatch** interface. Most scripting languages supported by Web browsers support late-binding only through **IDispatch**. If the required functionality is only exposed on another interface, the components will probably need to be modified.

Internet and Intranet Connections

If HTML is used for business reasons, the user layer might need to be coded for a variety of browsers. A user layer based on HTML must be served to users through a TCP/IP network connection, so development decisions will also be affected by:

- The types of connections implemented by users.
- The number of connections implemented.
- The variety of connection speeds at which users will access the product.

An array of connection types with differing bandwidth capabilities are available:

- Analog modems, up to 53 Kbps download
- ISDN modems, up to 112 Kbps download
- Cable modems, up to 10 Mbps burst download
- DSL modems, up to 6 Mbps download
- T1 and similar telecom connections, 1.5 Mbps and up
- Satellite dishes, up to 10 Mbps burst download
- Corporate networks, typically 10 Mbps or 100 Mbps shared Ethernet download

Selecting a User Service Layer Architecture

Choosing the appropriate UI within the user service layer can be a difficult task. Looking at these considerations can help lead the team toward creating a native application or Web-based application UI. Often, the team will choose to implement both types of interfaces for the application.

Native Application User Service Layer

Applications that require operating system client support are generally classified as *native applications*. On today's Windows platforms, native applications use operating system APIs to provide programmatic functionality. The Win32 API is typically used for 32-bit applications on Windows systems such as Windows 95, Windows 98, Windows NT, and Windows 2000. Thus, if the team has a well-defined target desktop, native applications can be created.

Because it encompasses a complete operating system, the Win32 environment allows developers a huge range of local computer control and precise UI capabilities. Developers can create specialized Win32-based applications available to a large audience. Additional technologies can be incorporated into operating systems and utilized by application components. Examples of such technologies are:

- DirectX multimedia.
- Open Database Connectivity (ODBC).
- OLE DB for Data Access.

Several languages, such as Microsoft Visual C++, Microsoft Visual Basic, and Microsoft Visual J++, can create native applications. In turn, these applications can be compiled and distributed to any number of systems. These languages create truly compiled applications, so if the UI requires a lot of intricate control or has a strong use of graphics, a native application will be the best choice.

Because application UIs require the use of specific functions from a given operating system, they are generally installed locally. This installation process allows for local high-bandwidth content and remote low-bandwidth content to be mixed during the application's use. For example, Microsoft Office applications can contain 120 megabytes of executable files and DLLs. However, data files and server applications can transfer much smaller pieces of information, thus saving significant network bandwidth. As most of the native applications that are created today require installation and configuration on the desktop systems, if the team will be continually changing the application, or the application executables are very large, a native application may not be the best choice.

The use of native applications also enables the easy incorporation of significant new technology. For example, Office 2000's new XML parsing capabilities can quickly be added to applications without having to create XML function libraries for each application. Thus to take full advantage of other native applications that can exist on the desktop, the team's application should also be a native application to provide the strongest interaction capabilities with other desktop applications.

Web-Based User Service Layer

Web-based UIs offer compelling user layer features with nearly universal distribution methods and ready-made rendering engines. Freely distributed Web browsers provide easily accessible application interfaces. These interfaces also help make application deployment more efficient. Initial deployment and subsequent upgrading is one of the hardest parts of producing an application. Using Web-based interfaces significantly reduces deployment and application maintenance time because the application doesn't have to be manually distributed to every individual user. Therefore, Web-based applications should be created when distribution, deployment, and continual application maintenance are significant issues for the team.

It is important to remember that Web-based interfaces are primarily designed as a method of displaying information on a screen. In the last couple years, the advent of scripting languages has introduced extensive programmatic and algorithmic capabilities to Web-based interfaces. Web-based navigation can be accomplished by "hotspots," or links can be included on each page to access and execute additional pages. These links can trigger the execution of code within the page or in a referenced file, as is often the case with new dynamic HTML (DHTML) Web-based interfaces. The control available to Web-based applications has significantly improved with the addition of client-side scripting and DHTML. If a lot of screen manipulation or calculations are required, Web-based interfaces are not the best solution.

Most of today's intranet systems are advanced enough to allow development using HTML 4.0, DHTML, and cascading style sheets. The target coding level will have been identified during the Envisioning Phase. All aspects of the application will have been tested in a variety of browsers using proof-of-concept systems created during the Planning Phase. Throughout the Planning and Development phases, developers should consider the range of connection types and determine how graphics, applets, components, and page loading speeds will affect development performance expectations.

Combination Native and Web-Based User Service Layer

The team should not consider the decision to create a native or Web-based UI as a mutually exclusive choice. As noted with the sample RMS application, applications can have both native and Web-based UIs. Each interface may be similar, or one can provide only specialized functions. Remember, even choosing two UIs means significant portions of the user services can be shared and reused by both interfaces. This is one of the benefits to creating a user service layer to provide the interaction between the UI and business objects.

Basics of Interface Design

This section is primarily taken from the *Microsoft Visual Basic 6.0 Programmer's Guide* (Microsoft, 1998).

Being an artist is not a prerequisite for creating a great UI. Most of the principles of UI design are the same as the basic design principles taught in any elementary art class. The design principles of composition, color, and so forth apply equally well to a computer screen, a sheet of paper, or a canvas.

Although programming tools make it easy to create a UI by simply dragging controls onto a screen-based form or Web page, a little planning up front can make a big difference in the usability of an application. The development team might consider designing UI elements on paper first, determining which control mechanisms are needed, the relative importance of the different elements, and the relationships between the control mechanisms.

These basic design principles apply equally well to a native application UI or a Web-based UI. The application code required to implement these principles may be radically different for native and Web-based applications; however, designing the UI for both types of applications is a similar process.

UI Elements

Several common elements are used in many implementations of UIs. These UI elements, when used properly, can help create the efficiency and productivity gains for the team's user community. Although these elements may look slightly different in a native interface than in a Web-based interface, they all function similarly in both environments.

Interface Styles

In the Windows-based application world, not all UIs look or behave the same. There are three main styles of UI:

- **Single-document interface (SDI)** An example of the SDI interface is the WordPad application included with Windows. In WordPad, only a single document can be open at a time; the document must be closed before another can be opened.

- **Multiple-document interface (MDI)** Applications such as Microsoft Word 2000 and Microsoft Excel 2000 are MDI interfaces. They allow multiple documents to be displayed at the same time, with each document displayed in its own window. An MDI application can usually be recognized by the inclusion of a Windows menu item with submenus for switching between windows or documents.

- **Explorer-style interface** The explorer-style interface is a single window containing two panes or regions, usually consisting of a tree or hierarchical view on the left and a display area on the right, as in the Microsoft Windows Explorer application.

- **Report interface** These can be considered an additional style of interface. Report information can be displayed in any type of graphical, row and column, or text format, or combination of formats. Many applications allow users to display reports or send them to a printer for hard-copy output.

In determining which interface style is best, the development team needs to look at the purpose of the application, as well as the work of the users. A simple clock application would be best suited to the SDI style, because it's not likely someone would need more than one clock open at a time. (In the case of this rare event, a second instance of the SDI application can be opened.) An application for processing insurance claims might lend itself to the MDI style, because a clerk is likely to be working on more than one claim at a time or might need to compare two claims. The Windows Explorer-style interface is being used for many new applications, because it lends itself to navigating or browsing through large numbers of documents, pictures, or files. Reports can provide a permanent record of the information at a particular point in time, and do not require direct interaction with the application to be useful to the user.

Dialog Box Control Mechanisms

Most applications need to directly communicate with the user. In Windows-based applications, dialog boxes prompt the user for data that the application needs to continue or to display information to the user. Dialog boxes are a specialized type of form that present information and generally require user interaction. Dialog boxes typically must be closed (hidden or unloaded) before the user can continue working with the application.

Applications must also present choices to their users, ranging from a simple yes/no option to selecting from a list containing hundreds of possibilities. Several controls can be useful in presenting choices. Table 7.1 summarizes a few of these controls and their appropriate usage.

Table 7.1   Controls and their usage

Control mechanism	Description
Label	Text that is displayed only.
Text box	Text that can be edited by the user. Text boxes are used to gather free-form information from the user. Text boxes are effectively used to gather numerical information as well as alphabetic information such as user IDs and passwords.
Command button	Typically rectangular buttons in a dialog box that carry out a command. When the button is chosen, it executes the appropriate action and typically looks as if it's being pushed in and released.
Check box	A small set of choices from which a user can choose one or more options. It indicates whether a particular condition is on or off, true or false, yes or no. When displayed in a group, check boxes work independently of each other; the user can select any number of check boxes at the same time.
Option button	A small set of options from which the user can choose just one. Option buttons should always work as part of a group; selecting one option button immediately clears all the other buttons in the group.
List box	A scrollable list of choices. Typically, the list of choices is displayed vertically in a single column, although multiple columns can be used as well. If the number of items exceeds what can be displayed in the box, scroll bars should be presented. Often multiple choices can be made from a single list by using the CTRL key to indicate multiple selections. Additionally, the box can drop down to display the list of choices.
Combo box	A scrollable list of choices along with a text edit field. Identical to a list box, except the user can either type information in the text box or choose the item from the list.
Slider control	A relative range that indicates the current position on a scale. These controls can be used to control program input, such as a volume control, or to adjust the colors in a picture.
Progress indicator	A percentage of a particular process that has been completed. These controls are useful as indicators that the application is performing work. If an excessive amount of working time is required, an estimate of the time remaining to complete the operation can also be supplied.

When requiring that the user make a choice, it is preferable to provide a default setting for the choice.

Composition

The composition or layout of each UI element not only influences its aesthetic appeal, but also has a tremendous impact on the usability of the application. Composition includes such factors as the following:

- Positioning of controls
- Consistency of elements
- Affordances
- Use of white space
- Simplicity of design

Positioning of Controls

In most interface designs, not all elements are equally important. Careful design ensures that users readily understand which elements are more important. These elements should appear in prominent locations, and less important, or less frequently accessed, elements should be relegated to less prominent locations.

Many languages are read from left to right and from top to bottom on a page. The same holds true for a computer screen. Most users' eyes are drawn to the upper left portion of the screen first, so the most important element should go there. For example, if the information on a form is related to a customer, the name field should be displayed where it will be seen first. Buttons, such as OK or Next, should be placed in the lower right portion of the screen, because users normally won't need these buttons until they have finished working with the form.

The grouping of elements and controls is also important. Information should be grouped logically according to function or relationship. For example, because their functions are related, buttons for navigating a database should be grouped together visually, rather than scattered throughout a form. The same applies to information; fields for a name and an address are generally grouped together, because they are closely related. In many cases, the relationships between controls can be reinforced with frames.

Often users move from one control area to another by pressing the TAB key. For input forms such as dialog boxes, maintaining a meaningful TAB order improves the user experience.

Consistency of UI Elements

Consistency is a virtue in UI design. A consistent look and feel creates harmony in an application—everything seems to fit together. A lack of consistency in the interface can be confusing, and can make an application seem chaotic, disorganized, and cheap, possibly even causing users to doubt the reliability of an application.

For visual consistency, the development team should establish a design strategy and style conventions in the early phases of the development process. Design elements such as the types of controls, standards for size and grouping of controls, and font choices should be established in advance. As discussed in Chapters 5 and 6, prototypes and proof-of-concept systems can be used to help make this type of design decision. Consistency in the following areas should be considered:

- **Type of control** Because a wide variety of controls is available for use in today's programming environments, it is tempting to use them all. This temptation must be avoided; instead, a subset of controls that best fits the application should be chosen. Although list box, combo box, grid, and tree controls can all be used to present lists of information, it's best to stick with a single style where possible.

- **Property settings** Consistency in the setting of properties for the controls is also important. For example, if a white background is used for editable text in one place, gray shouldn't be used in another place without a good reason.

- **Type of form** Consistency between different forms in the application is important to usability. If a grey background and three-dimensional effect is used for one form and a white background and two-dimensional effect is used for another, the forms will appear to be unrelated.

Affordances

Affordances give visual clues about the function of a visual element. Although the term may be unfamiliar, examples of affordances are everywhere. For example, a bicycle handgrip that has depressions where fingers should be placed makes it obvious that it is meant to be gripped. Push buttons, knobs, and light switches are all affordances, because their purpose can be discerned just by looking at them.

A UI should make ample use of affordances. For instance, three-dimensional effects on command buttons indicate to users that the buttons are meant to be pushed. If a command button has a flat border, this affordance is lost, and it is no longer clear to users that the button is a command button. However, the team might decide that flat buttons are more appropriate for a particular type of application, such as a multimedia application. Breaking with convention is acceptable as long as consistency is maintained throughout the application.

Another example of a common affordance is the text box. Users expect that a box with a border and a white background will contain editable text. Although it's possible to display a text box with no border, doing so makes the box look like a label that is not editable.

Use of White Space

The use of *white space* in a UI can help to emphasize elements and improve usability. White space doesn't necessarily have to be white in color; the term refers to the use of blank space between and around information on a form. Too many controls and information can lead to a cluttered interface, making it difficult to find individual fields, controls, or information. Incorporating white space in the application design emphasizes the form's design elements.

Consistent spacing between controls and alignment of vertical and horizontal elements can also make the design more usable. Text in a magazine is arranged in orderly columns with even spacing between lines to make it easier to read; similarly, an orderly interface is easier to read.

Design Simplicity

Perhaps the most important principle of interface design is that of simplicity. If an application's interface looks difficult, the application is probably difficult to use. From an aesthetic standpoint, a clean, simple design is always preferable.

A common pitfall in interface design is to try and model the interface after real-world artifacts. For example, suppose the team has been asked to create an application for completing insurance forms. A natural reaction is to design an interface that exactly duplicates the paper insurance form on screen. This strategy has several problems, including:

- The shape and dimensions of a paper form are different than those of a screen.
- Duplicating a form pretty much limits the team to text boxes and check boxes.
- There is no real benefit to the user.

A far better approach is to design the UI specifically for the application, perhaps providing a printed duplicate (with print preview) of the original paper form. By creating logical groupings of fields from the original form and using a tabbed interface or several linked forms, all the information can be presented without requiring users to scroll. Other options include:

- Using control mechanisms, such a list box preloaded with choices, to reduce the amount of typing required of users.
- Moving infrequently used functions to their own form.
- Providing defaults so that users are not forced to make a choice every time they use an option. (A mechanism must be provided to override the default.)
- Simplifying complex or infrequent tasks with wizards.

Observational testing of the application is the best way to test for simplicity. If a typical user can't immediately accomplish a desired task without assistance, a redesign may be in order.

Color and Images

The use of color in the interface can add visual appeal, but it's easy to overuse it. With many displays now capable of displaying millions of colors, it's often tempting to use as many as possible. Color, like the other basic design principles, can be problematic if not carefully considered in the initial design.

Preference for colors varies widely; the user's taste may not be the same as the team's preferences. Colors can evoke strong emotions, and certain colors have cultural significance. It's usually best to stay conservative, using softer, more neutral colors.

Choice of colors is influenced by the intended audience, as well as by the tone or mood the application designers are trying to convey. Bright reds, greens, and yellows might be appropriate for a children's application, but would hardly evoke an impression of fiscal responsibility in a banking application.

Small amounts of bright color can be used effectively to emphasize or draw attention to an important area. However, the number of colors used in an application should be limited, and the color scheme should be consistent. It's best to stick with a standard 16-color palette if possible, because dithering can cause some colors outside this palette range to disappear when viewed on a 16-color display.

Another consideration in the use of color is color-blindness. Many people are unable to tell the difference between different combinations of primary colors, such as red and green. To someone with this condition, red text on a green background is invisible.

Images and Icons

The use of pictures and icons can add visual interest to the application, but careful design is essential. Images can convey information efficiently without the need for text, but different people perceive images differently.

Toolbars with icons that represent various functions are a useful interface device, but if users can't readily identify the function represented by the icons, they can be counterproductive. When designing toolbar icons, it's important to follow the standards already established for other applications. For example, many applications use a sheet of paper with a folded corner to represent a New File icon. Although there may be a better metaphor for this function, representing it differently could confuse users.

It's also important to consider the cultural significance of images. Many programs use a picture of a rural-style mailbox with a flag to represent mail functions. This is primarily an American icon; users in other countries or cultures probably won't recognize it as a mailbox.

When designing icons and images, the best rule is "Keep them simple." Complex pictures with a lot of colors don't degrade well when they are displayed as a 16-by-16-pixel toolbar icon, or when displayed at high screen resolutions.

Fonts

Because text is often used to communicate information, selecting fonts that are easily read at different resolutions and on different types of displays is an important part of designing the UI. It's best to stick with simple fonts where possible. Script and other decorative fonts generally look better in print than on the screen, and they can be difficult to read at smaller point sizes.

Generally, the standard Windows fonts, such as Arial, Times New Roman, or System should be used. Otherwise, the team must distribute the selected font with the application, because if the application is used on a computer that doesn't have the selected font installed, the system will make a substitution that might change the appearance of the application.

Note When designing for an international audience, it is important to investigate what fonts that audience is likely to have available. Also, the team needs to consider text expansion, because text strings can take up to 50 percent more space in some languages.

Again, design consistency is important when choosing fonts. In most cases, no more than two fonts at two or three different point sizes should be used in a single application. Too many fonts can leave the application looking like a pieced-together ransom note.

Usability

Ultimately users determine the usability of any application. Interface design is an iterative process, and rarely is the first pass at an application's UI design going to yield a perfect interface. Involving users early in the design process creates a better, more usable interface with less effort.

What Is a Good UI?

A good place to start when designing a UI is to look at some of the best-selling applications. Much research, effort, and resources are expended on the usability of these applications. They have many things in common, such as toolbars, status bars, ToolTips, context-sensitive menus, and tabbed dialog boxes.

The team's own experience as users of software will also yield some insight into good UI design. By thinking about what works and what doesn't, and about how what doesn't work can be modified, the team can identify examples to emulate and examples to avoid. However, it's important to recognize that the personal likes and dislikes of a small team might not match those of the users by validating ideas with user prototypes.

Additionally, most successful applications provide choices to accommodate varying user preferences. For instance, Windows Explorer allows users to copy files with menus, keyboard commands, or drag-and-drop functions. Providing options broadens the appeal of the application; at a minimum, all functions must be accessible by both mouse and keyboard.

Windows UI Guidelines

One of the main advantages of the Windows operating systems is that they present a common interface across all applications. Users who can work with one Windows-based application can easily learn another one that uses the same basic interface, but can't as easily learn one that strays too far from the established interface guidelines.

Menus are a good example of this common interface. Most Windows-based applications follow the standard of positioning a File menu at the left end of the menu bar and a Help menu at the right end, with optional menus such as Edit and Tools in between. It can be argued that Documents would be a better name than File, or that the Help menu should come first. There's nothing to prevent the team from breaking with the standard, but doing so can confuse users and decrease the usability of the application.

The placement of commands is also important. For example, users expect to find the Copy, Cut, and Paste commands on the Edit menu; moving them to the File menu would be confusing. It's best not to deviate from the established guidelines without very solid reasons.

Discoverability of Features

One of the key concepts in usability testing is that of *discoverability*. If users can't discover how to use a feature (or even that the feature exists), that feature is worthless. For example, many Windows 3.1 users were never aware that the ALT, TAB key combination could be used to switch between open applications. There was no clue anywhere in the interface to help users discover this feature.

To test the discoverability of a feature, the team should ask users to perform a task without explaining how to do it. If they can't accomplish the task, or if several attempts are necessary to accomplish it, the discoverability of that feature needs work.

Navigation

All computer users can become familiar with menu-based navigation systems. Like many of the UI elements, consistent use of a menuing system is most important. As with other usability issues, the team should use the Windows standards to improve usability through discovery. With the improvement of browser scripting, Web-based applications can take on the same menuing styles as the classic native application menu systems. Additionally, native applications can use the link and page metaphors of Web-based applications to improve navigation throughout the application. Once again, simplicity and consistency are the key points to designing an application navigation system.

User Assistance Model

No matter how great the UI, there will be times that a user needs assistance. The user assistance model for the application should include online help and printed documentation, and it may include user assistance devices, such as ToolTips, status bars, "What's This?" help, and wizards.

The user assistance model should be designed early in the development process, just like any other part of the application. The model's features will vary depending on the complexity of the application and the sophistication of the intended audience.

Creating the UI

As the team designs and determines the look of the UI and the type of interface to create, the development team will have to create actual UI for the application. As discussed in Chapter 5, the team should rely on prototypes to work with the user community to test and design the UI. Once the design is created, as discussed in Chapter 6 during the Planning phase, the team can take advantage of the Integrated Development Environment (IDE) to simplify the implementation process for native and Web-based applications. The IDE provide wizards, templates, and screen painters to help the team rapidly create the UI, which in turn interacts with the other portions of the user service layer.

Implementing a Native User Service Layer

Creating native UI applications varies significantly between development languages. Within the Microsoft IDE, UIs can be created with Visual Basic, Visual C++, or Visual J++. These UIs often rely on controls, code libraries, and operating system APIs supplied as part of the development language. As many multi-layer applications are being implemented with Web-based interfaces, we will not spend a significant time discussing creating native application UIs. However, for additional information, several other books can be used as references, such as the *Microsoft Visual Basic 6.0 Programmer's Guide* (Microsoft, 1998), *Microsoft Visual C++ 6.0 Programmer's Guide* (Microsoft, 1998), *Desktop Applications for Microsoft Visual Basic 6.0* (Microsoft, 1999), *Desktop Applications for Microsoft Visual C++ 6.0* (Microsoft, 1999), *Visual Basic 6.0 Win32 API Tutorial* (Wrox Press, 1998), and *Essential Guide to User Interface Design: An Introduction to GUI Design Principles and Techniques* (John Wiley and Sons, 1996).

Implementing a Web-Based User Service Layer

Like any other enterprise application, an Internet-based application must often generate dynamic displays from one or more data sources. To help with the creation of this type of application, the development team can use the ASP component of IIS. With the release of IIS 4.0, ASP is also integrated with MTS.

Caution A common error made by many new ASP developers is implementing too much business layer logic within ASP scripts. To scale applications and simplify script coding, developers should remember to implement business logic blocks as business-layer COM components.

Overview of ASP

In an Internet application, a Web browser displays an HTML-page-based user service layer. Requests from this layer transmit via HTTP to a Web server. In response to these requests from the client Web browser, ASP pages activate on the Web server. The ASP pages can dynamically generate HTML pages to be returned to the requesting browser. These ASP pages can be used to generate UI code to format and control the look and feel of the Web pages, thus ASP would be considered part of the user service layer. Also, the ASP pages can contain server-side script code that implements business logic, thus ASP pages can be part of the business service layer. However, the ASP pages should contain server-side script code that uses middle-tier business objects to do much of the work. The business objects might in turn call data access objects to access data sources in the data access service layer. Alternatively, the HTML and client-side script code used to generate the user service layer might be located within the ASP pages. Either way, ASP straddles the line between the user service layer and the business service layer.

Benefits of ASP

ASP offers developers several advantages by addressing a number of issues and complications that arise during the development of high-quality, high-performance Web sites.

Familiar Programming Model

A major advantage of ASP is its familiar programming model, which closely resembles HTML but is augmented with scripting. Server-side scripts can be written in any language, as long as a corresponding scripting engine is available. IIS includes scripting engines for Visual Basic Script and Microsoft JScript, which is based on (ECMA) script.

In general, server-side ASP code should defer complex algorithms to COM components, and code that simply calls multiple COM objects to perform work should be placed in a COM component. Because ASP script code is interpreted at run time, less script interpretation results in more effective development performance. On a technical level, ASP code can use only the **IDispatch** interface to access Automation components. Business objects are compiled and can usually take advantage of vtable-binding, generally providing improved performance over ASP code's use of **IDispatch**. Additionally, business objects can be reused in other applications, such as a Win32-bit client version.

Security

ASP runs on a Web server and controls exactly what gets sent back to the Web client, thereby protecting intellectual property—data or code. Client computers cannot track the data's location or the origin of the generated HTML. This protective mechanism provides a layer of security abstraction that many applications can utilize with an appropriate design.

Browser and Display Variations

ASP tackles the problem created by wide client browser variation. For instance, different browsers provide different levels of support for different HTML versions and standards, including DHTML, and some browsers support proprietary extensions to HTML or DHTML. Some browsers support Java applets, some support ActiveX controls, and some don't support client-side components at all. Some browsers support client-side scripting through JavaScript or Visual Basic Scripting Edition, and others don't support any client-side scripting.

In addition to browser differences, the wide variation in screen resolution and display colors can make it difficult to create Web pages that work well for all users.

Dynamic Content

ASP also addresses the need to generate Web content dynamically, as well as statically. Dynamic content is normally generated from one or more server-side data sources, which should not be directly accessed by client computers. For one thing, per-client connections don't scale very well. More importantly, security issues arise when random Internet users are given access to corporate databases. As a result, Internet applications are usually structured so that a secured server-side application can generate HTML pages containing data to be displayed.

Whenever a Web client needs more data, the Web server receives a new request, and the server-side application then generates a new Web page.

ASP alleviates dynamic content issues by mixing server-side scripts and client-side content. Accessing an ASP page triggers execution of server-side scripts on a server. When these scripts are executed, an HTTP response is generated and sent back to the client. Server-side scripts can control the HTML statements (coded in .asp files) included in such responses; or these scripts can generate HTML statements on the fly. ASP pages provide a straightforward manner in which to handle various browser capabilities and to display conditionally different information according to the features supported by the requesting client.

With the advent of Java applets, ActiveX controls, DHTML, and ASP pages, it is now possible to write client-side Web applications that maintain some connection to a server. Instead of forcing a new page to be generated whenever more data is needed, data is transferred between scripted client-side components and a server-side application. Internal data sources do not need to be exposed on the Internet because they are accessed only by server-side applications.

Automation Components

ASP provides several standard Automation components to help with common Web tasks, such as determining browser characteristics, parsing parameters and cookies in a page request, or sharing information between pages in the application. ASP's support of Automation components, which are compatible with server-side scripts, makes it relatively easy to write pages to process HTML forms. In addition, complex operations can be coded once in custom components, and later reused in many server-side applications.

ASP and MTS

ASP provides a powerful way of bridging the gap between client-side presentation logic and server-side business logic in three-tier Internet applications. With IIS 4.0, ASP is fully integrated with MTS. MTS provides process, thread, and other resource management services to IIS and ASP applications, and allows pages in an ASP application to be marked as transactional, giving each page all the benefits of transactions.

The server-side script in an ASP page is often considered the first layer of business logic. This layer might use several COM objects to satisfy a request. Transactions can be used to help ensure that resources are updated correctly when multiple objects work together to fulfill a client request. IIS 4.0 allows any ASP page to be processed within a transaction. When a page is processed, a new transaction is created. All the objects created within the page are automatically enlisted in the transaction, if appropriate, by MTS. The transaction terminates when the entire file has been interpreted and any server-side scripts have executed. If the transaction aborts, all of the resources in the transaction roll back to the values they had before page processing began. Because the development team is creating a Web-based application's design, this roll back capability is particularly useful for pages that update databases.

IIS uses MTS to manage server application processes. Each application, denoted by a unique virtual directory, can be configured to run in the main IIS process or in a specific MTS process. Such a process can improve overall server reliability. If one application fails, only that application is shut down and restarted. Shutting down the application does not negatively affect other applications, or more importantly, the entire Web server.

Separating applications into individual processes also helps with server maintenance. If an application needs to be updated, only that application process needs to be shut down, and the entire Web server, as well as other server applications, can continue to run.

MTS manages all application processes. However, an IIS configuration setting can create a specific IIS application. An IIS application's management is encapsulated by a COM component called the *Web Application Manager* (WAM) before being controlled by MTS. The WAM is responsible for loading the ASP run-time and other DLLs, and communicates with these DLLs whenever an HTTP request is received. Whether running in IIS or in another process, each application contains an instance of the WAM object. When IIS is configured to run an application separately, developers can call on MTS administrative objects to:

- Create a new MTS package.
- Generate a new globally unique identifier (GUID).
- Add a WAM to a package using a new GUID.
- Configure the package to run in a separate process.

Applications configured to run in IIS are registered in a default MTS in-process package. When IIS receives an HTTP request, it determines whether or not the requested Uniform Resource Locator (URL) is designated as an IIS application. If so, IIS looks in its internal WAM map to locate the correct WAM object. If the application isn't running, its WAM won't exist and will have to be created. IIS creates the WAM object using the application-specific GUID generated at registration time. At this point, MTS starts a new process, if necessary, and begins managing objects and resources for the application. If the requested URL is not part of an application, it is processed within the default IIS application space.

ASP Application Specifics

As we discussed, ASP pages can be used to call the business objects from the server and return Web pages to the client. ASP pages contain a combination of directives, script, and text. Directives and script are delimited using the characters "<%" and "%>". The <SCRIPT> tag can be used to mark a block of server-side script. Any element other than a directive or server-side script is displayed as-is in the Web page returned to the client.

ASP page scripts are executed when the page request is received from the client. Objects created by the scripts exist only for the duration of page processing, unless explicitly saved in Session or Application variables. Saving objects in these variables may limit scalability or affect dynamic load balancing, and these implications should be considered carefully before saving objects.

Within the scope of a page, developers can create whatever objects they need to perform page work. However, as we've already said, as much business logic as possible should be encapsulated in components, rather than using script code. Server-side script should focus mainly on calling business objects and creating Web pages to be returned to the client computer.

When transactions are used, the page processing defines the transaction boundary for all objects created by the page. If any object aborts a transaction, an error page can be returned instead of the requested page. To mark a page as transactional, use the TRANSACTION directive in the first line of the page's code, as shown here:

```
<%@LANGUAGE="VBSCRIPT" TRANSACTION=REQUIRED%>
```

The **OnTransactionCommit** and **OnTransactionAbort** events can be used to return different information to the client, depending on whether the transaction committed or aborted.

The **CreateObject** method is used in a server-side script to create objects, ensuring that the objects are created within proper transaction context, and that access to ASP-intrinsic objects, such as **Response** and **Request**, is available. To abort a transaction from within a server-side script, call the **ObjectContext SetAbort** method.

Using Client-Side Components

ActiveX components are small COM components sent to the client from the ASP pages. Client-side ActiveX components can be used with client-side scripts to perform user service and business services. Using an ActiveX component with client-side scripting is no different than using remote business objects. (We discuss remote data objects in further detail in Chapter 9.) However, if developers are creating components to be used from client-side applications, they need to pay special attention to the code security and download issues described earlier.

When using Internet Component Download to download and install client-side application components, the components should be packaged in a self-installing executable or .cab file, according to guidelines in the Microsoft Platform Sofware Development Kit (SDK) Internet Component Download documentation. The downloadable file should be digitally signed so that users can verify that the file comes from a trusted source and has not been violated. All DLLs on which components rely should be included or referenced in the download package. Development tool documentation should identify the DLLs required by tool-generated components. Such documentation could also provide instructions on how to package these components for downloading.

Regardless of whether or not these components are downloaded, verify that they are safe for scripting and initializing. As mentioned, some browser configurations may prevent unsafe components from being created or scripted. Registry entries can be used to mark components as safe for scripting and initialization, or the **IObjectSafety** interface detailed in the Platform SDK can be implemented.

Accessing a Native Application

The key point to remember in accessing native applications is the application relies heavily on the underlying operating system. For Windows applications, the application's executables, DLL, and additional application code must be accessible and known to the client operating system. The application is typically started using an icon or through the operating system's program menus. For the application to be accessible, it is critical the application's installation and configuration routines are executed properly on the desktop computer.

Accessing a Web-Based Application

It is important to understand some basics of Web server and browser access. Most Web applications are accessed through a browser and a display name in the form of a URL. The display name leads the browser to an IP address, typically by means of a Domain Name Server (DNS) lookup. After the IP address is located, a TCP/IP session is established with the Web server using an HTTP communication protocol.

With older browsers or those not using HTTP 1.1 or later, each picture, page, control, and applet are separate HTTP requests, and therefore separate sessions. Each time a session is established, it requires processing, time, and bandwidth overhead. Browsers using HTTP 1.1 or later can be configured to perform multiple HTTP requests within a single session, thereby decreasing load time and communication overhead.

The client computer stores the resolved DNS name and the appropriate TCP/IP address in the computer's memory for a fixed period of time (determined by the user). The next time the URL is requested, the browser first looks in memory for the appropriate IP address. If the name is no longer stored in the client computer's memory, the DNS name lookup is retriggered.

Accessing Redundant Web-Based User Services

In the early days of statically written Web pages, scaling Web servers was a simple process. Mirror sites hosting identical content would be created on two or more Web servers. Each Web server had its own TCP/IP address, as shown in Figure 7.1. A DNS naming technique called *round-robin DNS* assigned all the TCP/IP addresses to a single display name. Each time the DNS server received a name request, it provided the TCP/IP address of the next server in an ongoing loop. Thus, access was evenly allocated across all servers, allowing these servers to share the request-processing load using a method known as *load balancing*. An additional result was that a client computer couldn't determine which server it would access when it requested the Web page's URL.

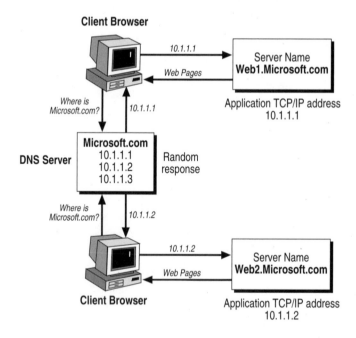

Figure 7.1   Web server configuration using Windows Load Balancing Service

Currently, dynamic pages and typical Web page scripting prevent this round-robin load balancing from working properly. Web servers maintain ongoing sessions, and many pages apply session variables that are used throughout a client computer's interaction with a Web server. Because a client computer might not always return to the same Web server over a specific period, round-robin load-balancing does not work with most session-oriented Web sites. If the client computer later accesses a different (mirrored) server, the mirrored server doesn't have any information about the client computer's previous session and might not recognize the authentication, causing a page request to fail.

A simple solution to this problem is to ensure that, for a period of time, a client always returns to the same server. With so-called *sticky connections*, the client computer resolves a URL to a single TCP/IP address allocated for all the Web servers. This central TCP/IP address is an intermediate address that controls specific servers to which actual page requests are sent. Logically, intermediary TCP/IP addressing resembles the diagram in Figure 7.2. Incoming requests are directed from the intermediate server to a new server. Repeat visitors are directed to their specifically allocated server.

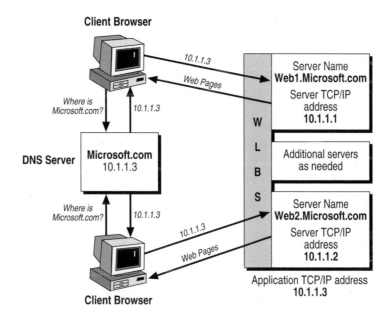

Figure 7.2   Adding Web servers to improve performance

Microsoft provides the Windows Load Balancing Service (WLBS) and Cisco Systems provides LocalDirector to maintain sticky connections for clients and to add fault tolerance. The WLBS system continually monitors Web servers to determine whether a server becomes non-functional, ensuring that page requests are not sent to a defunct server. To add additional Web server processing, a new mirror server is configured and simply added to the Web server WLBS cluster.

These scaling technologies allow the Web-based UI to continually increase the number of concurrent clients being served without requiring a significant re-design of the Web-based application code.

Connecting the User and Business Service Layers

In multi-layer application design, each layer must be able to communicate with its neighbors. Thus, the user service layer and business service layer must be able to pass control to each other, as well as pass information and data. Objects can be used within a user service layer as well as within the business service layer. Additionally, many mistakenly think the UI and user service layer are the only portions of an application that can affect the desktop computer. Often business objects are distributed to the desktop client computers along with the user service layer.

Making Business Objects Available to Client Computers

Components must be properly configured for object creation to work. To start with, developers must either provide a CLSID and the remote server name in a call to **CoCreateInstanceEx** to create the object or install some information in the client computer's registry. To access components using Visual Basic and most scripting languages, this information would include the object's **ProgID**, **CLSID**, and **RemoteServerName** registry entries.

Note For business objects running in MTS environments, the easiest way to provide this information is to run the client install program on each client computer. (For additional information on MTS see Chapter 8.) The client install program also takes care of installing and registering any type libraries or proxy/stub DLLs required to use vtable-binding or late-binding to access components during development.

The <OBJECT> tag is used on a Web page to automatically download the client install program, using the Internet Component Download service. The <OBJECT> tag CODEBASE parameter points the browser to the location of the program. To automatically install required remote component registry entries from a Web page using Internet Component Download, the <OBJECT> tag must be used to create the object; script code cannot download and install component information.

In addition to the general registration process for Internet components, code safety issues must be considered when using ActiveX controls or business objects from Web pages. Internet Component Download install programs should be digitally signed. Depending on the users' particular browser settings, a browser may prevent unsigned install programs from being downloaded. The digital signature lets browsers determine the install program's origin, and detect whether or not the install program has been violated.

Note The Platform SDK contains information about, as well as tools for, creating signed packages for download. Some development tools, such as Visual Basic, also provide packaging and deployment tools used for signing packages.

ActiveX Components should be marked as:

- **Safe for scripting** Users are notified that client-side scripts won't use the application's components to harm user computers or obtain unauthorized information.

- **Safe for initializing** Users are notified that the Web page's controls will not harm the user's computer.

The easiest way to perform this action for both scripting and initializing is to add the following subkeys to the registry under a component's CLSID:

```
Implemented  Categories\{7DD95801-9882-11CF-9FA9-00AA006C42C4}
Implemented  Categories\{7DD95802-9882-11CF-9FA9-00AA006C42C4}
```

If components aren't marked as safe for scripting and initializing, a browser can't create objects or make method calls to objects, depending on individual browser settings.

Accessing Business Objects in Native Applications

For native Win32 applications, the mechanics of accessing remote business objects with DCOM really aren't much different from those for accessing any other COM component. (We discuss DCOM is further detail in Chapter 8.) Developers simply call **CoCreateInstance**, **CoCreateInstanceEx**, or the equivalent object creation mechanism provided by the development language being used. After a DCOM-based object is created, method calls can be made as usual.

Note The object context's **CreateInstance** method should be used only to create MTS-hosted objects from within the MTS environment. **CreateInstance** should not be used to create remote business objects from applications running on users' computers. Such applications are base clients, running outside the MTS environment.

Native client applications should acquire and hold interface pointers to MTS-based business objects rather than recreate objects each time they are needed, largely to avoid the expense of locating remote servers and establishing communication sessions between computers. Typically, an application creates objects during its initialization, or when a specific portion of the application is first accessed.

Interface pointers returned from object creation should be stored in application variables for future use. These pointers don't need to be released until the application in which they are stored shuts down, unless the application receives a communication error during a method call. Such a communication error could indicate that the remote server computer is unavailable. Releasing and reacquiring the interface pointers allows the application to take advantage of MTS fail-over support on the server.

Accessing Business Objects in Web-Based Applications

COM objects can be created on a Web page using:

- **The HTML <OBJECT> tag** Objects are created during page rendering. This technique is normally used for visual objects, such as ActiveX controls.
- **Script code** Objects are created only when the script is executed.

These two methods of creating COM objects work for both client-side and remote COM objects. Client-side script code is used to call methods on objects, regardless of how the objects were created. The script code provides access to the methods and properties exposed by the objects' **IDispatch** interfaces.

When using the <OBJECT> tag, the business object's ClassID can be specified and given an ID so that the object can be accessed from client-side script code. The following <OBJECT> tag can be used to create an instance of a component:

```
<OBJECT ID="objCustomer"
    CLASSID="clsid:6FED8869-EAC5-11D1-80F4-00C04FD61196">
</OBJECT>
```

The exact script code used to create objects depends on the scripting language used. In VBScript, the **CreateObject** function is called, as shown here:

```
<SCRIPT LANGUAGE="VBScript">
    Dim objCustomer
    Set objCustomer = CreateObject("bus_CustomerC.Customer")
Do other program logic.
    Set objCustomer = Nothing
</SCRIPT>
```

In JScript, the **ActiveXObject** object is used, as shown here:

```
<SCRIPT LANGUAGE="JScript">
    var objCustomer;
    objCustomer = new ActiveXObject("bus_CustomerC.Customer");
Do other program logic.
    objCustomer = "";
</SCRIPT>
```

After the object is created, the object methods can be accessed through script code, using the object ID as the variable's name, as shown in the following example:

```
<SCRIPT LANGUAGE="VBScript">
    Dim rsCustomer
    Set rsCustomer = objCustomer.GetByEmail("someone@microsoft.com")
</SCRIPT>
```

Accessing Remote Objects Using RDS

Another option for accessing remote objects from client computers is to use RDS to call objects via DCOM or HTTP. RDS can be helpful for accessing remote objects from Web pages. However, like most scripting languages used in Web page development, it can access methods only on an **IDispatch** interface exposed by a set of components.

To use business objects with RDS over DCOM, they must be marked as safe for scripting and initializing, as described earlier. The client computer needs only a registry entry mapping the component's **ProgID** to its CLSID.

To use business objects with RDS over HTTP, their **ProgIDs** must be added to the **ADCLaunch** registry key on the server computer, as follows:

```
HKEY_LOCAL_MACHINE\SYSTEM\CurrentControlSet\Services\W3SVC\Parameters\ADCLaunch
```

The **RDS.Dataspace** object is used to invoke business objects. The following code fragment shows how a Web page could create a remote object and call its **GetByEmail** method using RDS over HTTP:

```
<SCRIPT LANGUAGE="VBScript">
    Dim rdsds, objCustomer, rsCustomer
    Set rdsds = CreateObject("RDS.Dataspace")
    Set objCustomer = rdsds.CreateObject("bus_CustomerC.Customer", _
                                    "http://webservername")
    Set rsCustomer = objCustomer.GetByEmail("someone@microsoft.com")
</SCRIPT>
```

The **DataSpace CreateObject** method generates a client-side proxy that calls methods on an object using **IDispatch** over DCOM or HTTP. One parameter specifies the **ProgID** of the object to be created. Another parameter specifies the object's server name. This parameter controls whether the object is called over DCOM or HTTP. If the server name is specified using the form \\machineName, DCOM is used. However, if the server name is specified using the form http://machineName, HTTP is used. HTTP over the Secure Sockets Layer (HTTPS) is also supported.

Note For more information about using RDS, including sample code, refer to the Microsoft Data Access SDK documentation included in the Platform SDK. The white paper *Remote Data Service in MDAC 2.0* by Kamaljit Bath is another excellent source of information; this white paper is available from the MSDN Web site at http://msdn.microsoft.com.

Using Data Binding

RDS can also be used to return disconnected ADO **Recordset** objects to client computers. In Internet Explorer 4.0 and later versions, DHTML data binding can be used to connect these **Recordset** objects to HTML elements on Web pages in development. Using data binding and client-side scripting allows users to browse through the **Recordset** objects without reconnecting directly to the to the Web server to retrieve additional records.

The data-binding support in Internet Explorer 4.x and later versions is not specific to any particular type of data. Internet Explorer will bind to any type of data for which there is a data source object (DSO). The DSO is responsible for transporting data between client and server computers, manipulating the data, and providing an object model for script access. The DHTML attributes DATASRC, DATAFLD, DATAFORMATAS, and DATAPAGESIZE are used to determine data origin, data fields bound to particular HTML elements, treatment of data as text or otherwise, and the number of records to be displayed on a page.

The **RDS.DataControl** object is a DSO for OLE DB **Rowset** objects and ADO **Recordset** objects. The **RDS.DataControl** object supports both two-tier and three-tier models of data access. In the two-tier model, data source information is embedded in the Web page, and each client gets its own connection to this data source. In the three-tier model, business objects are used to return a disconnected **Recordset** to the client, which is in turn attached to a **DataControl** object.

Visual Studio 6.0 supports data binding to ADO **Recordset** objects. Developers can use the ADO **Data Control** object to establish a connection between data-bound controls and a **Recordset** object. First, an ADO **Data Control** object is created. This object's **Recordset** property is then set to a **Recordset** object returned from business objects. The **DataSource** property of each data-bound control on a form or in a dialog box is set to the ADO **Data Control** object. The **Recordset** object can also be attached directly to each data-bound control using the **DataSource** property.

Summary

We began the chapter by discussing important considerations for the team determining the UI and user service implementation such as security, desktop operating system, client browsers, and distributed communication.

We also looked at the basics of a functional UI design. We recommended simplify and consistency as the primary guiding factors. Basic elements of the UI and their usage we also discussed. In designing the UI we provided several key areas of consideration such as the applications composition, usability, and user assistance model.

After looking at the UI design, we discussed key criteria for determining the type of application the team can create. These native and Web-based application characteristics were discussed as well as how these types of applications can be create and assessed. We concluded our discussion by looking at the interaction of the user service and business service layers.

Review

1. What is UI composition?
2. What is usability?
3. List some common issues encountered when designing the user service layer.
4. How can COM objects be used in the user service layer?
5. How does ASP fit in the user, business, and data access layers?

C H A P T E R   8

Business Service Layer Technologies

About This Chapter

Business objects tend to encapsulate corporate business rules and application-specific operations. Once the components are designed as described in Chapters 2 and 6, implementing them should be a fairly mechanical coding exercise. However, some specific issues may need to be addressed during the design process to ensure that business objects work well, particularly within the Microsoft Transaction Server (MTS) environment. This chapter focuses on such issues as:

- Using an object context to manage state.
- Using explicitly defined interfaces when possible.
- Composing functionality.
- Maintaining state across transaction boundaries.
- Propagating errors.
- Programmatically controlling security.

These issues are more common to business objects than to data objects.

In addition, this chapter examines using the Microsoft Component Object Model (COM) within the business service of an application's physical design. Business rules and processes are first integrated into a physical design that effectively uses COM technologies. Component-specific network technologies and environmental impacts are then integrated into the physical design.

The majority of this chapter's information is based on our own experience, together with the following sources:

- Mary Kirtland's *Designing Component-Based Solutions*
- Speeches and white papers from the Microsoft COM group

Upon completion, you will be able to:

- Understand the Microsoft Component Object Model (COM).
- Analyze the role of COM in logical and physical design models.
- Understand COM capabilities in transactional processing using MTS.
- Understand how objects are used throughout a network and enterprise.
- Analyze environmental impacts that affect the business service layer to derive an optimal physical design.

Overview of Business Services

As discussed in Chapter 6, before business services (also called the *business layer*) can be implemented, design documents must include a good preliminary specification of the needed main classes, or *business objects*, and how these business objects are to be packaged into components. As we examine business objects and their implementations, the following key design points should be considered:

- Regardless of how the information they use is actually stored, business objects encapsulate real-world business operations.
- Business objects control sequencing and enforcement of business rules, as well as the transactional integrity of the operations they perform.
- Each business object method should perform exactly one unit of work; each unit of work should in turn be implemented in exactly one method.
- Calling methods on business and data objects enables higher-level operations.
- Whether or not a particular caller is transactional, business objects should work properly.
- Business objects called *directly from* a presentation layer should not retain per-object state across method calls. Business objects called *within* a presentation layer can retain per-object state within a transaction boundary (a boundary between services layers).
- Minimizing network traffic between remote presentation layers and business objects is important; therefore, business objects should be network-friendly.
- Role-based security should be used to restrict access to business objects, as they are the gatekeepers that control data access.
- Transaction models, such as those within MTS, provide a straightforward model for handling errors generated within business object methods.

Based on the design points mentioned above, business object implementations will likely be important company assets for use in many applications.

Component Object Model (COM)

To facilitate understanding of Microsoft business service technologies, we'll examine COM, which is the foundation of many of the technologies we will discuss in this book. This chapter is not intended as an exhaustive discussion of COM, but we will briefly review some of the basic concepts developers should know before they begin their application architectures. Recommendations for further reading are listed in the bibliography.

Note Another leading object model and implementation in the computer industry is Common Object Request Broker Architecture (CORBA). For CORBA-specific information, we recommend Alan Pope's *The CORBA Reference Guide* (Addison-Wesley, 1998).

Why COM?

The fundamental goal of COM is to enable developers to create applications assembled from pre-built parts, or components. Components are the physical binary implementations of the business object. For example, an order-entry application could use a data-entry grid component to simplify entering ordered items into the application. Another component could look up a customer's city and state by entering the customer's ZIP code or postal code. Yet another component could calculate the order's sales tax. To make such a component-based application a reality, several technical challenges must be met.

The first technical challenge is how to locate the component on a computer or network and, once located, to execute the component. The locating of components is also referenced as a directory service for the components. If no such standards exist, overhead costs of learning to use components is very high. Additionally, the costs and inconsistencies of coding logic to locate additional components and create objects would present significant barriers to reusing pre-built components. In conjunction with these standard mechanisms used for internally created components, applications must also be available to identify and execute vendor-created components.

The second technical challenge is to provide standards for the application to interact with the components. Again, if no standards exist, the overhead cost of learning how to use such objects creates a barrier to reusing code. Ideally, a standard mechanism for object interaction would not distinguish the location of any given object, whether the object exists within its own application's process, within another process on the application's host computer, or within a different process on another computer altogether. Inter-process and remote communications usually require tremendously complex coding within an application. Providing standards for object interaction will allow application and component developers to spend less time creating such complex code.

The third technical challenge is executing true language independence, a complex challenge for any object model. Every element involved in a particular object—memory allocation, method names, parameter types, calling conventions, and so on—must be defined in such a way that the object can be created in one programming language and used by another. Application developers should not need to spend valuable time or energy worrying which programming languages or tools are used to create a desired component. Without wide support from development languages and tools, many different models will fragment the component market. This fragmentation raises the costs of identifying, purchasing, and developing components that are operable only in certain environments.

Finally, an ongoing challenge is in maintaining the potential to create newer versions of applications and components. Applications developed at different times can implement identical components, and thus cause usage conflicts, when running on a given computer. As developers continue to upgrade components to maintain function in the ever-changing world of computer technology, version compatibility must be maintained. These ongoing upgrades can involve fixing problems in existing component features, adding new functionality to existing components themselves, or creating new components altogether.

The following subsections review elements and terminology of COM that are commonly used in application development.

Objects

"Object" is one of the most overloaded terms in programming. As with most object-oriented models, COM objects are run-time instances of a particular class, with the class representing a real-world entity. We'll define the exact meaning of classes later in this chapter; conceptually, however, classes are types of objects. For example, based on their characteristics, classes could define a **Customer**, **Order**, or **SalesTaxCalculator**. Thus, each **Customer** object would represent a specific instance of a real-world customer; each **Order** object a specific instance of an order; and so on.

An object usually contains an identity, a state, and a type of behavior. Identity is the unique name or label distinguishing one object from any other. State represents data associated with a particular object. Behavior is a set of methods called to query or manipulate an object's state.

To help clarify these concepts, let's examine C++ objects, which are run-time instances of C++ classes. A C++ class defines member variables and methods that apply only to objects of this particular class. Upon a particular object's creation, a contiguous block of memory becomes allocated for member variables; the allocated memory's address in effect becomes the object's identity and the memory block's contents become the object's state. Located elsewhere in memory, method implementation code defines the object's behavior.

Most language-based object models are similar to that of C++, but the COM object model is somewhat different. Recall that two challenges faced by COM are language- and location-independence. When developers begin to examine inter-process and remote communications, memory addresses are not sufficient to identify objects. In addition, compatibility among all programming languages and tools regarding memory layout for object member variables is nearly impossible.

Accounting for these potential complications, COM approaches objects in a different manner than C++. In COM, the notion of an object's public interface and its implementation are completely separate. Applications can interact with COM objects only through the object's public interfaces using a COM-defined interface pointer. Since all interactions must go through the interface pointer, COM ignores an object's state location and memory inner workings. Additionally, since an interface pointer is the only means through which an application references a given object, the object's identity must relate to that pointer.

Interfaces

Understanding interfaces is essential to understanding COM. A COM interface is a collection of logically related operations that define a particular behavior. When developers define an interface, they provide specifications only for a set of operations, but not for implementations. Interface definitions represent a contract between a caller and an implementer: if a component implements a particular interface, the caller can expect the component to obey the interface specification. Such a specification includes a strict definition of interface method syntax, as well as a definition of interface semantics.

To be defined as a COM interface, such an interface must satisfy the following requirements:

- A unique identifier must identify the interface.
- The interface must ultimately derive from the special interface **IUnknown**.
- Once published, the interface must be immutable. In other words, the interface can't be changed.

COM Identifiers

Unique COM identifiers are needed to locate components, and also to reference each interface. Providing a unique identifier to cite each interface could involve using a string identifier, which could cause several problems.

The most critical issue raised by performing this action is the difficulty of guaranteeing the selection of a truly unique identifier. Even when a naming convention is imposed, there is a possibility that another developer elsewhere in the world will use the same identifier for a different purpose. To guarantee uniqueness, prefixes could be issued from a central authority—for example, one prefix per company. Each company would, in turn, need a central registry of names to prevent any duplicates within the company. To impose such a method on string identifiers seems much too complicated.

Instead of using string identifiers, COM implements globally unique identifiers (GUIDs, pronounced "goo-ids" or "gwids"), which are 128-bit system-generated integers that uniquely identify components. The algorithm used to generate GUIDs is statistically guaranteed to generate unique identification numbers.

Note According to the COM specification, GUIDs can be generated at the rate of 10,000,000 per second per computer for the next 3,240 years without risk of duplication.

GUIDs can be generated using a tool such as GUIDGEN, which accompanies the Microsoft Platform Software Development Kit (SDK). GUIDGEN calls the system application programming interface (API) function **CoCreateGuid** to generate the GUID, then provides several output options. For example, the following GUID was generated using the static const output option, and is suitable for inclusion in a C++ source file:

```
// {45D3F4B0-DB76-11d1-AA06-0040052510F1}
static const GUID GUID_Sample = { 0x45d3f4b0, 0xdb76, 0x11d1,
    { 0xaa, 0x6, 0x0, 0x40, 0x5, 0x25, 0x10, 0xf1 } };
```

The first line in the code example shown above is a comment showing how a GUID appears in string form; GUIDs are normally presented to users in this string form. The second and third lines in the code example above define the GUID as a constant that can be used in C++ code.

Note Most development tools automate the process of creating skeleton COM components. Such tools also generate appropriate GUIDs for developers in a format that the skeleton COM code can recognize.

Every interface is identified by a GUID. Whenever we need to uniquely identify an interface to COM, we use its GUID, which we call an interface identification (IID). The IID can be complex numerical figures such as {45D3F4B0-DB76-11d1-AA06-0040052510F1} or {45D3F4B1-DB76-11d1-AA06-0040052510F1}.

To simplify IID standards for use in source code, every interface should also have a string name. Conventionally, these string names usually begin with the letter "I"—for example, **IComputeSalesTax**. String names aren't guaranteed to be unique, but it's unlikely that two different interfaces with an identical string name would be used in one source code file.

Defining Interfaces

Concern may arise over how to define interfaces so that component developers know how to implement them and application developers know how to use them. COM does not rigidly distinguish interface definitions, as long as both component and application developers can agree on the definitions. In practice, COM interfaces are usually defined using the Interface Definition Language (IDL).

Similar to C++, IDL is a language that describes the exact syntax of an interface. Interface definitions begin with an interface keyword; interface attributes are contained in square brackets preceding the interface keyword. An object attribute indicates that COM IDL extensions should be used, and a UUID attribute (see the following note) specifies the IID for the interface being defined.

Note The attribute is named UUID because COM IDL is based on the Open Software Foundation's Distributed Computing Environment (DCE) IDL, which uses the term "universally unique identifier" (UUID) instead of GUID.

Not all development languages will support all data types that can be specified using IDL. Most interfaces use a fairly restricted set of data types. We discuss this limitation in more detail later in this chapter. COM methods can have any number of parameters and arbitrarily complex data types. Beside simple types such as a name and data type, developers can specify additional attributes for each IDL parameter. These attributes provide clues about how data should be copied from one place to another. IDL is a convenient text format for documenting the interface syntax. Once the IDL code is written, it can be compiled using the Microsoft IDL (MIDL) compiler to generate the following equivalent interface definition representations, which are useful to development tools:

- **Header file** Header files define the IDL types that can be used to declare interface pointer variables, or to derive an implementation class for an interface. Header files can be included in a C or C++ program.

- **Type library** Type libraries are binary representations of IDL code. Development languages, such as Microsoft Visual Basic, read the type library to determine the syntax of the interfaces described in the type library.

- **Source code for a proxy/stub DLL** This source code implements proxy/stub DLLs used for inter-process and remote communication.

While not difficult to use, IDL is still new to many developers; thus most development languages and tools offer assistance. Some systems, such as Visual Basic, completely hide IDL by allowing developers to define interfaces directly in the system's syntax while the system itself generates a type library for the interface. Other tools generate the IDL file automatically, usually by providing a wizard or similar automated guide to help developers define an interface and its methods; after the interface and its methods have been defined, the tools generate the correct IDL syntax.

Defining interfaces using IDL is a preliminary step toward language independence, but not a complete solution. Given an IDL file, or an equivalent header file or type library, an interface or client application implementation can be coded, as long as it is done in any language recognizing the interface's types used. To ensure communication between the implementation developed and the client computer, both client and implementation must agree on what an interface pointer would represent, and how that pointer intermediates method calls.

COM as a Binary Standard

COM, as a binary standard for object interaction, addresses many component challenges. COM is a binary standard because:

- It is part specification-oriented.
- It is part implementation-oriented.

COM is part specification-based in that it defines objects in a language- and location-independent manner, as well as how to locate and identify components, and also create objects. A COM component's interface can be recognized with the IDL, or equivalent header file or type library.

COM is also part implementation-based in that it provides system services that locate components and load them into memory. Additionally, COM can perform inter-process and remote communications as well as other needed tasks. COM defines the exact binary representation of an interface. Any programming language or tool that supports COM must create object interfaces that correspond to this standard binary representation.

The client's interface pointer is actually a pointer to a table of more pointers. The table of pointers is called the vtable. Each pointer in the vtable points to the binary code for an interface method in exactly the same manner as in a C++ virtual function table.

A specific pointer to a vtable is appropriately called a *vtable pointer*. Each COM object contains a vtable pointer for each interface it supports. A client requesting an interface pointer to an object obtains *a pointer to* an appropriate vtable pointer, *not* the vtable pointer itself. The vtable pointer needs an additional pointer to support an interface because the component needs a way to identify the object on which it should be working.

When a COM object is created, a single block of memory is usually allocated for both vtable pointers as well as any internal data members that the object needs. The component recognizes the relationship between the locations of both the vtable pointer and the object's entire memory block; thus, this component can identify its appropriate object. By using the interface pointer, COM further specifies that the first parameter passed to each method call is a pointer to the particular object mentioned.

Fortunately, most COM-supportive programming languages and tools automatically map interface pointers and vtables to equivalent concepts in the languages themselves. For example, C++ interfaces are equivalent to abstract base classes. These interfaces can be implemented by deriving a particular class from the abstract base class. Calling COM methods through an interface pointer is exactly like calling C++ methods through an object pointer. As another example, Visual Basic interfaces are almost completely hidden within the Visual Basic language itself. An interface can be implemented by using the **implements** keyword and thereby implementing the interface's methods. To use a COM object, declare an interface type object variable, create the object, and make function calls as normal.

Combined with a common interpretation of interface definitions, the binary standard for interfaces provides language independence as well as the potential for complete location independence. As mentioned, it's ideal to make in-process, inter-process, and remote calls identical on the client computer. Within a single process, the interface pointer can direct itself to the original vtable pointer and call methods directly. Although such a technique probably wouldn't work across different processes or computers, the interface pointer could be redirected to point to a proxy vtable pointer. The client-side proxy would presumably recognize methods in which to make inter-process or remote calls to an equivalent server-side object, or stub; in turn, that particular object would make in-process calls to the original object. To clients and components, method calls would appear identical.

The IUnknown Interface

A vtable contains three methods—**QueryInterface**, **AddRef**, and **Release**—not defined by the developer for a COM component interface. The **IUnknown** interface provides these three methods, and also defines fundamental behavior for COM interfaces. Clients can rely on this fundamental behavior because all COM interfaces derive from **IUnknown**. **IUnknown** helps resolve the technical challenge of providing a standard means to interact with objects, and additionally provides three important features: interface navigation, interface versioning, and object lifetime management.

Interface Navigation

Interface navigation is provided by the **QueryInterface** method. As mentioned previously, COM objects can support more than one interface. For example, if developers have one interface pointer to an object and desire another, they can request it from the object using the **QueryInterface** method. Because all interfaces derive from **IUnknown**, every interface conveniently supports **QueryInterface**.

To use **QueryInterface**, a client chooses an IID it wants to pass to an object. If it supports that interface, the object passes back the interface pointer. If not, the object returns an error. **QueryInterface** is an extraordinarily powerful mechanism that allows independently created clients and components to negotiate a common communication method. **QueryInterface** is also the key to solving the challenge of versioning, which is discussed in greater detail in the following paragraphs.

Interface Versioning

Because components and applications can be built and published independently, an interface that has been published is immutable—no changes to syntax or semantics are allowed. Changing a published interface is not permitted; even changes to an interface's number of methods could cause damage. For instance, a new client application could erroneously read an interface as containing five methods, and unsuccessfully attempt to call an obsolete component containing only four methods, thus a program error would occur. COM interfaces are therefore immutable to avoid such conflicts.

Now that we have said an interface cannot be changed, a new interface must actually be defined to "version" an interface. Existing clients are probably incompatible with new interfaces, since the original interface continues to exist, so these clients are unaffected by whether or not components implement the interfaces. New clients can implement support for new interfaces and access new features when the clients communicate with new components. If a new client happens to access an older component, it can use **QueryInterface** to safely detect that the component does not support the new interface and avoid using the new features.

In summary, once a COM interface is defined it cannot be changed, so to create a new version, the new interface is added to the component and the previous interface is also maintained.

Object Lifetime Management

Assuming that an object has been created on a client computer holding an interface pointer to the object, it seems logical that this object could be destroyed on the client on which it was created. However, the process of destroying an object that is no longer needed is complicated. For instance, one client can use **QueryInterface** to obtain multiple interface pointers to a single object. This client may not be able to track when it had finished using all interface pointers needed to safely destroy the object. Another client could potentially need to use the object after it was marked for deletion. No single client can distinguish when all clients have finished using the object except the object itself—with some assistance from each client.

To address the issues involved in destroying an object, **IUnknown** provides a third feature—*object lifetime management,* commonly referred to as reference counting—which tracks the number of clients using an interface. When a new interface pointer to an object is created, the object's reference count must be

incremented by calling **IUnknown AddRef**. A client computer that has finished
using an interface pointer calls **IUnknown Release** to *decrement* the object's
reference count. When the reference count is set to zero, the object destroys itself upon determining that its use is complete. Hence the object lifetime management feature neatly solves the problems of both a single client with multiple
interface pointers as well as multiple independent clients. With this feature
implemented, the client computer's only tasks are to create an object to get an
interface pointer, use the pointer to make method calls, and release the pointer
using **IUnknown Release**.

Classes

When considering classes, it should be remembered that all COM objects are
instances of COM classes. A COM class is simply a named implementation of
one or more COM interfaces. A COM class is named using a class identifier
(CLSID), which is a type of GUID. Like IIDs, CLSIDs are guaranteed to be
unique, but are difficult to use. Therefore, COM classes can also have string
names, called *programmatic identifiers* (ProgID).

Every COM class has an associated *class object,* also known as a class factory,
which has the ability to create instances of a single COM class. The COM specification defines a standard API function for creating class objects
(**CoGetClassObject**), and a standard interface for communicating with class
objects (**IClassFactory**). Thus, clients need only one mechanism to create any
type of COM object. The most important method of **IClassFactory** is
CreateInstance, which creates an object and returns a specified interface
pointer. A client can create a COM object simply by calling **CoGetClassObject**
to capture an **IClassFactory** interface pointer. Similarly, a client can create such
an object by calling **IClassFactory CreateInstance** to send an interface pointer
to the object, then releasing the **IClassFactory** interface pointer. Because this
procedure occurs often in COM applications, COM provides a wrapper function
that lets developers perform this procedure with one call: **CoCreateInstanceEx**.

COM classes differ from most language-based classes in that, once an object has
been created, its class is irrelevant to the client. All interaction with the object
occurs through public interface pointers, which don't recognize the private
implementation class used to create the object. This rigorous separation of interface and implementation is a key feature of COM. This "black box" concept
greatly simplifies the client coding effort because the client need not know how
the component works, just that they do work.

Components

A *COM component* is a binary unit of software that can be used to create COM
objects. For a given CLSID, a component will include the COM class, the code
to implement the class object, and usually the code needed to create appropriate
entries in a system registry.

Note Although components are sometimes called servers, we avoid confusion with server computers by maintaining the original term, "component," through-out this chapter.

The Microsoft Windows 95, Windows 98, and Microsoft Windows NT platforms allow three basic packaging methods for COM components: Windows services, executable files, or DLLs. Components are built as Windows services in situations where the components must always be running, even if no one is logged on to the host computer. Windows executable files are often used where an application provides a UI in addition to furnishing COM objects. Microsoft Word is an example of a COM component built as an executable file. In most other scenarios, components are packaged as DLLs. In particular, most components used to construct three-service layered applications will be packaged as DLLs. The Microsoft ActiveX controls used in a presentation layer are DLLs, as are all business service components that run within the MTS environment.

Another way to categorize components is by their location relative to the client, as described in the three categories listed below:

- **In-process components** These components run within the same process as the client. All in-process components are implemented as DLLs.

- **Local components** Local components run in separate processes, all on the client computer. A local component can be an executable file or a Windows service.

- **Remote components** Remote components operate on computers entirely separate from the client. Remote components can be executable files, Windows services, or DLLs. To run a DLL component remotely, a remote computer would implement a *surrogate process,* or an application run on a remote computer capable of running DLL components. Both COM and MTS provide standard surrogates for DLL components.

For the remainder of this section relating to COM, we will focus on components implemented as DLLs, as these are most prevalent in N-tier, or service-layered, applications.

DLL Component Structure

In addition to implementing COM classes and class objects provided by all types of components, DLL components are expected to implement four well-known entry points:

- **DllGetClassObject** returns an interface pointer to a class object for a specified component-implemented CLSID.

- **DllCanUnloadNow** indicates whether any objects created by a component are still active. If so, the DLL needs to remain in memory; otherwise, the DLL can be unloaded, allowing for computer resource conservation.

- **DllRegisterServer** writes all registry entries required for all COM classes implemented in the component.

- **DllUnregisterServer** removes all registry entries created by **DllRegisterServer**.

The COM run time calls **DllGetClassObject** and **DllCanUnloadNow**; applications should never need to call these functions directly. Installation programs and developer tools usually call **DllRegisterServer** and **DllUnregisterServer**.

Threading

COM supports multiple threading models for components. A *threading model* defines on which threads a component's objects can run, and also specifies how COM will synchronize access to the objects. On the Windows 95, Windows 98, and Windows NT platforms, COM components run in a multi-threaded environment. Components must be written to run correctly in such an environment.

All COM threading models are based on the notion of apartments. An *apartment* is an execution context for objects. Every object resides in exactly one apartment for its entire lifetime; one or more apartments reside within each process. All threads in a given process must be associated with an apartment before making COM calls, by calling **CoInitialize** or **CoInitializeEx**.

All calls to an object are made in the object's apartment. If the application responsible for calling runs in a different apartment, COM synchronizes access to the object's apartment. In addition, cross-apartment calls must be marshaled when using a *single-threaded apartment* (STA) model. More fully detailed in the "Remote Activation and Marshaling" section later in this chapter, *marshaling* essentially means that COM intercepts a call, packages the call stack into a standard format, does some work, and then converts the package back to a method call in the object's apartment. In-process, cross-apartment calls can substantially impact performance, highlighting the importance of understanding COM threading models.

In Windows 95, Windows 98, and Windows NT 4.0, COM supports two types of apartments. A single-threaded apartment (STA) is associated with one thread for the lifetime of an apartment. Such an apartment is created when a thread calls **CoInitialize** or **CoInitializeEx**. One process can have multiple STAs; the first STA created is the main STA. Each process can also have one *multi-threaded apartment*. Multiple threads can be associated with a multi-threaded apartment model. The registry key **ThreadModel**=FREE denotes a multi-threaded apartment model, also referred to as a *free-threaded model*.

By default, if the registry key **ThreadModel** is not set, an STA has a single thread associated with it for its entire lifetime, and apartment model objects residing in an STA will never be accessed concurrently, as they will always run on one thread. No matter how many objects are in this apartment, only one method call will execute at a time, and only a single instance of each particular object may exist in the STA at any given point in time. Thus, object developers are helped considerably as it eliminates the need to synchronize access to per-object state; if necessary, thread-local storage can be used. To provide better scalability, the registry key **ThreadModel**=Apartment can be set to allow multiple instances of an object to exist in an STA at any point in time. To implement this apartment value, the component's global data and DLL entry points must be coded as thread safe.

Synchronization in the STA is based on Windows messages. Calls are queued as special messages and processed by a COM-created hidden window. As a result, threads associated with an STA must have a *message pump*, which is a special program loop that retrieves Windows messages from the current thread's message queue, translates them, and dispatches the messages to other parts of the application. If the thread does not have a message pump, no calls will be processed. The STA synchronization model does not prevent re-entrance; it just provides thread safety. This model is exactly the same as that used by window procedures. During method calls to other apartments or processes, COM continues to pump messages so that the STA can process incoming calls and ensure that the thread's windows are responsive. Called objects can call to other objects in the STA without fear of deadlock.

Components complying with the apartment model are easy to write, but concurrency constraints can create an unacceptable performance bottleneck. In this case, such components may need to support the free-threaded model. COM does not synchronize access to objects in the multi-threaded apartment. Threads are dynamically allocated as needed to service all concurrent calls into the multi-threaded apartment. Thus, it is possible for free-threaded objects to be accessed concurrently by multiple threads, which can improve performance.

Writing thread-safe code can be difficult. Both global variables and per-object state must be protected. Developers must also be concerned as to whether functions from run-time or statically linked libraries are thread-safe. COM provides an important advantage in that it provides a choice of threading models when writing code. COM also resolves any mismatches between an object and caller-supported threading models.

This feature is particularly interesting for in-process components. In-process components normally use their client process threads instead of creating new threads. For the client process to create a COM object, it must have already called **CoInitialize** or **CoInitializeEx** to establish the apartment associated with the calling thread. But then how does COM ensure that the caller's apartment is compatible with the threading model supported by the created object? When a component is created, it specifies the threading model it supports using a named registry value on the **InprocServer32** key, as shown here:

```
HKCR\CLSID\{45D3F4B1-DB76-11d1-AA06-0040052510F1}\InprocServer32
   @="salestax.dll"
   ThreadingModel="Apartment"
```

COM uses the **ThreadingModel** value to determine which apartment an object will be created in, as shown in Table 8.1. For example, if the caller's apartment is an STA and the component's **ThreadingModel** is Apartment, the object will be created in the caller's STA. All calls from caller to object will be direct calls; no marshaling is needed. If the caller's apartment is a multi-threaded apartment and the component's **ThreadingModel** is Apartment, the object will be created in a new STA. All calls from caller to object will be marshaled.

Table 8.1   In-process server threading model options

	Caller's apartment		
ThreadingModel value	Main single-threaded apartment	Single-threaded apartment	Multi-threaded apartment
Unspecified	Main STA	Main STA	Main STA
Apartment	Main STA	Calling STA	New STA created
Free	Multi-threaded apartment	Multi-threaded apartment	Multi-threaded apartment
Both	Main STA	Calling STA	Multi-threaded apartment

Most applications and components available today either support the apartment model or are single-threaded (that is, they use the main STA). Apartment model components offer a nice balance of ease of development and performance. As discussed in more detail later in this chapter, MTS provides features to help apartment model components scale to support large numbers of users.

COM Programming Model

The programming model specified by COM is simple and powerful. Sometimes it's difficult to see the basic model's simplicity and elegance underneath all the services built on top of it. So we won't talk about any of those services here; instead, we'll focus on the programming model itself.

COM, OLE, and ActiveX

Developers might be more familiar with OLE and ActiveX than with COM, and might be confused about what technologies these terms refer to and how they are related. This wouldn't be surprising: Microsoft has changed its definitions of these terms over the past couple of years even though the technologies themselves have not changed. Here's a quick run-down:

- **COM** The fundamental component object model, introduced in 1992. The COM specification is available on the Microsoft Web site (at www.microsoft.com/com/resources/specs.ASP), and only those items defined in the specification are part of COM proper.

- **OLE** Built on top of COM and the mechanism used for compound documents. An example of using OLE is when a Microsoft Excel spreadsheet is inserted into a Word document.

- **ActiveX** Originally introduced with Microsoft's COM-based Internet technologies in 1996; essentially a marketing label used to identify these technologies. Then things got a little crazy, and everything COM-based got grouped under the ActiveX umbrella. That just confused everyone. Today some degree of normalcy has returned and the term ActiveX is used only when referring to ActiveX controls, a specific technology built on top of COM for programmatic controls. When developers put a control on a Visual Basic form or embed an <OBJECT> tag in an HTML page, they use ActiveX controls.

Automation

In covering the essentials of COM, we've learned that a common characteristic of COM objects and interfaces is that client applications must recognize the COM interfaces they will use when they are built. A client application can't create a random COM object and use interfaces possibly exposed by that object; the application can use only the interfaces it recognizes at build time.

While this scenario works well for many applications, it is often helpful to determine at run time what objects may be used, and their corresponding interfaces. This capability is provided by Automation, originally developed to provide a means for macro and scripting languages to programmatically control applications. Word and Excel macros are examples of Automation in action. As of this book's publication, both Word and Excel use a common macro scripting language, Microsoft Visual Basic for Applications. General-purpose scripting languages such as Visual Basic for Applications can't contain built-in knowledge of every interface possibly exposed by an object, so Automation performs this role for these applications.

The IDispatch Interface

Automation defines a standard COM interface, **IDispatch**, for programmatic access to an object. By implementing **IDispatch**, components can expose any number of functions to clients. Clients access all functionality through a single well-known function, **IDispatch Invoke**, as shown in Figure 8.1.

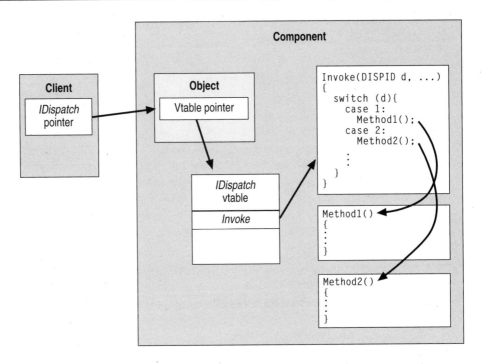

Figure 8.1 Invoking an Automation method using IDispatch

In its simplest form, late binding, Automation lets clients call objects without any prior knowledge of methods exposed by the objects. A client application creates an object as it usually would and requests the **IDispatch** interface. To access the object's functionality, the client calls the **IDispatch GetIDsOfNames** method with the text name of a function it intends to call. If the function is supported, a *dispatch ID* (DISPID), or a number identifying the function, will be returned. The client then packages all parameters to the function in a standard data structure, and calls **IDispatch Invoke**, passing in the DISPID and the parameter data structure.

When the object receives a call to **Invoke**, usually a method, it uses the DISPID as a key to determine which internal function to call. The object pulls apart the parameter data structure to build the method call to the internal function. If the correct parameters aren't available, the **Invoke** method can return immediately, without risking a component failure due to a poorly formatted method call. After the internal function completes its work, the return value and/or any error information is packaged into standard data structures, and returned as **[out]** parameters from the **Invoke** call.

This process is complicated if all the required "plumbing" has to be built. However, this process is enormously useful for interpreted languages. To use Automation-aware objects, an interpreter (sometimes called a *script engine*) needs to recognize how to create objects, call methods through **IDispatch**, detect errors, and destroy objects. Such an interpreter doesn't need to construct stack frames for different calling conventions, interpret interface pointers, or determine which functions an object exposes. All of these functions can be hidden within the interpreter itself, leaving a simple programming model for the script author.

On the component side, most of the plumbing can be hidden as well. Most COM-aware development tools create Automation-aware components by default. If the language itself is COM-aware, as Visual Basic is, details of implementing **IDispatch** can be hidden entirely, so only the exposed functions need to be implemented. If a particular framework provides COM support, the framework usually implements standard **IDispatch** and defines a data-driven mechanism for hooking up DISPIDs to internal methods. Again, the developer needs to implement only the actual functions.

The flexibility of late binding involves a price. First, all parameters passed to **Invoke** must be the **VARIANT** type. A **VARIANT** contains a value and a tag that identifies the value's type. Automation defines a set of types that can be placed in **VARIANT**s. If a particular set of data is not one of these types, it will need to be converted before developers can pass it as a parameter to an **Automation** method.

Note In practice, this **VARIANT** limitation is usually not a problem as the set of types supported by Automation is fairly extensive. Windows NT 4.0 Service Pack 4, Windows 98, and Windows 2000 are expected to add user-defined structures to the set of Automation types.

Second, objects can expose only one **IDispatch** interface at a time. While it is possible to expose additional **IDispatch**-based interfaces using different IIDs, in practice, no scripting languages can access these interfaces. Therefore, most Automation-aware objects expose a single programmatic interface for clients to use. This quality can impact development application design, particularly if security constraints are in place.

Finally, considerable overhead is associated with late binding. Every method call results in two calls to the object—one call to **GetIDsOfNames** to find the DISPID, and another call to **Invoke**. Overhead is also associated with packaging and unpackaging parameters passed into and out of **Invoke**. Generally, this overhead is acceptable in interpreted environments, but possibly not acceptable to all other clients.

Type Libraries

Because they are usually compiled, many client applications do not need the absolute run-time flexibility offered by late binding. In these scenarios, the required objects and methods are identified during the development process.

Rather than call **GetIDsOfNames** and risk overhead, DISPIDs for methods can be hard-coded into applications, in another form of Automation called *early binding*. This form of Automation involves binding the necessary components into the client application at build time. For early binding to work, development environments must have a way to determine the DISPIDs of methods being called. Ideally, the development environment could determine whether correct parameters were being passed to methods, and thus eliminate a multitude of application errors. Essentially, the development tool needs a complete description of component-exposed methods. Such a description would be provided by type information, usually stored in a type library associated with each component.

Dispinterfaces

As with normal COM interfaces, IDL can be used to define Automation interfaces. Automation defines a set of standard interfaces for creating and browsing type information. However, instead of using the **interface** keyword, the **dispinterface** keyword is used. This keyword indicates that the interface will be implemented using **IDispatch**; therefore, only Automation types can be used. The methods defined for the **dispinterface** will not appear in the interface's vtable.

With **dispinterface** keywords, developers can explicitly distinguish properties from methods—a property represents an attribute; a method represents an action. For example, a **Rectangle dispinterface** could have **Height** and **Width** properties and a **Move** method. Each property is implemented as a set of accessor functions: one function reads the property and an optional function writes the property. Both functions have the same DISPID; a flag is passed to **IDispatch Invoke** to indicate whether a read or write operation is requested. This capability is useful for Automation-aware languages, which can coat properties in syntactical sugar to make the objects easier to use. For example, in Microsoft Visual Basic Scripting Edition (VBScript), properties almost identically resemble variables, as shown here:

```
set rect = CreateObject("Shapes.Rectangle")
rect.Left = 10
rect.Top = 10
rect.Height = 30
rect.Width = rect.Height
```

As mentioned, it is rarely necessary to hand-code interface definitions in IDL. Development environments such as Visual Basic let developers define interfaces in standard language syntax and create the type library directly. Other development environments provide wizards to help define methods and properties on interfaces. The wizards generate correctly formatted IDL, which can be compiled using MIDL to generate a type library.

Dual Interfaces

Early binding is a substantial improvement over late binding for compiled clients. However, if a client is written in a development language that supports vtable binding, calling **IDispatch Invoke** seems to allow for much unneeded overhead. To address this concern, Automation supports *dual interfaces,* which are interfaces with characteristics of both vtable-based interfaces and **dispinterface**s.

Dual interfaces are defined using the **interface** keyword in IDL. All dual interfaces have the **dual** attribute, which indicates that parameter types in interface methods must be Automation types. In addition, all dual interfaces are derived from **IDispatch**. Methods defined in a dual interface are part of its vtable, so clients that understand vtable binding can make direct calls to the methods. But the interface also provides the **Invoke** method; therefore, clients that exclusively understand either early binding or late binding can also use the interface. The **Invoke** method implementation still uses the DISPID to decide which method to call.

For components that expose a programmatic interface, there is little reason not to define an interface as a dual interface. As of this book's publication, almost every COM-aware development tool can use dual interfaces, and most tools that let developers create COM components generate dual interfaces by default. Client applications that can take advantage of vtable-binding get improved performance with essentially no extra work for both component and application developers. Dual interfaces can also use the Automation marshaler, eliminating the need to install a custom proxy/stub DLL on client computers for such interfaces.

COM Support in Distributed Environments

As previously examined in the COM programming model, COM components can run on remote computers with little or no extra effort from the programming model perspective. COM's location transparency extends across apartments, processes, and computers. Some practical matters must be considered when communicating across computer boundaries. In this section, we'll discuss Distributed COM (DCOM), and also how location transparency operates.

Note Technically, *DCOM* refers specifically to the wire protocol for making COM calls between two computers. However, the term *DCOM* is often used to refer to the entire concept of COM communication across computers. Our discussion in this section focuses on what should be understood, on a general level, about how distributed applications based on COM operate.

Cross-computer COM calls introduce several issues that wouldn't normally be considered in a single-computer scenario. First, for security reasons, it may not be desirable to allow universal access for components installed on a particular computer. Second, users allowed to access such components—or on a larger scale, to access their own computers in which the components would reside—need to be educated as to the proper care of those components.

COM Security

The COM security model defines a standard means for COM objects to interact with operating system-provided security services. The COM security model is independent of the specific security services that may be available.

COM security primarily addresses two issues: who is allowed to launch components, and how calls are secured through interface pointers by providing activation security and call security.

Activation Security

The server computer's Service Control Manager (SCM) applies activation security whenever it receives a request to activate an object. *Activating an object* means either creating a new object or getting an interface pointer to a published object, such as a registered class object or an object in the running object table. We won't cover published objects in this book; instead, we'll focus on activation security as it applies to creating new objects.

The SCM uses information in the registry (or information obtained dynamically from published objects) to determine whether an activation request should be allowed. First, the SCM checks a computer-wide setting to determine whether any remote activation requests are permitted. If the computer-wide check succeeds, the SCM looks for component-specific security settings. We'll discuss these settings in more detail in the Registration Revisited section later in this section.

In essence, the registry can contain an access control list (ACL) that indicates which users can activate specific components. The SCM checks the client's identity against the ACL to decide whether the activation request can proceed. If there is no component-specific setting, the SCM looks at a default ACL.

If the access check succeeds, the SCM will launch the component, if necessary, and activate the object, otherwise access is denied. The SCM uses information in the registry to determine the security context, user identity, which the object should use to run. This identity becomes the client identity for any activation requests the object may make.

Call Security

Once an interface pointer to an object is obtained, a client can make calls to the object. COM also applies security to each method call through an interface pointer. Per-call security has two separate aspects. The first aspect is caller authentication and authorization, which is virtually identical to the activation security check described in the previous section, except that a different ACL is used and the component and client have moderate control over how often the check is performed. The other aspect relates to data integrity and privacy—that is, ensuring that network packets containing COM method calls have not been violated, and also preventing data in the packets from being read during transmission.

As is imaginable, performing security checks on every method call can have considerable overhead costs and involve unnecessary and redundant work. Thus, COM lets applications configure when and how to apply per-call security. Both client and server applications can establish process-wide defaults for per-call security by calling the **CoInitializeSecurity** function. Settings involved in calling this function include an ACL for authorization checks and an authentication level that determines how often authentication is performed, as well as whether data integrity and/or privacy should be enforced. If an application does not explicitly call **CoInitializeSecurity**, the COM run time will call this function, using information from the registry and on the application's behalf, before any objects are activated. As with activation security settings, COM will first look for component-specific settings; if COM does not find any component-specific settings, the default settings for COM components are applied.

In addition to setting per-call security at a process level, applications and components can tune security settings on individual interfaces and method calls using the standard **IClientSecurity** and **IServerSecurity** interfaces. Using these interfaces represents a more advanced technique than those found in this book. For additional information see the two titles by Guy and Henry Eddon, *Inside Distributed COM* (Microsoft Press, 1998) and *Inside COM+* (Microsoft Press, September 1999). For many applications, process-wide settings are sufficient. As we later discuss, MTS offers a role-based security abstraction on top of the COM security model that further simplifies securing access to components.

Registration Revisited

COM security relies on a number of registry entries. On Windows and Windows NT, these settings are usually configured using the DCOM configuration tool, DCOMCNFG.EXE, shown in Figure 8.2. DCOMCNFG lets developers set computer-wide and per-application settings involving actual registry keys.

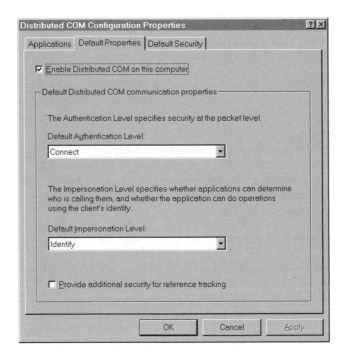

Figure 8.2   DCOM configuration tool used to configure DCOM security

Several key DCOM settings can be configured at the computer level. These settings are stored as values under the registry key HKEY_LOCAL_MACHINE \Software\Microsoft\Ole. Table 8.2 lists the major values, their purpose, and how to set them using DCOMCNFG. The values specified using DCOMCNFG will be used by default if no application-specific values are provided.

Table 8.2   Computer-wide DCOMCNFG registry entries

Registry value	Purpose	Configuration
EnableDCOM	Global activation policy for computers	On the **Default Properties** tab, select the **Enable Distributed COM On This Computer** check box.
LegacyAuthenticationLevel	Default authentication level applied to network packets	On the **Default Properties** tab, select a setting from the **Default Authentication Level** combo box.
DefaultLaunchPermission	Default ACL for activation security	On the **Default Security** tab, click **Edit Default** in the **Default Launch Permissions** area to edit which users have launch permission.
DefaultAccessPermission	Default ACL for per-call security	On the **Default Security** tab, click **Edit Default** in the **Default Access Permissions** area to edit which users have access permission.

DCOMCNFG also allows settings for specific applications to be specified. In COM, an application is nothing more than an identified process that hosts one or more components. Applications are identified by GUIDs, called AppIDs.

With the AppID key in place, DCOMCNFG can be used to establish security settings on a per-application basis. These settings will be used if the application does not call **CoInitializeSecurity** explicitly. The per-application settings are stored as named values under the **HKEY_CLASSES_ROOT\APPID\\{appid-guid}** registry key for the application on the server computer. Table 8.3 lists the security values, their purposes, and how to set them using DCOMCNFG's Application Properties window. To open the Application Properties window, select an application to configure in the **Applications** list box on the **Applications** tab, and then click the **Properties** button.

Table 8.3 Per-application DCOM security configuration registry entries

Registry value	Purpose	Configuration
RunAs	Identity used to run the server process	On the **Identity** tab, select the user account to use to run the application.
LaunchPermission	ACL for activation security	On the **Security** tab, select the **Use Default Launch Permissions** check box, or select the **Use Custom Launch Permissions** check box and click **Edit** to select specific user accounts to give launch permission to.
AccessPermission	ACL for per-call security	On the **Security** tab, select the **Use Default Access Permissions** check box, or select the **Use Custom Access Permissions** check box and click **Edit** to select user accounts that will have access permission.
AuthenticationLevel	Authentication level applied to network packets. (Windows NT Service Pack 4 or greater)	On the **General** tab, select a value from the **Authentication Level** drop-down list box to set the per-application authentication level.

Note It's important to register an AppID for DLL components that will be used remotely because DCOMCNFG can not be used to modify component settings unless the components have an AppID.

In addition to security settings, the registry also contains information about the component's location. On the server computer, this information is usually written to the registry by the component when it is installed. All that's needed on the server computer is the path to the COM component, stored under the **InprocServer32** or **LocalServer32** key for each CLSID. If the component runs as a service, some additional entries are needed.

It is also necessary to put information in the registry of remote client computers for those computers to be able to request remote objects, unless client applications are written to specify the server computer name when **CoCreateInstanceEx** is called. In particular, the client computer needs an AppID with a **RemoteServerName** value. The client may also need registry entries for proxy/stub DLLs used to marshal interfaces exposed by the objects. The remote component itself can't write the registry information because it isn't installed on the client computer.

There are two common ways to create the client-side registry entries on Windows computers. If no proxy/stub DLLs are required by the component, a .reg file containing the registry settings can be distributed to client computers and merged into the local registry. Otherwise, an installation program can be distributed that would write appropriate registry entries and install any proxy/stub DLLs required for the components to work correctly. In some cases, the installation program or .reg file will create the AppID key, but it won't specify where the component is located. If this is the case, DCOMCNFG can be used on the client to set the AppID's **RemoteServerName** value.

Remote Activation and Marshaling

With the security and component location information in place, objects can be created remotely. Let's look at how this process works.

As previously mentioned, creating objects is simple: an **IClassFactory** pointer is first directed to a class object, then **IClassFactory CreateInstance** is called to direct an interface pointer to an object that has been created. The SCM is responsible for locating the class object.

In creating remote objects, two SCMs locate class objects: the client computer SCM detects that a remote object has been requested and contacts the server computer SCM. The server computer SCM locates the class object as it normally would, then returns the interface pointer to the client computer SCM (assuming that all security checks pass).

The client computer SCM detects that a remote object has been requested in one of two methods. In one method, an application can specify a remote server computer name in the call to create an object. In a second method, when the SCM looks in the registry for component location information, the SCM might be pointed to a remote computer (typically, by using the **RemoteServerName** value on the AppID). Using either method, the client SCM ends up with a computer name, which in turn communicates with the SCM on that computer to retrieve the interface pointer. Once the interface pointer to the object is passed back to the client application, the application makes regular method calls through the interface pointer. The client's application is simply responsible for calling an in-process object—this is the beauty of location transparency.

Multitudes of mechanisms can be designed to create the illusion of an in-process call and can be located within the application's code. The actual interface pointer from the remote computer can't be handed to the client application; the memory address in that pointer has no meaning on the client computer. Instead, the client application is handed an interface pointer to a proxy object, which is in effect an in-process object. This object must do whatever is necessary to communicate with a corresponding stub object in the component's process.

A client application making a method call actually calls a method in the proxy. In what is known as *marshaling,* this proxy takes parameters passed to the method and packages them in a standard format.

Next, the proxy sends a request via an appropriate communication mechanism to the component process. The component process hands the request to the stub, which unpackages the parameters and calls the method on the real object. This process is called *unmarshaling*. After the method completes, any return values are passed back using the same process in reverse.

One of COM's goals is to hide the complexity of cross-computer and cross-process communication; proxy and stub objects perform exactly this process. Marshaling occurs not just across computers, but also across processes and apartments. Typically, implementations of proxies and stubs are generated automatically from IDL interface definitions using the MIDL compiler. These DLLs call system functions that encapsulate all details of marshaling and unmarshaling calls, as well as actual call request details. If a cross-computer call is requested, COM uses a remote procedure call (RPC) to make the call. If a cross-process call is requested, a lighter-weight inter-process communication mechanism called Lightweight RPC (LRPC) is used. If a cross-apartment call is requested, COM switches apartment contexts and synchronizes access appropriately—all automatically.

Normally, developers need only ensure that proxy/stub DLLs are installed and registered on appropriate computers. For a given interface, the proxy/stub DLL must be registered on all computers that use that particular interface. The proxy/stub DLLs generated by MIDL can be built to be self-registering, so developers only need to run REGSVR32 on the DLL to define the correct registry entries.

Packaging with MTS

Packages are a set of COM classes that perform related application functions. They are also the primary administrative units in MTS that define process and security boundaries.

Two types of packages are available in MTS: *library packages* and *server packages*. A library package runs in the process of the client that uses its COM classes. A server package runs as a separate MTS-managed process. Each COM class can be installed in only one package on a given computer. A package can be installed on multiple computers to distribute the workload for large numbers of clients.

Note It is possible for a component to include multiple COM classes installed in different packages. In general, this practice should be avoided. COM classes in a single component usually have interdependencies that may work only if the classes' objects run in the same process. In addition, splitting classes across packages complicates administration and maintenance.

By default, the MTS administrative tools install all COM classes in a component into a single MTS package. The MTS administrative tools also use the term "component" synonymously with COM's definition of "COM class." For consistency with the MTS administrative tools (UI) and documentation, we'll assume that, when discussing packaging, all COM classes in a component are installed in the same package. Furthermore, we'll refer to performing administrative tasks on components rather than on COM classes.

In physical terms, a package is a collection of DLLs and MTS catalog entries. The MTS catalog stores configuration information for packages, components, interfaces, roles, and so on. This information supplements the registry entries defined by COM. In MTS 2.0, the catalog is implemented using the Windows system registry. When developers create a package and add components to it using MTS administrative tools, they are adding information to the MTS catalog.

To facilitate moving packages from one computer to another, MTS allows all information about a package to be saved to a file, as shown in Figure 8.3. Such package files, which have the extension .pak, are text files containing all catalog entries for a package and its roles, components, and interfaces. Package files do not contain the components' DLLs, but they do contain references to all DLLs so that MTS administrative tools can locate and register the DLLs appropriately.

To enable MTS to use packaged components, each component must be implemented as a DLL. The component must implement the **DllRegisterServer** function, registering the component's CLSIDs, ProgIDs, interfaces, type library, and any other registry entries the component requires for proper operation. MTS will call this function to register the component when the package is installed on a server computer. A type library must describe all COM classes and interfaces in the component. Most programming tools that support COM produce components meeting these requirements.

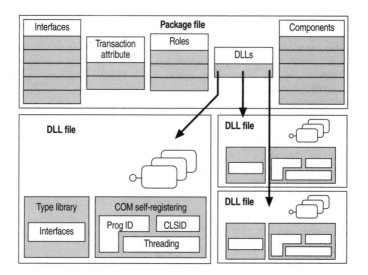

Figure 8.3 Exported MTS package file

Designing MTS Packages

The starting point for package design is the physical design, as discussed in Chapter 6. During the application design phase, the primary goal was to document any constraints imposed by application requirements, such as requiring authorization checks on calls into particular components or requiring certain components to run on a particular computer. It was not necessary, or even desirable, to have the entire physical design completed before implementing components. As applications are implemented, their physical design should be refined, with components placed into packages and any package deployment constraints documented. These four issues should be kept in mind when deciding how to package components:

- Activation
- Shared resources
- Fault isolation
- Security isolation

We look at each of these issues in detail in the following sections.

Activation

An application servers' components can be activated in one of two ways: in the client's process or in a package-specific MTS-managed process. We've already seen that MTS library packages are used to run the components in the client's process. Note that the term "client" in this sense is a different component or application running on the same computer on which the library package is installed, rather than a user application. Library packages do not support declarative security, nor do they offer the benefits of process isolation. Thus, library packages are typically used for utility components that might be used by multiple applications. Library packages are also useful when separate process overhead is undesirable and authorization checks are not required.

MTS server packages are used to run components in a separate MTS-managed process. MTS server packages also support declarative security, resource pooling, and so on. Most MTS packages are server packages. Application components are grouped into packages based on common resource usage, security requirements, and fault isolation needs.

Deciding how many packages are needed in an application is a balancing act. With many packages, system administrators have a lot of flexibility in deploying their applications. However, each MTS server package requires a certain amount of overhead to manage resource pools, shared properties, and so on. In addition, inter-process COM calls are much more expensive than in-process COM calls within a single apartment. And too many packages make system management tough. At this point in their application development, developers should create packages they think they need based on resource usage, security, and fault isolation. During performance testing, developers can adjust how components are allocated to packages if they find that process overhead or inter-process calls are a bottleneck.

Shared Resources

Components that use the same resources, such as databases, should be grouped together in a single MTS server package. Remember that MTS manages resource pools on a per-process basis. Each MTS server package gets its own thread pool, database connection pool, Shared Property Manager (SPM), and so on. If two components using the same database are located in separate MTS server packages, they can not pool database connections. If the components are in the same MTS server package, they can pool connections. This capability can greatly improve developed application performance and scalability. Similarly, components in separate MTS server packages can not share properties by using the SPM. Components that need to share properties must be in the same package to ensure correct application operation.

The location of resources should also be considered when designing packages. In general, components should be deployed as close as possible to the resources they use, particularly data stores, to help reduce network traffic within applications. For example, if two data stores used by applications might be located on different computers, consider putting the data objects that use each data store in separate packages. This arrangement gives system administrators the flexibility to install each package near the data store it uses. Any deployment recommendations or requirements, such as locating a package and a data store on the same computer, should be noted in the physical design documentation distributed with each application.

Fault Isolation

Separating components into different packages will also ensure that a fault in one component does not cause other components to fail. MTS will terminate a process whenever it detects internal corruption. Exceptions within a component can also force an MTS server process to terminate. Any transient state maintained in running objects or the SPM will be lost. If an application has components that maintain transient state, consider placing those components in a separate server package. Components should also be isolated during quality-assurance testing.

Security Isolation

MTS server packages are units of trust for MTS. Calls into a package can be secured. Calls within the package are trusted. Thus, application security requirements have a big impact on package design. If calls into a component must be authorized, clients and components must be allocated into different packages. Only components that can safely call each other without requiring an authorization check should be allocated into one package.

MTS security roles are defined on a per-package basis. If multiple components use the same roles, consider placing them in the same package. Generally, this method of grouping is safe, since components can be called by the same set of users, and should be trusted to call each other. Placing components that use the same roles in one package simplifies administration, since the system administrator does not need to remember to populate the role in multiple packages.

In addition, an MTS server package runs as a particular identity, and all components in the package run as the package identity. Components that need to run as different user identities should be in separate packages. Components might need to run as different identities because they should have different access rights to some resource or in order to maintain an audit trail. Although the exact identity each server package will run as cannot generally be defined during development, document any recommendations along with the permissions required by package components. For example, if a data object in a given package requires read/write access to a particular data store, document that fact.

Implementing COM in an MTS Environment

Let's examine the general concepts behind components that will run within the MTS environment. The four major tasks of implementing such components are:

- Write single-user, in-process COM components.
- Use explicit interfaces to define objects' public interfaces.
- Use **ObjectContext** methods to tell MTS when object state can be reclaimed.
- Use transactions to manage errors.

All components that run in the MTS environment must be implemented as in-process components. Each component must provide a class factory for each COM class in the component, as well as a type library that describes all COM classes and their interfaces.

In addition to these requirements, MTS components should be written as single-user components. The MTS Executive, mtxex.dll, provides thread management services, so developers don't need to cover multithreading issues in their components. In fact, threads should not be created on their own within their components. Components should simply be written as if one caller at a time will use them.

Recall that every in-process COM component has a **ThreadingModel** registry value associated with it; this registry value describes how the component's objects will be assigned to threads during execution. If a **ThreadingModel** value is not specified, the component uses the single-threaded apartment (STA) model. Thus, all objects will execute on the containing process main thread. COM synchronizes access to all objects on the main thread, so this approach is not very scalable. In addition, single-threaded stateful objects are prone to deadlock. However, if non-reentrant libraries are used within components, the STA model may need to be used.

A more suitable choice for MTS components is to use the apartment-threading model, by setting the registry key **ThreadModel**=Apartment. Remember that in the apartment-threading model, each object is assigned to a single thread for its entire lifetime, but multiple instances of the object can be created at once in any number of STAs. The component's global data and DLL entry points must be thread safe and protected from concurrent updates. This approach improves scalability without overly complicating their component implementation. It's not necessary to implement fully thread-safe components that support the free-threaded model; if these components are implemented, they must not create any threads on their own. Fortunately, every COM programming tool currently available can generate, at the push of a button, skeleton code that meets these requirements.

Note What about Java and COM? Java is a good language for implementing COM components. With the COM support provided by the Microsoft Virtual Machine for Java and Microsoft Visual J++, developers can easily create components from Java classes. MTS even provides a package to help developers access its features from Java: com.ms.mtx. The details of how developers code their components will vary. For additional information about writing components in Java, Paul Stafford's "Writing Microsoft Transaction Server Components in Java," available in the Microsoft Developer Network (MSDN) Library, is highly recommended.

The default behavior provided by COM programming tools is adequate for most components needed in a three-service layered application. If these defaults are used, developers can spend more time focusing on application-specific logic, and save hand-coding the basic COM component infrastructure for times when performance requirements cannot be met with the default code provided by their tools. Since COM is a binary standard, developers can change the implementation of any component without affecting its clients, as long as the public interface is not changed—even to the extent of changing implementation languages. In this book, we use the standard COM implementations provided by Microsoft Visual Studio tools. For information about hand-tuning components, or to learn more about how COM works, many books detailing the writing of COM components, especially for C++ developers, are available such as David Kryuglinski's *Programming Visual C++*, Fifth Edition and Guy and Henry Eddon's *Inside Distributed COM* (Microsoft Press, 1998).

Once basic in-process component framework is in place, COM class implementations can be added to the framework. Each COM class exposes its behavior through one or more COM interfaces. Some programming tools, such as Visual Basic, allow methods and properties to be exposed directly on the class and internally convert these methods and properties to a COM interface. Try to avoid this practice; always define COM interfaces explicitly by referring to the IDL. As mentioned, COM interfaces represent a contract between the caller and the object being called, and once published these interfaces must not be changed. When interface definition is mixed with implementation, changes could be made to interfaces without a full understanding of the possible consequences. Defining interfaces separately also helps when multiple developers are working on an application. Test objects that expose the interfaces can be created quickly to verify that interface-reliant client code works correctly.

In addition to the actual work of the method, each interface method implementation has two requirements. First, MTS must be notified when the object's state is finished. Second, errors must be handled within their objects, and MTS must be notified whether or not the method was successful. The Object Context associated with each object must be used. The **IObjectContext SetComplete** method indicates that an object has completed its work successfully. The **IObjectContext SetAbort** method indicates the object encountered an error.

When **SetAbort** is called, if the object is participating in a transaction, that transaction will fail and managed resources will be rolled back to their state prior to the transaction. This is an extraordinarily powerful mechanism for handling errors when many independently implemented objects are working together to perform some higher-level functionality requested by a client. If any one object can't complete its work, the entire request fails.

Since most objects will not retain state across method calls, the basic structure of each method will look something like the following pseudocode:

```
MyMethod(…)
    On Error Goto ErrorHandler
    CtxObject = GetObjectContext()

    Do work
    If error condition then
        Raise error

    CtxObject.SetComplete
    Return success

ErrorHandler:
    CtxObject.SetAbort
    Return error
```

Note In addition to calling **SetAbort** when an error occurs, a normal COM error should be returned. Clients then have the information they need to decide whether to continue doing work. **SetAbort** does not have any effect until the containing transaction ends.

These basic ideas apply to both data objects and business objects. With the basic component framework and a skeleton implementation of each class in place, we can turn our attention to the interesting part: implementing the application logic.

Basic Windows NT Application Services

Windows NT provides many of the services that were once the domain of the application developer, including:

- System services to ensure that separate applications are protected from each other on the system at all times.
- Memory management.
- Virtual memory services.
- File caching.

In the following sections, we discuss Windows NT architecture, and how applications interact with each other to utilize these services.

User Mode and Kernel Mode

Windows NT architecture is separated into a *user mode* and a *kernel mode*. Windows NT controls access to the memory on the system as well as access to all hardware. Applications running in user mode have no direct access to the hardware; they must communicate with the Windows NT Executive Service running in kernel mode to gain access to resources such as files, printers, communication ports, or even the processor.

Figure 8.4 shows Windows NT architecture and how applications behave and gain access to system resources.

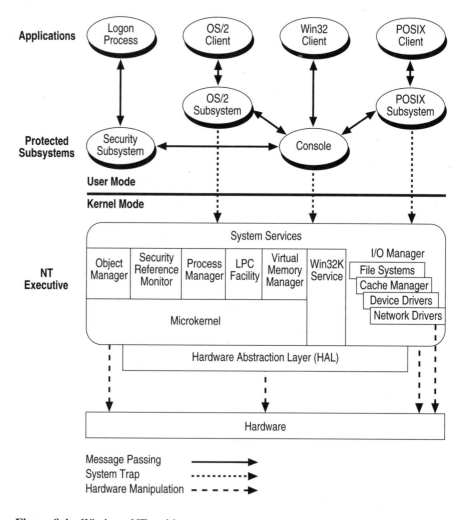

Figure 8.4 Windows NT architecture

The Executive Service controls access to all resources. The I/O Manager is the heart of access to resources such as files, system devices, and the network. The Virtual Memory Manager is responsible for managing the computer's memory and setting up protected memory areas for each application running in user mode. The microkernel provides such basic services as interrupt handling and thread scheduling.

User mode contains applications and user processes. There is only one way for information to pass from user mode to kernel mode: through the Executive Service. This means that there is no other way for an application to bypass security on the Windows NT system or compromise the complete control that Windows NT has over the physical resources on the workstation.

User mode is composed of several subsystems where applications reside. These in turn send and receive messages from the Executive Service. The subsystems include OS/2 and POSIX, and the security subsystem.

In Figure 8.4, a Win32 application communicates with the proper subsystem through messaging to gain access to the required resources. The subsystem is responsible for passing requests to the Windows NT Executive to be fulfilled. The Executive Service first assures that the operation is safe (not something that would disrupt the system or violate system integrity) and then completes the operation.

Virtual Memory

The Windows NT Executive Service also manages memory. The Virtual Memory Manager provides applications with memory, and manages virtual memory and the Windows NT pagefile. Each application has its own dedicated memory address. Different operating systems allow applications to access different amounts of memory:

- **Windows NT Server 4.0** Windows NT 4.0 grants 4 gigabytes (GB) of memory for each application. The application itself has a 2 GB addressable memory space.

- **Windows NT Server 4.0 Enterprise Edition** Windows NT 4.0 Enterprise Edition offers 4-GB memory tuning, which allows applications to address 3 GB of memory.

- **Windows 2000 Server** Windows 2000 Server will add support for the Enterprise Memory Architecture, which can provide up to 64 GB of addressable memory for an application that is "large-memory aware."

The virtual memory process, shown in Figure 8.5, works as follows:

1. An application submits a request to store data in memory.

2. When an application issues a call for a memory location, the Virtual Memory Manager maps the request to a non-conflicting memory address. The Virtual Memory Manager intercepts the request, determines how many pages are needed to fulfill the request, and then maps unused physical memory to empty address spaces in the application's virtual memory space. The Virtual Memory Manager hides the organization of physical memory from the application.

3. If there isn't enough unused physical memory available, the Virtual Memory Manager uses *demand paging* to find pages of RAM that haven't been used recently, and then copies that data to the paging file (pagefile.sys) on the hard disk. The newly freed RAM is remapped to fill the application's request.

4. When the data stored in pagefile.sys is needed, the pages are copied back into RAM. The new RAM location is mapped back to the same virtual address required by the application.

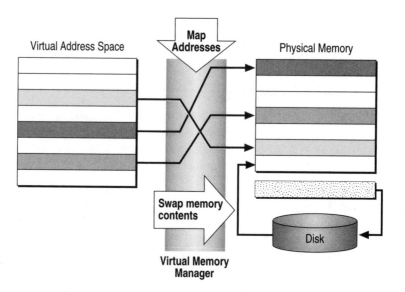

Figure 8.5 Virtual memory process

Cooperative Multitasking

Multitasking refers to the ability of multiple applications and processes to run at what appears to be the same time on a single system with a single processor. There are two types of multitasking systems: cooperative and pre-emptive.

The Windows 3.1 family of products is based on the concept of cooperative multitasking. The operating system grants each application access to the processor and system resources; it's up to that application to relinquish control of those resources for other applications to use. Clearly, a poorly written application that doesn't multitask well can easily bring the system to a halt, since that application is never forced to relinquish processor control.

Pre-Emptive Multitasking

The multitasking model used in the Windows 95, Windows 98, Windows NT and Windows 2000 families relies on pre-emptive multitasking. In a pre-emptively multitasked system, the system itself takes full control of the processor. In the case of Windows NT, the Executive Service controls the processor and resources at all times, not the applications. The Executive Service then grants access to the processor and other resources when necessary. Since the Windows NT Executive Service always controls hardware resources, such as the processor, it does not allow a single application or process to take control of the processor time and not relinquish it. For the application developer this means that it's no longer necessary to design an application to perform in a cooperatively multitasked environment, because this function is managed by the operating system.

Multithreading

In a multithreaded application, a single process or application can run several tasks at once. The Windows NT Executive Service grants each thread a slice of processor time. For example, a spreadsheet program may have an option that allows a recalculation to be done on a spreadsheet. By using multiple threads, the spreadsheet program can recalculate the spreadsheet in one thread and still allow the user to update other portions of the spreadsheet in another thread. Otherwise, to continue working, the user will have to wait until the recalculation is complete. Figure 8.6 illustrates both a single-threaded and a multithreaded process.

Single-Threaded Process

Multithreaded Process

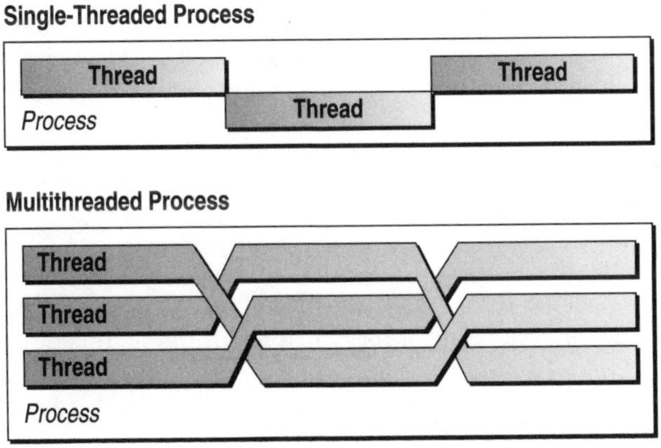

Figure 8.6   Multithreading in Windows NT

Windows 2000 COM+ Services

In the preceding sections, we have looked at the Microsoft technologies that can be used to build component-based three-service layered distributed applications. Central to the Microsoft strategy is a programming model based on COM and on MTS. In September 1997, Microsoft announced that COM and MTS would be unified in the future. The name given to this unified set of component services is COM+. The initial release of COM+ will appear in Windows 2000. We'll take a brief look at the features expected to appear in COM+ 1.0 and how COM+ will affect distributed application development.

Caution At the time this chapter was written, Windows 2000 and COM+ 1.0 were still in beta release; some details might change prior to release.

In COM+, all objects, remote or local, are created in the same manner. COM+ is built on a general-purpose activation and interception architecture that lets COM+ associate an object context with every object as it's created, and also allows COM+ to intercept calls to the objects created. During activation, COM+ will use attributes stored with the component or in application configuration information to determine which services, if any, the object uses. These services are built on the activation and interception architecture. COM+ keeps track of which services are in use and determines whether a call to the object requires work on the part of any of the services. If so, the services are automatically invoked at the appropriate point in the call. Instead of using a separate context wrapper to intercept calls, as MTS does, COM+ merges interception into the normal proxy/stub architecture already used to detect calls across apartment, process, or computer boundaries.

Although the architecture is general and all objects have an associated context, only classes implemented in DLL servers can be configured to use the COM+ services. Classes that are configured to use the COM+ services are known as configured classes; all other classes are known as unconfigured classes. Configured classes are hosted by the new COM+ surrogate, which merges the features of the COM and MTS surrogates and uses the standard COM surrogate architecture.

Unified Programming Model

What the unified architecture means for developers is that they can use all objects the same way, regardless of whether they use COM+ services. In MTS, to ensure that context information flows from one object to another, the object context **CreateInstance** method must be used. In COM+, the normal object creation

API functions, such as **CoCreateInstanceEx** or Visual Basic's **CreateObject**, may be used. Thus code such as this:

```
Dim ctxObject As ObjectContext
Dim subObject As IMyInterface
Set ctxObject = GetObjectContext()
Set subObject = ctxObject.CreateInstance("MyComponentProgID")
```

would be replaced by code such as this:

```
Dim subObject As IMyInterface
Set subObject = CreateObject("MyComponentProgID")
```

In addition, COM+ supports a more general moniker-based creation mechanism. *Monikers* are basically COM objects that provide an inherent naming standard. Developers provide a string name; the moniker then locates the object. While monikers have always been part of COM, COM+ adds a standard moniker that identifies how to create new monikers. The moniker-based method is useful as it can be extended at any time to support new features. Such an extension is possible by simply installing a new moniker component and informing developers about string names compatible with the new moniker. On the other hand, extending a system function like **CoCreateInstanceEx** to support new features is difficult. With the new moniker, new objects can be created by writing code such as this:

```
Dim subObject As IMyInterface
Set subObject = GetObject("new:MyComponentProgID")
```

Other than these changes to object creation, developers of MTS-based three-service layered applications won't notice any major changes in writing COM+ applications. COM+ 1.0 is geared toward writing multi-service layer applications; the programming model it promotes is essentially that of MTS. Components implementing COM+ services must meet the same requirements as they would for running in MTS. All existing MTS components will operate without change in COM+.

As in MTS, COM+ emphasizes a declarative, attribute-based model for accessing services. Developers can set attributes using the COM+ administrative services. Attributes and other metadata about each class are stored in a component library, which supplements the information available in the component's type library. When a component is registered with COM+, information from the component library is cached in a registration database that COM+ uses during activation to determine how to create an object.

The goal of the component library is to make components completely self-describing, including all the required registration information. The information in the component library can be used by the COM+ registration service to register components, eliminating the need to write registration code that directly manipulates registry entries under HKEY_CLASSES_ROOT. Because most of this code is automatically generated by development tools, this feature probably won't affect developers until their tools are updated to support COM+. For compatibility with existing components, COM+ will support components that register themselves under HKEY_CLASSES_ROOT as well as components that use the new COM+ registration mechanisms.

As mentioned, every COM+ object has an associated object context, which is associated with the object at creation time. Every COM+ object also contains a set of attribute-value pairs that describe the object's execution environment. The exact set of attributes maintained in the object context depends on how the object's class is configured. COM+ uses the object context to determine when specific services must be invoked. The object context is maintained by COM+ itself, based on the service attributes specified for components, classes, and interfaces, as well as the context of the object's caller. The object context attribute values can not be controlled at run time; however, developers may query the object context and call the methods it provides to access COM+ services programmatically.

Primary COM+ Services

COM+ is a combination of the COM specification and the addition of COM Services. The primary new and improved services are:

- Servers
- Transactions
- Security
- Administration
- Load balancing
- Queued components
- Events
- In-memory database

More information about these services is presented in Case Study 9.

Summary

COM's essential goal is to let developers assemble applications from pre-built parts, or components, irrespective of component location or development language used to implement the components. The COM model is defined so that components and applications can evolve independently over time.

The COM programming model is based on objects, interfaces, classes, and components. COM objects are instances of COM classes, which are named implementations of one or more COM interfaces. An interface defines a set of related methods; it represents a contract between the client and the implementer of the interface. All COM interfaces derive from the fundamental interface **IUnknown**. **IUnknown** provides object lifetime management and interface navigation features. COM components are binary units of software that can be used to create COM objects. Components include COM classes, an implementation of a class object used to create instances of each class, and code to create the registry entries needed to locate the classes. Most components available today, including many system services provided by Windows, are Automation-aware components that expose dual interfaces. These components are accessible to almost every development language and programming environment, including scripting languages. COM provides the basic building blocks of the three-service layer Windows DNA application.

Review

1. What is the COM specification?

2. How can COM work across computers?

3. How does MTS handle security?

4. What is COM+?

5. What are the primary services in COM+ 1.0?

CASE STUDY 7

Introducing COM+

The information provided in this case study is taken from the Microsoft white paper *Designing COM+ Applications*, supplied by the COM+ team.

"Dan, I'm glad I ran into you."

"Bill, somehow I don't believe this was a chance encounter."

"Well, you're right." Bill smiled glumly. "The other day, when we met with the Enterprise Architecture team, I said the RMS application would not use the new version of COM being released with Windows 2000. We're still not using COM+, but we're using a lot of the technology that it's based on. I've been getting lots of questions from the development team about this new stuff. We're not sure our design for RMS will work in the COM+ world."

"Bill, you're starting to sound like one of your young, hot-shot, super geeks. There is always some about-to-be-released technology that will change the world. Somehow, the world always survives. Why do you think COM+ would have that much effect on RMS?"

"Well I'm sure my team would love to save the world, but we'll just settle for saving the company. You now how a big part of MSF is versioned releases? We're just trying to make sure our design is solid for now and later."

Dan paused as he realized the positive effect MSF was having on the development team. "I guess you *can* teach an old dog new tricks. You're right. You know, I was at an executive briefing last year where I heard a great presentation on COM+. I made a few friends on that trip; I'll see what I can do."

Time to Learn

People were dragging chairs into the conference room. "Larger crowd today," thought Dan. "Tim will have to fight for doughnuts."

Just then, an announcement blared over the intercom. "The doughnuts have entered the building." In walked Tim and Bill, carrying ten large boxes.

"Hey boss-man, we brought a few extra to share today!" Tim yelled, as everyone dashed to grab a doughnut.

"Looks like we're going to need them; there sure are a lot of people interested in COM+," laughed Dan.

"Well, when you sent the video conference invite, I think it was forwarded to a few people around the company. Several of us have been using the *Designing Component-Based Applications* book, and we're excited to hear what the author has to say."

Just then, a giant video picture of Mary Kirtland displayed on the wall. "Hi, Mary," said Dan. "The gang's all here." Everyone took a seat.

"Thanks, Dan. Good to see you again. I guess I'll just get started."

Overview of COM+

"Hi, I'm Mary Kirtland. I'm a Program Manager with the COM+ Services team, and I'm going to talk about designing COM+ applications.

"First, I'll give a bit of background information about some Application Services we use with COM+ to build Windows DNA applications. Then we'll look at some specifics of how you go about the process of designing an application that uses COM+ technologies.

"Initially, though, I'll give you some background on Windows DNA. Windows DNA is a three-tier architecture that helps developers build distributed applications, from the user service layer through business logic, and finally to the data service layer. Windows DNA gives us a framework for thinking about how to build applications and how Microsoft technologies fit into them. COM+ fits in the Application Services that are provided by the operating system and are used to primarily build the business logic of your application. There's a little bit of overlap with the user and data layers, but COM+ primarily involves business logic.

"The first key thing about Windows DNA is that it is a three-tier application architecture, which we believe is the best way to build scalable distributed applications. The second key thing is that Windows DNA enables you to build your applications from components.

"Basically, components are reusable binary pieces of software that provide services to an application. Components give you a way to build up your application in increments, and they also enable you to modify your application over time. At this point, we're not specifically talking about COM or COM+ components. When we refer to components, we mean anything that you can reuse as a unit of distribution. Eventually, you'll pick COM and COM+ services for some parts of your application.

"The main enablers of Windows DNA are tools that help you build these components and eliminate some extraneous or non-specific work. An example is providing a framework for building the component infrastructure itself. You'll also need to have middleware services on which you can depend, and that provide transactions or security support. In addition, you'll want these services to save you time by providing auxiliary but necessary tools for you to use your systems properly. Finally, it's rare that you'll have an application that can exist without having to communicate with anything else. To facilitate in this communication process, Windows DNA can interoperate with your existing data and applications.

"The main Application Service that we're concerned with here is COM+. This is the run-time environment for COM components. COM+ provides a way for you to declare services or interest in services that you want. Microsoft provides the infrastructure that makes COM+ services work. A key element of this infrastructure is the Distributed Transaction Coordinator (DTC), which lets you compose components into larger units of functionality. Using DTC, you can make sure the resources that need to be updated as a group, are updated either all at once or not at all (even if there are multiple components used to build up that functionality unit). Microsoft also provides administrative tools that make it a little easier to deploy and package applications built of many components.

"Basically speaking, COM+ is the evolution of COM, which has been around for a long time, and also of MTS, which shipped with Windows NT 4 in the Option Pack. Microsoft combines COM and MTS into a single programming model, COM+, which ships with Windows 2000. Most of the information I'll discuss in this presentation also applies to developing applications for MTS. So if your applications must also work on Windows NT 4, or if you have clients with no access to Windows 2000 capabilities, many of the same principles I'll discuss here will apply also to MTS.

"Other key services that we use in conjunction with COM+ are Internet Information Server, and in particular Active Server Pages, or ASP pages, where ASP pages are used to dynamically construct HTML that targets Internet clients. Components encapsulate much of the work that you'll do within these ASP pages, and you'll use script commands to trigger actions on the components. You should use HTML to provide information about how you want your application to look and to be displayed to users in a platform-neutral way.

"Another Application Service that's available is Microsoft Message Queue Server. MSMQ allows you to send messages in a standard infrastructure that you can define. It also enables you to see what the message format looks like. MSMQ ultimately provides a great way to combine applications that aren't necessarily implemented in conjunction with one another. Another advantage of MSMQ is that you can guarantee that a message will be delivered exactly once. You can also make sure that the message gets routed through the least expensive mechanism, and you can assign priorities to your messages. So there's a lot more flexibility with MSMQ messages than with DCOM messages.

"To give you a bit of history, with COM, Microsoft introduced the notion of objects and interfaces. The key element in COM is that all access to an object is through its interfaces. Microsoft provides a standard object called a *class factory*, which is a means of creating other objects you want to interact with. Each object exposes a standard interface called IUnknown, which allows access to other interfaces that each object might expose. The classes that implement particular objects are combined into binary units of code called *COM components*. These components primarily include registration code that helps publish information about the COM components to a particular computer. COM components also provide information about how objects can be packaged object together and hooked into your computer's underlying operating system.

"With MTS, Microsoft added a few new elements, primarily declarative programming and state management. With declarative programming, you have the basic components, and you talk to them in the same way via interfaces. Clients get interface pointers, and they talk through those interface pointers to an object. You can specify information at the component, class, interface, and, with COM+, method level that indicates how you want to apply services to a particular component. Attributes could be, for example, simple requests or permissions allowed to users.

"Based on these attributes, and also on some information about the client computer, you can create a context in which the objects are going to operate. A context basically provides a safe environment for your objects. The object context also provides information about the transaction to which the object belongs, the security context, and additional data that the operating system and the MTS environment need to know to make sure that services are applied to the objects correctly. If you then create a subcomponent, or sub-object, from a given object, you should create contexts for those, too, by examining the attributes of a newly requested object, and also the context information for each current object. Attributes and context information are then combined to create a context for the new object.

"The ultimate direction in which Microsoft is moving with COM+ is to make the notion of attributes and context a fundamental part of the programming model. Instead of calling an API to access a particular service, in which you might call an initialization API and then call another API that provides instructions on configuring a service, you would simply declare an attribute. In other words, you would specify a desired action, and the system would determine how to execute that action for you.

"Another much-discussed aspect of MTS is state management. We often talk about MTS as promoting stateless objects, and that's not the ideal way to think about it. You should consider where your state will be. The key idea is that you shouldn't maintain per-object state across the transaction boundary, because you don't want to leak information from one transaction to another. You want to make sure that the information remains correct and consistent.

"You should also consider different types of state information. Rather than keeping state within each object, you may want to keep it with the client. Whenever the client needs to provide information to a particular object or component, the client can pass the information in its call to a particular interface method. You can still keep state in each object, as member variables; for example, you can keep state in a C++ class or in a Visual Basic class. But once again, you shouldn't assume that your state will be maintained across the transaction boundary. Thus, as long as the lifetime of your object is less than the lifetime of the transaction, you'll be just fine.

"If you need to maintain state across a transaction boundary, but you don't always want to pass it over from the client, you can keep it in shared transient state. You can also use shared transient state for information that applies to multiple clients. Microsoft provides a service called Shared Property Manager that can help you achieve shared transient states. To illustrate how Shared Property Manager works, imagine a location on a server computer in which you want to collect and track information. In this instance, you'd most likely pass, from your client, a key that requests the state you want. Otherwise, you'd want your objects to locate a key and request a state out of the shared location. You can also keep state information in a persistent store, like a database, to get the most flexibility and scalability. Then you can read it in only when you need it. If you can reuse or share the connections to that persistent state, you can get high scalability rates.

"Another important programming model aspect, from a component developer's point of view, is that you can indicate that you're done with the per-object state that you have in a particular object. You can make such an indication when your method call returns by calling the **SetComplete** and **SetAbort** methods. This procedure lets MTS know that it can reclaim the object, destroy it, and free up any server resources that might be associated with that object.

"As I mentioned, COM+ is the evolution of COM and MTS, or rather the result of the combining of the two to make an improved programming model. I want to emphasize that the basic programming models of COM+ and MTS are identical. A couple of years ago, Microsoft defined COM+ as a way to change how programmers build components. In Windows 2000 currently, Microsoft presents COM+ as much more of an evolutionary path than simply a new way of building components. The way that developers writing components is exactly the same as it was for MTS and COM as separate entities. With COM+, you'll still need to write in-process components and expose interfaces. Also, if you want to use automation, you have to implement **IDispatch** and registration code. Ultimately, whatever functions you've had to perform previously, you'll still need to do with COM+ in Windows 2000.

"However, there are some new services that you can use to expand the range and the types of applications that you can build. I'll briefly go through each of these items and talk about where you might want to use it in just a minute.

"There are also improvements to the existing MTS services. For example, if you're accustomed to using transactions and JIT activation in MTS, or if you don't need a transaction or JIT, the new COM+ Transaction Services can alleviate these issues. Microsoft has factored the services out so that you can choose which ones you want. If you don't want JIT, you can still get role-based security, for example. The role-based security has been improved to provide more information about the entire chain of callers. Overall, COM+ simply makes things easier for you, even if you're using the same services that were available in MTS.

Examples of COM+-Based Application Architecture

"An example of a high-level application architecture that you might use in COM+ is a prototypical, simple application with a FAT client and a Win32, or native, client. This application will communicate with a business service layer and an application data service layer running COM+ on Windows 2000. This application also has a number of components operating in the COM+ environment. These two layers communicate using DCOM, enabling the Win32 application to request a particular type of object and create it. An interface pointer will be passed, and the user service layer and business logic will communicate directly. These business objects can, in turn, use other objects. In many cases, the business objects will use data objects that encapsulate access to particular data stores. For example, ADO might be used to share SQL Server and also the data object communicating with SQL Server. There are several different options and types of stores that you can use for this type of data access. However, ADO is the easiest, most flexible option, from a programming perspective. It's a high-level and easy to understand model that can be accessed from scripts and components in almost any programming language. Later in this presentation, we'll talk about some alternatives to ADO and their varying degrees of flexibility.

"Another type of application that has recently become common is Web-based applications. In Web-based applications, IIS, probably in conjunction with ASP pages, acts as the part of the business layer that directly communicates with the user services, or the program that the user can access. In many cases, this user service layer is written using HTML, or perhaps dynamic HTML, or DHTML, and perhaps using some client-side components to aid in constructing logic that you might want to run in your user service layer. Instead of using DCOM to communicate between the Web-based application and IIS, you would use HTTP. In this case, you'd get a typical HTTP response request used to communicate between the user service layer and the ASP pages. The ASP pages then call business objects to do some of the work. ASP pages are interpreted today, so if you have lengthy work that you might want to reuse in multiple environments, it's really important that you take it out of script code and encapsulate it within a component. As I mentioned, these business objects can communicate with the data objects, which in turn will communicate with the data tier.

"Another aspect of applications that you might want to consider is having two independently developed applications that don't really have any explicit dependencies on each other, but sometimes need to collaborate and share information. A common example used in this context is order entry and shipping. When an order is placed, it will eventually need to be shipped. But you don't need to tie up the order entry process, waiting for confirmation that the order will be shipped, when it will be shipped, who will do the boxing, and so on. What you could do to prevent order tie-ups is use messaging to pass information from one application to another. In this scenario, you would have a front end that communicates to an application and does some work. That application, in turn, sends a message to a message queue; MSMQ would then be responsible for sending it to other applications that may use the message. Each application can communicate with its data store, and in some instances, may also communicate with the same data store.

Expanded Range of Design Choices

"Now let's look at the major features that help expand your range of design choices are Queued Components, Loosely Coupled Events or LCE, the In-Memory Database or IMDB, Transactional Shared Property Manager, object pooling, and dynamic load balancing.

Queued Components

"Queued Components is a new feature of COM+ that wraps message queuing behind the normal COM programming model. Instead of explicitly writing code to send a message to a queue, parse this message, and send it to the correct receiving application, you would simply expose a designated component's interface so that it can be queued. No time dependence is needed to receive the message and return a response. But, if an application calls a method from a queued client—one that understands how to do queuing—eventually the application will receive the message and understand how to process it. Regardless of its appearance, the message should be available to perform some work. This is the way that you would get asynchronous or time-independent behavior in COM+.

"If you want to determine how to work through a lengthy operation, or how to reduce the total time for a client request to return a response back to the client, you should try to move part of the processing out of the real-time client and application interaction timeline. We recommend that you send a message to a queued component, have it perform some work, and maybe update a data store with some status information. Otherwise, you could send another message back to a specialist application that knows how to complete the operation that you're performing out of line.

"At this point, you'll have to make a development decision about whether or not you want to change the message format. If you want to maintain the format, Queued Components is advantageous because you don't have to learn the MSMQ API. You would simply use the familiar COM programming model. On the other hand, if you want to change the message format—perhaps you need to communicate with an external application that has a defined message format—then you would need to use the MSMQ APIs directly.

Loosely Coupled Events (LCE)

"Another way that you can combine unfamiliar applications is to use LCE, Microsoft's publish-and-subscribe event model. This model works well with Queued Components. In the typical implementation of LCE, your application would be tied up from the time you launch an event until the time the recipients receive the message and return a response. If you don't want to wait for all subscribers to finish processing a particular event, you would use Queued Components to take that processing out of line. You would launch an event using a message, which would allow the event system to do work at its leisure.

"One advantage of LCE is that, unlike connection points in ActiveX controls, LCE allows persistent subscriptions, which don't have to be implemented within every component. So there's no logic managing the subscription within your components; the system performs subscription management for you.

"However, if you consider using LCE, you should keep in mind that its one limitation is its inability to perform true multicast. For example, if you have tens of thousands of subscribers to every event, LCE is probably not the mechanism that you want to use. On the other hand, if you have a handful or a fairly limited number of subscribers, then you can use LCE to broadcast information efficiently. Microsoft also provides a means for parallel firing, in which separate threads are sent to the trigger events of each subscriber as quickly as possible. Although this procedure is not true multicast, it does give you a way to send information to a number of subscribers, without waiting for each one to complete processing. Again, this is an ideal way to combine unrelated elements when they are developed.

"One of the key uses for this parallel firing is monitoring. In monitoring, you would instrument your components to trigger explicit events about unusual occurrences, such as access violations. If you have elements that need to be audited, you might want to fire those off. If you see that resources are being constrained, or that a problem is causing the system to perform worse than it does normally, you might want to fire off an event. Then you can have a separately developed monitoring application watch for particular events so that you can try to solve any problems that arise. The component doesn't distinguish what element performs the work, or when, or how—the component only alerts you to a potential problem.

In-Memory Database (IMDB)

"Another feature in COM+ that was previously unavailable in MTS is IMDB, which is essentially a data cache that helps you retrieve data from data stores and move it closer to your business objects. IMDB is geared toward read-mostly scenarios, where you have a table of data such as ZIP codes, cities, and states—information that doesn't change often. You retrieve the information from the data store, get it onto your application server—your middle tier where some business logic is happening—and then access the data out of memory quickly. Because memory is inexpensive, you have a readily available means to reduce network traffic back to your data store. For items that are read-mostly, rather than perform a query multiple times, you would simply cache the information into main memory and use it from there. IMDB is optimized for read-mostly scenarios because a distributed cache coordinator is not available in the version that ships with Windows 2000. So a separate cache on every computer reads a set of data out of the data store. Data changes have to go through the IMDB layer.

"It's important to note that you can't update the database and have it propagate back to every information cache possible. If you intend to change data, you have to make sure that a single computer will handle the necessary changes. Alternatively, you could provide a mechanism that can refresh the cached information, regardless of how many copies there are. But you'd have to implement the refresh mechanism yourself, because it's not built into IMDB in the initial version. You can, however, use it as a write-through cache. So, if you can work on one computer—you've partitioned your data and you've partitioned your client, so that every client and every data change is only going to happen on one computer—you can run the information through IMDB and then pass it on to the data store at a later time.

Transactional Shared Property Manager

"In MTS, the Shared Property Manager provided a way to manage the shared transient state that you might need to maintain across transaction boundaries, or between components, or between clients. In COM+, we introduced Transactional Shared Property Manager, which is built on top of IMDB because it uses the familiar Shared Property Manager interfaces to access IMDB functionality. You now have a choice of using IMDB directly through either OLE DB or ADO to implement a database approach. Also, you can use the object-based approach of the Shared Property Manager interfaces to access your state information. A benefit of the Shared Property Manager in COM+ is that it's computer-wide, not per-process. So in COM+, you can share information across several COM+ applications, whereas in MTS, all information was specific to a particular process or server package.

"Again, you'll need to manage data that's maintained across transactions, but doesn't necessarily need to be kept in a persistent store. Transactional Shared Property Manager is ideal for data hot spots such as Web page counters or IDs that you need to generate frequently. These Web elements would otherwise require that the database be updated every time a new number was needed or information needed to be stored away. The updates could cause the data store to be overwhelmed, causing performance to suffer. Transactional Shared Property Manager enables you to cache information into your computer's main memory to perform updates and then write the updates out to the database on an as-needed basis. This way, you avoid having to update your database every time you want to access particular data.

Object Pooling

"At one time, MTS was going to provide a feature that would emulate pooling objects. The idea was that MTS would create objects before the applications needed them and keep them on reserve. When these objects were needed, MTS would retrieve them quickly, rather than forcing users to create and initialize new objects. Unfortunately this feature never materialized. Every time applications deactivated an object, the object was destroyed by MTS. The next time users tried to recreate or access the object, a new physical object would be created on the server.

"COM+ now supports object pooling, which will allow applications to build a pool of similar objects, per-process. The objects can be put in the pool, and when an application asks for a particular object or calls a method on an object that has been deactivated, COM+ first looks in the pool. If there's a potential problem, the application should quickly remove it from the pool.

"If you have objects that are expensive to create, object pooling is a great way to create objects in the background before they are required for use and then quickly access them. Object pooling also allows you to control the maximum number of objects that can be created. Otherwise, if 10,000 clients request a particular object, COM+ would try to create the 10,000 objects, whether the physical computer systems were able to support them or not. With object pooling, you can also designate a maximum number of objects to be created, to help you manage resource usage on your server.

"A disadvantage of object pooling is that objects in a pool can't have thread affinity, and seemingly 90 percent of objects ever created to date *do* have thread affinity. For example, every Visual Basic component has thread affinity. If you use Visual Basic versions 5.0 or 6.0 to build your components, your components can't support object pooling. In future versions of COM+, this restriction will hopefully be eliminated so that you can use any language to build components that support pooling. Until then, you will be able to use the 6.0 versions of Visual C++ or Visual J++ to build objects that can be pooled.

"When implementing object pooling, you should remember three important conditions. One, if you're familiar with threading models, you must remember to support the free-threaded model, the neutral model, or both models at once, to access objects that support pooling. Second, object pooling is not beneficial if you apply it blindly. Third, object pooling does not always guarantee optimal performance.

"Considering these conditions, you should research your performance requirements to see if they are met without object pooling, and then evaluate whether you derive any benefits at all from activating object pooling. You may want to build a simple version of your component, particularly if you're a Visual Basic programmer (recall that Visual Basic doesn't support object pooling), to see if the component meets your performance requirements. If it doesn't, consider implementing the component using another language and then enabling pooling to see if that gives you the performance benefits that you need.

"Object pooling will most likely benefit organizations in which object creation costs (and initialization costs for particular components) are extremely high, or in which resources are scarce enough to necessitate components automatically creating objects.

Dynamic Load Balancing

"With MTS, when you want to scale up to support large numbers of clients, additional computers are needed. So multiple copies of a particular application or a package run on separate computers, and load is balanced across those computers in a static fashion. Particular clients always target one computer, or DNS round robin arbitrarily associates a particular request with a particular computer. In essence, it is difficult to maintain a configuration, particularly as the number of clients gets larger. Also, MTS is not sensitive to issues such as a particular computer failing. So if a client is constantly targeting one computer and that computer fails or goes off-line, the client is stuck. There's no way for the client to determine which computers to target to finish its work.

"COM+ adds genuine dynamic load balancing, where you specify a group of computers that all have identical components installed and then enable the client to access any of those computers based on an algorithm that runs on a router computer. The algorithm used in COM+ in Windows 2000 is a response-time algorithm. This algorithm collects statistics in the background and determines which computer is likely to give optimal performance when an object is created.

"Load balancing doesn't happen every time a component or an object is activated and deactivated. This is actually beneficial, because a load balancing operation on every activation with stateless components results in excessive overhead per call. If you just do the load balancing when you create the object, from that point on, the client, or a particular computer where the object was created, can communicate directly. So every time there's a particular method call, the method call just goes to the same computer, activates an object on that computer, does its work, and returns. That tends to give better performance than if you actually did a load balance on every single method call.

"The main reasons you perform load balancing in this manner are, first, to improve scalability, and second, to give additional availability when a particular computer is offline. Having this computer offline is acceptable because you can simply use another computer in the COM+ load-balancing cluster. Most COM+ components that you write are going to be load-balanceable. What you must watch for are any implicit computer affinities—in other words, dependence on a particular path, a particular server name, or state information that you're keeping on a particular computer. You need to make sure that, if the application gets routed to a different computer, it can still operate if state information is not available.

"At this point, we've covered different Application Services and the new features of COM+ at a high-level. For the remainder of my presentation, we'll examine the things you need to consider and the questions you need to ask when designing your applications.

Application Design Considerations

"When designing an application, you first have to determine the specific business problems you're trying to solve. When you've identified these problems, you have to determine the functional requirements. For example, you might create use cases and scenarios help clarify what an application needs to do from a user's perspective.

"You also need to outline the business objectives and non-functional requirements associated with your application. Business objectives are often the priorities you need to focus on. You must also support an expanding number of clients and have systems in place to handle the growing number of calls. The business objectives can give you performance information and requirements that tell you what you need to do to satisfy the customers who will use your application. You might also be faced with significant financial constraints in running your application; for example, customers with fewer resources might have to use their existing computers or be able to upgrade only to less-expensive systems rather than more costly ones. You might also encounter platform conflicts between client and server; for example, an organization might be running Windows 2000 on server computers and Windows 98 with Internet Explorer 5.0 on client computers. Operating system conflicts such as this one could heavily impact your application design. Your application's development could also be affected by your customer's choice of Web browser; for example, Netscape Navigator or Internet Explorer.

"The primary non-functional requirement is performance. Often developers want fast, optimal performance in their applications, so they set high performance requirements. In reality, it's a good idea to consider the specific response time that users expect. Also, you should gauge the number of clients needed and the amount of time the system needs to be available for the application. This information should have actual numbers, so the system performance can be tested against the build requirements. In this way, particularly with components, you can build a prototype application, do some testing, determine the location of bottlenecks, and then selectively tune or optimize the application's implementation to meet performance requirements, rather than blindly optimizing everything.

"Other constraints or requirements that you need to watch for concern deployment. You rarely have the opportunity to build an application completely from scratch. Usually, you need to communicate with an existing database or even multiple databases and existing applications. These databases and applications are going to operate on certain computers and communicate in certain ways with the computers. In most cases, you may not be able to change them.

"Topology constraints may also hinder an application's development. What type of network do you have? You may not have the flexibility or control to change the network or Internet connections to accommodate your application. Rather, you must make your application accommodate the topology.

"Security is another important non-functional requirement, involving protecting access not only to a particular program, but also to data. For example, are there certain types of data or certain rows of data in a database that no one should have access to? If so, you want to say that these particular user accounts and the detailed information in them can only be accessed by the account manager for those accounts. If you're the account manager for some other account, all you can do is get a summary of the information—perhaps the name of the account and who the account manager is. But you can get detailed information about your own accounts. Another way to restrict access is to say that a particular person is not allowed to modify information, but they are allowed to read it.

"Another question you need to ask yourself is whether the data needs to be protected in some way, such as with encryption. Are there any constraints on passing the information around in the normal, human, readable form? For example, you might not want to pass credit card numbers around as plain text. Instead, you might want to encrypt it in some fashion. The system can do that at a low level—for example, using RPC packet encryption—but those methods have a high overhead, and it's difficult to specify them with a fine granularity in the COM+ programming model. At the application level, you can specify that, for this interface, this particular method will be encrypted, and here's what you have to do to un-encrypt it before you can use it. So in some cases, it's much better to do this type of data protection at the application level, where you can define it as part of the contract between a client and a component, than it is to rely on the underlying infrastructure to just blindly protect all the data that's going across the network.

"You should also think about how the work of the application is divided up into transactions and workflows. Does a particular sequence of things have to happen in a particular order? What triggers the end of one operation and the beginning of another? Do some things need to happen as a unit? For example, if I'm making a withdrawal or transfer from my account in my bank, I want to make sure that, when I make a payment, money both comes out of my account and goes into the payee's account. I don't want money to be taken from my account and not to go anywhere. If it doesn't make it to the payee, I want to make sure it doesn't come out of my account either.

"It's important to think about the information that has to be treated as blocks, even when you are at a high or abstract level of design. Why? Because you don't have ultimate flexibility when it comes to specifying some of these constraints on a per-method or a per-method call level. So you need to think about the transaction requirements of particular methods, and about how they group together, when you're figuring out what methods go in a particular interface, what interfaces go in a particular component, and what components get packaged together. Even though these requirements aren't directly tied to any particular scenario, they end up impacting your design.

"After you've defined functional and non-functional requirements, you can begin modeling. You can also start to consider which logical objects you will include in your system, how these objects will fit together, which objects you can store, and which services you'll use to build your application. When you've got an idea of the core concepts and how they work together, you can refine them until you have defined components that you can implement.

"I know that many of you use object technologies, as well as object-oriented analysis and design, to logically model a problem. Although these techniques are perfectly acceptable, object-oriented analysis and design are not always ideal for designing components. Typically, when you perform logical modeling from an object perspective, you focus on the concepts and elements of your system. You also determine how these concepts and elements operate.

"When you examine your model from a component design perspective, you're typically performing a more service-oriented analysis. It's not always easy to judge exactly which objects ought to own a service. Several objects can work together to determine how to implement a particular service. So when you're doing a pure object-based design, you can lose sight of how certain objects might be grouped into components. In other words, you shouldn't always try to elicit a pure object-based model, because you will have to change it when you begin to build your COM components.

Objects in the COM+ Environment

"You'll see two typical types of objects running within a COM+ environment: business objects and data objects. Let's look at business objects first.

"Business objects encapsulate real world business operations. It's important that these operations be specified one place. For example, some objects might encapsulate a particular business rule. You don't want a business rule to be located in multiple places, because if the rule changes, it's hard to update the system. Other objects might be control objects. They basically enforce the sequencing of rules and the make sure that other objects are called to apply specific rules. Often the control objects are the ones that interact directly with the user service layer.

"When you take your initial cut at making a business object, you want to avoid trying to be all things to all the people who might ever want to use this object. Instead, you look at the known clients—the people who want to use this object today—and you provide the functionality that those clients need. Now you might think 'I've got a 'create new invoice' operation and an 'update invoice' operation, and I've got a query operation. It would be nice for my users to be able to delete an invoice or to mark it as paid as well.' In this case, it's probably worthwhile to flesh out the set of operations that are exposed by the object. But you shouldn't dream up potential clients who might do something a little bit differently. You probably want to get one version of the object out for the known client and if another client comes along, you can add a new interface or design a new object that meets the new client's needs.

"Another thing you want to do is make your methods fine-grained, meaning that they should do one thing and do it very well. Methods that do one thing and objects that do a cohesive set of related things are much easier to reuse than methods and objects that do a lot of things. For one thing, there is the weight factor: You're reluctant to load a 'kitchen sink' object into memory to use it. For another thing, a complicated operation may be applicable only to the client that's using it. You're going to get the most reuse if you break things up into separate steps and separate methods.

"You have to think carefully about how you're going to pass state information around in business objects. Ask yourself these questions: 'How do I get information into the object? Am I going to keep the information on the server or do I need to pass it in from the client? Do I need to get the information from a data store or will it come from the user service layer?' The way you talk to the business objects affects the look of the interfaces. If the information is kept on the client, you probably are going to end up with methods that have a lot of parameters to take all the information from the client tier and move it into the business object. The business object will use that information to complete one method; it will do its work, and it'll go away. If, on the other hand, the information is kept in a data store, typically the client presents some key information that the business object uses to retrieve the information from the store or from a transient shared area. The object uses the information to do its work and then returns the result back to the caller.

"In the case of a few high-level business objects, you will probably keep a lot of per-object state information. Typically you do this for internal business objects that are not directly accessed by the user service layer and that you know are going to be used only within the context of one transaction. For example, you might do this when you're building a master record with several detail records—say, an invoice with multiple items on it. When you're finished, you want to hand the invoice off to a data object to store. So one method says create the invoice and then add items to it one by one. As long as everything is done within the context of one transaction, this is a perfectly fine design, and you can keep the state information about that invoice within a particular object. If, on the other hand, you expect the user to pass information about one item at a time over to the business object, you don't want to keep that information in the per-object state, because then you have to keep this business object alive on the server, tying up resources, until the user decides he or she is done. Users have an annoying tendency to wander off before they've completed their work, and this poor business object would be sitting there, waiting to find out when it's done. So then you end up having to design things like timeouts and other things to clean up your resources. It's much easier just to say, 'Here's all the information; now do some work.' That's typically the approach that you'll see when you're going from the user service layer to the business service layer.

"You need to think about how the object methods or services that you want to implement at the business layer will work together. What things use the same resources? What things share responsibilities? What things work together to form one transaction? (These are typically packaged together into a higher-level operation.) If possible, you want to make sure that things that use the same resources are located in the same business object, and things that share the same transactional requirements are either located in the same package or have their transactional setting configured in such a way that they can work together to build that higher-level behavior.

"You also need to look at security requirements. This was a bit harder with MTS than it is with COM+ in Windows 2000, because you could not set security in MTS on a particular method. You could give certain types of users access to a particular component and to individual interfaces, but you couldn't restrict access to a particular method. You can restrict access to methods with COM+, but you will probably still want to group methods that have similar security requirements in a particular interface or a particular component. You should also think about the issue of data protection. Can you pass information around in plain text, or do you need to encrypt it? That's going to impact the interface design for these business objects, particularly any that talk to the outside world.

"Now let's take a look at the other primary type of object, data objects. You want your data objects to do is be responsible for the accuracy and consistency of a particular type of data. This ensures that the responsibility for that particular type of data is in one place. If something goes wrong with that data, you know where to go and look for problems. If you distribute the responsibility for checking the data across multiple objects and then just assume that the data is OK, you can end up with a corrupted data store. Or you have inconsistent information in different places in the data store, which is hard to correct. So the data objects are the last line of defense. They're responsible for making sure that your company's data doesn't get corrupted. Now they may, in turn, use system services to ensure that the data is in a consistent state. For example, you might want to use rules within an SQL Server database to make sure that you have referential integrity, or that deleting data in one place also deletes it in another. But for the most part, you want to make sure that responsibility for ensuring correctness is not at some higher level of the program—that it isn't spread out in your business objects.

"So what do you need to keep in mind about data objects? Well, again, there's the issue of where you're going to put the state. Here's where this whole argument about stateless and stateful objects really gets confusing for a lot of people who are thinking about using MTS or COM+. Typically, a data object is only in operation, or only in memory, during the lifetime of one transaction. Remember, the rule in MTS and COM+ is that you can't share state across transactions. But within a particular transaction, it's perfectly OK. So you might want to have a data object that is stateful, that you can set particular properties of, and that you can call individual methods to build up composite data. Then you would have a save method or something similar to indicate when it was time to write that information out to the store. Or you might use the same approach you would typically use for a business object, where you pass all the information into the data object at one time, it does some processing to ensure that the data's OK, and then just passes it on to the data store. Then the object goes away as soon as the transaction is completed. The key point I'm trying to make here is that you need to choose whether to design your interfaces so that you maintain information from one method call to another within a transaction, or whether to design them so that all the information is passed to the data object on a per-method basis.

"The typical behaviors of data objects are create, read, update and delete. If your objects need to be protected in any way, you need to decide whether you want the update, create, and delete operations in the same interface or the same component as the read operations. The operations that change the database might have different transactional requirements than the operations that just do a query. In both MTS and COM+, you can set the transactional level—the type of transaction support you want—only at the component level. If all the operations are in a particular component, you are going to get the transactional behavior that's specified. In that case, you might want to set your transactional settings to 'supports transaction,' and then make sure that any business objects that are doing queries don't have an enclosing transaction. Then they can do a query without

the overhead of doing a full transaction. Any business objects that are doing update operations should have an enclosing transaction that the data objects will fit
into. You might also choose to separate things so that you've got a cleaner separation when you're trying to restrict access. Then you can allow certain people to
query but not also do updates.

"As with business objects, you should think about which services in your data
objects use similar resources. For example, you want to keep services that talk to
a similar database or the same database table in one data object. You want to
make sure that you're able to share connections to a database. Connections are
expensive in using system recourses, and they're limited in number. So it's important that you be able to share access as much as possible. As I mentioned before, transactional behavior is really the key when you're doing data object
design. Transactions are expensive, so if you don't need them—if you're updating only one table and you can rely on the underlying data store to do the work,
or if you're not doing any updates at all—maybe this particular object doesn't
need transaction. On the other hand, if you're updating multiple things, or you
can't rely on the containing component to do transactions correctly, you might
want to require a transaction. So even though it's really easy to say, 'I want a
transaction,' and all the work of setting it up is done for you, you still need to
think about where you want transactions. Microsoft isn't getting rid of the need
to think about that part of design; we're just making it easier to implement.

"Another thing you have to think about is who is allowed to do various operations on your data object, so that you can split the operations into methods that
have particular role-based security applied to them. For even greater security,
you might want to split off into separate interfaces, different approaches that you
can take, depending on what platforms you need to support and what kind of errors your clients are willing to accept.

"One of the things you might want to watch out for with dividing things up into
multiple interfaces on a particular component is that script clients can only access the default **IDispatch** interface for a particular object. So if you have divided up the behavior of an object into multiple interfaces, the script client might
not be able to get to all of the services. That can be good or bad. You must make
sure that the services you want everyone to have access to are on the primary
interface. With COM+, you can selectively set the security settings on particular
methods, even for the dispatch interface, so you can cause them to get a security
error when they make a call. But you can't hide the fact that a particular method
is there. If you really want to hide a method, you split it off into a separate interface, or maybe even a separate component.

"You need to decide who will use the data objects and whether they will be used
directly from the user service layer. Are they going to be used by business objects
that you trust? Do you want to have to rely on the behavior of a particular object?
If not, you will want to make sure that all the responsibility for the data is encapsulated within the data object. And you also need to think about the language that the
clients are written in. If you have clients that are using script languages and can

access only **IDispatch**, you need to make sure that all of your functionality is provided through that default automation interface.

"So just a quick note on some things that you might want to think about for the user service layer. The user service layer usually contains ActiveX controls or automation components, depending on whether you've got a physical display or you're just doing some background processing. They usually run in-process, so they will typically be running within a browser environment, or within the context of a containing Win32 application.

"When you're building an application that relies on client-side components, one of the things that you need to watch out for is that the components may need to be installed over the Internet. That introduces some complications. When you're installing components to run in a browser environment, they need to be safe for encryption and safe for initialization; otherwise some clients may not even be able to get the objects created in their browser. They've got their security settings set so that they don't enable objects to be created within a particular page. By marking your objects as safe, you increase the chances that they'll let the objects be created.

"The other thing to watch out for is that user service layer objects are almost always accessed from script clients, meaning that you have to provide your programmatic interfaces through the default **IDispatch**. If you want to split things off into separate, well-defined interfaces with tight type definitions, that's fine. But you'll also want to create some sort of façade that provides the information that the script clients need through the default **IDispatch** interface. Now, there is a raging argument within the COM developer community about whether programmatic interfaces should be dual interfaces. A dual interface gives you both a custom aspect and the **IDispatch** component. If you have only one programmatic interface, I would say that you might as well make it a dual interface so that late-bound clients can access it through the fastest possible method, which is the custom part of the interface. Meanwhile the script clients can access it through **IDispatch**. If you have only **IDispatch**, everybody gets the slow way. If you have only the custom part, your script clients are out of luck. If you have multiple programmatic interfaces, things become kind of complicated, because even though they're all dual interfaces, only one dispatch interface is ever going to be looked at by your script clients. So you might want to decide that the default interface should either be a dual interface or a pure **IDispatch** interface that script clients can use.

"You also need to decide whether to do property-based or method-based interfaces. Property-based interfaces are perfectly fine at the user service layer, because you're working in-process. When you're going across the network connection, you should typically use a method-based approach, because you want to try to minimize the number of network roundtrips. For example, suppose you set the color, the size, and other attributes of an object. Those properties are then accessed through a script interface, based on **IDispatch**.

Connecting Components

"A lot of discussions about component-based design focus on how to design the components. But you also need to know how to connect the components. That's just as important as how to design the components in the first place. So I'm going to talk a little bit about how you connect the different physical nodes and logical nodes within your application.

"The first connection issue I'm going to look at is data access. The key is to use good principles of encapsulation and abstraction to hide the details of the data layer from your business objects. These details include such things as where data is stored, the physical structure, and the physical schema of the database. Use the data objects to present a nice, neat, logical model that business objects can work on. You don't want the business objects to have the responsibility of remembering where the data is, or what the physical data schema is, or what the best ways to access the data are. Get that information encapsulated in a data object.

"So what are some ways that you can implement access to the information in the data access service layer? There are several things to think about when you're picking a data access technology. We have a lot of them, including DAO, RDO, ODBC, OLE DB, ADO—in fact, you could probably pick any letter and add DA to it, and come up with an acronym for a data access technology. So how do you pick a particular technology? You look at things like ease of development. This could be important if you have a short development life cycle, or your developers are relatively new to this particular set of technologies. You might want to pick the access technology that has the best tools support or one that is easiest for your developers to work with, because you want to make it easy to build these particular types of components. On the other hand, ease of development tends to conflict with high performance, so programs that are easy to write might not meet the most demanding performance requirements. Then you need to look at whether you can get acceptable performance out of this component with the particular data access technology that you want to use. If you can't, then you might want to look at a slightly higher performing technology.

"You also have to think about the long-term impacts of picking these technologies. Are you going to be able to reuse this component in different situations? Are people going to be available to update the component if you have problems? And there might be other considerations that are important to your particular company. The key thing is to think about the non-functional requirements and business objectives and how everything fits into the overall enterprise structure and development standards, and use that information to pick the technology you use.

"Some of the options are whether to use a native data access API or something like OLE DB or ADO. These have greatly different ease of development standards, different tools support standards, and different flexibility. If you use a native API and you later change the underlying data store, your data object will need to be rewritten. But if you're using either OLE DB or ADO, you might be able to update some configuration information instead of having to change the code very much.

"You also might look at the difference between using dynamic SQL and using stored procedures. Stored procedures are probably going to give you much higher performance, but building query strings with dynamic SQL might give you more flexibility. In addition, stored procedures are typically specific to a particular database. So, again, if you think the data store might change or you need to support multiple data stores, you might want to keep that information in dynamic SQL statements.

"With COM+, you need to ask whether you go directly to the data store or use IMDB as a local cache for data. Are you mostly reading this information? Do you have one store where you can do updates? Or do you have to have some type of interactive development?

"You also need to think about communication with the external users of your system—both people and other programs. The protocol that you use to communicate with an external program or external user is determined by the kinds of user interface you want to present. If you're using a Web browser interface to present information to a user, then the communication protocol might be HTTP, because HTTP requests return HTML that naturally goes into the browser. But if you are talking directly to a WIN32 application, you might decide to use DCOM to communicate between the program and components that are running the business tier.

"You also need to think about firewall considerations and security issues. DCOM is good at communicating over TCP, but in most situations, it depends on a trusted domain relationship between caller and callee. Also it doesn't work really well through all firewalls. So in those situations, you might use an HTTP-based approach to get through the firewall and communicate with a Web server, and then have the server-side processing in the Web server communicate with the data objects.

"Some constraints might come from the operating system. For example, if you need to talk to an IBM mainframe, there are only certain protocols you can use. You need to think about the locations of the things that are communicating. Are they close together? Are they connected by a slow link? Is it a dial-up line? Is it a high-speed data connection? Your answers to these questions will help you define the protocol that you use to communicate between two tiers.

"As I mentioned before, two of your options are HTTP and DCOM. But you can also look at Remote Data Services, which gives you the ability to use either HTTP or DCOM through a COM component. This can be a nice option for accessing business objects and data without having to choose up-front either HTTP or DCOM.

"You should also think about messaging using MSMQ, or potentially using MSMQ in conjunction with IBM's MQ Series or some other messaging technology through a bridge. Then there are lower-level protocols such as RPC and sockets. But then you need to consider whether picking a particular option will affect whether you can build your application in a timely manner.

"I mentioned a while back that one of the things that you can do to improve performance is to eliminate some of the out-of-band work or independent operations, rather than tying them all together in one, big, synchronous operation. COM is synchronous: You make a method call, and you wait until you get a response. It's also tightly coupled, in the sense that the client knows what interface it's calling, goes to a particular object, and gets a response back from a particular interface method. But suppose your application doesn't need a synchronous response. You just want to say, "Here's some information; go process it at your leisure." In that case, you really want to consider using MSMQ or Queued Components, depending on whether you need to specify the message format or not.

"You might also want to develop your application as an independent silo that provides information that somebody might be interested in some day. In that case, you might consider using events, or you might consider publishing a message format that people could pick up. You might also combine these together in different ways, using Queued Components with LCE, for example.

"When you design parts of your application to work independently, you need to think about how you get status information back to the caller. If an operation has been working for some period of time, how do you let the caller know that it's done? You could send an asynchronous message back, or you could pull some status information from a data table. You also have to figure out how to recover from operations that are partially completed. For example, you order something and you get a message that the order has been placed, so you assume that the stuff that your order will be shipped eventually. What happens if the shipping department is not able to ship a particular item to you? The department has to have a recovery mechanism that says, "We're going to delay shipping this item for a while. If you don't want this particular product anymore, please let us know, and we'll cancel your order." Some business logic has to happen to recover from that partially completed operation.

"You also need to worry about security. Are you going to be able to communicate between these nodes, and do you have to protect the information that's being passed back and forth between them?

"After you've kind of figured out the big picture—here are the components we want, or here are the services we need to provide—how do you actually group them into the components that you're going to implement? First you pick classes that implement particular interfaces. Then you group the classes into components, which are the physical packages that you're going to install in a

COM+ application. In most cases, you're going to have one class per component, but in some cases, several classes that all work together can be grouped into one component. Then you need to group the components into applications and processes.

"Now you have to think about the units of trust and the units of deployment. You do security checks when you cross into an application, but everything within a particular application is trusted. Each application is deployed as a block, so if you want to put two different components on two different computers, you need to make sure that those components are in separate COM+ applications. If you need a security check, you need to make sure that the call into that component crosses an application boundary. An additional complication is that today each class can be part of only one application per computer. So we have two types of applications: one that runs in an independent process, and one that runs in its caller's process. That gives you a way to build up a library application.

"You have to think about where you want things to be activated—on a particular computer, for example. Which components share resources and should probably be in the same process? You want to make sure that you are taking advantage of the underlying pooling operations provided by the system, which are typically per-process. You might also want to make sure that, if a particular component fails in such a way that it crashes, you don't bring down the rest of your system. That would be a good reason to put a process boundary around a component or set of components, to make sure that they can't cause the rest of the system to fail.

"I've already mentioned security isolation—assigning components to separate applications if you need a security check. You also need to assign applications and processes to particular computers. How you do that will depend partially on your deployment constraints. You're also going to have to tune everything based on your performance requirements. You may need to implement load balancing to get the scalability you want.

"What this all boils down to is: you shouldn't make decisions too early. You want to maintain flexibility in how you assign components to applications and processes as long as possible. On the other hand, you need to build any known constraints into your application up-front. You don't want to maintain flexibility and then have the application break because it was installed in a way that didn't meet the constraints you assumed when you built the application. So put in the flexibility you think you're going to need, but make sure that you have constrained the places that should not be flexible.

"Well that pretty much wraps it up, Dan. Sorry I've got to run, but I hope that helps your team get a better idea of COM+ and application design."

"Absolutely, Mary. Judging by the grins on everyone's faces, they're really going to like this new stuff." Dan brought the meeting to a close.

Bill walked over to the VCR and gingerly removed the tape, handling it as though it was precious gold. "This was great Dan, I'm going to make a few copies for my development team. They won't need to rent video tapes for a month; they can just watch this one again."

"Yeah, yeah, you developers always do things the hard way," said Tim not wanting to pass up the opportunity for a good dig. "I streamed this out to our new Microsoft NetShow server, so we can just stream it to everyone's browser. They can watch it day and night."

As Dan ducked out of the room, he shouted, "Well, it sounds like this was sage advice. I'll leave it to you guys to figure out the details. Let's go get this application shipped."

C H A P T E R   9

Data Service Layer Technologies

About This Chapter

This chapter examines design issues related to data requirements, including how to implement data access services within an application. We explore characteristics of different data access technologies, and discuss how to best use each access technology. Furthermore, we discuss normalizing data and data integrity, as well as identify how business rules can affect application data and where these rules are implemented. We'll examine technologies that provide data access to legacy data system stores and Enterprise Resource Planning (ERP) applications such as SAP AG's product SAP R/3. Finally, we'll review COM+ In-Memory Database (IMDB) features that can improve data access performance.

The principles and guidelines we provide in this chapter are based on our own experience with the creation of application architectures and the implementation of enterprise applications, together with the following sources:

- *Visual Studio Developing for the Enterprise*, the documentation for Visual Studio, Version 6.0
- Microsoft Enterprise Integration Group
- The MSDN article *The SAP DCOM Component Connector*
- Mary Kirtland's *Designing Component-Based Applications*

Upon completion, you will be able to:

- Identify Microsoft data access technologies.
- Distinguish between the characteristics of relational and non-relational databases.
- Identify data modeling characteristics.
- Understand the basics of normalizing data models.
- Identify the most ideal data access technologies to be applied to different types of applications.

- Identify technologies that provide data access to host-based systems.
- Detail DCOM connectivity to SAP.
- Enumerate COM+ IMDB features.

What Is the Data Service Layer?

More than ever, organizations are tasked with providing data in an increasingly diverse manner. Not long ago, most information was held on a mainframe and in various database management systems (DBMSs). Now an organization's important information can also be found in locations such as mail stores, file systems, Web-based text, and graphical files.

As organizations seek to gain maximum advantage from data and information distributed throughout their departments and divisions, they can attack the problem of disparate data sources by putting all the data in a single data store. With this *universal storage approach*, a single data store holds any and all kinds of data.

Universal Storage

Universal storage solves the problem of multiple access methods by allowing only one type of data store. However, universal storage presents a huge technical challenge as far as writing a data store that can efficiently store and retrieve any type of data is concerned. Universal storage also fails to address the handling of existing data terabytes stored in another location, as the cost of converting data to the universal store would be enormous. In addition, the possibility of the universal store's single point of failure poses an additional risk.

Realistically, the Microsoft Open Database Connectivity (ODBC) approach of providing a common access method seems more feasible than that of universal storage. However, the common access method must encompass all types of data, rather than limiting itself to relational database tables and SQL queries as in ODBC.

Application Programming Interfaces (APIs)

Application program interfaces (APIs) are sets of commands that applications use to request and execute lower-level services performed by a computer's operating system. In this section, we discuss methods of manipulating various data sources through different data access interfaces. Each database vendor provides a vendor-specific API to ease database access. Non-DBMS data can be accessed through data-specific APIs, such as the Microsoft Windows NT Directory Service

API (ADSI), the Messaging API (MAPI) for accessing mail data, and file system APIs. By using a native access method for each data store, developers can use the full power of each store. However, this procedure requires that developers know how to use each access method, and developers must have a detailed understanding of API functions associated with each data store to use API access methods. If developers must maintain access to several data stores, and consequently must learn all the data access methods involved, organizational costs for training alone can become quite high.

Instead of using native data access methods, developers can choose to use a generic, vendor-neutral API such as the ODBC interface. Using this type of interface is advantageous in that developers need to learn only one API to access a wide range of DBMSs. Applications then can simultaneously access data from multiple DBMSs.

Universal Data Access

The Microsoft Universal Data Architecture (UDA) is designed to provide high-performance access to any type of data—structured or unstructured, relational or non-relational—stored anywhere in an enterprise. UDA defines a set of COM interfaces that actualize the concept of accessing data. UDA is based on OLE DB, a set of COM interfaces for building database components. OLE DB allows data stores to expose their native functionality without making nonrelational data appear relational. OLE DB also provides a way for generic service components, such as specialized query processors, to augment features of simpler data providers. Because OLE DB is optimized for efficient data access rather than ease of use, UDA also defines an application-level programming interface, or Microsoft ActiveX Data Objects (ADO). ADO exposes dual interfaces to easily be used with scripting languages as well as with C++, Microsoft Visual Basic, and other development tools. We discuss ADO more thoroughly in the ADO section later in this chapter.

UDA is a platform, application, and tools initiative that defines and delivers both standards and technologies tailored to providing enterprise data access. It is a key element in the Microsoft foundation for application development. In addition, UDA provides high-performance access to a variety of information resources, including relational and non-relational data, and an easy-to-use programming interface that is tool-independent and language-independent.

UDA doesn't require expensive and time-consuming movement of data into a single data store, nor does it require commitment to a single vendor's products. UDA features broad industry support and works with all major established database products. UDA has its origins in standard interfaces, such as ODBC, Remote Data Objects (RDO), and Data Access Objects (DAO), but it significantly extends functionality of these well-known and well-tested technologies.

UDA-Based Access Components

Microsoft Data Access Components (MDAC) provides a UDA implementation that includes ADO as well as an OLE DB provider for ODBC. This capability enables ADO to access any database that has an ODBC driver—in effect, all major database platforms. OLE DB providers are also available for other types of stores, such as the Microsoft Exchange mail store, Windows NT Directory Services, and Microsoft Windows file system using Microsoft Index Server. As shown in Figure 9.1, developers can write applications for existing or new data and for structured or unstructured data, using ADO as the single data access mechanism, regardless of the data's location.

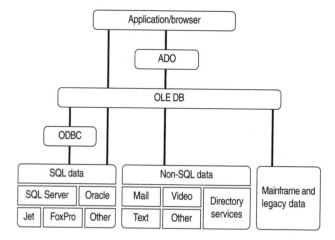

Figure 9.1   Microsoft's UDA design

Data Modeling

Data modeling is the process of identifying, documenting, and implementing data requirements for an application. Data modeling involves reviewing existing models and processes to determine if the data models can be reused. Data modeling also involves creating new data models and processes to suit a team's application requirements. The major events in data modeling are typically:

- Identifying data and associated processes (for example, the data's logical design).
- Defining data types, sizes, and defaults.
- Ensuring data integrity by using business rules and validation checks.
- Defining operational processes, such as security reviews and backups.
- Choosing a data storage technology, such as relational, hierarchical, or indexed.

It's important to understand that data modeling often involves unexpected organizational management. For example, data ownership, along with the implied responsibility of data maintenance, accuracy, and timeliness, is often challenged by new insights into the specific data elements to be maintained by particular organizations. Data design often forces an organization to recognize how enterprise data systems are interdependent. Data design also encourages efficiency, cost savings, and strategic opportunities, which arise because of coordinated data planning.

Note As discussed in Chapter 6, gathering information typically begins with requirements and progresses with Conceptual Design's use cases and usage scenarios and Logical Design's object, user, and service designs.

Identifying Data

Data describes a real-world information resource important to applications. It describes the people, products, items, customers, assets, records, and—ultimately—the data structures that applications categorize, organize, and maintain.

Identifying data is an iterative process. At first, the development team may pinpoint several vague, high-level details about how the application must handle its information. As the team's knowledge of the application's intended business process expands, the team fills in more details. The description for each data item typically includes:

- Name.
- General description.
- Ownership (who is responsible).
- Data characteristics.
- Logical events, processes, and relationships (how and when the data is created, modified, and used).

Part of the data design process is to specify how each data item should be quantified. Some typical data specifications, or attributes, are:

- Location (address, country, warehouse bin)
- Physical (weight, dimension, volume, color, material, texture)
- Conceptual (name, rank, serial number)
- Relational (assemblies consisting of subassemblies, authors who write multiple books)
- Value (currency, esteem)

The process of identifying data can involve interviews, analysis of existing data structures, document preparation, and peer reviews. The eventual result is a documented, conceptual view of an application's data that answers the questions of "Who, what, where, when, and how?" Generally, this is an early-stage exploration of how various departments, organizations, and applications need to research data.

Defining Data

As the team learns more about the application's data structures, it can group selected data items together and assign certain information details that describe the data's characteristics and relationships. A general approach to defining data includes:

- Defining tables, rows, and columns.
- Inserting index keys.
- Creating table relations.
- Assigning data types.

Defining Tables, Rows, and Columns

Regardless of how an application's data is physically stored, the data is typically organized into multiple tables or files, each having a set of rows or records, and columns or fields, similar to a spreadsheet's rows and columns (see Table 9.1). Each row in the table contains information about a particular person, product, item, customer, asset, or related item.

Table 9.1   Example of a People table

Row	Name	Address	Phone
1	Dan Shelly	100 Microsoft Way	(xxx) xxx-xxxx
2	Tim O'Brien	100 Microsoft Way	(xxx) xxx-xxxx
3	Marilou Moris	100 Microsoft Way	(xxx) xxx-xxxx
4	Jane Clayton	100 Microsoft Way	(xxx) xxx-xxxx

Inserting Index Keys

An *index key* is a special field that provides an index for fast retrieval. Such a key can be unique or non-unique, depending on whether duplicates are allowed. An index key can be designated as the *primary key,* making it the unique identifier for each table row. Keys should be used when applications need direct access to certain rows. For example, in Table 9.2 an author's identification number (Au_id) is the table's primary key because Au_id uniquely identifies only one author. A query using Au_id will provide extremely fast retrieval of the author's information.

Table 9.2   Example of an Author table

Authors table
Au_id (key)
Au_name
Au_Address
Au_Phone

Creating Table Relations

A database is usually composed of several tables rather than just one. These tables are often related to one another in various ways. For instance, a Titles table for library books could list the International Standard Book Number (ISBN), title, and year a particular book was published. In a database such as this one, it would also be useful to identify the publisher for each title. Rather than repeating all publisher information for each title in the Titles table, a relationship with a separate Publishers table can be established by including the publisher's identification (Pu_id) as a *foreign key* in the Titles table, as shown in Table 9.3.

Table 9.3   Example of related Titles and Publishers tables

Titles table	Publishers table
Ti_isbn (key)	Pu_id
Ti_title	Pu_name
Ti_yearpublished	Pu_address
Pu_id (foreign key)	Pu_phone

The relationship as demonstrated in this table is a *one-to-many relationship*. A single row in the Titles table is related to just one publisher in the Publishers table, but a single row in the Publishers table can be related to one or more records in the Titles table. As shown in Figure 9.2, relationships can be *one-to-one*, *one-to-many*, and *many-to-many*.

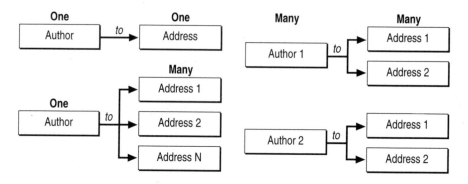

Figure 9.2   One-to-one, one-to-many, and many-to-many data relationships

It's worth noting that although a relationship has been identified as existing between the Titles and Publishers tables, no commitment has been made as to how that relationship will be managed. Depending on the final implementation, the development team might meet this management challenge by using table joins and foreign key constraints available with Microsoft SQL Server, or by writing custom code to read file structures directly and handle referential integrity inside application business objects.

Assigning Data Types

A data type is a named data category characterized by a set of values, a way to denote the set of values, and several implied operations that can interpret and manipulate the set of values. Data types can be:

- **Intrinsic** This data type is provided by a database. For example, SQL Server provides intrinsic data types such as integer, datetime, bit, char, and varchar.

- **Derived** This data type is defined using the Data Modeling Language (DML) provided by a database. A derived data type is built from available intrinsic data types or previously defined derived data types. Developers typically provide a name and structure for the derived data type. With derived data types, consistent use of special data types can be assured for selected columns, variables, and parameters.

Data types are important because they assure that an assigned data value is the correct type and within the acceptable range of values. Different data storage technologies and development languages support a variety of data types, such as character, variable character, integer, double integers, floating point numbers, bit fields, and binary fields.

While assigning data types, the development team should be sure that the data-type range fits the data to be stored, and will continue to fit it in the future. For example, with SQL Server an application can handle a maximum of 255 customer records if "tinyint" is chosen as a data type for customer identification, but more than two billion customer records if "integer" is chosen. As another example, if a single character is chosen as the customer service code, an expansion to two characters could create maintenance havoc. Every component and routine that accesses the service code would have to be examined and potentially updated.

Space can be saved in a database and table join operations can be improved by choosing appropriate data types for fields. As a general rule, the smallest data type appropriate for data in a field should be chosen.

While assigning data types, the development team should consider:

- Allowable maximums and minimums.
- Default values.
- Empty (or NULL) values.
- Anticipated growth.
- Expected and, when possible, unexpected changes.

In a relational database environment, data types help enforce the business rules. For example, dollars can't be mathematically added to colors. Although no one would ever program this mathematical process intentionally, a relational database identifies the data type mismatch and automatically denies database queries that attempt the impossible.

Ensuring Data Integrity

Data integrity involves actual values stored and used in an application's data structures. An application must exert deliberate control over every process that uses data to ensure continued correct information.

Developers can ensure data integrity through careful implementation of several key concepts, including:

- Normalizing data.
- Defining business rules for data access.
- Providing referential integrity.
- Validating data.

Normalizing Data

A database designer must refine and structure data to eliminate unnecessary duplication and provide a rapid search path to all necessary information. This process of refining tables, keys, columns, and relationships to create an efficient database is called *normalization*. Data normalization applies to relational as well as indexed files.

Normalization is a complex process with many specific rules and different levels of intensity. In its full definition, normalization is the process of discarding repeating groups, minimizing redundancy, eliminating composite keys for partial dependency, and separating non-key attributes. In simple terms, rules for normalization can be summed up as follows: "Each attribute (column) must be a fact about the key, the whole key, and nothing but the key." In other words, each table should describe only one type of entity (such as a person, place, customer order, or product item).

Some benefits of normalization are:

- **Data integrity** There is no redundant, neglected data.
- **Optimized queries** Normalized tables produce rapid, efficient joins.
- **Faster index creation and sorting** Tables have few columns.
- **Faster updating** There are fewer indexes per table.
- **Improved concurrency resolution** Table locks will affect less data.

Most simple databases can be normalized by following a simple rule: Tables containing duplicate information should be divided into separate tables to eliminate redundancy. For example, suppose a bookseller has developed a new application that helps track information about each book. This application might include the following data:

- Author name
- Author address
- Author phone
- Title
- ISBN
- Year published
- Publisher name
- Publisher address
- Publisher phone

The bookseller could create a single table with a field for each data item. However, such a table would contain many redundancies. For example, many authors have written more than one book for a single publisher, so the publisher information for each author would be repeated multiple times. If these fields were included in a single table, confusing duplication of entries would most likely occur. Using normalization principles, the data should be broken into four groups as shown in Table 9.4.

Table 9.4   Normalized Authors, AuthorsTitles, Titles, and Publishers tables

Authors table	AuthorsTitles table	Titles table	Publishers table
Au_id (key)	Au_id (foreign key)	Ti_isbn (key)	Pu_id (key)
Au_name	Ti_isbn (foreign key)	Ti_title	Pu_name
Au_address		Ti_yearpublished	Pu_address
Au_phone		Pu_id (foreign key)	Pu_phone

The keys provide a means of establishing table relationships. For example, the AuthorsTitles table creates a many-to-many relationship between the Authors and Titles tables (many authors might write many titles). Using the AuthorsTitles table, a query can find the ISBN of every book number an author wrote (using Au_id), and also determine which author wrote a certain book (using Ti_isbn).

Rather than create a separate AuthorsTitles table, the Au_id attribute could be added to the Titles table. Such an option is neither superior nor inferior to the previous example; it's simply a design tradeoff in which developers must evaluate their applications' expected query types, potential multi-user concurrency issues, and a possible performance issue of three indexes on one table.

Defining Business Rules for Data Access

Developers can use business rules to provide correct and consistent control of their applications' data access. Furthermore, subsequent applications should be expected to use the business rules set with the initial application, and thereby benefit from the built-in process dependencies and relationships already provided. In general, business rules that perform data access must be designed thoughtfully to provide self-contained, carefully coordinated processes.

Applications require data access business rules under the following circumstances:

- Inserting, updating, deleting, and viewing data
- Validating data
- Controlling data security
- Handling multi-source data access
- Providing application-based referential integrity

A business rule can be used each time an application inserts, updates, deletes, or views data. Business rules implemented in this manner provide concise control over data that can be updated. For example, if an application applies new sales orders to an invoice file, a business rule should automatically check the customer's credit limit before accepting and inserting sales order line items.

Data integrity is the process of verifying field values and validating related file values. In other words, data integrity verifies that numeric fields are genuinely number-based and within range, and also checks to see if particular relationships exist in their appropriate files. By putting all data validation routines into business rules, applications can guarantee correct data and easily adapt to future requirements.

Applications may require data access security to control access privileges for those permitted to use organizational applications. Business rules are an excellent way to manage data access privileges.

If a particular application needs to trace a complex chain of records as preparation for a decision process, a business rule can be used to simplify multi-source access. Such a business rule would automatically locate all required data stores and repackage them for easy use. For example, suppose an application needs to determine maximum possible payout for a single procedure in a multi-line healthcare claim. Inspecting the current line item involves searching the beneficiary's entire claim history for prior use of that line item's identical procedure. Additionally, lifetime and current year-to-date limits must be checked to determine the allowable amount. This multi-source access presents an excellent opportunity to create a reusable business rule that consistently and correctly handles the checking process.

One of the most common uses for business rules is handling the referential integrity processes for indexed files. Because indexed files such as those indexed using the virtual storage access method (VSAM) are typically controlled by the data storage engines, an application must provide custom code to handle constraints, foreign key deletions, and other common referential integrity issues. Application-based referential integrity can also be appropriate for relational databases, especially in situations where available triggers, constraints, and stored procedures are either inadequate or too complicated.

Providing Referential Integrity

For referential integrity to be maintained, a foreign key in any referencing table must always refer to a valid row in the table referenced. Referential integrity ensures that the relationship between two tables remains synchronized during updates and deletes. For example, suppose that an application contains both a Titles and Publishers table as shown in Table 9.5. Referential integrity requires that these two tables be synchronized. In other words, each publisher identification (Pu_id) in the Titles table must also exist in the Publishers table. The application cannot simply delete the Pu_id row from the Publishers table, because the Pu_id in the Titles table would lack a reference. However, it would be permissible to delete the Pu_id row from the Publishers table, and also delete every row in the Titles table that has an identical Pu_id. Such an action would maintain referential integrity for the two tables.

Table 9.5   Example Titles and Publishers tables

Titles table	Publishers table
Ti_isbn (key)	Pu_id (key)
Ti_title	Pu_name
Ti_yearpublished	Pu_address
Pu_id	Pu_phone

In a similar manner, the application can't simply add a row to the Titles table without a valid Pu_id already in the Publishers table. To do so would require bad data in the Pu_id field. Therefore, the application must ensure a valid Publishers row before inserting the related Titles row.

The actual implementation of referential integrity depends entirely on the data storage engine, as well as the application's design requirements. Historically, applications using mainframe VSAM files would use application code to handle referential integrity. Even if an application uses SQL Server or Oracle, the development team shouldn't necessarily use triggers, foreign keys, constraints, and cascading delete functions to maintain referential integrity. Instead, referential issues might be handled using application-based code.

Note Typically, application-based referential issues can be implemented most efficiently within data access objects and services. Occasionally, referential issues are handled within business layer objects and services.

Validating Data

Data validation guarantees that every data value is correct and accurate. Data validation can be designed into an application by using several different mechanisms: UI code, application code, database constraints, and business rules. Several types of data validation are possible:

- **Data type validation** One of the simplest forms of validating data, this type provides answers to such questions as "Is the string alphabetic?" and "Is the number numeric?" Usually such simple validations can be handled through the application's user interface.

- **Range checking** As an extension of simple type validation, range checking ensures that a provided value is within allowable minimums and maximums. For example, a character data type service code might allow only the Roman alphabetic letters A through Z. All other characters would be invalid. As with data type validation, an application's interface can typically provide necessary range validation, although a business rule could also be created to handle range validation.

- **Code checking** Code checking can be complicated and typically requires a lookup table. For example, when creating an application that calculates sales tax, the development team might need to create a validation table to hold the authorized, regional tax codes. This validation table could be part of a business rule, or it could be implemented directly in the application's database for query lookup.

- **Complex validation** When simple file and lookup validation are insufficient, complex validation can be used. This type of validation is best handled with business rules. For example, a healthcare-related application could read a single claim with a billed amount of $123.57, but the allowable amount may depend on a year-to-date rolling accumulation capped at $1,500 (not to exceed the lifetime policy maximum of $100,000). In this situation, data validation extends beyond the immediate data entry screen to one of careful evaluation of how to pay this claim based on the policy limits and year-to-date accruals.

Caution Be careful when creating applications that require *localization*, or distribution with different language code sets. Much of the data validation can be moved into a resource file that can be swapped into the application depending on the localization.

In older file structures, data is unfortunately often corrupted. (For instance, numeric fields might be blank or contain non-numeric characters.) As developers build enterprise applications, they may want to build a testing utility to verify that every field in every record of the files their applications use is correct. If not, these applications may provide unpredictable results.

Defining Operational Processes

Regular operation processes to protect data integrity are the backbone of applications. Every application requires ongoing maintenance activities, including:

- Maintaining databases.
- Providing data backups.

Maintaining Databases

If a development team is responsible for maintaining databases, the team will need to periodically perform a number of database-oriented tasks. For relational databases, these tasks include clearing the log file, checking memory and procedure cache peak loads, compressing file size, and validating links between tables and index pages. For hierarchical databases, these tasks include checking for broken links by walking the data structure thoroughly through all subordinate records. For VSAM files, the team will need to perform a rebuild with additional pre-allocated index positions for future expansion, based on the file's historical growth trends.

Note If the team is using SQL Server, developers can use the Database Consistency Checker (DBCC) to analyze and repair various aspects of a SQL Server database and installation.

Providing Data Backups

Backups are crucial to applications in case developers need to recover data due to corruption or another catastrophic event. Several backup choices are available, including:

- Dumping.
- Mirroring.
- Replicating.

Dumping involves copying data to an external device, such as a disk or tape, using a specialized format. Because dumping provides a snapshot of an entire database, changes made after dumping are lost (unless developers supplement the dump with transaction logs). Dumping is a popular method of handling data recovery. Developers using dumping for data recovery purposes should be sure to minimally perform it nightly.

Most relational databases (including SQL Server) provide *mirroring,* an alternative to dumping that involves continuously copying all transactions on one device to its duplicate, or mirror, device. Once mirroring is set up, it is generally seamless and maintenance-free. The primary benefit of mirroring is that recovery from a single device failure is virtually instantaneous. Those implementing mirroring should take caution, however; if the network connection to the mirroring computer becomes corrupted, many databases will cease to function. Even when implementing mirroring, developers should still perform periodic dumps to be safe.

Note Another technology for data fault tolerance is clustering, which is similar in concept to mirroring. Clustering connects two separate computers to a single data store. Clustering database servers can eliminate the physical hardware failure points of a single computer but typically do not provide a backup of the data.

By *replicating,* or using *replication,* developers can copy all or portions of their databases to any number of remote computers. Besides providing a means to backup data, replication has other benefits as well—developers can distribute their data throughout a network, balancing the workload and minimizing the risk of catastrophic failure. Replication is primarily a tool for keeping data consistent among distributed databases, and is not generally recognized as a way to provide database backups.

Choosing a Data Storage Technology

Developers have many options for defining a database and storing their application's data. Among the most popular are indexed, hierarchical, and relational data storage technologies. These types of data storage differ not only in that they physically manage storage and retrieval of data, but also in conceptual models they present to users and developers.

Indexed databases, such as VSAM, which provide extremely fast data retrieval, are suitable for sequential lists, random retrieval, and complex file relationships. Developers can easily read a VSAM file from beginning to end, or simply retrieve specific records using an index key. Indexed databases typically provide only data storage and retrieval. Developers' application code must handle referential integrity and data validation processes to accommodate what indexed databases can not provide.

A hierarchical database is especially useful for implementing inverted tree structures, such as bills of material or organizational ranking structures. Hierarchical data access is extraordinarily fast, because these data structures are directly linked. One interesting feature of a hierarchical database is that referential integrity is built-in. However, implementation of hierarchical databases often requires an experienced systems programmer to compensate for these databases' deficiencies in modeling complex relationships.

Relational databases have generally become the de facto standard for database storage. Relational databases are preferred because the relational model has a high usability factor, and also provides a standard interface, SQL, that allows numerous database tools and products to work together in a consistent and readable manner. Additionally, relational databases typically provide mechanisms for handling referential integrity, data validation, and a host of administrative processes to set up and maintain application data.

If a team designs an enterprise application, the application's developers may use existing mainframe databases, including relational, VSAM, and AS/400 files. With SNA Server, a team can seamlessly use mainframe and distributed databases on a network. This integration of mainframe and distributed data with Windows-based applications means that developers have many choices for data storage technologies.

Microsoft Data Access Components (MDAC)

After completing application design, developers should have access to conceptual design documents that contain a sufficient model of needed data objects. Additionally, the project team will presumably have defined several specific data and data connectivity requirements. With these requirements, the team should be able to approximate how these objects will be grouped into components. As developers attempt to implement these components, they should keep the following key design points regarding data objects in mind:

- Accuracy, completeness, and consistency of data rely on the data objects that own such data.

- Data objects should operate correctly whether or not the objects' callers are transactional.

- Developers should carefully consider how their data objects are to be used, and also consider the expense of data access before retaining state across method calls. This point is particularly important, as data objects can not retain state across transaction boundaries.

- The fewer network round-trips required to use a data object, the better—data objects should thus be network-friendly. Additionally, typically the fewer round-trips the better the application performance.

Every data store provides a native access method. Each database vendor provides a vendor-specific API to ease database access. As mentioned, non-DBMS data can be accessed through data-specific APIs, such as the Windows NT Directory Service API or MAPI, for accessing mail data, or via file system APIs. By using the native access method for each data store, developers can use each store's full power. However, such technique requires developers to learn how to use each access method. Furthermore, developers must understand the API functions and their most efficient uses, and also learn how to use diagnostic and configuration tools associated with data stores. The project team should be aware that costs of training developers on all data access APIs used within an organization can be high.

Distributed application developers face two fundamental technical challenges related to data access. First, developers rarely have the opportunity to start from the beginning, regarding data access. Most applications need to access existing data, which can be stored in a variety of formats. For instance, some of this information could be stored in DBMSs; other data could be stored in less structured forms. Many DBMSs are on the market, including mainframe databases such as Information Management Systems (IMS) and DB2, server databases such as Oracle and SQL Server, and desktop databases such as Microsoft Access and Paradox. It is possible for multiple DBMSs to be in use with a single application. Non-DBMS data can be stored in text files, indexed sequential access method (ISAM) files, spreadsheets, e-mail messages, or any application-specific file. Somehow, distributed application developers must integrate such disparate data sources into a unified view for application users.

A second challenge related to data access is that distributed applications naturally involve accessing remote data sources. In most cases, users implementing applications to examine data are working on different computers than the computers on which data is stored. Therefore, it's important that efficient mechanisms for accessing remote data are in place, to minimize network traffic generated by applications. This point becomes increasingly critical as applications scale to reach thousands or millions of users, many connected to computers through relatively expensive network bandwidth over wide area network (WAN) connections or throughput constrained modem connections.

MDAC components are:

- **ADO** Application-level programming interface to data.
- **Remote Data Service (RDS)** Client-side caching engine; formerly known as Advanced Data Connector (ADC).
- **Microsoft OLE DB provider for ODBC** Access provider for ODBC databases, via OLE DB.
- **ODBC driver manager** The DLL that implements the ODBC API and directs calls to the appropriate ODBC drivers.
- **ODBC drivers** Database drivers for SQL Server, Access, and Oracle.

Open Database Connectivity (ODBC)

Instead of using native data access methods, developers can choose to use a generic, vendor-neutral API such as the Microsoft ODBC interface. ODBC is a C programming language interface for accessing data in a DBMS using SQL. An ODBC driver manager provides the programming interface and run-time components developers need to locate DBMS-specific drivers. The DBMS vendor typically supplies ODBC drivers. These drivers translate generic calls from the ODBC driver manager into calls to the native data access method.

The primary advantage of using ODBC is that developers need to learn only one API to access a wide range of DBMSs. Applications can access data from multiple DBMSs simultaneously. In fact, application developers do not need to target a specific DBMS—the exact DBMS to be used can be decided upon application deployment.

Unfortunately, there are several drawbacks to the ODBC approach. First, an ODBC driver must be present for every data store developers want to access. These drivers must support SQL queries, even if the database does not use SQL for its native query language. Second, the ODBC API treats all data in the form of relational tables. Both constraints can cause problems for unstructured and non-relational data stores. Finally, the ODBC API is a standard, controlled by a committee. In other words, regardless of the underlying DBMS's capabilities, the ODBC driver can expose only functionality that is part of the standard. Modifying the API is a complex process. The committee must agree to the proposed change, specify how ODBC drivers should implement the proposed function(s), and specify how applications or the driver manager can detect whether a given driver supports the new specification. Drivers must be updated, and applications must ensure that new drivers are installed or that applications are written carefully against older drivers.

In practice, ODBC is a widely used mechanism for database access and an appropriate solution for applications that work only with traditional relational databases. Most major DBMS vendors support ODBC. However, as applications move beyond relational DBMSs (RDBMS), a more comprehensive solution is needed.

OLE DB

OLE DB specifies a set of COM interfaces for data management. These interfaces are defined so that data providers can implement different support levels, based on underlying data store capabilities. Because OLE DB is COM-based, it can easily be extended; resulting extensions are implemented as new interfaces. Clients can use the standard COM **QueryInterface** method to determine whether specific features are supported either on a particular computer, or by a particular data store. This capability improves upon function-based APIs defined by ODBC.

Figure 9.3 shows the high-level OLE DB architecture, which consists of three major elements: data consumers, service components, and data providers.

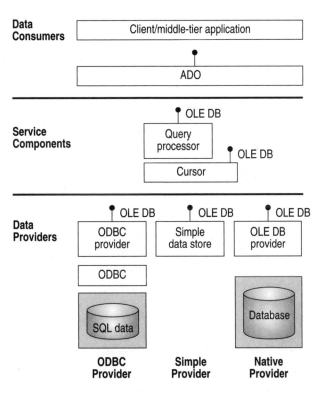

Figure 9.3 OLE DB architecture

Data consumers are COM components that access data using OLE DB providers. OLE DB service providers are COM components that encapsulate a specialized data management function, such as query processing, cursor management, or transaction management. OLE DB is designed so that these service components can be implemented independently from data providers, which are in turn delivered as stand-alone products and plugged in as needed. For example, simple data providers may provide a way only to retrieve—but not query, sort, or filter—all information from its data source.

A *service component* may implement SQL query processing for any data provider. If a consumer wanted to perform a SQL query on data from a simple data provider, the service component could then execute the query.

OLE DB *data providers* are COM components responsible for providing information from data stores to the outside world. With the use of this procedure, all data is exposed in the form of virtual tables, or rowsets. Internally, providers will make calls to an underlying data store using its native data access method or a generic API, such as ODBC.

The OLE DB object model consists of seven core components, shown in Figure 9.4. These objects are implemented by data providers or service components and used by data consumers.

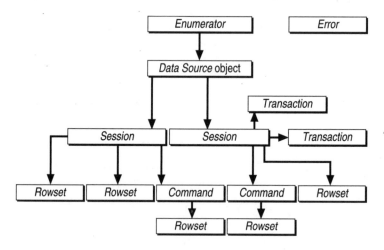

Figure 9.4   OLE DB object model

In the OLE DB object model, an **Enumerator** object locates a data source. Data consumers that aren't accustomed to a specific data source use an **Enumerator** object to retrieve a list of names of available data sources and subordinate **Enumerator** objects. For example, in a file system, each file could correspond to a data source and each subdirectory could correspond to a subordinate **Enumerator** object. The data consumer searches the list of names for a data source to use, moving through the subordinate **Enumerator** objects as necessary. Once a data source is selected by name, a **Data Source** object can be created.

A **Data Source** object knows how to connect to a data store type, such as a file or a DBMS. Each OLE DB provider implements a **Data Source** component class with a unique CLSID. A data consumer can either create a specific Data Source directly, by calling **CoCreateInstance**, using the Data Source's CLSID, or it can use an **Enumerator** object to search for a data source to use. Although each **Data Source** class has a unique CLSID, all classes are required to expose a certain set of OLE DB interfaces. This requirement is important, as a consumer can standardize the use of any available data source. Data consumers specify the name of the data source to which they want to connect, as well as provide any authentication information, through the **Data Source** object. Once a **Data Source** object is created, it can reveal the underlying data provider's capabilities.

Developers create **Session** objects using a **Data Source** object. A **Session** represents a particular connection to a data source. A **Session** object's primary function is to define transaction boundaries. **Session** objects are also responsible for creating **Command** and **Rowset** objects, which are the primary objects for which to access data through OLE DB. A **Data Source** object can be associated with multiple **Session** objects.

If an OLE DB provider supports queries, it must implement **Command** objects. **Command** objects are generated by **Session** objects, and are responsible for preparing and executing text commands. Multiple **Command** objects can be associated with a single **Session** object. Developers should keep in mind that OLE DB doesn't distinguish among command languages used; **Command** objects must simply understand commands and translate them into calls to the underlying data provider when the commands are executed.

Commands that return data create **Rowset** objects. **Rowset** objects can also be created directly by **Session** objects. A **Rowset** simply represents tabular data. **Rowsets** are used extensively by OLE DB. All **Rowsets** are required to implement a core set of OLE DB interfaces. These interfaces allow consumers to sequentially traverse the rows in the **Rowset**, get information about **Rowset** columns, bind **Rowset** columns to data variables, and get information about the **Rowset** as a whole. Implementing additional OLE DB interfaces supports additional features, such as updating the **Rowset** object or accessing specific rows directly.

The OLE DB object model also includes an **Error** object. Any other OLE DB object can create error objects. They contain rich error information that can not be conveyed through the simple HRESULT returned by COM methods. OLE DB **Error** objects build on a standard error-handling mechanism, **IErrorInfo**, defined by Automation. OLE DB extends this error-handling mechanism to permit multiple error records that a single call returns, and also to permit providers to return provider-specific error messages.

The OLE DB object model provides a powerful, flexible mechanism for consumers to access any data type uniformly. OLE DB defines a rich, component-based model that lets data providers implement as much functionality as the providers are able to support, including sequential access, simple rowsets, and full DBMS functionality. This model gives developers the option of writing generic data access components that use only the most basic functionality. Using this model, developers may also write components (optimized for a specific DBMS) that use a single programming model.

ActiveX Data Objects (ADO)

The OLE DB object model exposes functionality through COM interfaces that are not Automation compatible, which means that OLE DB cannot be used directly from many programming languages and tools, such as Microsoft Active Server Pages. Thus, UDA also defines the application-level programming interface ADO. All ADO interfaces are dual interfaces, so any COM-aware programming language or tool can use them. ADO is the recommended way to access data stores in multi-service layer applications, also commonly referred to as Microsoft Windows DNA applications.

ADO Object Model

The ADO object model is shown in Figure 9.5. ADO is built on top of OLE DB, so developers will see many similarities to the OLE DB object model. ADO was also designed to be familiar to developers who have used earlier Microsoft data access object models such as DAO and RDO. Unlike DAO and RDO, the ADO object model is not hierarchical. Except for **Error** and **Field** objects, all objects can be created independently, making it easy to reuse objects in different contexts. Creating objects independently also allows for several ways to accomplish a particular programming task.

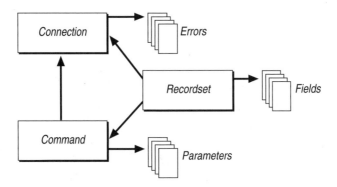

Figure 9.5   ADO object model

Note Microsoft has introduced several object models for data access over the years. DAO consists of Automation objects for accessing the Microsoft Jet database engine used by Access as well as ISAM and ODBC databases. RDO consists of Automation objects for accessing relational ODBC data sources. These technologies are supported "in-the-box" by Visual Basic 5.0. However, while these technologies will continue to be supported, future development efforts should focus on ADO.

The **Connection** object represents a unique session to a data store. The **Connection** object is essentially a combination of the **Data Source** and **Session** objects in OLE DB. **Connection** objects expose an **Execute** method that lets developers perform simple tasks with a minimal amount of effort. Alternatively, **Connection** objects can be attached to **Command** and **Recordset** objects, which also offer methods to access data from the data store.

Command objects in ADO are equivalent to OLE DB **Command** objects—both provide a means to prepare and execute parameterized commands against the data source. Preparing a command lets developers save a processed form of the command that can be executed quickly. A **Command** object has a **Parameters** collection, which contains one or more **Parameter** objects, each representing a command-specific parameter. ADO **Command** objects are available only when the underlying OLE DB provider implements OLE DB **Command** objects.

Recordset objects are the basis of ADO. Like OLE DB **Rowset** objects, they represent tabular data from a data source. **Connection** and **Command** methods that return data from the data store return read-only **Recordset** objects that can be accessed sequentially. More flexible **Recordset** objects can be created directly by programmers, connected to **Connection** and (optionally) **Command**

objects, and populated by calling various **Recordset** methods. **Recordset** objects support a variety of options for controlling the amount of data retrieved from a data source at a given time. Other available options control the type and duration of locks placed on the underlying data source, and also specify when updates are applied to the data store.

Although **Recordset** object refers to the overall construct of a set of rows and columns. At a granular level, a **Recordset** refers to a set of columns associated with a specific row, which is also the current row. Individual columns of the **Recordset** are accessed through its **Fields** collection, with one **Field** object for every column. Associated with every **Recordset** object is a cursor. In database terms, a cursor is the software that returns rows of data to an application. The cursor in a **Recordset** object indicates the current position in the **Recordset** and determines what row will be returned next. ADO supports several cursor types, ranging from simple forward-only cursors, to cursors that let developers move to any row, to cursors that let developers view changes made by other users as developers move through the **Recordset** object.

Programming with ADO

The ADO object model contains the seven objects listed in Table 9.6.

Table 9.6   Objects contained in the ADO object model

Object	Description
Connection	Manages a connection to a data source.
Command	Defines a specific command to execute against a data source.
Recordset	Represents a set of records from a data source or the results of an executed command.
Field	Represents a column of data with a common data type. A **Recordset** object has a **Fields** collection, with one **Field** object per column in the **Recordset**.
Parameter	Represents a parameter associated with a **Command** object based on a parameterized query or stored procedure. A **Command** object has a **Parameters** collection, with one **Parameter** object per command parameter.
Property	Represents a dynamic characteristic of an ADO object defined by the OLE DB provider. **Connection**, **Command**, **Recordset**, and **Field** objects have **Properties** collections, with one **Property** object per dynamically defined characteristic.
Error	Contains details about data access errors for a single operation. A **Connection** object has an **Errors** collection, with one **Error** object per OLE DB provider error.

Connections

Developers use a **Connection** object to set up a connection with a data source. When the object is used with an ODBC data source, developers establish a connection by passing either a data source name (DSN), user ID, and password or a DSN filename to the **Connection** object's **Open** method.

Data objects should generally access data sources using a fixed identity, rather than using the client's identity. This technique greatly simplifies administration and makes it possible to efficiently pool database connections across multiple client requests. If developers need to restrict access to a database, they can restrict access to business objects with which clients interact, or to the data objects themselves.

The most straightforward and flexible way to specify parameters for the **Connection** object's **Open** method is to include a DSN filename in development source code and then specify the data source, user ID, and password in the DSN file. This technique lets a system administrator modify the data source or account access information without requiring source code changes to components.

The **Connection** object specifies the type of database access desired by the developer. Developers would use the **Mode** property to indicate a read-only, write-only, or read/write connection, and also the type of sharing to be permitted so the team's database will be protected. Developers must set the **Mode** property before opening a connection.

Typically, developers open a connection immediately before accessing the database, then subsequently close this connection as soon as possible, rather than retain a connection for an object's lifetime. This approach is acceptable despite the expense of creating database connections, because the ODBC 3.0 driver manager contains exceptional connection pooling services. For each connection request, the driver manager first examines the pool for an acceptable unused connection. If it finds a connection, the driver manager returns it; otherwise, the manager creates a new connection. If the connection remains idle for a specified period (by default, 60 seconds), the connections driver manager disconnects it from the database and removes it from the pool. Currently, only free memory and the number of database connections available limit the ODBC connection pool size. The only alternative for controlling the pool size is to set the ODBC pooling time-out value based on an estimated connection rate.

The driver manager does not reuse a connection that was established using a different user identity. Developers thus should connect to databases using a fixed identity within their data objects. If developers use the client's identity, every unique client will require a unique database connection, eliminating a key scalability benefit of three-service layer architecture and Microsoft Transaction Server (MTS). Developers also can not reuse connections across process boundaries. As we discussed in Chapter 8, components that access the same data sources should run within the same process so that connections can be reused.

If developers examine **Connection** object methods in the ADO documentation, the **BeginTrans**, **CommitTrans**, and **RollbackTrans** methods, related to transaction processing, will occur. Components running in the MTS environment should never use these three methods. Instead, developers should let MTS manage transactions through **ObjectContext** and use the **ObjectContext**, **SetComplete**, and **SetAbort** methods to elicit the transaction outcome.

Accessing Data

Using ADO, data can be accessed using three elements: the **Connection Execute** method as well as the **Command** and **Recordset** objects. Developers can use the **Connection Execute** method to execute a specified command against a data source. When used with an ODBC data source, commands can be SQL statements or nonparameterized stored procedures. Any results are returned as a Recordset object with a read-only, forward-only cursor. We'll discuss cursors in more detail in the "Recordset Objects" section below.

Note Stored procedures can provide a great performance boost, especially for complex data access operations. However, developers should use stored procedures only for data access. Business logic should be implemented in business objects.

Developers can use **Command** objects to execute parameterized stored procedures and commands or to save a compiled version of a command that will be executed multiple times. Developers also establish a connection to a data source by setting the **Command ActiveConnection** property. Developers should specify such a command using the **CommandText** property, and execute this command using the **Execute** method. Any results are returned as a Recordset with a read-only, forward-only cursor. If developers have a parameterized command, they should specify such parameters in the **Command** object's **Parameters** collection. To compile a command for speedy reuse, developers set the **Prepared** property.

Finally, developers can manipulate data directly using **Recordset** objects. Creating a **Recordset** object and using its methods directly is the most flexible way to manipulate data.

Recordset Objects

When developers use ADO, they will almost always manipulate data exclusively through **Recordset** objects. Developers get either a **Recordset** as the return value from a **Connection** or **Command Execute** call, or developers create their own Recordsets.

A **Recordset** object comprises a set of rows and columns. As mentioned, at any given time, a **Recordset** refers to the set of columns associated with the current specific row. The **Recordset**'s individual columns can be accessed through the

Fields collection. Developers move through the rows of a **Recordset** by using the object's associated cursor.

Recordset objects are tremendously useful for three-service layer applications. State on a server should not be shared across method calls; rather, server states should connect to a database, retrieve data, disconnect, and return all data to the caller. Disconnected **Recordset** objects can accomplish such a process through ADO.

Recordset Locking

Recordset objects also support a variety of lock types. Whenever records in a **Recordset** are being updated, a lock must be put on those records. The following **LockType** property values specify what types of locks are placed on records during editing:

- **adLockOptimistic** Optimistic locking applies locks record by record, but only when the **Update** method is called.

- **adLockPessimistic** Pessimistic locking applies locks record by record, at the time the record is read.

- **adLockBatchOptimistic** Batch optimistic locking applies locks to the entire **Recordset** object, but only when the **UpdateBatch** method is called.

- **adLockReadOnly** Read-only locking is the default. When this lock type is specified, developers cannot update data in the **Recordset** object.

Note The **Recordset** object provides a set of methods for moving through its rows. The **MoveNext** and **MovePrevious** methods move forward and backward through the Recordset, one record at a time. Developers can use the **BOF** and **EOF** properties to detect when they have reached the beginning or end of a **Recordset** object. For a **Recordset** object that supports dynamic positioning, **MoveFirst** and **MoveLast** are available. For a **Recordset** object that supports bookmarks, developers can use the **Bookmark** property to return a unique identifier for a current record in the **Recordset** object. At a later time, developers can set the **Bookmark** property to return to that particular record. **Recordset** objects also provide methods to move to specific records by ordinal number.

The most common way to populate a **Recordset** object that developers create is to attach it to a **Connection** object using the **ActiveConnection** property, then by calling the **Recordset Open** method. Developers can also populate a **Recordset** object programmatically, if the data does not derive from an OLE DB data source.

ADO Cursor Types

ADO supports the following four cursor types:

- **Dynamic cursor** Enables developers to view additions, changes, and deletions made by other users. All types of movement through the **Recordset** object that don't rely on bookmarks are permitted. Bookmarks are supported if the OLE DB provider supports them.

- **Keyset cursor** Similar to a dynamic cursor, except that developers can't see records added by other users and developers can't access records deleted by other users. Keyset cursors always support bookmarks.

- **Static cursor** Provides a static copy for a set of records. Developers cannot see additions, changes, or deletions made by other users. Static cursors always support bookmarks, and thus permit any type of movement through the **Recordset** object.

- **Forward-only cursor** Similar to a static cursor, but allows developers only to scroll forward through the **Recordset** object.

The **Recordset** object features available to developers depend on the cursor type specified when the **Recordset** object is opened.

Note Not every OLE DB provider supports every cursor type. When developers use the OLE DB provider for ODBC, the cursor types available to developers depend on types supported by the underlying ODBC driver for a database. The SQL Server ODBC driver supports all four cursor types.

Disconnected Recordset

Disconnected **Recordset** objects use optimistic locking; developers can manipulate these objects on the client using a client-side cursor library. (In this context, "client" refers to either the presentation or business layer.) Disconnected batch updates are supported through the **UpdateBatch** method. Using the **UpdateBatch** method requires extreme care, because another client may risk updating several records while these records are being modified on a different client. When the batch update is applied, developers will receive errors for the conflicting updates. In this case, developers need to define, as part of their component interfaces, how partial updates will be handled—will they generate transaction failures, or will the client need to handle the error?

To create a disconnected **Recordset** object, before opening the connection, developers should set the **CursorLocation** property on either the **Connection** or the **Recordset** object to **adUseClient**. The developers should then retrieve the data and release the **ActiveConnection**. If developers want to allow the client to modify the information, they should create the **Recordset** object using batch optimistic locking (**adLockBatchOptimistic**) and either a static (**adOpenStatic**) or a keyset (**adOpenKeyset**) cursor.

Recordset Fields

As mentioned, columns of the current row in a **Recordset** object are accessed using the **Fields** collection. Developers can access a field by its name or by a numeric index. When developers use an ODBC data source, the field name corresponds to its name in a SQL SELECT statement. The numeric index is thereby determined by the field's position in the SQL SELECT statement. Once developers have a **Field** object, they can get or set information about this object using its properties. The most commonly used property is **Value**, which can be used to retrieve or set the field's data value.

Two special methods on the **Field** object—**GetChunk** and **AppendChunk**—are available to handle long binary or character data. Developers can use **GetChunk** to retrieve a data portion and **AppendChunk** to write a data portion. Developers can determine whether they need to use these methods by examining the **Field** object's **Attributes** property.

Handling Errors

Any ADO operation can generate errors, so it's important to handle those errors within method calls. Such error handling consists of two steps performed by ADO: returning error codes for each method call, then supporting the standard COM error reporting mechanism, **IErrorInfo**. Specific OLE DB provider errors, such as native database error codes or ODBC error codes, are stored in the **Errors** collection associated with a **Connection** object. One ADO call can generate multiple errors in the **Errors** collection. It is recommended that developers walk through the **Errors** collection to retrieve substantial error information about database failures.

ADO clears the **ErrorInfo** object before it makes a call that could potentially generate errors. However, the **Errors** collection is cleared and repopulated only when the OLE DB provider generates a new error, or when the **Clear** method is called. Some methods and properties can generate warning messages in the **Errors** collection without halting program execution. Before calling these methods or properties, developers should clear the **Errors** collection so that they can read the **Count** property to determine whether any warnings were generated. **Methods** that can generate warnings include **Recordset Resync**, **UpdateBatch**, and **CancelBatch**. The **Recordset Filter** property can also generate warnings.

Remote Data Service (RDS)

Although ADO recordsets offer access to only one row of data at a time, recordsets do not necessarily access the underlying data store every time the cursor moves. Internally, a **Recordset** can cache multiple rows of data. This caching capability is an important part of building scalable distributed applications.

We'll consider a scenario in which thousands of users access an online store over the Internet. The catalog of items for sale is most likely maintained in a database. If each user maintains a unique connection to the database for the entire time the user browses the store, the number of database connections available on the database server strictly limits the number of simultaneous shoppers. On the other hand, if database connections are used only while blocks of data are read from the database, a single connection can support many users. In addition, if a large block of data can be sent back to each user's computer, the user can browse a catalog with fewer database server accesses. The latter scenario not only can reduce network traffic; it could also make the online store more responsive for the user.

The MDAC technologies that help make this scenario a reality are ADO disconnected **Recordset** objects and RDS. The RDS architecture is shown in Figure 9.6.

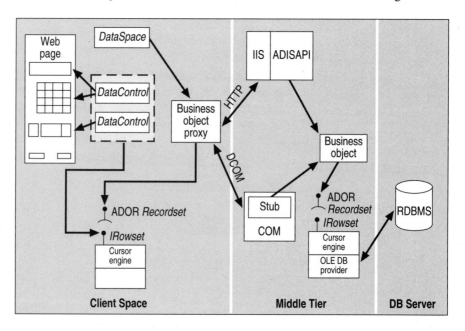

Figure 9.6 RDS architecture

A disconnected **Recordset** object has simply been dissociated from its **Connection** object. Disconnected **Recordset** objects do not retain locks on the underlying data store. Instead, all data for all rows is cached within the **Recordset** object. If a **Recordset** is modified and the changes are saved back to the data store, OLE DB checks each modified row for conflicting updates in the data store. In other words, OLE DB checks whether the row has been modified since the **Recordset** object was cached. If so, a conflict is reported to the application so that the application can handle the conflict properly.

RDS provides a client-side cursor engine for disconnected recordsets. It also provides a very efficient service for marshaling recordsets between computers, over either the Internet or an intranet. This means that a server application can generate a set of data and copy it to a client application, which can browse the data as if it were connected to the actual data store. RDS also provides a way to bind **Recordset** objects to data-bound controls, which can greatly simplify writing this type of client application.

RDS provides three components to help developers write applications: **RDS.DataControl**, **RDSServer.DataFactory**, and **RDS.DataSpace**. An **RDS.DataControl** object is used to bind data-bound ActiveX controls to **Recordset** objects. Client applications use **RDS.DataControl** to browse or modify a Recordset. **RDSServer.DataFactory** is essentially a generic business object for communicating with data sources. It contains no business rules or other application-specific logic.

The **Recordset** object itself is obtained in one of two ways. First, the **Recordset** object can be created implicitly by **RDS.DataControl**. Properties of **RDS.DataControl** are set that identify the data server and query to be used. When the **Refresh** method is called, an **RDSServer.DataFactory** object is used behind the scenes to create the **Recordset** object. Second, custom business objects that return disconnected recordsets can be defined. **RDS.DataSpace** objects are used to create client-side proxies to these business objects. The client-side proxy does whatever is necessary to communicate with the business object. Once the proxy has been created, the application can call whatever method returns a **Recordset** object; it then sets the **Recordset** property of **RDS.DataControl**.

This book exclusively endorses the second method. Middle-service business objects will use data objects to create ADO disconnected recordsets. These **Recordset** objects will be passed back to the presentation layer using RDS. Presentation-layer client applications will use RDS to bind the **Recordset** objects to data-bound controls.

In intranet scenarios, DCOM can be used to transfer **Recordsets** between client and server computers. In Internet scenarios, however, HTTP will normally be used. In this case, RDS provides services to manage the HTTP communication. An Internet Server API (ISAPI) extension, Advanced Data ISAPI (ADISAPI), is installed on the Web server. ADISAPI does the work required to handle requests for Recordsets from client-side business object proxies. It creates server-side objects, calls the methods required to generate the **Recordset** objects, and converts the data to an efficient form for transmission back to the client. ADISAPI and the business object proxies handle all details of actually transmitting the data via HTTP.

Choosing the Right Data Access Technology

Almost all applications require some form of data access. For standalone desktop applications, local data access is typically easy to implement with little or no programming effort. For enterprise applications, data access is considerably more complex, often involving remote data sources with different data formats and storage mechanisms.

Developers often ask the question, "Which data access technology should I use to build this enterprise application?" To answer this question, developers need to keep two critical points in mind: the importance of code reuse and developers' ability to implement the chosen interface. Often, developers implement an exotic data access solution in a quest for better performance or more control, only to create an application that is an expensive maintenance burden. The newer data access technologies typically reduce development time, simplify code, and yet still provide high performance while exposing all required functionality.

Developers can effectively use virtually all of the Microsoft data access technologies in most situations. Nevertheless, each data access technology has its relative strengths. If their applications require data access, developers will want to understand the unique data access implementation and usage issues specific to each data access method.

When to Use ADO

ADO is Microsoft's premier data access technology. The ADO data access technology and its partner OLE DB comprise the recommended solution for all data access. If their team is developing a new application, developers should definitely use ADO.

If the team is considering migration to ADO, they have to decide if characteristics and benefits of ADO are enough to justify the cost of converting existing software. Older code written in RDO and DAO will not automatically convert to ADO code. However, whatever solutions developers previously developed using other data access strategies can definitely be implemented using ADO. In the long run, ADO should be used.

When to Use RDO

If the team has an RDO application that works well today, there's no reason to change it. If the application needs to be extended to access other kinds of data, consider reengineering to use ADO. As mentioned above, new applications should use ADO.

When to Use ODBCDirect

ODBCDirect is an acceptable choice if the application must run queries or stored procedures against an ODBC relational database, or if our application needs only the specific capabilities of ODBC, such as batch updates or asynchronous queries. However, every feature in ODBCDirect is also available in ADO.

If developers have a working knowledge of ODBCDirect and have large amounts of existing ODBCDirect code, or just need to extend an existing application that already uses it, ODBCDirect will still work for the application. The drawback is that ODBCDirect cannot provide all data access if the application requires other types of non-ODBC data sources. Eventually, the team could take advantage of design, coding, and performance benefits provided by ADO.

When to Use DAO

DAO is the only data access technology that supports 16-bit operations. If the application must run within a 16-bit environment, DAO is the only logical choice.

If the application must access both native Microsoft Jet and ODBC resources, DAO will work; however OLE DB or ADO will provide faster access and require fewer resources.

If the team is experienced in using DAO and has large amounts of existing DAO code, or just needs to extend an existing application that uses a Microsoft Jet database, DAO may still work for the application. Once again, the drawback comes as an application requires other types of data sources, and DAO cannot provide data access. Eventually, the team will want to take advantage of ADO.

When to Use ODBC

Several factors influence choosing the ODBC approach, including a requirement of high performance, more granular control over the interface, and a small footprint.

The ODBC API is considerably harder to code than the object-based interfaces, but provides a finer degree of control over the data source. Unlike other data access technologies (such as ADO, RDO, or ODBCDirect), the ODBC API has not been made "bullet proof." While it's fairly easy to create ODBC errors during development, the ODBC API provides excellent error handling with detailed error messages. In general, developing, debugging, and supporting an ODBC API application requires a tremendous amount of knowledge, experience, and many lines of code. As a general rule, developers prefer to access data by using a simpler, higher-level object interface such as ADO.

ODBC is not suitable for nonrelational data such as ISAM (Indexed Sequential Access Method) data because it has no interfaces for seeking records, setting ranges, or browsing indexes. ODBC simply was not designed to access ISAM data. While developers can use the Microsoft Jet ODBC driver to handle ISAM and the native Microsoft Jet engine data, what is really happening is that the Microsoft Jet database engine converts the ISAM data to relational data and then provides limited ISAM functionality. Performance in this situation is slow due to the extra layer imposed by the Microsoft Jet engine.

If the application requires very fast access to existing ODBC data, and if developers are willing to write many lines of complex code (or already have a log of ODBC code available for reuse), ODBC can be a good choice.

Choosing a Data Access Strategy

A project team needs to consider the following questions before choosing a data access technology:

- **Is the development team creating a new design, or modifying an existing application that uses obsolete data access technology?** For a modification, it's tempting to continue with the application's former data access methods, which in the short term seems like a reasonable and cost-effective decision. However, the downside involves programming difficulty as the application stretches toward new and different data sources. For a new design, developers should use ADO.

- **Where is the data? Is it on the Web, on a remote server, or simply stored locally on user systems?** If the data is simply stored on users' local systems, the need to build a separate server to manage the data might be overkill. If the data is remote, what about connection management? What happens when the application can not connect? Should the application be using an asynchronous data access technology such as ADO or RDO?

- **What are the developers trained to use? Do they already have experience with ADO, RDO, DAO, or ODBC? Is it worth the modest one-time cost and effort to train the entire staff to use ADO?** If the team begins using ADO, can developers reasonably anticipate a maintenance cost reduction in the near future?

- **Does an application require data access to both relational and nonrelational data sources? Do developers have an OLE DB provider for each?** If so, use ADO.

- **Are developers planning to use MTS?** If this is the case, developers need to choose one of the data access technologies that can be executed on the server and act as a "resource manager" (an MTS term for a component that implements its set of resource manager interfaces). For example, ADO, RDO, and ODBC can act as MTS resource managers. The DAO interface is not capable of being a resource manger. The team should also consider if the component must be thread safe, such as with ADO and RDO, since this is a requirement for most MTS-managed components if developers expect reasonable resource use and performance.

- **Does every application already use the ODBC API?** If developers continue with ODBC, how will their applications access other kinds of data sources in the future?

Developers can use differing data access technologies to implement useful data access and application communication strategies; such strategies are listed in Table 9.7.

Table 9.7   Key characteristics for data access technologies

Best choice is...	If the application requires...	Remarks
ADO	Mainframe data or program communications	With Microsoft SNA Server, developers can set up OLE DB data providers for mainframe data sources such as VSAM, CICS, IMS, and AS/400 files.
	Reengineering	For existing applications, developers should consider reengineering with ADO. As an alternative, developers could continue with previous data access methods.
	New development	For all new development, use Microsoft's ADO data access technology.
	Uniform access to a variety of data sources and data types	ADO is a common interface for all data access requirements.
	Fast development	ADO helps minimize development cost because it is uniform, consistent, and easy to use. The team can be trained once and benefit continuously thereafter.
	High performance	ADO provides rapid performance.
	Web: Internet Information Service's (IIS) Active Server Pages (ASP)	If the application uses IIS with ASP to generate browser-independent HTML from databases, use ADO.
OLE DB	Custom File Access	The team can write custom OLE DB data providers for virtually any data source. Once written, ADO can then be used as the data access technology.
RDO	Fast access to existing ODBC data	RDO is very fast.
ODBCDirect	Access to ODBC data	ODBCDirect provides a performance improvement over the older DAO data access technology.
DAO	Enhancements to existing data access	DAO provides a consistent programming model for DAO situations where some of the data access services must be provided using Microsoft Jet. If developers already have large amounts of DAO code and are willing to overlook the design, coding, and performance benefits provided by ADO, there's no reason to change it.
	Running within a 16-bit environment	DAO is the only choice.
ODBC API	Fast access to existing ODBC data	If the team is willing to develop and maintain complex code using the ODBC API, this is a good choice.

Accessing Host-Based Data

Many organizations have their data tied up in different hardware and software platforms. While it may not be feasible or advantageous to move that data to a centralized location, there is profit in making distributed data appear as though it can be accessed from a single data source. This strategy fits in well with the multiple service programming model that allows programmers to modify their client-based applications without having to understand the particulars of where the data is stored.

ADO for the AS/400 and VSAM

This section covers ADO's role in allowing Windows-based systems to communicate with VSAM and AS/400 systems, as illustrated in Figure 9.7. To describe how this ability works, developers need to have a basic understanding of how AS/400 and mainframe systems communicate. First, we'll briefly introduce how the communication occurs. Then, we'll describe the method IBM systems use to communicate, DDM (Distributed Data Management) and how OLE DB interacts with DDM to expose data through Microsoft SNA Server.

Most computer systems use data storage, data management, and data access methods that are unique to that system. This causes issues of interoperability when information systems professionals require different systems to share data or allow users to access data across multiple systems simultaneously. Added to this problem are the issues of networking and connecting disparate systems such as SNA Server and Windows NT.

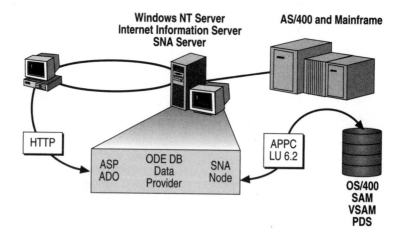

Figure 9.7   Accessing AS/400 data

IBM devised the Distributed Data Management (DDM) architecture to provide a standardized method for data access between multiple similar hardware, dissimilar hardware systems, and multiple operating systems. DDM supports three types of data storage types: records, byte streams, and relational databases.

As mentioned, Microsoft devised OLE DB to provide a set of data access interfaces to enable multiple data stores to work seamlessly together. Independent software vendors implement OLE DB in their data providers to integrate disparate data storage, data management, and data access systems.

As noted in Figure 9.7, Microsoft has developed the OLE DB Provider for AS/400 and VSAM, an OLE DB data provider for accessing SNA data sources using DDM. This provider complies with Level 4 of the IBM DDM architecture and the OLE DB architecture. The OLE DB Provider uses SNA Server, the reliable platform for host integration as the networking bridge between the SNA host and Windows NT operating systems.

The Microsoft OLE DB Provider for AS/400 and VSAM supports the following features:

- Set attributes and a record description of a host file (column information).

- Position to the beginning record or the ending record in a file.

- Navigate to the previous or next record in a file.

- Seek to a record based on an index.

- Lock files and records.

- Change records in a file.

- Insert new records and delete records in a file.

- Preserve file and record attributes.

DDM and OLE DB

A DDM process takes place between two computer systems: the first is the source system, where the program requesting the data resides; the second is the target system, where the data resides.

File access using DDM and OLE DB involves the source application first being written to acquire data records. These data records originate from a host file using a specific data source location that is embedded in an initialization string. The ADO run-time DLLs respond to the source application's request for an open connection by communicating with the OLE DB data provider using the information specified in the initialization string. As seen in Figure 9.8, the OLE DB Provider for AS/400 and VSAM interprets the OLE DB requests and translates them to DDM commands. The initialization string will specify the Advanced Program to Program Communication (APPC) logical units (LU) alias on an SNA

Server computer, code page conversion, user ID, and password. The provider uses WinAPPC and SNA Server for host connectivity.

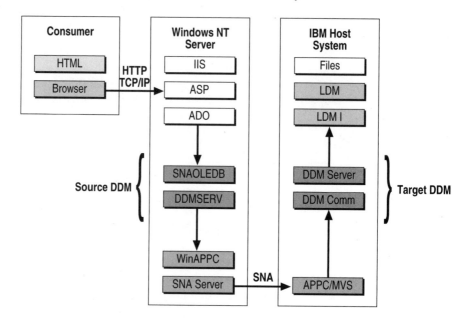

Figure 9.8   OLE DB access with APPC

The DDM architecture and APPC protocol takes care of issues related to security, error handling, resource locking, and flow control. When the source DDM server receives the data, it is converted from DDM to OLE DB data types native to the source system.

To read and write records within a host file, the computer application must know the record format—primarily the field size and field data format. However, on the mainframe, only the length of the records within the file is described to the system. The system has no knowledge of field definitions within the file. Mainframe files are often referred to as record-level or program-described files. Mainframe application developers embed the record format of host data files as part of the application program. The OLE DB Provider for AS/400 and VSAM accesses host record files outside of the host application. In other words, no field-level descriptions, or metadata, exist to describe the host records. The OLE DB Provider works around this problem by reading a locally stored computer file that contains the metadata mapping for the host file. The computer application developer creates this local file, which is called a host column description (HCD) file. The HCD file contains a file identifier (name), host data type (length, precision, scale), computer data type (OLE DB data type), and host CCSID (code page). With this information, the OLE DB Provider can transform the host data record into a computer data record composed of individual information fields. Additionally, the OLE DB Provider converts the host data from host EBCDIC to UNICODE, then to the target computer ANSI code page using the National Language Support API.

Files in OS/400 can be either record-level or field-level described, where the fields in the file are described to the operating system. Field-level described files are often referred to as externally described files. The OS/400 keeps a record of the field-level descriptions available for use by any application. Traditionally, AS/400 developers have used the system-stored field-level record descriptions. This reduces the amount of programming required to define records. Application programmers utilize three primary elements to describe fields within a file to the AS/400 operating system: Data Description Specification (DDS), Interactive Data Definition Utility (IDDU), and SQL. Through all of these elements, the field is described by common attributes such as name, alias, length, data type, data validity restrictions, and text description. Use of a local HCD file is not necessary to describe the record format for data stored in the AS/400, because the Microsoft OLE DB Provider for AS/400 and VSAM uses DDM commands to retrieve the record description. Optionally, a computer application developer can use an HCD file to access AS/400 program-described, otherwise known as AS/400 flat files.

Microsoft OLE DB Provider supports the following objects for AS/400 and VSAM:

- **Enumerator**
- **DataSource**
- **Session**
- **Rowset**
- **Command**
- **View**
- **Index**
- **ErrorObject**

The **Transaction** and **TransactionOptions** objects are not supported.

Microsoft ADO Provider supports the following objects for AS/400 and VSAM:

- **Connection**
- **Recordset**
- **Field**
- **Command**
- **Parameter**
- **Collection**
- **Error**

COMTI and Mainframe Data Integration

This section details how Windows clients can integrate well with mainframe environments such as CICS and IMS using Microsoft's Component Transaction Integrator (COMTI). COMTI is a feature of SNA Server 4.0. Working in conjunction with MTS, COMTI makes CICS and IMS programs appear as typical MTS components that can be used with other MTS components for building distributed applications. COMTI brings drag-and-drop simplicity to developing sophisticated applications that integrate Web transaction environments with mainframe transaction environments.

The basis of this new technology is the COMTI Component Builder. The Component Builder provides a COBOL Wizard which helps the developer determine what data definitions are needed from the COBOL program, and generates a component library (.tlb file) that contains the corresponding automation interface definition. Because of the strong integration with MTS, when the component library is dragged and dropped into the MTS Explorer (or MMC snap-in), a COM object is created that can invoke a mainframe transaction. This allows developers to build applications using Active Server technologies that can easily include mainframe transaction programs (TP). Similarly, mainframe developers can easily make mainframe TPs available to Windows-based Internet and intranet applications. Developers do not have to learn new APIs, nor do they have to program custom interfaces for each application and mainframe platform. Because COM Transaction Integrator for CICS and IMS does all of its processing on the Windows NT Server, there is no COMTI executable code required to run on the mainframe, and developers are not required to rewrite most mainframe COBOL programs. Client applications simply make method calls to an Automation server, and mainframe TPs simply respond as if called by another mainframe program.

COMTI saves time and effort spent programming a specialized interface with the mainframe. As a generic proxy for the mainframe, COMTI intercepts object method calls and redirects those calls to the appropriate mainframe program; it also handles the return of all output parameters and return values from the mainframe. When COMTI intercepts the method call, it converts and formats the method's parameters from the representation understandable by the Windows NT platform into the representation understandable by mainframe Transaction Programs (TPs). All COMTI processing is done on Windows NT Server, and no executable code is required to run on the mainframe. COMTI uses standard communication protocols (for example, LU6.2, provided by SNA Server) for communicating between Windows NT Server and the mainframe.

COMTI provides an interface between Automation components and mainframe-based applications. Running on Windows NT Server, COMTI-created components appear as simple Automation servers that developers can easily add to their application. Behind the scenes, COMTI functions as a proxy that communicates with an application program running on IBM's Multiple Virtual Storage (MVS) operating system.

Applications that run in part on Windows platforms and in part on the mainframe are distributed applications. COMTI supports all distributed applications that adhere to the Automation and distributed COM (DCOM) specifications, although not all parts of the application have to adhere to these standards.

A client application uses COMTI to access a transaction process (TP) running on the mainframe. The specific TPs supported in COMTI are IBM's Customer Information Control System (CICS) and IBM's Information Management System (IMS). An example of this type of distributed application might be simply reading a DB2 database on the mainframe to update data in a SQL Server database on Windows NT Server.

The client application can be running on Windows NT Server, Windows NT Workstation, Windows 95/98, or on any other platform that supports DCOM. Because DCOM is language-independent, developers can build their client application using the languages and tools with which they are most familiar, including Visual Basic, Visual Basic for Applications, Visual C++, Visual J++, Delphi, Powerbuilder, and Microfocus Object COBOL. That client can then easily make calls to the COMTI Automation object (or any other Automation objects) registered on Windows NT Server.

COMTI Makes It Easier to Extend Transactions

Although COMTI can be used with simple mainframe data accessing applications, it becomes an even more powerful tool by allowing developers to extend transactions from the Windows NT Server environment to the mainframe. Windows-based applications that use MTS can include CICS applications in MTS-coordinated transactions (with SNA Server 4.0 SP2, COMTI includes IMS transactions now that IBM provides Sync Level 2 support for IMS via IMS 6.0). COMTI integrates seamlessly with MTS so that:

- Windows developers can easily describe, execute, and administer special MTS objects that access CICS or IMS Transaction Programs (TPs).

- Mainframe developers can easily make mainframe TPs available to Windows-based Internet and intranet applications.

- MTS component designers can easily include mainframe applications within the scope of MTS, two-phase commit (2PC) transactions.

Developers using MTS in their applications can decide which parts of the application require a transaction and which parts don't. COMTI extends this choice to the mainframe as well, by handling both calls that require transactions and calls that do not. For applications that require full integration between Windows-based two-phase commit and mainframe-based Sync Level 2 transactions, COMTI provides all the necessary functionality. COMTI does this without requiring developers to change the client application, without placing executable code on the mainframe, and with little or no change to the mainframe TPs. The client application does not need to distinguish between the COMTI component and any other MTS component reference.

COMTI has two visible interfaces:

- The COMTI Management Console
- The Component Builder

The COMTI run-time proxy provides the Automation server interface for each COMTI-created component and communicates with the mainframe programs. The run time does not have a visible interface.

The COMTI Management Console collects information about the user's environment and configures COMTI for the Windows NT Server and for the MVS mainframe TP environment.

The Component Builder (CB) provides application developers an easy to use, GUI tool for creating the Windows-based component libraries (.tlb files). The CB also allows developers to either start from or create the COBOL data declarations used in the mainframe CICS and IMS programs. The CB is a stand-alone tool that does not require that any language, such as Visual Basic or C++, be installed on the same computer.

At run time, COMTI intercepts method invocations for a COMTI component library and provides the actual conversion and formatting of the parameters and sends and receives them to and from the appropriate mainframe program. COMTI uses the component created by the developer using CB at design time to transform the parameter data being passed between Automation and the mainframe transaction program. COMTI also integrates with MTS and Microsoft Distributed Transaction Coordinator to provide two-phase commit (2PC) transaction support.

The Component Builder isn't required on a deployment computer. The run-time proxy and COMTI Management Console are required on a deployment computer.

Differences Between Windows and Mainframe Terminology

The term "transaction" is defined differently depending upon the computing environment. A transaction in the MTS environment is a set of actions coordinated by the Distributed Transaction Coordinator (DTC) as an atomic unit of work. In contrast, a transaction in the CICS environment has a more general meaning. Any CICS program that uses APPC with another CICS program is referred to as a "Transaction Program" (TP). APPC is a set of protocols developed by IBM specifically for peer-to-peer networking among mainframes, AS/400s, 3174 cluster controllers, and other intelligent devices. A TP can provide any type of service, including terminal interaction, data transfer, database query, and database updates.

For a TP to communicate directly with another TP using APPC, the two programs must first establish an LU6.2 conversation with each other. LU6.2 is the de facto standard for distributed transaction processing in the mainframe environment and is used by both CICS and IMS subsystems. One program can interact with another program at one of three levels of synchronization:

- Sync Level 0 has no message integrity beyond sequence numbers to detect lost or duplicate messages.
- Sync Level 1 supports the CONFIRM-CONFIRMED verbs that allow end-to-end acknowledgment for client and server.
- Sync Level 2 supports the SYNCPT verb that provides ACID (atomicity, consistency, isolation, and durability) properties across distributed transactions via two-phase (2PC) commit.

Of the three sync levels, only Sync Level 2 provides the same guarantees provided by an MTS transaction. Thus, in the CICS and IMS environment, the term "transaction program" may or may not imply the use of 2PC. The term simply refers to the program itself. It is only when the term "transaction" is qualified as Sync Level 2 that the MTS developer and the mainframe developer can be sure that they are referring to the same thing. Likewise, a "Sync Level 2 transaction" would theoretically ensure that both the Windows and mainframe developers are working congruently.

COMTI supports both Sync Level 0 and Sync Level 2 conversations. If a method invocation is part of a DTC coordinated transaction, COMTI uses Sync Level 2 to communicate with CICS. If a method invocation is not part of a DTC coordinated transaction, then COMTI uses Sync Level 0.

DCOM Connector for SAP

SAP is a proprietary system designed to run line-of-business applications to manage a large variety business functions. This means that users must work with proprietary interfaces to manage SAP data. SAP, which is an integrated product, allows corporations to graphically map and manage their business processes into an integrated whole.

One of the latest versions of SAP, R/3, is object oriented. This allows SAP system designers to create COM interfaces to support a variety of programmable interfaces supported by COM via the DCOM Connector for SAP. The DCOM Connector for SAP aids in integrating the functionality contained in distributed environments.

The run-time instances of business objects or remote functions provided in the R/3 application are available in MTS as COM objects using the DCOM Connector. The DCOM Connector is installed in the MTS in the form of components within a package and allows developers to create and administer COM objects.

The SAP R/3 DCOM connector is fashioned around the multi-service layer architecture and contains an R/3 application server that exposes the SAP business objects and remote functions that can be called from components within MTS. These objects and functions are mapped through COM via a DLL. Clients can make calls to those components through MTS, which communicates with the R/3 application server and makes the communication transparent to the client application.

In the DCOM Component Connector, ABAP objects (BAPIs) are mapped onto COM interfaces and visa versa. (ABAP stands for Advanced Business Application Programming Interface.) BAPIs is a term used to represent objects that have a guarantee not to change. It stands for a well-defined interface to processes and data of business application systems. Also, the SAP Business Object Repository (BOR) is integrated with the Microsoft Repository (XML Repositories). The solution is scalable because the components can be installed and distributed as often as needed and connections are pooled to R/3's Remote Function Calls (RFCs). When Windows NT clients are used, security is provided in the context of MTS. Optionally, Windows NT user IDs can be mapped to R/3 security for a single logon. All Tables and Structures are represented as ADO recordsets. There is automatic marshaling via RDS. At the core, OLE DB is used to and from map ABAP tables. ADO is the interface to OLE DB. The DCOM Connector automatically generates proxy and stub components for objects. The next version of the DCOM Connector will support 2PC and outbound calls, and requires COM+ Services.

The DCOM Component Connector provides the following benefits for corporations:

- **A new dimension of openness** The DCOM Component Connector provides interoperability between R/3 objects and COM objects across a heterogeneous network through well-defined business interfaces. It exposes R/3's mature business processes and business objects to open DCOM access, making it easier to complement and extend R/3 using Microsoft tools—for example, to create new front ends or to extended business processes.

- **Leverage existing programming skills** With the DCOM Component Connector, developers have the choice of either extending the Business Framework by using software components written with SAP tools (ABAP Objects) or COM tools (Visual Studio, Visual Basic, Visual C++, and Visual J++). This leverages existing investments in training, people, and in the huge market for pre-built COM components.

- **Eased integration** The integration of R/3 Business Components with third-party products, legacy systems, and homegrown applications has become much easier with the DCOM Component Connector. Now even distributed transactions of several systems containing several databases are possible.

- **Evolutionary approach** The DCOM Component Connector works even if R/3 itself does not run on a Windows NT platform. This allows corporations to save costs by leveraging their existing infrastructure. And through the built-in scalability of multiple servers in every service layer (MTS and R/3 Application Server), this solution is able to grow with developers' needs.

COM+ In-Memory Database (IMDB)

A new feature in COM+ is the In-Memory Database (IMDB), a database that maintains its tables in memory. There are several reasons why having such a database might be useful.

Many applications need to retrieve fairly static data from persistent tables. For example, an application might use a table of valid ZIP codes and the corresponding city, state, and area code to automatically fill in the city and state fields of a data entry form when the user enters a ZIP code. A business object might use the table to validate the phone number for a given address. This table will be large, and retrieving it from a persistent database over and over again will lead to performance problems. By using IMDB as a cache for the persistent database, the table can be loaded once from the persistent database into an IMDB database. Data objects would be configured to retrieve information from the IMDB database rather than the persistent database. Because memory is relatively cheap, this approach can be an inexpensive way to improve the performance of developers' applications.

While caching is primarily useful for read-only data, it can also be used for read/write scenarios. This technique can be useful when an application's data objects reside on a different computer than the database server. To reduce the network traffic involved in reading and writing the database, an IMDB cache can be configured on the data object server computer. Data objects can read and write to the IMDB. Updated records are propagated back to the persistent store when transactions commit. This approach works particularly well when the database can be partitioned such that only one computer is updating a particular subset of records through the cache.

IMDB also offers a powerful alternative to the Shared Property Manager (SPM) for managing shared transient state. Unlike the SPM, IMDB can be used to share information across server processes. Because IMDB is an OLE DB provider, ADO can be used to access information stored in an IMDB database. Developers are more likely to be familiar with the ADO interfaces than the SPM interfaces, making it easier to implement shared transient state.

Figure 9.9 shows how IMDB works. The COM Explorer is used to configure the IMDB server process to run on a particular computer. This process runs as a Windows NT service. The IMDB server process is responsible for managing IMDB tables and interacting with any underlying persistent databases. The database tables are kept in shared memory; the COM Explorer can be used to configure how much memory is set aside for these tables. IMDB also provides a proxy, which is an OLE DB provider that runs in each client process. The proxy can interact directly with the IMDB tables for read-only scenarios, but it must go through the server process for read/write scenarios or to request locks on the data.

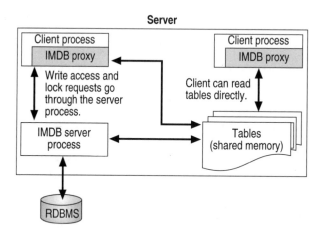

Figure 9.9   Accessing the COM+ IMDB

Caution In COM+ 1.0, IMDB is limited to a single computer. If information is cached from a persistent database to an IMDB database running on multiple computers, there is no coordination across computers. Likewise, transient state managed by an IMDB database is local to a computer. However, future versions of IMDB are expected to include a distributed cache coordinator and a lock manager, to enable coordination across computers.

IMDB imposes some restrictions on the types of database tables it supports. In particular, the tables must have primary keys, and all changes to the tables must be performed by the IMDB. This means that some database features such as auto-increment fields, time-stamp fields, and triggers cannot be used in an IMDB database. In addition, IMDB does not provide a query processor and does not permit tables to be partially loaded from a persistent store; instead, the entire table must be loaded. The table can be sorted and filtered using ADO **Recordset** objects.

Despite these restrictions, using IMDB from components is straightforward. Developers can use either OLE DB or ADO to access IMDB tables. To do so, developers provide a DSN to establish the database connection and then use normal OLE DB or ADO methods. The DSN is configured using the COM Explorer. Developers also use the COM Explorer to map the IMDB data source to a persistent data source and to define which tables, if any, are loaded from the persistent data source when the IMDB server process starts.

Summary

UDA is Microsoft's strategy for providing a common data access method for all types of data, regardless of where the data is. UDA is based on OLE DB, a system-level component architecture for data management. UDA also defines an application-level programming interface for data access, ADO. ADO can be used from any programming language or tool that supports COM.

UDA is implemented by MDAC. MDAC includes ADO, an OLE DB provider for ODBC, as well as several ODBC components. In the ADO programming model, data is manipulated using **Recordset** objects. ADO is the recommended data access technology for all new application development.

Data objects represent the data access service of an application. They are responsible for the accuracy, completeness, and consistency of the data they own. They should work correctly whether or not their clients are transactional. Data objects for MTS are in-process COM components.

The application's data access has several important characteristics that ensure data integrity, such as normalization, use of business rules, and referential integrity.

New data access technologies such as COMTI for host data access, SAP DCOM connector for ERP access, and COM+ IMDB provide excellent capabilities for simplifying the team's data access requirements.

Review

1. What is the UDA?

2. Which data access components are available from Microsoft?

3. What is the recommended Data Access Component?

4. How can applications access host-based data with COM?

5. What is COM+ IMDB?

C H A P T E R   1 0

Testing and the Production Channel

About This Chapter

After a project begins, it is important for the developers to have the appropriate working environment. This chapter begins by explaining how to build a working environment that supports development, testing, certification, and production. We refer to this life cycle as the *production channel*, and we describe it using real-life examples. We explain the goals of the production channel, which are to provide appropriate application testing within a controlled environment while protecting the production environment of the organization from unnecessary interruption.

We also look in greater detail at testing, and we recommend several ways to execute and monitor tests. Then we discuss ways to scale out an application's production environment by adding servers to the physical implementation.

Finally, we examine ways to classify program faults and failures, discuss the larger issue of product bugs, and describe methods of tracking, classifying, and resolving known bug problems.

The principles and guidelines we provide in this chapter are based on our own experience with the creation of application architectures and the implementation of modern applications, together with the following sources:

- Microsoft Solutions Framework
- The MSF *Principles of Application Development* course # 1516
- Mary Kirtland's *Designing Component-Based Applications*

Upon completion, you will be able to:

- Identify the stages of a production life cycle.
- Apply appropriate security measures to the development environment.

- Understand the benefits of the development, testing, certification, and production life cycle.
- Describe a typical day in the production channel.
- Identify performance requirements.
- Explain how to perform software testing and application tuning.
- Understand the process of bug management.

Managing the Development Environment

Because today's systems are complex and critical, the development team must have a solid environment in which to work. Managing the application development environment is often just as important as managing the project itself. This environment should be isolated from the working environment of the organization, which we call the *production environment*, because of the potential for negative impact both on the organization's daily work and on the direction of the application development.

As a critical aspect of management, a change control system must be in place during both the development and maintenance periods to ensure that changes to a new application don't adversely affect the organization's production environment and the users that rely on its stability for daily operations. For example, in the early days of Web development, when Web pages usually consisted of only text and pictures, it was easy to make changes to them. However, today's Web pages are much more complex, and many are full-fledged application environments that must be maintained and available at all times. Downtime on a Web site can mean lost revenues or can cause bad will when customers are unable to access necessary resources. It's no longer acceptable for a Web site to be unavailable while someone tracks down the change that caused the site to stop working properly, ascertains who made the change and why, and fixes the problem.

A change control system that is not enforced is useless. The development team must put policies in place that prevent control procedures from being circumvented. For example, no one should be able to make direct changes to an application in the production environment without first applying that change within a testing and certification environment. The process for making changes must be well thought-out, well understood, and as automated as possible.

Production Channel

Application projects can go through at least four distinct stages, which comprise a life cycle called the *production channel*. These stages are:

- Development
- Testing
- Certification
- Production

Each of these stages is supported by a specified team of people and computer systems. Neither the people nor the systems should overlap between stages. A set of rules should be developed to determine when and how specific changes to the application progress through the production channel. By following these procedures, any problems will be discovered in the testing or certification stage, rather than in the production stage.

Development

First and most important, all changes occur on the development systems. If this basic policy is not established in the beginning, the entire process is likely to fail. This policy should not be compromised and should be enforced throughout the system. Developers will often be tempted to skirt around the policy when a critical change is needed or when going through the entire rollover process is too inconvenient. However, even the smallest and most innocent change can have unexpected and destructive consequences. Creating a policy and sticking to it ensures that the entire process is successful.

Testing

Each project should have a comprehensive test plan that encompasses the major functionality of the application and ensures that everything works properly. After the application is modified on the development systems, the changes are sent to the testing systems. This "sending" process may be nothing more than a batch file or a button on a Web page activated by whoever has been assigned this responsibility and has the proper access rights to initiate this "rollover." On the testing systems, a series of tests determine whether the application is still working properly after the changes.

The testing stage concentrates on functionality and usability issues, and can be carried out on a wide variety of machines and environments.

Certification

When basic testing is complete, the application is rolled over to the certification systems. A person or group of people then test it thoroughly to determine whether any bugs or problems remain to be fixed before the application is sent to the production server. This certification testing is much more thorough than the tests carried out on the testing systems and should include coverage, usage, and performance validation, which we discuss in detail later in this chapter. The certification team may perform integration checks with other systems that interact with the application, such as applications that share business COM objects or the production database. In addition, the certification team may check that the application can handle normal working stress by simulating the loads that are expected in the production environment.

The certification stage concentrates on performance and integration with existing systems. The certification environment should be fully functional, and be configured to resemble the production configuration as closely as possible. In particular, it should reproduce any multiple-network protocols, COM transports, domains, or firewalls that restrict access to particular computers. Items such as database connectivity must be configured on the certification servers the same way they are on the production servers.

Note Testing and certification require people as well as systems. There is no reason to have a certification system if no one is available to test the application while it is on this system.

Production

The project is rolled over to the production server or servers only after the test plan has been completed and the application is proven stable. The advantages of a smoothly operating production channel are greater flexibility and scalability. For example, if certification tests determined that another production server is required to meet demand, the additional server can be configured and added. The only modification needed is to configure the application's systems on the new server.

In the meantime, the development team may already be working on the next version of the application on the development server.

Change Control Process

Developing a change control process and establishing policies are relatively easy compared with the task of enforcing them. Fortunately, Microsoft Windows NT and Microsoft Windows 2000 have built-in features to ensure that everyone follows the rules. Figure 10.1 shows the NT file system (NTFS) permissions that are appropriate for developers through the four production-channel stages. Obviously, the developers need full access to the source files on the Development server because they make the changes there. However, they are given limited access to the same files on the Testing, Certification, and Production servers so that they can't change the files without going through the change control process.

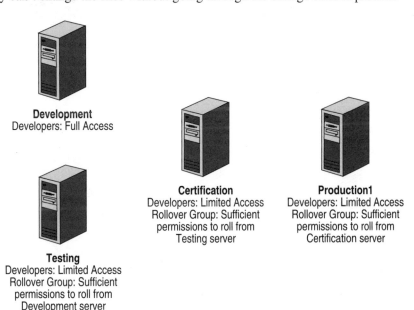

Development
Developers: Full Access

Certification
Developers: Limited Access
Rollover Group: Sufficient
permissions to roll from
Testing server

Production1
Developers: Limited Access
Rollover Group: Sufficient
permissions to roll from
Certification server

Testing
Developers: Limited Access
Rollover Group: Sufficient
permissions to roll from
Development server

Figure 10.1 Developers' system permissions in the production channel stages

Figure 10.2 shows a simplified view of the production channel that culminates in rollover to three production servers. To illustrate the potential for problems if a change control process is not followed, suppose a company has a working Web site for which it is designing a Web-based application using Active Server Pages (ASP), COM business objects, and an SQL data server. The application has several informational Web pages containing text and graphics, including a picture of a lion.

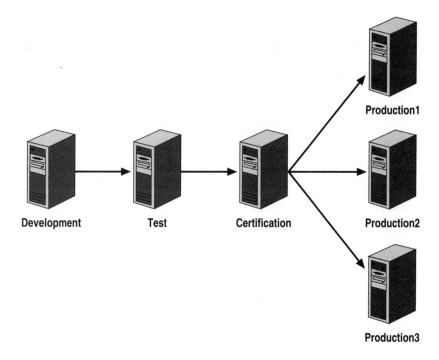

Figure 10.2   Simplified production channel rollover process

Suppose that a developer decides that this picture is no longer needed, connects to the production Web servers, removes the link to the picture from the page, and deletes the picture from the servers, without realizing that another developer has linked to the same lion picture from a different page. Because the lion picture is no longer available, that page and any other pages linked to the picture display an error message.

Taking this scenario one step further, suppose the developer removes the picture from only the Production1 and Production2 servers, not from Production3. Now the production environment is inconsistent. A user who connects to the Web site via the Production3 server will see the lion picture, whereas a user who connects via Production1 or Production2 will not.

In the above example, removing the picture causes a minor inconvenience for a few people. The impact is potentially much greater if the same kind of unregulated change results in the deletion of a compiled business object. Any pages that use the business object will be out of service, and critical business processes may be affected. Even if the developer changes the business object instead of deleting it, other portions of the Web application might be adversely affected.

Sizing the Production Channel

When many developers are working on the same project, it quickly becomes obvious why a staged production channel is important, especially with Web-based applications. However, setting up a production channel is just as important if only one person is responsible for the entire application. The production channel enforces discipline, requires that changes to the application be tested before it is deployed in the production environment, and can provide the means to roll back changes if necessary.

The production channel example we have provided is very basic. Often an application will have multiple components such as Web pages, business objects, and data, and will be deployed on multiple servers, such as Web servers, indexing servers, transaction and queuing servers, and database servers. For the most accurate testing, each server should be emulated in the certification stage of the production channel so that the certification environment exactly mimics the production environment. As Figure 10.3 shows, the certification environment can also be scaled down for smaller applications or organizations.

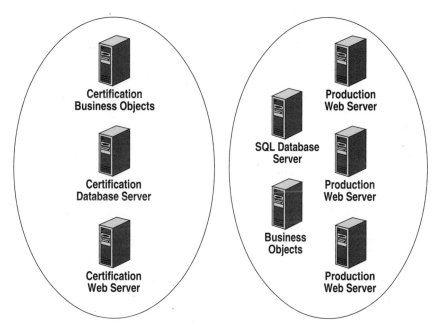

Figure 10.3 Scaling down the certification environment

In small environments, the certification database may be physically stored on the production database server, but it should be a separate database that mimics the live data used in the production system. Production data should never be manipulated during certification.

In some circumstances, the entire certification environment might need to be located on a single computer. However, if the production environment consists of multiple computers, inter-computer connectivity won't be adequately tested by this certification configuration. Running multiple certification servers that are configured the same way as the production servers is more likely to identify and resolve connectivity issues, such as database connections, so that the application can be rolled smoothly to production.

Caution Conducting performance tests that generate large amounts of network traffic on production networks can interrupt normal operation. Before executing these tests, the feasibility of isolating the testing and certification networks from the production network should be seriously considered.

Testing Enterprise Applications

Testing is the process of exercising the software under controlled conditions and assessing the result. The controlled conditions should involve normal and abnormal data and events. Testing should strive to introduce the unexpected to determine how the system will react.

Ultimately, the role of testing is not just to find bugs, but to assure quality. Because the ultimate definition of quality is "meeting the customer's needs by solving the business problem," the testing process should support that goal by validating what needs to be done and verifying that it is being done correctly.

The testing process is not limited to the Stabilizing Phase of the MSF Development Process Model, but is also an integral part of the Developing Phase. At the Project Plan Approved Milestone (at the end of the Planning Phase), the project team establishes a baseline for the test plan and begins work on the more detailed testing specifications that describe how individual features will be tested. The testing specification is baselined at the Scope Complete Milestone (at the end of the Developing Phase), because at that point the feature set should not grow or change.

During the Developing Phase, *coverage testing* attempts to thoroughly test each feature of the product as well as the actual code base of the product in a relatively closed environment. During the Stabilizing Phase, testing shifts from coverage testing to *usage testing*, which validates that application's fulfillment of the use cases and usage scenarios developed during the Envisioning Phase. This stage of testing usually includes involving actual users of the product in beta tests, and preferably occurs in the application's production environment. Tolerance for bugs decreases as testing progresses through the Stabilizing Phase, and because the focus is on shipping during this phase, being able to successfully manage bugs is paramount.

Because of the multiple dependencies within a distributed application environment, testing requirements for this type of application are extensive. Each dependency, Web page, component, and database, as well as elements such as the GUI code, middleware, and network infrastructure, must be tested not only for functionality but also for compatibility in multiple configurations.

The best way to test a distributed enterprise application is using a bottom-up approach. Each component is tested individually outside the MTS environment. When the basic functionality of a component is working, the component is tested within MTS on a single computer. Finally, the application as a whole is tested in the distributed enterprise environment.

Component–Level Testing

The first step is to test each component individually, outside the MTS environment (the same kind of unit testing that is done for any other kind of code). The easiest way to test components is to write a simple test harness that exercises all the functionality exposed by the COM classes. Scripting languages and rapid application development (RAD) tools, such as Microsoft Visual Basic Script and Microsoft Visual Basic, are great ways to build simple test harnesses. Multithread test harnesses can be used to make sure that the component has no concurrency problems. The goal is to verify that the application logic of each component works correctly, before the component is placed in the distributed application environment. Many programming tools provide only limited support for debugging components running within MTS, so the more bugs that can be eliminated up front, the better.

One potential problem with testing a component outside the MTS environment is that the component's code typically uses the object context. When a component runs outside the MTS environment, the object context is not available. If the release version of the component might run both within and outside the MTS environment, the object context must be checked to see whether it exists at run time before any method calls are made. If the released version always runs within MTS, checking for the object context before every method call may not be necessary. In this case, conditional compilation is a useful approach if the programming language being used supports it.

The disadvantage of this approach is that a special version of each component must be built to run outside MTS. There is a slight risk that the application logic might be correct in this version and incorrect in the version build for MTS, but it is the best approach available for testing components written in languages such as Microsoft Visual C++ or Microsoft Visual Basic outside the MTS environment.

Local Integration Testing

After the components have been tested outside MTS, they should be tested again within MTS on a single computer, beginning with single, independent components and gradually building up to the entire application. Testing on a single computer eliminates network errors and reduces security problems while the application is being constructed. Getting the entire application working on a single computer verifies correct transactional behavior and security checking before the application is set up across a distributed environment.

Initial testing should focus on whether transactions interact as expected. After the normal code paths are validated, the error paths should be executed. Appropriate calling of **SetAbort**, **SetComplete**, **EnableCommit**, and **DisableCommit** should be verified, including whether the correct error codes are being returned and whether errors are being handled correctly in the clients. In some cases, the original component won't be able to reproduce all the errors, and it may be necessary to build a special test version that uses the same interfaces but does produce the errors so that all the error paths are exercised.

To reduce the initial configuration work of setting up a test environment, all components should be running in the security context of the interactive user with authorization checking disabled. When the application has been validated in this environment, the components should be tested to make sure they work for a particular user with authorization checking enabled. Finally, any role-based security checks, declarative or programmatic, should be verified to ensure that they work as expected.

Debugging Tools

If a component doesn't execute as anticipated, it may need to be executed in a debugger so that each line of code can be examined. Primary concerns are developing components with debug information and configuring the debugger so that the MTS surrogate is correctly launched.

Traces allow viewing of output information as the component is executing. This information is primarily useful when the code is not executing in the debugger or the source code is not available. However, traces can cause problems if a component does not have access to the interactive user's desktop and a message box is displayed where it can't be seen or closed.

Return values from all COM method calls should be checked to determine whether COM is reporting information about the system or about specific errors generated by the component. For example, COM may report access violations and communication errors in the method return value when the component is executing in a distributed or secure environment.

Data Access Testing

If data access components are not able to access their data sources, database management system (DBMS) tools and the tools provided by ODBC should be used to track down the problem. If SQL Server is being used, connecting to a database, issuing queries, and so on can be tested with the SQL Enterprise Manager. The SQL Trace program can be used to watch operations against the database. Also useful are the Visual Data Tools and SQL debugging feature of Microsoft Visual Studio Enterprise Edition.

If a data source is accessed via ODBC, the data source driver may allow use of the ODBC driver manager to test data source access with a particular data source name (DSN). ODBC also provides a trace facility that can help troubleshoot ODBC errors. Trace messages are written to a log file that can be examined for details of the ODBC commands that were executed.

If data sources can be accessed manually but not from MTS components, data source compatibility with MTS must be verified. In particular, the ODBC drivers must support MTS. If data sources can be accessed from within MTS but transactions aren't working correctly, the Microsoft Distributed Transaction Coordinator (MS DTC) might not be running or might not be properly configured on all computers involved in the transaction.

Integration Testing

When the application is working on one computer, it should be tested in a distributed environment before being released for deployment. At this point, the testing is done within the certification environment. In general, MTS applications should not require any special coding to work in these scenarios, but setting up a certification environment is a great way to test package settings and deployment instructions before an application is actually deployed.

Integration testing should start with a simple deployment and build up to more complex deployments. For example, the application should be tested without a firewall in place before it is tested with the firewall. In addition, the application should be tested both with a single client and with multiple concurrent clients, either using multiple-client computers or a test harness that simulates multiple clients.

The techniques described for local testing also apply to distributed testing. Most administrative tools available with Windows NT allow administrators to operate on remote machines as well as local machines. For example, event logs for multiple machines can be viewed from a single workstation. However, some techniques apply specifically to the distributed environment. If the application works locally but objects cannot be created remotely, network connectivity between the computers may be interrupted or DCOM may not be enabled. Checking the event log will indicate whether security problems are preventing object creation or access.

The exact mechanism used to test network connectivity depends on the network protocols available between computers. If TCP/IP is used for DCOM communication, the Ping utility can be used to determine whether a particular computer can be reached, but does not guarantee communication via DCOM. The DCOM Configuration utility, DCOMCNFG.EXE, can be used to determine whether DCOM is enabled on a particular machine. This test is particularly important on Microsoft Windows 95 and Windows 98 clients, where DCOM is not enabled by default.

If the application's basic COM or MTS functionality is being troublesome, the test computers should be examined to ensure that they are in good working order.

Performance Validation

As illustrated in Figure 10.4, defining the necessary level of performance is a critical first step in the validation process. After the requirements have been defined, a set of tests for measuring performance can be identified. These tests should be conducted at various points during the development process to ensure that performance is within striking distance of requirements. As the application approaches completion, performance can be validated in the context of a test environment that resembles the one in which the application will ultimately be deployed. If the tests indicate that performance requirements are not being met, a series of controlled experiments should be conducted to locate performance bottlenecks. The bottlenecks can then be removed and testing can be repeated until the requirements are met.

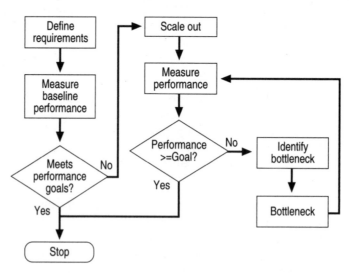

Figure 10.4   The performance validation process

Defining Performance Requirements

Performance requirements should be defined up front, before development and debugging begins. To define a good performance requirement, project constraints must be identified, services to be performed by the application must be determined, and the load on the application must be specified. This information can then be used to select appropriate metrics and determine specific performance goals that must be achieved.

Identifying Constraints

Some aspects of a project cannot be changed to improve performance. There may be constraints on the schedule or on the choice of development tools or technologies. For example, the application might need to be deployed by a certain date to meet contractual obligations. The development team might have Visual Basic expertise but no expertise in Visual C++, making it impractical to develop components using Visual C++. Hardware constraints might be a factor, particularly for user workstations. Whatever the constraints are, they must be documented. These are the factors to be held constant during performance tuning. If satisfactory performance cannot be achieved within these constraints, they may have to be revisited by management or the customer.

The aspects of the project that are not constrained can be modified during the tuning process to see whether performance can be improved. For example, can components be implemented in a different language? Can different data access technologies be used? Are transactions really needed? Can computers be added to the application topology? These questions can help identify ways to remove bottlenecks in the system.

Determining Services

Applications typically provide one or more services that correspond to use cases and usage scenarios. Usually each scenario can be described as a set of transactions. Even if transactions are not involved, a sequence of interactions with the user takes place for each scenario. The semantics of each performance-sensitive scenario (what the user does and what the application service does in response) should be defined precisely, including how the service accesses databases and other system services. These definitions drive the tests that measure performance.

In addition to defining which services should be measured, how often these services are used must be specified. Accurate estimates of the usage of various application services helps create tests that closely mimic the expected usage of the system, improving the accuracy of performance test results.

Specifying the Load

A common way to measure the load on an application is to identify the number of clients that will use the application. A related measure is *think time*, which is the elapsed time between receiving a reply to one request and submitting the next request. For example, if it takes about 60 seconds for a user to enter all the information required for a Web-based time-entry form, 60 seconds is the think time for the Time Entry scenario.

Load variance over time must be considered. For some applications, the load remains fairly constant, while for other applications, the load may vary. For example, a payment processing application will have a heavier load during the week when payments are due. An insurance claims application will have a heavier load when a natural disaster, such as a hurricane or tornado, occurs. A help desk application will have a heavier load in the month following the release of a software upgrade. Information about how the load varies over time can be used to determine the peak and average system loads. Performance requirements can then be based on either or both of these measures.

Defining Metrics and Goals

When constraints, services, and load have been identified, the specific performance goals, or requirements, for the application need to be defined. The first step is to select the specific metrics to be measured. Common metrics include:

- **Total system throughput** Measured in transactions per second (TPS). This quantity is measured for a given mix of service requests (that is, transactions) and a given user load.

- **Response time** The elapsed time between submitting a request and receiving a reply. Response time metrics are often specified as a percentile—for example, "95 percent of all requests must respond in less than one second."

After the appropriate metrics have been selected, the required values for those metrics must be specified. These values should be realistic measures of the necessary performance of the application—"as fast as possible" is almost never a good metric. A simple way to determine the TPS requirement is to divide the number of clients by the think time. For example, if on average an application needs to support 1200 simultaneous clients with a 60-second think time, a value of 20 TPS (1200/60) can be specified as the average load. Response-time measures should take user expectations into account. For example, suppose that after users submit a form, they should wait no longer than 5 seconds before they can assume that the application is not working correctly. The response time requirement would then be specified as 95 percent response within 5 seconds over a 28.8 KB modem connection (the lowest possible denominator).

Measuring Performance

After specific performance requirements have been identified, testing can begin to determine whether the application meets those requirements. It is important to eliminate as many variables as possible from the tests. For example, bugs in the code can create the appearance of a performance problem. To accurately compare the results from different performance test passes, the application must be working correctly. It is especially important to retest application functionality if modifications have been made to the implementation of a component of the application as part of the tuning process. The application must pass its functional tests before its performance is tested. In addition to application changes, unexpected changes can occur in hardware, network traffic, software configuration, system services, and so on. Both types of change must be controlled.

To correctly tune performance, accurate and complete records of each test pass must be maintained. Records should include:

- The exact system configuration, especially any changes from previous test passes.
- Both the raw data and the calculated results from performance monitoring tools.

These records not only help determine whether performance goals have been met, but also help identify the potential causes of performance problems down the road.

Exactly the same set of performance tests should be run during each test pass; otherwise, it is not possible to discern whether any difference in results is due to changes in the tests rather than to changes in the application. Automating as much of the performance test set as possible helps eliminate operator differences.

Defining Performance Tests

During performance testing, values for the metrics specified in the performance goals are measured and recorded. Think time, transaction mix, and any other performance metrics must also be met. Within these constraints, the testing should be as realistic as possible. For example, the application should be tested to determine how it performs when many clients are accessing it simultaneously. Multiple clients can be simulated in a reproducible manner using a multi-threaded test application, in which each thread represents one client. If the application accesses a database, the database should contain a realistic number of records, and the test should use random (but valid) values for data entry. If the test database is too small, the effects of caching in the database server will yield unrealistic test results. The results might also be unrealistic if data is entered or accessed in unrealistic ways. For example, it's unlikely that new data would be created in alphabetical order on the primary key.

The MTS Performance Toolkit provides sample test harnesses that can be used as models for building automated test harnesses for applications. These sample test harnesses demonstrate how to collect TPS and response-time metrics, as well as how to simulate multiple clients using multiple threads. Usually, test harnesses need to accept user-specified input parameters, such as the transaction mix, think time, number of clients, and so on. However, the rules for creating realistic random data will probably be encoded within the test harness itself.

After a test harness has been created to drive the application, all the invariant conditions for running the tests should be documented. At the very least, these conditions should include the input parameters required to run the test harness. How to set up a "clean" database for running the test—that is, a database that does not contain changes made by a previous test pass—should also be documented, as well as the computer configurations used for the test. Usually, the test harness should be run on a separate computer from the MTS application, because this setup more closely approximates a production environment.

Determining Baseline Performance

After performance goals have been defined and performance tests have been developed, the tests should be run once to establish a baseline. The more closely the certification environment resembles the production environment, the greater the likelihood that the application will perform acceptably after deployment. Therefore, it's important to have a realistic certification environment right from the beginning.

With luck, the baseline performance will meet performance goals, and the application won't need any tuning. More likely, the baseline performance will not be satisfactory. However, documenting the initial test environment and the baseline results provides a solid foundation for tuning efforts.

Identifying and Eliminating Bottlenecks

If performance requirements are not met after the application is scaled out (as discussed in Chapter 2), or if scaling out is not an option, data from the test results should be analyzed to identify bottlenecks in the system and form a hypothesis about their cause. Sometimes the test data is not sufficient to form a hypothesis, and additional tests must be run using other performance-monitoring tools to isolate the cause of the bottleneck. Commonly used tools for monitoring the performance of MTS-based applications include the following:

- **Microsoft Windows Task Manager** The Performance tab of the **Task Manager** dialog box, shown in Figure 10.5, provides information about CPU and memory usage on a particular computer. The Processes tab provides information about CPU and memory usage by all the processes on that computer. You can use this information to determine at a high level where bottlenecks might be located.

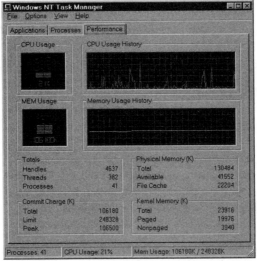

Figure 10.5   The Performance tab of the Task Manager dialog box

- **The Transaction Statistics pane in MTS Explorer** If an application uses transactions, the Transaction Statistics pane in MTS Explorer, shown in Figure 10.6, can be used to collect high-level information about the application's performance. How many transactions commit or abort during a test pass can be determined, as well as the minimum, maximum, and average response times. These response times are for transactions only, not for an entire end-to-end scenario, and do not distinguish between different types of applications in the system. However, this information can be used to get a rough idea of how distributed transactions impact the application's overall performance.

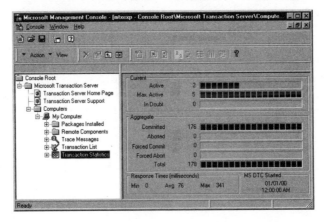

Figure 10.6   MTS Explorer Transaction Statistics pane

- **Microsoft Windows Performance Monitor (PerfMon)** This GUI application, shown in Figure 10.7, is a useful tool for identifying bottlenecks and suggesting possible causes. It allows various performance counters on a Windows NT system to be observed. Performance counters measure the throughput, queue lengths, congestion, and other metrics associated with devices and applications.

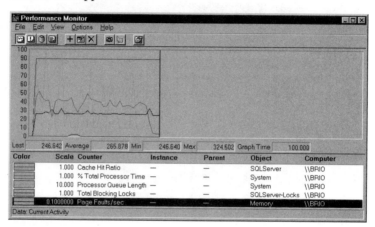

Figure 10.7 Microsoft Windows Performance Monitor

- **Visual Studio Analyzer** This program, which is included with Microsoft Visual Studio 6.0, can also be used to monitor performance counters. In addition, it can be used to monitor events related to the application's components and communication between components. Both COM and MTS fire events that the Visual Studio Analyzer can capture, thus helping to identify performance bottlenecks related to component implementations. For example, method calls that are consistently slow can be identified.

Note Visual Studio 6.0 provides extensive documentation on using the Visual Studio Analyzer.

Although MTS does not currently provide any performance counters per se, counters for devices such as memory, disks, and the CPU can be used to identify many bottlenecks. System applications such as SQL Server also provide performance counters that can help identify bottlenecks.

The most common performance problems in MTS applications are due to insufficient RAM, insufficient processor capacity, disk access bottlenecks, and database hotspots. Table 10.1 describes a set of performance counters that can be used to identify these common bottlenecks.

Table 10.1 Performance counters for identifying common bottlenecks

Performance counter	Description	Common bottleneck
Memory: Page Faults/Second	Number of page faults in the processor	Sustained page fault rates over 5/sec indicate that the system has insufficient RAM.
Physical Disk: % Disk Time	Percentage of elapsed time that selected disk drive is busy servicing read or write requests	Percentages over 85%, in conjunction with Average Disk Queue Length over 2, might indicate disk bottlenecks, if insufficient RAM is not causing the disk activity.
Physical Disk: Average Disk Queue Length	Average number of read and write requests queued up during the sampling interval	Queue lengths over 2, in conjunction with % Disk Time over 85%, might indicate disk bottlenecks, if insufficient RAM is not causing the disk activity.
System: % Total Processor Time	Percentage of time processors are busy doing useful work	Percentages consistently over 80% indicate CPU bottlenecks.
System: Processor Queue Length	Instantaneous count of the number of threads queued up waiting for processor cycles	Queue lengths greater than 2 generally indicate processor congestion.
SQL Server: Cache Hit Ratio	Percentage of time that SQL Server finds data in its cache	Percentages less than 80% indicate that insufficient RAM has been allocated to SQL Server.
SQL Server-Locks: Total Blocking Locks	Number of locks blocking other processes	High counts can indicate database hot spots.

Note Many other performance counters are available. For additional information, see the Windows NT Performance Monitor and the *Microsoft Windows NT Workstation 4.0 Resource Kit*.

After data has been collected using various performance monitoring tools, any bottlenecks should be pinpointed and possible causes identified. Solutions need to be devised and implemented based on hypotheses about the causes of the bottlenecks. Sometimes this process is easy, but often the performance data does not give a clear indication of how the problem might be fixed. In this case, experiments must be conducted that change one aspect of the application or test environment at a time so that the impact of the change on performance can be observed. If the change has no impact or makes performance worse, that change must be undone and another solution tried.

Common Bottlenecks

Developers who have experience with performance tuning begin to see common problems and solutions. The performance group on the Microsoft COM team has identified several common bottlenecks that are commonly seen in MTS-based applications. These bottlenecks and some of the experiments done to identify them are described in the MTS Performance Toolkit. In this section, we look at some of the more common bottlenecks and how to work around them.

SQL Server Bottlenecks

Both the communication protocol and the login credentials used for SQL Server connections can be tuned to provide better performance.

Client Protocols

The default client protocol for SQL Server is the named pipe communication protocol. However, better performance and higher scalability can be achieved using TCP/IP as the client protocol. To use this protocol, TCP/IP Sockets must first be enabled in SQL Server using the SQL Server Setup program. Then for each system that runs components that access SQL Server, the SQL Client Configuration Utility can be used to specify TCP/IP Sockets as the default network on the Net Library tab. SQL Server must be stopped and restarted before the changes will take effect.

System Administrator Login

When the system administrator login is used to access SQL Server, the master database is written to in every transaction. However, the application probably does not use the master database. To avoid the overhead of accessing the master database, a specific login can be created for the application, with the database accessed by the application as the default database. This login can then be used for all data source names (DSNs) or connection strings in the application.

Data Access Bottlenecks

Accessing data is an expensive process, and ways can almost always be found to improve data access performance. This section describes a few of the data access "gotchas" to look out for.

File DSNs

File DSNs provide an easy way for developers to define the database they need to access. However, File DSNs have very poor performance because the system must continually open and read the .dsn file to determine the database connection parameters. Substantially better performance can be achieved using the following alternatives:

- **User DSNs or System DSNs** These can be created using the ODBC Data Source Administrator. User or System DSNs might make system administration a little more complex, because the .dsn file can no longer simply be copied from one place to another. However, the performance gains typically outweigh the increased administration costs.

- **Inline connection strings** Components can be modified to directly specify the connection string rather than using a DSN when opening ADO Connection or Recordset objects. This technique reduces the administrative impact, but components might need to be rebuilt the database configuration changes.

ADO and OLE DB Performance

Early versions of ADO and OLE DB scale poorly in multi-threaded clients that use connection pooling, particularly on multiple-processor computers. This shortcoming can greatly affect the performance of MTS components and ASP pages. Microsoft Data Access Components (MDAC) 2.0 and later versions contain fixes for this problem, so these versions should be used if possible. Other possible workarounds are:

- Scale out the application so that MTS components are hosted on multiple servers.
- Modify components that are bottlenecks to use ODBC directly.

Late-Binding to Data Access Components

As we've seen in earlier chapters, late binding to COM components is inherently slower than vtable binding or early binding, because late binding must make multiple calls through the IDispatch interface for each method call in the client. In addition, packaging method call parameters into the data structures required by the IDispatch **Invoke** method has a cost in terms of performance. If supported by the development tool being used, early binding or vtable binding improves application performance.

MS DTC Log Device

The MS DTC writes log records for every transaction. If the log is stored on a slow hard drive, it can create a bottleneck. The performance of an application that uses transactions can easily be improved by configuring the MS DTC to store its log on a dedicated, fast drive with a high-speed controller.

Multiple MS DTCs

By default, each server running SQL Server and MTS uses a local MS DTC. The overhead of communicating between all the MS DTCs can have an impact on an application's performance. Configuring the system to use a single MS DTC reduces this bottleneck. A remote MS DTC can be set up by stopping the MS DTC service, removing the MS DTC service from the local computer, and then using the MS DTC Control Panel applet to point to the computer on which the MS DTC is running.

Other MTS Bottlenecks

The MTS Performance Toolkit provides a more complete list of potential bottlenecks. We'll look at just two more examples: accessing the system registry and dynamic memory allocation.

Accessing the System Registry

Reading the system registry is an expensive process. If the registry is used to store configuration information for the application, components and applications should read the information only once. Components can then store the information in the Shared Property Manager (SPM) so that it is readily accessible to all objects in the process. Applications can store the relevant information in local variables.

Dynamic Memory Allocation

Dynamic memory allocation is another expensive process that should be eliminated if possible. Allocation is especially expensive when heaps are created and destroyed. Microsoft Visual Basic 5.0 is particularly troublesome because it releases and re-creates project heap space even when the heap space can be reused.

Scaling the Production Environment

In this section, we look at some of the most common deployment configurations for applications that use IIS for the front-end user interface, MTS for business objects, and SQL Server for the database server. Most of our discussion also applies to applications that are not Web-based using IIS.

Configuration #1: Single Node

In the first configuration, shown in Figure 10.8, IIS, SQL Server, and the MTS application are all installed on a single server, or *node*. All clients communicate with that node. This configuration is the most straightforward one to deploy and administer. There are no special security issues or firewalls to worry about because the entire server application runs on one computer.

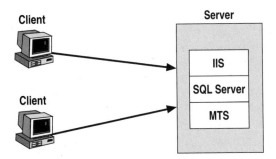

Figure 10.8   Deploying the application to a single node

Because there are no cross-server calls between IIS, MTS, and SQL Server, performance is good for individual clients. If the MTS application is configured to run in-process, performance is even better. The tradeoff is that in-process MTS applications do not participate in role-based security.

An additional tradeoff is that this configuration can support only a limited number of users. Adding memory, high-performance storage devices, or processors to the node allows more users to be supported, but at some point the limit of available hardware will be reached. Then the application will need to be deployed on multiple servers in order to support additional users. Thus, the single-node configuration is most useful for applications with a small user load.

Configuration #2: IIS on a Separate Node

In the second configuration, IIS runs on one server and SQL Server and the MTS application run on a second server. Web clients communicate with the IIS server. This configuration provides faster response for static pages and simple ASP, because more computer resources can be dedicated to IIS. Because MTS and SQL Server are running on the same machine, performance of data objects and the business objects that use them should also be good. Another advantage is that with two servers, the application can scale to larger numbers of users than with a single node.

This approach does have some drawbacks. Calls from ASP-based Web pages to MTS components are cross-server calls, which are inherently slower than local calls and can cause performance bottlenecks. Having the two servers on opposite sides of a firewall can also cause difficulties, depending on the type of firewall separating the servers and on corporate policies regarding traffic through the firewall.

Configuration #2 is useful for applications that consist primarily of static Web pages and simple ASP, with limited use of MTS components and SQL Server databases. If the IIS server is not able to support the user load, the IIS site can be replicated to multiple computers and Windows Load Balancing Service can be used to distribute client requests across the replicated servers.

A disadvantage of this configuration is that all the IIS servers communicate with a single MTS/SQL Server computer, which can become a performance bottleneck as user load increases.

Configuration #3: SQL Server on a Separate Node

In the third configuration, IIS and the MTS application run on one server and SQL Server runs on a second server, as shown in Figure 10.9. Clients communicate with the IIS/MTS server. Because there are no cross-server calls between IIS and MTS, response time for Web pages and the components they use is good. If security and process isolation are not required and the MTS application is configured to run in-process, performance is even better. The application can scale to support more clients than in the single-node configuration.

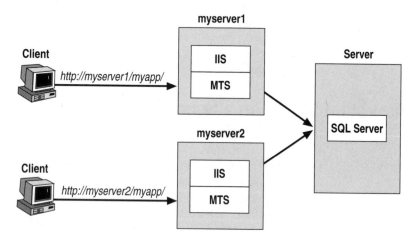

Figure 10.9   Using Windows Load Balancing Service to distribute client requests

The disadvantage is that all calls to SQL Server are cross-server calls. Because database calls typically involve a lot of disk I/O and data processing on the SQL Server computer, these calls are fairly slow anyway (compared to a component method call), so the extra cost of cross-server calls might not cause any problems. However, it is important to verify that cross-server calls do not cause a bottleneck that prevents the application from achieving its performance requirements. The ODBC connection pool time-out might need to be adjusted to account for the longer connection setup time over the network.

As with Configuration #2, Configuration #3 might run into difficulties if the servers are on opposite sides of a firewall. Additionally, better performance might be attained by using TCP/IP as the communications protocol for SQL Server. Depending on the type of firewall separating the servers and on corporate policies regarding traffic through the firewall, configuring access to SQL Server through the firewall over TCP/IP can range from simple to impossible. Packet-filtering firewalls that allow specification of the TCP/IP ports to be opened might be the most successful solution.

Configuration #3 is useful for applications with low to moderate user load that access existing databases running on dedicated servers or databases that must be isolated from the Internet. Applications that need to support higher user load might be able to use a variation of this configuration in which the IIS/MTS server is replicated on multiple server machines and Windows Load Balancing Service is used to distribute client requests across the replicated servers. In addition, because all database requests are directed to a single SQL Server computer, the limit on the user load that can be supported will eventually be reached.

Configuration #4: Each Database on a Separate Node

At some point, any configuration that places an application or the databases it uses on a single server will not be able to handle all user requests with acceptable performance. To support higher user load, the application and databases might need to be partitioned.

Several techniques can be used to partition the application and databases. In Configuration #4, the SQL Server databases used by the application are hosted on multiple servers, as shown in Figure 10.10. Each server can host one or more of the databases, but each database is hosted on only one server. MTS application packages are installed on the servers closest to the data they use. This partitioning complicates deployment a little, because each computer that makes calls to components needs to know where the MTS components it uses are deployed.

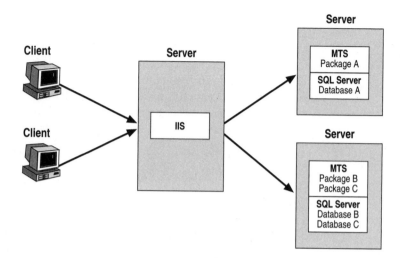

Figure 10.10   Placing SQL Server databases on separate nodes

If the application uses transactions that access multiple databases, a high percentage of the transactions might be distributed in this configuration. Distributed transactions are slower than transactions on a single computer, because the MS DTC must communicate with all the computers to coordinate the transaction. However, the increase in the completion time per transaction is usually an acceptable tradeoff, because the average time per transaction for large user loads is likely to decrease. Additionally, because IIS is running on a separate computer from MTS/SQL Server, the performance and firewall issues mentioned earlier for Configuration #2 will be of concern for this configuration. Again, the increase in the time to complete a single method call or the administrative complexities of passing through a firewall are usually acceptable because larger user loads can be supported. Potential topologies should be carefully tested to ensure that the application's performance requirements are met.

Configuration #5: Partitioned Database

If the application uses a single database and its tables can't be restructured into multiple databases, or if the application uses multiple databases but can't meet performance goals with each database on a separate server, the situation is more complicated. In these instances, multiple copies of a single logical database might need to be created, with each copy installed on a separate server. SQL Server replication can be used to propagate changes from one copy to another.

Configuration #5 is useful when a clear mapping exists between application users and subsets of the data values stored in the database. For example, all users in a particular geographical location might update a local copy of the database. Periodically, these updates can be replicated to a master database at company headquarters so that users who perform operations across geographical locations have access to all the data they need. A portion of the database key value (the value used to identify a specific record) would depend on the geographical location to prevent collisions between updates from different sites.

In one variation of this configuration, the database is partitioned but the application is not. The MTS application packages are installed on a single server, and the components contain code to determine which database server to use for any particular operation. For most situations, this variation isn't particularly useful because any changes to the database configuration are likely to require changes to the components.

In another variation, the MTS application is replicated to each database server. The components use configuration information about the server to determine what data values are valid inputs for that computer. (Otherwise, each server would need customized versions of the components.) Client computers or IIS servers are configured to point to particular database servers. For example, all client computers at a particular site might point to a local IIS server that in turn points to a specific server that has the MTS application and SQL Server database installed. This variation, which is shown in Figure 10.11, can be useful for geographically distributed deployments.

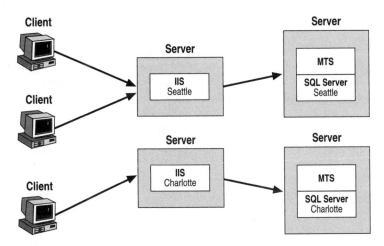

Figure 10.11   Using a specific IIS server to access a geographically partitioned database

Configuration #6: Partitioned Application

The application might need to be partitioned in addition to the database. With this configuration, each MTS application package is deployed to a different database. The most common way to partition applications is by functionality. For example, Figure 10.12 shows the business objects installed on the IIS server and the data objects installed near the data they access. Performance with this configuration should be quite good, as the calls from ASP pages to business objects and the calls from data objects to SQL Server databases are local. Only the calls between business objects and data objects are cross-server calls.

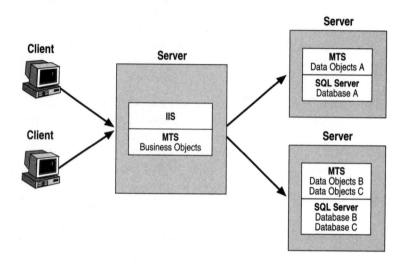

Figure 10.12   Partitioning an application

This configuration has many possible variations that are combinations of features discussed for other configurations. As database partitioning, replication, load balancing, and so on are added to the configuration, deployment and administration become increasingly complex. The benefit is that the application can support a very large user load. When complex configurations are used, application performance must be tested using the methods described in Chapter 13 to ensure that performance requirements are met.

Fault Tolerance

If an application has stringent reliability or availability requirements, the application packages can be deployed on a cluster (a group of physical computers that acts as a single logical computer). One physical computer is online, at any given time, providing services to clients. If that computer fails, another automatically takes over. Microsoft Cluster Server (MSCS) provides the services for coordinating actions within a cluster consisting of two computers.

Bug Management

The information in this section is taken directly from the MSF *Principles of Application Development* course # 1516.

A *bug* is anything that needs to be addressed and resolved before an application is released. Despite the widely held perception that all bugs are defects, they are not. Defects are a category of bugs, but a bug is any issue that arises from using the application that is being developed. Examples of bugs include:

- Enhancement requests.
- Suggestions that are out of scope for the release.
- Issues that arise over user preferences.
- Unavoidable design consequences.
- Defects.

Bug tracking processes encompass such issues as bug reporting, prioritization, assignment, resolution, and closure. Understanding the exact status of the application at all times is fundamental to the Stabilizing Phase. Bug tracking and its output is the process that provides this exact status. Bugs have to be tracked and managed so that the project team can make necessary tradeoff decisions during the Stabilizing Phase. A large part of stabilizing is managing tradeoff decisions about what the team will fix and what it won't. The team must classify bugs in terms of their priority and their risk so that it can determine the proper form of resolution.

Tracking

Before the bug tracking process begins, some sort of bug repository, typically a database, must be established. Newly found bugs are reported by entering them into the database. Each tester enters the bugs they find. Newly identified bugs should be automatically categorized as active.

As bugs are reported, the Development team leader prioritizes and assigns them to specific developers for resolution. In the Stabilizing Phase, the Development team leader might personally resolve the bugs that will not be fixed.

For each bug that requires a development-based resolution, a developer typically resolves it by fixing it. The developer then tests the fix to ensure that it has been effected and that no new bugs have been introduced in the process. When the active bug has been resolved, its status changes to reflect the method of resolution. Next, a tester must ensure the quality of the fix and ascertain that no new bugs have been introduced. If a new bug has been introduced, the tester enters it into the bug database, thus starting the cycle all over again. If the fix did not successfully resolve the original bug, the Development team leader reactivates the bug. Only when a bug has been successfully resolved is it finally closed. Instead of fixing the bug, the team can always decide to document the bug as part of the released product. Thus, the team chooses to postpone fixing the bug until after the product release.

Classification

Bug classification provides a way of identifying priorities and risk. Classifying bugs encompasses two important issues: severity, which addresses the impact of the bug on the overall application if it is not fixed, and priority, which measures the bug's importance to the stability of the application. It is not enough to report bugs; they must be classified to become actionable.

Typical severity level classifications are:

- **Severity 1: System crash** This class of bug causes the system to crash, hang, or otherwise stop working, with the risk of total data loss.
- **Severity 2: Major problem** This class of bug represents a serious defect in the software function, but does not necessarily risk total system failure or data loss.
- **Severity 3: Minor problem** This class of bug represents a defect in the function of the software, but not one with much risk of lost data or work.
- **Severity 4: Trivial** This class of bug represents what is primarily a minor cosmetic problem, which most users are unlikely to notice.

Typical priority level classifications are:

- **Priority 1: Highest priority** A show-stopping bug. The application cannot ship, and the team may not be able to achieve the next interim milestone.
- **Priority 2: High priority** A major bug. The application cannot ship, but the team may be able to achieve the next interim milestone.
- **Priority 3: Medium priority** The application can ship, and the team can achieve interim milestones. These bugs are low enough in priority that they tend to be fixed only if there is enough time at the end of the project and fixing them does not create a significant risk.
- **Priority 4: Low priority** Low priority bugs typically are enhancement requests and bugs that are not worth fixing.

Resolution

Resolving a bug is not the final step in bug tracking. It's an interim step towards closure. Closure occurs only after a tester determines that fixing the bug did not create another problem and that the bug is unlikely to surface again.

Bugs are typically resolved as:

- **Fixed** The developer has fixed the bug, tested the fix, checked in the code, assigned the fix to a product release number, and assigned the bug back to the tester who reported it.

- **Duplicated** The bug is a duplicate of another one that is already in the bug database. The duplicate bug is resolved, closed, and linked to the original bug.

- **Postponed** The bug will not be fixed in the current release, but might be fixed in a subsequent one. This designation is used when the team sees value in fixing the bug but does not have the time or resources to correct it.

- **By design** The behavior reported is intentional and is called out in the Functional Specification.

- **Can't reproduce** The developer can't verify the existence of the bug with any level of consistency.

- **Won't fix** The bug will not be fixed in the current release because the team does not think it's worth the effort, or the management or customer has deemed it unimportant.

Summary

Developing complex applications is difficult. This difficulty should not be increased by having an inadequate production channel. We discussed the stability and manageability benefits that result when a production channel is implemented that provides an orderly handoff from development systems, to test systems, to certification systems, to production systems. We also discussed several considerations for testing enterprise applications.

Before an application is scaled out, the current performance should be analyzed. We discussed how to define performance requirements, define performance metrics and goals, and conduct performance tests. We recommended establishing an initial performance baseline against which to measure the results of performance enhancements. We also discussed several techniques for scaling out a typical Web-based application in a production environment.

Finally, we discussed the process of bug management, and reviewed how to track, classify, and resolve bug issues throughout a project.

Review

1. What are the stages of the production channel?
2. What are some advantages of the production channel?
3. What are key areas to consider when defining performance requirements?
4. What is a performance baseline?
5. What are the two categories of testing?
6. What are the stages of bug management?

Testing RMS

"Oh, man!"

Dan Shelly could not believe his eyes. Another network error message had popped up on his screen. "That's the third one this morning! What is going on down there?"

He opened My Computer to check his mapped drives, trying to track which server was down. "Oh, great! That new one we put in for the AutoCAD folks. Boy, am I going to hear about this!" He thought for a moment, then stood up and grabbed his planner and notepad. "Might as well head down to the server area and see what's going on. Certainly not going to get anything else done here."

When he got to the large, glassed-in room that held the bulk of Ferguson and Bardell's server farm, Tim O'Brien, the Network Manager, was already seated in front of the newest server, a quad-processor behemoth with an outboard RAID 5 array and massive amounts of memory. Tim was working feverishly at a command prompt, while off to one side, Bill Pardi was offering unsolicited advice. As Dan entered the room, Tim sat back with a defeated look. "No go, Bill," he said. "Whatever Sam put on here has munged the registry big-time. I'll probably have to go to the backups."

"Hi guys," said Dan, affecting a cheery tone. "What's going on? Are we having fun yet?"

Bill was defensive. "We're having some problems with the new CAD server, and Tim and I are trying to see what can be done about them." Dan didn't let on that he knew what was going on. "Really?" he said. "I didn't know Tim called on you for network advice, Bill. Do you know what's causing the problem?"

Before Bill could say anything else, Tim looked up from the console. "Aw, Bill, quit your acting. Dan won't kill us. He'll only *want* to kill us." He turned to Dan. "The truth is that the developers needed to test some of the components they were building, and they wanted to run another load-simulation script on them. Because we've talked about getting another server like this one for the RMS project, they asked if they could install the components on here. I didn't want to do it, but they said that the components worked fine on their own machines and that no one would notice if they put them on the CAD box. So I said 'Yes.' The installation went okay, but when they started their tests, the box went down. We got it up again twice, but it looks like the third time is the charm. I'll try restoring the registry from last night, but if that doesn't work, I'll probably have to rebuild it using yesterday's backups."

Dan kept his voice level. "So let me get this straight." He turned to Bill. "Your developers needed to test some components, so you told them to put them on a *production* server?" He turned back to Tim. "And you *let* them?" Tim nodded glumly. Bill started to say something, but Dan held up a hand. "I don't want to hear it, Bill. We'll talk about this another time, another place. For now, you and I are going to leave so Tim can get this box back up as fast as possible. I'm tired of getting error messages while I'm working."

Tim and Bill looked puzzled and anxious. "Why are you getting error messages?" asked Tim. "You don't use this server."

"Didn't either one of you wonder why I was down here so soon after the server went down?" Dan asked. "Did you think it was just coincidence? I don't advertise the fact, but I map drives to every one of our servers every week. It's how I test performance and check whether our security policies are being followed. Today happened to be the day I mapped to this server."

Just then the three of them noticed Jim Stewart leaning against the door with his arms folded and a calm but stern look on his face.

"Jim! Not often we see you in this neck of the woods," said Dan. "Come and join us." He moved slightly to one side, blocking Jim's view of the console. "So, what are you doing down here?"

"Calculating," said Jim dryly. "Uh-oh," thought Dan, "here's trouble." Tim asked innocently, "Calculating what?"

"Calculating just how much this downed server is costing me," said Jim, his voice dropping in both pitch and temperature. "I can actually calculate it two or three different ways. Want to know how?"

"Not particularly," thought Dan, but he knew they were in far enough that the only way out was to keep going to the other side, so he said, "Sure, Jim, tell us how it looks to you."

As if he were teaching a college class, Jim said, "There's the wasted salary method. That's the easiest, because I know the hourly salary figure for every department, so I just multiply that for the affected departments by the hours the server is down. Then, there's the lost revenues method." He began to pace up and down. "I hate it when he paces," thought Dan, but he said nothing.

"Lost revenues are somewhat harder to calculate, because they vary month by month. But I can take the total profit for the year for a department, divide it by the number of hours to get an hourly rate, and use that.

"Finally, there is the opportunity cost method. What work did we lose by not getting this work done so that our resources were available to sell to someone else? This cost is pretty much speculative but can often yield rather spectacular results."

By this time, the knot in Dan's stomach had grown to about the size of a cantaloupe, and both Bill and Tim looked pretty sick. Not wanting to ask, but knowing he had to, Dan said, "And what numbers do you come up with for the CAD server, Jim?"

Jim stopped pacing and looked first at Dan, then at Bill and Tim. His voice rose. "Best as I can figure it, lost salaries work out to about $1,300 an hour. Lost revenues look like somewhere between $4,000 and $5,000 an hour. And opportunity costs? Let's just say, higher than that. Bottom line is, if you keep this server down the rest of the day, you're going to cost Ferguson and Bardell at least $25,000. So what are you doing about it?"

Dan affected a calmness he did not feel. "Jim, we've got one of the best in the business trying to fix it. I was going to talk with Bill later about what caused this, but I think now would be the best time, and I want you to be in on it. So why don't we all adjourn to the small conference room down the hall, and leave Tim to stop the dollars from going down the drain."

What's Needed and Why

When they got to the conference room, Jim wanted answers. "Now tell me what happened. Why is that server down?"

Dan explained the situation in a few sentences. Jim turned on Bill. "Your people already have the most expensive machines in the company! Isn't that enough?"

"No, it's not!" Bill retorted. He had been getting more and more upset throughout Jim's tirade and was determined to have his say.

"It's not like it used to be, Jim. Once upon a time, we wrote stand-alone applications that we would compile and test at our own machines. We needed the big boxes to speed up the compiling time, so we wouldn't waste a morning watching a computer churn through Clipper code, for instance. But once the compile was done, we could test the app locally using database files on our own computers. If it worked there, we simply put it on the network and told everyone how to get to it and run it. For the really incompetent ones, we might write a batch file and put the app in their login scripts.

"But we don't write that way anymore. We break our applications into components, and some bits go on the user's computer and some go on a server. We use back-end databases that servers have to run, and we tie those servers to other servers running Web hosting applications, and security packages, and electronic commerce, and data warehouses, and who knows what else."

Bill went to the whiteboard, grabbed a marker, and drew some boxes on the board. Then he connected them with lines and turned to Dan. "And now, we've added another piece to the puzzle, or rather a *bunch* of new pieces. We're writing N-tier, which means we've got a user layer, and a business services layer, and a data access layer. We need MTS, and SQL Server, and IIS, and each of them should really be running on its own server. But in the development area, we don't have these apps set up on their own boxes, so what can we do? Either we don't test until we roll the app out, or we test on the production systems because they are the only systems running the services we need."

When Bill paused for a moment, Dan stepped in. "Bill, you come from a mainframe environment, so you know the value of the four-step development environment. Why haven't you implemented it at Ferguson and Bardell?"

"One simple reason—*dinero*," said Bill, rubbing his thumb and fingers together and looking at Jim. "Every year we submit a budget request for a stand-alone testing lab, but the executive committee always cuts it from the final budget." Bill shrugged. "The old IT Director reported to the CFO and had to rely on the CFO to argue his case to the executive committee, so there was never anyone on that committee who understood the need."

"Point made, and point taken," said Jim, nodding. "You are absolutely right. I never understood the need until now. Of course," he said, looking at both Bill and Dan, "Until now, I never was invited to IT meetings, either."

"Point made, and point taken," said Bill. He turned to Dan. "So where do we go from here? I don't want to be responsible for any more lost revenue, and I suspect you don't either."

"First of all," Dan said, "I want you to send out a memo—and I want it sent *today*—that no one in development is to touch a production machine for testing purposes, no matter how urgent the test is or how trivial it seems. I'll follow up with a memo to the entire company, explaining why some machines are designated as production machines and listing all the machines we are giving that designation. I'll also have Tim double-check our security settings and procedures on those machines to make sure that well-meaning people can't take a server down accidentally."

After a moment's thought, he continued. "When we've shut the production barn doors, we need to figure out what we need for a test barn. We want to balance need with cost, though, so I'm not sure just what direction to go."

"Dan, what's the four-step development environment you mentioned a few minutes ago?" Jim asked.

"Basically, it consists of four different levels of isolation and criticality," said Dan. He erased Bill's drawing from the whiteboard and drew four new boxes, which he labeled *Dev*, *Test*, *Cert*, and *Prod*. "The developer builds a new app, or a part of one, or a new version of an old one, on his or her own computer. That's the Dev box, for *development*. When the developer thinks the app is ready, he installs in on a test computer that mimics the normal operating environment of the company. That's the Test box. In some companies, a testing group within the development department takes over at this point and walks the application through the testing process.

"If the app runs OK in the simple test environment, it is moved to another computer where it is thoroughly tested, including testing for load issues, response times, and interaction with other production-level applications. That's the Cert box, for *certification*. And when it passes all the tests thrown at it in the certification stage, it is put on a production machine. That's the Prod box." Dan put down his marker. "I've simplified the process a great deal. Ideally, it should include security settings at each level so that the people from the level before and after can't bypass the process, as well as a clearly defined documentation and change control process. The bottom line, though, is two-fold: Testing is never done on a production machine, and nothing is ever installed that hasn't been tested beyond the developer's machine."

"The problem is," added Bill, "that to do testing the way it should be done, you need a testing environment that mimics your production environment at each level. Whatever services you are running in Production should be present in Certification, and, if you're testing N-tier applications, you'll need them all in Testing as well. It can be expensive to set it all up, and you need one or more people to run and maintain it."

Jim looked at the board and rubbed his chin. "Bill, I used to think IT was always looking for new toys to spend the company's money on. I still think some IT people are like that. But since I've been working with the RMS project, I've come to realize that you and Dan just want to build the most professional IT organization you can. And when you can get his mind off the doughnuts, I think Tim wants the same thing, too."

He walked back and forth a few times. "It sounds to me as if a top-notch testing lab would take some space. Am I right?" Bill nodded. "Have you ever looked at that space on 34?" Jim asked Dan.

"You mean the old executive dining room? I thought the telemarketing group was taking that."

"They are," said Jim. "In fact, they're moving next week. But that is going to free up their space…"

"...which is right above us!" Bill exclaimed. "Wow, that would be perfect: near, but still isolated."

"Now, you can't have all of it," cautioned Jim. "I've promised some of it to the sales folks. But I think you could take half of it without a problem. Would that work?"

"We'll make it work, Jim," said Dan. "Not to seem ungrateful, but space is only part of the equation. What are we going to put in that space?"

"Can you get me a realistic proposal for a top-quality testing lab by the end of the week?" asked Jim. "I can't promise we can do it all, but I think the business case is certainly there." He grinned. "Especially if I recite some revenue numbers."

"How about if we make it a phased proposal," suggested Dan. "The first phase what we need to test RMS, the second phase later this year, and the final phase next spring? That way we spread out the pain some, with the bulk of it coming after everyone has seen the success of RMS."

Jim looked at Dan and smiled. "You know, you've got a streak of politician in you. That's an excellent suggestion. Write it that way, and you and I will present it to the Old Man together. He can be crusty, but he also understands that you have to spend money now to make—or save—money later. You'll get your lab."

CHAPTER 1 1

Application Security

About This Chapter

With the advent of distributed applications, it's becoming important to implement effective security to counteract the increased exposure and complexity of the software. Greater opportunities to manipulate data on local computers or across the network mean that application developers need to have a basic awareness of protocols and applications that use security today to help them design and create applications for tomorrow.

We begin this chapter by looking at different security-related protocols. We then look at the basic security concepts of authentication, which involves identifying users precisely and reliably when they log onto the system and when they access any resource within it; and encryption, which stores and passes information from one place to another so that it can't be read by anyone who intercepts it. We also discuss access control, which determines what users are allowed to accomplish, and auditing, which records what goes on inside the operating system as users request and work with the resources it makes available to them. Finally, we take a look at log files, event logs, and distributed environments.

The principles and guidelines we provide in this chapter are based on our own experience with the creation of application architectures and the implementation of modern applications, together with the following sources:

- Mary Kirtland's *Designing Component-Based Applications*
- The Microsoft Mastering Series Group's *Mastering Enterprise Development Using Microsoft Visual Basic 6* courseware
- Microsoft Visual InterDev online Help
- Microsoft Windows NT Workstation 4.0 Resource Kit
- Microsoft Internet Information Server 4.0 online Help
- Microsoft Technet's article #Q102716, "User Authentication with Windows NT"

- The Microsoft PBS Web team's white paper *Secure Networking Using Windows 2000 Distributed Security Services*
- Mark Bieter's white paper *Internet Information Server Security Overview*
- http://www.microsoft.com/ntserver/security/exec/feature/WebSecurity.asp
- http://home.netscape.com/eng/ssl3/draft302.txt

Upon completion, you will be able to:

- Understand how to implement application security requirements.
- Identify security authentication methods.
- Understand basic authentication capabilities of Web services.
- Identify security access methods.
- Identify different methods of encrypting information.
- Understand the benefits of application auditing.
- Identify methods for application auditing.

Authentication Security

The best security system is only as safe as its authentication scheme. Although many secure applications exist, users can jeopardize efforts to secure applications by using generic passwords such as 1234, not using any passwords at all, or writing passwords and leaving them in places where they can easily be discovered. Remedies such as password dictionary check or minimum password lengths are available to safeguard potentially unsecured applications; however, not all application security problems can be solved programmatically. Assuming that steps will be taken to exclude reckless password behavior on the part of users, in this section we take a look at the security process of *authentication,* which involves identifying and validating users, and potentially revalidating users as an ongoing process.

Windows NT Authentication

Windows NT users are authenticated by the MSV1_0 Authentication Package that corresponds to MSV1_0.DLL in Windows NT's <systemroot>\SYSTEM32 directory. Conceptually, MSV1_0 is split into two halves. The top half is responsible for receiving the logon request and determining whether the request is to the local or remote Windows NT computer. If the request is local, MSV1_0 passes the logon information to the bottom half of MSV1_0. The bottom half of MSV1_0 in turn authenticates the user by referencing the local security database. However, if the logon request is to a remote Windows NT computer, the top half of MSV1_0 passes the logon information to the local computer's

Netlogon service. The Netlogon service in turn passes the logon information to the remote Windows NT computer's bottom half of MSV1_0. When the Netlogon services of two computers communicate, challenge/response occurs. Challenge/response doesn't occur with local logons. The request is answered and returned to the top half of the local Windows NT computer's MSV1_0 through the respective Netlogon services.

Note We focus mainly on network authentication as it relates to Windows NT LAN Manager (NTLM) security over the network via challenge/response. However, MSV1_0 also supports interactive logons, service logons, and network logons. All forms of logon through the MSV1_0 Authentication Package pass the name of the domain containing the user account, the name of the user account, and some function of the user password. These various types of logon differ in the way the password is represented. For interactive logons and service logons, the client logging on is physically on the computer running the top half of the MSV1_0 Authentication Package. In this case, the clear (unencrypted) text password is sent into the top half of the MSV1_0 Authentication Package. The top half of the MSV Authentication Package converts the clear text password to both a LAN Manager password and a Windows NT password before sending it on to either the Netlogon service or the lower half. The lower half queries the passwords from the Security Account Manager (SAM) and compares the passwords to ensure they are identical.

The following steps are an example of how a user might log on locally or remotely to a Windows NT system:

1. Press CTRL+ALT+DEL to display the Windows NT Security logon dialog box. Pressing this key combination before logging on protects against Trojan Horse-type programs that impersonate the operating system and manipulate users into disclosing their username and password.

2. Provide a username and password to enable the logon process to call the Local Security Authority (LSA).

3. The Local Security Authority runs the MSV1_0 Authentication Package.

4. The authentication package checks the user accounts database to see whether the account is local. If it is, the username and password are verified against those held in the user accounts database. If it is not, the requested logon is forwarded to the Windows NT Netlogon service. The Netlogon service on the local computer communicates with the Netlogon service of the remote Windows NT system (in this example, a domain controller). Here, the upper half of MSV1_0 on the local computer communicates with the lower half of MSV1_0 on the remote computer, initiating a challenge/response.

5. When the account is validated either locally or remotely, the SAM (which owns the user accounts database) returns the user's security ID (SID) and the security IDs of any global groups to which the user belongs.

6. The authentication package creates a logon session and then passes the logon session and the security IDs associated with the user to the Local Security Authority.

7. If the logon is rejected, the logon session is deleted, and an error is returned to the logon process.

8. If the logon is accepted, an access token is created, containing the user's security ID and the security IDs of the Everyone group and any other groups to which the user belongs. It also contains user rights assigned to the collective security IDs. This access token is returned to the logon process with a Success status.

9. The logon session calls the Win32 subsystem to create a process and attach the access token to the process, thus creating a *subject* for the user account.

10. For an interactive Windows NT session, the Win32 subsystem starts a shell process (that is, starts the desktop) for the user.

After the validation process, the user's shell process is given an access token. For Windows NT 4.0, the token is associated with Explorer.exe. The information in this access token is a reflection of anything the user does or by any process that runs on the user's behalf.

Kerberos Authentication

Kerberos authentication was developed within the think tanks of MIT. It is a ticket-, session-, and trust-based authentication scheme. The Kerberos Authentication included in Windows 2000 is based on Kerberos v5. When compared with the Windows NT domain strategy, the Kerberos authentication protocol provides the following benefits:

- **Faster server authentication performance during initial connection establishment** The application server doesn't have to connect to the domain controller to authenticate the client, so applications servers can scale better when handling a large number of client requests.

- **Delegation of authentication for multi-tier client/server applications and architectures** When a client connects to a server, the server impersonates the client on that system. But if the server needs to make a network connection to another network server to complete the client transaction, the Kerberos protocol allows delegation of authentication for the first server to connect on behalf of the client to another server. The delegation also allows the second server to impersonate the client.

Note Applications that use process access permissions can take advantage of additional security providers on Microsoft Windows 2000 and can use *delegate-level impersonation* and *cloaking* to affect the security credentials used during method calls. Delegate-level impersonation is established by the client process and allows a server to impersonate the client and to pass the client's credentials to remote computers. Previously, servers could impersonate the client only to access local resources. Cloaking is used to hide an intermediate server's identity from a destination server. For example, if Client A calls Server B, which then calls Server C on Client A's behalf, and Server B has cloaking enabled, Client A's identity will be used for calls to Server C.

- **Transitive trust relationships for inter-domain authentication** Users can authenticate to domains anywhere in the domain tree because each domain's authentication services trust the tickets issued by other authentication services in the tree. Transitive trust simplifies domain management for large networks with multiple domains.

- **Authentication between heterogeneous systems (even Internet-based systems)** Users can validate once and access many different systems on different operating system platforms. For example, Windows 2000 security can be utilized between Windows 2000 and UNIX or mainframe environments, provided the correct Microsoft COM libraries are being utilized on the UNIX or mainframe systems. Users don't have to be running Windows 2000 to be authenticated by a Windows 2000/Kerberos domain.

Note The transition from the NTLM authentication used in Windows NT 4.0 to Kerberos domain authentication can be very smooth. Windows 2000 services support client or server connection using either security protocol. The transition from enterprise-based services using Kerberos authentication to Internet-based services using public-key authentication (discussed later in this chapter) is mostly transparent to the user.

Web-Based Authentication

Almost every Web browser on the market supports a basic form of authentication that involves sending a username and password in clear text over the Internet or an intranet. Unfortunately, this basic authentication allows this information to be stolen by others. Because organizations need to provide secure access to information on their networks and servers, user authentication is an important aspect of a Web server. In addition to the security provided by Windows NT, Microsoft Internet Information Server (IIS) 4.0 includes additional security features that Windows NT uses to correctly identify users, determine their level of access, and create a secure Internet connection.

In this section, we first describe the IIS 4.0 authentication technology. Then we discuss Microsoft's Secure Channel technology, which is used to protect networked data from prying eyes when communicating in Internet or intranet environments after users have been authenticated.

Windows NT Challenge/Response Support

IIS 4.0 provides support for the Windows NT challenge/response authentication, which uses a cryptographic technique to authenticate the password. The actual password is never sent across the network, so it cannot be captured by an unauthenticated source. Challenge/response is supported by Microsoft Internet Explorer 2.0 and later versions.

When Windows NT challenge/response authentication is enabled, the user's Internet Explorer browser proves its knowledge of the password through a cryptographic exchange with the Web server. If the authentication exchange succeeds in identifying the user, the user is not prompted for account information. However, if the authentication exchange initially fails to identify the user, Internet Explorer prompts the user for a Windows NT account username and password, which it processes using the same Windows NT challenge/response method. Internet Explorer continues to prompt the user until the user enters a valid username and password or closes the prompt dialog box.

Note Windows NT challenge/response authentication takes precedence over basic authentication. If the user's Web browser supports both authentication methods, it chooses Windows NT challenge/response authentication.

Cookies

Web applications can use simple cookie mechanisms to track and identify users. Cookies are small files sent from the server to the user's computer, where they are stored locally. These identification cookies typically contain a globally unique identifier (GUID) that can be requested and queried by a Web server. Although cookies provide a simple means of identifying users, they should not be used when the information being accessed is considered confidential or private. A cookie can be intercepted in transit, or even copied from a user's computer, and anyone can then use it to represent himself or herself as the cookie's user. Although the concept of stealing cookies is similar to that of stealing logon usernames and passwords, cookies are technically much easier to "borrow."

Digital Certificates

Digital certificates give users a secure method of logging onto a Web site without having to remember logon usernames and passwords. IIS supports the use of X.509 certificates for access control. Certificates verify identity in much the same way as driver's licenses or corporate identification cards do. They are issued by a trusted certificate authority, either a department within an organization or a public company such as VeriSign or Entrust. How rigorously IIS checks identities or credentials when issuing a certificate depends upon the level of security—or trust—required for the information or application being accessed.

Certificate-based client authentication requires a protocol that can handle certificates at both the client end and the server end, as well as the appropriate requests and replies.

Server Certificates

Unique digital identifications, called *server certificates*, form the basis of a Web server's Secure Sockets Layer (SSL) security features. Server certificates, obtained from a trusted, third-party organization, provide a way for users to authenticate the identity of a Web site. The server certificate contains detailed identification information, such as the name of the organization affiliated with the server content, the name of the organization that issued the certificate, and a unique identification file called a *public key*. This information helps to assure users about the authenticity of Web server content and the integrity of the secured HTTP connection. The public key, along with another privately held key, form the SSL *key pair*. A Web server utilizes the key pair to negotiate a secure TCP/IP connection with the user's Web browser. (Although the key pair serves a vital role in establishing a secure link, the key pair is not directly used for data encryption.)

Client Certificates

With SSL, a Web server can also authenticate users by checking the contents of their *client certificates*. These encrypted files are similar to conventional forms of identification such as driver's licenses or passports. A typical client certificate contains detailed identification information about a user and the organization that issued the certificate. Each user enters a password when signing his or her certificate, and this password is required every time the certificate is activated for use. As with a driver's license, mere possession of a certificate does not constitute proof of ownership. Only the owner of the certificate should know the password because it is the key to verifying access.

Certificate Mapping

This method maps the client certificate to the Windows NT server user account and requires a copy of the certificate. The Web server has a client certificate-mapping feature that authenticates users who log on with client certificates, without requiring the use of basic or Windows NT challenge/response authentication. A certificate mapping relates the contents of the user's client certificate to a corresponding Windows NT account, which is a file that defines the rights and access policies of the user. After a mapping is created and enabled for a particular user, each time that user logs on with his or her client certificate, the Web server automatically connects, or maps, that user to the appropriate Windows NT account.

This approach is ideal when the Web site issues its own certificates using a certificate server, such as Microsoft Certificate Server, which is included in the Windows NT 4.0 Option Pack.

Wildcard Mapping

When using wildcard mapping, the IIS server doesn't need to possess the client certificate, but instead authenticates the user based on information stored in the certificate, such as "SubjectName." IIS 4.0 also includes a Microsoft ActiveX component that automates the wildcard mapping using an Active Server Page (ASP). For example, a business could set up an ASP page that asks users whether they want to map their certificate to their Windows NT Server user account. If a user chooses to do so, the information in the certificate is mapped to the appropriate Windows NT Server user account.

IIS 4.0 can authenticate users who log on with a client certificate by creating mappings that relate the information contained in the certificate to a Windows NT user account. Using the Web server's certificate mapping feature, IIS 4.0 can either map a specific user's client certificate to an account (a one-to-one mapping), or map multiple certificates to an account. To map multiple certificates, wildcard-matching rules must be defined that create a mapping by verifying only whether a certificate contains certain items of information. For example, to map all users who log on with client certificates issued by a particular organization, a wildcard-matching rule could be defined that automatically maps any certificate issued by that organization to a single user account, rather than creating a separate mapping for each client certificate.

Programmatic Use of Certificates

Client authentication in IIS 4.0 goes beyond pure authentication and access control. Information in the certificate is exposed to both ASP and Internet Information Server Application Programming Interface (ISAPI) applications. As a result, developers try to create custom ASP and ISAPI applications that can serve personalized content, control access, or query databases based on the information fields in the client certificate. Developers can use client certificate authentication, along with SSL encryption, to implement a very tamper-resistant method for verifying user identity.

Microsoft Certificate Server

Internet Information Server 4.0 Option Pack contains certificate management features available through Microsoft Certificate Server, and standard cryptographic API functions available through Microsoft's CryptoAPI, which we discuss later in this chapter. Certificate Server has the following features:

- Accepts standard PKCS #10 certificate requests.
- Issues X-509 version 1 and version 3 certificates in PKCS#7 format.
- Issues SSL client and server certificates.

- Issues Secure Multipurpose Internet Mail Extensions (S/MIME) certificates.
- Issues Secure Electronic Transactions (SET)-compliant certificates.
- Supports open interfaces that enable writing of modules to support custom formats.

SQL Server Authentication

In this section, we discuss the various types of security available with Microsoft SQL Server, including standard security, integrated security, and mixed security.

Standard Security

Standard security uses SQL Server's own logon validation process for all connections. Connections validated by SQL Server are referred to as *non-trusted connections*. Standard security is useful in network environments with a variety of clients, some of which may not support *trusted connections,* which we discuss below. Also, standard security provides backward compatibility for older versions of SQL Server.

Integrated Security

Integrated security allows SQL Server to use Windows NT authentication mechanisms to validate SQL Server logons for all connections. Connections validated by Windows NT Server and accepted by SQL Server are referred to as *trusted connections*. Only trusted connections are allowed. Integrated security should be used in network environments where all clients support trusted connections. The clients of SQL Server in a three-tier application are MTS components.

Note With Windows NT 4.0, MTS components must be authenticated by a domain controller. Authentication of a component by a domain controller over the network adds extra traffic and therefore extra expense. With Windows 2000, Kerberos helps hold down traffic by carrying information that allows direct component authentication without taking a trip to the domain controller.

When the SQL Server logon security mode is set to integrated, an MTS component's login is validated as follows:

1. To access SQL Server, a component first obtains a valid Windows NT user account. MTS components use the Windows NT user account specified in the component's MTS package's **Identity** property. When the user account is in a domain, the username and password are validated by the domain controller's security accounts database when the MTS package executable launches via LAN Manager security. However, if the user account is located in a workgroup, the username and password are validated by the local security accounts database.

2. The component connects to SQL Server, and SQL Server looks in the syslogins table for a mapping to a SQL Server logon ID. This mapping is created as part of the configuration process based on whether a logon exists, a logon does not exist, or neither a logon nor a default logon exists. If the logon exists, the component is logged onto SQL Server with the privileges associated with that logon ID. If the logon does not exist, the component is logged onto SQL Server using the default SQL Server logon ID, which is usually a guest account. However, if the component's account has administrator privileges on Windows NT, the user will also have administrator privileges within SQL. Finally, if the logon does not exist and there is no default logon ID, the component is denied access to SQL Server.

3. Once the logon process is complete, access to individual SQL Server tables is managed through permissions granted within an SQL Server database.

Mixed Security

When mixed security is used, SQL Server validates logon requests using either integrated or standard security methods. Both trusted connections (as used by integrated security) and non-trusted connections (as used by standard security) are supported. Mixed security is useful in network environments that have a mixed client base. For those clients that support trusted connections, Windows NT validates logons. For clients that support only non-trusted connections, SQL Server validates logons.

When a server's login security mode is set to mixed, a component's logon is validated as follows:

- When a component attempts to log onto the server over a trusted connection, SQL Server examines the logon name. If this logon name matches the component's network username, or if the logon name is blank or contains spaces, SQL Server uses the Windows NT integrated logon rules (as for integrated security).

- If the requested logon name is any other value, the component must supply the correct SQL Server password, and SQL Server uses its own logon validation process (as for standard security). If the logon attempt is not over a trusted connection, the component must supply the correct logon ID and password to establish the connection, and SQL Server uses its own logon validation process (standard security).

Note Integrated or mixed security is recommended for enterprise solutions using Windows NT Server, MTS, and SQL Server. Integrated security makes management of logons easier because accounts can be administrated from one source in Windows NT. Also, developers can avoid coding logon IDs and passwords into their components or placing them in ODBC DSNs. Any logon changes under standard security forces components to be recompiled or ODBC DSNs to be tracked down and updated.

Using SQL Authentication with Objects

As we've said, SQL Server requires a logon ID and password. We'll now demonstrate how a component can implement such a security measure.

A component supplies its logon either through the **ConnectionString** property of the ADO Connection object, or as a Connection String parameter to the Open method of the **Connection** or **Recordset** objects. If a component supplies a logon ID and password, the component connects using standard security. If the component does not supply a logon ID and password, the component connects using integrated security, and within MTS, the component's package identity is used as the logon.

If the connection is through an OLE DB provider, the provider must be notified that integrated security is to be used. The logon ID or password should not be provided, but instead the **Trusted_Connection** attribute should be set as shown in the following code:

```
Dim conn as ADODB.Connection
Set conn = New ADODB.Connection
conn.Provider = "SQLOLEDB"
conn.ConnectionSTring= "Data Source=MYSERVER;' & _
 "Initial  Catalog=Pubs;Trusted_Connection=Yes"
conn.Open
```

Encryption

Beyond securing files and directories against unauthorized access, developers need to effectively protect sensitive information transmitted over a network from all forms of interception and tampering. This is particularly important with information transmitted over the Internet. Today, users visiting commercial Web sites are sometimes reluctant to supply sensitive information, such as a credit card or bank account number, for fear that computer vandals will intercept this information. To address this type of security concern, we'll take a look at several methods developers can use to encrypt sensitive information.

Security-Related Protocols

Security-related protocols contain built-in authentication and encryption mechanisms. All applications need to do to utilize these mechanisms is incorporate the protocol.

Developers may find it helpful to understand in which Open Systems Interconnection (OSI) layer the protocol is functioning to understand the scope of security the protocol provides. Where the protocol function determines the scope of data that it protects, ranging from a single application to a complete network. For example, protocols functioning at the application layer implement security on a per-application basis. Hypertext Transfer Protocol Secure (HTTPS) and NTLM are examples of protocols that operate in the OSI application layer. Some protocols create tunnels, or virtual connections, that allow network communication to occur between network devices. Point-to-Point Tunneling Protocol (PPTP) and Layer 2 Tunneling Protocol (L2TP) are examples of protocols used to create virtual connections for virtual private networks. PPTP and L2TP operate at the OSI datalink and network layers.

Another important issue to keep in mind is that security-related protocols are effective only because of the way they encrypt authentication information and data. Table 11.1 shows the security-related protocols we'll be discussing throughout this chapter, including their relation to the OSI layers and the methods they use to encrypt information.

Table 11.1   Security-related protocols

Protocol	OSI Layer	Authentication	Encryption	Transport
L2TP	Datalink	CHAP, PAP, MS-CHAP	RC4, DES	IP, IPX, NetBEUI
PPTP	Datalink	CHAP, PAP, MS-CHAP	RC4	IP, IPX, NetBEUI
HTTP/SSL	Application	X.509	RC2, RC4, DES	IP
IPSEC	Network	HMAC-MD5, HMAC-SHA, DH	DES	IP
SMB/NTLM	Application	Challenge/response	DES, MD4	IP, IPX, NetBEUI

Secure Sockets Layer (SSL)

IIS 4.0 provides privacy, integrity, and authentication in point-to-point communications through Microsoft's Secure Channel technology. In particular, the SSL 3.0 protocol, implemented as a Web server security feature, provides a secure and virtually impervious way of establishing an encrypted communication link with users. SSL guarantees the authenticity of Web content, while reliably verifying the identity of users accessing restricted Web sites.

Note IIS 4.0 also supports the Private Communication Technology (PCT) 1.0 protocol. Similar to SSL, PCT 1.0 includes hardy and efficient encryption features for securing communications.

With SSL, the server and the user's Web browser engage in a negotiating exchange that involves the certificate and the key pair to determine the level of encryption required for securing communications. The server and the browser set up an encrypted session that only they can understand. This exchange requires that both the server and the browser be equipped with compatible encryption and decryption capabilities. The end result of the exchange involves the creation (usually by the browser) of an encryption key, or *session key*. Both the server and the browser use the session key to encrypt and decrypt transmitted information. The session key's degree of encryption, or *strength*, is measured in *bits*. The greater the number of bits comprising the session key, the greater the level of encryption and security. The server's session key is typically 40-bits to 128-bits.

Keys are created in pairs consisting of a public key and a private key. The public key is given to anyone (and is often made available though a public agency, such as a certificate authority). The private key is kept and safeguarded by the key requestor. Both keys are required for any exchange of information. To configure SSL on the Web server, a key must be generated and configured to work with the Web server. The IIS Key Manager is used to generate the key pair request and to activate the generated key. A secure server key can be created from the key request file using Microsoft Certificate Server or by using the key request file to obtain a key from a third-party provider such as VeriSign or Entrust.

Theoretically SSL can transparently secure any TCP/IP-based protocol running on any port if either the browser client or Web server know the other is using SSL. However, in practice, separate port numbers have been reserved for each protocol commonly secured by SSL so that packet-filtering firewalls can allow secured traffic through.

Internet Explorer encrypts data—such as HTML forms containing private information—by using the server's public key. The encrypted data is sent to the server, which decrypts the data using its private key. (The data can be decrypted only with this private key.)

Encrypting only communication that contains private data, such as credit card numbers, addresses, or company records, is the most effective use of SSL. Because SSL uses a computer's processor to encrypt data, it takes much longer to retrieve and send data from SSL-enabled directories. In an SSL-enabled directory, place only those pages that have or will receive sensitive information. Also, keep the content of pages in an SSL-enabled directory free from unnecessary elements because every item on the page will be encrypted, including simple graphics. Every element on the page increases the time it takes to transmit the data.

SSL, IIS 4.0, and Microsoft Proxy Server

SSL was designed to eliminate "man-in-the-middle" attacks, where an entity might try to step between the client and the server. As a result, SSL does not work directly with proxy servers, and to incorporate the SSL protocol with proxy servers, such as Microsoft Proxy Server, developers must allow direct access through an unrestricted proxy server port. Then, the client can communicate directly with the server using SSL. Of course, SSL must be set up properly on the hosting server, and allowing direct access does create additional security concerns. For example, if Microsoft Proxy Server 2.0 is installed on the IIS 4.0 computer, Web Publishing must be enabled. In addition, if Packet Filtering is being used, a packet filter for TCP Port 443 must be added. Enabling Web Publishing allows Web clients to directly communicate with the Web server. Additionally, creating a filter for port 443 on the proxy server allows SSL traffic to be sent directly to the Web server so that it can communicate directly and securely with the client.

Server Gated Cryptography

Server Gated Cryptography (SGC) is an extension to the SSL security protocol that allows financial institutions to provide secure Web services for their customers, no matter where they might be, without the need to change Web browser or server software. SGC allows international banks to build computer infrastructures based on the Microsoft BackOffice family that interoperate with a range of popular client software, including Internet Explorer versions 3.02, 4.0, and 5.0, Microsoft Money 98, and Netscape Navigator 4.0. SGC is included in all of Microsoft's current Web client and server software, and previous versions of these products can be upgraded by downloading a file from the Microsoft SGC Web page at www.microsoft.com/security/tech/sgc/. Microsoft's SGC product is fully compatible with Netscape's SGC product.

For online banking to be secure, both the bank and the customer must be able to verify that each is who they say they are. For example, a bank wants to protect John Smith's banking information from anyone except for John Smith. Likewise, John Smith wants proof that he is genuinely communicating with his bank, and not with a software criminal or other individual wishing to violate his account.

SGC leaves it to the bank to determine how to verify users' identities, but most choose to require that the customer provide a user ID and a password at the start of each online banking session. SGC requires that the bank prove its identity to the customer's software using a digital certificate. Like any other digital certificate, the bank's certificate is a collection of data that uniquely identifies its owner. The certificate is generated by a trusted third-party organization that is in the business of issuing certificates. By using public key cryptography, this certificate authority ensures that, although anyone can read the certificates that it issues, only it can create them after carefully checking the recipient's identity. Certificates are cryptographically protected against counterfeiting, forgery, or modification.

Until now, strong encryption products have been unavailable to the worldwide banking industry. U.S. export laws regarding cryptographic software have prevented banks and other financial institutions from providing security to their World Wide Web services using the high-security products available in North

America. Unlike SSL, which must be produced in both an exportable version that uses a 40-bit cryptographic key and a North American version that uses a 128-bit key, a single version of SGC that uses a 128-bit key worldwide can be produced. This development is a result of a U.S. Department of Commerce decision to license the export of strong cryptographic products in cases where it is possible to restrict them to financial institutions.

To obtain an SGC digital certificate, a bank must prove that it is a bona fide financial institution. This is usually done by providing a Dun & Bradstreet DUNS number or an American Banking Association number, but also can be done by submitting documents from a state, provincial, or national government verifying that the institution has been chartered as a bank. This level of proof is necessary to ensure compliance with the U.S. Department of Commerce provision that only financial institutions be granted license to export SGC. A full listing of the certificate authorities that provide digital certificates for use with SGC is available on the Microsoft SGC Web page.

Once issued, the certificate is installed in exactly the same way as an SSL certificate in the bank's Web server software. Each time an SGC customer starts a session with the bank's server, the bank's server automatically sends its certificate to the customer. The exchange happens behind the scenes, and neither party has to take any action. When the bank provides its digital certificate to the customer's software, the software checks that the certificate is valid and that it vouches for the bank's identity. Once this has been done, the banking session can begin.

SGC enables Web client and server software to dynamically determine the encryption level of an SSL session. It is implemented as an extension to the SSL protocol and its successor, the Transport Layer Security (TLS) protocol. To use SGC, both the client and server must be running software that implements SGC. When a customer connects to an SGC-secured Web site, the browser software and the Web server software initiate a normal SSL connection. During the "handshake" portion of the session, the client checks the server's digital certificate and looks for special data in the certificate that indicates the server can participate in an SGC session. If the special data is not in the certificate, the client negotiates a normal SSL session using a 40-bit key. However, if the special data is in the certificate, the client resets the handshake and negotiates a session using one of the following crypto algorithms and a corresponding key:

- 128-bit RC4
- 128-bit RC2
- 56-bit DES
- 3Key 3DES (pending final approval by the U.S. Department of Commerce)

CryptoAPI

CryptoAPI, which ships as part of Windows NT 4.0 and Internet Explorer 3.0 and later, was designed to take the task of cryptography off the shoulders of developers. It includes the Cryptographic Service Provider (CSP) interface, which makes accessing cryptography easier by allowing developers to change the strength and type of their cryptography without modifying application code.

CryptoAPI frees applications from having to do their own encryption. It provides extensible, exportable, system-level access to common cryptographic functions such as encryption, hashing, and digital signatures. Any application written with CryptoAPI can use certificates that support the X.509 standard. This standard enables any standards-compliant application or system to access the Web server from any platform, including the UNIX and Macintosh platforms.

Access Security

Access security is an important part of the application's architecture. In simple terms, access security is about who gets to use the application and how they get to use it. With a secure application, both the user and the application are confident they are exchanging information within authentic circumstances. Applications must ensure the privacy of sensitive user information, and also protect the architectural components and services that run the application from unauthorized tampering or eavesdropping by the user.

For an application to be secure, each application service must be available only to qualified users. At the same time, every component, service, and supporting file must be protected from unauthorized viewing, tampering, or modification. The best way to protect the application's architectural elements and processes is with the built-in security services provides by the Windows NT and Windows 2000 operating systems. Windows NT and Windows 2000 prevent unauthorized access and tampering by providing user access control, resource and service protection, and audit ability.

Windows NT Access Security

Anything that can be done in Windows NT involves some type of security check. If someone attempts to access a file, a security check occurs. If someone tries to log onto a workstation, a security check occurs. These security checks also include access by other Windows NT computers. For example, if another computer attempts to access a data file or other resource, a security check occurs.

Note When Windows NT is used as a desktop operating system, these security checks are generally invisible because in most situations users log onto their own computers with administrator privileges and never encounter any permission issues.

The Windows operating system provides a number of primary security functions to control access to enterprise applications, including those listed in Table 11.2.

Table 11.2   Primary Windows NT security functions

Function	Description	Discussed in this section
User and group management	Controls network logon and logoff rights, both local and remote, for users, groups and administrators.	User Access Control
Security policy definitions	Defines user and group rights (such as password aging, default access permissions, and audit policies).	User Access Control
File and object access	Protects files and directories, including removable media. This includes protecting the files that make up the operating systems.	File Protection
Registry access	Protects registry settings from remote tampering.	Windows NT Registry Security

With these Windows NT security functions, applications can control access to all Windows NT object types, including all of the application's objects, services, and resources. The list of securable object types is extensive, and includes:

- Local or remote NTFS files and directories.
- Processes and threads.
- Named and anonymous pipes.
- Console screen buffers.
- File-mapping objects.
- Access tokens.
- Mail slots.
- Registry keys.
- Local or remote printers.
- Windows NT network shares.
- Windows NT services.
- Inter-process synchronization objects.

The application may not be concerned with access permissions for each of these objects. However, for a difficult security implementation, it's useful to know that the application can not only define these permissions as administrator, but can also set and check object access permissions programmatically.

Knowing how Windows NT security works is important when protecting enterprise applications. Because IIS allows Web browsers to access files on a Windows NT system, it is especially important to understand the unique security requirements of a Web application. (We discuss the specifics of Web-based application security in a later section.)

User Access Control

Applications can use four Windows NT functions to control user access: user accounts, user groups, user rights policies and permissions, and program access control.

User Accounts

An application can control user access by using an authentication scheme, such as Windows NT challenge/response. If users can't log on to the network, they can't run the application.

Specifically when using Windows NT authentication, user accounts are the keys to Windows NT security. Every user who has access to a Windows NT system has a user account consisting of a name, password, and other logon parameters. With the Windows NT User Manager, administrators can establish, delete, or disable user accounts.

Note It is preferable to disable Windows NT user accounts instead of deleting them. A disabled account cannot be used to gain access to the network. If a Windows NT account is deleted, all reference to it is removed from the system, which can seriously impede administrators who are trying to determine what a user could do and access, and can invalidate specific audit references.

Administrators (and other people with the correct permissions, such as Account Operators) can create as many accounts as needed and then restrict user access to applications and Windows NT resources on a per-account basis. This means that properly configured user accounts play a significant role in allowing users access to applications and operating system resources.

Generally, specific applications do not request the Windows NT security administrator to add or change network logon accounts. But as a first line of protection, Windows NT authentication is available if the application needs it.

Note Programmatic access to the Windows NT SAM database can be made through the Active Directory Security Interface (ADSI), the Active User Object (AUO), Lightweight Directory Access Protocol (LDAP), and the ActiveX Data Object (ADO).

User Groups

Another way to limit access to an application is by collecting users into groups. A user group is a set of users who have identical network rights.

Note Collections of users with the identical user rights and group memberships are often referred to as *roles*.

Grouping user accounts simplifies user-access administration. User groups also make it easier to grant multiple users access to a designated network resource, because all that must be done is to grant a specific access permission to the group (instead of to each individual user).

Defining user groups creates the application's security model, which specifies which groups have access to which application permissions. To develop such a security model, the application's use cases can be used to:

- Identify the system's participants (referred to as *actors* in UML).
- List the data and resource access operations that each participant needs (often captured in the use case diagrams, activity diagrams, and usage scenarios).
- Group users according to their participation to set access permissions.

For example, a set of user groups based on levels of permissions could be Public, Private, Confidential, Secret, and Top Secret.

User Rights Policy and Permissions

User rights policy controls the rights granted to user groups and individual accounts. User rights policy also specifies restrictions, such as password expiration and lockout duration. Permissions apply to specific securable resource objects, such as files, directories, and services.

Note For most security-conscious environments, password expiration should be set no higher than every 45 days, and the minimum password length should be eight characters.

User-access rights can control network resources and services, such as "logging onto a server", "running resources as services", or "backing up and restoring data." Setting control via user rights policy is accomplished by first assigning specific users to a group, then using Windows NT User Manager to grant the user or group permissions to the securable resource objects. These permissions help to specify who can use securable resource objects and under what conditions. With careful coordination of user and group access rights, enterprise applications can easily leverage Windows NT security to control user access.

Program Access Control

Applications can also control access by programmatically limiting access rights to certain users or groups. For example, selected component interfaces can be assigned to certain users, thereby preventing others from using the component's method. Security modules operating as "gatekeepers" for any component's method can be created as part of the application.

However, program access control can require a lot of administration. If the access control is "hard coded" into the objects, each time the access permissions need to be changed, the component must typically be rebuilt and redistributed. A better choice is to leverage the access security built into MTS. MTS significantly simplifies the administration of component access privileges, uses the access permissions already set up with user and group accounts, and abstracts the security from the actual components.

File Protection

Developers can protect files through the capabilities of two file systems offered by Microsoft operating systems: File Allocation Table (FAT) and the Windows NT File System (NTFS). If developers are concerned with truly controlling access to files, they should use only NTFS. FAT does not provide adequate security measures.

Applying NTFS File Permissions

An application might have many different kinds of non-database support files and folders, including .ini, .txt, .prf, or other special files that maintain program information. If the application has support files that need protection, specific and explicit permissions such as No Access, Read, Change, and Full Control can be applied.

To set access permissions for a file, the following conditions must be met:

- Use a secure file system (NTFS).
- Own the object.
- Have object change permission.
- Have full control of the object.

The most common approach to setting file access permissions is to use Windows NT Explorer. Windows NT Explorer can easily set file permissions on a file-by-file basis or for the entire folder (including all files contained within that folder).

Another tool for setting file permissions is the Cacls.exe utility. This command-line, batch mode utility displays or modifies access control lists. Cacls.exe has limited functionality: It can only grant or deny Read, Change, and Full Control permissions.

Note One additional benefit of Cacls.exe is its ability to append a new permission to the permissions that already exist for a file, directory, or subdirectories. For example, the Tester group could be added to the groups that have Full Control permission for a directory and its subdirectories. The subdirectories could also have different permissions already associated with their files.

For an enterprise application (such as a Web site) that is exposed to external user access, it's not unusual to first protect all of the files on the entire server where the application resides, and then apply specific Windows NT file permissions where access is needed.

Caution Use extreme caution when changing the permissions for the root directory as well as for the Windows NT system files. Careless administrators can create permission problems that prevent users from logging onto their computers.

Distributed Component Protection

If the application uses distributed COM (DCOM), the components that are deployed and registered also need to be secured. In the context of remote component deployment, security means configuring each component's access and launch permissions and protecting the component from tampering.

Security for creating remote objects is important because of the simplicity of DCOM. Whether a client uses a local ActiveX component or the same component running on a remote computer is determined by the client computer's Windows Registry entry for the component. The default configuration of DCOM allows only computer administrators to access and launch objects from a remote client. After the components are distributed, registered, and NTFS file permissions are applied, access and launch permissions can be configured.

Object permissions can be configured with the DCOMCNFG utility. With DCOMCNFG, DCOM-specific settings in the registry are defined that specify where the component runs and who can launch and access the object.

For more information on using DCOMCNFG to configure object access and launch permissions, search for *DCOMCNFG* in the MSDN Library.

Operating System Services Protection

Windows NT protects all of its services by allowing only its own kernel mode components to directly access operating system resources. User processes can't directly access these resources. When the application requests an operating system service, the Windows NT security system performs a validation check of the service permissions. If the service access permission matches the requesting user, the service is provided.

With Windows NT, explicit access control can be set for every operating system service. These operating system objects include processes, threads, shares, files, folders, and devices.

Windows NT Registry Security

The initialization and configuration information used by an enterprise application is typically stored in the registry. For example, the configuration information for an application's distributed components is kept in the registry. Because the default Windows NT workstation setup for the Registry Editor allows administrators to have remote access, external tampering could put the application's registry data at risk.

Take the following steps to protect the application's registry information:

- Protect the registry files.
- Restrict network access to the registry on each workstation that uses the application.

Note For Windows NT 4.x, the registry files are in the SystemRoot\System32\ Config directory. By default, the SystemRoot directory is \WINNT.

The default operating system installation on Windows NT workstations lets any administrator have remote access to the registry from another computer. If the winreg key does not appear in the registry, any user who can connect to the computer can also connect to the registry and damage the configuration information.

Note The default Windows NT Workstation installation does not define the winreg key and remote registry access is allowed by default. However, Windows NT Server does define this key and allows only the administrator to remotely access the registry.

To restrict network access to the registry, the following key should be created on each workstation that uses the application:

HKEY_LOCAL_MACHINE\SYSTEM\CurrentcontrolSet\Control\Secure PipeServers\winreg

Then the registry permissions of the winreg key should be edited to grant or revoke specific access privileges.

Caution It is important to check with the network administrator before coding these registry settings into the application and component installations, as these settings may conflict with other security measures being taken by the organization.

ASP and HTML Page Security

The primary function of IIS is to download, under controlled access conditions, HTML and ASP pages from the local server to the remote browsers. Access to the application's Web pages and graphics can be limited by setting directory and file permissions for files such as those with .htm, .asp, .gif, and .jpg extensions.

Access to certain pages can be controlled programmatically by establishing user-level permissions in a Session object. The logon name and password provided by the user should be validated against a database. More secure and robust applications use the built-in security groups within Windows NT and check permissions against the Windows NT account database.

Note Windows NT 4.x has a practical limit of 50,000 to 100,000 users. Third-party products, as well as Microsoft Site Server's Membership system, provide excellent security systems for Web sites with larger user communities (millions of users). With Windows 2000, the Active Directory provides additional security and scalability for very large Web communities.

Setting Web Server Permissions

The Web server's permissions can be configured to limit how users view, run, and use ASP pages. These Web server permissions apply to all users and do not differentiate between user accounts. A very basic setup would be to:

- Enable the Read permissions for virtual directories containing .asp files without scripts.

- Enable Read and Script permissions for virtual directories containing .asp and .htm files that contain scripts.

- Enable Read and Execute permissions for virtual directories containing both .asp and other executable files, such as .exe and .dll files, which require the Execute permission to run.

After these general Web server permissions have been applied to the virtual directories, either securing the ASP and HTML pages or using TCP/IP access restrictions can specify additional access limitations at the individual file level.

MTS Application and Data Security

In a three-tier or N-tier application, users no longer access data directly from their client application. Instead, users access components from the middle tier running on MTS. This splitting of access from user to component and from component to data involves two types of security:

- **Application security** This involves authorizing user access to the application code within the MTS packages. Developers should implement application security in the business service layer.
- **Data security** This involves authorizing MTS packages for access to the data. Developers should implement data security in the data service layer.

Security Isolation

Server packages are the units of trust for MTS. Calls into a package can be secured. Calls within the package are trusted. Thus, application security requirements have a big impact on package design. If calls into a component must be authorized, the clients and the component must be located in different packages. Only components that can safely call each other without requiring an authorization check should be located in the same package.

MTS roles are defined on a per-package basis. Multiple components that use the same roles can be placed in the same package. Generally, this grouping is safe. Because the components can be called by the same set of users, they should be trusted to call each other. Placing components that use the same roles in one package simplifies administration because the system administrator does not need to remember to populate the role in multiple packages.

In addition, a server package runs as a particular identity, and all components in the package run as the package identity. However, some components in the package might need to run as different identities because they need different access rights to some resource or in order to maintain an audit trail. Components that need to run as different user identities should be located in separate packages. Although the exact identity each server package will run as generally can't be defined during development, any identity recommendations, along with the permissions required by package components, should be documented. For example, if a data object in a given package requires read/write access to a particular data store, the fact that the identity used to run that package must have read/write access to the data store should be documented.

Benefits of MTS Roles

Roles are a key security feature of MTS. Roles within the MTS N-tier model provide the following benefits:

- **Encapsulated access** Database access can be totally encapsulated by MTS components because users do not access the database directly.

- **Connection pooling** MTS can utilize connection pooling because multiple concurrent connections can be accessed between the database and MTS. Utilizing concurrent connections dramatically improves application scalability.

- **Streamlined security** Database security administration can be streamlined because application user accounts don't need to be managed at the database level. Instead, package identities can be assigned database access which is much more efficient and manageable.

- **Inter-package authentication** MTS security can authenticate package-to-package calls without the need for additional logons or sessions.

Declarative Security

To implement this security within Windows NT, user groups that represent the appropriate categories for application security need to be defined. Within MTS, roles are defined for a set of components within an MTS package. When the multi-service layer solution is implemented, Windows NT user groups are assigned to the appropriate MTS role. This way, users and groups are not directly associated with the data, and changing user security involves simply modifying the user groups that have access to the MTS packages. This implementation of MTS security is called *declarative security*.

Note Traditionally, components were written to impersonate the client running the initial application that was retrieving the data. However, this method runs contrary to multi-service layer application design, where application security is separated from data security. With MTS, package identities should be set for each package, and all components running in the package share this identity. Package identities allow developers to associate a Windows NT user with the package.

Programmatic Security

Security can be programmed directly into MTS components. This *programmatic security* provides more granular security within the components. For example, multiple groups can be assigned to a role for a component, and the groups can be programmatically accessed within the component to further manipulate security.

MTS makes programmatic security available within its components using two methods within the **ObjectContext** object:

- **IsSecurityEnabled** Developers can query the **IsSecurityEnabled** method to return a true value meaning that security is enabled or a false value meaning that it is not.

- **IsCallerRole** Developers can query the **IsCallerRole** method to return a true or false value. This method determines whether a caller is a member of a role by accepting a string value of the role's name and comparing it with the current user account. After the comparison, **IsCallerRole** returns either a true value meaning the user is contained in the role or a false value meaning the user is not.

Note By default, error checking should be implemented to deny access if errors occur.

Enabling MTS Security

MTS contains a system package that is automatically installed with MTS. MTS uses the components contained within the system package for internal functions. For MTS security to work, it must be properly enabled and a valid Windows NT user must be assigned to the Administrator role for this system package.

MTS security is enabled at two levels: the package level and the component level. Both levels have only two settings: enabled or disabled. The package-level setting takes precedence over the component-level setting. For example, if security is disabled at the package level, all component security is disabled. However, if package-level security is enabled, component-level security may be selectively disabled.

Note It is important to keep in mind that security is triggered when a component from one package calls a component from another package. However, security is not triggered when components call one another in the same package.

SQL Server Access Permissions

Regardless of whether a component uses standard or integrated security to make a connection, SQL Server identifies the connection using the logon. Being allowed to make a connection does not mean that the component has permissions to perform any operations on the database. The component's permissions depend on its logon.

Each logon is mapped to a set of permissions for each database object. The permissions are either enabled or disabled. For example, suppose a particular user's logon contains **Select** permissions on the **Authors** table. These permissions allow the specified user to perform **Select** statements only on the **Authors** table. If this user has no **Select** permissions on the **Employees** table, the user cannot get any data from that table.

Permissions must be granted to a logon before any components using that logon can access databases or the objects inside those databases. The permissions describe the capabilities of each logon. The permissions also designate which statements a logon can issue against database tables, such as **Select**, **Insert**, **Update**, and **Delete**. In addition, the permissions determine whether or not a logon can execute specific stored procedures.

If a logon has execute permissions on a stored procedure, that logon may run the stored procedure. The stored procedure runs even if it performs actions for which the logon has no permissions. For example, a particular user's logon may be required to execute permissions on a stored procedure named **AddCustomer**. Even though this particular user does not have Insert permissions on the **Customers** table, the **AddCustomer** stored procedure can successfully execute an **Insert** statement to add a new customer.

Auditing

Auditing is an important step in effective security management. Unfortunately, many applications do not incorporate simple auditing techniques that can provide a tracking mechanism to identify security breaches. In addition to security auditing, simple auditing can operate as application monitoring to help determine what an application is doing and who did what with the application.

> **Caution** Those new to incorporating auditing into applications should be forewarned: Auditing can be expensive because it can utilize extensive processing and storage resources. Also, auditing is an intrusive process that, when overzealously implemented, can cripple an application's performance. The application development team must determine an appropriate level of auditing to reach a medium between governing the working application and allowing the application freedom to simply operate unencumbered.

A common way to address this concern is to emulate the designers of Windows NT. Within Windows NT, seemingly everything that can occur on a system can be audited into a Windows Event Log. However, as shipped Windows NT does not activate most auditing features by default. These features can be activated when system administrators think it is necessary. Minimal information is always recorded in the Event Log, such as System or Application Errors, or the start-up of certain application services.

One way to categorize auditing events that can be incorporated into applications is to group them by the following headings:

- **Information** Informational messages enable applications to pass along state knowledge, such as noting that a computers data storage has reached 750 MB. Messages can also communicate the application is functioning correctly.

- **Success** Incorporating success messages (for example, notifying users that an application service has successfully begun at a particular date or time) can provide reassurances to administrators as well as allow automated monitoring systems to check for successful entries.

- **Warning** Warning messages typically signify problems that may arise. Warning messages could alert users to unexpected events in an application. When users receive warning messages, they should perform a follow-up to determine if additional action is required to solve the problem being addressed.

- **Failure** If an action cannot be properly completed, the application should make a permanent record in the form of a failure message. The development team should not rely upon users to report that they have been receiving error messages, as such the application should track important client or server errors. From a security point of view, it is important to capture failure messages that result when an application reports that access to a particular system was denied. These access failures are the first line of defense against unwanted software violations. For example, 42,000 failed data requests in a one-minute period can signify a potential security breach, as well as a significant problem with the application.

Log Files

Writing text files that act as log files is a simple way to provide auditing. Text files can be written from all common programming languages, as well as through ADO and ODBC. It is recommended programming practice to allow system administrators to determine where log files are physically located. The application can request a log file directory during installation and store the location within the application's registry setting.

Event Logs

The logs created by the Windows NT event logging service are accessible from the Windows event viewer. They are separated into three different logs: a security log, a system log, and an application log. Support for these logs can be incorporated into applications to ensure that information is written into the appropriate event log. The event logs are physically located in the Windows NT Systemroot\System32\Config directory in the appevent.evt, secevent.evt, and sysevent.evt files. Server administrators should secure access to these files to prevent tampering, as well as prevent software criminals from trying to cover the tracks of their illegal system access.

Windows NT provides several interfaces for controlling auditing. As mentioned, most auditing is disabled by default, but can occur for:

- **Windows NT system auditing** System auditing includes user logon and logoff, object access, file and object access, use of user rights, user and group management, security policy changes, system restart and shutdown, and Process Tracking.

- **File and directory auditing** This type of auditing can be set to determine the success and/or failure of read, write, execute, delete, change-permission, and take-ownership actions.

- **Registry auditing** Auditing within the registry includes success and failure actions that query values, set values, create subkeys, enumerate subkeys, notify, create link, delete, write DAC, and read control.

Caution An excessive amount of auditing can adversely impact system performance. For additional information on how to set auditing values, refer to *Microsoft Windows NT 4.0 Security, Audit, and Control* (Microsoft Press, 1998).

For ongoing monitoring of applications, the project team can build Windows NT performance counter capabilities into the application. As discussed previously, the Windows NT Performance Monitor provides excellent real-time information regarding how an application is functioning. Additional counter information specific to the application can be reported to the performance monitoring system by including the appropriate performance interfaces. For additional information on incorporating performance monitor interfaces, refer to the *Microsoft Windows NT Workstation 4.0 Resource Kit* (Microsoft Press, 1996).

Distributed Environments

The way Windows NT 4.0 authenticates users directly affects how the use of distributed applications should be audited. For example, with Windows NT authentication, a token gets passed only from point A to point B. When B wants to access something, B's security token is used to access C. The effect is not transitive, meaning if C trusts A, and A trusts B, C does NOT inherently trust B. (Kerberos security, on the other hand, is transitive.) To successfully build auditing into Windows NT 4.0 distributed N-tier environments, developers need to understand this underlying method of authentication.

Obviously, developers need to audit for errors. However, the following items can also be audited for:

- Success events.
- Failure events.
- Object access monitoring.

- Database access monitoring.
- Runtime diagnostics.
- Development diagnostics.
- Usage monitoring.

When developers create an audit trail for object security, they generally want to know who was trying to use the application. To determine who is using an application, the programmatic security services provided by MTS must be implemented. For example, developers could create audit objects to implement an audit trail originating from the presentation tier and ending at the data tier. MTS programmatic services also enable developers to perform more sophisticated security checks in components, rather than simply checking role membership.

Most security needs—even programmatic security—can be met by using role-based security. For example, when designing a banking application, developers may have a business rule enabling a bank teller to authorize withdrawals of up to $500 from a particular user's account, but larger withdrawals must be authorized by a manager. In this case, the **Withdraw** method implementation needs to take different actions depending on the caller's role. The object context methods **IsSecurityEnabled** and **IsCallerInRole** can be used to handle this procedure.

In rare instances in which role-based security is insufficient, MTS provides the **ISecurityProperty** interface, which can be used to access Windows NT user identities. The object context is queried to obtain an **ISecurityProperty** interface pointer, and then one of the following four methods is called to obtain a security identifier (SID):

- **GetDirectCallerSID** returns the SID of the external process that called the currently executing method.
- **GetDirectCreatorSID** returns the SID of the external process that created the currently executing object.
- **GetOriginalCallerSID** returns the SID of the base client process that initiated the sequence of calls from which the call to the current object originated.
- **GetOriginalCreatorSID** returns the SID of the base client process that initiated the current activity.

A SID is a Windows structure containing information about a particular user and any groups to which the user belongs. The Windows API must be used to parse a SID. The SID's information can be used to restrict access to components or to obtain information for auditing and logging. When a SID obtained from the **ISecurityProperty** interface is no longer needed, **ReleaseSID** should be called to release the SID.

SIDs are not easily accessible from Visual Basic, so MTS also provides a **SecurityProperty** object. The **SecurityProperty** object is defined in the MTS type library. A reference to the object can be obtained using the Security property of the object context, as shown in the following code example:

```
Dim secProperty as SecurityProperty

Set secProperty = GetObjectContext.Security
```

The **SecurityProperty** object provides access to usernames only, not to the entire SID. Fortunately, the username is all that's generally need for auditing or logging.

Just as they can audit object security programmatically, developers can audit database security by building in parameters, such as a username, that is passed to stored procedures in the database. Later, the database can record the username in the appropriate table using an additional stored procedure or trigger.

Summary

Application security can be divided into four categories: authentication, encryption, access, and auditing.

We discussed how authentication begins the user interaction and initial interactive security system for applications. Developers must identify and validate users, as well as determine what role they play within the application. Several application authentication mechanisms are available to Windows NT based applications, such as Windows NT Authentication and Kerberos. In addition, many Web-based types of authentication such as basic authentication, Windows NT challenge/response, cookies, and the use of digital certificates can be used by applications. SQL Server's three authentication methods of standard, integrated, and mixed security can also be used within applications.

Information can be encrypted when it is being transferred between the applications users, services, and data stores via several security-related protocols and methods such as SSL and Microsoft's CrytoAPI.

Once an application recognizes a particular user, the application must allow the user access only to the appropriate areas through such security measures as controlling access to system services, files, components, and the Windows NT Registry. Web- and MTS-based applications can pose different access security issues for the teams applications.

Finally, we looked at how to audit who is doing what with an application. We identified several categories of audit entries, and discussed logging entries into log files and the Windows NT event service logs.

Review

1. What is authentication?
2. What are several methods for Web-based authentication?
3. What is encryption?
4. What is access security?
5. Why should applications provide auditing services?
6. Which Windows NT services provide mechanisms for auditing?

C H A P T E R   1 2

Development Deliverables

About This Chapter

This chapter discusses how to move from the Planning Phase to the Developing Phase in the Microsoft Solutions Framework (MSF) Development Process Model, using the application's Functional Specification and design. As many applications suffer from poor implementation, the transition between these two phases must emphasize the importance of writing solid application code.

An application comes alive during the Developing Phase, but not without potential difficulties. In this chapter, we'll examine the creation process, including how the various team roles function during development. We'll explore testing, bug tracking, and the "zero-defect mindset," and also show how the project team makes effective trade-offs. In addition, we'll discuss how multi-layer application designs can be implemented as monolithic, client/server, or distributed as multi-layer applications. Finally, we'll explore the end of the Developing Phase, when the Scope Complete Milestone is reached, and all product features and original code are incorporated into the application.

The principles and guidelines provided in this chapter are based on our own experience in creating application architectures and implementing of enterprise applications, along with the following resources:

- Microsoft Solutions Framework
- Jim McCarthy's *Dynamics of Software Development*
- Steve Maguire's *Debugging the Development Process*
- Steve McConnell's *Software Project Survival Guide*
- Mary Kirtland's *Designing Component-Based Applications*

The majority of information in this chapter is derived from the MSF Development Process Model and is based on the MSF *Principles of Application Development* course #1516.

Upon completion, you will be able to:

- Identify interim milestones and deliverables that lead to the Scope Complete and First Use milestones.

- Understand the roles played by individual team members during the Developing Phase.

- Apply a zero-defect mindset to development projects.

- Understand the testing process's impact on software quality.

- Understand the bug-tracking process.

Overview of the Developing Phase

The Developing Phase is the third of the four phases of the MSF Development Process Model. The Developing Phase follows the Planning Phase, which is completed with the Project Plan Approved Milestone. To this point, the team has focused on product vision, product architecture, and project planning. During the Developing Phase, the team's focus changes to project execution.

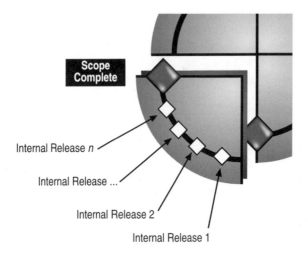

Figure 12.1   The Developing Phase

The team may ask, "How can we successfully implement our development process to ship the right product on time?" The answer to this question lies in a common understanding of the product vision. To further enhance the development process, the team should weigh this understanding of the vision with realistic limits for developing a functional software product. Developers should then implement the product defined by the project team.

As noted in Figure 12.1, the Development implementation leads to application coding being completed and initially released to the project team, resulting in the Scope Complete Milestone. This milestone of the Developing Phase has the following characteristics:

- All product features are implemented, even if not fully optimized.
- The product has passed basic testing and the current list of bugs has been addressed, although not necessarily fixed.
- Team members and key stakeholders agree that the included features meet the product vision and design, and have been successfully implemented.
- User performance materials are baselined and ready for testing and stabilization.

The Developing Phase contains many small similiarities to the other phases of the MSF Process Model. For example, results of the Planning Phase efforts would produce the following revised deliverables:

- Functional Specification
- Master Project Plan
- Master Project Schedule
- Master Risk Assessment Document

Where these deliverables are the output for the Project Plan Approved Milestone, they become the input and tools for the Developing Phase. The Planning deliverables are used as a forecast to quantify the implementation of the development process. These Planning deliverables should not be viewed as completely static; they are baselined and should be used as a guide in the Developing Phase. The deliverables for completing the Developing Phase will include revised versions of the Planning Phase deliverables, as well as the following:

- Source code and executables
- User performance materials
- Testing elements

In this chapter, we'll discuss how to incorporate Project Plan Approved Milestone deliverables into the Developing Phase so that a team can begin to create a software product and reach the Scope Complete Milestone. Specific interim milestones can help continue the team's progress through the Developing Phase.

Often called "getting the real work done" on a development project, the true focus of the Developing Phase is building the product solution.

Planning Feeds the Developing Phase Deliverable

Architecting the product properly during the Planning Phase provides the context to *implement* the product during the Developing Phase. In the *Software Project Survival Guide* (Microsoft Press, 1998), Steve McConnell describes the transition between the two phases using the terms *upstream* and *downstream*. Application architecture work through the Planning Phase moves upstream, leading to the Developing Phase. Product work implementing the design moves downstream beginning at the Developing Phase and ending at the product release point. If a team's early upstream work is sound, the team members know exactly what needs to be implemented. If the upstream architecture is unsound, pieces derived from this architecture will significantly impede the project.

The Master Project Schedule describes the expected implementation schedule for the Developing Phase. The Functional Specification provides the Conceptual, Logical, and Physical application designs, the foundation for physical code implementation. The project's risk assessment and management must continue to be proactively managed as the risk's probability and impact fluctuate throughout the project. Also during the Developing Phase, the team will implement the Development Plan incrementally, using interim milestones as mentioned.

For example, in moving from Envisioning to Planning and into Development, one logical architectural requirement may map to a dozen physical design templates, which may, in turn, be able to map to hundreds of lines of actual code. In moving from design to coding, the team certainly can't implement all features, services, and object code at once—the code must be implemented in manageable portions. As each code segment is integrated, it will be combined with the others to form the complete application.

Each new compilation of the application can be made available as an interim product release during the Developing Phase. At some point during the product development, these interim releases are made externally available in the form of alpha and beta product releases.

Development Process

Within the MSF Development Process, the true significance of the Developing Phase is the project team and stakeholders' agreement that the planned feature set as implemented meets all expectations. Additionally, stakeholders and project team members must agree that all features included in the product have been completed, and that the product as a whole has been developed appropriately.

Who Does What During Development?

During the Developing Phase, all team members should focus on their particular roles as well as continue to identify and manage risks. Each role has primary responsibilities that combine to provide the necessary project coverage to successfully complete the Developing Phase. These responsibilities are as follows:

- **Product Management** Product managers are responsible for managing customer expectations. They also continue plans for channeling product information to customers and external stakeholders. Product managers also prepare customers for alpha and beta releases.

- **Program Management** Program managers facilitate communication between all the project teams, and coordinate the interim milestone releases across the entire team. Program managers are also responsible for several of the phases' deliverables, such as revisions of the Functional Specification, Master Project Plan, Master Project Schedule, and Master Risk Assessment Document.

- **Development** Developers create all code necessary to implement all product features. They also provide initial functional testing of code and features. The Development team is responsible for creating the baselined code for the interim alpha and beta releases as well as the baselined scope complete product release.

- **User Education** The User Education team conducts initial product usability testing and begins user performance testing. This team coordinates the user community for alpha and beta product releases. User Education team members additionally create initial user performance materials to support the product, such as help wizards, online training materials, and formal user training courses. The User Education team is ultimately responsible for the Developing Phase's baselined user and support documentation deliverables.

- **Testing** Testers create detailed test specifications, plans, cases, data, and scripts to conduct initial functional testing. These testing elements are executed during the Developing Phase to validate the interim internal, alpha, and beta releases. Testing's primary role is identifying and tracking bugs as the team moves toward the scope complete product release. The Testing team is also responsible for documenting the product testing process, from start to finish.

- **Logistics Management** Logistics managers provide internal team operations support. They also create operations support materials and documentation, as well as deploy and support initial product alpha and beta releases.

Several general steps should take place throughout the Developing Phase. As mentioned with the Envisioning Phase steps, these steps are not intended as imperatives, but merely guidelines. The step names are for simplification only, and can be modified for a team's specific project.

Step #1: Analysis and Rationalization

At this point in the development process, the team should have identified a solid plan of action with few variables. Thus, the Developing Phase should not necessitate a significant amount of additional research; the phase should primarily begin with the analysis of the current application design.

Within the Development team, the design and project schedule should be analyzed to identify specific resources to be applied to the coding process. By looking at feature buckets, performed as part of the Planning Phase's design process, the Development team can identify coding teams responsible for particular product features. In determining the coding teams, the Development team can also consider the packaging of the application into service layers (also part of the design process). Coding teams can be created based on differing skills required by languages and tools to implement specific code within the user, business, and data access service layers.

The Testing team should examine the product design to determine who will conduct the types of tests, and further review the use cases to verify that the proper usability testing will occur. The Testing team should have identified an exhaustive set of test scenarios based on use cases, physical design, and non-functional requirements, such as application and user performance metrics during the planning phase, and now must determine how to execute these test scenarios.

Finally, as discussed later in this chapter, the project team will release multiple versions of the product during the Developing Phase. With each release, feedback from users, as well as the Testing and Logistics Management teams, must be analyzed to determine the current product release's successes and failures. Any issues and bugs existing in the product should be pinpointed for causes and product locations, and then be resolved appropriately.

Step #2: Implementation

The next step in the Developing Phase is for the source code development team to implement the application design. However, there are other artifacts (or documents) that must be delivered at the Scope Complete Milestone. The User

Education team must create user- and application-support artifacts, which must exist to ensure a successful product release. Although many teams focus solely on traditional user and installation documents, the User Education team can focus on online help and tutorials as well as program wizards to improve user and support experiences.

Step #3: Validation

Validation is a full team effort; however, throughout the Developing Phase validation is particularly the responsibility of the Development and Testing teams. The ongoing usability testing, performance validation, bug tracking, and zero-defect quality mindset all drive the validation step.

Because multiple product releases occur throughout the Developing Phase, there are many instances in which at least a portion of the team will focus on validating the current deliverables. For efficiency in validating the application code, the Development and Testing teams should automate as much of the testing process as possible.

Ongoing Risk Management Process

The risk management process begins during the Envisioning Phase and continues through the entire product lifecycle. As a deliverable for the Planning Phase, the Master Risk Assessment Document is continually revised using the five-step process shown in Figure 12.2 on the next page. It should come as no surprise that the team would continue to manage and track the status of the various risks from the Planning Phase's revised Master Risk Assessment Document. Again, for each risk, the project team should answer the following questions:

- Has the team done anything to mitigate the risk?
- Has the risk changed due to forces outside the team's control?
- As a result of either team efforts or outside forces, has there been a change in either the probability or the impact of the risk? If so, what is the change in the risk's exposure rating, and therefore in its priority?
- Have any of the contingency triggers been removed?
- Based on answers to the questions above, what should be the team's next course of action?

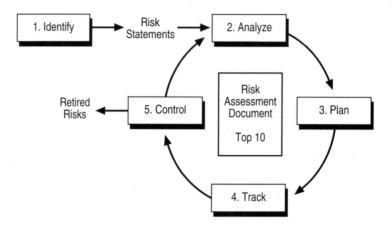

Figure 12.2   Risk assessment revisited

We continue to emphasize risk management to stress its importance in completing a project successfully. Risk management should be an ongoing and dynamic process. Practicing risk management throughout a project is a vital part of the MSF approach to project management. During the Developing Phase, the project team should reevaluate the project's top ten risks and execute mitigation plans, as well as executing the contingency plans for realized risks.

Scope Complete Milestone and Its Deliverables

The Developing Phase's primary goal is to reach the Scope Complete Milestone. The seven deliverables required to meet this milestone are:

- **Revised Functional Specification** This deliverable updates the design to reflect the developed product. The revised Functional Specification reflects any agreed-to changes occurring in the design during the Developing Phase. This specification can also identify new features that the team may consider for future versions.

- **Revised Master Project Plan** This document shows how the team plans to execute the last stage of the development process, the Stabilization Phase, including deliverables the team intends to deploy. The Revised Master Project Plan reflects any changes that occurred during the Developing Phase.

- **Revised Master Project Schedule** This schedule outlines the time required for the Stabilization Phase and its deliverables. Like the Revised Master Project Plan, this schedule reflects any changes that occurred during the Developing Phase.

- **Revised Master Risk Assessment Document** This document shows possible risks to the project, and outlines how the team plans to handle each risk. The revised Master Risk Assessment contains both preexisting risks and newly identified risks. This assessment also describes risk management plans and their progress to date.

- **Source code and executables** This set of deliverables is a feature complete release of the actual application. The source code and executables represent the application with all the product features complete and signify the team's first shot at a release candidate.

- **User performance and support materials** These materials document how the application works, for both users and support teams. Artifacts that support user performance range from product wizards to user documentation and classroom training materials. Additionally, artifacts for operations teams that will support the application in production will describe how the application is installed, configured, administered, and used.

- **Testing elements** This set of deliverables describes how the application will be validated, and what application elements are to be tested, during the Stabilization Phase. Testing elements are test plans, specifications, cases, and scripts that cover the full feature set of the newly baselined product. The Testing team should create automated test scripts for use in the Developing and Stabilization Phases.

Interim Milestones

To accomplish its project goals successfully, the team must set interim product delivery milestones to work toward throughout the phase by breaking the Developing Phase into manageable portions. During the Developing Phase, interim milestones encourage a product-shipping mindset. While the team may choose to include other milestones, basic interim milestones during the Developing Phase are typically represented as one or more of the following: internal release, alpha release and beta release, which lead to the Scope Complete milestone's product deliverable.

Interim milestones primarily measure the progress of building a product. Code creation is often done by different teams in parallel and in segments for different product features, so the team needs a way to measure progress as a whole. To provide solid boundaries for interim milestones, internal releases force the product team to synchronize the code at a product level. This synchronization process is sometimes called *integration testing*.

Typically, internal releases on medium-size projects are one to three months apart and on large projects two to four months apart. However, the number and frequency of releases will vary depending on the project's size and duration.

The team should also try to achieve user interface and database freeze points during development. Although not formal interim milestones, these points are ideally accomplished early in the Developing Phase. Deliverables, such as user education training documents, can have strong dependency on the user interface to create the user support and training material. Also, the feature teams often begin implementing functionality in connection with the database structure early in the Developing Phase. Thus, the earlier in the Developing Phase the user interface and database design can be frozen, will result in fewer changes to the dependant documentation and code.

The Developing Phase typically acts as an iterative process to reach a well-defined end result. Specific interim releases can have goals for the product team, such as testing a particular feature, portion of the user interface, or product deployment capabilities. Some product releases may be externally focused toward customers and users. Early releases should incorporate high-priority product features to ensure that the team can deliver such features. Early internal releases can address high-risk architectural areas to determine feasibility or identify development changes required to minimize the cost and effect of design changes.

Breaking up large projects helps the team focus on more actionable subsets that can direct daily progress. Any minor corrective actions occurring early in the development process can also decrease the cost of changes. The product mindset of internal and external releases can increase quality by providing a more stable base for new development and allowing the team to fix bugs closer to the time at which they occur rather than toward the end of the project.

Internal Product Releases

Internal releases are similar to the overall product concept of versioned releases. Both involve incrementally adding functionality to a known baseline. These internal releases also help the team stabilize the product, achieve quality goals, and practice shipping the product. When a team uses internal releases during the developing cycle, it is essentially establishing a known baseline, which provides a further measuring tool. The team can then compare the functional specification implementation with the actual product's business need, and additionally identify design issues not discovered during the Planning Phase.

Internal releases happen throughout the entire Developing Phase. Each release is designed to expand on previous releases, as noted in Figure 12.3. This independence gives an additional benefit of viewing each release as a self-contained product, which further encourages the product mindset during the development process. Reviewing the results of an internal release is a necessary part of turning the team into a learning organization that repeats best practices and learns from mistakes.

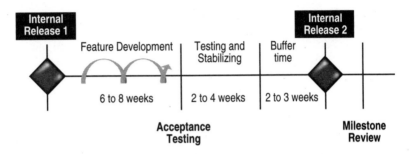

Figure 12.3   Internal releases during the Developing Phase

Each internal release has a *quality bar* that must be reached before the team can achieve the internal milestone. A quality bar is a quality level measurement that the team has clearly stated and must achieve for the internal release. Each internal release has a small Stabilizing Phase, during which the team can bring the product up to quality standards and practice the stabilizing process.

As the project team develops the product, it uses successive internal releases to incrementally add feature subsets until the product is complete. With each internal release, the overall development scope increases until the entire product is complete. If a team hasn't planned properly during the Planning Phase, it will be much more difficult to separate its development into interim releases, and to implement each successive release.

External Product Releases

Although this practice does not strictly adhere to MSF, we recommend that external product releases also occur during the Developing Phase. These releases help synchronize the coding process with the other project team members' responsibilities. These external releases demonstrate successful execution of the project plan to customers, users, and other external project stakeholders.

Depending on the project's size and duration, an alpha release or set of releases is rarely feature-code complete. An alpha release enables the project team to practice its ability to fully release a product, and also begins to test other product-related deliverables, such as user and operations support materials.

Beta external releases are typically very close to feature-code complete and typically without any performance enhancements.

Revised Functional Specification

As the Planning Phase's primary deliverable, the Functional Specification is the paramount input resource for the Developing Phase. The Functional Specification is the compass that guides the project downstream. While a team can't plot the exact course for the project, the team can use the Functional Specification as a guide. Interim milestones are tools that can be used to make the Functional Specification a reality while revising it as needed.

Reviewing the Functional Specification

The revised Functional Specification doesn't have to be perfectly integrated with the interim milestones. However, the Functional Specification does need to mirror the reality of any differences between the delivered application and the original functional specification before the Scope Complete Milestone can occur.

The team should not be surprised if new changes result from the implementation of the interim milestones. As you may recall, one of the goals of the Functional Specification is to help provide team consensus. Again, just as the project team reviews the original Functional Specification, changes to the Functional Specification should also be reviewed for the following reasons:

- Everyone with a stake in the Functional Specification is allowed to take part in creating it.
- A variety of people are involved in making sure that audience needs are met.
- The Functional Specification serves as a method of communicating what is going to be built.
- A forum for negotiating and achieving buy-in is provided.

Revising the Functional Specification encourages association of design into reality to assure the team that business needs are being met. Each team role can review the Functional Specification using the criteria in Table 12.1.

Table 12.1   Reviewing the Functional Specification

Team role	Role in reviewing the Functional Specification
Customer	Functionality of software product created in interim milestones meets business needs.
Product Management	Solution meets known requirements or Functional Specification is reviewed and revised to match changes to requirements.
Program Management	Team responsibilities and schedules are realistic. Program Managers believe that responsibilities for each specified function are clear, and that committed schedules are realistic.
Development	Implement features in the solution based on Functional Specification requirements. Re-evaluate risks on a daily basis to ensure that implementation is achievable. Issues that arise should be discussed with the team and documented where changes need to occur with the Functional Specification and scheduling. Ideally, adequate planning has been done and changes will be marginal.
Testing	The ultimate goal for testing in the Planning Phase was to have a defined strategy for test platforms, scripts, and data and commits to testing all aspects of the Functional Specification. In the Developing Phase, testing should align its goals with the interim milestones decided upon by the team. Testing can only test what the development team has built.
User Education	Partake in alpha and beta tests to ensure that the product features are usable, though not necessarily bug-free. Users should be provided with adequate information on how to work with the product, although formal help files and documentation may not be available during the Developing Phase.
Logistics Management	Work with alpha and beta testing to support and deploy the product. As the product is deployed, the Logistics team can provide information needed to change the Functional Specification to insure a smoother product deployment.

As an example of revising the Functional Specification, let's examine the development of the model Resource Management System (RMS) application. During the development of the RMS application, a problem was discovered using the Web client, ADO Disconnected **Recordset Objects**, and Windows NT security. When using a Disconnected **Recordset Object**, the user's security ID was not being passed properly to the middle layer business objects in MTS. The team was forced to make slight changes to the application's architecture. Although the Web client and ADO Disconnected Recordset were tested during the Planning Phase's proof-of-concept, the integration of Windows NT security was not included in the proof-of-concept. Thus, the design problem was not discovered until the Developing Phase. Fortunately, during completion of the Development Phase, a software patch was released to resolve the problem. Unfortunately, the patch was not released in time to be implemented into the team's first release of the application. Thus, the RMS team identified a design change for the product's next version.

Revised Master Project Plan

The Master Project Plan needs to be updated to match planned implementation details against reality. While the Master Project Plan shouldn't be used to manage the project's day-to-day needs, the plan serves as a "big picture" to tell the team where the project is heading.

As the project evolves, team and work role plans will continue to be carried out, execution of tasks will be updated with the plan, and efforts to integrate the plan into the product will continue to be synchronized. The overall owners of the Master Project Plan are the Program Managers. Each team role develops and maintains its own realistic project plan within the overall Master Project Plan. The development, test, training, user support, communications, and deployment plans are updated to reflect changes caused by details found in implementation.

Revised Master Project Schedule

The Master Project Schedule contains information on the following schedules:

- Development
- Internal and external product ship dates
- Test
- Training
- User support
- Communications
- Deployment

The development schedule is the driving force during the Developing Phase; therefore, the other schedules should integrate at the interim milestones. Ultimately, a revision of the Master Project Schedule results from changes occurring in any of the project schedules.

During the Planning Phase, and as part of the development schedule details, the team can create *release dates* for interim milestones to give the team a tangible target to pursue. During the Developing Phase, when the various teams target interim milestones, changes to the schedules should be noted and passed to

Program Management. Program Management must assess how individual updates will effect the overall schedule and work with the other team roles to determine the affect to the overall project. When conflicts arise, Program Management is responsible for driving the tradeoff decisions that will affect the schedule. Once the decisions are made, the updated schedules are compiled into a revised Master Project Schedule.

Revised Master Risk Assessment Document

The Master Risk Assessment Document is first created as a deliverable during the Envisioning Phase. This document is owned by the Program Management team, which also has responsibility for ensuring that the revision is complete and accurate. The revised Master Risk Assessment Document represents additional detailed risk assessments from various team members. The team can use this aggregated version of lower-level assessments to get an overall view of risks.

The Master Risk Assessment Document will help synchronize risk assessments across a team. This assessment will also aid in prioritizing the team's decisions about risk management. Risk management is still handled by the individual team roles responsible for given risks.

Source Code and Executables

The source code and executables represent a team's code- and feature-complete delivery. As long as the code produced by programmers begins to meet the functional requirements, the quality of the code being produced should also be considered.

Efficiency in developing the source code and executables is critical for delivery of a timely product. Unfortunately, however, many teams sacrifice code quality when rushing to finish a program by a particular deadline. It is important to remember that high code quality must be maintained throughout the project, even under tight deadlines; the project may cost more in the long run if developers cut corners on source code in the short-term interests of saving money by hurrying through the application's development.

Although management must take responsibility for compromising quality for meeting deadlines, programmers can also lower the quality bar in the interest of saving time. If no one ever monitors the quality of code that programmers write, it should be no surprise that the code quality could deteriorate.

To minimize chances of sacrificing quality to save time, the team should set standards that:

- Force developers to maintain a methodical and disciplined approach to coding, regardless of pressure to take shortcuts.
- Remind developers constantly that code's internal quality is important.

The decision to use standards and implement a review process to ensure that such standards are being used will affect the way that programmers approach coding. By making it clear that such standards are mandatory rules, not optional guidelines, the team will ensure that its members will realize that meeting standards is an integral part of their jobs rather than a corollary if convenient.

Coding standards have traditionally focused on the following topics:

- Naming
- Layout
- Commenting
- Coding dos and don'ts

The emphasis on such topics is usually on writing *shareable code*—that is, code that other programmers can read and reuse easily. Shareable code is beneficial, even if one programmer exclusively works with the code. When returning to shareable code three months after the initial development effort, the programmer will be more likely to be able to recognize and work with the code again.

Another goal of traditional coding standards is to assist in making the code more robust. For example, such coding standards should mandate error handling, prohibit **GoTo** statements, and so on. Program elements, files, functions, variables, and constants must all follow naming conventions. Such requirements aid in project organization. Also, prefixing elements to indicate the data type, as in Hungarian notation, is commonplace.

User Performance and Support Elements

Elements that support user performance range from in-product wizards to user documentation and classroom training materials. Together the team should focus on building the product as described in the Functional Specification, and on working with users to ensure product reliability from one internal release to another.

As Steve Maguire noted in *Debugging the Development Process* (Microsoft Press, 1994):

> If users think that you're on the right track when reading the documentation, it goes a long way towards assisting the programmer in writing the code. Programmers need to program with the users in mind when they implement their code. Also, if the programmer thinks a task is not intuitive or slow, it's likely that the user will also.

When testing the product's functionality during interim milestones, beta testers should not use the portions of the application that do not meet the quality bar desired for the product's code. One or two malfunctioning parts of the application may give a negative impression to testers for overall functionality. In beta testing, ideals aren't always going to be met. Therefore, the objectives for testing need to be clearly stated so that beta testers know specifically what to test and what to ignore.

Testing Elements

In this section, we'll discuss various testing tools that can be used to help design and develop a solid product. We'll discuss integrated milestone testing and review the zero-defect mindset, code reviews, and the daily build.

Integrated Milestone Testing

The testing process is not limited to the Stabilizing Phase, but is an integral part of the development process as well. At the Project Plan Approved Milestone, the team baselines the test plan and begins work on a more detailed test specification that describes how the team will test individual features.

The test specification is finished at the Scope Complete Milestone because, at that point, the feature set should not grow further. Because the Scope Complete Milestone represents a feature-complete baseline product, the team can consider the product to be in alpha form for the Stabilizing Phase. This alpha product should not be confused with the alpha and beta testing performed in the Developing Phase's interim milestones. Interim milestones in the Developing Phase also contain a subset of actions to be performed during the Stabilizing Phase.

The transition between the Developing Phase and the Stabilizing Phase is characterized by the transition from coverage to usage testing. Following are examples of types of coverage testing that might be done on a typical project.

- **Unit and functional tests** These make up the majority of manual testing. Check-in, build verification, and regression tests tend to be automated, because they are run repeatedly throughout the development process. Developers with the goal of discovering bugs perform unit tests before testers find the bugs.

- **Functional tests** These focus on making sure that features are present and functioning properly.

- **Check-in tests** These are quick, automated tests that developers perform before checking in code.

Additional testing includes:

- **Build verification tests** These are run after the daily build to verify that the product has been built successfully. Build verification tests are also often referred to as *smoke tests*.

- **Regression tests** These are automated tests that run after the daily build to ensure that the code has not regressed in quality.

Following are examples of *usage testing* that might be done on a typical project:

- **Configuration tests** These confirm that a product runs on the target hardware and software.

- **Compatibility tests** These involve examining how a program interacts with other programs, potentially even previous versions of the principal program being tested.

- **Stress tests** These focus on pushing a product to its limits. Conditions tested include load memory capacity, potential for full disks, high network traffic, and high numbers of users.

- **Performance tests** These document how quickly the product performs. Configuration, compatibility, and stress testing may also play a role in performance testing.

- **Documentation and help file tests** These focus on errors in documentation and help files, including content defects as well as product deviations.

Alpha tests are the first internal uses of the product as a whole by external resources. *Beta tests* are product trials conducted by a subset of external users to discover issues that the product team did not find. Despite the widely held perception that all bugs are defects, *defects* are actually a class of bugs. On the other hand, a *bug* is any issue that arises from using the product being developed.

As we previously discussed, classifying bugs helps in identifying priorities and risks and to prepare the team to resolve the bugs. *Severity* and *priority* are the two main issues for classifying bugs. *Severity* relates to the impact of the bug on the overall product if the bug is not fixed; *priority* is simply the team's measure of the bug's importance to product stability.

Typical severity-level classifications are:

- **Severity 1** System failure; a bug that causes the system to fail or risk total data loss.

- **Severity 2** Major problem; a bug that represents a serious defect in software function, but does not necessarily risk total system failure or data loss.

- **Severity 3** Minor problem; a bug that represents a defect in software function, but without much risk of lost data or work.

- **Severity 4** Trivial; a bug that represents a primarily cosmetic problem, which most users are unlikely to notice.

Typical priority-level classifications are:

- **Priority 1** Highest priority; with these "showstopping" bugs, the product cannot ship, and often, the team cannot achieve the next interim milestone.

- **Priority 2** High priority; with these major bugs, the product cannot ship, but the team may be able to achieve the next interim milestone.

- **Priority 3** Medium priority; with these bugs, the product can ship, and the team can also achieve interim milestones. These bugs are low enough in priority that they tend to be fixed only if there is enough time near the end of the project, and if fixing them does not create a significant risk.

- **Priority 4** Low priority; with these bugs, testers typically make enhancement requests. Bugs with such low priority are often negligible and not worth fixing.

Typically, a product cannot ship with known severity 1 or priority 1 bugs.

Resolving a bug is an interim step toward *closure,* which occurs only after a tester determines that fixing the bug did not create another problem. Closure also occurs if a tester determines that a particular bug is unlikely to surface again.

Bugs are typically resolved as:

- **Fixed** The developer has fixed the bug, tested the fix, checked in the code, assigned the fix to a release number, and assigned the bug back to the tester who reported it.

- **Duplicated** The bug reported is a duplicate of another bug already recorded in the bug database. The duplicate bug should be closed and linked to the original bug.

- **Postponed** The bug will not be fixed in the current release, but might be fixed in a subsequent one. This designation should be used when the team sees value in fixing the bug, but does not have the time or resources to correct it during the current release being tested.

- **By design** The behavior reported in a particular bug is intentional and acknowledged in the Functional Specification.

- **Can't reproduce** The developer can't verify the existence of the bug with any level of consistency.

- **Won't fix** The bug will not be fixed in the current release, because the team does not think fixing the bug is worth any effort.

Zero-Defect Mindset

As discussed earlier, a *zero-defect mindset* for the entire project team is a critical success factor for the product. Also, a zero-defect mindset represents the team's commitment to achieve a quality product, specifically by building the quality into the product at the time the team does the work.

Having a zero-defect mindset does not mean developing a product with absolutely no defects. The zero-defect mindset is simply a goal to which the team can aspire. Likewise, *zero-defect deliverables* do not necessarily have any defects, but do meet a predetermined quality bar. *Zero-defect milestones,* in turn, require the product to meet a predetermined level of quality before such milestones can be achieved.

The central benefit of a zero-defect mindset is that it gives quality a high priority and visibility in the project. Because high quality is a basic customer need, a by-product of the zero-defect mindset is a focus on meeting customer needs.

The Daily Build

Although it can be difficult to implement, executing a daily build provides great benefits. A daily build is simply compiling and integrating the application's source code into a deliverable executable. As the name implies, the daily build should occur every day. In practice, however, the daily build concept can be applied in a slightly longer time frame, but should not exceed a three- to four-day time period. In *Dynamics of Software Development*, Jim McCarthy notes:

> *It's easy to be delusional when you're creating software but, in the face of the daily build, much potential for fantasy is harmlessly discharged.*

One of the strengths of a daily build is that it's available publicly to anyone on the project team wanting to assess the progress of a project. This build indicates progress by identifying that the product is moving forward as a whole rather than simply in individual pieces.

The build provides the definitive status of team and product progress by allowing the team to examine the product holistically with little room for interpretation. As Jim McCarthy mentions in *Dynamics of Software Development*, the daily build serves as the heartbeat of the project:

> *If the daily build fails ... the 'heartbeat' monitors start to screech insistently demanding emergency attention.*

He continues by saying that a weak pulse indicates a struggling project, whereas a strong pulse serves to reassure the team.

The concept of a daily build has many benefits, but fundamentally, a daily build gives the product life during the development process. Another benefit of the daily build lies in the act of putting the product's pieces together while exposing elements that aren't working properly. Pieces that don't fit properly into the product highlight the product's integration issues. Building their own pieces into the product forces team members to synchronize their efforts.

Yet another benefit lies in having the team test each daily build to determine product status and quality. Team and customer morale improves when they see the product's progress from build to build. The frequency of daily builds can also benefit the team by enabling team members to pinpoint the source of a defect more efficiently. Frequent builds also enable team members to maintain synchronization more easily.

Summary

Although considered an art by many, learning to create and code great applications can be done. In the preceding chapters, we have discussed many techniques that teams can use during the Developing Phase. The actual Developing Phase uses these technologies to reach its Scope Complete Milestone.

The Scope Complete Milestone signifies that a team is ready to put the finishing touches on a product. All features will have been created; therefore, the team is now ready to move into the Stabilizing Phase. Through this phase, the team's risk management skills will continue to be exercised to help create the desired product.

Review

1. What are the seven deliverables of the Developing Phase?

2. What are interim product releases?

3. What are the benefits of interim product releases?

4. What are three ways a bug can be resolved?

5. When is a team ready to move to the Stabilizing Phase?

C A S E   S T U D Y   9

Developing RMS

"Alright, everyone, let's review. How are we doing?"

It was Monday, April 26th, and the team was one week into the Developing Phase. Other than the problem with the AutoCAD server, it had been a good week. Everyone had gotten their usual refreshments and taken their places around the conference table, and the Agenda Building item had been covered.

"How are we doing?" Dan repeated. "Let's take it by team roles, so we can look at each of our focuses as we go." He placed a transparency showing each team role and the focus it was to have during the Developing Phase on the overhead projector. Then he turned back to the group.

Product Management Report

"Jane, let's start with you. As Product Management, your focus is managing customer expectations, executing your communications plan, and getting ready for the first beta. How's all of that going?"

"Very well, actually," said Jane, turning to the checklist in her project binder. "I liked the way you put it last week when we kicked off the Developing Phase— 'making sure customers expect what they will get and that they get what they expect.' I've already run one update on the RMS project in our company newsletter, and we have an RMS page on the company intranet, linked off the IT section on the home page. Jim and I have sent memos to all the managers who will be using the administration client, telling them RMS is coming and giving them a rough idea of when to expect it and what to expect. I've also chosen two test groups for Bill and his folks to use: a small one for the first test pool and a larger one for the second."

There were nods of affirmation around the table as Dan said, "Sounds like you are right on schedule with your plan, Jane. Just one question: What are you doing about the lack of accounting functionality? I know there were a number of people in your own group looking forward to that, and they are bound to be disappointed."

FERGUSON AND BARDELL
ENGINEERING • ARCHITECTURE • PROJECT MANAGEMENT

The RMS Project
Meeting Agenda

Meeting Date: April 26, 1999   **Purpose:** Developing 3

I.   Agenda Building

II.   Update by Team Roles
   - Product Management
   - Program Management
   - User Education
   - Logistics
   - Development
   - Testing

III.   Q&A

IV.   Wrap-Up: Path-Forward Assignments

"We've met it head-on," said Jane emphatically. "I just didn't think any 'happy-face' talk would work, because most of these people have heard that sort of thing before and don't believe it when you try it. We simply told them that there wasn't time to put the accounting functionality in the first version, but that we will try to get it in the next version, which we hope will be out before the end of the year. Some of them were skeptical, but since we were already giving them more information than they had ever had before, they decided to reserve judgement." She turned to Bill. "We've got to deliver on Version 2, though, or our name is mud."

"Hey, I just work here," said Bill, holding up his hands. He gestured toward Dan. "Talk to the boss-man—he signs my check."

"Actually, Jane signs your check, with a stamp," said Dan with a chuckle. "Mine too, in fact. So I'd say Version 2 of RMS is a sure thing."

Jane laughed. "Glad to know who's really got the power in here," she said.

Program Management Report

"Moving right along," said Dan, looking at the transparency. "Program Management is me, and I also have three basic things on my plate during the Developing Phase: project tracking, team communication and coordination, and beta planning." Leaning on the conference table, he looked around the group. "Folks, I need some feedback here. I decided to change to one-on-one meetings with each of you instead of team meetings during the Developing Phase, with only a weekly team meeting to allow us to check our work. I was hoping that the one-on-one meetings would be more efficient and more effective, since I could focus exclusively on what one person was doing and not waste the time of the other team members.

"I've been meeting with each of you for a week, now, and I need to know if you have found it helpful. Do you prefer this change, or would you rather go back to always meeting as a group?"

Because no one wanted to be the first to respond, the group fell silent. Finally, Marta said, "I can't speak for the others, but I prefer the one-on-one meetings." Others in the room nodded in agreement as Marta continued. "I felt that the two meetings you and I had last week were very productive. I came out of them knowing much more clearly what you wanted out of my role on the team, and yet we took less time than the team meetings would have. I think it was a good change."

"I think I know why the one-on-one meetings work now, but wouldn't have worked earlier," Marilou said "When we were doing the Envisioning and the Planning Phases, we needed to be together to build a common vision and a common plan. We needed to hear each other's viewpoints, to make tradeoffs, to stir one another's creativity. We also needed to build a team spirit." She paused a moment, then continued. "Now that we're in the 'building' part of the project, we each have our own tasks. We don't necessarily need to be together to do this work. But we need to maintain that team spirit, and we need to affirm one another as we each slog through the work ahead. I think that the balance of one-on-one meetings and a weekly team meeting is just what we need during this phase of the project."

"Well-said," Bill agreed, without looking up from the table.

Tim added, "Your e-mail updates are also a good idea, since we aren't meeting together as much." He grinned. "It's a shame you can't send doughnuts through e-mail, though."

Dan smiled. "Next time I get a mailing from Microsoft, I'll see if that feature is scheduled for any future releases of Exchange."

User Education Report

He looked at the role list on the transparency. "I want to save Bill and Marta for last, so let's go to User Ed. Marilou, how's your work progressing?"

Looking in her project binder, Marilou said, "As you noted in our Developing Phase kick-off last week, Dan, my role is responsible for developing the elements of user support, like documentation and reference cards. I'm also responsible for doing product usability testing."

She pulled a small binder out of her bag. "Here is the beginning of the user documentation. I met with the development team last Friday. They walked me through what they had, and we did some screen captures. I worked on the documentation for those over the weekend." She turned to Bill. "Bill, I can't finish the documentation until you tell me we've got a freeze on the visual interfaces and give me the final screen shots. Is that going to happen soon?"

"I think so," he replied, looking at the project schedule in front of him. "We're supposed to be done with an alpha version this Wednesday. I'll check with the team to see if the interfaces will be frozen by then, and I'll send you an e-mail. If it is, we can get together Thursday morning."

Marilou nodded. "That'd be great."

Dan asked, "What about usability testing?"

"I'm working with Marta on writing some usability test scripts," said Marilou, "but we can't really finish until we get to the first beta." She looked at her notes. "I'm also working with you and Jane to plan the beta testing, which you already know."

Dan nodded. "Sounds good, Marilou. I'm glad you're doing the documentation, because you'll also be doing the user training for the managers. Jane showed me the documentation you did for some special classes, and I must say I'm impressed."

Logistics Management Report

He turned to Tim. "Let's jump to you, big boy. Have you helped take down any more servers?" He ducked as Tim threw a doughnut hole his way.

"No I haven't, and you can be sure I'm keeping Bill and all his minions as far from the production servers as possible," said Tim testily.

"What's this all about?" asked Jane.

"Just a lab class for our Network Manager and our Development Director, with a helping hand from your boss," said Dan, grinning. "I think everyone involved learned something, and that's all we need to say about it." Turning serious, he asked, "How is the new testing lab coming, anyway?"

"Well, we don't have the new machines in yet, but we've taken some spare equipment and moved it up there," Tim said. "And I've got one of my folks up there today doing some wiring and set up. If the new machines come in next week like we think, they should be up and ready for the first beta."

"Excellent, Tim. Hope the timing works out." Dan looked at his notes, then asked, "How is the operational support documentation coming?"

Tim looked stricken. "Oops … I knew there was something I'd forgotten." He said humbly, "Sorry, Dan—I haven't touched it."

Dan nodded. "That's OK, Tim; you've still got plenty of time, and actually, you can't do your documentation until the test system is up and running and the development team freezes the deployment." Making a note on his planner, he continued, "Assuming they hit their schedule, you'll need to have a draft of the support documentation in two weeks. Can you do that?" Tim nodded.

Development Report

Dan turned to Bill. "Okay, Chief, the floor's yours. Tell us how the actual work is going on the RMS application—or should I say applications?"

Bill opened the binder in front of him on the table. About 3 inches thick, it was divided into code listing, screen shots, and project plans and schedules. He pulled out a four-page Gantt chart covered with check marks and scribbles.

"Beth and Sam have been doing the bulk of the work on the project, but they've had some help from about four other people in the department. Basically, we've divided the work as follows: Beth is doing the business layer on the SQL side, the Win32 client in Visual Basic, and the Web-based Outlook interface. Sam is doing the business layer on the Exchange side, the database design and the data access layers, and the Web interface for the timesheets.

"Our order of work has been to design the SQL database first, then do all the business objects. Once we've got the business objects built, we could build outward in both directions at once, doing both the data access layer and the presentation or user layer. As of today, we've completed almost all of the business objects, and have some of the other objects done as well." He looked at Marilou. "The order of work we've chosen is why I can't be sure when we'll freeze the interface; it's one of the last things we do. What I can do, though, is see if Sam and Beth can do a good cut at the clients before they move to the data layer."

Marilou nodded, and Dan asked, "Have you made many changes to the design we did in the Planning Phase?"

"Nothing of great consequence," said Bill, flipping to another section of his binder. "The most significant changes have been new methods we've had to add that we didn't think of then. For example, managers approve timesheets. We had a method for employees to submit timesheets for approval, but nothing for a manager to ask for all submitted timesheets at once for review. So we added it and updated the design document."

"What about MTS?" asked Marilou. "Are you using very many transactions?"

"All over the business layer," Bill replied. "The basic rule is that anytime we write data, either new or changed, to the SQL database, we wrap it in a transaction."

"I know transactions in my area," said Jane, "but I'm not sure what MTS is."

"Microsoft Transaction Server," said Marilou, who then gave a short but effective explanation of transactions and their use in RMS. When she finished, Bill said, "That's twice this morning you've explained something so well that even I understood it, Marilou. You do pretty well for a trainer."

"That's *Ms.* Trainer to you, Chief," said Marilou with a grin.

"Don't forget, Bill," said Dan, "you and Ms. Trainer here are supposed to be working closely during the Developing Phase. I'm guessing by some of the comments this morning that she's somewhat out of the loop. Would that be true?"

Bill looked flustered. "I guess you would say that. I was just moving the work forward like I always have."

"I understand," said Dan calmly, "and I don't want to get in the way of the work. But, the reason User Ed is supposed to work with you is to accelerate both the production of the training and support materials and to shorten the feedback loop. Marilou's a pro, as you've already seen. She's not going to step on your toes, at least not unless they really need it, and even then I'd bet the end result will be a better product, which I know you want, Bill. When we get done today, get with Marilou and be sure she knows when your next team meetings are so she can attend."

Bill seemed all set for a retort, but taking note of the tone in Dan's voice, he sighed instead. "Sounds like just more bureaucracy to me, but since we're doing it by the book, we might as well go all the way with it."

"Thanks, Bill," said Dan. "You're right, I do want to do this exactly by the book, both as a training exercise and to prove to everyone that MSF can work. We can adjust it on future projects as we see the need; for now, though, we want to learn it the right way."

Testing Report

He looked at his notes. "I saved Testing for last, because I wanted to take some time to share with everyone else what we are doing here. Marta, why don't you outline what we are doing about testing RMS?"

Marta pulled some notes from her bag. "As most of you know, writing software is not something I have done a great deal of in the past, she said. "So, it was with some trepidation that I agreed to accept the Testing role on this team."

"We remember," Tim said dryly.

Marta continued, "Dan has given me some excellent coaching, and has also helped coordinate the relationship between the Testing role and the Development role. Additionally, Bill has been a big help, even though I'm not sure he has always agreed with my being on the team."

"Nothing personal, Marta," said Bill quickly. "You're a competent and intelligent worker, best as I can tell. I just think usability testing should be the responsibility of the development folks. But, since Dan sees it differently, I figured we might as well make the most of it."

"So what did the old curmudgeon do to help you out, Marta?" asked Tim with a grin.

"He and Dan came up with the idea of assigning a programmer to help me with the Testing role. This person is not one of the people working on building RMS, but is another member of the staff who acts as a technical assistant to me. I draw up the plans and am responsible for tracking the results and reporting to the team, while Mike—that's his name—helps with the actual testing. Or at least, the part of the testing that falls to us."

"I thought all testing was done by you," said Jane.

"Actually, no," said Marta. She turned to Dan. "I've prepared some transparencies that explain more of the process, if you don't mind."

"Not at all," said Dan. "It's all yours."

Marta described the difference between usage testing and coverage testing, and the subtypes of each. She explained that unit testing was the developers' responsibility, and that the developers were also doing functional tests. "Once they complete a feature set, though, they give it to us to validate that the function works," she said.

"How can they do that if not all the objects are complete?" asked Tim.

"They use stub procedures in the objects, which simply return without causing an error," Marta replied. "Sometimes they put in a message box, just so we know the stub actually got called. It's not as critical in RMS as it might be in a much larger project, because we'll be retesting everything when we do usage testing, and if we find anything then, the application is small enough that it won't be difficult to track down the offending object or component."

Tim looked at Bill. "Marta's got 'Build verification tests' listed, but I don't remember you or the others talking about doing daily builds. Are you?"

"Nope," said Bill, leaning back in his chair. "That's one of those ivory-tower things you read about, but very few development teams actually do. We tried it earlier this year on another project, and it became obvious very quickly that you have to adjust the frequency of builds to fit your project. For RMS, we're doing a build about every three days."

"And again," said Marta, "because the project is so small, we're not doing regression testing, either."

"Then what, exactly, is it that you and Mike are working on?" asked Jane. "I mean, it sounds like the developers are doing most of the work right now."

"They are," said Marta, smiling. "That's the approach we all decided on. If you remember, the Testing role doesn't really come to the forefront until the Stabilizing Phase. For now, we are preparing our test scripts as best we can, as well as running everything the developers give us through our test harness so we can get a head start on stress and performance testing. Mike and I are also working on our bug database."

Bill sat up straight. "Bug database? You hadn't mentioned that to me. What's that about?"

"Wait a minute, Bill, before we talk about bugs," said Dan. "I want to hear more about the test harness. Marta mentioned it in passing one day, but I want to hear the details. Then we'll learn about all the bugs in RMS."

"The test harness is pretty cool, I think," said Marta with a smile. "Mike wrote it over a weekend, and I was impressed, but he said it was not much different from others that were available. Basically, it is an automated component tester. We simply enter the name of the DLL, the method we want, any parameters it is expecting, and how many times we want it to be called in a row, and the test harness calls the component that many times and logs the results to a file. It also keeps track of things like memory usage, disk activity, and some other stuff, and writes those to the file after whatever number of repetitions we set. As long as we know the interface contract, we can test any object we want, automatically. Mike wants to expand it to test entire feature sets, but he hasn't had time yet. We've been testing all the components as the developers give them to us."

"Any problems yet?" asked Marilou.

"No, Bill's people seems to write pretty error-free code," said Marta.

"That's exactly right, and that's why you don't need any bug-tracking database!" said Bill heatedly. Glaring at Dan, he continued, "I think it's an insult to Sam, Beth, and the others working on RMS for Marta and Mike to even mention tracking bugs, much less to build a database to track them. Why, she herself said that she's getting error-free code!"

"Yes, but it's possible for code to be error-free and still contain bugs," said Dan.

Bill looked at the others as if to see whether they agreed that their leader had gone crazy. Then he turned back to Dan. "That's impossible! How can you have bugs in error-free code?"

"What's the definition of a bug?" Dan asked Marta.

"Any issue arising from the use of the product," Marta replied without hesitation.

"Is it necessarily a defect?"

"No, although it might be."

"What should be done about all such issues arising from the use of the product?"

"They should be reviewed and addressed prior to the release of the product."

"What are some examples of bugs that are not defects?"

Marta ticked the statements on her fingers as she spoke. "Enhancement requests; suggestions that are out of scope for the release; issues that arise over user preferences; and unavoidable design consequences."

"So you see, Bill," said Dan as he moved to the whiteboard, "you can write perfect, but not bug-free, code. It is the job of the Testing role, along with you and the rest of the RMS team, to deal with all issues in one way or another." Dan drew a circle on the board. "Here's the bug-tracking process. It's a lot like the risk-tracking process. It begins with the tester—Marta, Mike, one of us, one of the beta testers—reporting an issue. The issue gets entered into the database. As the development lead, Bill, you give it a priority rating and severity rating. You then assign the bug to a developer to resolve. Once the developer thinks the bug is resolved, he sends it back to the tester to see if it truly is resolved. If it is, the bug is retired. If it isn't, the tester reports it again and starts the process over." Dan turned to Marta. "Do you have the transparency that shows the priority and severity classifications?" She nodded and handed it to Dan, who put it on the overhead projector.

"As you can see, we classify all issues according to these ratings." He wrote the words *quality bar* on the board. "The quality bar is what the Testing role deems an acceptable quality for us to release the product. What is our quality bar for RMS, Marta?"

"No Severity 1 or 2 bugs and no Priority 1 or 2 bugs," said Marta without hesitation.

"So, as you can see," said Dan as he sat back down, "ultimately the Testing role determines whether or not we ship on time, or even at all. If the Testing folks say we haven't hit the mark, then we go back and do it again. It's a big responsibility, but it is the key to a quality product. That work begins during Developing, but finishes during Stabilizing. Any questions?"

"Just one," said Bill in a low tone. "What if we disagree with what Testing says? What if my people feel like they've hit the mark?"

"Then we bring it to the project team and we work it out here," said Dan evenly. "And remember, Bill, Testing's goal is the same as yours, and mine, and all of ours—to produce the very best application we can given the constraints we set in the beginning."

Problem Solving

Dan was sitting in his office when Bill poked his head in. "Knock, knock...anybody home?"

"Come on in," said Dan. "What's up, Chief?"

"I have an apology and a question," said Bill. "Do you have time for either?"

Dan moved out from behind his desk and took one of the two chairs facing it, then motioned for Bill to take the other. "Don't know about any need for an apology, Bill, but I always have time for my Director of Development. What's on your mind?"

Bill fidgeted for a moment, then said, "I want to apologize for some of my comments this morning. I think I was too gruff or blunt, as usual, and it wasn't called for."

"Apology accepted, Bill," said Dan, "although frankly, I'm not sure it was as bad as you seem to think."

"Probably because you're all getting used to it," said Bill with a dry laugh. "That doesn't make it right, though, and I felt like I needed to say something to you about it."

"So what's causing you to feel so tense, Chief? I would have thought that by now you would have realized that we're all on the same team."

"I do when I stop to think about it. Part of it is the new ways of doing things on this project, and part of it is the tight schedule we're working on. You said yourself that we're working under the gun. Now that we're actually building RMS, all of us in development are really feeling the heat, me especially. And that leads to my question."

"Shoot."

Bill hesitated, took a deep breath, and said, "You know we've got Beth and Sam as the primary developers on the project. Well, I've run into a problem that I don't know how to solve, and I want your advice."

Dan waited for Bill to continue. "I guess the best way to put it is that both Sam and Beth are slowing us up, but in different ways. I'm afraid if I don't figure out how to deal with them, we're going to miss our target dates."

Dan whistled. "That's a problem, all right. I'm glad you came to see me about it, although I certainly wouldn't have expected this. I mean, Sam and Beth are both excellent programmers. What sort of problem could make them both turn into stumbling blocks?"

"It's kind of strange, really," said Bill. "They are almost mirror images of each other. Let's start with Sam.

"Sam is an excellent programmer, with what I call a 'programmer's mind.' He usually comes up with creative solutions, ones that other programmers look at and realize they would never have thought of. That's his strong suit—his ability to find creative ways to solve the programming challenge. He just seems to sense intuitively how an app should fit together. As a result, he is also one of our fastest coders."

"So what's the problem?" asked Dan, puzzled.

"He's sloppy, plain and simple," said Bill. "Once he has figured out the proper algorithm, he just doesn't care about the grunge work of writing all the supporting code and such. He makes careless, stupid mistakes, then doesn't take the time to double-check his code. We're having to go back and clean up his work after he thinks it's finished, and it is slowing us down."

"I've known people like that at other companies," said Dan. "What's the problem with Beth, then? I have a hard time imagining her writing sloppy code."

"No, she writes immaculate code, and that's exactly the problem," said Bill. When he saw Dan's confusion, he continued, "She writes perfect code, Dan, but she takes forever to do it. She turns out one component for every four of Sam's. When she finishes her pieces of the project, they will be documented to the hilt and will have everything lined up perfectly and working smoothly—but she won't finish, at the rate she's going, until sometime in 2001. I just don't know what to do."

"Hmmm." Dan got up, walked over to the window and looked out for a moment. Then he turned and leaned against the windowsill. "You know, Bill, this isn't unusual. Programmers often fall into one of these camps—either the creative genius too busy writing code to be bothered with details, or the detail-oriented by-the-book type who writes more comments than code and is scared to let his or her creative juices loose. The key, of course, is to get them to cross-pollinate." He thought a moment more, then snapped his fingers. "That's it!"

"What's it?"

"Cross-pollination, of course. It's the only way."

"I don't know, Dan," said Bill, "I think Sam may already have a girlfriend."

"No, not like that," said Dan, laughing. "I mean we've got to get their good habits to rub off on each other, while at the same time keeping the bad habits in check. Here's what you do." Dan outlined his plan.

Bill looked at him in admiration. "You know, that's one of the best ideas I've ever heard. I've always wanted to do something like it, but I never would have thought of it in just this way. I see now why those IT folks at your old firm thought so highly of you."

Dan looked surprised. "How do you know what they think of me?"

Bill smiled as he rose to leave. "You're not the only one with contacts in other companies, you know."

Regression Testing

"Come on in, both of you," said Dan. Marta and Mike walked into his office and sat at the small conference table as Dan brought his notepad over and joined them. "How is the testing going, Marta?"

"Well, here is the chart showing all the items to be tested and the results," said Marta as she handed Dan a number of pages stapled together.

"Wow, this is impressive, Marta," exclaimed Dan as he perused the various pages. "How did you produce this? It looks like an Access report."

"It is, sir," said Mike. "As we put more and more pieces through the test harness, and as we began testing features, it was getting too confusing tracking them on paper or on a whiteboard. So, I built a simple Access database. Also, I modified the test harness to write the final results of its tests directly to the Access database, so that we can compare results over time if we test something more than once."

"Cheap regression testing—good idea," commented Dan approvingly. "I see you've also listed your target metrics."

"Yes, it didn't seem prudent to do any sort of performance testing without also having something to compare against."

Dan continued looking through the numbers and notes, taking in the various tests and their results. He suddenly stopped and looked up at Marta. "What is this circled test on page four? It looks like a pretty significant miss of the mark."

"That's the problem we want to talk with you about, Dan. The test you're looking at is the new method Bill mentioned at our last full team meeting. Remember, the one about listing timesheets to be reviewed?"

Dan nodded. "Sure, I remember. Didn't seem like any big deal at the time. What's this performance gap I think I see, if I'm reading the chart correctly?"

Marta shifted uncomfortably in her chair, and then looked at Mike. "Why don't you explain it, Mike? I don't want to let my lack of understanding get someone else in trouble."

Before Mike could say anything, Dan said, "No, Marta, you're the head of Testing, and it's your job to present the problem calmly and clearly so we can deal with it. If you've mistested, we'll find that out only by examining the problem directly. And if you're right, you've done your job and kept us from delivering a bad product. So, you tell me, not Mike. What's the problem here?"

Marta took the chart and pointed to the last set of numbers. "When we started doing the testing, we didn't set metrics for individual objects, we just recorded the results. When we started testing features, though, Mike and I set target metrics for response time, based on what we thought was reasonable."

"Sounds good to me. Go on."

"For the feature of calling up all the timesheets to be reviewed, we set a target metric of 5 seconds for the record set to appear. That's the number you see in this column."

"Got it. Then this next number must be the result of the test, correct?"

Marta nodded. "That's right. As you can see, the result set came back in approximately 2 seconds."

Dan looked confused. "So what's the problem? They hit the metric with room to spare. I must be missing something."

Mike shook his head. "No, sir, you're not missing anything; there's another test we haven't told you about yet."

Dan smiled. "In other words, 'shut up and let us finish.'"

Mike grinned. "I wasn't going to put it that way, but as usual, you have correctly assessed the situation."

Dan laughed out loud. "I've been accused of having some politician in me, Mike, but I believe you have me beat. Alright, I'll be quiet, and you tell me about the other test."

Marta took control of the conversation again. "The results for the first test are based on the test data Bill and his team are using in their daily work, Dan. Mike and I wondered, though, what might happen with a larger data set. After all, Ferguson and Bardell has over 800 employees, so a year's worth of timesheets comes to over 40,000 rows of header information, not to mention the individual timesheet line items. We decided to find out."

"So," continued Mike, "I created a copy of the SQL database, then created about 30,000 sample timesheets with some random data in each one. Took me about an hour to figure out how to do it so that I could guarantee enough randomness to make the tests meaningful. Then, we tested the feature against the substitute database."

"And," concluded Marta, "the results were different. Significantly so, in fact. That's the number you see in the last column."

"Fifteen seconds?!" Dan couldn't believe his eyes. "That's horrendous! Why, with response like that, some of our users will assume their machine is locked up and reboot it. We can't live with that." He stopped and looked at Marta. "But, I still don't understand why this is your problem. It seems to me that this is a problem for Bill's crew."

Marta looked even more troubled. "It would be, if they were willing to accept it."

"Ah, I see," said Dan quietly. He paused a moment, then asked, "So which is it, they deny the results are valid or they think the metric is unrealistic?"

"Both," said Mike, his shoulders slumping slightly. "Even after I explained the testing procedure to Sam, he said I didn't know what I was talking about. They claim that the metric should be more like 10 seconds, and that the new machine we'll be using for SQL Server will get the results down to that."

Dan thought for a minute, then said, "I think a 10-second response time is at the outer limits of acceptable, especially when you consider that we'll be at 1200 employees by this time next year. Their comment about the new server, though, may be valid." He sat back in his chair, his chin on his chest, thinking through options. Finally, he said, "Here's what I would do if I were you." Picking up his notepad, he listed several steps for them to take. When he finished, he turned to Marta. "Do these make sense to you? Do you think they will work for you?"

She looked at the list dejectedly. "We can try them. I'm not sure what Bill will do, though."

"He's not a crazed grizzly, Marta; he's just a protective mama bear who looks out for his cubs. Show him the truth, though, and he will come around. Just ignore the growling."

Scope Complete Milestone

"Wow, eclairs!"

Tim moved straight to the credenza and grabbed a pastry in each hand. "What's the occasion, boss-man? You finally break 100 hitting the little ball with the big stick?"

"No, Doughnut Dude, that's not it at all, even though I *did* break 100 last weekend," said Dan as the rest of the team gathered in the big conference room.

Jane snorted. "Aren't you awake yet, Tim, or have you really forgotten that today is the Scope Complete Milestone meeting?"

Tim exclaimed, "Whoa, that's right! I did forget." As Bill came into the room, Tim thrust an eclair at him. "Congratulations, Chief!"

Bill looked at the mangled pastry in disgust while the rest of the group laughed. "No thanks, Tim; you eat mine for me. Looks like you've already got a good start on it."

"Don't mind if I do." Tim downed the eclair in one bite.

"Alright, everyone, let's get started. Dan looked at the agenda in front of him. "As usual, the first item is Agenda Building. Does anyone have anything to add today?"

FERGUSON AND BARDELL
ENGINEERING • ARCHITECTURE • PROJECT MANAGEMENT

The RMS Project
Meeting Agenda

Meeting Date: May 7, 1999   **Purpose:** Scope Complete Milestone

I.   Agenda Building

II.   Review of Releases
   • Alpha release
   • Beta release

III.   Review of Deliverables

IV.   Review and Agreement on Key Points

V.   Go/No-Go decision

VI.   Q&A

VII.   Wrap-Up: Path-Forward Assignments

CHICAGO • DETROIT • MILWAUKEE • CINCINNATI • INDIANAPOLIS • LOUISVILLE

"I do," said Bill quietly. "I've got something I'd like to say when we finish the agenda today."

"Alright, Bill," said Dan as he added Bill's name to the bottom of the page, thinking, "I wonder what that's about."

While all attendees opened their project binders, Dan continued. "As Jane has already noted, today is supposed to be the day we hit the Scope Complete Milestone. Let's begin by reviewing the two internal releases we've done."

The team spent about 30 minutes discussing the alpha and beta releases of RMS. The alpha had been distributed only to members of the project team, and the beta had been released to a small group of users enlisted by Jane and Marilou. Overall, both releases had gone well, with the beta release revealing some especially important issues to be addressed.

"You know, Dan, that was sort of sneaky, what you had Marta do with the beta," said Bill, looking up at Dan with a slight smile. Marta looked at Bill, uncertain where this was going.

"What do you mean, Bill?" said Dan innocently, even though he knew exactly what Bill was referring to. "I don't recall doing anything sneaky."

"Oh, *you* didn't do it," replied Bill. He looked at Marta as he said, "You just had her and Mike do it."

"Well, Bill, it seemed to be the only way to get you and Sam to realize Marta was right," said Dan. He was wondering whether Bill was about to deliver some sort of angry declamation or biting commentary, when Bill grinned somewhat ruefully and said, "Well, it certainly was effective. Got my attention, as well as Sam's. Pretty effective, yes sir."

"Would somebody clue the rest of us in on this big trick Dan had Marta pull on you?" asked Jane.

Dan and Marta both started to explain, but Bill cut them off. "Here's the scoop. Marta and Mike, in one of their tests, thought they found some response times that were below standard, especially in the timesheet review feature. They tried to tell Sam and me about them, but we blew them off, saying that their metric was unreasonable and that a better box would take care of it. So, they bided their time until the beta pilot group was working with the Win32 client, and then they sprang their trap."

"It wasn't a trap," said Dan. "We just wanted the beta to be as realistic as possible."

"Well, it certainly was realistic, down to the phone calls and e-mails I started getting!" said Bill with that same rueful smile. "After we had installed the beta RMS app on the pilot group's machines, Marta, Mike, and Tim switched the back-end SQL database to one they had prepared with 50,000 timesheets in it.

The response time blew up to about 13 seconds, and the users blew up at Sam and me."

"What about the faster box as the answer?" asked Jane.

"They took care of that, too," said Bill. "I went over to complain, thinking they were still using that P-100 we'd been testing with. Turns out Dan had called in a favor from our hardware guy, and he'd brought over a brand-new quad processor box that was four or five times the box we had originally spec'ed. So, it clearly wasn't the box. Sam and I had to admit that the response time was too slow, and the code was the problem."

"I'm really sorry, Bill, but I just couldn't see any other way to convince you," said Marta, obviously distraught.

Bill scowled. "Now you listen here, young lady. You did exactly what you should have done. Sometimes the only way to convince a hard-head like me is to let me lie in the bed I've made. Don't ever apologize for doing your job." He paused, then continued, "Reminds me of when I helped put in one of the first real-time gunnery computers. We had a gunnery chief who didn't trust these new-fangled devices and always argued with us when we showed him the gunnery numbers the computer put out. One day we ran the computation, and he told us we were wrong and we were tired of his attitude. So I asked him which numbers he wanted us to use, his or the computer's. Of course, he was on the spot, so the only thing he could say was to use his numbers. We overshot the target so badly we almost hit a destroyer." Bill laughed at the memory. "He realized his stubbornness came close to causing a catastrophe. He's not the only sea dog who needed to learn that lesson."

Jane smiled and patted Bill on the arm. "At least you learned it."

"Enough mushy stuff, said Tim. "I want to hear what happened next!"

Bill laughed. "Well, after Sam and I each got an earful from every one of the beta testers, we decided we'd better look at the code. Turned out, in his hurry he had used a particularly inefficient method of getting the record set. It didn't show up with a small table, but popped right up whenever the table grew beyond 10,000 rows. He changed the way the method worked, and the response time dropped to under 5 seconds."

Everyone clapped as Bill shook hands with Marta, who was obviously relieved. "I'm sure glad that turned out as well as it did," she said. "Now I've got a question for you, Bill.

"Mike and I noticed that at one point Sam was turning out code much faster than Beth, but that it wasn't always very good code. Some of our test harness trials failed, and it was almost always Sam's code that was the culprit. Then, we began to notice a change, until by last week Beth had caught up to Sam in quantity and Sam had almost caught Beth in quality. What happened?"

Bill and Dan exchanged looks. "Sorry, professional management secret," said Dan. "No can share. That's why Bill and I get paid the big bucks."

"Hey, no fair!" exclaimed Tim. "I want the big bucks too; remember, I'm the one with the student loans that I'll be repaying till 2020! Cough it up, guys."

Bill leaned forward conspiratorially. "Two words, Tim: *code review.*"

"Code review?" said Marilou. "I thought we talked about a third-party review and decided we didn't have the time."

"I didn't say third-party, did I?" replied Bill. "This was second-party review." Then he chuckled. "Actually, it was Dan's idea. And it worked like a charm."

"Very simple, really," said Dan. "I told Bill to have Sam and Beth start each day by reviewing each other's code from the day before. Beth saw how much more code Sam was turning out, and her output picked up immediately. Sam saw how much cleaner and mistake-free Beth's code was, and his quality started picking up. Neither wanted to be shown up by the other. In the end, we included the code written by the other contributors to the project, and rotated the reviews. It didn't add that much time to the project, and it greatly improved both quantity and quality." He looked at Bill and said, "Of course, it only worked because we have good people working in development, who want to do the best work they can. That's a commentary on their manager and his ability to hire, train, and retain good workers."

Bill nodded his thanks. "So, are we there? Have we hit Scope Complete?"

Dan moved to the overhead and said, "Let's look at the deliverables and the objectives and see if we're there." The team worked through the deliverables list, checking off each one as the documents were placed on the conference table. Finally, Dan said, "OK, it looks as if we've covered all the deliverables. How about the objectives? Can someone call them out so we can see if we agree on them?"

Jane began. "Agreement on the planned feature set, and whether or not it has actually been developed." She picked up the revised Functional Spec and read off each feature set. The team discussed whether they and the users agreed that the feature set should be part of Version 1, and whether or not the beta reflected the feature appropriately.

When they had worked through all the feature sets, Dan said, "Alright, it looks like we feel the current version hits all the feature sets. Now what, Jane?"

Jane looked at her notes. "Baseline materials to support user performance."

"How about it, Marilou and Jane?" asked Dan. "Have we got all we need to support the users?"

Marilou nodded. "I was worried about it at first, because it looked like I would never get a frozen user interface to work from. But when you put me into the dev team meetings, I was able to start getting what I needed sooner, and in the end we hit the schedule, although it was close."

"Good," said Dan. "I'm glad that worked out." He turned to Tim. "What about you, Tim? Are you and your staff ready to roll out all the pieces of RMS?"

Tim nodded. "Yes, we've got a pretty good set of support documents, if I do say so myself. And of course, the incident with the AutoCAD server pushed us to another level of professionalism as far as test beds and production servers are concerned. We have added a number of topics to our overall network management notebooks, and my staff is much more aware of the logistics issues involved in rolling out a new application. I think we're ready for the next phase."

"Which leads us," said Jane, "to the last point: the stabilization process, including application pilots and additional testing."

"And that means Marta and Tim," said Dan. "Are you both ready for the next phase, since you two drive that phase together?"

Marta nodded. "I wouldn't have believed it when we started, but I actually feel confident about our testing methodology, and I also feel confident in my grasp of the issues. Tim and I have already met to plan the work, and we believe we are ready."

"Excellent," said Dan as he closed his notebook. He looked at the team members one by one. "The final mark of the Scope Complete Milestone is that we have a product that is ready for testing and has no additional feature code to be written. It may have bugs, as we discussed earlier, but there is nothing standing in the way of handing it over to the stabilizing crew. Are we there?"

Each person nodded, and Bill said, "I think we've written a very strong version. Sam, Beth, and I agree that we're ready to hand it off. In fact," he continued as he reached into his bag and brought out a CD-ROM, "we burned a final copy of the Win32 client last night for Marta and Tim. It isn't the final release, yet, but it's looking pretty golden to us." He handed it to Marta and said, "Test it in good health."

"Thanks, Bill. Here's hoping we don't find anything that needs changing."

"If you do, don't hesitate to come right to us and tell us. We don't want to hit any destroyers." Bill turned to Dan. "I asked for a moment at the end of the agenda. Are we done?"

Dan started to nod, but Jane interrupted him. "Wait a minute. We can't be done with this milestone. Our customer isn't here for it."

"That's right," said Marilou, "no Jim. Where is he, anyway?"

"I forgot to tell you," said Dan. "He and I met yesterday afternoon late, and we went over the same points that we just went over this morning. He had already seen the beta, and feels that it meets the aims and goals for Version 1. He told me he thought it was good to go, but that the final decision was up to us this morning."

"Sounds like the trust level is going up," said Tim. "That's a good thing, I think."

"In fact," replied Dan, "Jim specifically said that if we were satisfied with it, especially Bill and I, that was good enough for him."

"And that leads to my item," said Bill. He looked at the members of the team before he continued. "As you all know, I've been pretty much of a naysayer throughout this whole process. I thought the MSF thing was just a bunch of needless overhead, and I resented having non-programmers involved in a development project. Well, I was wrong."

He paused as if to let that statement sink in for a moment, and then continued. "In the beginning, Dan said that his goal was to make the development department look good. It remains to be seen whether that comes to pass. But what I'm convinced of, now, is that doing development this way ensures we won't look *bad*. The Envisioning Phase makes sure we build what the user really needs. The Planning Phase helps us be realistic about that and not make promises we can't keep. And doing the Developing Phase as we have, with a team working together to cover all the bases, has kept us from making a big code boo-boo that wouldn't have shown up until about a year from now, when we hit table sizes as big as we tested for last week. The long and the short of it is, I've seen how this process keeps my folks and me from failing. That is worth a lot to me. If we look good when it's over, that will just be icing on the cake."

After a moment of silence, Dan said, "Bill, thanks for those comments. I had never thought about it, but I think you are exactly right. Doing development this way is a good insurance policy. My goal, though, is still to make you and your people the heroes when we're done. We'll see if we hit that goal."

Leaning back in his chair, Tim said, "Well, all this feel-good talk reminds me of eclairs—mushy and sweet! Mmmphh!" Tim shoved the last eclair into his mouth.

P A R T   4

Shipping the Product

C H A P T E R   1 3

Product Stabilization

About This Chapter

In this chapter, we will discuss the Stabilizing Phase of the MSF Development Process, and how the team must move from the earlier phases of product creation to the final stages of shipping the product.

The final stages of shipping a product can often be summarized by Charles Dickens' comment, "These are the times that try men's souls." We will discuss the evolutionary cycle the team will progress through to move from the Developing Phase's Scope Complete Milestone to the Stabilizing Phase's Release Milestone. We summarize this phase's effort as four primary steps: fix the bugs, synchronize all product deliverables, ship the release, and extensively test the release. Leading up to the Release Milestone, we identify several key interim milestones that are reached by the continual iteration of these steps.

This chapter also covers some guidelines for the deployment of an application after the product is released. From the preplanning phases though pilot testing, support, and troubleshooting, we explore efficient ways to get the application to users with as little negative impact as possible on them, their systems, and networks.

The principles and guidelines provided in this chapter are based on our own experiences with creating application architectures and implementing enterprise applications, as well as on the following resources:

- Microsoft Solutions Framework
- *Microsoft Windows 98 Resource Kit*
- Microsoft white paper *Technical Overview: Clustering and Windows NT Load Balancing Services (WLBS)*
- Microsoft Official Courseware *Administering Systems Management Server 2.0*, course #827a

Upon completion, you will be able to:

- Understand each team role's responsibilities in shipping the final release.
- Identify the steps in the process of stabilizing an application.
- Understand the incremental process of shipping the right product.
- Identify the deliverables for a Final Product release.
- Understand methods for deploying a product.
- List some of the tools that facilitate the deployment process.

Overview of Stabilization

Once the team has completed the product's source code with the Developing Phase's Scope Complete Milestone, the Stabilizing Phase must prepare the product for release to the customer. As mentioned in Chapter 12, the Developing Phase's Scope Complete Milestone product release is a product that has implemented all product features and completed basic functional testing. Although the team has been focused on shipping the right product at the right time throughout the project, the team should become acutely aware of this during the Stabilizing Phase. Figure 13.1 illustrates that the Stabilizing Phase is when the product must be completed in order to reach the Release Milestone.

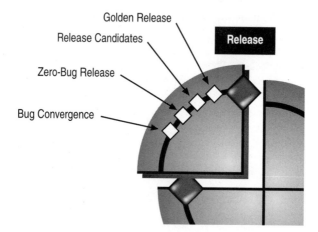

Figure 13.1   The Stabilizing Phase and Product Release milestone

During the Stabilizing Phase, the team may ship multiple external product releases while driving toward the final product release. During these interim releases, the team will primarily focus on testing to identify bugs, and fixing the bugs that are identified. A significant interim milestone that signifies the team is getting close to releasing a product is generally referred to as the zero-bug release (ZBR). ZBR is the first interim product release in which all active bugs have been resolved in some manner, whether fixed, postponed, or deemed unimportant. Once an interim release is shipped, extensive testing must occur to determine whether the product is ready, at which point the team can declare victory and classify the release as the Final Product Release.

The Stabilizing Phase is also characterized by the completion of all the other product support elements, including user performance artifacts, installation and configuration guides, and operations support staff training programs. These artifacts and processes must also be tested and released before the product can be released. Only after all the application code and related materials are ready for release can the team say they have reached their goal of shipping the right product at the right time.

Stabilization Process

The stabilization process is completed, as are the other phases of the project, by the entire project team. Each team member must execute his or her responsibilities with the primary goal of shipping the product. The somewhat frantic final days of the development process, when the team is pushing very hard to get the product out the door, is often referred to as the *end-game*. Within project teams, many stories can be related about activities and heroics during this end-game crunch time, which demonstrate the team's complete commitment to releasing the product.

Unlike the other phases of the development process, this phase is not characterized by the action steps; rather, it is characterized by the interim releases. The same steps are repeated within each interim release: fix the bugs, synchronize all product deliverables, ship the release, and extensively test the release. Eventually, the team will determine that a release is ready for prime time, and that will be the Final Product Release.

Who Does What During Stabilization?

Although the team works together to achieve the Release Milestone that marks the end of the Stabilizing Phase, individual team roles have their own focuses during this phase. Because the primary emphasis is on shipping the release, every role focuses on something to do with shipping the product.

Table 13.1 identifies some specific team role responsibilities for the Stabilizing Phase. The lead for each team role ensures that these responsibilities are carried out and communicates with the rest of the project team.

Table 13.1   Team roles and Stabilizing Phase responsibilities

Role	Responsibilities
Product Management	Coordinate interim product releases with the customer. Plan for the Product Launch.
Program Management	Manage Beta and Pilot product releases. Maintain the project schedule. Drive the sign-off process from the customer along with the operations and support groups for the final product release.
Development	Focus on finding, reporting and fixing bugs. Ensure product integration is completed and succesfully tested.
User Education	Ensure the user support materials are ready to ship. Designate and coordinate trainers and user training for the interim release sites. Designate and coordinate trainers and training for product release with the customer, end users, operations, and support groups.
Testing	Execute the test plan. Find, report, and classify the application bugs. Close bugs and verify they are properly resolved. Heighten focus on usability, installation, and configuration testing.
Logistics Management	Interim product release installation, configuration, deployment, and support. Plan released product deployment. Provide training to the operations and support groups, including the Help Desk team.

Interim Milestones

Unlike the previous phases that can be characterized by steps, the Stabilizing Phase is better characterized by its interim milestones. Each interim milestone functions as a product release. These product releases continue in an iterative fashion until the team determines that the final product release has been created. At each of these interim releases, the team synchronizes and ships all the product deliverables. With each successive interim release, the product is tested, bugs are tracked, and corrections are made. The final product release decision is a shared responsibility across the project team leads, the customer, and the operations and support groups.

Milestone #1: Interim Releases as Bugs Converge

As discussed in Chapter 12, the team can release the interim product releases to portions of the user community to provide additional testing. During the Stabilizing Phase, the team should see a downward trend in the number of reported bugs. This downward trend signifies that the application is becoming more stable. Although there are often peaks and valleys in the number of reported bugs, overall the team should see a downward trend that is manifested over time, not necessarily at each fixed point in time.

Milestone #2: Zero-Bug Release

ZBR is the first point in the project when the development team finally catches up to the testing team, and there are no active bugs, or no bug is active for more than a specified length of time (usually 72 hours). It is to be expected that the bug count will increase after this product release, but the development team will continue to fight to get to ZBR with each successive interim product release. Reaching ZBR is a strong indication that the team is in the final stages of shipping the product, and the end-game is in full swing.

Milestone #3: Release Candidates

When the team thinks the product is potentially ready for final release, a release candidate is built. Each release candidate includes all the elements required in a shippable product, and has no active bugs. The team will perform highly intensive testing against the release candidate to flush out any final show-stopping bugs. This intensive testing determines whether the release candidate will become the final product release, or if the team must generate a new release candidate with the appropriate fixes. It is unlikely that the first release candidate will be the one that ships, as show-stopping bugs are often found in the first release candidates.

Milestone #4: Final Product Release

The final product release is the release candidate that all the key stakeholders, team members, and customers agree is the version that will be shipped. This is the release that is shipped in the box, and on which no further development or testing is conducted. Determining which release is the final product release is a difficult decision. Ultimately the answer is about shipping the right product at the right time. Does this product fully meet the needs of the customer? Other key release considerations are the bug report data, the results of the release candidate testing, and the supportability of the product. As with most major decisions, there are many inherent risks, but the decision will be made as a team effort.

Ongoing Risk Management Process

During the initial phase of deployment planning, it's essential to identify possible risks, anticipate how they might affect the deployment, and explore mitigation measures. Successfully identifying these risks helps the team avoid delays and feel prepared to face potential complications.

It's important to review and update the Master Risk Assessment Document during each phase of development because, over time, new risks come to the fore while others recede. Table 13.2 is a simplified example of the type of risk matrix that might be developed in connection with the deployment process.

Table 13.2   Sample deployment risk management matrix

Description	Risk impact	Risk probability	Mitigation
If the Help Desk is understaffed, overtaxed, or undertrained, the deployment timeline will be affected.	Medium	High	To minimize the effect on the deployment, either slow it down to reduce the load on the Help Desk or increase the Help Desk staff. Proper training on deployment issues will reduce the time it takes them to handle individual calls, reducing their load.
If the support staff is understaffed, overtaxed, or undertrained, the product release and its subsequent deployment will be affected.	Medium	High	To minimize the effect on the deployment, either slow it down to reduce the load on the support staff or increase the support staff. Proper training on deployment issues will reduce the time it takes them to handle individual user issues, reducing their load.
If members of the logistics team do not have the authority to make changes to the deployment or the application, the deployment timeline will be lengthened.	High	Medium	Program Management will need to facilitate tradeoffs between the logistics team and the development team in order to effect changes to the application.
If network connectivity between the distribution servers becomes inoperable, the deployment will cease.	Medium	Low	To ensure distribution of the source code to the distribution servers, the connection must be corrected. Alternatively, the source code could be distributed via CD-ROM.
If network connectivity between the distribution server and the users becomes inoperable, the deployment will cease.	Medium	Low	To ensure deployment of the application, the connection must be corrected. Alternatively, a CD-ROM deployment method could be used.
If the server load from the deployment is too high, the installation timeframe per installation can become unacceptable.	Medium	Low	To reduce installation time and return the number of daily deployments to the client machines.
If users have difficulty with the new application, its usage will decrease.	Low	High	To reduce users' frustrations with the new application, increase the amount of training or the type of training systems.

Release Milestone and Its Deliverables

Achieving the Release Milestone is the final goal for the project team. It marks the point where the team has finished all work on the product, so the product, product elements, and product artifacts are ready to be shipped. This is also the transition point at which the team relinquishes ownership of the application and the operations and support organization takes over for deployment, maintenance, and ongoing product support. At the project level, the Release Milestone signifies that the team has accomplished the project-level vision for the product. Don't forget, this milestone is also a time for celebration—the goal has been reached.

When the Stabilizing Phase is complete, the project team reaches the Release milestone. The deliverables of this milestone provide valuable information for the deployment and use of the application in the production environment.

The six deliverables required to meet the Release Milestone are:

- **Final product release** The source code and executables, as described above.
- **Product release notes** The documents containing release information and late changes.
- **User and support performance artifacts** The final release of supporting information.
- **Testing results** The bug status and database for future projects.
- **Project archives** All relevant product information created during the development process, whether or not it shipped with the product.
- **Project documents** All stages of the product documentation including the major milestone releases.

Release Notes

Every product seems to have a set of last-minute changes or issues that the customer, user, and their support teams should be aware of. Creating a simple document that outlines these issues and acts to communicate important application or compatibility issues can help to alleviate problems that may be encountered by the product deployment team.

User and Support Performance Artifacts

The user performance artifacts can take many forms such as Help files, wizards, how-to guides, and training materials. The primary focus of these user performance artifacts is twofold: to prepare the user community for the product release, and to assist the user community after the product release. Creating and releasing a product that the user does not know how to use, does not know how to learn to use, and does not know who to learn from can turn even the most successful project into a disaster. The following sections discuss some of the primary responsibilities of the User Education team:

Application Documentation

The key to a well-accepted deployment lies in the documentation an organization provides for its users. The project team might want to announce in advance that the application is nearing completion and to give those curious users a location where they might find some preliminary material to read. It's crucial that documentation is in place and ready to be accessed when this location is announced. The documentation may be in paper form, or it may be posted on a Web site for easy accessibility.

It's a good idea to precede the full documentation with a page highlighting the application's main capabilities. When the project team is about a quarter of the way through deployment, it might want to post a Frequently Asked Questions (FAQ) document to the Web site. The FAQ should be updated on a regular basis. When compiling the FAQ, the team might want to ask users to submit samples of documents they intend to use with the application and then gear the FAQ to those samples. This involvement gives users a feeling of participation in the process.

Training and Training Documentation

As part of the stabilizing process, the project team can implement a training plan with documentation. This training may be self-paced training, formal classroom training, or informal one-on-one training, depending on the size of the deployment and the complexity of the application. Whether the initial training is formal or informal, additional training should follow after the user community has used the application.

Support Documentation

System documentation can have multiple parts, depending on the application. Server-based documentation may be required if the application consists of a database engine and data. This documentation can be broken down into specific documents containing the changes and updates to the installation, system configurations, and ongoing configuration. For example, a document describing the disaster recovery process for the database should be created. (Disaster recovery might consist of an automatic process that stops the database engine during low access periods and copies the data to a backup location.) It is also appropriate to document the usage of an enterprise utility to back up the database. Waiting until a failure to verify a backup and restoration plan is highly inadvisable.

Depending on the architecture of the application, tuning opportunities may arise on multi-tier systems as the application enters the production environment. These tuning parameters should be tested during the interim releases, and the tuning suggestions and methodology should be incorporated in the system documentation. The team should provide a matrix or table format in the documentation to summarize these tuning parameters.

Client documentation should also be created that contains the specifics of how the application installation on the client is performed and the default settings made during the installation. This support document should be created during the Developing Phase and finalized during the Stabilizing Phase. Any modifications to the default installation should be noted in this documentation. Additionally, for a multi-layer application, it may be advantageous to create a high-level document describing how the three layers interact.

Testing Results

The application's testing results should be collected and stored in a permanent archive. These results may be used to determine new features for new product versions, as well as to lend help to the support and maintenance teams.

Project Archives

The project's artifacts as well as the final deliverables for each product milestone should be permanently archived. These artifacts may be used to set guidelines for future projects and also to provide a historical record of this application's development process.

Product Deployment

A variety of deployment tools are available for presenting the application setup routine to the client workstation. Tools such as Microsoft Systems Management Server (SMS), logon scripts, e-mail distributions, and Web-based advertisements are available to aid in this process. The choice of the deployment tool depends on the application being deployed, the environment, the pace of deployment, and the expected skill level of the users. Each of these deployment methods will be discussed in detail later in this chapter.

Regardless of the deployment tools used to distribute the product, just as we discussed with developing the product, the deployment will fail unless it is planned properly. Creating a deployment plan and testing the plan before sending the product to the user community will help ensure a smooth transition for the product from the development process into the use and maintenance phases of the product's lifecycle.

Deploying the application by means of an e-mail distribution or Web-based advertisement requires somewhat more experienced users and a longer deployment timeline to allow each user to initialize the installation. Some methods allow for increasing user permissions on the local client more easily than others. If users have local administrative permissions or the computers are not tightly controlled, permissions are not an issue.

Using logon scripts to perform a deployment can be a very simple, effective, and quick method. This method does, however, require some interaction with users in that they need to log off and log on to initialize the script. This method also may not give users enough local permissions to perform the installation. If the local computer is not tightly controlled with permissions, logon scripts should work well.

Using SMS as the deployment method of choice eliminates some of the problems we've discussed. SMS does not require users to log off and log on to initialize the installation, as it takes care of the initialization itself. SMS can also modify users' local permissions to get around local client systems that may be locked. The need for users to understand the deployment process is minimized because the system administrator determines and controls the deployment process. SMS makes managing the distribution easier by automating issues such as the targeting and scheduling of the distribution and the notification of clients about the details of an upcoming release.

Planning the Product Deployment

In the deployment of any software application, there is some risk of incompatibility between the new application and a user's existing software, operating system configurations, or hardware drivers. Planning and testing of the application deployment are essential steps in the overall development process, forming the yardstick by which the success of the project can be measured.

Planning takes into consideration the human and technical resources needed to deploy the application, from staff who will support the users throughout the deployment period to the network circuits that will deliver the application source code to the client's workstation. The planning goal is to define the resources needed for all aspects of deployment, and to estimate as accurately as possible the usage and schedules of those resources.

Testing measures this usage in a controlled environment, such as a computer lab or a pilot group on the production network. The metrics collected from the testing may indicate a need to make adjustments to the resources for the actual deployment. Success in one or two areas of the deployment does not necessarily indicate overall success. For instance, an application setup routine may install flawlessly, but lack of experience on the part of users could create problems, such as an unacceptable load on the Help Desk support staff.

Planning and testing are invaluable processes that should not be skipped, because they always provide some insight into the deployment process.

Dealing with multifaceted and dispersed locations adds complexity to an application deployment. A deployment plan must be created that takes into account locations, organization, connection speeds, server load, and deployment timelines. For deployment, organizations and users should be categorized based on different structures such as physical location, departmental organization, and network topologies.

Location

Organizations and users are often categorized by physical location, but they can also be subdivided according to which server is used as their primary logon validation server.

The easiest system to plan for is a deployment that is based on physical location, whereby each location has its own logon validation and file server. This server can be used as the distribution point for the application to that location. When each physical location does not have its own file server, connection speeds must be evaluated to determine which server should be used for the application's distribution point.

The team must take great care to consolidate clients into distribution groups according to their location breakdown, and it needs to be aware of several issues when deploying an application to multiple physical locations. In the initial phase of deploying the application source code, the deployment can be limited to a small number of distribution points. In large-scale deployment, it's critical that the source code be sent to the application distribution points a minimum of one week before the deployment to clients. This lead time provides enough leeway to confirm that the source code arrived successfully at the distribution points and allows time for resending if necessary. Once the real deployment process begins, the team must take care to ensure that the application is deployed only to clients where the source code is available.

Organization

Organizing a deployment by department can create some additional complications during application deployment. A company may want to deploy an application to everyone in a department even if that department spans several physical locations and possibly several security domains. Careful deployment decisions must be made when dealing with such a situation. The department's clients should be grouped into multiple deployment groups based on their physical location and their application distribution server. It may even be necessary to break the target group into different client groups or different network connectivity groups. When the application is actually deployed, it's important that all the clients in all the department's groups receive the application within the same time frame. Before sending the application, the team should verify that each of the distribution sources is in place and that the connectivity to the various clients exists.

Connection Speeds

Connection speeds are probably the easiest item to overlook when deploying an application, but one of the most important items for ensuring a successful and timely application deployment. Two types of connections can significantly affect deployment:

- The connection speed between the original application source server and the remote application distribution points used by the actual deployment process.
- The connection speed between the distribution point and the client computers.

When planning the distribution of the source code from the original source location to the application distribution point, it's important to identify the slowest connection link. With proper planning, this distribution can take place at low network volume operating times and should have minimal effect on overall network operations. If network connection speeds are very slow, the source distribution should be planned for a weekend or an extended low-network-utilization period. If the application is large and the connections are extremely slow, we suggest that the code be distributed by an alternative method, such as a portable hard drive, CD-ROM image, or other large portable media.

Server Load

In conjunction with the connection speed, the team must consider the load that the deployment will create on distribution points. This load should be monitored to ensure that the normal daily tasks of the server can be carried out without degradation. Other items that might need to be compensated for are databases, domain controllers, e-mail servers, file servers, and Web servers.

As the number of connections to the application distribution point increases, the installation speed typically decreases. Having adequate processor speed, sufficient RAM, and adequate connection speed on the distribution servers can minimize this effect. To alleviate some load on the server, the number of deployments by the server can be reduced in specific time periods.

Deployment Timeline

When deploying a large application, the deployment timeline must be planned in detail and then modified based on testing. Gathering deployment and installation statistics during the initial stages of deployment testing is crucial in determining a realistic deployment timeline. These statistics should include:

- Connection speeds to the distribution points and from the distribution points to the clients.
- The distribution server load.
- The quantity of distributions during each phase of the deployment.

One source of information that is often overlooked is the volume of Help Desk calls generated by an application deployment. Some calls are simply for information about the deployment schedule and others are for instructional help. These calls need to be closely monitored to determine whether the deployment timeline is too aggressive or whether unforeseen issues are arising in the deployment process. A manageable volume of Help Desk calls is a positive sign that the deployment process can move forward and that the number of installations per time period can be increased.

Software, Data Setup, and Conversion

After the installation of the application has been verified, the users will need a way to migrate or convert existing data from earlier versions or from other data sources. This process will vary depending on the application, but many tools exist to facilitate migration and data conversion.

It is important to make the process as automated and painless as possible. Three methods to consider are:

- **Upward compatibility** The easiest migration is when the new application handles old data directly without any intervention. In this case, users simply open their old documents in the new application.

- **Common format** This method requires that the old data be saved in a format that both the old and new applications can handle. This process is usually straightforward once the common format is identified. Users can convert their files to this common format if their knowledge level and time allows, but it is sometimes more effective to create an automated process to convert all the files to the common format. (Automatic conversion may present a challenge if the files to be converted are dispersed among multiple servers and be even more of a challenge if they are dispersed among multiple workstations.)

- **Specialized application** An application can be created to convert old data to a format that the new application can handle. (The conversion application could perform double-duty by removing extraneous information from the old data files.) If the new application accesses databases or data warehouses, it may be useful to convert data from flat files, relational databases, and other formats using the Microsoft Data Transformation Services. This utility is provided with Microsoft SQL Server 7.0 and provides an easy way to convert, manipulate, and validate data being transferred from one data store to another. The data conversion destination is not limited to SQL Server databases, but can also handle third-party platform destinations.

During a managed deployment process, documents already opened in the new application may need to be used on a computer to which the new application has not yet been deployed. The best way to avoid this problem is to deploy the application on a department-by-department basis.

Whichever migration method is selected, its process must be clearly communicated to the users, especially if they are expected to complete the process on an as-needed basis.

Interim Product Release Deployment

In deploying the interim product releases, it should be assumed that the installation process itself has progressed to the point of zero defects. To have zero defects, the installation process must correctly identify and handle multiple versions of the operating systems that are used throughout the organization. The process must install the correct .dll files, .ini files, or other files required by each version of the application and the target user's desktop operating system. Care must be taken to deliver all of the correct files with each product release, as users testing the product must be able to receive subsequent releases to the same desktop computer.

In deploying the interim releases, the team must also test the interactions of the application with the applications already installed on the client's system. Troubleshooting in this area of deployment can be difficult because of the wide variety of applications being used, and separate testing is often required. Full testing of all the applications would take considerable time, and the team may find it necessary to prioritize, testing only the most widely used applications.

Previous product installations, along with the interim product release deployments, allow the team to forecast the load on the organization's support staff and Help Desk. This part of the deployment process directly affects how quickly and when deployment takes place. The team should allocate time for educating the support staff and Help Desk staff about how to assist in the deployment process and resolve simple issues. This education may be in the form of an instructional paper distributed to staff, or in a meeting to allow a two-way discussion about what to expect. Whichever means is used, it's critical to the success of the deployment that the Help Desk load be forecasted in advance, and that a team approach to the deployment be adopted.

By providing some training, a team can drastically reduce the number of support calls they receive and enhance users' acceptance of the deployment. Training users on the application helps separate the deployment installation questions from the application usage questions. It may even be possible to route support calls related to application-training issues separately from general support problems.

Deployment Methods

There are numerous way to deploy a product. We'll discuss several effective methods for product deployment such as Microsoft's Systems Management Server (SMS), logon script distribution, e-mail distribution, and Web-based distribution.

Systems Management Server

The most effective deployment system is SMS, which enables system administrators to handle the distribution and organization of the deployment in a controlled and preplanned manner. SMS also frees users of the responsibility of deployment, which can even be performed without the users' knowledge or intervention.

When building an SMS deployment system to handle a specific application, several factors must be considered. The extent of the deployment and the size of the application being deployed greatly affects the system and how it handles the distribution. A properly developed SMS system disperses distribution servers according to the location of the clients and the speed of the network. The process of building the deployment mechanism within an SMS system requires organization of the client systems into specific groups, based on features such as physical locality, department, or client operating systems. Figure 13.2 shows the flow of an application package and advertisement instructions from the master source at the SMS site server to a local distribution point source and the client access point. The targeted clients poll the client access point periodically and connect to install the package at the specified time.

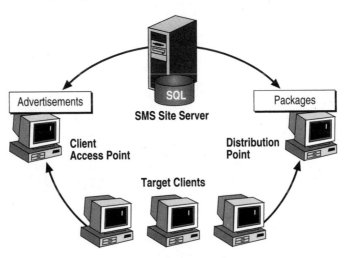

Figure 13.2   SMS software distribution process

During the testing phase of the SMS deployment system, a note should be made of the time required to distribute the application code from the source to the distribution points. It's highly recommended that a variety of speed connections be tested, from the fastest to the slowest. Collecting data during this test distribution helps to calculate the time that will be required to fully distribute the application source code. Testing multiple installations from the same distribution point is necessary in order to obtain the server load information. This data can be used to determine the total number of installations a distribution point can handle.

Another item worth evaluating during the testing process is how the test users react to the installation. This information can be helpful in estimating how many Help Desk calls to expect.

Logon Scripts for Deployment

Another method of distributing applications is via logon scripts. Logon scripts are effective in distributing applications to the general public, but some safeguards must be in place. Some factors to take into consideration when using logon scripts include:

- The possibility of repetitive installations.
- Whether the application installation requires only a single installation per computer or an installation for each user of the computer.
- How deployment to specific groups, other than those in Windows NT groups, should be controlled.
- Whether shortcuts need to be created at the user level for a machine-level installation.

The logon-script deployment of applications is primarily controlled by system administrators, but users must still log off and log on to receive the distribution. When creating the logon-script system, proper groupings and scripting conditions should be implemented. The installation script should be able to recognize the various client operating systems. Groupings should be created to control the deployment of the application. The application portion of the logon script should have the built-in intelligence to recognize whether the machine has previously been updated. The script should also handle the creation of user-level shortcuts, and recognize how to avoid multiple installations.

Testing of a logon-script deployment system is fairly straightforward in that users need to be added only to the testing group. After the group membership has been updated, the test users can log off and then log on to have the implementation take place. The script installation process should be logged to allow for intelligent modifications to the deployment script. Information should also be gathered to help determine whether additional load is created in the morning hours by the logon process and the typical high volume of system usage during this period.

E-Mail Distribution for Deployment

Another way to deploy applications that may be appropriate for some organizations is via e-mail. The following considerations are specific, though not necessarily unique, to deployment by e-mail:

- Using this form of deployment requires additional intelligence that must be built into the application installation package.

- The installation package must be able to determine the client operating system.

- The installation process must be able to accommodate multiple source servers.

- The e-mail system must be able to handle clients who are performing the task over a remote access server (RAS) or slow wide area network (WAN) connection.

- This form of deployment must also establish policies for installing applications across a dial-up networking connection that might be performed on personal home equipment.

- The application could also be created so that it is small enough to be contained within an e-mail message.

The one large flaw with using e-mail as a deployment method is that it relies on the user to initiate installation by opening the message. To circumvent this, the e-mail deployment system can be designed to automatically launch the installation, which would prevent cancellations caused by the user deleting the message.

During the testing phase of an e-mail deployment system, statistics should be gathered on the success of the installation, the likelihood or number of cancellations, and the time required to install. As with the logon-script system, an increased load will be experienced during the early morning hours because of new incoming e-mail.

Web-Based Deployment

Web-based deployment is another viable means of distributing applications. Like the other methods, this one needs to handle multiple distribution servers. This method also relies on users to check the Web location on a regular basis and then initialize the installation. If the application is needed and the knowledge level of users is adequate, a Web-based application may be the best option for an organization. The Web application page must be accessible to all employees who will need the application; creating a simple yet effective page that all users can understand is a key factor in the success of this method.

We suggest that the team work with users of varying skill levels to test a Web-based installation. Input from them on page layout and ease of use during the testing phase reduces the number of Help Desk calls. A logging system should be put in place to determine on which computers the application has been installed.

Production Support

Creating a load-balanced fault-tolerance system can increase the application's uptime.

Windows NT Load Balancing Service (WLBS) can be implemented to create redundancy and fault-tolerance in a Web-based database application system. WLBS allows front-end Web access to have redundancy and can load-balance up to 32 servers, meaning that if a server goes offline, the load is automatically redistributed to the remaining servers. When the offline server recovers and rejoins the WLBS system, the load of the system is then redistributed.

Clustering on the database servers can also be used to allow fault-tolerance on the database engines. Clustering of the database engine servers makes it possible to reduce the load on each server. If a failure occurs on one server, its load is redirected to another clustered server. Under normal working conditions, the cluster separates the database processes and allows for faster access to the shared data drives.

Testing of the fault tolerance system should be done during the deployment testing or the pilot testing periods to ensure good performance.

Data Migration and Coexistence Issues

Some application deployment issues are generated when a system is converted from one server operating system to another. For example, organizations converting from Novell NetWare file servers to Microsoft Windows NT servers find that the application deployment process must handle a transition period until all client applications are converted to the new system. This often means maintaining data access for both platforms. If a limited number of people maintain and update the data, the application should be deployed to their computers either first or last. Then the data should be duplicated between the new system and the old system in a timely manner, until the total deployment is complete. If a large number of people can change the data, a gateway system should be implemented from the new system to the old system to help maintain accurate data access. After the completion of the deployment, the gateway system or data duplication can cease, and the application can be fully switched to its permanent configuration and file server operating system.

Summary

In this chapter, we have stressed the importance of the Stabilizing Phase in shipping the product, as well as how to deploy the product after the Release Milestone is reached.

We discussed how to complete the Stabilizing Phase to ensure that the right product is shipped at the right time. It was suggested that this phase iterates four primary steps: fix the bugs, synchronize all product deliverables, ship the release, and extensively test the release. Each iteration is classified as an interim release. Each interim release will bring the team closer to attaining the phase's Release Milestone.

We discussed three stages of the deployment process: planning, testing, and deploying. Proper planning simplifies the deployment process and improves the impact of the application on the user community. As discussed extensively throughout this book, once a plan is created it should be incrementally tested. Finally, the implementation of the deployment plan moves the completed product from the hands of the customer to the systems of the user.

Review

1. What is the primary goal of the Stabilizing Phase?

2. How does the team incrementally reach the Release Milestone?

3. What are the primary steps of the Stabilizing Phase?

4. What are the primary interim releases of the Stabilizing Phase?

5. What are the deliverables of the Stabilizing Phase?

6. What are some of the deployment methods that can be used within an organization?

C H A P T E R   1 4

Project Review

About This Chapter

An old saying notes that "the road to destruction is paved with good intentions." Despite having the best of intentions, some firms never take the time to conduct an organized review of a project once it is complete. As a result, many of these firms end up living with out-of-control development projects.

In this chapter, we will discuss the value of a formal project review. This discussion relates to projects that have recently been completed, and to the ongoing growth and improvement of an organization's development process. We'll examine the relationship between the project review and the Capability Maturity Model for Software, and also show a project review's importance in providing feedback on an organization's best practices.

Next, we'll examine the practical considerations of conducting a project review: when to schedule a project review, who should attend, and the proper physical setting for conducting a project review. We'll demonstrate how to prepare for and run the actual meeting. We'll show various ways to gather and document the information. Finally, we'll discuss the possibility of utilizing a project review team for large projects.

The principles and guidelines provided in this chapter are based on our own experiences with creating application architectures and implementing enterprise applications, as well as on the following resources:

- Microsoft Solutions Framework
- Dempsey, Dvorak, and Meehan's "Escaping the IT Abyss," *The McKinsey Quarterly*
- Mark C. Paulk, Charles V. Weber, Bill Curtis, and Mary Beth Chrissis' *The Capability Maturity Model: Guidelines for Improving the Software Process*
- Dr. Joyce Statz's white paper *Microsoft Solutions Framework and the Capability Maturity Model*

Upon completion, you will be able to:

- Describe the benefits of a project review.
- Evaluate the relationship between a project review and the Software Capability Maturity Model.
- Identify some practical considerations involved in project reviews.

Case for Project Review

In an article titled "Escaping the IT Abyss," Dempsey et al. tell us the role in which project reviews play in the most effective IT organizations:

> *Reviewing overall IT performance helps you to distill lessons that will help you do better next time. Most companies claim to perform reviews, but few do so effectively. They may complain that they can't review big projects properly because "Most of the original people are gone or have moved on to different efforts," as one CIO told us, or because "The scope of the project has changed many times over the years," as another explained. Both these objections can be addressed if projects are kept short, given clear objectives, required to produce regular deliverables, and monitored continuously.*
>
> *In the best IT companies, business people drive the projects and are on the hook for the results. Hard benefits are budgeted for, and results are measured at every stage. Post-implementation review is easier, since all the milestone results are available to help managers weigh outcomes against objectives. Lessons learned are built into subsequent projects.*

As the quoted passage above implies, only by examining the past can organizations adequately prepare for the future. For example, an individual interviewing for a job claims to have twenty years of experience in a particular field. Following the interview, one of the interviewers asks the candidate if the individual indeed has twenty years of experience, or only one year of experience twenty times. If organizations do not contemplate and learn from both successes and failures, progress will be slow, or even non-existent.

An initial post-project review, or *postmortem,* is recommended as a starting point for the entire project review process. A project review as a whole is a post-milestone review meeting that formalizes the process of learning from past experience. A thorough project review should carefully analyze the project to identify strengths and weaknesses of the each development phases. Post-project reviews begin the process of incorporating best practices into an organization's development process so that the project team learns to identify and confront potential risks in future projects.

Benefits of Project Reviews

Numerous benefits, both individual and corporate, arise from conducting project reviews. As mentioned earlier, the most important benefits are self-examination, reflection, and resulting growth through the incorporation of best practices. These benefits ideally occur for both the individual and the organization. Additional benefits of project reviews are that they:

- **Provide project closure** Closure is important if team members have spent time and energy on the completed project, and will begin another project immediately. Project closure is particularly important if the project team will soon dissolve. Official project closure will also help the team members to move on to something new.

- **Provide a final outlet for team communication** A project review can be cathartic for team members who have strong feelings about particular aspects of a project. If not expressed in a controlled manner and setting, team members may express such feelings later in less desirable circumstances, places, or means. In sharing their thoughts, team members should focus on the team's actions rather than on the individuals; furthermore, such a communication outlet should *never* be used to place blame or point fingers at any individuals or groups.

- **Address the team's morale** Project reviews may actually enhance team morale by allowing teammates to share positive as well as negative feelings, and also to offer praise throughout the team. Traditionally, software development has often been somewhat of a solitary effort; the software development team approach addressed in this book lends itself to shared responsibilities as well as shared praise for a successful project.

- **Set best-practice baselines** Future teams may also benefit from project reviews by accessing the current team's perception of the project's strengths and weaknesses. Such perceptions can provide the basis for creating best-practice baselines for software development within an organization. Project teams should remember the framework concept, which suggests that organizations must modify their practices to find the best methods and executions for their particular projects. In the early stages of developing a best-practice baseline, a good exercise for all development team members is simply to read project reviews from their organization's previous projects. To simplify access, these baselines should be gathered into a single location, often referred to as a best-practice guide or process library.

- **Establish feedback loops** All the project review output can be combined into a best-practice baseline and should be used as *input* for subsequent projects. Organizations should apply project review insights to improve future projects. Such a feedback loop marks an organization as being dedicated to improvement. Feedback loops are key features of the Capability Maturity Model for Software.

Capability Maturity Models

Dr. Joyce Statz of TeraQuest provided the Capability Maturity Model for Software information upon which this section is based. Since the mid-1980s, Carnegie Mellon University has provided several studies and models that describe organizations' progressions from "infancy" to "maturity." The Capability Maturity Model (CMM) for Software is one of several such models. CMMs support evolving capability for developing software, managing people, acquiring software, personal software process, and systems engineering. Many of these models share common features, although content and intended audiences vary.

Each model provides a structured view of its focus area, generally in a five-layer progression of increasingly sophisticated practices. Most CMMs intend to incrementally improve an organization's overall capability. Each layer of the CMM provides a baseline for improvement in established practices, as well as a basis for the next layer of mature practices. The CMM for Software comprises five layers, which are described in Table 14.1.

Table 14.1   Five levels of CMM for Software

Level	Focus	Key process areas
5: Optimizing	Continuous process improvement	Defect prevention Technology change management Process change management
4: Managed	Product and process quality	Quantitative process management Software quality management
3: Defined	Defined engineering process	Organizational process focus Organizational process definition Integrated software management Software product engineering Inter-group coordination Training program Peer reviews
2: Repeatable	Project management and commitment process	Requirements management Project planning Project tracking and oversight Software subcontract management Software quality assurance Software configuration management
1: Initial	Heroes	Extraordinary effort

A complete discussion of the CMM is outside the scope of this book. Nevertheless, it is worthwhile to note that the Microsoft Solutions Framework is an excellent guide for organizations in following the progress from the initial stages of Level 1 to the higher maturity levels. For additional information on the CMM for Software, please refer to Mark C. Paulk, Charles V. Weber, Bill Curtis, and Mary Beth Chrissis' *The Capability Maturity Model: Guidelines for Improving the Software Process* (Addison-Wesley, 1995).

Our purpose in briefly discussing the CMM is to demonstrate the importance of project reviews in evolving an organization to a more efficient CMM maturity level. One characteristic of a CMM Level 1 organization is reinventing processes for each project. By conducting project reviews and implementing the reviews' results as standard practices, such an organization can avoid this inefficient, but common, problem.

Two key challenges for CMM Level 2 organizations are accurate project planning and effective project tracking. Using project reviews to compare plans with actual events and timelines enables such a team to hone its estimating and tracking skills. Over time, this organization can create an increasingly realistic sense of time and resources that project tasks require. Without a project review, it is likely that this team will repeatedly overestimate or underestimate project schedules and resources.

In the white paper *Microsoft Solutions Framework and the Capability Maturity Model,* Dr. Statz points out that project reviews are critical to reaching Level 3, as noted below:

> *Although most Level 2 organizational discipline is seen at a project level, members of an individual project can usually find good practices that could be useful in another project. Leveraging those best practices across the organization and defining processes that can be tailored to each project is the heart of Level 3 of the CMM.*

> *Project teams generally accumulate a rich process history as they complete their project. They should keep this data in a repository for use by other project teams on future projects. The organization will develop an appreciation for common processes and advisors who can help tailor those processes.*

At Levels 4 and 5, the fundamental purpose of the project review is to facilitate the feedback loop. As the team identifies problems, it can change its processes to eliminate or mitigate such problems in future projects.

The CMM for Software provides a solid measure of a development organization's effectiveness and maturity. The project review is a key tool in organizations' efforts to improve development processes and progress to more efficient levels of software development maturity.

Project Review Considerations

Most project reviews have several common characteristics. Though not exhaustive, the following list identifies several issues that teams should consider when planning project reviews:

- Timing
- Formality
- Length
- Setting
- Attendees

When to Conduct a Project Review

A post-project review should logically take place after a project is completed. However, the process of analyzing and learning from completed work is valuable at any stage of a project. The major project milestones presented by the MSF Development Process, particularly after the Developing Phase's Scope Complete Milestone, are also appropriate times to apply project review principles and conduct formal project reviews.

While no rules dictate when to schedule an end-of-project review, it's best to conduct it within a short time after the project is complete. If the review is scheduled too soon, team members tend to focus their discussions too heavily on the latter part of the project. Additionally, the team members may still feel emotionally and mentally too close to the project to analyze it objectively. If the review is postponed for too long, the team is likely to forget the project's specific details. Additionally, after extremely long periods, the project's difficult and frustrating elements tend to fade in their significance.

Table 14.2 provides several simple recommendations for how long to wait after the product ships to conduct a project review, while considering various project characteristics.

Table 14.2   Recommendations for when to conduct a project review

Project characteristic	Two weeks after shipping	Five weeks after shipping
Scope of project	Small	Large
Length of project	Short (days to 3 months)	Long (3 months to years)
Energy level of team members	Low	High
Team member availability	Some working on other projects	All working on other projects

Formality of Project Reviews

Project review formality can vary from project to project. A small group can meet to informally discuss project issues, or a formal project review team can research these issues closely, and then present a set of organized results.

Ideally, a project review should be a formal, well-planned event with a set of objectives, a specific meeting agenda, and a well-defined process. Although helpful in building morale, informal project review meetings tend not to capture optimal best-practice lessons crucial to project review success.

Because participants arrive prepared, formal project reviews also enable teams to focus discussion on learning points, as opposed to turning the project review into an unfocused complaint session.

Time Frames for the Review Process

While project reviews often involve meetings and daylong events, it's ideal to keep a single review meeting to two hours or less. Setting an appropriate time frame for a project review may involve separating the process into a series of several meetings. In this way, each meeting may focus on a particular area or point in the project's development process. It is important to note that much of the review preparation work should be done before the actual meeting.

Proper Settings for Reviews

Conducting project reviews in an appropriate physical environment will have a positive impact on review success and team morale. Arranging a room with a round table or circle of tables is suggested, as this arrangement allows team members to communicate on an equal level with one another, with no individual dominating "the head of the table." The room should be large enough to comfortably seat all team members; if conflict is likely, the room should allow extra space, as feeling cramped can elevate bad feelings among teammates.

A blame-free environment is crucial for targeting the real project issues. If people feel threatened, they'll put their energy into defending themselves rather than honestly examining the project's strengths and weaknesses objectively. The focus should remain on the development process and team actions as a whole, not on individual participants in the project.

Who Should Attend?

Typically, anyone involved in the project—even if only for a small percent of the time—should participate in the project review. If at all possible, it's ultimately most beneficial to gather all team members for the project review process to allow everyone involved to have input.

However, if inviting all team members makes the review group inconveniently large, a suggested alternative is conducting mini-project reviews by dividing people into groups responsible for specific project elements. Representatives from each mini-project review can then attend a final, comprehensive project review.

Preparation for a Project Review Meeting

The basic agenda for any project review should cover the following questions:

- How did the project schedule work for the team?
- How effectively were resources applied to the project?
- What strengths and weaknesses of each project phase can team members identify?
- What did not work well on the project?
- What suggestions can team members make to improve the overall process?
- What recommendations would team members make for future projects?

The questions listed above do not necessarily have to be addressed in any particular order in the project review process; however, they are essential starting points for any project review. Typically, Program Management should arrange the project review process and timeline before the actual review process takes place, and add any additional questions or issues, tailored specifically to the project, to cover in the review.

All team members involved in the project should feel free to reflect on their involvement, roles, percent of time spent on the project, dates involved, and so forth. Typically, the project review timeline acts as a vehicle to focus people on the entire project, rather than the final project stages or their exclusive roles in the project.

For most projects, the process and agenda should be distributed a week in advance, along with recommended issues for the team to contemplate when preparing for the actual review. The team members may want to respond before the actual meeting or meetings to allow Program Management to further organize the project review and distribute a project observation list.

For a small or informal review process, the team may simply consider a review agenda and mention their observations at a single review meeting. It is beneficial for the team to look over reviews from earlier projects, to help set the team's expectations.

Facilitating the Meeting

It is often beneficial to have an individual outside of the project team facilitate the review meeting. Otherwise, the Program Management team lead should identify a facilitator for any review meetings, as Program Management is ultimately responsible for facilitating the review process.

The facilitator should maintain order and structure in the meeting, and also ensure that the team members remain focused and do not personally attack one another. The facilitator should also make sure that all agenda items are covered, that everyone is equally involved in discussions, and that the meeting is conducted within the appropriate time frame.

Recording the Discussion

Ideally, the project review discussion should be recorded so that all team members can observe what's being written. Large sheets of flipchart paper taped on the meeting room's walls, computers, and whiteboards can all be effective means of recording the meeting.

Recording the discussion is effective because everyone involved focuses on the information itself instead of on one another, helping keep the discussion on track. Creating new documents during a review meeting is also excellent in facilitating the meeting because they offer an alternative means for which to handle unrelated topics or tangents—the recorder simply writes off-subject ideas on a separate sheet of paper. That way, valid ideas aren't lost, but they don't defocus the team's discussions pertinent to the set agenda, either.

In addition, recording comments prompts team members to voice their thoughts more concisely and to avoid repeating issues already documented. Lastly, it's often beneficial to provide an objective recorder not directly involved with the project. Thus, the recorder can focus on capturing information, while not necessarily analyzing thoughts as they are presented.

Organizing a Project Review Team

Program Management may choose to organize a project review team when planning a review for larger projects. The team approach works especially well when several project teams are involved in a large project.

Program Management may use a variety of tactics in organizing a project review team. For instance, functional discipline groups can be created: one for development, one for testing, one for user education, and one for program management. Another example of a project review team is a multifunctional group comprised of members from each functional discipline, based on the particular development process phases.

Project Review Preparation

Upon its organization, a project review team should meet separately, prior to the actual review meetings. The product team leads and managers should also attend this preliminary review team meeting to determine the project review schedule and goals. During this preliminary meeting, the attendees should identify all groups and individuals needed for the actual project review.

Gathering Information

In gathering information for a project review team, the entire project team responds by e-mail with comments about the project's strengths and weaknesses, and also with improvement suggestions for the next milestone or release. The project review team should concurrently interview team members in preparation for one or more project review meetings.

Analyzing

The project review team should ensure that all pertinent information generated before and during the project review is gathered and analyzed.

Developing Recommendations

To develop recommendations, the project review team should prioritize each action item and issue identified as a strength or weakness based upon its effectiveness at reaching the project team's goals. Such resulting recommendations should focus only on high-priority items and issues.

Problems, items, and issues that pose project weaknesses should be studied carefully. If best practices exist to address such weaknesses, the project review team should list these best practices as recommended solutions. For problems with no known best-practice solution, the project review team should determine alternatives for solving the problems.

Presenting and Reviewing Recommendations

As a final step in the preliminary review process, the project review team should present a summary of all findings and recommendations to the management and project teams. All additions, revisions, and corrections should be recorded for inclusion in the project's final report. The project team as a whole should select the recommendation or recommendations to be accepted to implement in the development process for the next milestone or release.

Capturing Feedback

As mentioned previously, documenting project review feedback is important for a future project's team members to use as a reference guide.

Before the actual project review takes place, an individual should be chosen to write the meeting's events into a document. Such a document should include the timeline, names of people involved, list of recommendations, and information recorded from the discussion. The document should not omit material from the information recorded during the meeting, or from e-mail collected by the project review team, because such information most accurately reflects team members' perceptions in the project review.

After the review document has been completed, all team members should have a chance to review the document before it is published, so they can propose changes if needed.

Accountability

One of the biggest mistakes teams make after a project review is filing the project review document away and never referring to it again. As we discussed, this is a mistake for organizations seeking to improve the efficiency and success for software development.

As each new project is begun, it is effective to review the recommendations from previous projects as a "self-check" for the new project. At various planned times throughout a newer project, it's effective to review the list of recommendations and evaluate as a group how the team is performing in those areas. Accountability makes time and effort of the project review more productive.

Summary

Project teams that don't conduct formal project reviews not only stop short of the finish line, they shortchange themselves and their organizations of valuable learning and growth opportunities. When conducted effectively, project reviews provide essential feedback into organizations. This feedback can then enable organizations to more rapidly improve their effectiveness. Learning from both successes and failures, then using project reviews to develop best practices for an organization's future projects, are investments that will return a dividend on all future software projects.

Review

1. List the benefits of a project review.

2. Discuss the relationship between project reviews and the CMM for Software.

3. List some practical considerations involved in project reviews.

4. Explain methods to conduct project reviews for large projects.

C A S E   S T U D Y   1 0

Shipping RMS

Dan poked his head around the corner of the cubicle where Marta, Mike, and Tim were working. "How many bugs today, Marta?"

Harried, Marta glanced at him briefly. "Eleven." She returned to her work.

"Top five still the same?" He hated to keep interrupting her, but at this stage of the project, he felt confronting her now was more effective than setting up a formal meeting later.

"Still the same."

"Stop by before you leave today, OK?"

"Got it." She kept her focus on the screen.

Dan left the testing area and headed back to his office. Some managers might have been offended, but he had been through similar levels of stress in earlier projects. "End-game is a pretty good name for this stage of a project," he thought. He had played some chess growing up, and he could still remember the intense concentration involved in the final moves to checkmate, as he tried to reach his goal without letting his opponent sneak up on him. "We know the moves we want to make, and we're trying to make them. What we don't know is whether or not a bug is going to rear up and bite us."

The team had reached bug convergence three days earlier. Fortunately, RMS was a small enough project that hitting bug convergence wasn't difficult, even considering the pilot release in progress. The test team had quickly discovered around 20 bugs, which the development team had reduced to 10 in one day. Subsequently, the rate of bug discovery had slowed substantially, although everyone by this point had begun to feel pressure to finalize the project.

However, during the past two days, the team hadn't made much progress at all in resolving the project's outstanding issues. In fact, no one could determine the causes of the top five bugs. Most frustrating was that several bugs seemed linked to the new server purchased exclusively for RMS.

When he got to his office, Dan checked the project charts on the wall. He had hoped they could reach the zero-bug release deadline by Thursday, but meeting that deadline was becoming less and less likely. Until now, the project team hadn't used any buffer time; maybe it was necessary now to take some buffer time from the bank. "It's too soon to decide," Dan told himself. "Wait till you see what Marta and the developers work out today."

Are We Ready for the Users?

Just then, Jane knocked at his office door. Marilou was peering over Jane's shoulder. "Come in, both of you. Have a seat."

The women joined Dan at his small conference table. "What's on your mind?" Dan asked.

Marilou spoke first. "I wanted to show you the documentation and Help files and see if you have any last-minute suggestions."

"And I'd like a project update to give to Jim and put on the intranet, but I didn't want to bother Marta or Tim," added Jane. "They both look pretty wound up."

"They're both under a lot of pressure right now," said Dan. "I'm afraid Marta is losing some of her newfound faith in our development team. The testers logged a set of bugs against the new server that no one can pinpoint." He looked at Marilou. "But that doesn't keep the rest of us from doing our jobs, huh? Let me see what you've got."

He flipped through Marilou's documents. "This is really good stuff, Marilou. Well organized, good use of screen shots, looks attractive. Great work!" He knew Marilou, with her background in technical writing and desktop publishing, would be able to put together excellent documentation for the project.

Dan continued to admire the documentation while Jane and Marilou waited silently for his final verdict. "I think this is good to go," Dan said finally. "My only concern is that you might want to wait until we reach the zero-bug interim milestone. That way, we can be fairly sure that we're not going to have to rip something out of these docs to take care of a bug."

"Good point. I'll tell the print shop to hold it for a day or so."

Jane looked worried. "Is it that much of an issue, Dan? One, I don't want to be the person to tell Jim. And two, our users won't like hearing that there's a delay."

"You don't need to say anything to anyone," Dan replied, "I'm a big believer in openness, but I also don't think it's wise to share either failures or successes on a development project until the project's finished. Sharing too much information can put false ideas in people's heads." Although managing customer and user expectations were fundamental to Jane's and Marilou's roles on the team, he didn't want either group to get alarmed. "Nobody needs to be told anything at this point. We should wait until we have something definite to tell them, or until we have to slip the schedule. If we ship the product late, at least we'll be shipping a bug-free product."

"I'm just telling people now that we're working to make sure the product has the best possible performance, and that seems to satisfy them for the time being," Marilou said. "Of course, if we have to change the feature set or slip the schedule substantially, we'll have to give them more details."

Dan nodded. "Agreed." He looked at Jane. "As for Jim, I would simply tell him that we've got a bug or two we're still working on, and we'll keep him posted." Dan knew that Jim would probably appreciate a brief update, considering that he was filling the demanding roles of both CFO and COO.

"Sounds good," Jane said. As they got up and walked toward Dan's door, she added, "Oh, and one more thing. Since we're not meeting as much while Testing and Development are pushing for the finish, I feel really uninformed. What's left?"

Dan pointed to a chart on his wall. "Basically, once we reach zero-bug release, we'll do a final internal release to make sure we're happy with the installation routine. We'll also do some intensive final testing. Then, we'll take the release candidate and run it on another set of user computers. We'll have the users work through the testing scripts that Marta and Mike wrote. Assuming no one finds any new bugs, and also assuming we've kept the bug list at zero and dealt with all risks in the Risk Assessment Document, we'll have a meeting to decide whether or not we're at the Release Milestone. If so, we'll declare RMS to be at Final Release, and Tim and his crew will do the roll-out."

"The physical roll-out," corrected Marilou. "We'll still have to do the business and logistical roll-outs."

"True," said Dan, smiling. "Thanks for reminding me."

"I thought I saw one more step on the project plan," put in Jane. "A project review, is it?"

Dan nodded, but before he could provide any more details on the project plan's final step, Marta and Tim walked up. Tim looked defeated, but Marta was agitated and distressed.

"Let's get out of here," Jane whispered, grabbing Marilou's arm and leading her hastily away.

A Fresh Look

As Marta bore down on him with Tim in tow, Dan assumed as calm an air as he could. "Hello there, guys. Long time no see."

Marta ignored both his tone and his greeting. "Dan, there's a problem, and it's just what I was afraid of! The code doesn't work, and no one can fix it, not Tim, or Bill, or Sam, or Beth, or Mike—and I don't know how to fix it myself! I can't handle all of this responsibility! I can't make sure it's done right." She was clearly exasperated. "What was I thinking? I knew I should have left when I tried, and not let everyone talk me into staying!"

Tim looked miserable. He corroborated Marta's judgement about the broken code. "I just don't understand it, Dan. The build worked fine in the test lab, but when we moved it to the multi-processor box, the response time actually went down. Now we're getting these weird error messages. This morning, the box actually blue-screened." He sighed. "The only thing I can think of is that there's something wrong with the SMP support. I guess we'll have to send this box back, move RMS to a regular box, and hope we can live with the speed."

Dan knew that he needed to take charge of the situation. "First of all, let's not have this conference in the hall. Come into my office, calm down, and let's talk." He ushered Tim and Marta into his office, shut the door, and sat with his teammates at his conference table.

Dan could tell that Marta and Tim were up against some common pitfalls of the Stabilizing Phase. "I understand why you're stressed, Marta. Trust me, everyone who works with computers has experienced it. Because you can't see everything going on inside the box, it can be horribly frustrating to track down problems like this one. You can't tell whether it's the hardware, the operating system, some obscure driver, or the software we wrote. But getting angry just muddies your thought processes even more."

He turned to his Network Manager. "And you, Tim, are doing two things you should never do: First, you're assuming too much, and second, you're grasping at straws. You should know better."

Tim's demeanor changed from defeated to angry, which is what Dan wanted. "What other choices do I have in a crisis like this?" he demanded.

"I don't know," said Dan, "because I don't have the background you and the others have had with this experience." Tim looked somewhat mollified as Dan continued. "What I do have is more experience doing troubleshooting. If you were a highly paid consultant, you'd have to approach problems systematically. If someone contacted you to check out this situation in another company, what would you want to check first?"

Tim thought for a moment. "Well…first I'd check all the hardware. I'd make sure the hardware was on the approved hardware list and do some research into anything about the hardware that I thought was unusual. Then I'd try to make sure the hardware was working properly."

"OK," Dan said encouragingly, "those are good general-purpose things to check. Now get more specific. Describe a specific case to me."

"Let me give it a try," said Marta. Her frustration was beginning to subside, and she was intrigued enough by the conversation to want to contribute her natural problem-solving tendencies. "We have a custom software application that interacts with certain services—say, MTS and SQL Server—on a Windows NT server. This application seems to run fine on one box, but either runs poorly or not at all on another box. The second box is an SMP box, which may or may not have anything to do with the problem."

"Can I jump in here?" asked Tim. Marta nodded. "When we tried to solve this problem, the box seemed to get less and less stable, especially after the blue screen came up this morning."

"Now," challenged Dan, "what strategy can you come up with for tackling this problem?"

"Well, to eliminate the SMP box as the source of the problem, we could get another SMP box, configure it like the one we have, and try running the application on the new one," said Marta.

"True, but unfortunately, that means a schedule slippage because we can't get another SMP box for at least a month," reminded Dan. He turned to Tim. "You mentioned that the box became more and more unstable? Any clues there, or anything you could check?"

"No, not that I can think of. We've got other SMP boxes, and they are all very stable."

"Anything different about this one?" asked Dan. "The build process, the patch levels, anything like that?"

"I checked the patches already," said Tim, "and they all looked OK, as far as I could tell. I didn't do the build—I had one of the guys do the build when the box came in." Tim thought for a moment. "The build…I wonder if…Hey, could I use your computer for a moment, Dan?"

"Of course."

Tim hurried over to Dan's computer. "Can I log you off and log myself in?" Dan nodded, and Tim logged in and opened several Windows programs.

Dan and Marta watched as Tim arranged the various windows on the screen. He scrolled through file listings and checked various file properties. After a few minutes, he snapped his fingers. "That's it!" Turning to Dan, Tim pointed at the screen. "That's the problem."

"What? What's the problem?" asked Marta, confused.

Dan thought he knew the answer, but wanted Tim to explain the details. "Come on, Tim, don't keep us in suspense."

"Look," said Tim, activating one file window. "This is a directory on the MTS server that's already in production." He switched to another window. "And this is the same directory on the new server. Notice anything?"

"The directories don't contain all the same files," said Marta.

"That's OK," said Tim. "Unless two servers are identical and loaded with exactly the same software, the directories won't be the same. There's another way they're different, but you can't see it in this view." He switched both windows to a detail view and then arranged them on the screen so that all the details were visible. "Now do you notice anything?"

"Some of the file dates aren't the same, even though the file names are," said Marta. "Is that important?"

"Sometimes it can be *very* important," said Dan, nodding to Tim, "It can mean that different versions of the software have been installed on the two servers. Usually, that doesn't matter. But if one program installs an older version of a file that is also used by another program, the other program may not function correctly."

"It can get really hairy with servers, what with patches, add-on software, and the like," said Tim. "I told my guy to be sure the box was current and that it had all the services and software it needed, but I never told him what order to install everything in, or which files to keep and which ones to overwrite. I just assumed he would know."

"There's that 'assume' word again," said Marta, grinning at Tim. "And you know what happens when you assume."

"OK, OK, I got it," said Tim, holding up his hands.

"So what do we do now?" asked Marta.

"Order in doughnuts," said Dan.

Marta looked puzzled. Tim explained, with a wry smile, "What he means, Marta, is that he knows a Network Manager who's going to learn not to assume anything by rebuilding a server tonight."

User Feedback

After Tim rebuilt the server, the Stabilizing Phase moved forward rapidly. The remaining bugs in the pilot release were cleaned up in a few days. Tim's Logistics Management team did a final internal release and worked with Marta to carry out the final internal testing.

When they were convinced that the application was ready, the project team did a limited rollout in the Chicago office over a weekend, testing the Win32 client further. At the same time, the IT staff members from the other offices connected to the Internet and submitted numerous mock timesheets.

The limited rollout was a success. No new bugs were discovered, and the installation routines worked without a hitch. The team was excited, but they knew that the final test was on Monday, when Marilou carried out her first two training classes.

On Monday, the RMS project team gathered in Dan's office, along with Sam and Beth. The group was scheduled to go to lunch just as they had after they finished the Planning Phase, but they had to wait for Marilou and Jim to return from the second training class, which was directed at managers using the Win32 client. Earlier, Marilou and Jim had overseen the first class, a general course on using the Web interface to work with timesheets.

Dan sat at his desk, fiddling with a pen. Sam, Beth, Tim, and Marta were playing cards at the small conference table, while Jane sat in a corner, reading. Bill paced back and forth, his arms folded over his chest.

"Bill, will you stop your pacing?" said Jane. "You're acting like an expectant father."

"At least we didn't have to bring a shower gift," Beth said. Everyone laughed, and even Bill smiled slightly.

"Don't worry about it, Bill," said Dan. "It's not like your career depends on this one application."

"That's true," said Bill, "but after that last high-profile project bombed, I'd like for this one to be a hit."

Dan walked to his office door and looked down the hall toward the elevators. "Well, looks like you'll know in a moment. Here they come."

Jim and Marilou walked in, and Marilou put her training materials on the credenza. When she turned to face the rest of the group, she had a somber look on her face. "She's usually pretty bubbly, especially after a class," thought Dan. "This looks bad."

"Well?" Bill was anxious to know the verdict. "What about it?"

"Let's go to lunch," sighed Jim, "We'll all feel better after we eat."

Amid protests from others in the group, Dan said, "I think we'd rather hear the managers' reaction first, Jim, even if it's bad." Everyone agreed.

Jane stepped forward to face her friend. "Marilou, no sugarcoating now, just tell me straight: What did they think?"

Marilou glanced at Jim, who nodded slowly. She threw up her arms. "They loved it!" She hugged Jane, while Jim stood laughing at the surprised looks on the others' faces.

"You stinkers!" Dan smiled amid the general celebration among the team members and shook hands with Jim. "You know your lunch bill will probably be higher," Dan joked, "We'll all want to pay you back for that little scare."

"Not a problem." Jim laughed again. "I'll gladly pay for lunch many times over to hear some of the great comments we heard today."

"Why the big response?" said Tim. "I mean, it's a good program and all, but it's not like we wrote the next version of Windows."

"It wasn't the program itself that generated most of the raves, although they did like it. They realized the difference the application will make in their work," said Jim, "but it was the *way* in which we did the program that impressed them the most. The project was done on time, on spec, and obviously written in response to their suggestions. They liked the level of communication we gave them, the way in which we handled the rollout, and the training.

"Most of all, though, they liked the fact that *we kept our word*. Almost everyone said over and over that we restored their faith in our IT department's ability to deliver." He turned to Bill. "They especially mentioned you, Bill. They knew that your folks did the actual writing, and they kept saying how they knew you'd give them a winner."

"But that's not fair!" said Bill, humbly. His hand swept the room. "Without all of us—all of *you*—we couldn't have pulled off this project."

"Don't sweat it, Chief." Dan punched Bill in the arm. "By putting together a good team and working a good system, we put out a good product. If you and your developers get most of the credit, that's alright." He looked at Bill slyly. "You can make it up to us by going back to work while we eat your share of lunch. OK?"

"No way!" said Bill, grinning. "We're tired of pizza and Jolt. Time for some other food groups."

As the group moved off for lunch, Marilou told Tim, "Speaking of food, I really liked the icon you gave the program. None of the managers got it, but I thought it was cute."

"Icon?" Bill was baffled. "The last time I looked, it was something like a timesheet."

"Oh no," Marilou grinned. "That got changed before the rollout to the managers' machines."

"Well, what is it now?" asked Dan.

"A doughnut."

"A doughnut!" shouted Bill. "Where did *that* come from?" Tim was hiding behind Sam. "You did it, didn't you?" Bill said, pointing a finger at Tim. "I'll show you a doughnut or two!"

Tim ran for the elevators, Bill close behind him. "Save us a place at the restaurant!" Jane yelled after them.

Reviewing the Project

Three weeks later, the team gathered again in Dan's office for the official RMS project review. The rest of the rollout had gone well, and the RMS application was in use throughout Ferguson and Bardell. Benefits were already becoming obvious, both in the assignment and scheduling of resources and in the increased efficiency of the timesheet process.

Bill opened the meeting. "This meeting is certainly fitting. We started this project differently than any other on which I've ever worked, and we're going to end it the same way, by doing something I've never done before. Why are we having a project review, anyway?" He leaned toward Jane and stage-whispered, "Watch this—Dan will have an overhead with a reason."

"Of course I will," said Dan, placing a transparency on the projector beside his chair. "Some of us actually know how to use PowerPoint."

Bill grimaced. "Ouch! OK, I'll be quiet."

"Actually, that's exactly what I *don't* want you to do," said Dan, turning on the overhead projector. "Here's the reason we are here, and why I don't want any of you to be quiet." He read from the transparency: "A project review is a means of formalizing the process of learning from past experience." He turned back to the group. "If we simply leave RMS and move on to the next project without reflecting on what was good and what was bad, what we did well and what we should do better or differently next time, we miss the opportunity to reinforce what we learned. The end of a project is what educators call a 'teachable moment,' and we want to take advantage of it."

"Well, I for one think we should move to a six-phase process, not just four," said Tim. "In fact, I've got a transparency that shows the six phases I have in mind. It's based on something put out by Russ Berne & Company in Oakland, New York." Tim placed his own transparency on the projector, and read each point. "One–Enthusiasm. Two–Disillusionment. Three–Panic. Four–Search for the Guilty. Five–Punishment of the Innocent. Six–Praise and Honors for the Non-Participants." Tim turned off the projector and removed his transparency as the others laughed.

"That's horrible, Tim," said Dan with a chuckle as Tim sat down. "Where did you get these six phases?"

"Oh, they're from a wall plaque my mom had around the house for years. When I was at her house a few weeks ago, I picked it up and brought it here. The plaque's hanging in my office now."

"Right next to your autographed poster?" said Jane with a grin. "You know, Dan, I think Tim's list is actually a good place to start."

Tim feigned shock. "Whoa—you mean I tried to do something funny and it actually has some value?"

"No, really," persisted Jane. "Those six phases were funny to us because they came so close to home. We've all seen—or been part of—projects that turned out just like that. By following the MSF Development Process and Development Team Models, and using the MSF Design Process, we made sure that RMS was exactly the opposite."

"Good point, Jane," said Dan. Then he addressed everyone. "Let's spend some time talking about what parts of the process we thought were especially helpful."

The team worked through the agenda, sometimes discussing calmly, sometimes arguing, sometimes trying to talk all at once, and sometimes listening carefully to one another. After three hours, Dan had covered ten pages of a legal pad with the group's primary points. He finally put down his pen and said, "That's good, gang. I think we have wrung the last ounce of reflection out of this project." Grimacing, he shook his hand. "Or the last bit of writing out of my fingers."

"Well, I hope you've got some strength left in that hand," said Bill gruffly, as he stood up across the table from Dan, "because you're going to need it."

Dan rose slowly to face him. The room grew quiet. "When we began, you said that your goal was to make us look like heroes. I just want to say, in front of everyone else on the team, that I think you are a real hero. Anyone who can take

FERGUSON AND BARDELL

ENGINEERING • ARCHITECTURE • PROJECT MANAGEMENT

The RMS Project
Meeting Agenda

Meeting Date: June 7, 1999   **Purpose:** Postmortem

I.   Agenda Building

II.   Purpose of Project Review (Postmortem)

III.   Project Schedule

IV.   Use of Resources

V.   Strengths and Weaknesses by Phase
- Envisioning
- Planning
- Developing
- Stabilizing

VI.   Possible Process Improvements

VII.   Recommendations for Future Projects

a team of people from extremely different backgrounds and show them how to use their skills to pull off a project like this one like we did is a man I'm proud to work for." He offered his hand to Dan, who modestly took it. Bill gave Dan a firm handshake.

"Thanks, Bill. Coming from someone with all the experience you have—well, that means a lot." He looked at the others. "My thanks to all of you. You've been a great team to work with."

"Don't make it sound like you'll never see any of us again," said Jane, gathering up her stuff. "After all, we've promised my people that Version 2 will include the accounting package, remember."

As the team dispersed, Dan made a note to e-mail Jim Stewart about the next round of RMS funding.

A P P E N D I X

Review Questions and Answers

Page 3

Chapter 1
Enterprise Architecture

1. What common IT challenges can an enterprise architecture address?

- **Deliver business value** Tightly align IT to business objectives.

- **Control costs** Squeeze every ounce of leverage from existing IT investments and make careful and informed future investments.

- **Sense and respond** Improve the cross-functional capabilities within the organization and extend those capabilities outside the organization to reach customers, suppliers, and stakeholders more effectively.

2. What are the primary goals of an enterprise architecture?

- Be logically consistent.

- Include both activities and coordinated projects.

- Progress from the current state to the desired future state.

- Address both current and projected business objectives and processes.

3. List the phases of enterprise architecture adoption.

- Envisioning

- Planning

- Developing

- Stabilizing

4. **Describe the four perspectives of the MSF Enterprise Architecture Model.**

   - **Business Perspective** Includes broad business strategies and plans for moving the organization from its current state to its desired future state. The Business Perspective describes how the business works.

   - **Application Perspective** Represents the services, information, and functionality that cross organizational boundaries, linking a variety of users to achieve common business objectives. The Application Perspective defines the enterprise application portfolio.

   - **Information Perspective** Describes what the organization needs to know to run its business processes and operations.

   - **Technology Perspective** Lays out the hardware and software supporting the organization. The Technology Perspective provides a logical, vendor-independent description of infrastructure and system components that is necessary to support the Application and Information Perspectives, and defines the set of technology standards and services needed to execute the business mission.

5. **How can applications be delivered while an enterprise architecture is under development?**

   The enterprise architecture should not be defined in a vacuum, but should reflect information discovered by actually building solutions. Using versioned releases that incorporate feedback from teams and users should result in progressive refinement of the architecture. Otherwise, a rapidly changing business environment could quickly overtake an organization's ability to both complete models at the enterprise level and deploy projects before business changes make the models invalid.

Page 43

Chapter 2
Enterprise Applications

1. **What is software architecture, and what are the characteristics of a good architecture?**

   Software architecture is a set of significant decisions about the organization of a software system. These decisions include:

   - The selection of the structural elements and interfaces comprising the system.
   - The system's behavior as determined by collaborations among those elements.
   - The combining of structural and behavioral elements into larger sub-systems.
   - The architectural style that guides the system's organization.

   A good software architecture has the following characteristics:

   - Resilient
   - Simple
   - Approachable
   - Clear separation of concerns
   - Balanced distribution of responsibilities
   - Balanced economic and technical constraints

2. **What are three ways of documenting software architecture?**

   - Unified Modeling Language
   - Design patterns
   - Design antipatterns

3. **What are the features of an enterprise application?**

   - **Complex** It is a multi-user, multi-developer, multi-component application that can utilize substantial data, employ extensive parallel processing, affect network-distributed resources, and require complex logic. It can be deployed across multiple platforms and inter-operate with many other applications, and it is long-lived.

   - **Business-oriented** Its purpose is to meet specific business requirements. It encodes business policies, processes, rules, and entities; is developed in a business organization; and is deployed in a manner responsive to business needs.

   - **Mission-critical** It is robust enough to sustain continuous operation. It must be extremely flexible for scalability and deployment, and allow for efficient maintenance, monitoring, and administration.

4. **What are design patterns and antipatterns?**

A design pattern is instructive information that captures the essential structure and insight of a successful family of proven solutions to a recurring problem that arises within a certain context and system of forces. It identifies the key aspects of a common design structure that make it useful for creating a reusable object-oriented design. Design patterns can be either generative or non-generative. Generative patterns can be used to solve engineering problems, whereas non-generative patterns are merely observed. Generative design patterns provide complete solutions to business and technical problems. They are primarily geared toward "green field" designs, meaning they are applied to new designs.

Design antipatterns are geared toward solving problems for which an inadequate solution is already in place. The best way to differentiate patterns and antipatterns is to say that patterns lead to an original solution for a set of criteria and forces, while antipatterns lead to a new solution when the current design is not working. Thus patterns are used when starting from scratch, and antipatterns are used to fix things that are broken.

5. **Identify five guiding software management principles.**
   - Alignment with business goals
   - Product mindset
   - Architecture-first
   - Design within context
   - Different languages for different project phases

6. **List the six submodels of the Enterprise Application Model.**
   - Business Model
   - User Model
   - Logical Model
   - Technology Model
   - Physical Model
   - Development Model

7. What is the MSF Application Model for Development?

The MSF Application Model for Development (MSF Application Model) provides a three-tier services-based approach to designing and developing software applications. It views an application at a logical level as a network of cooperative, distributed, and reusable services that support a business solution. Application services are units of application logic that include methods for implementing an operation, function, or transformation. These services should be:

- Accessed through a published interface.
- Driven by the interface specification.
- Focusing value toward the customer, not the provider.
- Mapped directly to actions.

The MSF Application Model describes applications as using three services: user, business, and data. These services allow for parallel development, better use of technology, easier maintenance and support, and flexibility in distributing the application's services. These user, business, and data services can reside anywhere in the environment, from a single desktop to servers and clients around the world.

Chapter 3
Project Teams

1. What are the six roles of the MSF Team Model for Application Development?

- Product Management
- Program Management
- Development
- Testing
- User Education
- Logistics Management

2. What are the focal points and responsibilities of each role?

- **Product Management** The job of this role is to respond to the customer's need or problem. The key contribution of this role is to drive the team to a shared vision of how to meet the need or solve the problem. Product Management answers the business-driven question, "Why are we doing this?" and ensures that all members of the team know and understand the answer. The key external goal of this role is customer satisfaction.

- **Program Management** The job of this role is to own and drive the development process. The leader of this role must understand the difference between being a leader and being a boss. The primary responsibility of the leader of the Program Management role is to move the project through the development process to ensure that the right product is delivered at the right time. The key external goal of this role is delivery within project constraints.

- **Development** The job of this role is to be technology consultants and product builders. Development determines exactly how to implement each feature, the actual architectural implementation, and how long the coding portion of the project will take to implement. Development does not determine which features to implement, but how to write the code for the product. The key external goal of this role is delivery to product specifications.

- **Testing** The job of this role is reality induction. Testing must be able to clearly articulate both what is currently wrong with the product, and what is currently right with it, so that the status of the product's development is accurately portrayed. Testing develops test strategies, plans, schedules, and scripts. The key external goal of this role is to make sure that the team knows and addresses all issues before releasing the product.

- **User Education** The job of this role is to enhance user performance so that users are as productive as possible with the product. To accomplish this goal, User Education acts as the advocate for the users of the product, much like Product Management acts as the customer advocate. However, this is a two-way street, because User Education also acts as the team's advocate to the users of the product. The key external goal of this role is enhanced user performance.

- **Logistics Management** The job of this role is to serve as the advocate for the operations, product support, help desk, and other delivery channel organizations. The key external goal for this role is smooth deployment and ongoing management of the product.

3. **How can the MSF Development Team Model be scaled for large and small projects?**

   Large projects call for organizational practices that formalize and streamline communication. All the ways to streamline communication rely on creating some kind of hierarchy; that is, creating small groups, which function as teams, and then appointing representatives from those groups to interact with each other and with management. To scale large projects, the project team can be divided into two kinds of subteams:

   - **Feature teams** These are small subteams that organize one or more members from each role into a matrix organization. These teams are then assigned a particular feature set and are responsible for all aspects of that feature set, including its design and schedule.

   - **Function teams** These exist within a role. They arise when a team or project is so large that it requires the people within a role to be grouped into teams based upon their functionality.

   Although the MSF Development Team Model consists of six roles, a team doesn't require a minimum of six people. In other words, it doesn't require one person per role. The key point is that the six goals have to be represented by the six roles on every team. Having at least one person per role helps to ensure that someone looks after the interests of each role, but not all projects can be approached in that fashion.

On smaller teams, one team member might have more than one role. Two principles guide this type of role sharing:

- **Single role for Development** Development team members should never be assigned to another role. The developers are the builders, and they should not be distracted from their main task. To give additional roles to the Development team only makes it more likely that schedules will slip due to these other responsibilities.

- **Conflict of interest** Roles that have intrinsic conflicts of interest should not be combined. For example, Product Management and Program Management have conflicting interests. Product Management wants to satisfy the customer whereas Program Management wants to deliver on time and on budget. If these roles are combined and the customer requests a change, the risk is that either the change will not get the consideration it deserves to maintain customer satisfaction, or that it will be accepted without understanding the impact on the project. Having different team members represent these roles helps to ensure that each perspective receives equal weight.

4. **What are the stages of development through which a team can progress?**

We view teams as progressing through the following stages:

- Awareness/concern
- Hope/optimism, willingness
- Identification of needs and solutions
- Supportive/caring behaviors
- Trusting/respectful relationships
- Team cohesiveness

The goal is to have all teams move to the last stage, team cohesiveness, where productivity is the highest.

5. **What two types of education improve a team member's effectiveness?**

- **Process education** Training in the process of developing software.
- **Technical education** Training in the actual languages and tools being used.

Chapter 4
Development Process

1. Briefly describe the Waterfall Model and the Spiral Model.

- **Waterfall Model** A project life cycle model that is primarily linear. It is an orderly, highly structured process based on the following well-defined development steps: system requirements, software requirements, analysis, program design, coding, system test, and operations.

- **Spiral Model** A project life cycle model that is primarily iterative. The stages of application development that make up this model are typically characterized as inception, elaboration, construction, and transition. Within each stage are five activity phases: requirements, design, implementation, deployment, and management. The Spiral Model's process is a continuous circle through the stages of development, with each stage requiring multiple revolutions through the five phases.

2. What are the workflows of the Unified Process?

The workflows of the Unified Process are five core processes that are continually executed during the four phases of the development process until the application is completed. Each circuit of the five workflow steps is called an iteration, and each iteration culminates in an internal product release. The workflows are:

- Requirements
- Analysis
- Design
- Implementation
- Testing

3. What are the phases and milestones of the Unified Process?

Because the Unified Process is based primarily on the Spiral Model, like that model, its four phases of development are Inception, Elaboration, Construction, and Transition. Each phase strives to achieve specific goals:

- **Inception Phase** Iterations focus on producing the business case. The Inception Phase's milestone is the Lifecycle Objective Milestone.

- **Elaboration Phase** Iterations are responsible for developing the baseline architecture. The Elaboration Phase's milestone is the Lifecycle Architecture Milestone.

- **Construction Phase** Iterations focus on creating the product with incremental releases of product builds and features. The Construction Phase's milestone is the Initial Operation Capability Milestone.

- **Transition Phase** Iterations ensure the product is ready for release to the user community. The Transition Phase's milestone is the Product Release Milestone.

4. **Discuss the objectives and purpose of each MSF phase.**

   - **Envisioning Phase** A shared vision of the project is built among all the key stakeholders. This vision should include a mutual understanding of the business needs being addressed, clearly identified solutions that meet the customer's expectations, and a solid estimation of the project constraints.

   - **Planning Phase** The application's architecture is defined. This application architecture is based on the Conceptual, Logical, and Physical Design Models. In addition, the three variables with which the team must work—schedule, resources, and features—are more clearly defined during the Planning Phase. By the end of this phase, the team has determined the schedule it will meet, the resources it will use, and the features it will build.

   - **Developing Phase** The most important task is to build the application. Iterations, which have been used during the earlier phases, become even more important during the Developing Phase. The team can expect to do multiple iterations of the application during this phase, typically named alpha, beta, and golden release candidate. Additionally, all known bugs should be addressed by the end of this phase. Addressing known bugs does not necessarily imply that all the bugs have been fixed; merely that they have been investigated. The goal of the Developing Phase is to deliver an application that meets all stated expectations and is ready for external testing.

   - **Stabilizing Phase** Significant performance and environmental testing occurs. All known issues are resolved before delivery, and any tasks needed for support and ongoing maintenance of the product are completed. This phase seeks to tie up the loose ends. Documentation, release notes, final "bug stomping," product hand-off, and product deployment are all part of this phase. The Stabilizing Phase starts when the team shifts its focus from code development to stabilizing the product and ends when the customer accepts the product as complete. A significant aspect of this phase is that the customer and users begin to pilot-test the product. This phase is also the training ground for the organization's operations and support teams. During this time, Logistics Management works to ensure a smooth transfer of product support to the organization's internal support groups, with the product release completing the transfer.

5. **List the deliverables for each phase of the MSF Development Process model.**

   - **Envisioning Phase** The Vision Document, the Master Risk Assessment Document, and the Project Structure Document. We also recommend that a prototype system be included with the deliverables for this milestone.

- **Planning Phase** The Functional Specification, the Master Project Plan, the Master Project Schedule, and an updated Master Risk Assessment Document. For most projects, another deliverable of this phase might be a proof-of-concept system that helps the team and stakeholders understand the application's architecture. Additionally, any significant design concerns can be tested with the proof-of-concept system before the Project Plan Approved Milestone is reached.

- **Developing Phase** The revised and completed Functional Specification, the updated Master Project Plan, Master Project Schedule, and Master Risk Assessment Document, source code and executables, initial performance support elements, and the Test Specification and test cases.

- **Stabilizing Phase** Golden release, release notes, performance support elements, test results and testing tools, source code and executables, project documents, milestone review.

6. **Discuss the benefits of versioned releases.**

   - **Communication** Promotes frequent and honest communication between the team and the customer. Each release reflects the best ideas of everyone involved.

   - **Earlier delivery** Enables the project team to deliver critical functionality earlier and to obtain feedback from the customer for future releases. When the customer knows (or senses) that future product releases will be delivered in a timely manner, the customer is much more receptive to deferring features to later releases.

   - **Closure** Forces closure on project issues. Using a versioned release allows the team to deal with a manageable number of issues during the Stabilizing Phase and to address all the issues before release.

   - **Goals** Sets clear, motivating goals for all team members. The team can easily manage each version's scope and quickly achieve results, so team members see rapid progress. Their role in determining the schedule helps ensure that their tasks are manageable, specific, and associated with a tangible result.

   - **Freedom and flexibility** Allows freedom and flexibility in the design process, enabling the team to be responsive to changes in the business environment. This freedom and flexibility reduces uncertainty and helps to manage the changes in project scope by allowing the team to vary features and schedules in relation to the overall plan. Features that become critical as a result of business changes can be designated as high priority for the next release. The early release becomes stable as the team starts work on the next one.

   - **Continuous and incremental feature delivery** Dictates a new set of features immediately following the release of the completed set. As a result, the team continues to add value for the project's customer and users.

7. Explain the concept of tradeoffs and the tradeoff triangle of project variables.

Every project presents three variables with which the team must work. These three variables—schedule, resources, and features—are illustrated in the tradeoff triangle.

The relationship between these three variables tends to be hazy at the beginning of the development process. At that point, the team has a rough idea of what to build, an estimate of available resources, and an approximate target delivery date. During the Planning Phase, the project elements represented in the triangle become more distinct. By the time the Planning Phase is complete, the team knows the nature of available resources, the product features, and the fixed ship date.

It's important to keep in mind that the three variables are interrelated. Changes on one side of the tradeoff triangle affect the other two sides. If the team understands and utilizes this concept, it has both the rationale and the motivation to take corrective action as changes occur during development.

Page 205

Chapter 5
Project Vision

1. What are the primary goals of the Envisioning Phase?

- Serve as an early form of planning.
- Establish clear communication and consensus from the beginning of the project.
- Help the team pull different perspectives into a common understanding.
- Provide the basis for future planning.
- Identify what the customer and key stakeholders deem essential for success.

2. What team roles are responsible for accomplishing envisioning goals?

- **Product Management** The primary driver for the Envisioning Phase. This role is responsible for delivering the Vision Document, managing customer expectations, and involving the customer in prototype development.
- **Program Management** Responsible for developing design goals, describing the solution concept, and outlining the project structure.
- **Development** Responsible for designing prototypes, outlining development options, and identifying implications of the vision.
- **Testing** Responsible for developing testing strategies, specifying acceptance criteria, designing a bug-tracking system, and designing a risk management system.
- **User Education** Responsible for identifying user performance needs and implications, managing user expectations, and involving users in prototype development.
- **Logistics Management** Responsible for identifying deployment implications and support implications of the product vision.

All roles are responsible for managing project risks.

3. What are the primary components of a Vision Document?

- A vision statement
- User research
- Competitive information
- Features and feature buckets
- A rough schedule

4. What are the benefits of using prototypes?

Clearly communicating the information learned from the customer and users is difficult. Information about business requirements must be communicated to team members with varying degrees of technical and business background, and information about how the product will solve the business problem must be communicated to the customer and users. To more easily accomplish this communication, a prototype application that demonstrates portions of the product's vision should be developed during the envisioning process and included in the Vision Approved Milestone deliverables. This prototype helps clarify existing ideas and helps draw out additional ideas from the team, the customer, and the product's users.

5. What are project risks?

Risk is the *possibility of suffering loss*. For a given project, this loss could be in the form of:

- Diminished product quality
- Increased costs
- Missed deadlines
- Complete failure to achieve the project's goals

6. What is risk management?

The identification and proactive mitigation of the risks a project might encounter, and the development of a system for managing those risks should they materialize during the project's life cycle.

Page 261

Chapter 6
Project Plan

1. Why do we need a Planning Phase?

The Envisioning Phase asks the question "Can we use technology to solve this business need, and if so, how?" The result is a common understanding of the problem and a common vision of the solution. The Planning Phase asks the question "Realistically, what will it take to reach the vision developed in the Envisioning Phase?" The result is a detailed plan to which both the customer and the project team can agree.

The Planning Phase is where the dreams of the Envisioning Phase are tested against reality. It's here that the hard questions are asked. The Planning Phase involves difficult, detailed work, and as a result a project team may be tempted to avoid it or rush it. The truth is that the work done in this phase will determine the success or failure of the project. It is better to face the truth now, on paper, than to face it later in a failed implementation. The common vision established in the Envisioning Phase has to go through the refining fire of the Planning Phase for the team to be sure that the vision is strong enough to bear up during the Developing and Stabilizing Phases.

2. Describe the three designs of the MSF Design Process.

The MSF Design Process consists of three distinct types of design work: conceptual, logical, and physical. Each of these generates a model of the same name: the Conceptual Design Model, the Logical Design Model, and the Physical Design Model. Each part of the process approaches the design task from a different perspective and defines the solution differently.

- **Conceptual Design Model** Views the problem from the perspective of the user and the business, and defines the problem in terms of scenarios.
- **Logical Design Model** Views the solution from the perspective of the project team, and defines the solution as a set of cooperating services.
- **Physical Design Model** Views the solution from the perspective of the developers, and defines the solution's services and technologies.

The goals of the three parts are:

- **Conceptual Design** Identify business needs and understand what users do and what they require. Conceptual Design generates scenarios that reflect complete and accurate requirements, by involving the customer, users, and other stakeholders.
- **Logical Design** Organize the solution and the communication among its elements. Logical Design takes the business problem identified in Conceptual Design scenarios and formulates an abstract model of the solution. In other words, Logical Design takes the scenarios from Conceptual Design and produces objects and services, user interface prototypes, and logical database design.

- **Physical Design** Apply real-world technology constraints, including implementation and performance considerations, to the outputs of Logical Design by specifying the details of the solution. The outputs of Logical Design are used to produce components, user interface specifications, and physical database design.

3. **What information is presented in a Functional Specification?**

- **Vision summary** What the team wants the product to be, justification for the product, and key high-level constraints. Based on the Vision Document from the Envisioning Phase.

- **Design goals** What the team wants to achieve with the product. Development will use these goals to make decisions on such issues as performance, reliability, timeliness, and possibly usability and accessibility. These goals were originally developed during the Envisioning Phase.

- **Requirements** What the customer, users, and stakeholders think the product must do. The requirements should be prioritized. Conflicting requirements should either be resolved or balanced in some way.

- **Usage summary** When the product will be used and who will use it. This is a high-level aggregation of the usage scenarios that were defined during the design process.

- **Features** What exactly the product does. A prioritized list of product features, including such things as potential user interface, application navigation, and detailed functionality.

- **Dependencies** What the product depends on. A description of external entities upon which the product might depend, including both high-level issues (such as interfacing to corporate systems) and low-level issues (such as a shared component).

- **Schedule summary** What the schedule is. A summary of the Master Project Schedule, identifying key interim milestones, deliverables, and the product ship date.

- **Risks** What the risks are. A list of risks that require external visibility or escalation.

- **Appendixes** What remains. A collection of the design process output that the team used to develop the Functional Specification.

4. What is a Master Project Plan?

The Master Project Plan gathers detailed plans from members of the project team to tell how the product will be built. The team then uses this collection of more-detailed deliverables to synchronize its work throughout the remainder of the project.

The purpose of a Master Project Plan is to:

- Consolidate feature team and role work plans.
- Describe how feature teams and roles will execute their tasks.
- Synchronize the plans across the team.

The overall owner of the Master Project Plan is Program Management, because this role is the primary coordinator of planning and process for the project. However, each role on the team is responsible for developing and maintaining its own realistic project plan within the overall plan.

Page 353

Chapter 7
User Service Layer Technologies

1. What is UI composition?

The layout of each UI element. It not only influences its aesthetic appeal, but also has a tremendous impact on the usability of the application. Composition includes such factors as:

- Positioning of controls
- Consistency of elements
- Affordances
- Use of white space
- Simplicity of design

2. What is usability?

How easily or effortlessly a particular application can be utilized by its intended users. Usability includes such issues as menu design, discoverability of features, navigation, and user assistance.

3. List some common issues encountered when designing the user service layer.

- Do any application requirements specify the type of UI?
- Do security issues, such as firewalls, impact communication between user workstations and server-side computers?
- What operating systems must be supported on user workstations?
- What Web browsers must be supported?
- Can COM components install and run on user workstations?
- Are remote COM components accessible from user workstations?

4. How can COM objects be used in the user service layer?

If the UI is a native application, installing and running COM components on user workstations probably isn't an issue. A Win32 application needs to be installed, but the COM components are simply treated as part of the application's installation routine. Things are somewhat more complicated for Web-based applications. Providing that a particular browser supports client-side COM components, the components usually download and automatically install on users' computers the first time the component is accessed.

ActiveX controls are COM objects that are sent from a Web server to execute on users' desktops with their browser. Some users, or the organizations for which they work, might worry about the security of automatically downloading and installing executable code on client computers. Some users might not allow any components to be downloaded to their computers. If Web-based applications must support such users or organizations, it is best not to use any client-side COM components (including ActiveX controls) unless the components are installed locally on the users' computers. Some users want to decide on a case-by-case basis whether to download and install particular components on their computers. In this case, developers might choose to use client-side COM components.

5. How does ASP fit in the user, business, and data access layers?

In an Internet application, a Web browser displays an HTML-page-based user service layer. Requests from this layer transmit via HTTP to a Web server. In response to these requests from the client Web browser, ASP pages activate on the Web server. The ASP pages can dynamically generate HTML pages to be returned to the requesting browser. These ASP pages can be used to generate user interface code to format and control the look and feel of the Web pages, thus ASP would be considered part of the user service layer. Also, the ASP pages can contain server-side script that implements business logic, thus ASP pages could be part of the business service layer. However, the ASP pages should contain server-side script that uses middle-tier business objects to do much of the work. The business objects might in turn call data access objects to access data sources in the data access service layer. Alternatively, the HTML and client-side script used to generate the user service layer might be located within the ASP pages. Either way, ASP straddles the line between the user service layer and the business service layer.

Chapter 8
Business Service Layer Technologies

1. What is the COM specification?

The specification document explaining COM and how it is implemented. Even though other technologies have been added to COM over the years (notably OLE and ActiveX), the fundamental component object model specification, introduced in 1992, remains the basis for COM. The COM specification is available on the Microsoft Web site (www.microsoft.com/com/resources/specs.ASP), and only those items defined in the specification are part of COM proper.

2. How can COM work across computers?

By utilizing the services provided by DCOM (Distributed COM). Technically, *DCOM* refers specifically to the wire protocol for making COM calls between two computers. However, the term *DCOM* is often used to refer to the entire concept of COM communication across computers.

3. How does MTS handle security?

MTS server packages are units of trust for MTS. Calls into a package can be secured. Calls within the package are trusted. Thus, application security requirements have a big impact on package design. If calls into a component must be authorized, clients and components must be allocated into different packages. Only components that can safely call each other without requiring an authorization check should be allocated into one package.

4. What is COM+?

Basically speaking, COM+ is the evolution of COM, which has been around for a long time, and also of MTS, which shipped with Windows NT 4 in the Option Pack. Microsoft combines COM and MTS into a single programming model, COM+, which ships with Windows 2000.

5. What are the primary services in COM+ 1.0?

- Servers
- Transactions
- Security
- Administration
- Load balancing
- Queued components
- Events
- In-memory database

Page 453

Chapter 9
Data Service Layer Technologies

1. What is the UDA?

The Microsoft Universal Data Architecture (UDA) is designed to provide high-performance access to any type of data—structured or unstructured, relational or non-relational—stored anywhere in an enterprise. UDA defines a set of COM interfaces that actualize the concept of accessing data. UDA is based on OLE DB, a set of COM interfaces for building database components. OLE DB allows data stores to expose their native functionality without making nonrelational data appear relational. OLE DB also provides a way for generic service components, such as specialized query processors, to augment features of simpler data providers. Because OLE DB is optimized for efficient data access rather than ease of use, UDA also defines an application-level programming interface, or Microsoft ActiveX Data Objects (ADO). ADO exposes dual interfaces to easily be used with scripting languages as well as with C++, Microsoft Visual Basic, and other development tools.

UDA is a platform, application, and tools initiative that defines and delivers both standards and technologies tailored to providing enterprise data access. It is a key element in the Microsoft foundation for application development. In addition, UDA provides high-performance access to a variety of information resources, including relational and non-relational data, and an easy-to-use programming interface that is tool-independent and language-independent.

2. Which data access components are available from Microsoft?

Microsoft Data Access Components (MDAC) provides a UDA implementation that includes ADO as well as an OLE DB provider for ODBC. This capability enables ADO to access any database that has an ODBC driver—in effect, all major database platforms. OLE DB providers are also available for other types of stores, such as the Microsoft Exchange mail store, Windows NT Directory Services, and Microsoft Windows file system using Microsoft Index Server.

3. What is the recommended Data Access Component?

ADO is Microsoft's premier data access technology. The ADO data access technology and its partner OLE DB comprise the recommended solution for all data access. A development team working on a new application should definitely use ADO.

4. How can applications access host-based data with COM?

By using the Microsoft OLE DB Provider for AS/400 and VSAM.

5. What is COM+ IMDB?

A new feature in COM+, the In-Memory Database, a database that maintains its tables in memory.

Page 501

Chapter 10
Testing and the Production Channel

1. What are the stages of the production channel?

- Development
- Testing
- Certification
- Production

2. What are some advantages of the production channel?

- Any problems will be discovered in the testing or certification stage, rather than in the production stage.
- Formal testing is always done.
- An organized process is used to introduce change.

3. What are key areas to consider when defining performance requirements?

- Project constraints must be identified.
- Services to be performed by the application must be determined.
- The load on the application must be specified.

4. What is a performance baseline?

The results of the initial performance tests.

5. What are the two categories of testing?

During the Developing Phase, *coverage testing* attempts to thoroughly test each feature of the product as well as the actual code base of the product in a relatively closed environment. During the Stabilizing Phase, testing shifts from coverage testing to *usage testing*, which validates the application's fulfillment of the use cases and usage scenarios developed during the Envisioning Phase. This stage of testing usually includes involving actual users of the product in beta tests, and preferably occurs in the application's production environment. Tolerance for bugs decreases as testing progresses through the Stabilizing Phase, and because the focus is on shipping during this phase, being able to successfully manage bugs is paramount.

6. What are the stages of bug management?

- Reporting
- Prioritization
- Assignment
- Resolution
- Closure

Page 539

Chapter 11
Application Security

1. What is authentication?

Identifying and validating users, and potentially revalidating users as an on-going process.

2. What are several methods for Web-based authentication?

- Windows NT Challenge/Response
- Cookies
- Digital certificates

3. What is encryption?

A means of protecting sensitive information transmitted over a network from all forms of interception and tampering by converting the data to random nonsense data, usually involving agreed-upon algorithms for transmission and reception.

4. What is access security?

In simple terms, access security is about who can use the application and how they can use it. With a secure application, both the user and the application are confident they are exchanging information within authentic circumstances. Applications must ensure the privacy of sensitive user information, and also protect the architectural components and services that run the application from unauthorized tampering or eavesdropping by the user. For an application to be secure, each application service must be available only to qualified users. At the same time, every component, service, and supporting file must be protected from unauthorized viewing, tampering, or modification.

5. Why should applications provide auditing services?

Auditing provides a tracking mechanism to identify security breaches. In addition to security auditing, simple auditing can operate as application monitoring to help determine what an application is doing and who did what with the application.

6. **Which Windows NT services provide mechanisms for auditing?**

   ■ **Windows NT system auditing** System auditing includes user logon and logoff, object access, file and object access, use of user rights, user and group management, security policy changes, system restart and shutdown, and Process Tracking.

   ■ **File and directory auditing** This type of auditing can be set to determine the success and/or failure of read, write, execute, delete, change-permission, and take-ownership actions.

   ■ **Registry auditing** Auditing within the registry can be set to determine the success and/or failure of query values, set values, create subkeys, enumerate subkeys, notify, create links, delete, write DAC, and read control.

Chapter 12
Development Deliverables

1. What are the seven deliverables of the Developing Phase?

- Revised Functional Specification
- Revised Master Project Plan
- Revised Master Project Schedule
- Revised Master Risk Assessment Document
- Source code and executables
- User performance materials
- Testing elements

2. What are interim product releases?

Releases of the product prior to the Scope Complete Milestone, typically called Internal, Alpha, and Beta.

3. What are the benefits of interim product releases?

- Break the Developing Phase into manageable portions.
- Encourage a product-shipping mindset.
- Provide a way for the team to measure progress as a whole.
- Force the product team to synchronize the code at a product level.
- Force the team to achieve user interface and database freeze points, thus resulting in fewer changes to the dependant documentation and code.
- Address high-risk architectural areas to determine feasibility or identify development changes required, thus minimizing the cost and effect of design changes.
- Help the team focus on more actionable subsets that can direct daily progress.
- Increase quality by providing a more stable base for new development.
- Allow the team to fix bugs closer to the time at which they occur rather than toward the end of the project.

4. **What are three ways a bug can be resolved?**

   Any three of the following:

   - **Fixed** The developer has fixed the bug, tested the fix, checked in the code, assigned the fix to a release number, and assigned the bug back to the tester who reported it.

   - **Duplicate** The bug reported is a duplicate of another bug already recorded in the bug database. The duplicate bug should be closed and linked to the original bug.

   - **Postponed** The bug will not be fixed in the current release, but might be fixed in a subsequent one. This designation should be used when the team sees value in fixing the bug, but does not have the time or resources to correct it during the current release being tested.

   - **By design** The behavior reported in a particular bug is intentional and acknowledged in the Functional Specification.

   - **Can't reproduce** The developer can't verify the existence of the bug with any level of consistency.

   - **Won't fix** The bug will not be fixed in the current release, because the team does not think fixing the bug is worth any effort.

5. **When is a team ready to move to the Stabilizing Phase?**

   - All product features are implemented, even if not fully optimized.

   - The product has passed basic testing and the current list of bugs has been addressed, although not necessarily fixed.

   - Team members and key stakeholders agree that the included features meet the product vision and design, and have been successfully implemented.

   - User performance materials are baselined and ready for testing and stabilization.

Page 617

Chapter 13
Product Stabilization

1. What is the primary goal of the Stabilizing Phase?

To prepare the product for release to the customer.

2. How does the team incrementally reach the Release Milestone?

During the Stabilizing Phase, the team may ship multiple external product releases while driving toward the final product release. During these interim releases, the team will primarily focus on testing to identify bugs, and fixing the bugs that are identified. A significant interim milestone that signifies the team is getting close to releasing a product is generally referred to as the zero-bug release (ZBR). ZBR is the first interim product release in which all active bugs have been resolved in some manner, whether fixed, postponed, or deemed unimportant. Once an interim release is shipped, extensive testing must occur to determine whether the product is ready, at which point the team can declare victory and classify the release as the Final Product Release.

3. What are the primary steps of the Stabilizing Phase?

Unlike the other phases of the development process, this phase is not characterized by action steps; rather, it is characterized by interim releases. The same steps are repeated within each interim release:

- Fix the bugs
- Synchronize all product deliverables
- Ship the release
- Extensively test the release

Eventually, the team will determine that a release is ready for prime time, and that will be the Final Product Release.

4. What are the primary interim releases of the Stabilizing Phase?

- One or more interim releases with a decreasing number of bugs
- Zero-bug release (ZBR)
- One or more release candidates
- Final Product Release

5. **What are the deliverables of the Stabilizing Phase?**

   - **Final product release** Source code and executables.

   - **Product release notes** Documents containing release information and late changes.

   - **User and support performance artifacts** The final release of supporting information.

   - **Testing results** The bug status and database for future projects.

   - **Project archives** All relevant product information created during the development process, whether or not it shipped with the product.

   - **Project documents** All stages of the product documentation including the major milestone releases.

6. **What are some of the deployment methods that can be used within an organization?**

   - Microsoft Systems Management Server (SMS)

   - Logon scripts

   - E-mail distributions

   - Web-based advertisements

Chapter 14
Project Review

1. List the benefits of a project review.

- **Provide project closure** Closure is important if team members have spent time and energy on the completed project, and will begin another project immediately. Project closure is particularly important if the project team will soon dissolve. Official project closure will also help the team members move on to something new.

- **Provide a final outlet for team communication** A project review can be cathartic for team members who have strong feelings about particular aspects of a project. If not expressed in a controlled manner and setting, team members may express such feelings later in less desirable circumstances, places, or means.

- **Address the team's morale** Project reviews may actually enhance team morale by allowing teammates to share positive as well as negative feelings, and also to offer praise throughout the team.

- **Set best-practice baselines** Future teams may also benefit from project reviews by accessing the current team's perception of the project's strengths and weaknesses. Such perceptions can provide the basis for creating best-practice baselines for software development within an organization.

- **Establish feedback loops** Ultimately, all the project review output can be combined into a best practice baseline and should be used as *input* for subsequent projects. Organizations should be able to apply project review insights for the purpose of improving future projects.

2. Discuss the relationship between project reviews and the CMM for Software.

Project reviews are important tools in evolving an organization to a more efficient CMM maturity level. One characteristic of a CMM Level 1 organization is reinventing processes for each project. By conducting project reviews and implementing the reviews' results as standard practices, an organization can avoid this inefficient, but common, problem.

Two key challenges for CMM Level 2 organizations are accurate project planning and effective project tracking. Using project reviews to compare plans with actual events and timelines enables an organization to hone its estimating and tracking skills. Over time, an organization at this level can create an increasingly realistic sense of time and resources that project tasks require.

Project reviews are critical to reaching CMM Level 3. Although most Level 2 organizational discipline is seen at a project level, members of an individual project can usually find good practices that could be useful in another project. Leveraging those best practices across the organization and defining processes that can be tailored to each project is the heart of Level 3. Project teams generally accumulate a rich process history as they complete their project. They should keep this data in a repository for use by other project teams on future projects. The organization will develop an appreciation for common processes and advisors who can help tailor those processes.

At CMM Levels 4 and 5, the fundamental purpose of the project review is to facilitate the feedback loop. As the team identifies problems, it can change its processes to eliminate or mitigate such problems in future projects.

3. List some practical considerations involved in project reviews.

- Timing
- Formality
- Length
- Setting
- Attendees

4. Explain methods to conduct project reviews for large projects.

Program Management may choose to organize a project review team when planning a review for larger projects. The team approach works especially well when several project teams are involved in a large project.

Program Management may use a variety of tactics in organizing a project review team. For instance, functional discipline groups can be created: one for development, one for testing, one for user education, and one for program management. Another example of a project review team is a multifunctional group comprised of members from each functional discipline, based on the particular development process phases.

Glossary

A

activity A collection of tasks within a particular process; where the work is done.

analyzing risk Converting risk data into risk decision-making information.

antipatterns *See* design patterns and antipatterns.

application A grouping of software for the purpose of solving a business problem.

application architecture The design and plan for building an application, as well as certain consistent styles of application construction.

Application Model One of the six core models of MSF. The MSF Application Model for Development (MSF Application Model) provides a three-tier services-based approach to designing and developing software applications. MSF views an application at a logical level as a network of co-operative, distributed, and reusable services that support a business solution. The model describes applications as using three services: user, business, and data.

Application Perspective Part of the Enterprise Application Model. The enterprise architecture from the point of view of the applications used to support business processes.

architecture A design and plan for building something; also, the style of that plan or design. *See also* enterprise architecture, application architecture.

architecture first An approach to IT planning and implementation that emphasizes basing such work on a well-thought-out, well-understood enterprise architecture. It represents a commitment that all three parts of the IT task—planning, building, and managing—are based on a coherent, higher-level architecture; that the architecture has been worked out before the start of the coding work; and that the architecture drives the work.

artifact Documents of all kinds that are generated as part of the project. *See also* deliverable.

B

best practice Refers to recommended procedures to follow. The term does not imply that best practices that will always produce successful results.

buffer Time added to a project schedule to help the project team accommodate unexpected problems and changes. It is typically created by setting an internal deadline that occurs sooner than the external one that has been publicized.

bug Any issue arising from the use of the product.

build strategy One of the four strategies designed to extricate an organization from the IT abyss. The build strategy endeavors to define a long-term infrastructure target that increases flexibility while maintaining cost levels.

business function Business functions are the highest level of what business processes are intended to accomplish. For example, financial management is a business function; accounts receivable is a related business process. *See also* business process, business process decomposition.

Business Perspective One of the four perspectives in the Enterprise Architecture Model. The business perspective views the enterprise architecture from the point of view of the business processes. It includes broad business strategies and plans for moving the organization from its current state to its desired future state. The business perspective describes how the business works. Subtopics might include the organization's high-level goals and objectives, the organization's products and services, business processes that embody the functions and the cross-functional activities performed by the organization, major organizational structures, and the interaction of all these elements.

business process A process is "a structured, measured set of activities designed to produce a specified output for a particular customer or market. It implies a strong emphasis on how work is done within an organization." (Davenport, Harvard Business Review, 1993). Business processes have customers and in most cases (but not always) cross-organizational boundaries.

business process decomposition A top-down hierarchical way of analyzing in detail an organization's business processes. The flow of analysis usually proceeds in the following order: function, process, activity, and task. Business rules and processes usually apply at the task level. *See also* business process.

C

candidate project list During the planning phase of the enterprise architecture, determining which IT projects to undertake requires complex tradeoffs in uncertain situations. The candidate project list helps IT planners to balance business needs and goals against technological possibilities and risks and prioritize projects for a versioned release of the enterprise architecture.

client/server architecture *See* two-tier architecture.

Conceptual Design The process of acquiring, documenting, validating, and optimizing business and user perspectives of the problem and the solution. Its purpose is to capture and understand business needs and user requirements in their proper context. The output of Conceptual Design is a set of information models, use cases, and usage scenarios that document the current and future states of the system. *See also* Logical Design, Physical Design, Design Process Model.

control strategy One of the four strategies designed to extricate an organization from the IT abyss. Organizations in the IT abyss attempt to get all IT under control by setting funding targets for future application and infrastructure spending.

controlling risk Addressing the results of risk tracking and the process as a whole.

critical success factors The activities, tasks, technology, funding, and milestone requirements that must be accomplished before an organization can reach its long-term goals and objectives. Similar to dependencies.

current state assessment An assessment of the actual present-day status of the organization's business processes, applications, information stores, and technological support made during the planning phase of the enterprise architecture.

customer-focused mindset A best practice or principle of a successful team, it means committing to understanding and solving the business problem, focusing on the alignment of business and technology, and involving the customer throughout the process.

D

deliverable A physical artifact created by the team, usually associated with reaching an interim or major milestone. It can be the only product or one of several products associated with that milestone.

design patterns and antipatterns A design pattern is instructive information that captures the essential structure and insight of a successful family of proven solutions to a recurring problem that arises within a certain context and system of forces. It identifies the key aspects of a common design structure that make it useful for creating a reusable object-oriented design. Design patterns can be either generative or non-generative. Generative patterns can be used to solve engineering problems, whereas non-generative patterns are merely observed. Generative design patterns provide complete solutions to business and technical problems. They are primarily geared toward "green field" designs, meaning they are applied to new designs.

A design antipattern is geared toward solving problems for which an inadequate solution is already in place. The best way to differentiate patterns and antipatterns is to say that patterns lead to an original solution for a set of criteria and forces, while antipatterns lead to a new solution when the current design is not working. Thus patterns are used when starting from scratch, and antipatterns are used to fix things that are broken.

Design Process Model One of the six core models of MSF. The MSF Design Process Model is based on three different phases—Conceptual, Logical, and Physical Design—that provide three different perspectives for three different audiences—users, the project team, and developers.

desired architecture The future envisioned state of the enterprise architecture.

Developing Phase The third of four distinct phases of the MSF Development Process Model, it is the period during which all projects for the versioned release are initiated. It culminates in the Scope Complete Milestone, indicating all projects have been started and preparations have been made for external testing and stabilization.

Development Process Model One of the six core models of MSF. The MSF Process Model for Application Development (MSF Development Process Model) is a project life-cycle model that is milestone-based, iterative, and flexible. It describes the phases, milestones, activities and deliverables of an application development project and their relationship to the roles of the MSF Development Team Model. It includes four phases (Envisioning, Planning, Developing, and Stabilizing), each with its own major milestone (Vision Approved, Project Plan Approved, Scope Complete, and Release). *See also* each of the phases and deliverables.

Development role One of six MSF team roles. It acts as technology consultant to the team and is responsible for actually writing the application.

Development Team Model One of the six core models of MSF. The MSF Team Model for Application Development (MSF Development Team Model) provides a flexible structure for organizing project teams. It emphasizes both clear roles and responsibilities and clear goals for team success, and it increases team member accountability through its team of peers approach. It consists of six roles: Product Management, Program Management, Development, User Education, Testing, and Logistics Management. *See also* each of the six roles, respectively.

digital nervous system Analogous to a biological nervous system in that it provides an organization with the information it needs. It supports basic business operations, prepares an organization to react to both planned and unplanned events, and helps to gain and/or maintain a competitive advantage.

E

Enterprise Application Model An architecture model for designing and building enterprise applications. The model consists of six submodels: Business, User, Logical, Technology, Physical, and Development.

enterprise architecture A structure that describes the organization's business activities, the applications and automation that support those business activities, the information necessary to carry out those business activities, and the technologies and infrastructure used to deliver the applications and information. It results in a logically consistent plan of activities and coordinated projects that guide the progression of an organization's application systems and infrastructure. The plan should move from the current state to a desired future state based on current and projected business objectives and processes.

Enterprise Architecture Model One of the six core models of MSF. The MSF Enterprise Architecture Model provides a consistent set of guidelines for rapidly building enterprise architecture through versioned releases. The model aligns information technology with business requirements through four perspectives: Business, Application, Information, and Technology.

enterprise architecture planning The process of working from a current state to an envisioned future state of the enterprise architecture. The process anticipates and plans for the obstacles that impede progress toward initiation of projects that will move the organization forward.

enterprise architecture process A rational way to make decisions that lead to action rather than reporting. Once this rational process is in place, you can focus on project selection and prioritization and "plan while building" rather than plan first and then build.

Envisioning Phase The first phase of the MSF Development Process Model, during which the project team is assembled and comes to agreement with the customer on the project vision and scope. The Envisioning Phase culminates in the Vision Approved Milestone.

execute strategy One of the four strategies designed to extricate an organization from the IT abyss. Organizations eager to leave the IT abyss focus on execution, in both operations and new development to reach competitive status as soon as possible.

extend strategy One of the four strategies designed to extricate an organization from the IT abyss. A strategy for organizations that aspire to lead and must focus their energies on identifying and testing new opportunities while continuing to drive performance.

F

feature team In large projects, a multidisciplinary subteam that is responsible for a particular feature set.

features One of the three sides of the tradeoff triangle, the other two being resources and schedule, it refers to the product and its quality.

four perspectives Together, they make up the Enterprise Architecture Model. MSF uses the acronym BAIT to refer to the four perspectives: Business, Application, Information, and Technology.

function team In large projects, a subteam within a role. They arise when a team or project is large enough that it requires the people within a role to be grouped into teams based on their functionality.

Functional Specification A deliverable that describes the solution in explicit detail.

G

gap analysis A study that is conducted to discover the gap between the current state and the desired state of the enterprise architecture.

goal What the business intends to accomplish or attain.

guideline A recommended course of action to achieve particular ends.

I

identifying risk Discovering and recognizing potential problems with the project.

information What the organization needs to know to run its business processes and operations. It includes standard data models, data management policies, and descriptions of the patterns of information consumption and production in the organization.

Information Perspective Part of the Enterprise Application Model. The enterprise architecture from the point of view of the information that the organization has stored for its use.

information store A database or other kind of repository where information in all of its forms is kept.

information technology (IT) The architecture, structures, and processes that are the core of an information systems strategy.

initial candidate project list *See* candidate project list.

interim milestone A point in time that signals a transition within a phase and helps to divide large projects into workable pieces. *See also* milestone, major milestone.

IT abyss A model that describes the gap between an enterprise and its ability to maximize value from its IT investments. The IT abyss is the most prominent feature of the IT landscape and represents the present state of an organization on the IT landscape chart, situated between past and future states. An organization's position relative to the abyss on the IT landscape chart determines which of four strategies it should adopt to help it get out of or across the IT abyss.

IT assets What the organization has, grouped in three main areas: application portfolio, technology infrastructure, and IT organization.

IT/business performance The organization's current performance, grouped in two main areas: spending and results.

IT diagnostic areas Enterprise architecture planners can evaluate an organization's current IT environment in three key diagnostic areas: IT assets (what the organization has), IT management processes (how things are done), and IT/business performance (current performance).

IT inventory A quick, high-level inventory across the enterprise, looking only at the details of the areas that the vision identifies as being of interest. The IT inventory of an organization can be divided into three categories:

- **Applications** Systems made up of executable software.
- **Information** Computerized data stores containing information, often accessed through a database management system.
- **Technology** Hardware, software, and electronic networks that support applications and data stores.

For analysis purposes, an organization's IT inventory also includes items that are planned or under development.

IT landscape A graphical representation of an organization's IT assets evaluation depicting past, present, and future performance. The IT abyss model describes varying levels of the IT landscape. Factors contributing to the IT abyss include IT assets, IT management processes, and IT business performance.

IT lifecycle The process of planning, building, and managing information technology.

IT management processes How the organization does things, grouped in five main areas: strategic direction-setting, technical direction-setting, funding, execution, and review.

L

Logical Design The process of describing a solution in terms of the organization, structure, syntax, and interaction of its parts from the perspective of the project team. The purpose of Logical Design is to apply the services-based organizing principles of the MSF Application Model, and to lay out the structure of the solution and the relationship among its parts. The output of Logical Design is a set of business objects with corresponding services, attributes, and relationships; a high-level user interface design; and a logical database design. *See also* Conceptual Design, Physical Design, Design Process Model.

Logistics Management role One of six MSF team roles. It is responsible for acting as advocate for the operations, product support, Help Desk, and other channel organizations.

M

major milestone Achieving a major milestone represents team and customer agreement to proceed and signals a transition from one phase into the next. *See also* milestone, interim milestone.

Microsoft Solutions Framework (MSF) A framework developed by Microsoft for planning, building, and managing distributed computing systems. MSF is a set of proven practices for organizing software development teams and project planning that can be applied to planning and implementing almost any form of computing technology.

milestone A point at which the team assesses progress and makes mid-course corrections. Milestones are review and synchronization points, not freeze points.

mitigating risk The practice of predicting and then taking steps to eliminate risk from a proposed course of action.

MSF *See* Microsoft Solutions Framework.

multi-layer architecture *See* N-tier architecture.

N

N-tier architecture An application architecture in which the presentation, business, and data tiers are logically separated. Also called three-tier architecture. "N-tier" is becoming the preferred term since it implies (correctly) that the logical separation of services can result in more than three tiers. *See also* two-tier architecture.

O

objective Represents what an organization wants to achieve in the long-term. *See also* goal.

P

patterns *See* design patterns and antipatterns.

phase One of four distinct divisions of the MSF Development Process Model, culminating in a major or external milestone.

Physical Design The process of describing the components, services, and technologies of the solution from the perspective of Development. Its purpose is to apply real-world technology constraints to Logical Design, including implementation and performance considerations. The output of Physical Design is a set of components, a user interface design for a particular platform, and a physical database design. *See also* Conceptual Design, Logical Design, Design Process Model.

plan, build, manage IT lifecycle The fundamental life cycle upon which MSF is based. Enterprise architecture focuses on the planning aspects of the MSF lifecycle.

Planning Phase The second phase of the MSF Development Process Model that culminates with the Project Plan Approved Milestone.

postmortem A formal process of reviewing what went right and what went wrong with a project as a way of learning for the future.

proactive analysis An evaluation of how new and unused technologies can be applied to the organization. In this approach, planners do not treat the boundaries of current business practices as limitations, but try to change business processes through a new application of technology in a way that adds value to the organization. The proactive approach means that IT professionals have to imagine future directions that the organization might take and look for ways to apply new or unexploited old technologies to business. *See also* reactive analysis.

process A collection of activities that yield a result, product, or service; usually a continuous operation.

process decomposition *See* business process decomposition.

Process Model *See* Development Process Model.

Product Management role One of six team roles in MSF. It acts as the customer advocate to the team and the team advocate to the customer.

product mindset A best practice or principle of a successful team, it means the team treats the work performed as a product, enabling it to use a versioned release strategy to prioritize features and address changes.

Program Management role One of six MSF team roles. It is responsible for driving the timely development of the solution. The program manager drives critical tradeoff decisions, facilitates team communication, and manages the schedule and resource allocation, but is not the "boss" as he or she might be in a traditional top-down project team.

Project Plan Approved Milestone The major milestone at the end of the Planning Phase that represents the point at which the project team, the customer, and key project stakeholders agree on the project deliverables. This milestone provides an opportunity to establish priorities and set expectations, and serves essentially as a contract between the project team and the customer.

R

reactive analysis A top-down approach in which the organization initiates no action unless an event of some kind threatens the status quo. Then an individual or a team is given the task of forestalling change or attempting to control change as the organization drifts toward another—usually unplanned-for—state.

Release Milestone The major milestone at the end of the Stabilizing Phase that represents the point at which the team has addressed all outstanding issues and ships the product, placing it in service. At the Release Milestone, responsibility for ongoing management and support of the product officially transfers from the project team to the operations and support groups.

resources One of three sides of the tradeoff triangle, the others being schedule and features, it includes people and money.

retiring risk Eliminating risk from the risk plan. One approach to retiring a risk is to archive the risk and its management plan (successful or otherwise) into a repository for use and reference by future projects. Conversely, risks can be simply removed from the risk management process after they have occurred or been resolved.

risk The possibility of loss or injury; a problem waiting to happen.

risk assessment Determining risk probability (the likelihood risk will occur) and risk impact (the severity of loss if the risk does occur).

Risk Assessment Document A consolidation of the team's risk management output in a single document.

risk contingency Addressing what to do if a risk occurs.

risk contingency trigger The criterion for executing a contingency plan.

risk exposure A quantification of the overall threat constituted by a risk, it is calculated by multiplying probability times impact.

risk impact The severity or magnitude of loss if a risk occurs.

risk management A proactive process of identifying, analyzing, and addressing risk.

Risk Management Model One of the six core models of MSF. The MSF Risk Management Model provides a structured and proactive way to manage project risks. It consists of five steps: identify, analyze, plan, track, and control.

risk planning Anticipating risks with consequences that an organization cannot accept. Risk planning involves examining how much is known about the risk, and if the organization can live with the consequences, or avoid the risk entirely. The plan can include a way to reduce the likelihood the risk will occur, and determine ways to reduce the impact should the risk occur.

risk probability The likelihood that a risk will occur.

risk source Where a risk can originate.

risk statement A condition-consequence statement that helps to clearly articulate risk.

S

scale A way of adjusting the scope of a planned project so that it matches a fixed ratio or actual need.

scale down To narrow the scope of a project or plan.

scale up To expand the scope of a project or plan.

scenario A single sequence of interactions between objects and actors. A scenario illustrates a particular instance of a use case and can show either the current state of the process or a desired future state. *See also* use case.

schedule One of three sides of the tradeoff triangle, the others being resources and features, it means time.

Scope Complete Milestone The major milestone at the end of the Developing Phase that represents the point when all features are complete and the product is ready for external testing and stabilization.

shared project vision A best practice or principle of a successful team, it means clearly understanding project goals and objectives, and understanding and buying into a vision that is held by all team members and the customer. It is important because it provides the team with a uniform sense of purpose, resolves conflicting and contradictory visions, clarifies project goals and objectives, and ensures that team members are working toward the same goal.

Spiral Model A project lifecycle model that is primarily iterative. The stages of application development that make up this model are typically characterized as inception, elaboration, construction, and transition. Within each stage are five activity phases: requirements, design, implementation, deployment, and management. The Spiral Model's process is a continual circle through the stages of development, with each stage requiring multiple revolutions through the five phases.

Stabilizing Phase The last of four distinct phases of the MSF Development Process Model, it is the period during which all team efforts are directed at addressing all issues derived from feedback. No new development occurs during this phase. It culminates in the Release Milestone, at which point responsibility for the product shifts to the operations team.

standard Established or prescribed course of action or procedure to be followed for specific situations, operations or business processes.

strengths, weaknesses, opportunities, threats Factors in an organization that may impact proposed solutions to enterprise architecture problems. Analyzing these factors may influence IT decisions. *See also* SWOT analysis.

SWOT analysis A way to evaluate strategies with respect to the organization's resources and environment.

T

Team Model *See* Development Team Model.

team of peers A fundamental concept, underlying the team model, which says each role on a project team brings a unique, valuable perspective to the team that must be equally valued.

Technology Perspective Part of the Enterprise Application Model. The enterprise architecture from the point of view of the technological infrastructure that supports the business processes.

Testing role One of six MSF team roles. It is responsible for making sure that all issues are known to the team and addressed prior to releasing or deploying.

three-tier architecture *See* N-tier architecture.

top ten risk list An identification of the ten top priority risks, taken from the risk assessment document.

tracking risk Monitoring the risks and their mitigation plans.

tradeoff triangle A triangle of project variables whose three sides are resources (people and money), schedule (time), and features (the product and its quality). It is used to make project tradeoffs. A change to one side requires that the team make a correction on one of the sides to maintain project balance, including potentially the same side on which the change first occurred.

two-tier architecture Also known as client/server architecture. In a two-tier architecture, a client process handles the data processing and presentation parts of the application. Data is stored on centrally administered server machines. Clients connect directly to the servers they need, often for the lifetime of the application's use. *See also* N-tier architecture.

U

undesired architecture The enterprise architecture that results when an organization does not attempt to plan for the future.

Unified Modeling Language (UML) A language used to model software systems. Its primary purpose is to help organizations visualize, specify, create, and document the artifacts of a software system. It evolved from several primary modeling languages that were prevalent in the late 1980s and 1990s. It consists of modeling elements, relationships, extensibility mechanisms, and diagrams.

Unified Process Model (UP) A life-cycle model used for the analysis, design, and implementation of enterprise applications. It requires extensive use of the Unified Modeling Language (UML) modeling, and is use-case driven, architecture-centric, iterative, incremental, risk-confronting, object-oriented, and layered. It is a repository for object-oriented system development patterns, objects, and code. *See also* workflows.

use case A behaviorally related sequence of interactions performed by an actor in a dialogue with a system to provide some measurable value to the actor. *See also* scenario.

User Education role One of six MSF team roles. It is responsible for acting as the advocate for the user of the product.

V

versioned release Providing the most critical functionality for a product in the first version and postponing other desirable features into later releases.

Vision Approved Milestone The major milestone at the end of the Envisioning Phase that represents the point at which the project team and the customer agree on the overall direction for the project, including what features and functionality the product will and will not include.

Vision Document A major milestone at the end of the Envisioning Phase that sets forth all the projects and goals for the next versioned release of the product.

Vision Statement A deliverable that expresses the long-term vision of the product and provides a context for decision-making.

W

Waterfall Model A project lifecycle model that is primarily linear. It is an orderly, highly structured process based on the following well-defined development steps: system requirements, software requirements, analysis, program design, coding, system test, and operations.

willingness to learn A best practice or principle of a successful team, it means committing to self-improvement through gathering and sharing knowledge and institutionalizing learning using such techniques as reviews and postmortems. It is important because it allows team members to benefit from mistakes, helps them repeat successes, and mandates time for the team to learn.

workflow Five core processes within the Unified Process model that are continually executed during the four phases of the development process until the application is completed. Each completion of the five workflow steps is called an iteration, and each iteration culminates in an internal product release. The workflows are requirements, analysis, design, implementation, and testing. *See also* Unified Process Model (UP).

Z

zero-defect mindset A best practice or principle of a successful team, it means committing to quality, performing work at the highest possible level of quality, and focusing on achieving the quality bar set by the team. It is important because it increases product stability, schedule predictability, and accountability.

Bibliography

Administering Systems Management Server 2.0 (Microsoft, 1998)

AntiPatterns: Refactoring Software, Architectures, and Projects in Crisis, William Brown, Raphael Malveau, Hays McCormick III, and Thomas Mowbray (John Wiley and Sons, 1998)

The Capability Maturity Model: Guidelines for Improving the Software Process, Mark C. Paulk, Charles V. Weber, Bill Curtis, and Mary Beth Chrissis (Addison-Wesley, 1995)

The CORBA Reference Guide, Alan Pope (Addison-Wesley, 1998)

Creating a Vision for Your Product, Laurie Litwack (Microsoft)

Debugging the Development Process, Steve Maguire (Microsoft Press, 1994)

Design Patterns: Elements of Reusable Object-Oriented Software, Erich Gamma, Richard Helm, Ralph Johnson, and John Vlissides (Addison-Wesley, 1995)

Designing Component-Based Applications, Mary Kirtland (Microsoft Press, 1998)

Desktop Applications for Microsoft Visual Basic 6.0 (Microsoft Press, 1999)

Desktop Applications for Microsoft Visual C++ 6.0 (Microsoft Press, 1999)

Dynamics of Software Development, Jim McCarthy (Microsoft Press, 1995)

"Escaping the IT Abyss," Dempsey, Dvorak, and Meehan, *The McKinsey Quarterly*, N.4 (1997)

Inside COM+, Guy and Henry Eddon (Microsoft Press, 1999)

Inside Distributed COM, Guy and Henry Eddon (Microsoft Press, 1998)

Internet Information Server Security Overview, Mark Bieter (Microsoft)

Mastering Enterprise Development Using Microsoft Visual Basic 6, Microsoft Mastering Series Group (Microsoft, 1998)

Microsoft Solutions Framework and the Capability Maturity Model, Dr. Joyce Statz (Microsoft/TeraQuest, 1999)

Microsoft Visual Basic 6.0 Programmer's Guide (Microsoft Press, 1998)

Microsoft Visual C++ 6.0 Programmer's Guide (Microsoft Press, 1998)

Microsoft Windows NT 4.0 Security, Audit, and Control (Microsoft Press, 1998)

Microsoft Windows NT Workstation Resource Kit (Microsoft Press, 1996)

A Pattern Language: Towns, Buildings, Construction, Christopher Alexander, Sara Ishikawa, and Murray Silverstein (Oxford University Press, 1977)

Pattern Languages of Program Design, James Coplien (Addison-Wesley, 1995)

Patterns and Software: Essential Concepts and Terminology, Brad Appleton (www.enteract.com/~bradapp/docs/patterns-intro.html, 1997)

Rapid Development: Taming Wild Software Schedules, Steve McConnell (Microsoft Press, 1996)

Remote Data Service in MDAC 2.0, Kamaljit Bath (Microsoft)

The SAP DCOM Component Connector (Microsoft, 1997)

Secure Networking Using Windows 2000 Distributed Security Services, Microsoft PBS Web Team (Microsoft)

Software Architecture: Perspectives on an Emerging Discipline, Mary Shaw (Prentice Hall, 1996)

Software Engineering Economics, Barry Boehm (Prentice Hall, 1981)

Software Project Management: A Unified Framework, Walker Royce (Addison-Wesley, 1998)

Software Project Survival Guide, Steve McConnell (Microsoft Press, 1998)

Software Risk Management, Ron Higuera and Yacov Haimes (Software Engineering Institute)

Succeeding with Objects, Adele Goldberg and Kenneth S. Rubin (Addison-Wesley, 1995)

Technical Overview: Clustering and Windows NT Load Balancing Services (Microsoft, 1998)

Theory and Practice of Object Systems, Dirk Riehle and Heinz Zullighoven (John Wiley and Sons)

The Timeless Way of Building, Christopher Alexander (Oxford University Press, 1970)

Tried and True Object Development: Practical Approaches with UML, Ari Jaaksi, Juha-Markus Aalto, Ari Aalto, and Kimmo Vatto (Cambridge University Press, 1999)

The Unified Modeling Language User Guide, Grady Booch, James Rumbaugh, and Ivar Jacobson (Addison-Wesley, 1998)

The Unified Software Development Process, Ivar Jacobson, Grady Booch, and James Rumbaugh (Addison-Wesley, 1999)

Index

The manuscript for this book was prepared and submitted to Microsoft Press in electronic form. Text files were prepared using Microsoft Word. Pages were composed by Online Training Solutions, Inc. (OTSI) using Adobe PageMaker 6.5, with text in Times and display type in Helvetica Narrow.

Editing, production, and graphic services for this book were provided by OTSI. The hard-working project team included:

Project Editors:	Joyce Cox
	Joan Lambert
Editorial Team:	Leslie Eliel
	Michelle Kenoyer
	Rachel Moorhead
	Gale Nelson
	Gabrielle Nonast
Production Team:	R.J. Cadranell
	Karen Lee
	Mary Rasmussen

Contact OTSI at:

- E-mail: joanl@otsiweb.com
- Web site: www.otsiweb.com

Real-world developer training
for results on the job—and on the exam.

The Microsoft Certified Solution Developer (MCSD) credential is the premium certification for professionals who design and develop custom business solutions with Microsoft development tools, technologies, and platforms. Now you can build the skills and knowledge tested on the MCSD exams—and on the job—with these official Microsoft training kits.

Each MCSD TRAINING KIT features a comprehensive training manual, lab exercises, reusable source code, and sample exam questions. Work through the system of self-paced lessons and hands-on labs to gain practical experience with essential development tasks. By the end of the course you've created a full-featured working application—and you're ready for the corresponding exam!

Desktop Applications with Microsoft® Visual Basic® 6.0: MCSD Training Kit
ISBN: 0-7356-0620-X
U.S.A. $69.99
U.K.   £64.99 [V.A.T. included]
Canada $104.99

Desktop Applications with Microsoft Visual C++® 6.0: MCSD Training Kit
ISBN: 0-7356-0795-8
U.S.A. $69.99
U.K.   £64.99 [V.A.T. included]
Canada $104.99

Distributed Applications with Microsoft Visual Basic 6.0: MCSD Training Kit
ISBN: 0-7356-0833-4
U.S.A. $69.99
U.K.   £64.99 [V.A.T. included]
Canada $104.99

Analyzing Requirements and Defining Solution Architectures: MCSD Training Kit
ISBN: 0-7356-0854-7
U.S.A. $69.99
U.K.   £64.99 [V.A.T. included]
Canada $104.99

Microsoft Press® products are available worldwide wherever quality computer books are sold. For more information, contact your book or computer retailer, software reseller, or local Microsoft Sales Office, or visit our Web site at mspress.microsoft.com. To locate your nearest source for Microsoft Press products, or to order directly, call 1-800-MSPRESS in the U.S. (in Canada, call 1-800-268-2222).

Prices and availability dates are subject to change.

mspress.microsoft.com

Masterful instruction.
Your pace.
Your place.

Master the tools of your trade with in-depth developer training—straight from the source. The award-winning MICROSOFT MASTERING series is now available in ready-anywhere book format. Work at your own pace through the practical, print-based lessons to master essential development concepts, and advance your technique through the interactive labs on CD-ROM. It's professional-level instruction—when and where you need it—for building real-world skills and real-world solutions.

MICROSOFT LICENSE AGREEMENT

Book Companion CD

IMPORTANT—READ CAREFULLY: This Microsoft End-User License Agreement ("EULA") is a legal agreement between you (either an individual or an entity) and Microsoft Corporation for the Microsoft product identified above, which includes computer software and may include associated media, printed materials, and "online" or electronic documentation ("SOFTWARE PRODUCT"). Any component included within the SOFTWARE PRODUCT that is accompanied by a separate End-User License Agreement shall be governed by such agreement and not the terms set forth below. By installing, copying, or otherwise using the SOFTWARE PRODUCT, you agree to be bound by the terms of this EULA. If you do not agree to the terms of this EULA, you are not authorized to install, copy, or otherwise use the SOFTWARE PRODUCT; you may, however, return the SOFTWARE PRODUCT, along with all printed materials and other items that form a part of the Microsoft product that includes the SOFTWARE PRODUCT, to the place you obtained them for a full refund.

SOFTWARE PRODUCT LICENSE

The SOFTWARE PRODUCT is protected by United States copyright laws and international copyright treaties, as well as other intellectual property laws and treaties. The SOFTWARE PRODUCT is licensed, not sold.

1. **GRANT OF LICENSE.** This EULA grants you the following rights:

   a. **Software Product.** You may install and use one copy of the SOFTWARE PRODUCT on a single computer. The primary user of the computer on which the SOFTWARE PRODUCT is installed may make a second copy for his or her exclusive use on a portable computer.

   b. **Storage/Network Use.** You may also store or install a copy of the SOFTWARE PRODUCT on a storage device, such as a network server, used only to install or run the SOFTWARE PRODUCT on your other computers over an internal network; however, you must acquire and dedicate a license for each separate computer on which the SOFTWARE PRODUCT is installed or run from the storage device. A license for the SOFTWARE PRODUCT may not be shared or used concurrently on different computers.

   c. **License Pak.** If you have acquired this EULA in a Microsoft License Pak, you may make the number of additional copies of the computer software portion of the SOFTWARE PRODUCT authorized on the printed copy of this EULA, and you may use each copy in the manner specified above. You are also entitled to make a corresponding number of secondary copies for portable computer use as specified above.

   d. **Sample Code.** Solely with respect to portions, if any, of the SOFTWARE PRODUCT that are identified within the SOFTWARE PRODUCT as sample code (the "SAMPLE CODE"):

      i. **Use and Modification.** Microsoft grants you the right to use and modify the source code version of the SAMPLE CODE, *provided* you comply with subsection (d)(iii) below. You may not distribute the SAMPLE CODE, or any modified version of the SAMPLE CODE, in source code form.

      ii. **Redistributable Files.** Provided you comply with subsection (d)(iii) below, Microsoft grants you a nonexclusive, royalty-free right to reproduce and distribute the object code version of the SAMPLE CODE and of any modified SAMPLE CODE, other than SAMPLE CODE, or any modified version thereof, designated as not redistributable in the Readme file that forms a part of the SOFTWARE PRODUCT (the "Non-Redistributable Sample Code"). All SAMPLE CODE other than the Non-Redistributable Sample Code is collectively referred to as the "REDISTRIBUTABLES."

      iii. **Redistribution Requirements.** If you redistribute the REDISTRIBUTABLES, you agree to: (i) distribute the REDISTRIBUTABLES in object code form only in conjunction with and as a part of your software application product; (ii) not use Microsoft's name, logo, or trademarks to market your software application product; (iii) include a valid copyright notice on your software application product; (iv) indemnify, hold harmless, and defend Microsoft from and against any claims or lawsuits, including attorney's fees, that arise or result from the use or distribution of your software application product; and (v) not permit further distribution of the REDISTRIBUTABLES by your end user. Contact Microsoft for the applicable royalties due and other licensing terms for all other uses and/or distribution of the REDISTRIBUTABLES.

2. **DESCRIPTION OF OTHER RIGHTS AND LIMITATIONS.**

   - **Limitations on Reverse Engineering, Decompilation, and Disassembly.** You may not reverse engineer, decompile, or disassemble the SOFTWARE PRODUCT, except and only to the extent that such activity is expressly permitted by applicable law notwithstanding this limitation.

   - **Separation of Components.** The SOFTWARE PRODUCT is licensed as a single product. Its component parts may not be separated for use on more than one computer.

   - **Rental.** You may not rent, lease, or lend the SOFTWARE PRODUCT.

   - **Support Services.** Microsoft may, but is not obligated to, provide you with support services related to the SOFTWARE PRODUCT ("Support Services"). Use of Support Services is governed by the Microsoft policies and programs described in the user manual, in "online" documentation, and/or in other Microsoft-provided materials. Any supplemental software code provided to you as part of the Support Services shall be considered part of the SOFTWARE PRODUCT and subject to the terms and conditions of this EULA. With respect to technical information you provide to Microsoft as part of the Support Services, Microsoft may use such information for its business purposes, including for product support and development. Microsoft will not utilize such technical information in a form that personally identifies you.

- **Software Transfer.** You may permanently transfer all of your rights under this EULA, provided you retain no copies, you transfer all of the SOFTWARE PRODUCT (including all component parts, the media and printed materials, any upgrades, this EULA, and, if applicable, the Certificate of Authenticity), **and** the recipient agrees to the terms of this EULA.

- **Termination.** Without prejudice to any other rights, Microsoft may terminate this EULA if you fail to comply with the terms and conditions of this EULA. In such event, you must destroy all copies of the SOFTWARE PRODUCT and all of its component parts.

3. **COPYRIGHT.** All title and copyrights in and to the SOFTWARE PRODUCT (including but not limited to any images, photographs, animations, video, audio, music, text, SAMPLE CODE, REDISTRIBUTABLES, and "applets" incorporated into the SOFTWARE PRODUCT) and any copies of the SOFTWARE PRODUCT are owned by Microsoft or its suppliers. The SOFTWARE PRODUCT is protected by copyright laws and international treaty provisions. Therefore, you must treat the SOFTWARE PRODUCT like any other copyrighted material **except** that you may install the SOFTWARE PRODUCT on a single computer provided you keep the original solely for backup or archival purposes. You may not copy the printed materials accompanying the SOFTWARE PRODUCT.

4. **U.S. GOVERNMENT RESTRICTED RIGHTS.** The SOFTWARE PRODUCT and documentation are provided with RESTRICTED RIGHTS. Use, duplication, or disclosure by the Government is subject to restrictions as set forth in subparagraph (c)(1)(ii) of the Rights in Technical Data and Computer Software clause at DFARS 252.227-7013 or subparagraphs (c)(1) and (2) of the Commercial Computer Software—Restricted Rights at 48 CFR 52.227-19, as applicable. Manufacturer is Microsoft Corporation/One Microsoft Way/Redmond, WA 98052-6399.

5. **EXPORT RESTRICTIONS.** You agree that you will not export or re-export the SOFTWARE PRODUCT, any part thereof, or any process or service that is the direct product of the SOFTWARE PRODUCT (the foregoing collectively referred to as the "Restricted Components"), to any country, person, entity, or end user subject to U.S. export restrictions. You specifically agree not to export or re-export any of the Restricted Components (i) to any country to which the U.S. has embargoed or restricted the export of goods or services, which currently include, but are not necessarily limited to, Cuba, Iran, Iraq, Libya, North Korea, Sudan, and Syria, or to any national of any such country, wherever located, who intends to transmit or transport the Restricted Components back to such country; (ii) to any end user who you know or have reason to know will utilize the Restricted Components in the design, development, or production of nuclear, chemical, or biological weapons; or (iii) to any end user who has been prohibited from participating in U.S. export transactions by any federal agency of the U.S. government. You warrant and represent that neither the BXA nor any other U.S. federal agency has suspended, revoked, or denied your export privileges.

DISCLAIMER OF WARRANTY

NO WARRANTIES OR CONDITIONS. MICROSOFT EXPRESSLY DISCLAIMS ANY WARRANTY OR CONDITION FOR THE SOFTWARE PRODUCT. THE SOFTWARE PRODUCT AND ANY RELATED DOCUMENTATION ARE PROVIDED "AS IS" WITHOUT WARRANTY OR CONDITION OF ANY KIND, EITHER EXPRESS OR IMPLIED, INCLUDING, WITHOUT LIMITATION, THE IMPLIED WARRANTIES OF MERCHANTABILITY, FITNESS FOR A PARTICULAR PURPOSE, OR NONINFRINGEMENT. THE ENTIRE RISK ARISING OUT OF USE OR PERFORMANCE OF THE SOFTWARE PRODUCT REMAINS WITH YOU.

LIMITATION OF LIABILITY. TO THE MAXIMUM EXTENT PERMITTED BY APPLICABLE LAW, IN NO EVENT SHALL MICROSOFT OR ITS SUPPLIERS BE LIABLE FOR ANY SPECIAL, INCIDENTAL, INDIRECT, OR CONSEQUENTIAL DAMAGES WHATSOEVER (INCLUDING, WITHOUT LIMITATION, DAMAGES FOR LOSS OF BUSINESS PROFITS, BUSINESS INTERRUPTION, LOSS OF BUSINESS INFORMATION, OR ANY OTHER PECUNIARY LOSS) ARISING OUT OF THE USE OF OR INABILITY TO USE THE SOFTWARE PRODUCT OR THE PROVISION OF OR FAILURE TO PROVIDE SUPPORT SERVICES, EVEN IF MICROSOFT HAS BEEN ADVISED OF THE POSSIBILITY OF SUCH DAMAGES. IN ANY CASE, MICROSOFT'S ENTIRE LIABILITY UNDER ANY PROVISION OF THIS EULA SHALL BE LIMITED TO THE GREATER OF THE AMOUNT ACTUALLY PAID BY YOU FOR THE SOFTWARE PRODUCT OR US$5.00; PROVIDED, HOWEVER, IF YOU HAVE ENTERED INTO A MICROSOFT SUPPORT SERVICES AGREEMENT, MICROSOFT'S ENTIRE LIABILITY REGARDING SUPPORT SERVICES SHALL BE GOVERNED BY THE TERMS OF THAT AGREEMENT. BECAUSE SOME STATES AND JURISDICTIONS DO NOT ALLOW THE EXCLUSION OR LIMITATION OF LIABILITY, THE ABOVE LIMITATION MAY NOT APPLY TO YOU.

MISCELLANEOUS

This EULA is governed by the laws of the State of Washington USA, except and only to the extent that applicable law mandates governing law of a different jurisdiction.

Should you have any questions concerning this EULA, or if you desire to contact Microsoft for any reason, please contact the Microsoft subsidiary serving your country, or write: Microsoft Sales Information Center/One Microsoft Way/Redmond, WA 98052-6399.

Register Today!

Return this
*Analyzing Requirements and
Defining Solution Architectures
MCSD Training Kit*
registration card today

Microsoft Press
mspress.microsoft.com

OWNER REGISTRATION CARD   **0-7356-0854-7**

Analyzing Requirements and Defining Solution Architectures MCSD Training Kit

FIRST NAME   MIDDLE INITIAL   LAST NAME

INSTITUTION OR COMPANY NAME

ADDRESS

CITY   STATE   ZIP

(   )

E-MAIL ADDRESS   PHONE NUMBER

U.S. and Canada addresses only. Fill in information above and mail postage-free.
Please mail only the bottom half of this page.

For information about Microsoft Press®
products, visit our Web site at
mspress.microsoft.com

Microsoft®Press